P9-CKZ-304

AMERICA'S HERITAGE

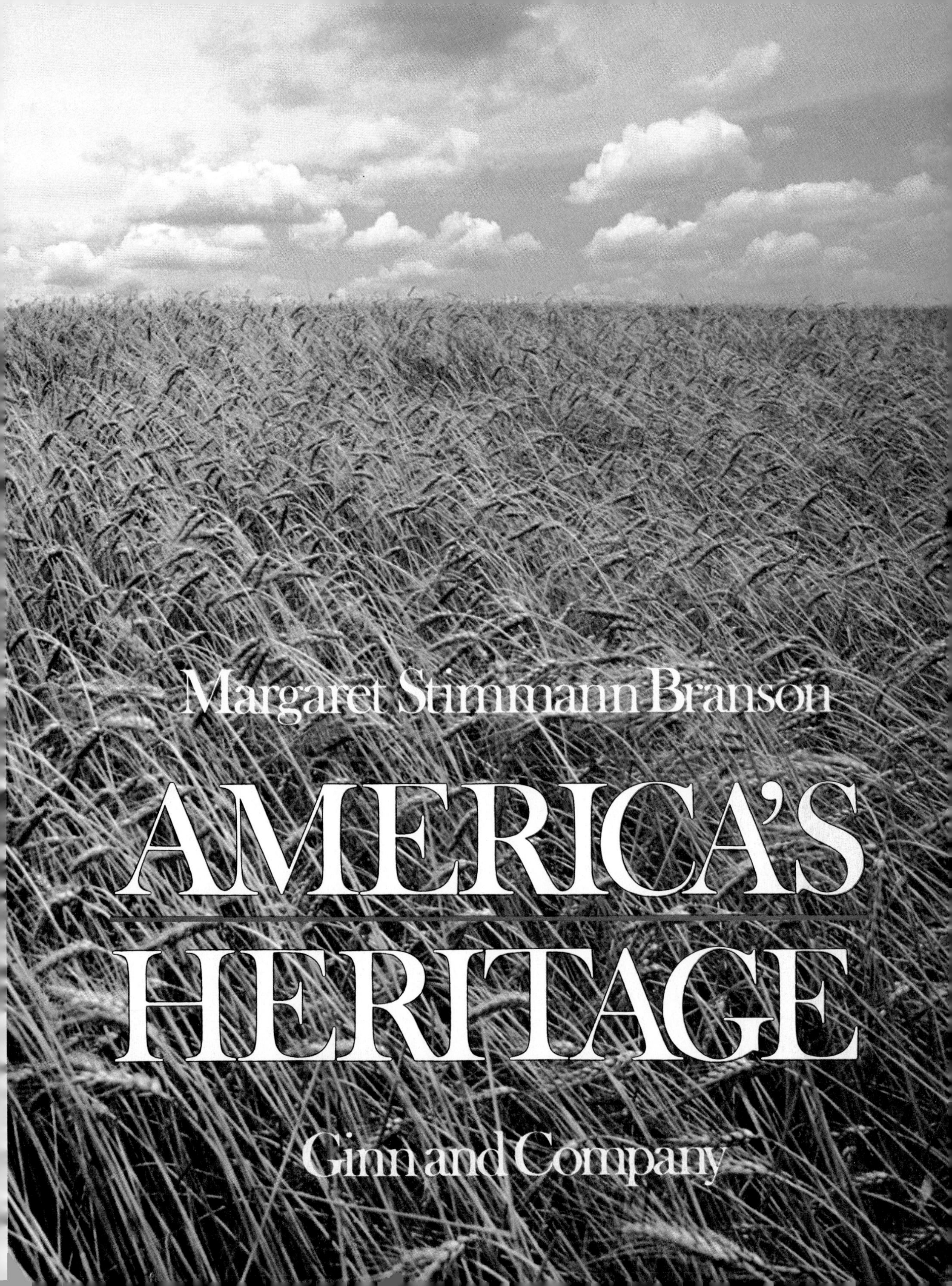

Margaret Stimmann Branson

AMERICA'S HERITAGE

Ginn and Company

For Tom and David

Design and Production: Blackbirch Graphics
Photo Research: Linda Sykes
Cartography: H. Shaw Borst, Inc.
Cover Design: Blackbirch Graphics

GINN AND COMPANY
Home Office: Lexington, Massachusetts 02163
0-663-37988-1

About the Author

Margaret Stimmann Branson, active and well-known writer and educator, is Associate Professor of Education at Holy Names College, Oakland, California. Dr. Branson has served as teacher, counselor, curriculum coordinator, vice principal, supervisor, and consultant, mostly in the Oakland, California, Public Schools.

Dr. Branson received her undergraduate degree from the University of the Pacific. She holds two Master's degrees: one from the University of California, Berkeley (Education), and one from Holy Names College (History). She received her Ed.D. from the University of San Francisco.

Author of numerous articles and textbooks, Dr. Branson is a member of the National, California, and Eastbay Councils for the Social Studies, The American Historical Association, and the Organization of American Historians.

Table of Contents

Maps and Charts

Unit One The Founding

# of America

The English Colonies Grow

4 The Colonies Win Freedom

5 Establishing a New Government

Chapter 1

Our Country Is Discovered and Explored

Pueblo Bonito National Monument, Chaco Canyon, Arizona

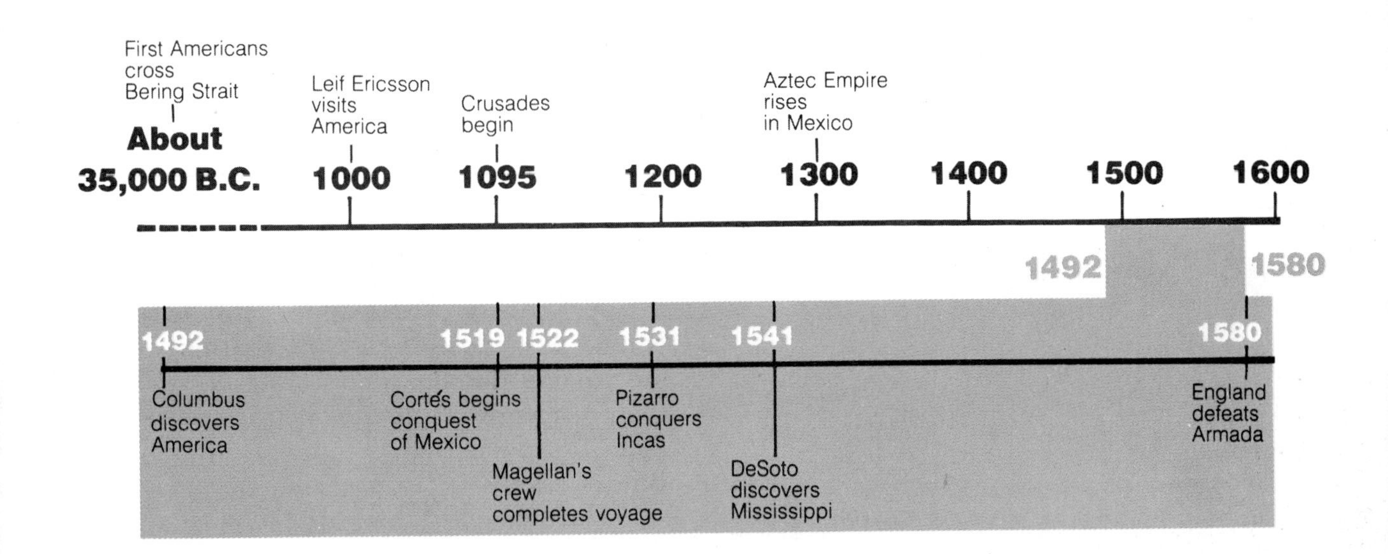

Part One

The First Americans

Who were the First Americans?

Many, many years ago—perhaps 35,000 years ago—life was very different than it is today. At that time, the earth was in the grip of the last Ice Age. There were few people anywhere in the world, and none lived in the Americas. People did live in Asia, however. And some of them wandered into North America.

The firstcomers did not know they had found a new continent. Like all Ice Age peoples, they were hunters. They had to move from place to place in search of their food. Sometimes they killed giant elephants called mammoths. Some of their spearpoints have been found in several places in North America. Scientists say these are about 30,000 years old.

Besides hunting, men and women of the Ice Age fished for their food. They also gathered wild fruits, roots, and seeds to eat. Farming had not yet been invented. Neither had writing. The firstcomers, therefore, did not leave any written records. But they did leave other evidence, which scientists can date and study.

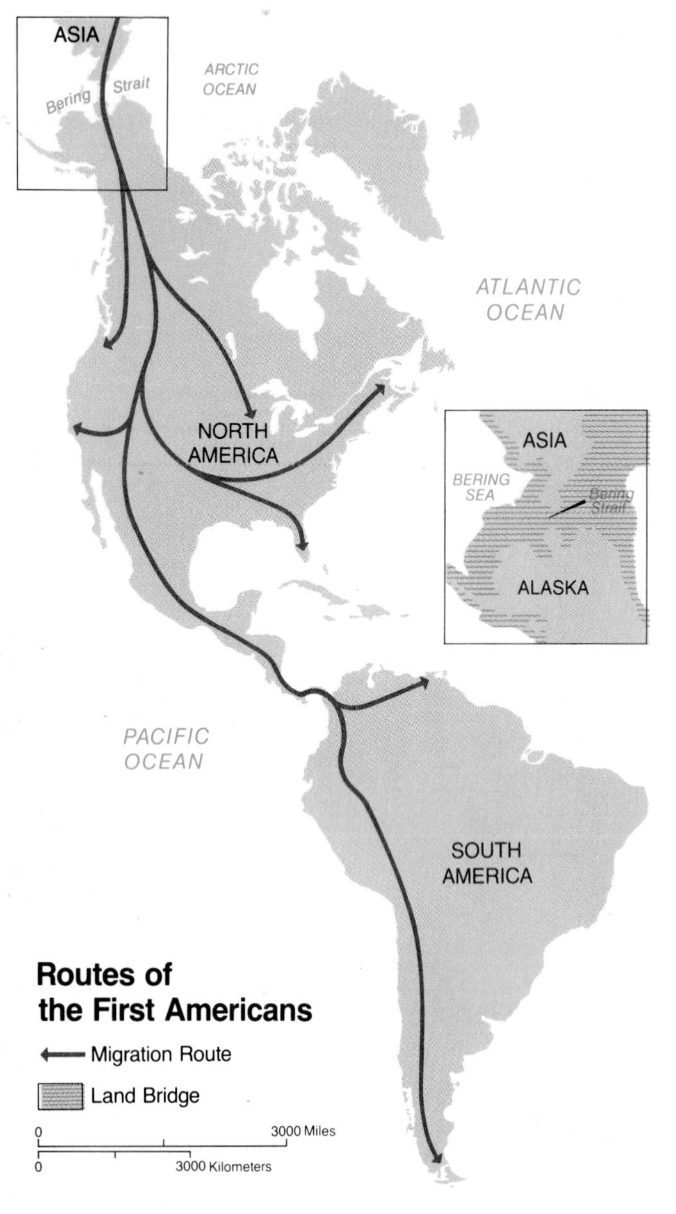

Routes of the First Americans

All of this evidence is important. Each item is like a piece to a giant jigsaw puzzle. We still do not have all of the pieces. Perhaps we never shall. But we now have enough to tell a fairly accurate story.

It is safe to say that the first Americans were Asians. But no one is sure just when the first group arrived. It was probably about 35,000 years ago. Other groups followed. Even so the peopling of America from Asia was a slow process. It may have gone on for 25,000 years.

Getting from Asia to America was not too difficult when the first peoples came. Look at the map on the left. Notice how close those two continents are to one another in the Far North. Only a narrow strip of water separates them. It now is called the Bering Strait. But thousands of years ago there was no water in that strait. Then a land bridge linked the continents. Those who wanted to come in search of food could just walk across the bridge.

As time went on, more and more Asians came. They spread out over the land. Slowly some bands made their way down the river valleys and along the eastern side of the Rocky Mountains. From there some moved onto the Great Plains. Others pushed on to the shores of the Atlantic Ocean. Still others kept moving south. A few even reached the very tip of South America. To this day their descendants are living in that cold, windswept land.

1. Why did people from Asia come to America?
2. When and how did they come?

Where did the First Americans settle?

For thousands of years the people who later came to be called Indians had the Americas all to themselves. Most of them finally settled in what is now Mexico and Central and South America. Over time their numbers grew. Twenty million or more Indians probably were living there when Europeans and Africans finally began to arrive.

In Mexico and Central and South

America, Indians developed three great civilizations.

The Aztecs, who lived in what is now Mexico, built large and beautiful cities. They built roadways, pyramids, irrigation systems, and temples.

The Maya settled farther south in what is today Central America. They, too, were great builders. In some of their special buildings they studied the sun, moon, and stars. In others they worshiped their rain, sun, and corn gods. The Maya developed a calendar and systems of arithmetic and writing. They also enjoyed playing games. One of their favorites was something like basketball. The object of the game was to put a ball through a hoop. The Mayan culture collapsed about A.D. 900. Scientists still do not know why.

The Incan center Machu Picchu was not destroyed by the Spanish because of its location high in the mountains above the Urubamba River in Peru. The stone head (right) is an example of Mayan carving.

This model of the central square of Tenochtitlán, the Aztec capital, shows some of the famous Aztec pyramids.

The Incan fortress (left) shows the great skill of their builders. No mortar was used to cement the stones. The feather mantle (above) shows the more delicate artistry of the Incas.

Still farther south, along the west coast of South America, lived the Incas. They ruled over a huge area. The Incas were skillful metal workers. From gold, silver, lead, and copper they made fine jewelry and other objects.

Like the Aztecs and the Maya, the Incas were great builders. They built with stone, but they did not have any mortar. Yet, they worked with such care that a knife blade couldn't fit between the stones.

Fewer Indians chose to remain in North America. Those who did were widely scattered. Over time, their numbers also grew. But no more than one million were living north of Mexico when Columbus arrived. Most of these—perhaps 750,000—were in what became the United States. (See map, page 7.)

3. Where and how did the Aztecs, Maya, and Incas live?

4. About how many Indians were living north of Mexico when Columbus arrived?

How did the Indians live?

The Indians were really many peoples. And their ways of living differed from place to place.

Take the matter of housing, for example. Some Indians liked to live in tall apartment-like buildings. Others used tents, thatched huts, or wooden houses.

Some Indians stayed in one place and became expert farmers. For example, the Hohokam, who lived in our Southwest, tapped the water of the Gila River. They built a series of mighty canals. They used water drawn from the canals to irrigate their crops.

Major Indian Tribes of North America about 1500
Culture Areas
Arctic
Subarctic
Northwest Coast
California
Plateau
Great Basin
Southwest
Great Plains
Northeast and Great Lakes
Southeast
Middle America
ARCTIC OCEAN
PACIFIC OCEAN
ATLANTIC OCEAN
HUDSON BAY
GULF OF MEXICO
ESKIMO
KOYUKON
INGALIK
TANANA
ALEUT
HAN
NABESNA
HARE
ATHENA
BEAR LAKE
TUTCHONE
MOUNTAIN
YELLOWKNIFE
DOGRIB
TLINGIT
TAHLTAN
KASKA
SLAVE
SEKANI
CHIPEWYAN
HAIDA
TSIMSHIAN
CARRIER
KWAKIUTL
CHILCOTIN
SHUSWAP
SARSI
KAIGANI (BLOOD)
CREE
NOOTKA
MONTAGNAIS
NASKAPI
BEOTHUK
SALISH
KUTENAI
SIKSIKA (BLACKFOOT)
PLAINS CREE
MICMAC
PUYALLUP
SPOKANE
COUER D'ALENE
ASSINIBOIN
OJIBWA
ALGONQUIN
FLATHEAD
OJIBWA (CHIPPEWA)
ABNAKI
PASSAMAQUODDY
CHINOOK
COOS
YAKIMA
NEZ PERCÉ
CAYUSE
CROW
HIDATSA
MANDAN
TILLAMOOK
KLAMATH
MENOMINEE
OTTAWA
HURON
MOHAWK
MOHICAN
PENOBSCOT
ONONDAGA
PENNACOOK
SHOSHONI-BANNOCK
TETON DAKOTA
SANTEE DAKOTA
CAYUGA
YUROK
YUKI
MODOC
NORTH PAIUTE
NORTH CHEYENNE
SAUK
FOX
POTAWATOMI
SENECA
MAHICAN
MASSACHUSET
ONEIDA
SIOUX
YANKTON DAKOTA
KICKAPOO
NARRAGANSET
PEQUOT
HUPA
POMO
MAIDU
MIWOK
OMAHA
PAWNEE
IOWA
SUSQUEHANNA
ERIE
DELAWARE
MIAMI
UTE
ARAPAHO
OTO
KANSA
ILLINOIS
NANTICOKE
MISSOURI
PAMUNKEY
POWHATAN
CHICKAHOMINY
MATTAPONY
SOUTH PAIUTE
PUEBLO
SOUTH CHEYENNE
SHAWNEE
SALINAN
CHUMASH
HOPI
MOHAVE
NAVAHO
JICARILLA APACHE
KIOWA
OSAGE
TUTELO
HAVASUPAI
ZUÑI
CHEROKEE
PAMLICO
QUAPAW
CATAWBA
CAHUILLA
YUMA
APACHE
WICHITA
CHICKASAW
CREEK
HICHITI
MARICOPA
PAPAGO
PIMA
COMANCHE
CADDO
ALABAMA
MESCALERO APACHE
CHOCTAW
OPATA
WACO
NATCHEZ
BILOXI
APALACHEE
SERI
LIPAN
CHITIMACHA
TIMUCUA
ATAKAPA
KARANKAWA
YAQUI
CONCHO
SEMINOLE
CALUSA
TARAHUMARA
COAHUILTEC
WAICURI
TAMAULIPEC
PERICU
ACAXEE
HUICHOL
TOLTEC
HUASTEC
TLAXCALAN
TOTONAC
YUCATAN MAYA
TARASCAN
AZTEC
MIXTEC
ZAPOTEC
QUICHE MAYA
0
1000 Kilometers

Light from the smokeholes shows where families would build their fires in this Huron longhouse. Many families of one clan lived in a longhouse. Each family had space near its own fire.

Many Indian tribes lived in tepees. A tepee is a tent made of hides stretched over a framework of poles. An opening at the top lets out smoke from the fire in the center. Tepees are warm in winter and cool in summer.

Other Indians moved from place to place. They depended upon fishing, hunting, and gathering for their food.

Among the Indians there may have been as many as a thousand different tribes. Some tribes had only a dozen members. Others numbered many hundreds. In certain tribes men or women could be named chiefs. Those chiefs enjoyed great powers. But in other tribes there were no chiefs. Decisions were made by voting.

Not only were there many tribes, but Indians also spoke many languages. Experts say the Indians of North America spoke at least 600 languages. Indians, therefore, often did not understand those from other tribes. That was especially true in California, where every tribe had its own language.

Women had special importance in some tribes. Among the Iroquois the women owned the longhouses, garden plots, and the tools used to farm them. They were responsible for peace and order in the longhouses. When a divorce took place, it was the woman who kept the children. When a mother died, her property went to her daughters, not to her sons. So powerful were women among the Iroquois that they appointed the chiefs.

5. In what ways did Indian tribes differ from one another?

There is rich variety in the Indian tribes of North America. The woman above was an Apache. Her photo was made in 1906.

Sitting Bull (above) was one of the last great chiefs of the Sioux. The moccasins (below) were made by Arikara Indians.

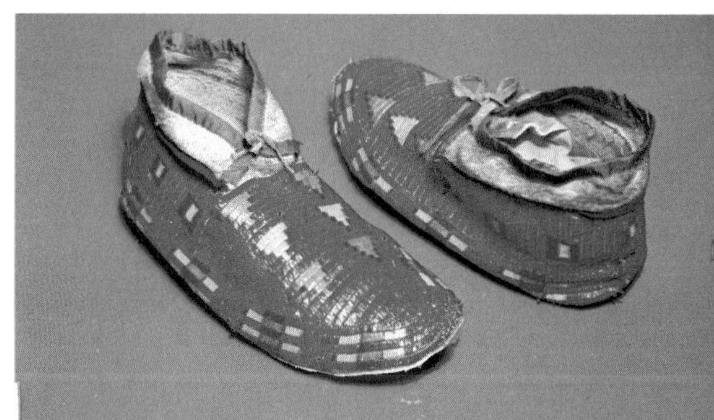

Pouches like the one below were decorated with moose hair by young Huron girls. The fringe was made from deer hair. The couple on the right are Tlingit Indians from the Pacific Northwest. They are wearing ceremonial costumes and holding a painting of the Thunderbird.

How did Indians feel about the land?

Indians valued the land. To them the earth was very special. It was sacred. When Indians talked of the land, they sometimes described it as "Beloved Mother" or "Kindly Great-Grandfather."

Indians never spoke of land as "yours" or "mine." They believed everyone should be able to use land. But no one should own it. That did not mean that one tribe would not drive another from its hunting grounds. They often did. But when a tribe moved away, the land was open to others to use. The tribe no longer claimed it.

Much of the trouble between Indians and the European settlers arose over the issue of land. Europeans who came to America were used to buying and selling land. They felt that a person could own land. They also believed that an owner could do whatever he or she pleased with that land. To Indians those ideas were unthinkable.

6. Describe the Indian attitude toward the land.

7. Why did quarrels about land often break out between Indians and Europeans?

Part Two

Setting the Stage for Exploration

Who were the first Europeans to discover America?

No one is really sure just when the first Asians reached North America. Neither is anyone sure when the first Europeans arrived. There is reason to believe that the Irish may have been first. But when or where they landed is uncertain. More is known about the coming of the Norse. *Norse* is the name by which people from Norway, Sweden, and Denmark once were known.

Leif Ericsson was a Norseman. He may have been the first European to discover America. He made the voyage about A.D. 1000, or almost one thousand years ago.

The Norse were great sailors. Men, women, children—and even their dogs—climbed into small, open boats

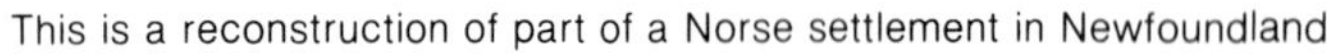
This is a reconstruction of part of a Norse settlement in Newfoundland

and set out across the seas. Those boats were propelled by oars and sails. They offered no protection from sun, wind, or rain. It was in such a small ship that Leif Ericsson came to America. He landed first near Labrador. Later he sailed south along the coast to Newfoundland. There he and his followers built a settlement. Remains of that settlement recently have been unearthed. (See photo, page 10.)

Some Norse tried to make their homes in Vinland, as Leif called the land he had discovered. But the Indians who lived there did not want them. Again and again the Indians attacked the settlers. After several years, they were able to drive the Norse away. Thus the Indians were left for another 500 years to enjoy the continent they first had found. You will read more about the Norse on pages 12-13.

1. When did Leif Ericsson discover America?

2. Why did the Norse leave Vinland?

What was Europe like one thousand years ago?

In Leif Ericsson's time there were no strong nations or governments in Europe, such as there are today. As a result, there was very little law or order. Police and law courts were few indeed. Robbers roamed through town and country, making travel dangerous.

Most Europeans in A.D. 1000 were farmers. They looked to rich landholders called nobles for protection. The nobles lived in castles surrounded by huge walls. Just outside the walls lived the farmers.

Fighting between the nobles was common. A noble would gather his knights around him and raid his neighbor's castle. When the farmers saw the attackers coming, they would run inside the walls. The raiders would burn down the farms and try to capture the castle. Life in those lawless times was hard for everyone, especially for the serfs. Unlike free farmers who owned their lands, serfs were men and women "bound to the soil." They were bought and sold with the land on which they were born. In exchange for protection in time of attack, the serfs had to give up their freedom and most of the crops they worked to produce.

Peasants work in the fields outside the walls of a beautiful medieval castle.

At That Time

The coast of Newfoundland was a welcome sight to the Norse explorers after their long trip across the Atlantic. The fish, berries, and wild wheat which the Norse found there were also welcome after days at sea.

Eric the Red, Leif the Lucky, Freydis the Fearless. Father, son, and daughter of the Norse family Ericsson. They were born in what today is Norway. But in their time the peoples of Scandinavia (Norway, Sweden, and Denmark) all called themselves *Norse*. Many Norse were seafarers. But few sailed as far from home as the Ericssons. Members of that family made the long, dangerous journey to America several times 500 years before Columbus.

The story of the Ericssons really begins with the father, Eric. He was called "the Red" because of the color of his hair. But he had a hot temper as well. Eric left Norway to escape punishment for accidentally killing someone. He went to live in Iceland. There he again got into trouble, so he left to go exploring. Sailing west, Eric found the world's largest island. He named it *Greenland* because he found a few grassy valleys amid that land of ice and snow. The next summer he returned to Iceland. He persuaded twelve or fifteen shiploads of people to return with him to Greenland and settle there.

One day an old sailor stopped to see Eric. He told him of land he had seen still farther west. It was "flat and wooded" country with no icy mountains. Eric listened carefully. He decided to look for that land, so he went back to Norway to get help. When he arrived, he learned that his son, Leif, had the same idea. In fact, Leif had already bought a *knarr*, or small, open boat. He had signed on a crew. Everything was ready. But on the day they sailed, Eric was thrown from his horse and had to stay home.

When he set out from Norway, Leif was a big, strapping fellow in his early twenties. He and his crew crossed the Atlantic in the summer of the year 1001. They visited several islands off the coast of Canada. Then they landed on Newfoundland. They built large houses with great fire pits and steam baths. There they spent a wonderful winter. The climate then was not nearly as cold as it is today. Salmon and halibut were plentiful. Some say the party even found grapes, or "vin," but that is doubtful.

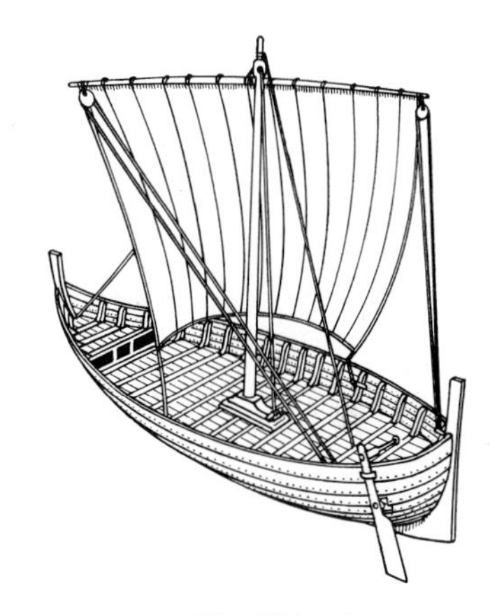

The Viking *knarr* was a sturdy craft used for long trips.

When the winter was over, Leif sailed home. He wanted to spread news of the wonderful land he had found. En route he rescued fifteen shipwrecked sailors stranded on a reef. This rescue earned him the nickname "the Lucky."

Despite tales of plenty, there was no great rush to go to "Vinland," as Leif called the land he had found. A journey across the north Atlantic in a small, open boat with only the stars to steer by was not for everyone. But Leif's brother, Thorvald, was eager to go. So, too, was his half-sister, Freydis. Together with 250 men and women they put to sea in three ships.

All might have been well if the Norse had been friendly with the people they found living in Vinland. Those people probably were either Indians or Eskimos, but the Norse called them "Skrellings." Time and again the Norse fought the Skrellings. In one pitched battle Freydis saved the day for the Norse. When it looked as though the men would retreat, Freydis took charge. She slapped some of them with her sword to make them return to battle. She screamed at the top of her lungs. The Skrellings were so startled that they broke off the attack. But it wasn't long before they were back in even greater numbers.

Realizing that they were few while the Skrellings were many, the Norse went home after a few years.

3. Why was life so hard for the serfs in A.D. 1000?

4. How did the nobles live?

What were the Crusades?

A series of religious wars called the *Crusades* helped Europe to recover from its period of lawlessness. In 1095 the Pope called on all Europeans to unite and march east to Asia to fight the Muslims. The Muslims controlled Christian holy places in the Middle East. To regain Jerusalem and other holy places, Europeans from many lands fought side by side.

The Crusades were failures as military campaigns. The Crusaders lost most of the battles. But they learned much from their experiences. The Easterners were better educated and more advanced than most Europeans. In the East there were beautiful cities where people lived happily and in peace. The eyes of the Crusaders opened wide at the new products and ideas they met.

5. What did the Crusaders learn in the East?

Where were the riches of the East?

The peoples of Asia traded with each other. Arab merchants traveled by ship, or overland by camel, to the Far East. In China, India, and the East Indies, they traded for spices, gold, silk, and fine cloth. Spices were important because they preserved food and made it taste better. In those days there were no refrigerators to keep food fresh.

When they saw oriental jewels and spices, Europeans decided they must get some for themselves. But these articles came from far away. Thousands of miles of ocean, deserts, and mountains separated Europe from the Far East. The

European merchants buy Oriental goods from Arab traders. The goods are being loaded on a ship for the long trip to Italy.

cost of carrying goods such distances was very high. Robbers and pirates often attacked the merchants who were trying to bring their precious goods to market.

6. From what countries of Asia did gold, silk, spices, and fine cloth come?

7. Why were Eastern goods expensive?

What changes took place in Europe after the Crusades?

The Europeans were not successful in the Crusades. After years of fighting, the Muslims still held Jerusalem. But the Europeans did learn a lot from their experiences. One thing they learned was that they wanted to trade with the East. To do this, they realized that they would have to bring law and order to their own lands. Some way would have to be found to make the nobles stop warring with one another.

Because they had the most to gain from trade with the East, merchants took the lead. When the Crusades were over, they refused to live inside castle walls.

Instead they moved to cities. They supported leaders who wanted to become kings. They insisted that everyone, including the nobles, obey the king. After gunpowder came into use about 1400, it was easier to force nobles to accept the king's authority. The king's armies could batter down castle walls with gunpowder.

As free farmers and serfs heard how much freer and better life was in the cities, they, too, began to move away from the castles. In the cities they found jobs making goods that could be traded for products from the East.

Over the years the power of the nobles decreased. The power of the merchants and the kings increased. Finally unified kingdoms such as France, England, and Spain came into being.

8. Why did European merchants support kings?

9. Why did free farmers and serfs move to the cities?

What was the effect of the printing press?

Printing was brought from China into Europe around 1450. Until this

Marco Polo leaves Venice on his journey to China in 1271. Polo spent seventeen years in China. When his story of his adventures was printed two centuries after his trip, it stirred European interest in trade with the East.

This Italian mariner's compass is the oldest known compass in the world. The invention of the compass made possible long voyages out of sight of land. The basic design of the compass is still the same today as it was in the 15th century when this compass was made.

time, books had to be copied by hand. So there were very few books—and very few readers. With the invention of the printing press, books became more plentiful and therefore cheaper. More people read the books and learned about the world around them.

The sails of a caravel could be moved to catch the wind.

Marco Polo wrote a very popular book. He was an Italian who had traveled all the way to China as a young man. He stayed there many years. Then Marco Polo returned with a fortune in gold and goods. The book he wrote about his adventures had an amazing effect. It made the people of Europe more eager than ever to obtain jewels and spices from the East.

10. How did the invention of printing affect reading?

11. Who was Marco Polo?

What conditions made longer voyages possible?

The growth of strong kingdoms restored law and order in Europe. Citizens obeyed their governments and were proud of their homelands. Money poured into the national treasuries. With some of this money, the kings sent out ships to explore unknown oceans.

Some new inventions helped explorers find their way. One of the most important was the compass. Until it came into use, sailors stayed close to land to avoid becoming lost. But with the compass, long voyages far from the sight of land became possible. A compass looks something like a watch. Instead of hands, however, it has a single needle. And instead of numbers, it has the directions north, east, south, and west on its dial.

Another important invention came from the Portuguese. They invented a new kind of ship. They called it the *caravel* (kar′ ə vel). It was built to sail at an angle or as close to the wind as a modern racing boat. Its sails filled, but they did not shake. Sailing close to the wind was important for making long journeys, because fair winds could not always be counted upon.

Each of those inventions was important. So, too, were the better maps and charts which the explorers were able to make. Taken together, all of those things made sailors more willing to venture far from home. The sailors felt there was less to fear.

12. What did kings do to encourage longer journeys?

13. How did new inventions reduce sailors' fears of the unknown?

Part Three

Finding and Naming America

Why did Europeans want a sea route to Asia?

Some Europeans traveled overland to Asia. But traveling by land was costly and dangerous. They hoped, therefore, to find a sea route. One ship could bring back a larger load than many pack animals—and with less cost and danger.

The Portuguese sent out many explorers in the effort to find a sea route to the Far East. Those explorers sailed south along the long coast of Africa. Then they turned east in the hope of finding India. But not until 1498 did one of them succeed. Vasco da Gama reached India in that year. His trip took almost two years. To get to India and return, he had to sail 24,000 miles (38,400 km).

Could a faster, shorter route to the Far East be found? An Italian navigator named Christopher Columbus thought so. He had a plan. He tried to interest others in his plan years before da Gama sailed for India. First he tried to interest the king of Portugal. The king and his advisers listened politely. But in the end they refused to furnish Columbus the ships and sailors he would need for the journey. Discouraged, Columbus left for Spain.

1. Who was the first European to sail around the coast of Africa?

2. Who thought he had a better plan for reaching the Far East?

What was Columbus's plan?

After the king of Portugal turned him down, Columbus went to Spain. There he hoped to interest King Ferdinand and Queen Isabella in his plan.

Ferdinand and Isabella were co-rulers. Isabella was the daughter of the king of Castile. She was a queen in her own right before she married Ferdinand of Aragon and they began their joint rule of Spain. So Isabella had power and wealth more than equal to that of her husband.

The king and queen listened politely to Columbus. But they decided they were too busy at the time. They had a war on their hands. Until it was settled, they could not consider Columbus's request. Besides, some of their advisers did not think Columbus's plan would work.

What Columbus proposed to do was to sail west in order to get to the Far East. If, as he believed, the world was round, he could reach Japan by sailing west. Perhaps he could, the king and queen's advisers agreed. But, they argued, the earth was much larger than Columbus believed it to be. And as it turned out, the advisers were right. But while arguments about the size of the earth went on, no one even suspected that the Americas lay between Europe and the Far East. They did not know that a whole "new world"—the Americas—would bar the way.

Discouraged after years of trying to get help from the Spanish, Columbus and his son, Diego, were ready to go to France. In fact they were on their way when a messenger from the queen overtook them. The messenger had good news. First, the war was over. Second, Queen Isabella had decided at last to help Columbus.

3. Why did Columbus think that he could sail west to the Far East?

This is a reproduction—with some modern spellings added—of the map which Columbus probably used in his voyage to the New World. It is called the Toscanelli map after the person who made it.

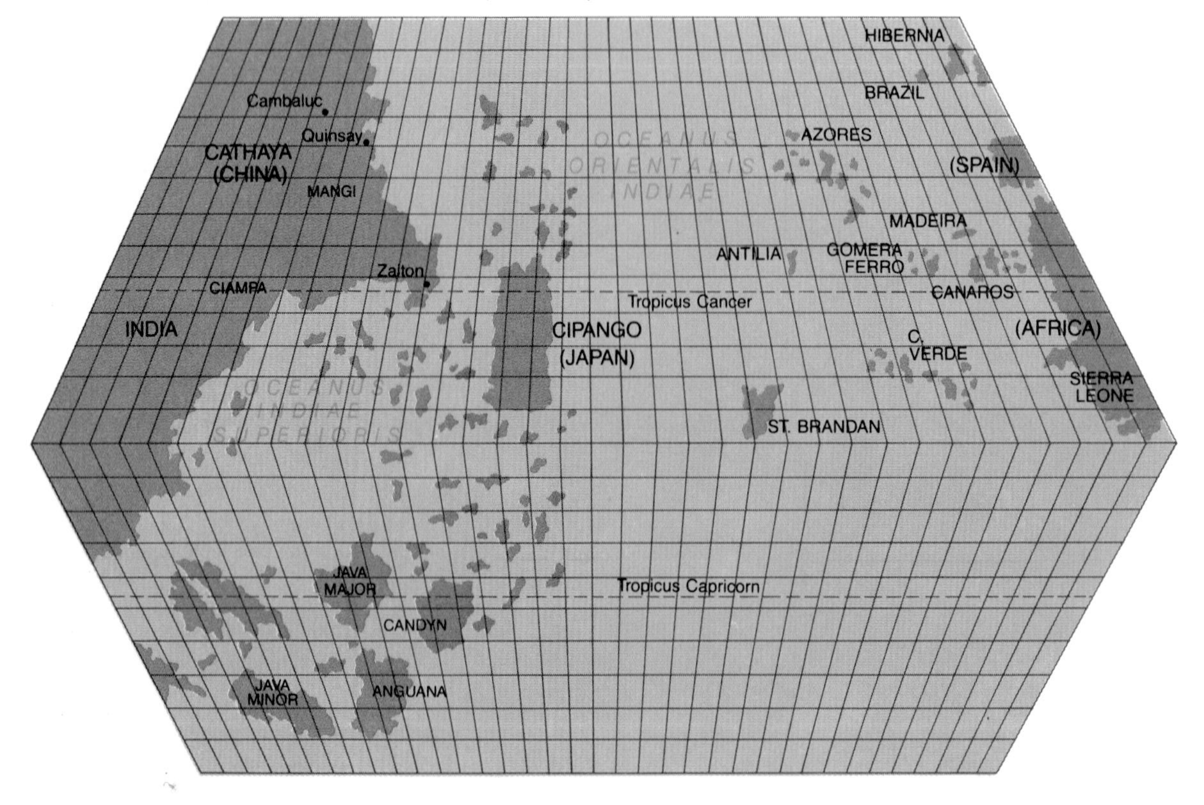

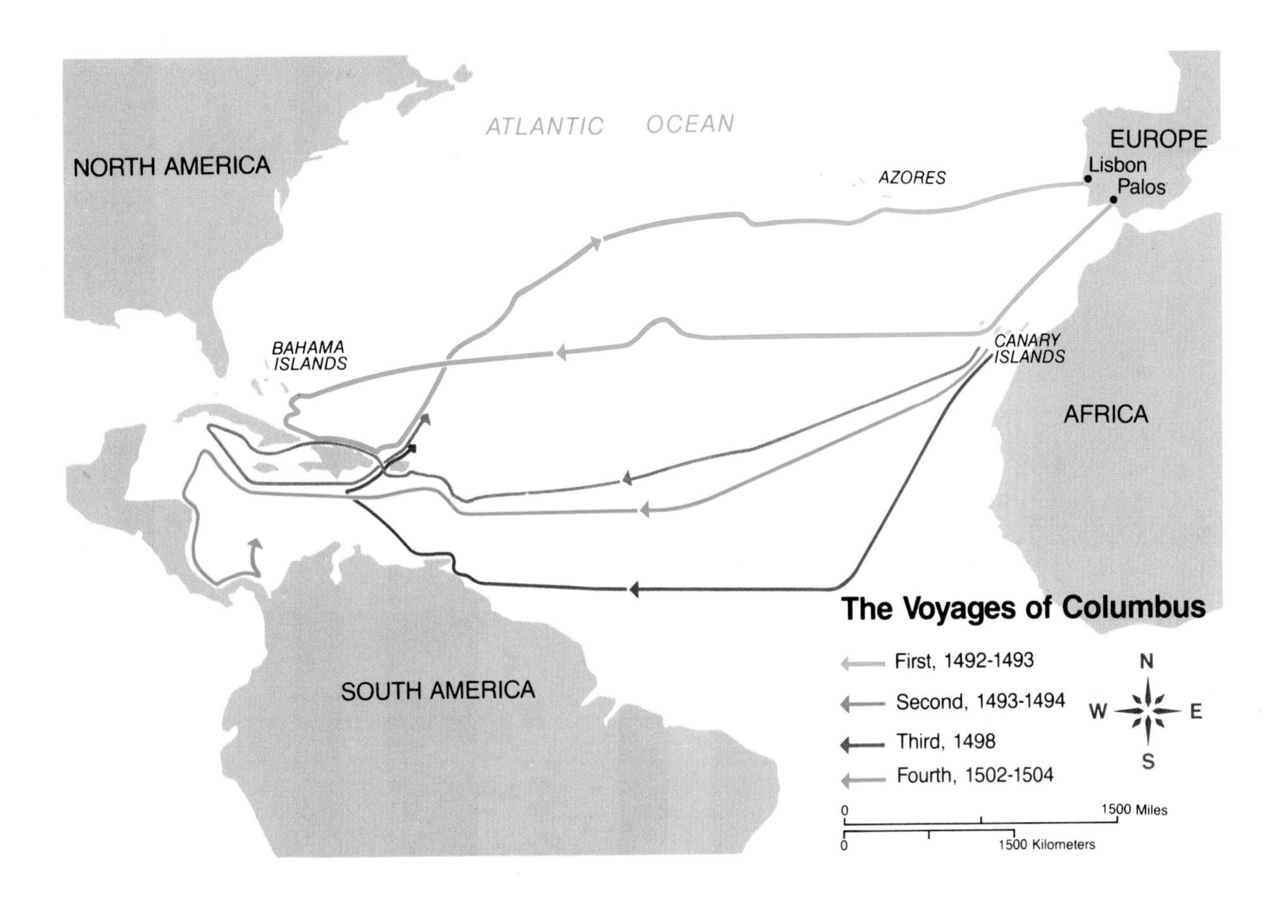

4. Why did Columbus and the king and queen's advisers argue? Who was right?

Who made the most important sea voyage in history?

Early in the morning of August 3, 1492, three small ships slipped out of the harbor at Palos, Spain. On the deck of the flagship, the *Santa Maria*, was the Captain General, Christopher Columbus. In the wake of the *Santa Maria* came two smaller ships, the *Pinta* and the *Niña*. There were 90 men in the party. They had started on what is said to have been the most important sea voyage in history.

Columbus was happy and full of confidence. The king and queen of Spain had promised to name him Admiral of the Ocean Sea when he returned. They also had promised him 10 percent of all the gold, silver, and jewels he brought back. They had even given him a letter of introduction. It was addressed to the "Grand Khan," the ruler of China. Columbus did not doubt that he would meet the Khan. He expected to be in Asia in a relatively short time. Columbus thought Asia was only about 2400 miles (3840 km) from Spain. He knew his ships could average about 140 miles (224 km) per day. So he thought the voyage would take about seventeen or eighteen days.

But the days at sea stretched into weeks. Columbus was mistaken. The world was larger than he had thought.

As weeks passed, the crew grew more worried. Several times the sailors

Historymaker

As the three ships of Columbus's fleet plowed through the seas, the *Pinta* took the lead. On the bow was a young lookout, Rodrigo de Traina. He thought the night had seemed unusually long. Gratefully he turned the fourth hourglass of his watch. He watched its sands trickle slowly down through the narrow neck. All was quiet, and he felt very alone. Then suddenly at 2 A.M., he was startled by some brightness ahead. He was sure it was a white cliff shining in the moonlight.

"Tierra! Tierra!" (Land! Land!), Rodrigo cried out excitedly.

Captain Martín Alonzo Pinzón stumbled out of his quarters. He wanted to make sure of this sighting for himself. There had been too many false reports on this long voyage. The crew was in an ugly mood, and this

This is the earliest known portrait of Columbus.

urged Columbus to turn around and head for home. Each time he encouraged them to keep going. Land was just ahead, he said. In an effort to show how sure he was, Columbus offered a prize to the first person to sight land. But not until their 69th day at sea did land come into view. And it was none too soon. By then the crew had threatened to seize the ship and sail back to Spain.

When Columbus stepped ashore on October 12, 1492, he thought he had found Asia. He was still many thousands of miles away from his goal, however. Instead he had landed in the Bahama Islands. Thinking that he had reached the East Indies, Columbus named the people who came to greet him "Indians."

5. Why did the sailors become worried during the voyage?

6. Why is Columbus's voyage called the most important sea journey in history? Do you think it was?

was not the time to arouse more false hopes. This time, however, the sighting was correct. Pinzón promptly fired the shot agreed upon as a signal for the good news.

Christopher Columbus heard the shot as he lay in his bunk on the flagship, *Santa Maria*. A special feeling came over him. He knew this day—October 12, 1492—would be an extraordinary one. It was the day for which he had worked for so many years. But even Columbus had no way of knowing that what was about to happen would change all of history.

It was still dark when the Captain General rose. (Columbus had not yet been named Admiral of the Ocean Sea.) He began to dress with great care. He wanted his appearance to be equal to the occasion. Columbus donned his finest red velvet coat. He decided to carry the royal flag of Spain in his hand. He would ask his seconds-in-command, the brothers Martín and Vicente Pinzón, to carry the ship's banner.

Properly dressed, Columbus proceeded to the bow of his flagship. He knew how eager the crew was to go ashore after weeks at sea. But Columbus had an actor's sense of timing. "Better to wait until the right moment," he said to himself. So he ordered his ships to sail back and forth outside the barrier reef.

From his vantage point, Columbus watched as people gathered on the shore of the island. It was a small island. He would call it San Salvador (Christ the Savior).

For hours the gentle Arawaks who gathered on the shore remained there. They gazed in wonder at the fleet of three ships in full sail off the coast of their homeland. Later Columbus was to write that the people he met were "very well made with very handsome bodies and good countenances [faces]."

It was just about noon before the Captain General decided that the right moment had come. Then, solemnly, thankfully, and with tears of joy glistening in his eyes, Columbus went ashore. Certain that he had arrived in the Indies, Columbus called the natives he met "Indos," or Indians.

That meeting was the first of many fateful encounters between Native Americans and Europeans. In all of history there is nothing to compare with the dramatic meetings between peoples of different cultures which have taken place time and time again in the Americas.

How did America get its name?

Since Columbus discovered a "new world," one would think that it would be named in his honor. But this did not happen for two reasons:

First, Columbus did not realize that he had touched on a New World. Only on his deathbed did he speak of finding "An Other World."

Second, Columbus was not popular in his later years. He died a despised and neglected man.

After his first voyage, Columbus returned to a hero's welcome. The king and queen of Spain declared a holiday in his honor. People lined the streets to cheer him. They gazed in wonder at the Indians he had brought back. They were amazed at the strange birds, fruits, and vegetables he had collected. Although they were disappointed that he had not come home with gold and spices, not much was said. Everyone was sure he would find riches on the next trip.

Columbus had no trouble getting help for a second trip. In fact, he returned to America with 17 ships and 1200 men. Many were settlers who intended to make their homes in "the Indies." Some were missionaries who went to teach Christianity to the Indians.

But things did not go well for Columbus and the settlement he tried to start. He proved to be a better sailor than a governor. He wanted the settlers to work. The soil was excellent. Food crops could be grown easily in a matter of weeks. But the Spanish had not come to grow crops or to trade fairly with the Indians. Most of them had come to find gold. But there was little gold to be found. So the settlers demanded gold from the Indians. The Spanish threatened the Indians at gunpoint. Some settlers stole whatever they wanted of the Indians' belongings. In a vain attempt to stop fighting between the Spanish and the Indians, Columbus required each native to bring a gold tribute. This was more than the natives could do because gold was rare. Next he divided up the land and the Indians who lived on it among the colonists. The Indians were forced to work for the benefit of the Spanish. Natives who refused were killed or shipped to Spain to be sold as slaves. News of the bad things which were happening reached the rulers of Spain. They were very disturbed. When Columbus returned to Spain in 1496, he got a polite but cool reception.

Columbus himself was very unhappy about the way things were turning out. Nevertheless, he tried to organize a third voyage.

But this time people were less willing to go. Some poor farmers signed on for the journey. So did draftees from the army and laborers who were promised wages of 14 cents per day. A few women and girls also decided to go along. They had to work for their passage. Still there were not enough people to fill Columbus's three ships. So a pardon was offered to criminals who would spend a year in "the Indies." Few of them took the offer, however.

Things went no better after Columbus returned to the New World for the third time. Some unhappy settlers returned to Spain. Others wrote letters complaining about the way Columbus and his two brothers treated them. Finally the rulers of Spain decided to send an official to look into their complaints. The official sent all three of the Columbus brothers home in chains.

For six weeks after his return, Columbus was kept in chains waiting to be heard in court. At last he was given a chance to present his side of the story. Many people turned against him. But Queen Isabella did not. She agreed that he should make a fourth voyage in 1498. This time he was to sail farther south. Ferdinand and Isabella wanted to be sure that he got to Asia. Columbus sailed along the coast of Central America as far south as Panama. Then, in 1504, he had to return to Spain in deep disappointment. He was 53 years old, an old man for those times.

Never again did Columbus return to the Americas. He spent his last two years in poor health. Those years were saddened by the death of Isabella in 1504. She had understood what he was trying to do. She had protected him against his enemies.

Columbus died on May 19, 1506, without realizing how much he really had accomplished.

If Columbus was ignorant of what he had done, others were not. Amerigo

Amerigo Vespucci, for whom America was named, made two trips to the New World. He wrote a vivid story about what he saw.

Vespucci (ve spü′ chē), another Italian sailing for Spain, claimed to have made some discoveries in the two Americas. What is more, he said that he had found a "new world," not the Indies. He published his claims in a booklet which he called *Mundis Novis*, which is Latin for "New World."

Amerigo's booklet happened to fall into the hands of a German mapmaker in 1512. He had been trying to think of a name for the two "new" continents. "Why not call them 'America' for Amerigo?" he said to himself. And that is the name by which they have been known ever since.

7. Why weren't the Americas named in honor of Columbus?

8. Why was the New World named for Amerigo Vespucci?

Part Four

Exploring the Americas

Which country took the lead in exploring the Americas?

Columbus did not succeed in finding a route through the Americas to the Far East. Europeans, however, were sure that there was one. They spent 150 years looking for it. Spain, the strongest nation in Europe, took the lead in exploring the New World.

Most of the early explorers, therefore, were Spaniards. Among them were a considerable number of black men who had moved to Spain from Africa.

The explorers looked for gold as well as for a water route across the Americas. When they came to the New World, they brought along their horses and donkeys. They often took cattle and pigs along, too, to use as food. Many of these animals escaped to form the wild herds later found on the western plains and in the southern forests of North America.

1. Why did Spain take the lead in exploring the Americas?

2. What two things were the early explorers looking for?

How did the Indians and the Spanish get along?

At first the Indians the Spanish met were friendly. But in time they came to fear and distrust the Spanish.

The Indians had good reason to fear the newcomers. Using guns, which the Indians had never seen before, the Spanish killed thousands of Indians. The

High up on the sheer wall of Canyon del Muerto in present-day Arizona, a Navaho artist made this pictograph of the coming of the Spanish.

Spanish captured other Indians and worked them to death as slaves. So cruel were the Spanish conquistadores (kon kwis′ tə dôr′ ēz), or conquerors, that some of their own priests cried out against them. One priest, Bartolomé de las Casas, worked among the Indians for fifty years. Finally he wrote a small but powerful book, *The Tears of the Indians*. In it he told of Indian suffering caused by the conquistadores. He appealed to the conscience of the world, but few people responded.

Life in the Americas was difficult for the Spanish explorers. They were far from home in a strange, new land. They had to leave their families behind. Daily they faced many kinds of dangers. The Indians greatly outnumbered them, and the Spaniards feared attack. Many died of disease and starvation.

Despite their problems, the Spanish rolled up a remarkable record. Within fifty years of Columbus's landing, they

Bartolomé de las Casas came to the New World as a planter. He became the first priest ordained in the Spanish colonies, and spent the rest of his life working to help the Indians.

had explored all the western coastline of the New World south of present-day Canada. They also had explored all of the eastern coastline south of Labrador. And they had mapped much of the interior as well. (See map, page 26.)

3. Why did the Indians come to fear and distrust the Spanish?

4. What kind of a record as explorers did the Spanish make?

Who were some of the most famous Spanish explorers?

1. Ponce de León (pons′ də lē′ ən) conquered Puerto Rico and became its governor. Indians there told him about a "fountain of youth" to the north. The Indians said that people who drank from this fountain regained their youth.

Juan Ponce de León, then 53 years old, hunted for the "fountain of youth." While doing so, he discovered and named Florida in 1513. But he never found the magic fountain.

2. Cortés (kôr tez′) was the greatest conqueror of them all. He heard that the land we now call Mexico was rich in gold and silver. With an army of 500 men, Hernando Cortés set out from Cuba in 1519 to conquer Mexico.

Mexico was ruled by the Aztec emperor. An Aztec belief helped Cortés. The Aztecs believed that, centuries before, a "light-skinned god" had lived among them. This god had gone away, but had promised to return some day to rule them. Could the white man Cortés be this "fair god"?

The ruler of the Aztecs was named Montezuma (mon′ tə zü′ mə). He lived in the capital city, a splendid place high in the mountains. The city was built on an island in a lake. Causeways connected the island with the mainland.

Cortés led his men into the island capital. Montezuma was not sure how to treat his godlike visitor. Cortés seized the chance to take Montezuma prisoner.

Later the Aztecs attacked the Spaniards furiously. Many men were killed on both sides, but Cortés finally won the struggle with his better weapons. In Mexico the Spanish conquerors gained treasures for Spain that matched those found by the Portuguese in the Far East. And Mexico became a Spanish colony.

3. De Soto. We know today that there was much gold and silver within the borders of the United States. But when Spanish explorers came looking for it more than 400 years ago, they could not find it.

Take Hernando de Soto, for instance. In 1539 this handsome and swaggering young conqueror was already rich. But he wanted still more gold and more adventure. So he bought ships and hired soldiers and sailed to Florida.

For months on end, de Soto and his men wandered through the present states of Florida, Georgia, the Carolinas, Tennessee, Alabama, and Mississippi. They did not find gold. But they did meet Indians who fought bravely against them.

In 1541, de Soto discovered North America's greatest river, the Mississippi. The Spaniards described the river as "of great depth" with "a strong current." Also, they said, "the water was always muddy, and timber and trees were continually flowing down."

A year later de Soto was no longer a handsome, confident conqueror. Instead, he was sick and discouraged from his long journey. He died in 1542, and his men buried him secretly in the Mississippi so that the Indians would not

HUDSON BAY
LABRADOR
NORTH AMERICA
NEWFOUNDLAND
ROCKY MOUNTAINS
GREAT LAKES
Missouri R.
Colorado R.
Ohio R.
Mississippi R.
Arkansas R.
GRAND CANYON
Santa Fe
Red R.
De Soto
ATLANTIC OCEAN
Coronado
Father Marcos-Estevanico
Rio Grande
St. Augustine
FLORIDA
Ponce de León
GULF OF MEXICO
AZTECS
Cortés
CUBA
Tenochtitlán (Mexico City)
Veracruz
HISPANIOLA
PUERTO RICO
CENTRAL AMERICA
CARIBBEAN SEA
PACIFIC OCEAN
N
W
E
S
Balboa
PANAMA
Early Spanish Explorations
Balboa 1513
Ponce de León 1513
Cortés 1519
Pizarro 1531-1533
Father Marcos-Estevanico 1535-1536
Coronado 1540-1542
De Soto 1539-1542
0
1500 Miles
0
1500 Kilometers
Amazon R.
INCAS
SOUTH AMERICA
Pizarro
Cuzco

Can you see why Father Marcos and Estevanico might have thought they were seeing cities of gold?

find his grave. De Soto's men then floated down the river on rafts. They finally reached safety in Mexico.

5. What area did Cortés conquer for Spain?
6. What great river did de Soto discover? In what year?

4. Pizarro (pi zär′ ō). In 1531 Francisco Pizarro, a hardhearted conquistador who could neither read nor write, led a small army into what is now the South American country of Peru. (See map, page 26.) Home of the Inca Indians, Peru was rich and civilized. The Incas welcomed the Spanish visitors into their midst. And, once again, the Spaniards struck first, taking the young Incan ruler prisoner.

Pizarro sent out an order to the people of Peru. He told them that he was keeping their emperor in a room. The Incas must fill this room with gold and silver, or their leader would be killed. From all over Peru, people came to the room with gold and jewels. Finally the room was filled with treasure.

Instead of letting the emperor go, Pizarro broke his promise. He had the emperor killed anyway, then took over Peru himself. The lawless and dishonest Pizarro was murdered a few years later. But the Spaniards held on to Peru for another 300 years.

5. Father Marcos, Estevanico (ās tā vän′ ē kō), and **Coronado**. North of Mexico, the Indians told the Spanish, lay the golden cities of Cibola (sē bol′ ə). Undreamed-of riches lay there for the taking. The Spaniards sent out a scouting party to look for the "golden cities."

Two of the party's leaders were Father Marcos, a Catholic priest, and Estevanico (Little Stephen), a black scout. Estevanico and Father Marcos pushed northward into what is now New Mexico.

For centuries Indians in the Southwest had lived in villages. Their homes were made of clay, sand, and stone. When the priest and the scout first saw one of these villages, they became very excited. Here were cities of gold! Perhaps the sunlight shone on the houses in such a way that they looked golden.

Under instructions from Father Marcos, Estevanico led an advance party toward Cibola. He dressed as an Indian medicine man. With him were two greyhound dogs and some friendly Indians. From time to time he sent back crosses to Father Marcos to show his progress. The larger the crosses, the closer Estevanico was to his goal.

When a signal in the form of a very large cross arrived, Father Marcos was overjoyed. Estevanico must have arrived at Cibola. But as time passed and no more crosses came, the priest became worried. What had happened?

Later an Indian who had been with Estevanico told Father Marcos the story. The party had been attacked, and "Little Stephen" had been killed by enemy Indians near Cibola.

Father Marcos returned to Mexico to make his report. Unfortunately the report glowed like gold. As a result, the Spanish sent another large army northward into what is now our United States.

The commander of that expedition was named Coronado. Unhappily he found no gold, but his men discovered the Grand Canyon and pushed all the way into present-day Kansas. (See map, page 26.)

Coronado was branded a failure. Yet he had really done very well for his king. The whole area west of the Mississippi River was claimed by Spain.

7. Who conquered Peru for the Spanish?

8. What were Father Marcos and Estevanico looking for?

9. What did Coronado do for the king of Spain?

Part Five

Discovering the Pacific

Who discovered the Pacific Ocean?

Balboa (bal bō′ə) was a Spaniard who stowed away on a ship sailing from Hispaniola to South America. (See map, page 26.) Hiding with him in a barrel was his dog, a bloodhound named Leoncico (lē ôn′ sē kō).

The ship carrying Balboa was wrecked near the coast of South America. He and his faithful dog swam safely to shore with the rest of the crew.

Balboa was a stowaway, but he was also a leader. The shipwrecked sailors looked to Balboa for help and advice. He had visited these shores before and knew the countryside.

A narrow strip of land called Panama connects the continents of North America and South America. To the east of the strip lies the Atlantic Ocean. West of Panama is the Pacific Ocean. (See map, page 26.)

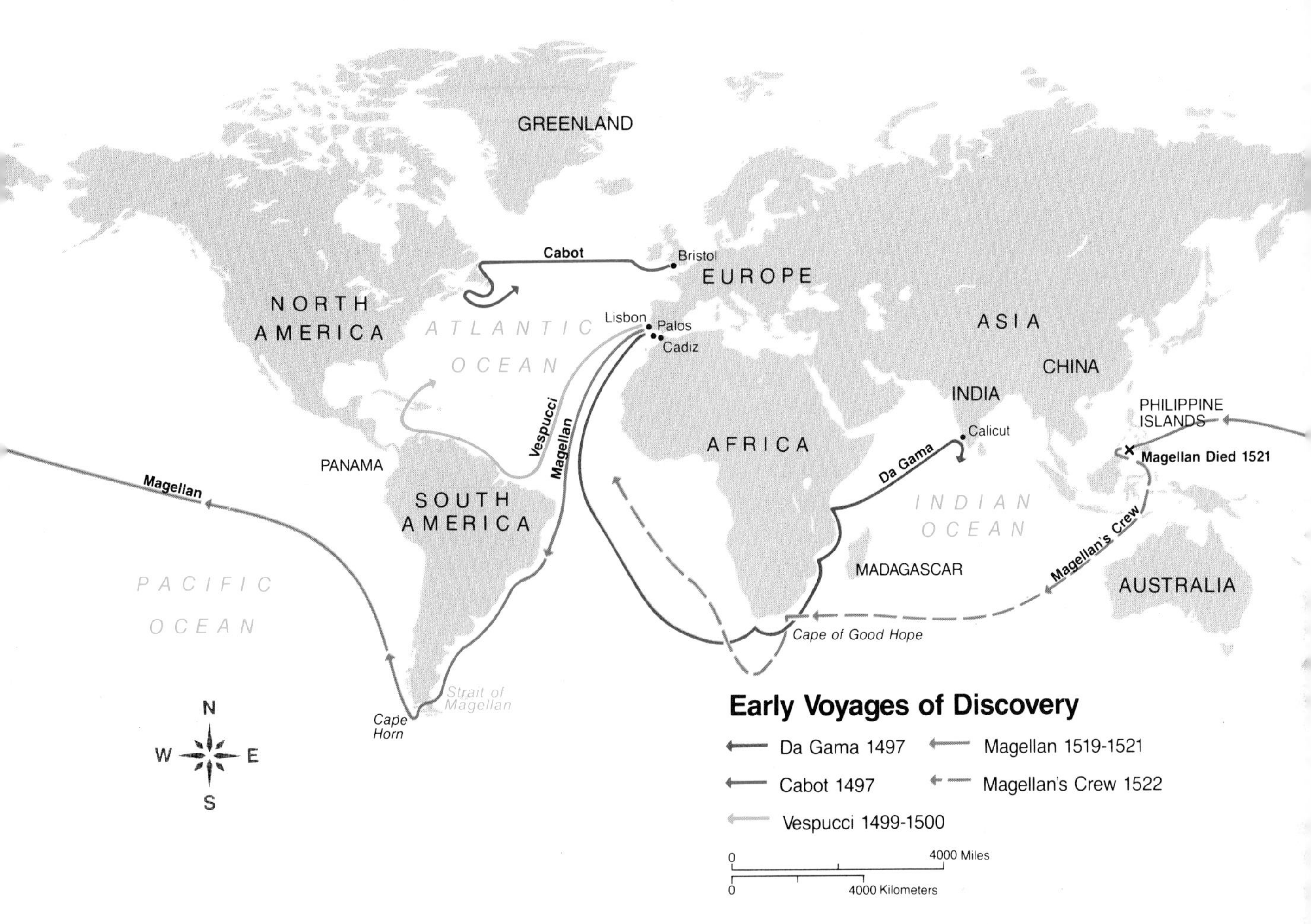

No European explorer had seen the Pacific Ocean until Balboa arrived in Panama. There, Indians told him of a huge, shining sea that stretched off to the west.

Taking a party of men and his dog with him, Balboa climbed up a steep mountain. In the party were thirty Africans and a group of Indians. From the mountain, Balboa could see the vast Pacific Ocean, which he claimed for Spain.

Balboa discovered the Pacific Ocean in 1513. Other Spaniards followed him, crossing over from the Atlantic to the wide Pacific.

New questions arose. What countries lay on the opposite shore of the Pacific? How far away was Asia? The answers were soon to be found.

1. What strip of land connects North America with South America?

2. What did Balboa discover?

Who first sailed across the Pacific Ocean?

Magellan (mə jel′ ən) was the leader of the first expedition to sail all the way around the world. It took three years for his crew to make this important voyage. (See map, above.)

Focus on Skills

To understand history, one must know geography. And to appreciate the story of the discovery and exploration of the Americas, one must know something about the hemispheres.

The new continents of North America and South America, discovered by Columbus and others, lie in the western half of the world. (See map, page 31.) This half of the globe is called the western hemisphere (hem′ ə sfir). The term *hemisphere* comes from the ancient Greek language. *Hemi* means half, and *sphere* means globe.

The continents of Asia, Australia, and most of Europe and Africa lie in the eastern half of the world. This is the eastern hemisphere.

The earth may also be divided into northern and southern hemispheres. These two hemispheres are divided by the equator, an imaginary line running horizontally around the center of the earth halfway between the North Pole and the South Pole. The half of the earth lying south of the equator is the southern hemisphere. The half of the earth north of the equator is the northern hemisphere.

Examine the two maps shown on page 31. By noting their details you should be able to answer the following questions easily.

1. Which is the western hemisphere? What continents lie in that hemisphere?
2. Which is the eastern hemisphere?
3. How much of Europe and Africa lie in the western hemisphere?
4. Which is the northern hemisphere? The southern hemisphere?
5. Which continents lie in both the northern and southern hemispheres?
6. Sometimes the northern and southern hemispheres are given different names. One is sometimes called the land hemisphere. Which do you think it is? Why? The other is sometimes called the water hemisphere. Which is it? Why do you think it bears that name?

Magellan left Spain in 1519. He sailed to South America. Then he rounded South America's tip and sailed thousands of miles across the Pacific Ocean. On the way, food ran out and the starving sailors had to eat rats. Magellan was killed in a battle he joined between tribes in the Philippine Islands. But the few sailors still alive continued the voyage. They sailed across the Indian Ocean and around the tip of Africa. They returned to Spain in 1522.

3. Where did the Magellan expedition sail?

What did Magellan's voyage prove?

The world learned much from Magellan's voyage. First, it proved once and for all that the earth is like a round ball. A ship or airplane can travel around it in one direction and come back to its starting point. Second, the voyage showed that the earth was larger than most people thought, because the Pacific was far wider than they imagined. As a matter of

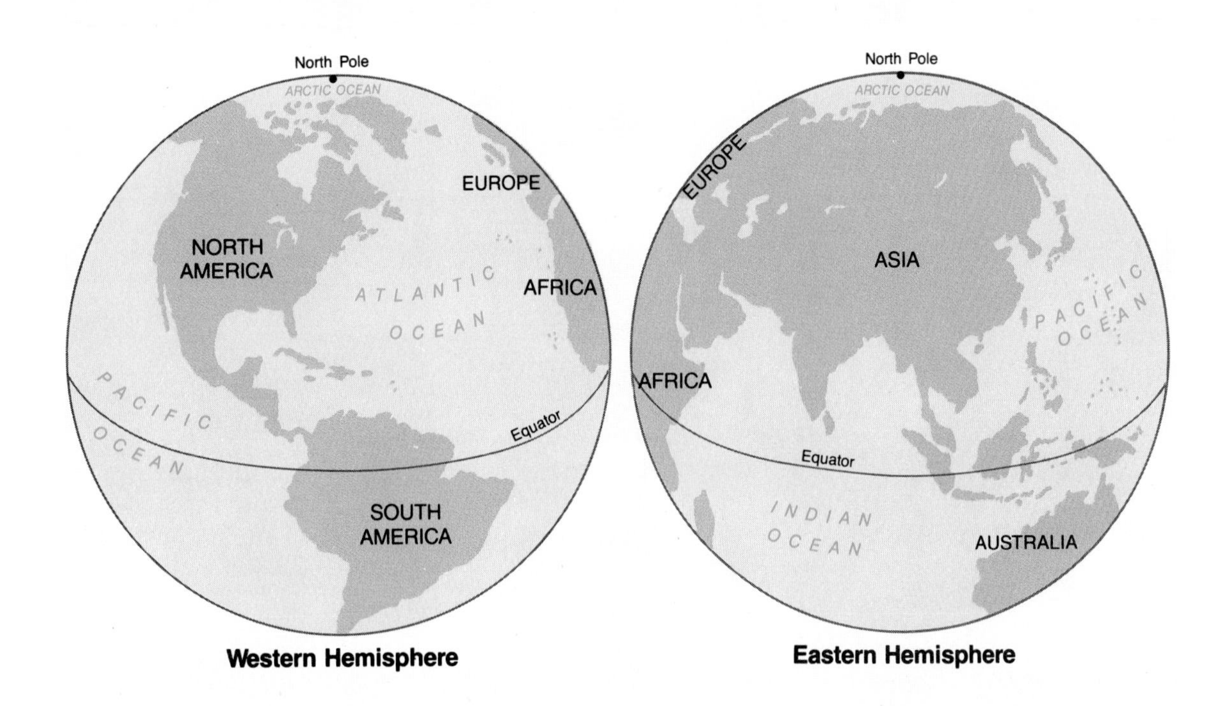

Western Hemisphere

Eastern Hemisphere

fact, the Pacific covers more than one-third of the whole surface of the earth.

Last, the voyage proved that North and South America are not part of Asia. It is true that North America and Asia almost touch at the Bering Strait. But south of the strait, the Pacific Ocean separates them by thousands of miles. For example, the distance between California and Japan is over 5000 miles (8000 km).

4. What three things did Magellan's voyage prove?

5. What great ocean lies between North America and Asia?

Part Six

England Challenges Spain

Who challenged Spain for the New World?

Spain took an early lead in discovering and settling the Americas. But other nations were in the race as well. Portugal and Holland sent explorers to the Americas. So, too, did France and England. In time England's navy became the best in the world. And England became Spain's greatest threat.

The Spanish called their great fleet the "Invincible Armada," because they were sure it could not be beaten. But storms and the faster, lighter English fleet sank almost half the Spanish ships.

As early as 1497 the English had sent John Cabot exploring. Cabot was an Italian, but he and his sons sailed for the king of England. Cabot traveled along the North Atlantic coast. He claimed the lands he saw for England. Off the coast of Newfoundland, Cabot made a big discovery. He found the rich fishing grounds called the Grand Banks. The French and the Portuguese lost no time getting to the Grand Banks to fish. In fact, they profited more from Cabot's discovery than did the English. To this day the Grand Banks are an important food source.

For many reasons the English did not follow up quickly on Cabot's voyages. But when Queen Elizabeth came to the throne in the middle 1500s things were to change. Elizabeth I was a remarkable and determined woman. She had made up her mind to defeat Spain and make England the strongest nation of Europe.

To defeat Spain, the queen sent out "Sea Dogs." These were bold sailors who raided Spanish treasure ships homeward bound for Europe. One of the most famous was Sir Francis Drake. Starting in 1577, Drake sailed around the world, as Magellan had done. But on his way, Drake robbed many Spanish ships of their gold. Drake also visited northern California and claimed it for England.

Dashing Sir Francis Drake was the most famous of the English "Sea Dogs." He sailed his ship, the *Golden Hind*, around the world and brought home much Spanish gold.

Spain's pride was hard hit by the Sea Dogs. War with England loomed.

1. Who were the "Sea Dogs"? Why did they raid Spanish ships?

2. What "Sea Dog" sailed around the world? What part of America did he visit?

How did Spain answer England?

In 1588 Spain gathered a huge fleet of ships called the Armada (är mä′ də). With this fleet the Spanish hoped to invade and conquer England. But the English were waiting for the enemy with smaller and faster ships. The Armada was ripped to pieces.

Spain never fully recovered from the loss of the Armada. Its sea power had been dealt a heavy blow. England, on the other hand, became the ruler of the seas. At this time the English turned to the New World and started to plant colonies there.

3. What was the Spanish Armada?

4. What nation became the ruler of the seas?

Queen Elizabeth I made England ruler of the seas and a leader among the states of Europe.

Building Your Vocabulary

Complete the following sentences by selecting the correct word from those listed on the right.

1. North America is in the western—?—.
2. The peoples of Norway, Sweden, and Denmark were called—?—.
3. The—?—were a series of religious wars.
4. A—?—is a ship specially designed to sail into the wind.
5. Spanish conquerors were called—?—.
6. The Aztecs, Maya, and Incas developed great—?—.
7. The Indians felt that the earth was—?—.

sacred
hemisphere
Crusades
Norse
conquistadores
caravel
civilizations

Recalling What You Have Learned

Match each item in Column A with the correct item in Column B.

Column A
1. Aztecs
2. Spain
3. Asia
4. Incas
5. Magellan
6. Isabella
7. Bering Strait
8. Iroquois
9. Amerigo Vespucci
10. de Soto

Column B
A. first round the world sea voyage
B. conquered by Cortés
C. America named in his honor
D. lived in what is now Peru
E. location of land bridge between Asia and America
F. sent Columbus on his first journey
G. women held key positions among these people
H. discovered Mississippi River
I. took the lead in exploring the Americas
J. continent from which First Americans came

Discussing the Important Ideas in This Chapter

1. Why was the peopling of the Americas a long, slow process?
2. Why is it incorrect to speak of the Indians as though they were all one people?
3. What effects did the Crusades have on European life?
4. Why did the Spanish take the lead in exploring the New World?
5. Sometimes it is said that "America

was not discovered once; it was discovered many times." Do you agree or disagree with this statement? Why or why not?
6. Why was Magellan's voyage important?
7. How did the arrival of the Spanish affect the Aztecs, the Incas, and the Maya?
8. Why was the defeat of the Spanish Armada a turning point in the history of the Americas?

Improving Your Map Skills

The map on page 18 may look very strange to you. It is like the map which Columbus may have used on his first voyage to America. Modern spelling has been added in some places. Compare this map to the one shown on page 590. Find five names that are the same on both maps. Point out three important differences between the two maps.

Improving Your Study Skills:
Research

When you want to find out more about a topic, there is an easy way to see if a book has information about the topic. You can use the book's index. Most textbooks, and many books of nonfiction have indexes. The index is found at the back of the book.

Suppose you want to know more about American Indians. First, look in the index of this textbook.

1. How is the information in the index arranged so that you can find what you need easily?
2. How many entries are there listed under the heading "Indians, American"?
3. What does the last line of the index section for "Indians, American" say?
4. Look for "Cherokee Indians" in the index. How many entries are there for "Cherokee Indians"?

Select one tribe from the list below. Go to your library and ask the librarian to help you find books about American Indians. Some good general books are:

The World of the American Indian, National Geographic Society, 1974.

American Heritage Book of Indians, American Heritage Publishing Company, 1961.

A Pictorial History of the American Indian, Oliver LaFarge, Crown Publishers, 1956.

Find three facts about the tribe you chose that you can share with the class. Use the indexes of the library books to help you.

Algonquin	Nez Percé
Delaware	Micmac
Iroquois	Seminole
Creek	Comanche
Cherokee	Zuñi
Sioux	Cheyenne
Apache	Chippewa

Chapter 2

Settlers in English America

Reconstructed village at Jamestown, Virginia

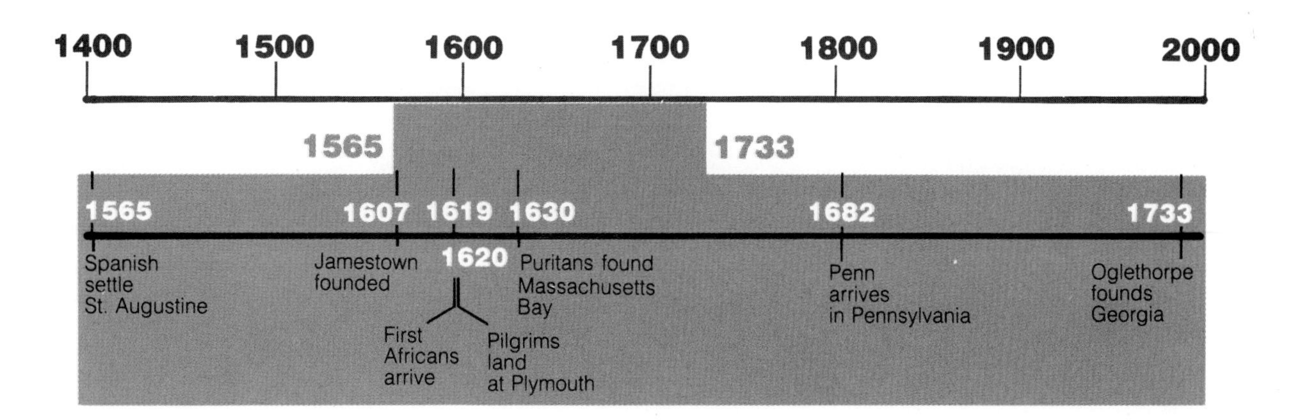

Part One

England Takes the Lead in Settling the Atlantic Seaboard

What did the country look like in 1600?

Where you now live was probably a very lonely place in 1600. Parts of North America were then so thick with forests that squirrels could jump from tree to tree for hundreds of miles without landing on the ground. Other parts of the land were empty plains and deserts. There were no cities or highways. The only towns were widely scattered Indian settlements. In addition, there were a few Spanish forts in what is now Florida. The best known fort was St. Augustine. It was founded in 1565. The fort was often attacked. It was frequently burned by the British and the French. Yet the tiny stronghold managed to survive. It claims the honor of being the oldest European settlement in the United States today.

Although North America, except for Mexico, was sparsely settled wilderness in 1600, some Europeans wanted to

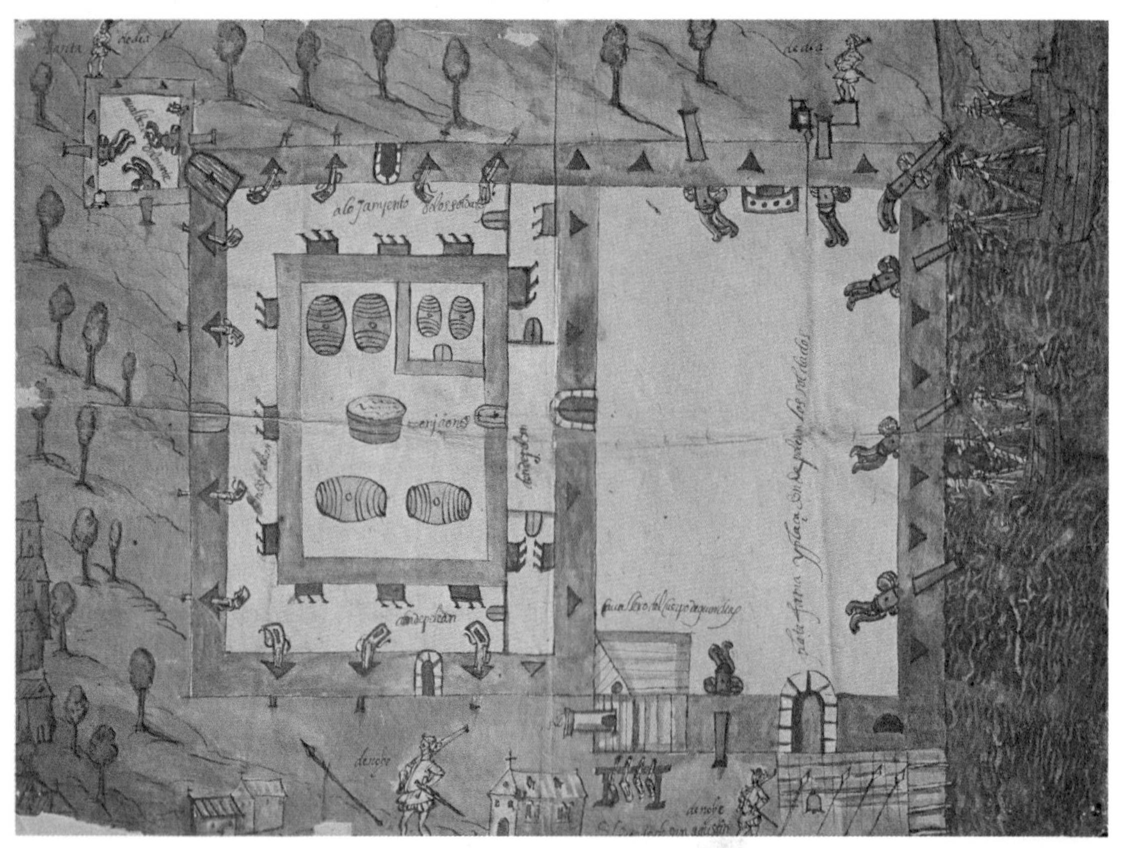

This early plan of the Spanish fort at St. Augustine, Florida, shows how the fort was defended. Notice the cannons, the posts for sentries, and the bells to sound the alarm in case of attack.

live there. And none among them were more eager than the English.

Why were English men and women willing to risk their lives to come to America? To answer that question we must examine conditions in England itself.

1. Describe the appearance of what is now the United States in 1600.

2. Name the oldest European settlement in the United States today.

What made people want to leave England for America?

England was a proud and strong nation in 1600. Its navy was second to none. England had defeated the Armada and made peace after a long war with its old enemy, Spain. The English enjoyed more liberty and had more rights than anyone else in Europe at that time. But many troubles lay beneath the nation's surface.

In the 16th century, religious struggles had broken out all over Europe. Nations were torn by religious differences. England broke away from the Roman Catholic Church. Then the English set up their own church, which was run by the government. But many people were unhappy with the new church. They wanted to worship in their own way.

Besides religion, there were other reasons why English people were ready to leave home. Many people could not find work. So the chance of finding great riches across the sea was tempting. For farmers who owned little or no land in England, acres of rich soil lay waiting in America. America was a land of opportunity. Many writers and political leaders urged English men and women to take advantage of that opportunity.

Some who urged others to go to the New World had selfish reasons. They believed that planting settlements in America would benefit those who stayed in England. England needed gold; perhaps the settlers could find it.

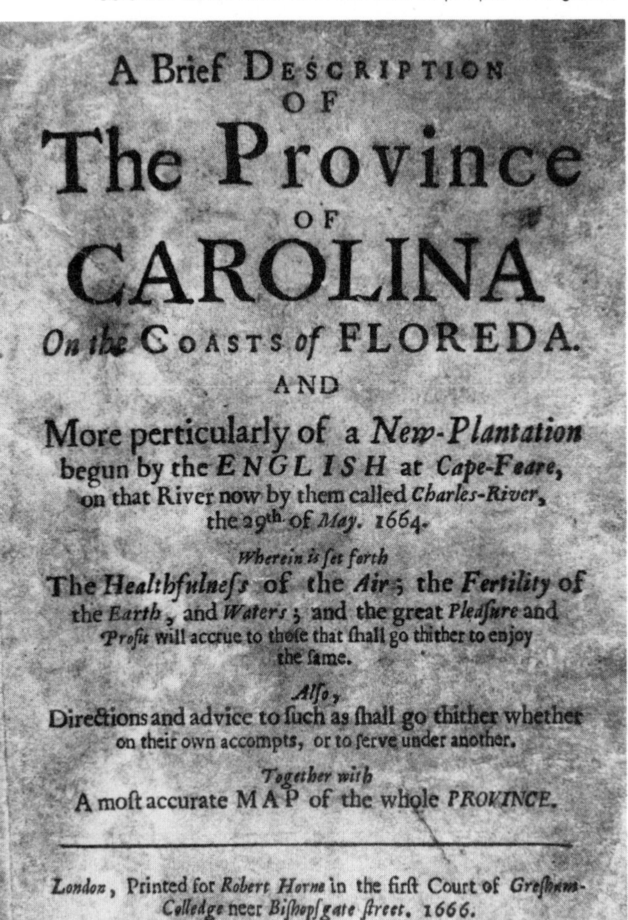

A Brief DESCRIPTION
OF
The Province
OF
CAROLINA
On the COASTS of FLOREDA.
AND
More perticularly of a *New-Plantation* begun by the *ENGLISH* at *Cape-Feare,* on that River now by them called *Charles-River,* the 29th. of *May.* 1664.

Wherein is ſet forth
The *Healthfulneſs* of the *Air*; the *Fertility* of the *Earth*, and *Waters*; and the great *Pleaſure* and *Profit* will accrue to thoſe that ſhall go thither to enjoy the ſame.

Alſo,
Directions and advice to ſuch as ſhall go thither whether on their own accompts, or to ſerve under another.

Together with
A moſt accurate MAP of the whole *PROVINCE.*

London, Printed for *Robert Horne* in the firſt Court of *Greſham-Colledge* neer *Biſhopſgate ſtreet.* 1666.

Colonies advertised their benefits to people in England.

Some people thought England was too crowded. They thought the New World could provide an outlet for its excess population. They urged the poor, the jobless, and orphans to settle in America.

England also needed *raw materials*, or materials which could be used to manufacture various products. Examples of raw materials which the English wanted were metals, lumber, tar (to waterproof ships), cotton, sugar, and other foodstuffs. The colonists could supply those raw materials. Then workers in England could turn them into finished products and sell them back to the settlers at a profit. The settlers would need iron pots, shoes, furniture, tools, and many other things. So colonies would provide a ready market for English goods.

3. Name three reasons why some English men and women were willing to go to the New World.

4. Why did certain English writers and political leaders hope that people would go to America?

When did the English first try to settle in America?

The first attempt to establish an English colony in America was made in 1585. One hundred men came to settle on Roanoke Island in what is now North Carolina. They looked for minerals but found none. Neither did they have any luck farming. One man, an artist, made some fine drawings of Indians which later became valuable sources of information. But that was the only good thing which happened. After the men had spent about ten months on the island, Sir Francis Drake, the Sea Dog, appeared on the coast with his fleet. He offered to take the colonists back to England. The

John White was a settler at Roanoke and the grandfather of Virginia Dare. He made many watercolors of the Indians, plants, and animals he saw in Virginia. Here are his drawings of a flying fish, a pineapple and a tortoise. White's work is prized both for its beauty and the information it gives us about early Virginia.

men were so discouraged, sick, and hungry that they accepted.

Two years later, another group of 117 settlers went to Roanoke. This time there were women and children, as well as men in the party. Later one of the couples had a daughter. Named Virginia Dare, she was the first child born in America to English colonists.

What happened to that colony is a mystery. When an English ship returned to check on the settlers they had vanished. So Roanoke is called the "Lost Colony."

Later the English were to have better luck in planting colonies. Between the years 1607 and 1733 they planted thirteen of them along the Atlantic coast from what now is Maine in the north to Georgia in the south. Those colonies would become the thirteen original states. In this chapter we are going to learn how each of them began. For convenience we shall divide them into three groups according to location: the Southern Colonies, New England, and the Middle Colonies.

5. What happened to the first two groups of settlers on Roanoke Island?

6. How many colonies did the English establish? Where were they located?

Part Two

The Southern Colonies

Which were the Southern Colonies?

Five of our present-day states once were part of the Southern Colonies. Among them was the very first colony planted by the English in America, as well as the last. Virginia claims the honor of being the first. Georgia was the last.

Look at the map on page 42. Locate Virginia and Georgia. Find the Carolinas—North and South—and Maryland. Those five colonies made up the southern group.

Even though these colonies were all in the South, they were not alike. Each was founded at a different time and for different reasons. Each developed in a different way.

1. Name the Southern Colonies.
2. Which was founded first? Which was founded last?

How and why was Virginia founded?

Some London merchants were eager to start a colony in the New World. So they formed a company, which they called the London Company. They raised money by selling shares of stock in the company. They bought ships and supplies. They recruited settlers, and they even paid the way for those who could not pay for themselves.

They needed, of course, to get the king's permission to found a colony. But that was no problem. The king was happy to grant the merchants' request.

On December 20, 1606, three small ships carrying 120 settlers sailed from London. During eighteen weeks at sea, fifteen settlers died.

When at last the settlers arrived in America, they made their way up the James River. They chose the site that became the first permanent English settlement. (See map, page 42.) They named it Jamestown, in honor of King James I.

But the settlers chose a poor place. The land was swampy and unhealthy. Two-thirds of the newcomers died within the first eight months. Those who survived did not try to farm. They spent their time hunting for gold. They quarreled with the Indians. They, too, might have lost their lives had it not been for their leader, Captain John Smith. His iron will and his ability to make friends with the Indians saved the small settlement.

According to tradition, Smith was captured by Indians and taken to the great Chief Powhatan. Powhatan ordered his warriors to put Smith to death. Powhatan's beloved young daughter was watching. She was only twelve or thirteen years old. Although her real name was Princess Matoaka, she is known in history by her nickname, Pocahontas (pō′ kə hon′ təs). Pocahontas rushed to Smith just as the clubs were about to fall. She threw her arms about him and begged her father to spare his life. Powhatan grudgingly agreed.

Whether or not the story is true, Smith did make friends with Powhatan. After that things gradually improved in Jamestown. The colony was able to survive, and in time to prosper, for several reasons:

First, Smith made the colonists forget "gold hunting" and get to work.

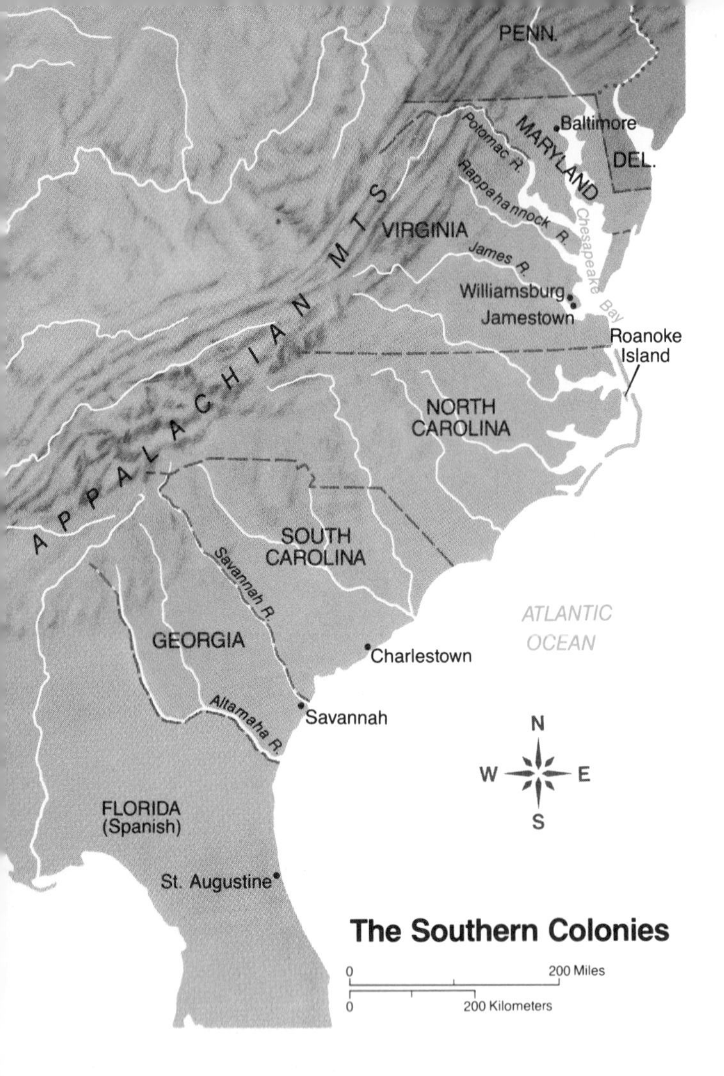

The Southern Colonies

This portrait of Pocahontas, or Rebecca Rolfe, was made while she was in England.

Second, the Indians brought food to help the settlers until they could grow their own.

Third, more settlers arrived from England. Families came. So, too, did a number of young, unmarried women. They were especially welcome. Those who agreed to marry were given the right to build homes. Unmarried persons, however, were required to live in barracks.

Finally, the colonists learned to grow tobacco. The Indians raised tobacco, and they introduced the colonists to it. The colonists did not like its taste. But one of the settlers, John Rolfe, could see that tobacco had possibilities as a cash crop. He began to experiment with it. He got some seeds from another area and tried growing them. Finally he produced a tobacco which Europeans not only liked, but craved. Within five years it became a major source of income for the colonists.

Rolfe married Pocahontas. After their young son, Thomas, was born, they went to visit England. There the Indian princess, now known as Rebecca Rolfe, was presented to the king and queen of England. She was greatly admired in London. But just as she was ready to return to America, she became ill. She died when she was just 22 years old.

3. Where was the first permanent English settlement?

4. Why was the colony able to survive?

What two systems did colonists use to try to solve the labor shortage?

In Virginia, as well as in other colonies, land was the major source of wealth. But before the land could be made to pay, it had to be cleared. Crops had to be planted, harvested, and taken to market. Trees had to be felled and made into lumber. Minerals had to be dug from the earth. To do all those things required workers. But there were not enough of them in the colonies. So the English tried two systems in an effort to solve the shortage of labor. The first system was called *indentures*. The second was *slavery*.

John Rolfe grew a mild tobacco from seeds brought from the West Indies. When it became popular in Europe, tobacco became the staple crop of the Virginia colony.

Indentures were agreements. In exchange for their passage to America, men, women, and children agreed to sell their labor for a certain number of years. Usually they had to work between four and seven years. Children, however, had to work until they were 18 or 21 years old. At the end of their indentures, servants were supposed to be given "freedom dues." Often that was land. Sometimes it was money, clothing, or tools. Only about 20 percent of the ex-servants ever collected their "freedom dues," however.

Indentures usually were signed with a ship's captain before the voyage. Then the captain delivered the servants to a port. People looking for workers came down to the ships. They looked over the servants offered and took their pick. It was not uncommon for whole families to sign such agreements and then find themselves sold in different ports. Sometimes they never saw one another again.

The indenture system had three major evils. First, many people were lured by false advertising. (See advertisement on page 39.) They were told that getting rich in America was easy. Second, the passage across the Atlantic was a nightmare. The indentured servants were crowded into the holds of ships. They did not have decent food or water. Death rates of 50 percent or more were common. Finally, the system was hardest on children. They brought high prices because they had to serve for longer periods of time. A kidnapping industry grew up in England. Orphans—and there were many—were swept up and sent off to America.

Recent research shows that many more persons came to America as indentured servants than once was thought. At least half—and probably more—of the

THREE POUNDS REWARD.

RUN AWAY from the Subſcriber, living at Warwick furnace, Minehole, on the 23d ult. an Iriſh ſervant man, named DENNIS M'CALLIN, about five feet eight inches high, nineteen years of age, has a freckled face, light coloured curly hair. Had on when he went away, an old felt hat, white and yellow ſtriped jacket, a new blue cloth coat, and buckſkin breeches; alſo, he took with him a bundle of ſhirts and ſtockings, and a pocket piſtol; likewiſe, a box containing gold rings, &c. Whoever takes up ſaid ſervant and ſecures him in any goal, ſo as his maſter may get him again, ſhall have the above reward and reaſonable charges paid by JAMES TODD.

N. B. All maſters of veſſels, and others, are forbid from harbouring or carrying him off, at their peril.

Unhappy indentured servants often ran away. If they were caught, they were made to serve longer.

white immigrants to the English colonies were indentured. Indentured servants were held in the colonies for more than 150 years, until long after the American Revolution.

Slavery forces a person to work without hope of freedom. Although slavery existed here for 250 years, just when and how it began is not clear. It developed over time. In the end it almost destroyed the United States. You will learn more about the system of slavery as you continue your study of American history.

John Rolfe noted in his diary that twenty Africans arrived in Virginia in 1619. Those Africans, brought against their will, were traded to planters for supplies. They were supposed to be treated like other indentured servants and given their freedom after a time. There is evidence that these first African arrivals were freed.

In 1624 one of the African couples in the original group had a son. The baby's name was William Tucker. He was the first black child born in the English colonies.

As years passed, the treatment of Africans began to change. By 1640 some blacks were still indentured servants. A few had been freed and had land of their own. But some blacks were serving for life. They were slaves.

Why was the system of slavery possible in the English colonies? There were three main reasons. First, Africans did not look like white immigrants. Their color made them easily recognizable, especially if they ran away. They could be returned to their masters more easily than white indentured servants, who also often ran away. Second, Africans did not worship as Europeans did. They were said to be "heathens," or non-Christians. They did not have the same legal protection as Christians. Third, there were few Africans in the colonies. They came from different areas. They did not speak one common language. So it was difficult for them to help one another.

There was no great rush to buy slaves. Slavery grew slowly. As late as 1670 there were about 8000 indentured servants in Virginia, but there were only about 2000 slaves. In time, however, the slave trade would increase tremendously, and it would become important in all of the Southern Colonies.

5. Explain the difference between an indentured servant and a slave.

6. Why was slavery possible in the English colonies?

How were seeds of self-government planted in Virginia?

The first seeds of self-government, or *democracy*, were planted in Virginia in 1619. It is interesting that the first Africans also arrived in 1619.

Before 1619 the London Company had sent governors to rule the Virginia colony with an iron hand. The Company owned all the land, buildings, and tools.

Settlers were required to bring all they produced to Company storehouses. In return, they got only as much as they needed to live on. The Company kept the rest. Naturally, the Company's rules were unpopular. Some settlers refused to contribute. Attracting new settlers became much more difficult. So in 1619 the Company was forced to change its ways. It introduced reforms which were very important. In time they were adopted by all of the other English colonies. Some of them are still part of our government today.

The colonists were given the right to make their own laws. The king chose the governor. But each village or settlement sent two representatives to meet with the governor and his council. In all there were 22 representatives who spoke for the settlers. This lawmaking group was called the *House of Burgesses*.

At first all white males over seventeen years of age could vote for members of the House of Burgesses. Later voting was restricted to property owners. For a time women could vote, if they had enough property.

In the towns, people were elected to handle daily problems. There were judges, sheriffs, and justices of the peace, for example. All of those were positions used in England. In fact, the whole idea behind the reforms in Virginia was that colonists were to be treated just as persons in England were. They no longer were to be treated as second-class citizens.

Serving in the House of Burgesses or as town officials gave colonists a lot of good experience. They learned how to govern themselves. They also began to think of serving in a political office as an honor and as a duty. Members of wealthy families, in particular, were eager to be chosen. When the colonies

Virginia's capitol building, where the House of Burgesses met, has been reconstructed in Williamsburg.

declared their independence, experience in government was to prove very valuable.

7. How did the Virginia colonists take part in their government?

Why was Carolina divided into two colonies?

King Charles I of England was forced off his throne for a time. Some friends helped him regain it. To show his appreciation, Charles gave them all of the land between Virginia and Florida. They returned the compliment by naming it Carolina. *Carolus* means "Charles" in Latin.

Carolina's new owners were proud and wealthy. They dreamed of a colony ruled by persons like themselves. So they divided Carolina into large plantations or estates. Each plantation was to be owned and governed by a landholder. In turn the landholders were to rent farms to settlers.

Farmers who did well were supposed to be given a voice in the government. But it did not always work out that way. Often the farmers were forced to take orders from the owners.

The small farmers who lived in the northern part of Carolina hated the landholders. They were fiercely independent. Many of them had moved there from Virginia long before King Charles made the land grant to his friends. During those years they raised tobacco. They also learned how to get tar from trees in the forests. Tar was used to make ships watertight. It was much in demand in Europe. The people of the north began to call themselves "Tarheels." They also began to think of themselves as very different from the people who lived farther south. In time they rebelled. They insisted that Carolina be divided. Naturally the landholders of the south were not very happy. But they had to give in to the Tarheels' demands. Carolina was divided into North and South Carolina in 1712.

But even before that split, something changed the way South Carolina developed. A sea captain arrived at Charles Town (later Charleston) with some rice seeds from Madagascar, a large island off the east coast of Africa. The hot, humid climate of the area around Charles Town proved ideal for rice. So landholders who had been trying to grow sugarcane began growing rice. They flooded the rich soil by using canals and streams. Naturally the flooded land attracted mosquitoes. The mosquitoes, in turn, carried a disease

The backcountry farmers of North Carolina often lived in cabins like this one.

Rice Hope was a famous plantation in South Carolina. Contrast the house in this illustration with the backcountry cabin on the preceding page. You can see why there were serious differences between the people of North and South Carolina.

called malaria. As you can imagine, almost no one wanted to work in the rice fields. So to get labor the owners began to buy slaves. As the demand for rice grew, so did the demand for slaves. Landholders came to believe that they could not do without them.

8. Why did North and South Carolina develop differently?
9. Why did demand for rice increase the demand for slaves?

Why did people first come to Maryland?

Religion played an important part in the settlement of many of the thirteen colonies. Nowhere was this more true than in Maryland. Maryland was founded by Roman Catholics.

Roman Catholics suffered greatly when England became Protestant. One of the few Catholics the king still liked was Lord Baltimore. This nobleman asked King Charles for land in America where Catholics would be admitted along with Protestants. The king granted some land to Lord Baltimore and his son.

In 1634 two small ships sailed into a wide bay on the Atlantic coast. Aboard these two ships, the *Ark* and the *Dove*, were about 200 colonists of both the Catholic and Protestant faiths. As soon as they landed, some priests celebrated the first mass said in the English colonies.

The new colony was named Maryland in honor of the queen of England. The settlers bought land from the Indians and began working hard in their fields planting crops. Within four months they sent a shipload of corn on the *Dove* to colonists in Boston. In return they received dried codfish. Maryland never suffered from hunger or disease as Virginia and other colonies did.

Protestants poured into Maryland until they greatly outnumbered the Catholics. Religious troubles broke out in the colony. To make matters worse for the Catholics, the neighboring colony of Virginia was strongly Protestant. Virginia claimed part of Maryland's territory. There was fighting along the border.

To stop those troubles, Lord Baltimore persuaded the colonists to take an important step. They passed the *Act of Toleration*, granting freedom of religion to all people of the Christian faith. The act saved Maryland's Catholics, although it did not help those who were not Christians.

For many years, the government of Maryland was controlled by Protestants. But Catholics had nothing to fear. They could worship in their own way. While the Act of Toleration was not perfect, it marked an important step toward religious freedom.

10. Why was Maryland able to avoid hunger?

11. Why is the Act of Toleration an important milestone in American history?

Lord Baltimore's son, shown here with his grandson, saw Maryland as a haven for people of all faiths.

When and why was Georgia colonized?

Georgia was the last of the thirteen English colonies to be settled. It was founded in 1733. Its founder was named James Oglethorpe (ō′ gəl thôrp).

Georgia was founded for two main reasons. First, it bordered on Florida, which belonged to Spain. Georgia was to be a buffer to keep Spain from attacking the other English colonies. Oglethorpe brought a small English army with him.

Second, Georgia was founded as a place where the English who had no money could get a new start. The laws of England were very strict about debt. Persons unable to repay just a small loan could be put in prison. They might stay there for years, because there would be no way they could earn money to pay back what they owed. Sending such persons to America made more sense than keeping them in jail in England.

Oglethorpe had great hopes for the Georgia colony. The settlers were given fair treatment, and slavery was forbidden at first. But the colony grew slowly. Too few people were willing to lead the hard, dangerous life that Oglethorpe asked of them. Georgia managed to keep going, but its laws were changed. Slavery was permitted, and slaves had to do the work that free people were unwilling to perform.

12. For what two reasons was Georgia founded?

13. Why did Georgia grow slowly?

Part Three

New England

Which four colonies were in New England?

The most northeastern part of the United States is called New England. Four colonies once claimed all of that area. The first to be founded was Massachusetts. Settlers landed there in 1620. The other three colonies were offshoots from Massachusetts. They were New Hampshire, Connecticut, and Rhode Island.

Look at those four colonies shown on the map on page 50. Which was the largest? Which had the shortest coastline? Which was the farthest south?

Now turn to the map of present-day United States on page 588. Compare that map with the one shown on page 50. Notice that six states today occupy the area which the four colonies once claimed. Vermont was carved from the western part of New Hampshire. Maine, now a separate state, was a part of Massachusetts until 1820.

1. Name the four colonies established in New England.

2. Which of them was founded first?

When and why did the Pilgrims come?

Perhaps the colonists best known to Americans today are those who settled at Plymouth, Massachusetts, in 1620. Today Americans celebrate Thanksgiving in their memory. They were the first group to arrive in New England. They were called Pilgrims—for good reasons. A *pilgrim* is a person who makes a journey, usually for religious purposes.

The Pilgrims came to America because they were not free to worship in England as they wished. England had an official church. It was the Church of England. The Pilgrims, however, objected to it. They said its buildings and its services were too "fancy." They preferred things which were "plain." They also believed that the Church of England was too rich and powerful. They felt that it had strayed from what they thought was the true message of the Bible. Because of their objections, the Pilgrims began to hold religious services in their own homes. They had to do so in secret because the king disapproved. In time, however, the king found out about their meetings. He ordered soldiers to break up the services. Many Pilgrims were arrested. All who refused to worship in the Church of England were outcasts.

Some of the outcasts moved to Holland. There they had religious freedom. But then they began to have other worries. They were afraid that their children were becoming too worldly. Their children were also becoming more Dutch than English. So the Pilgrims asked some English merchants to send them to America. In the wilderness they would establish a "godly" colony far from the evil influences of Europe.

The merchants agreed. In 1620 over 100 men, women, and children sailed for the New World on a ship called the *Mayflower*. Only about thirty members of the group on that voyage were Pilgrims. The other passengers were people looking for wealth and adventure. Some of them were religious, some not especially so.

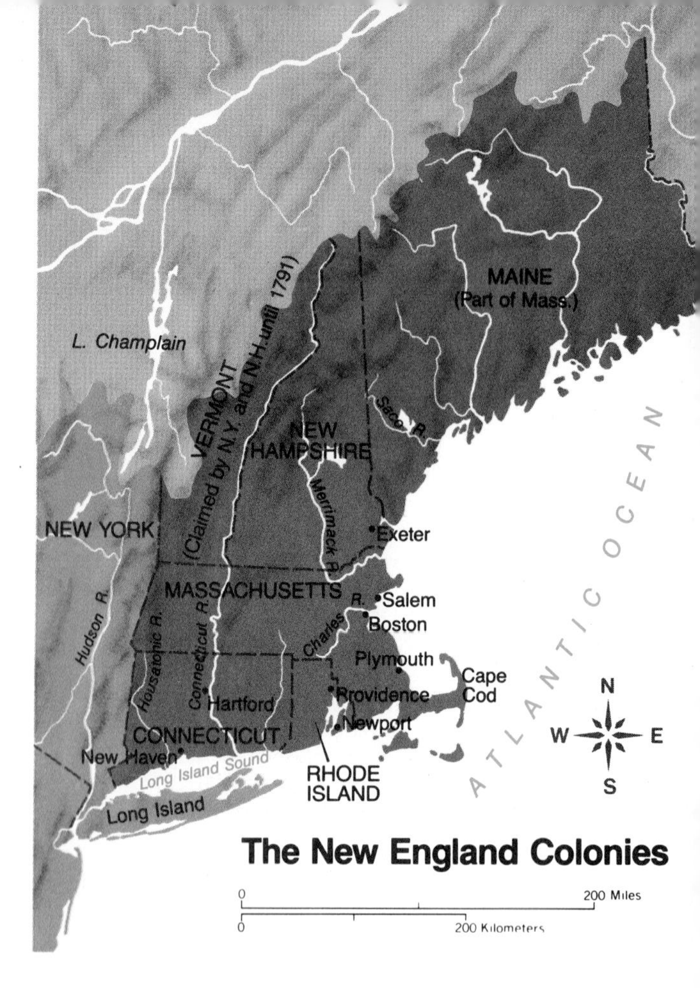

The New England Colonies

The *Mayflower* was a fairly large ship for its time. The vessel sailed from Plymouth, England, in September 1620. It arrived at Massachusetts in late November after a voyage of 65 days. There were storms along the way, and the ship may have been blown off its course. In any case, the *Mayflower* landed far north of the English settlements in Virginia. (See map, page 68.) Originally the Pilgrims had intended to make their new home somewhere in Virginia.

When the Pilgrims first saw the New England coast, they were disappointed. It was winter. The weather was bad. The skies were dark. The forests looked forbidding. But they quickly reassured each other.

Before going ashore, they held a meeting in the ship's cabin. They made some promises to one another. Those promises were written into an agreement called the *Mayflower Compact*. It required Pilgrims and non-Pilgrims to obey laws passed by the majority.

Armed with the Mayflower Compact, their plan for governing the new settlement, they went ashore. They named the place where they landed Plymouth.

3. Why did the Pilgrims come to America?

4. What was the Mayflower Compact?

How successful was the new colony?

The Plymouth colony was a success, although the Pilgrims suffered terribly from disease at first. In fact, only 44 of them lived through the winter of 1620-1621. At one time only seven in the whole colony were well enough to bury their dead in frosty graves.

When the *Mayflower* sailed back to England in the spring of 1621, not a Pilgrim left. One of them wrote for all in his diary. He said, "It is not with us as with other men, whom small things can discourage."

In addition to their own courage and hard work, the men and women of Plymouth owed some of their success to the Indians.

When the spring arrived, neighboring Indians appeared. Two of them, Samoset and Squanto, could even speak English! Samoset, an Algonquin, had learned the language from fishermen along the coast of Maine. Squanto had once visited Europe with English fishermen and spent several years there. On his return he joined the Wampanoag tribe.

The Indians helped the settlers. They showed them how to plant crops by fertilizing the land with dead fish. The Pilgrims made a treaty of friendship with Massasoit (mas′ ə soit), the neighboring Indian chief. For many years there was no war.

Plymouth colony continued as an independent unit from 1620 to 1691. Then it was absorbed into the largest and most important settlement, the Massachusetts Bay Colony.

5. Who was Squanto? Who was Samoset?

6. Why was the Plymouth Colony able to succeed?

The *Mayflower II*, thought to closely resemble its namesake, sailed the Atlantic in 54 days in 1957.

Why did the Puritans come to Massachusetts?

Ten years after the Pilgrims left for America, a group of English merchants formed the Massachusetts Bay Company to settle around Boston. The Boston colonists were called *Puritans*, because they wanted to purify, or make pure, the English church. Religion meant more to the Puritans than anything else in their lives.

In the summer of 1630 almost 1000 Puritans and other colonists arrived in Massachusetts. Ten years later their population had grown to 20,000.

The Massachusetts Bay Colony got off to a good start. The Puritans had learned from other colonies' mistakes. They sent a scouting party ahead to pick the best location for their settlement. They got reports about the land. They even made up a checklist for those planning to come to America so that they would bring along enough food, medicine, tools, and other supplies. Thus when the settlers arrived they were prepared. As a result the Puritans did not suffer as did the first people at Jamestown and Plymouth.

The Puritans believed that they were on a special mission. They intended to build "a city upon a hill," a society that would attract world-wide attention. That attention was not to come because of wealth or beauty. It was to come because the "city on a hill" would show others how to live in harmony with the truths of the Bible as the Puritans understood them.

Because the Puritans wanted better to understand God's will, they spent much time in their churches. They also looked for messages from heaven in thunderstorms, dreams, accidents, or strange happenings of any kind.

The Puritans were hard workers. They built towns throughout the colony.

THE INCONVENIENCIES THAT HAVE HAPPENED TO SOME PERSONS WHICH HAVE TRANSPORTED THEMSELVES

from *England* to *Virginia*, vvithout prouisions necessary to sustaine themselues, hath *greatly hindred the Progresse of that noble Plantation: For preuention of the like disorders* heereafter, that no man suffer, either through ignorance or misinformation; it is thought requisite to publish this short declaration: wherein is contained a particular of such necessaries, *as either priuate families or single persons shall haue cause to furnish themselues with, for their better support at their first landing in* Virginia; *whereby also greater numbers may receiue in part, directions how to prouide themselues.*

Apparrell.

Apparrell for one man, and so after the rate for more.

Apparrell	li.	s.	d.
One Monmouth Cap	00	01	10
Three falling bands	—	01	03
Three shirts	—	07	06
One waste-coate	—	02	02
One suite of Canuase	—	07	06
One suite of Frize	—	10	00
One suite of Cloth	—	15	00
Three paire of Irish stockins	—	04	—
Foure paire of shooes	—	08	08
One paire of garters	—	00	10
One doozen of points	—	00	03
One paire of Canuase sheets	—	08	00
Seuen ells of Canuase, to make a bed and boulster, to be filled in *Virginia* 8.s. One Rug for a bed 8.s. which with the bed seruing for two men, halfe is	—	08	00
Fiue ells coorse Canuase, to make a bed at Sea for two men, to be filled with straw, iiij.s. One coorse Rug at Sea for two men, will cost vj.s. is for one	—	05	00
	04	00	00

Victuall.

For a whole yeere for one man, and so for more after the rate.

Victuall	li.	s.	d.
Eight bushels of Meale	02	00	00
Two bushels of pease at 3.s.	—	06	00
Two bushels of Oatemeale 4.s. 6.d.	—	09	00
One gallon of *Aquauitæ*	—	02	06
One gallon of Oyle	—	03	06
Two gallons of Vineger 1.s.	—	02	00
	03	03	00

Armes.

For one man, but if halfe of your men haue armour it is sufficient so that all haue Peeces and swords.

Armes	li.	s.	d.
One Armour compleat, light	—	17	00
One long Peece, fiue foot or fiue and a halfe, neere Musket bore	01	02	—
One sword	—	05	—
One belt	—	01	—
One bandaleere	—	01	06
Twenty pound of powder	—	18	00
Sixty pound of shot or lead, Pistoll and Goose shot	—	05	00
	03	09	06

Tooles.

For a family of 6. persons and so after the rate for more.

Tooles	li.	s.	d.
Fiue broad howes at 2.s. a piece	—	10	—
Fiue narrow howes at 16.d. a piece	—	06	08
Two broad Axes at 3.s. 8.d. a piece	—	07	04
Fiue felling Axes at 18.d. a piece	—	07	06
Two steele hand sawes at 16.d. a piece	—	02	08
Two two-hand-sawes at 5.s. a piece	—	10	—
One whip-saw, set and filed with box, file, and wrest	—	10	—
Two hammers 12.d. a piece	—	02	00
Three shouels 18.d. a piece	—	04	06
Two spades at 18.d. a piece	—	03	—
Two augers 6.d. a piece	—	01	00
Sixe chissels 6.d. a piece	—	03	00
Two percers stocked 4.d. a piece	—	00	08
Three gimlets 2.d. a piece	—	00	06
Two hatchets 21.d. a piece	—	03	06
Two froues to cleaue pale 18.d.	—	03	00
Two hand-bills 20. a piece	—	03	04
One grindlestone 4.s.	—	04	00
Nailes of all sorts to the value of	02	00	—
Two Pickaxes	—	03	—
	06	02	08

Houshold Implements.

For a family of 6. persons, and so for more or lesse after the rate.

Houshold Implements	li.	s.	d.
One Iron Pot	00	07	—
One kettle	—	06	—
One large frying-pan	—	02	06
One gridiron	—	01	06
Two skillets	—	05	—
One spit	—	02	—
Platters, dishes, spoones of wood	—	04	—
	01	08	00

	li.	s.	d.
For Suger, Spice, and fruit, and at Sea for 6. men	00	12	06
So the full charge of Apparrell, Victuall, Armes, Tooles, and houshold stuffe, and after this rate for each person, will amount vnto about the summe of	12	10	—
The passage of each man is	06	00	—
The fraight of these prouisions for a man, will bee about halfe a Tun, which is	01	10	—
So the whole charge will amount to about	20	00	00

Nets, bookes, lines, and a tent must be added, if the number of people be greater, as also some kine.

And this is the vsuall proportion that the Virginia *Company doe bestow vpon their Tenants which they send.*

Whosoeuer transports himselfe or any other at his owne charge vnto *Virginia*, shall for each person so transported before Midsummer 1625. haue to him and his heires for euer fifty Acres of Land vpon a first, and fifty Acres vpon a second diuision.

Imprinted at London by FELIX KYNGSTON. 1622.

This 1622 English handbill advises settlers to avoid "inconveniences" by taking the proper equipment to the colonies.

Each town was laid out according to a similar plan. Two or three acres (about 1 ha) were left in the center to serve as the village common, or pasture land, for all of the cows, sheep, and goats. A school and a church were always placed where everyone in the town could reach them easily. The remaining land was divided into lots. One lot was given to each family. Other lots were kept in reserve so that newcomers would have a place where they could build homes. On the edge of the town were strips of land belonging to each family. On that land they could grow their crops. Nearby was a common woodlot, with trees for everyone.

7. What special hopes for their colony did the Puritans have?
8. What plan was followed for building new towns?

John Winthrop's practical nature and strong will served the Massachusetts Bay Colony well.

Who were some of the important Puritans?

John Winthrop was the single most important Puritan leader. He was 42 years old when he left England at the head of the "Great Migration." That was the name given to the first large group of settlers in the Massachusetts Bay Colony.

Winthrop was a well-educated man, a lawyer, and a gifted speaker. He was able to convince his followers that they were "saints," or special people who had been chosen for an important mission. Winthrop thought the "saints" would build a new paradise on earth in the New World. They would drive away all evils and any "false teachers."

Winthrop was also a very practical man and a good governor in many ways. In fact, he served as governor twelve times. Winthrop always was concerned about his people's well-being and about their morale. He kept a diary which has proved to be an important source of information about colonial times. And he even found time to write a two-volume *History of New England.*

The best known woman in Massachusetts Bay Colony was the poet Anne Bradstreet. At sixteen she married Simon Bradstreet and came with him and her father to New England. Her father was one of the leaders of the Great Migration. He took great pains with her education. In addition to writing poetry, she raised a large family. Several of her books were published in England during her lifetime. But not until after her death, in 1672, were any published in America.

Her poems are important because they give us a glimpse into colonial times. She wrote about many subjects. Among them were the seasons, family life, religion, and town life. She also wrote many love lyrics about her husband to whom she was devoted. And she has even described for us her feelings when their house burned down.

9. Who was John Winthrop? What contributions did he make?

10. Why are Anne Bradstreet's poems important?

Why did settlers go to Connecticut?

Connecticut was settled by people who first had made their homes in Massachusetts. It was really an offshoot of the Massachusetts Bay Colony.

People decided to leave Massachusetts for three main reasons. Some of the people who left Massachusetts were pioneers. They went because they had heard of the rich farm land along the Connecticut River. They wanted to make new homes there where they thought farming would be easier and more profitable than it was in the rocky soil of Massachusetts.

Others went when they heard that the Dutch were moving into the area. In fact, the Dutch did build a fort on the Connecticut River to support their claim to that rich farming region. So some men and women left Massachusetts Bay and built a fort just upstream from the Dutch. They were determined that Connecticut was to be kept for the English.

Still others moved to Connecticut for religious reasons, and they proved to be the most important group.

Perhaps the best known of the settlers who came for religious reasons was Thomas Hooker. For several years Hooker preached in a church near Boston. He attracted a small but loyal group of followers. Hooker's ideas were not popular with Puritan leaders, however. For one thing, Hooker thought that the church had too much power in the Massachusetts Bay Colony. He said that all the colonists should vote, not just church members. The Puritan leaders disagreed. Finally Hooker made up his mind to leave. In 1636 he and 35 families who believed as he did packed their belongings and headed southwest. They founded a settlement at Hartford.

Hooker and his followers were not the only people who moved to Connecticut for religious reasons. There were other groups as well. They, too, established settlements. In time, the settlers decided that they needed to organize a government for Connecticut. Representatives met. They drew up a written set of rules, or a constitution, which they called *The Fundamental Orders*. It was an important step toward democracy because it gave control of the government to the people instead of to the church. But it was not a completely democratic constitution. Only "freemen" were given power. Freemen were white males who were not indentured.

11. For what three reasons did people move to Connecticut?

12. Why were The Fundamental Orders a step toward democracy?

Why were Rhode Island and New Hampshire established?

Rhode Island was founded in 1636, the same year as Connecticut. In many ways, its story is like that of Connecticut.

Rhode Island's founder was Roger Williams, a Massachusetts clergyman like Hooker. Also like Hooker, Williams disagreed with the Puritans, but much more violently. Williams declared that in any nation the church and the state should be separate. In other words, the church should mind its own business, while the government should run the affairs of state. The church should not tell the government what do do.

This idea of separation of church and state has been practiced in the United States since its founding in 1789. But it was a new idea in 1636 when Roger Williams preached it. The Puritans became furious.

To make matters worse, Williams said that the colonists should pay the Indians for their land instead of simply taking it away from them. After the Puritans ordered his arrest, Williams fled southward through an icy Massachusetts winter. Sheltered by friendly Narragansett Indians, he and his followers founded what is now the city of Providence.

The Puritans protested the actions of Williams to the English government. Far from punishing Williams, the English praised him and recognized his rule over the new colony. In time, people of many beliefs, including Roman Catholics and Jews, were welcomed to Rhode Island.

Just two years after Roger Williams arrived in Rhode Island, another small group came in search of religious liberty. They were followers of Anne Hutchinson. She was banished from the Massachusetts Bay Colony because of her outspoken and forceful leadership.

For many years Anne Hutchinson played an important role in Boston. She liked people, and they respected her both

This statue of Anne Hutchinson stands on the grounds of the Massachusetts State House in Boston.

for her nursing skills and her keen mind. Despite the fact that she had a large family to care for, she always found time to tend the sick and to assist women in childbirth. But she gave most of her time to the church and to her religious studies. If women had been allowed to be ministers, she surely would have been one. But since she could not preach from a pulpit, she held meetings in her home. At those meetings she often criticized what various ministers had said in their sermons.

In time Puritan leaders began to worry about Mrs. Hutchinson's large following. They disliked some of her ideas. Finally they ordered her to keep silent. But she would not. They brought her to trial and demanded that she admit

Historymaker

When 27-year-old Roger Williams and his wife, Mary, arrived in Boston in 1631, their future looked bright. Williams already had made quite a reputation for himself both as a lawyer and as an exciting preacher. For that reason he was offered a choice job in the Massachusetts Bay Colony. The Puritan leaders invited him to become minister of the most important church in their colony.

To everyone's surprise, Williams turned down the job. He said he could not agree with many of the Puritans' ideas. And that is when his troubles began. From then on they grew. Just four years after they had arrived, Williams, his wife, and their newborn child, whom they named "Free-borne," were ordered to leave Massachusetts. In the midst of a bitter winter, they and five loyal friends set out for Rhode Island.

Why was Williams banished? He had not committed any crime. He had not harmed anyone. On the contrary, he was one of the most friendly and beloved of all the leaders in the colonies. Williams, however, did hold ideas which then were considered "new and dangerous." The Puritans warned him to keep those ideas to himself. But he would not. Time and again he spoke his mind in town meetings and from the pulpits of churches in the colony. To all who would listen—and many did—he kept saying:

People should not be punished for what they believed.

If people wanted to give money to the church, that was fine. But they should not be forced to pay taxes to support any church.

All colonists ought to be eligible for public office. Church membership should not be a requirement.

Colonists ought to be able to make their own laws and choose their own leaders in free elections.

The land belonged to the Indians. If settlers wanted land, they should buy it. They did not have the right to take land.

The more Roger Williams talked about his ideas, the more nervous Puritan leaders became.

"This man has a 'windmill' in his head," one of the Puritans exploded.

"Williams is dangerous," said another. "If he is not silenced, he soon will have all of the Colony in flames."

"Let's put him on the next ship bound for England," suggested a third.

The uproar Williams caused was hard on Governor John Winthrop. He liked Williams. He realized that the young preacher had a keen mind and that he was a leader. Massachusetts needed people like that. So Winthrop talked to Williams privately. He tried to persuade him to be less outspoken. He also explained that he wanted Williams to stay in the Colony. But he

Roger Williams is welcomed by the Narragansett Indians.

couldn't do his job if Williams kept on speaking out against the Puritans' beliefs.

Williams listened to his friend. Then he said he was sorry, but he could not agree to keep silent. He had to do what he thought was right. He would go on talking about the need for religious and political freedom. He would continue to stand up for the Indians and their rights.

When Williams refused to give in, the General Court ordered him to get out of Massachusetts Bay Colony within six weeks. He and a small band of followers moved into Rhode Island. There Canonicus, chief of the Narragansetts, welcomed them and gave them shelter through the winter. Later, Canonicus sold Williams the land on which he founded present-day Providence. In time that small settlement grew, and it became the capital of Rhode Island.

Back in Boston, Puritan leaders laughed about the "goings on" in "Little Rhody." As more and more discontented people moved there, they began calling it "Rogue's Island." They said it would come to no good. But they were wrong.

Rhode Island became a lighthouse among the colonies. There people could enjoy complete freedom of religion. Jews, Catholics, Quakers, and nonbelievers—all were welcomed and allowed to worship or not as they pleased. No one was required to pay taxes to support any religion.

In Rhode Island settlers also enjoyed political freedom. They made their own laws. They chose their own leaders in frequent elections. They could think, write, and speak about their own beliefs without fear of punishment.

Today we take for granted the kinds of religious and political freedom for which Roger Williams once had to fight. It is hard to realize that when he proposed them he was far, far ahead of his time.

publicly that her teachings were wrong. Again she refused. In November 1637, they took away her membership in the church and ordered her to leave the colony. At the time she was awaiting the birth of another child. The court agreed that she could remain in Boston until her baby was born, but then she would have to go. Her husband and some followers went on ahead to Rhode Island.

In the spring of 1638, Mrs. Hutchinson and her children left for the new settlement. Later the Hutchinsons left Rhode Island and moved to Long Island. There, a year after their arrival, all but the youngest daughter were killed by Indians.

One of Mrs. Hutchinson's closest friends was also banished. He was the Reverend John Wheelwright. He, too, thought people should be free to think and to practice religion as they saw fit. Wheelwright led his followers into New Hampshire and established a settlement at Exeter in 1638.

13. Why did Roger Williams and Anne Hutchinson go to Rhode Island?

14. Who settled in New Hampshire? Why?

Part Four

The Middle Colonies

Which were the Middle Colonies?

Examine the map on page 59. Notice the names of four present-day states. They are New York, New Jersey, Pennsylvania, and Delaware. Once those states were called the Middle Colonies. A glance at the map will tell you why. To the north lay the New England Colonies. To the south were the Southern Colonies. So the Middle Colonies were the four which were sandwiched between their neighbors.

1. Why were New York, New Jersey, Pennsylvania, and Delaware called the Middle Colonies?

Who settled the New York Colony?

The Dutch, not the English, were the first colonists of New York. They had sent an explorer named Henry Hudson to look for a passage to the Far East early in the 1600s. Hudson did not succeed, of course, because no such passage existed. But he did discover and explore an important river which now bears his name. (See map, page 59.)

Hudson's discoveries attracted the interest of the Dutch West India Company. It established a colony called New Netherland in 1626. The colony stretched 150 miles (240 km) up the Hudson River and spilled over into what are now the states of Connecticut and New Jersey. (See map, page 59). It also included Manhattan Island, which the company bought from the Canarsie Indians for just $24 worth of trading goods.

The Dutch were eager for settlers to come to the new colony. But they did not attract many, even though they offered large tracts of land on the Hudson to those who would bring settlers. The trouble was that the Dutch did not treat newcomers well. They sent one bad governor after another from Holland. The last of them was a man named Peter Stuyvesant. He was known for his fierce

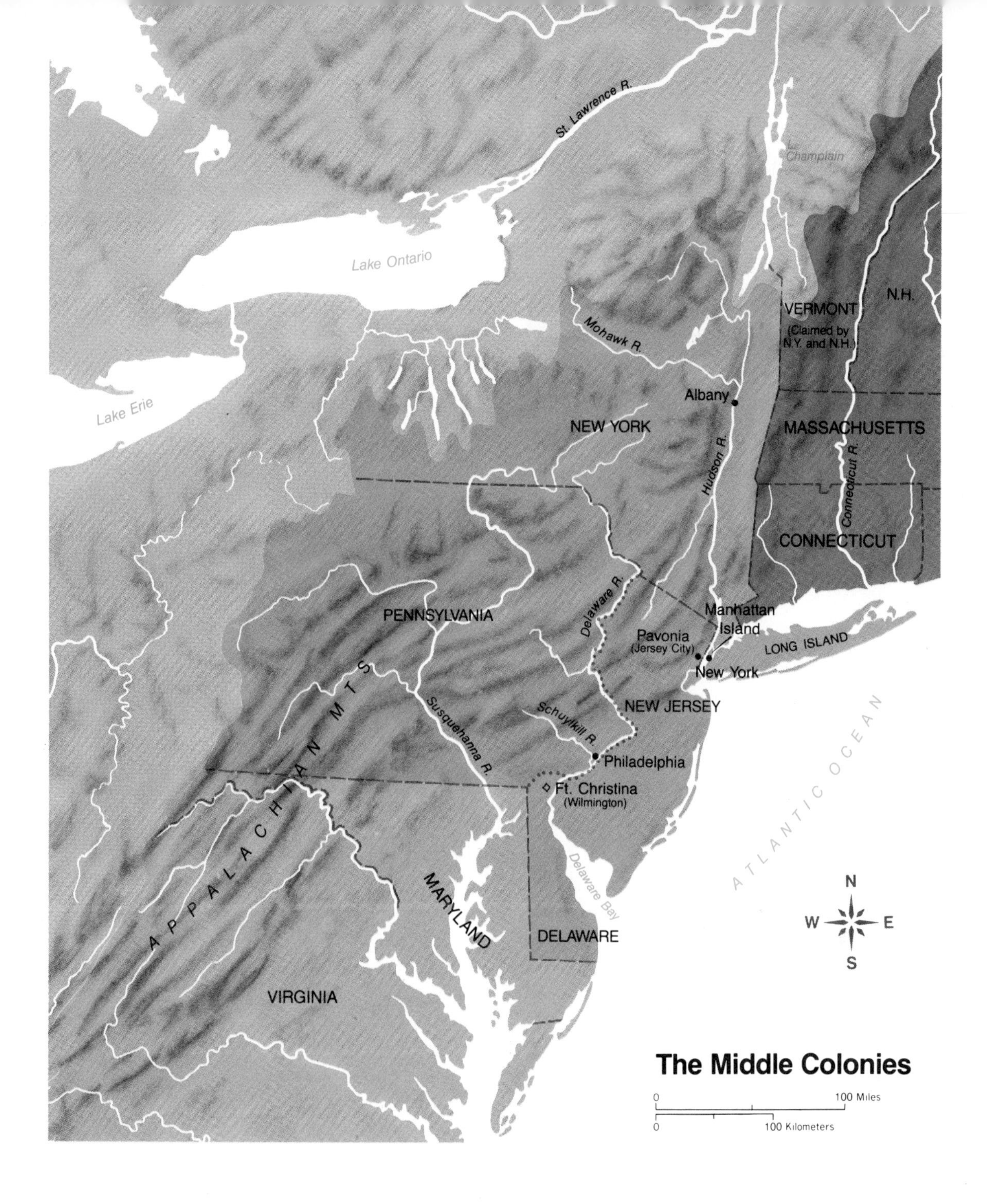

temper and for his wooden leg. Stuyvesant was especially hated by the people he ruled.

Meanwhile, the English were settling to the north and south. The English were trade rivals of the Dutch. They made no secret of the fact that they would like to drive out the Dutch. And in 1664 they finally were able to do it. They sent a fleet of ships to New Amsterdam, as New York City then was called. They ordered the governor to surrender.

Fierce Peter Stuyvesant once said that if anyone dared to oppose his rule as governor of New Netherland, "I will make him a foot shorter and send the pieces to Holland."

Governor Stuyvesant ordered his people to fight. But they refused. He grew angry. He swore and stamped his wooden leg and demanded that they defend the colony. But his temper tantrum was in vain. The settlers said they would just as soon be ruled by the English as by their own cruel masters.

When New Netherland surrendered, the king of England gave it to his brother, the duke of York. The duke renamed New Netherland for himself. It thus became New York. New Amsterdam was renamed New York City.

2. When and where did the Dutch establish a colony?

3. Why were the English able to take over from the Dutch?

How was New Jersey founded?

Soon after New Amsterdam was settled, some Dutch colonists set up a trading post where Jersey City is today. A few years later they pushed on to the Delaware River. There they built a fort and made a settlement around it.

When the English forced the Dutch to surrender in 1664, they divided what had been New Netherland. As you know, part of it became New York. The duke of York gave to friends the land west of the Hudson to the Delaware River. One of those friends had been governor of the English island of Jersey. He chose the name New Jersey in honor of that small island.

New Jersey grew rapidly. Because the land was good for farming, settlers streamed in. Soon they began to build roads. By 1650 they had completed the first "highway" in what is now the United States. About 100 years later they built the first lighthouse in America.

4. How did New Jersey become an English colony?

Who founded Delaware?

Several groups were involved in the founding of Delaware. The first were the Delaware Indians. They were three closely related tribes who were friendly to most Europeans. They welcomed Dutch traders and enjoyed trading furs with them for other goods. When the Dutch established a settlement in their midst, the Delawares did not object. But after a short while, for reasons not completely known, the Delawares drove the Dutch away.

On the heels of the Dutch came a small band of settlers from Sweden. At that time, Sweden was a much larger country than it is today. It included

Finland, so that some of the people who came were Finns. These newcomers were more successful. They had been sent by Swedish merchants in 1638 to build a fort on the Delaware River near what is now Wilmington. The settlers built Fort Christina, and in time they established other settlements as well. They called their new homeland New Sweden.

The people of New Sweden soon taught their neighbors an important lesson. They built their homes by cutting down trees and notching their ends. Then they put the tree limbs together into what was called a log cabin. It was a kind of shelter until then unknown in the Americas. The log cabin quickly became very popular.

For a few years the Swedish colony got along well. Johan Printz was its governor. Printz could really throw his weight around. He weighed 400 pounds (180 kg)! But Governor Stuyvesant had been eyeing the small colony. He wanted to take it over for the Dutch. He sent some warships and 700 soldiers against New Sweden. There were more soldiers in the Dutch force than there were settlers in New Sweden. It was impossible for them to resist, so they surrendered without firing a shot.

Not long after the Dutch forced New Sweden to surrender, the English took over New Netherland. So the English also claimed New Sweden. They gave it a new name. They called it Delaware, but not in honor of the Indians, as you might think. The colony was named for Lord De La Warr who had explored Delaware Bay two years after Henry Hudson had been there. In 1682 Delaware became part of Pennsylvania. Delaware was given its own assembly in 1702. But it remained the property of the Penn family until after the American Revolution. (See page 63.)

At the simple Quaker service, anyone so inspired may speak to the group. This painting shows a colonial Quaker meeting.

5. Which different groups of people played a part in the early history of Delaware?

Why was Pennsylvania a "Holy Experiment"?

Pennsylvania was founded by one of the most remarkable and best loved persons in American history. He was William Penn.

Penn was born in England, the son of an admiral. He was rich and well-educated. He might have done well there except for one thing. While he was in college, he joined a religious group called the Society of Friends, or Quakers. Quakers held strong beliefs. They believed that all persons were of equal worth, no matter what their sex, color, or position in life. So the Friends would not bow down to anyone, including kings. They also thought that a person's religious beliefs were a private matter. How someone wanted to worship God was nobody else's business.

Further, Quakers believed that wars were wrong. Under no circumstances would they fight in them. As you can imagine, such ideas made them very unpopular at the time. As a matter of fact, thousands of Quakers, including Penn, were thrown into jail for their beliefs.

As it happened, the king of England owed Penn's family a large sum of money. As usual, the king was short on cash, so he offered Penn a large piece of land lying north of Maryland instead. Penn accepted the land as payment. He named it Pennsylvania in honor of his father. As long as he owned the land, said Penn, it would be open to people of all beliefs. It would be a land of freedom and of brotherhood.

William Penn arrived in America in 1682 to plan the building of Pennsylvania's chief city. Its name was *Philadelphia*, meaning "City of Brotherly Love." Penn met with the Indians under an elm tree. He carried no weapons and called everyone "Friend," as was the Quaker custom. Penn paid the Indians for land and made a peace treaty with them. The treaty was never broken.

The peaceful settling of Pennsylvania was called the "Holy Experiment." In a pamphlet written in German, French, and Dutch, Penn invited colonists of all different faiths and nationalities to come to Pennsylvania. Quakers, Presbyterians, Catholics, and Jews answered him from all parts of Europe. Germany, torn by religious wars, sent many colonists. Blacks arrived from neighboring colonies. Penn offered the newcomers cheap, fertile land and a voice in the colony's government. From the first, the Friends strongly opposed slavery. Quaker teachers were especially anxious to help educate the blacks.

In the years that followed, Pennsylvania became the richest colony in North America. Philadelphia was its most glittering city, the "unofficial capital" of the English colonies.

Penn, unfortunately, did not do as well himself. He fell into debt. He was

William Penn and some followers make a treaty with the Indians. This painting was made by Edward Hicks, a Quaker preacher, in the 19th century. Hicks is one of America's most famous "primitive," or self-taught, painters.

Focus on Skills

When the term "colonial times" is used it refers to a period of about 170 years. Colonial times began with the first permanent settlement in Jamestown, Virginia, in 1607. They ended in 1776 when the settlers said they were no longer colonists. They were citizens of the free and independent nation of the United States.

Show that you understand the order in which events happened in early America. On a separate sheet of paper, copy the time line shown below.

Put brackets [ ] around the years which represent colonial times, or the years that the thirteen colonies belonged to England.

Place the number of each of the following events on the time line with its date.

1. the first Africans arrive in Virginia
2. the Pilgrims land at Plymouth
3. Puritans found Massachusetts Bay
4. Rhode Island founded
5. Wheelwright founds Exeter, New Hampshire
6. English take over New Netherland
7. Swedes settle in Delaware
8. Carolina divided into two colonies
9. Settlers arrive in Maryland
10. Oglethorpe founds Georgia
11. Hooker moves to Connecticut
12. House of Burgesses founded

imprisoned in England because he could not pay what he owed to others. Finally he had a series of strokes which left him unable to carry on the business of the colony. All his good work might have been undone had it not been for his remarkable second wife, Hannah Callowhill Penn.

Hannah Penn was the only child of two successful merchants. They taught her how to keep accounts and how to run a business. Her knowledge and skills proved very important for Pennsylvania. Although she spent most of her life in England, Hannah and a stepdaughter did come to America for two years. She managed the Penn farm in Bucks County. During that time she learned about the problems of the colony.

Prior to his death in 1718, Penn wrote a will saying that Hannah alone was to be in charge after his death. He had great confidence in her abilities. He also knew she was a good Quaker who shared his values.

Penn's confidence in his wife was well placed. She managed to keep the colony growing and the colonists contented. Pennsylvania remained in the hands of the Penn family until the American Revolution.

6. Why did people from many parts of the world and from other colonies come to Pennsylvania?

7. In what ways did William and Hannah Penn contribute to the success of Pennsylvania?

Building Your Vocabulary

Match each item in Column A with the correct item in Column B.

Column A	Column B
1. raw materials	A. forced labor without hope of freedom
2. colony	B. person who makes a religious journey
3. indentured servant	C. an agreement or contract
4. slavery	D. a member of the Society of Friends
5. democracy	E. person who agreed to work in exchange for passage to the New World
6. pilgrim	F. an overseas settlement
7. compact	G. things which can be manufactured into finished products
8. Quaker	H. self-government
9. colonist	I. opponent or competitor
10. rival	J. settler

Recalling What You Have Learned

Choose the one best answer for each item.

1. The name of the "Lost Colony" was (a) St. Augustine. (b) Jamestown. (c) Roanoke. (d) New Sweden.
2. Writers and political leaders in England were eager to plant colonies in the New World because they (a) wanted gold. (b) thought England was over-populated. (c) hoped to get raw materials. (d) all of these reasons.
3. Which one of the following was not a Southern Colony? (a) Virginia (b) South Carolina (c) Florida (d) Georgia
4. An Indian princess who helped the Jamestown settlers was (a) Squanto. (b) Massasoit. (c) Pocahontas. (d) Samoset.
5. Freedom of religion was promised the peoples of Maryland by (a) the Mayflower Compact. (b) the House of Burgesses. (c) the Act of Toleration. (d) The Fundamental Orders.
6. Which of the following was not in New England? (a) New York (b) Massachusetts (c) Rhode Island (d) New Hampshire
7. Puritans got their name because they wanted to (a) find pure gold. (b) purify the church. (c) prevent harm to the Indians. (d) travel to distant places.
8. Which of the following was not a leader of a New England colony? (a) Roger Williams (b) John Winthrop (c) Peter Stuyvesant (d) Anne Hutchinson
9. Which of the following was not a Middle Colony? (a) New York (b) New Jersey (c) Delaware (d) North Carolina
10. The colony called a "Holy Experiment" was (a) South Carolina. (b) Pennsylvania. (c) Connecticut. (d) Virginia.

Discussing the Important Ideas in This Chapter

1. Why were the English able to take the lead in colonizing North America?
2. Explain the difference between the system of indentures and slavery.
3. What great hopes led to the settlement of Georgia and Maryland?
4. What did the Puritans mean when they said they wanted to "build a city upon a hill" in New England?
5. How did Indians help the English settlers?
6. What were some of the steps colonists took toward achieving greater self-government, or democracy?

Improving Your Map Skills

On a separate sheet of paper draw a map like the one shown on the right. Make the map you draw several times larger, however.

1. Print the name of each colony on your map.
2. Indicate the three groups of colonies in the following ways:
   a. Lightly shade in the New England Colonies;
   b. Draw light lines across the Middle Colonies;
   c. Put a series of widely spaced dots in the Southern Colonies.

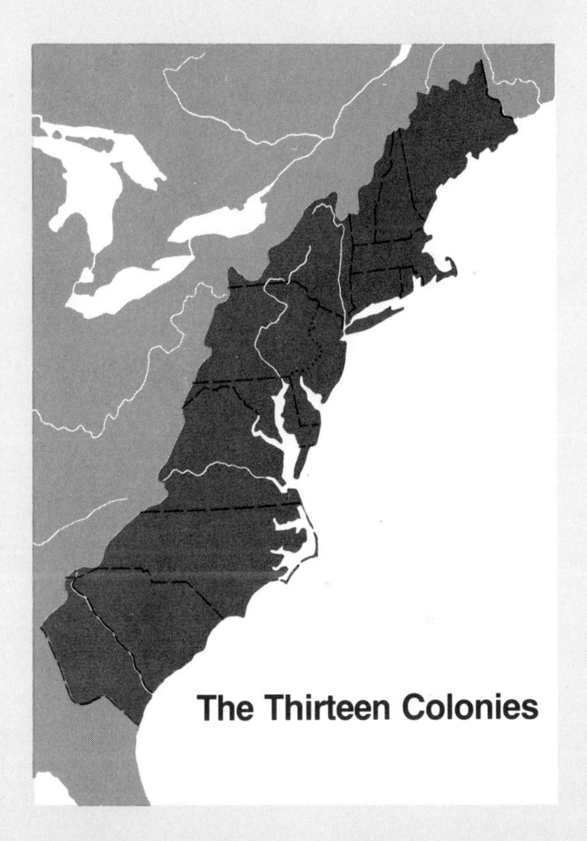
The Thirteen Colonies

Improving Your Study Skills: *Writing*

Write a "headline" which could have been used to describe each of the following important events in the colonies. (An example would be something like this: ROANOKE DISAPPEARS; NO TRACE OF SETTLERS FOUND)

1. Pocahontas saves the life of Captain John Smith of Jamestown by pleading for his life with her father.
2. Roger Williams, John Wheelwright, and Anne Hutchinson are forced to leave the Massachusetts Bay Colony.
3. The first Africans arrive in Jamestown to be sold as indentured servants.
4. Representatives of settlers in Connecticut draw up a written set of rules to all people of the Christian faith.
5. Representatives of settlers in Connecticut draw up a written set of rules called Fundamental Orders which gives control of government to all freemen instead of to the church.

Chapter 3

The English Colonies Grow

Kitchen of the Jethro Coffin House, Nantucket, Massachusetts

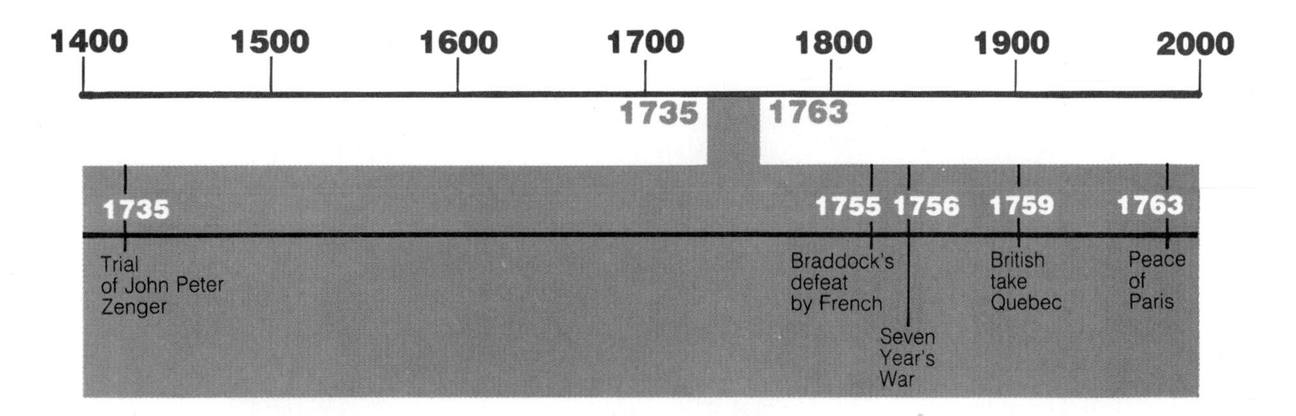

Part One

Making a Living in New England

How many people worked on the land?

Earning a living was not easy in colonial America. Almost every man, woman, and child lived and worked on a farm. Even the few townspeople regularly spent some time working on the land.

Today fewer than five out of every one hundred Americans are farmers. In colonial times about 97 out of every 100 people farmed. During the last 300 years, however, more than just the numbers have changed. The ways in which people meet their needs have also changed.

In this chapter we are going to learn how the colonists provided some of the *goods* and *services* they needed. *Goods* are products which can be seen and touched. For example, shoes, wool, sugar, guns, and wagons are goods. *Services* are tasks which people perform for one another. When people teach, cut hair, deliver mail, or prepare meals they provide services.

Historians, as you know, have divided the English colonies into three

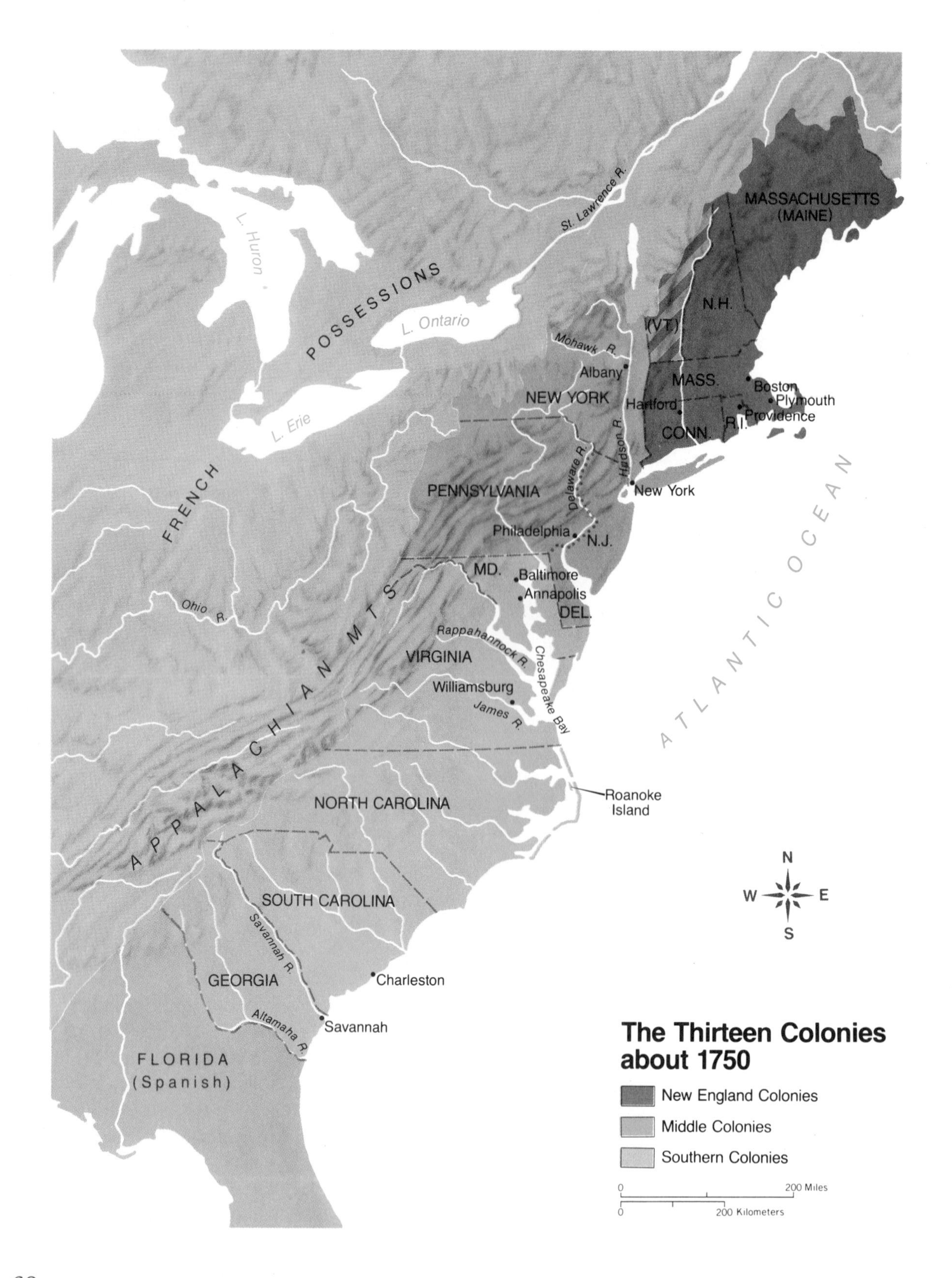

MASSACHUSETTS (MAINE)
N.H.
(VT.)
MASS.
CONN.
R.I.
Boston
Plymouth
Providence
Hartford
Albany
NEW YORK
New York
PENNSYLVANIA
Philadelphia
N.J.
MD.
Baltimore
Annapolis
DEL.
VIRGINIA
Williamsburg
NORTH CAROLINA
Roanoke Island
SOUTH CAROLINA
Charleston
GEORGIA
Savannah
FLORIDA (Spanish)
FRENCH POSSESSIONS
APPALACHIAN MTS
ATLANTIC OCEAN
L. Huron
L. Ontario
L. Erie
St. Lawrence R.
Mohawk R.
Hudson R.
Delaware R.
Ohio R.
Rappahannock R.
Chesapeake Bay
James R.
Savannah R.
Altamaha R.
N
W
E
S
The Thirteen Colonies about 1750
New England Colonies
Middle Colonies
Southern Colonies
0
200 Miles
0
200 Kilometers

separate groups because of their location. The three areas in colonial America were the New England Colonies, the Middle Colonies, and the Southern Colonies. As we soon shall see, life was indeed different in each of these areas.

1. About how many Americans were farmers in colonial times? How many are today?

2. What is the difference between goods and services?

How did geography affect the way New Englanders lived?

Geography is the study of earth, its natural resources, and its peoples. *Natural resources* are things found in nature which are useful for human industry. Examples are soil, water, forests, minerals, and harbors. How people earn their living often depends upon where they live and what natural resources are found in that region. Certainly that was true in colonial New England.

In New England the land is hilly, while the soil is thin and rocky. At times the climate is damp and cold. Farming was not easy for the settlers. So they turned to one of their most important natural resources, their forests. They learned to use that natural resource in many ways. Trees provided lumber for building houses, ships, and other products.

With the growth of the colonies on the Atlantic Coast, shipbuilding became an important business. All vessels were then made of wood. Some of the ships made in New England were sold to English merchants. Others were used by the colonists themselves for carrying on trade.

New Englanders also used wood to make furniture which sold for high prices. Another useful item made from lumber was the barrel. Barrels were used to ship products.

The barrel maker was important to the colonists.

To some New Englanders, the forests were home. These people were trappers and traders who obtained animal furs from the Indians. The fur business was very important. Furs brought high prices abroad. There, hats and clothes made of fur were in demand.

3. Why was farming difficult in New England?

4. Why were the forests an important natural resource?

Why did people turn toward the sea and to trade?

Treasure is usually found in the form of gold or silver. But New Englanders found it in—of all things—*codfish*! New England's thin and rocky soil yielded few rich crops. But off its seacoast were millions of cod and other

Codfish caught off the coast of Newfoundland are brought to land, cleaned, and dried. Codfish were so important to the economy of New England that for years a wooden carving of a codfish hung in the Massachusetts State House.

valuable fish ready for the taking. Thus fish, along with lumber, became another important natural resource. Thousands of New England settlers made their living by fishing.

Since ships went to sea for days or weeks at a time, methods had to be found to keep the fish from spoiling. Fish were dried, salted, or pickled in barrels. Then they could be carried great distances and sold to the colonists or to customers in other countries.

In a manner of speaking, New England's settlers finally faced east toward the ocean instead of west toward their frontiers. Farming continued in New England, of course, as it does to this day. But the main interest of the region was the sea and foreign trade.

New England sailors traveled to ports all over the world. They carried cargoes of fish and lumber, which often brought huge profits.

Many sea captains became wealthy, especially those who took part in what is called the "Triangular Trade." (Study map, page 71.) Such a trip often began in New England. A ship would leave a port such as Boston loaded with weapons, axes, beads, and barrels of rum. The slave traders of Africa wanted these products.

The ship would then sail across the ocean to the west coast of Africa and trade its cargo for slaves. From Africa it crossed the Atlantic again to the West Indies. There the slaves were sold, and the ship took on a load of sugar and molasses.

The last leg of the triangle brought the ship back to New England. The sugar and molasses were made into rum. The ship was then ready to repeat its journey to Africa and the West Indies.

In time the slave trade would create many problems. But when it began, few colonists expressed disapproval.

5. Why did fishing and sailing become important occupations for New Englanders?

6. What was the Triangular Trade?

What kinds of work did blacks do in New England?

Not many blacks lived in colonial New England. They numbered only about 2 percent of the population. But both free blacks and slaves left their mark on history. Free blacks were those who bought their freedom from their owners, or had it given to them.

One of the most outstanding free blacks was Paul Cuffe. Early in life he developed an interest in trade. In 1775 when he was just 16 years old he got a job on a whaling ship. Almost ten years later he slowly began building and sailing his own vessels. He owned a 69-ton schooner, *The Ranger*, as well as a number of smaller ships.

After the American Revolution, Cuffe became a wealthy man. He bought land. Cuffe built a school in Westport, Massachusetts, and gave it to the town. He also helped build a meetinghouse for the Society of Friends (Quakers). Cuffe himself was a Quaker.

Cuffe used his ships to carry 38 free blacks back to their homeland in Africa. He hoped to help all those who wanted to return to Africa. But the project proved to be too expensive for one person. Cuffe

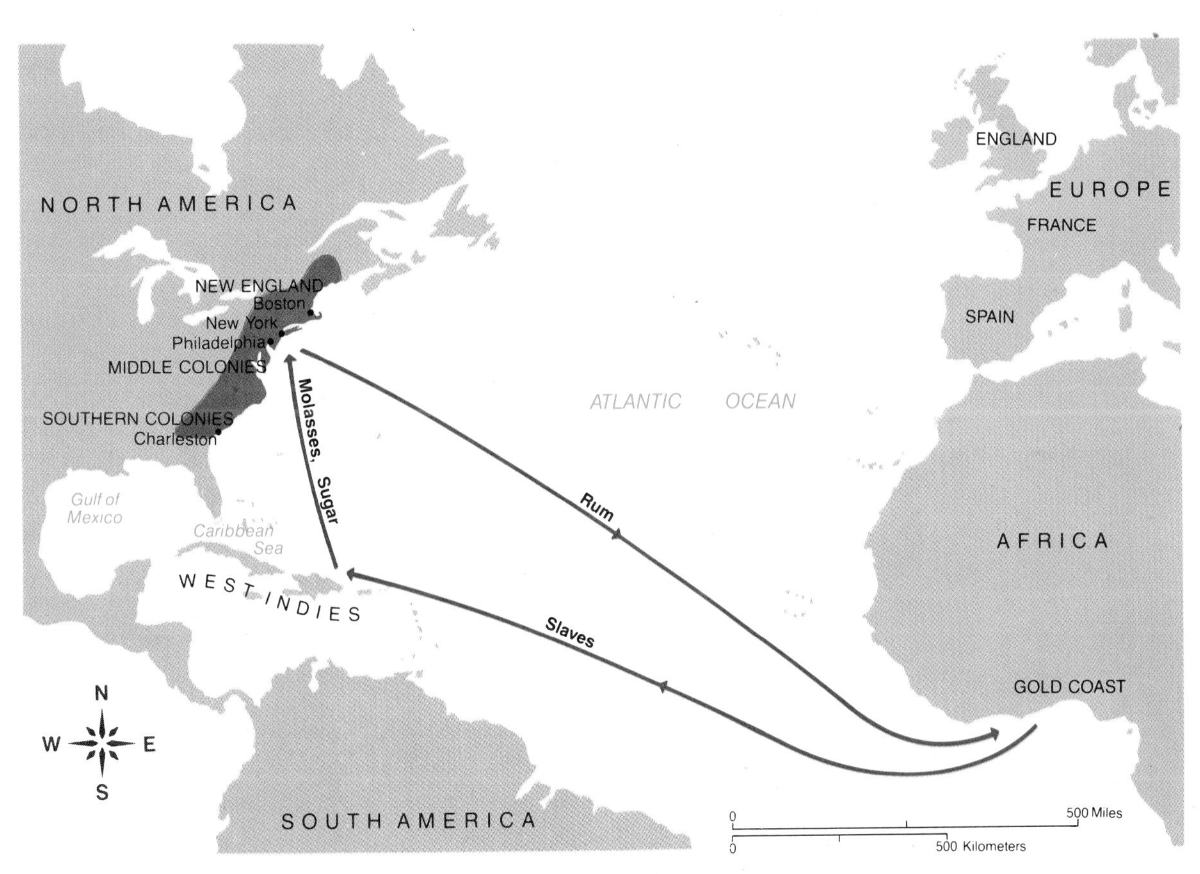

Triangular Trade

Thirteen Colonies

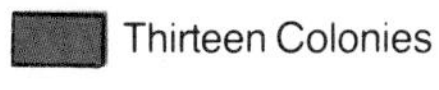 The Triangular Trade

The engraving above shows Paul Cuffe and one of his ships. Below is the engraving of Phillis Wheatley which appeared on the title page of her book of poems printed in 1773. Wheatley's poem on the death of George Whitfield, a minister, was printed as a broadside, or handbill, in 1770. At that time Wheatley was only 17 years old and had been in America only 9 years. The sale of this poem launched her career.

couldn't interest others in helping him pay for it.

Most free blacks did not do nearly as well as Cuffe. Life in New England was not easy for them. Black storekeepers, for example, were allowed to make only small amounts of money. As one traveler from France put it: "The whites do not like to give [blacks] credit to undertake any extensive commerce, nor even give them means of a common education."

New England slaves served in all kinds of jobs. Some were artisans and carpenters. Some were servants. Perhaps the best known servant was Phillis Wheatley, who wrote fine poetry. Her verse was published and admired by readers both in the colonies and in Europe. Wheatley was set free by her owners.

7. What kinds of work did free blacks do in New England? What did slaves do?

8. Who were Paul Cuffe and Phillis Wheatley?

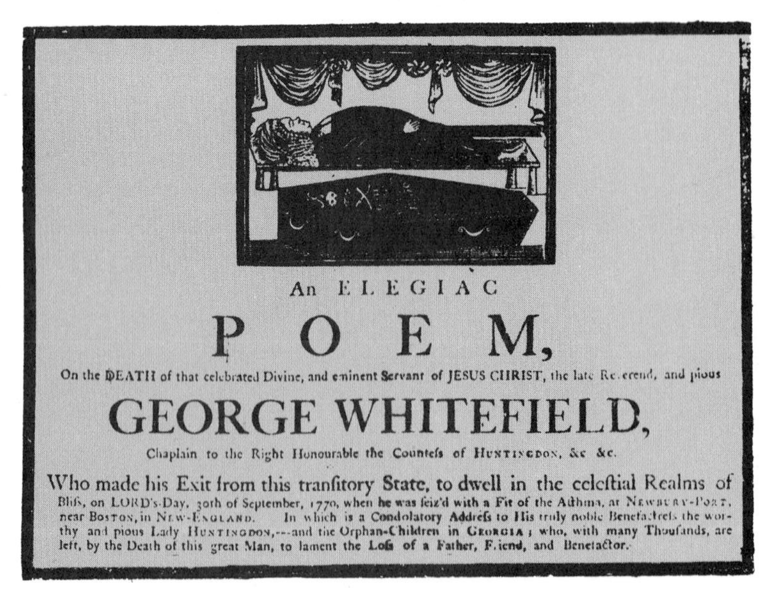

An ELEGIAC

POEM,

On the DEATH of that celebrated Divine, and eminent Servant of JESUS CHRIST, the late Reverend, and pious

GEORGE WHITEFIELD,

Chaplain to the Right Honourable the Countess of HUNTINGDON, &c &c.

Who made his Exit from this transitory State, to dwell in the celestial Realms of Bliss, on LORD's-Day, 30th of September, 1770, when he was seiz'd with a Fit of the Asthma, at NEWBURY-PORT, near BOSTON, in NEW-ENGLAND. In which is a Condolatory Address to His truly noble Benefactress the worthy and pious Lady HUNTINGDON,---and the Orphan-Children in GEORGIA; who, with many Thousands, are left, by the Death of this great Man, to lament the Loss of a Father, Friend, and Benefactor.

Part Two

Living in the Middle Colonies

Why were the Middle Colonies called America's "bread basket"?

Along the middle Atlantic coast runs a strip of flat land, or plain. Here, in the Middle Colonies, the soil was very rich. The land was perfect for growing wheat and other cereal crops. For this reason, the Middle Colonies were known as the "bread basket of the New World."

In addition to rich soil, farmers in the Middle Colonies had another blessing. Large, deep rivers flowed past their fields. (See map, page 59). These rivers were the highways which many farmers used to ship their goods to market. Meat and grain from the Middle Colonies were sold along the Atlantic coast, in the West Indies, and in Europe.

In the Middle Colonies, farms were of all sizes. Some were very large and were called *estates*. There were also many small farms. Besides wheat, farmers raised oats, barley, hogs, cows, sheep, and horses.

Owners of the big estates lived in beautiful homes, many of them built of brick. The owners rented parts of their land to settlers. Large numbers of indentured servants (page 43) also worked on the estates. Many of these servants were Germans and Scotch-Irish.

Small farms were worked by their owners. German landowners produced fine gardens, orchards, and livestock (farm animals). Most of the Germans were peace-loving folk who wished to be left alone among themselves. Scotch-Irish often settled along the frontier on the edge of the wilderness. Many Scotch-Irish farmers were also hunters and soldiers.

1. What crops were produced in the Middle Colonies?

2. Why were the large, deep rivers of the Middle Colonies an advantage to farmers?

Why did manufacturing and trade also become important?

Manufacturing and trade grew to be as important as farming in the Middle Colonies.

The Middle Colonies contained iron, which was made into stoves, nails, and iron parts for ships and wagons. Other goods manufactured were cloth, bricks, barrels, and wagons. Shipbuilding was a busy industry.

Many of these goods and much of the farm produce funneled into Philadelphia and New York City. They were the two largest cities in colonial times. Both were busy seaports and trading centers on the Atlantic coast. (See map, page 68.)

Merchants in New York City and Philadelphia bought farm goods and other products from the Middle Colonies. These goods were loaded in ships and sent abroad to be sold. With the profits from sales, the merchants bought products from Europe. These goods were shipped back to New York City and Philadelphia to be sold in the colonies. Thus the docks at these two great trading centers were always busy with ships coming and going.

Women took an active part in the trade of the Middle Colonies. Many women ran shops, taverns, even foundries. A number of women owned news-

Once this painting of a farm at the foot of the Catskill Mountains in New York State hung over the mantle of the house it depicts. The farm was typical of the Middle Colonies.

papers. Many were printers. Seven of the official printers for colonial governments were women.

Being in business was not always easy for women in colonial America. Sometimes "she-merchants," as they often called themselves, were not treated fairly. An advertisement which a group of women placed in a New York City newspaper in 1733 explained the kinds of problems they faced.

We, widows of this city, have had a meeting as our case is something deplorable. We beg you will give it place in your weekly journal, that we may be relieved. It is as follows:

We are housekeepers, pay our taxes, carry on trade and most of us are she-merchants. As we . . . contribute to the support of the government, we ought to be entitled to some of the sweets of it.

Despite the problems of these "she-merchants," most merchants in New York City and Philadelphia did very well. Some grew quite rich.

3. Why did New York City and Philadelphia become great trading centers?

4. What part did women take in the business life of the Middle Colonies?

Part Three

Living in the Southern Colonies

In what two ways did farming develop in the South?

In the South, the weather is warmer than in New England or the Middle Colonies. There are long, hot summers and mild winters. The land along the coast is flat. Inland are hills and high mountains.

Farming in the Old South was carried on in two ways. First, there were the large farms, or plantations. Spreading over thousands of acres, the plantations were much like the estates in the Middle Colonies. The big difference was that plantations were worked by slaves, not indentured servants or hired workers. Cotton, rice, and tobacco were raised on plantations.

Second, there were small farms. They were found everywhere in the South, but especially in the hilly, western, wooded country. There, the struggling pioneer farmers cut clearings out of the wilderness. These people were the Germans and Scotch-Irish, whom we have already met in the Middle Colonies.

Beautiful cities such as Charleston and Savannah developed in the South. But these cities did not grow into huge trade centers as did Philadelphia and New York City. The reason was that the plantations carried on a great deal of trade themselves.

Plantations were located on or near the coast, often along rivers. Each plantation was a small town in itself. There were homes and cabins for workers and slaves. There were buildings where household goods like soap and candles were made. And there were sheds where products to be traded were stored.

Large plantations had their own docks on rivers or harbors. From these docks trading ships sailed back and forth to other colonies, or to Europe.

1. Name the two kinds of agriculture found in the South.

2. Why was a plantation like a small town?

Why did slavery increase in the South?

The first Africans to arrive in the English colonies in 1619 were probably indentured servants. Slavery grew slowly, as you have learned. (See page 44.) But by 1700 things had begun to change. More and more blacks were brought from Africa to be sold as slaves. The greatest demand for slaves was in the South. Slaves were needed to work the great plantations that were growing up along the coastal lowlands. By 1720 blacks outnumbered whites by more than two to one in South Carolina. In the heavily settled plantation areas surrounding Charleston, there were three times as many blacks as whites.

One reason African slaves were in such demand was that they were good farmers. They knew how to farm the lowlands because the climate and soil were like those of their homelands. Slaves were able to recognize many useful plants which they found growing in the South. They taught their masters how to make those plants grow. They also knew how to raise cattle in the hot, humid climate. It was the slaves who really introduced cattle raising in the Carolina wilderness.

Slaves worked not only in the fields, but at skilled jobs as well. They helped build homes and cabins. They worked as carpenters, sawyers, and ironworkers. Some were servants in plantation houses. And a few held "white collar" jobs, such as clerks or medical assistants.

3. Why did slaves from Africa prove to be good farmers in the South?

4. What kinds of skilled work did slaves perform?

How were slaves brought to America and how were they treated?

African slaves were sometimes victims of their own chiefs and of Arab traders living along the African coast. For a price, chiefs sold their own people (or sometimes prisoners captured in battle) to traders. In turn, the traders sold them at a higher price to the owners of slave ships. The slaves were chained together and packed into the bottoms of dirty, foul-smelling vessels. There was little air or food on the long voyage across the Atlantic, and many Africans died. The very sick were often thrown overboard to drown.

Slaves had no rights in colonial America. They were looked upon as property instead of as human beings.

At That Time

Eliza Lucas Pinckney lived in South Carolina from 1722-1793. She was a very successful plantation manager and the mother of two sons who became famous when the United States gained its independence. Fortunately she kept a "letter-book." It contains copies of letters she sent to others and also copies of business papers. The following picture of her and her times is based on this book and other sources.

Once Eliza Pinckney taught her neighbors to grow indigo, it became an important crop in South Carolina.

Afraid? Perhaps I should have been. But I wasn't. I was excited and happy to become a planter, even though I was only sixteen years old at the time.

My father, George Lucas, was a British army officer. In 1738, he was called to serve in another country. So he had to leave South Carolina. Of course I was sorry to see him go. My father was also my teacher and my friend. He must have had a lot of faith in me because he left me in complete charge of our three plantations. In addition to managing them, I had to care for my sick mother and a younger sister.

Ever since I was a little girl, I've loved plants. Nothing gives me more pleasure than working with them. I try to make them produce better. I also experiment with new plants never before grown in the South. Sometimes my experiments succeed. They did in the case of indigo. (Indigo is a plant from which blue dye is made.) The first time I planted indigo, frost killed all of the plants. Worms destroyed my second planting. At last, however, I developed a strong plant strain. I raised a good crop, but I did not harvest it. Instead I let that entire planting go to seed. Then I carefully gathered all of the seeds. I shared them with my neighbors. They, too, began to plant indigo. In time it became South Carolina's chief money-making crop. The first free school for children outside Charleston was built with money made from indigo.

When I tried to raise silkworms, I did not succeed. I had hoped to produce silk from which fine cloth could be made. Despite all my efforts, I only produced enough silk to make three dresses.

While I was a planter, I sometimes left my work to visit friends. Often I went to Charleston to stay with Judge and Mrs. Charles Pinckney. When Mrs. Pinckney died, the judge asked me to marry him. He was twenty years older than I, but that did not matter. We shared thirteen happy years together. Some of them were spent in England. Then my husband died very suddenly. I was left a widow with three young children to care for.

I did not have much time to sit and feel sorry for myself. My husband had owned seven plantations. I owned the three which once were my father's. So as a young widow I became responsible for all ten plantations and for the 300 slaves who worked on them.

My working days are long ones. But no matter how busy the day is, I find time for music, reading, and studying. Over the years, I've studied French, shorthand, and the law.

Although I own ten plantations, I have many worries. I'm especially worried about all of my debts. It is a constant struggle to pay all the bills and to provide for the needs of all the slaves. Whenever I'm upset, I go into the fields to work among the plants. Throughout my life, they have been my chief source of joy.

A young British officer painted this watercolor of the hold of a slave ship in 1846. Horrible conditions like this were the rule from the beginning of the slave trade.

They could not vote. They could not protest against the treatment they received. They had almost no hope of freedom.

When blacks were sold at slave auctions, families were often split up. Children were separated from their parents. Discipline ranged from affection and kindness to downright brutality. Many slaves were whipped for daring to refuse to obey orders.

Even so, not all African slaves in England's thirteen American colonies found life entirely bad. In some cases they bought their own freedom or were granted it by their masters. Thousands of free blacks had their own farms. Some free blacks managed to buy members of their families out of slavery.

5. How were Africans captured and brought to America?

6. Describe the way in which slaves were treated.

How did education and religion develop in the South?

Education in the Old South was mainly for the rich. Because there were few towns, there were few schools. The children of plantation owners studied under private teachers, or tutors. For those who lived on small farms or on the frontier, there was little or no regular schooling. The teaching of slaves was mostly forbidden. Plantation owners believed that education would make them more restless under slave conditions.

Sons of the wealthy often went to college in England. In 1693 a college was founded in Virginia. Named William and Mary, in honor of England's king and queen, it is the second oldest college in the United States. (The first college was founded in Cambridge, Massachusetts, in 1636. It is now Harvard University.)

For the most part, Southerners were not strict and serious about religion.

They had not tried to break away from the Church of England, as the Puritans had done. Southerners went to church, but they enjoyed sports and entertainment, too. Dancing and horse racing were popular pastimes enjoyed by rich and poor alike.

As the Southern Colonies grew, people of many different religions settled there. French Protestants, driven from their homeland, moved to Charleston and other towns on the coast. Quakers also arrived in large numbers. To the west, the Scotch-Irish on the frontier were strong Presbyterians. Small groups of Jews settled in Charleston and Savannah.

Baptist and Methodist preachers rode on horseback from town to town to spread their teachings. Many blacks became Christians. Religion finally became a strong force in the South. But, unlike early New England, people of different faiths managed to live together peacefully.

7. Why were there few schools in the Southern Colonies?

8. What religions were found in the South?

Part Four

Daily Life in the Thirteen Colonies

How did the settlers supply themselves with clothes?

In colonial times garments often were handed down through two or even three generations. It was not unusual for a girl to wear a dress that had been made for her grandmother. Clothes were all handmade. Further, they were very costly. In the year 1650, for example, a man's best suit or a woman's best dress was worth as much as a cow or a half-dozen goats.

In colonial times most clothing was made from wool, linen, or leather. Obtaining any of these materials was far from easy. To get wool, for example, colonists first had to raise the sheep. Then the sheep had to be sheared. Next the fleece had to be washed and combed before it could be spun into thread.

Spinning fleece into thread on a wool wheel was hard work. Look at the picture on the right. Notice the large wool wheel. It usually was about six and

A woman does the work of a colonial spinner at Old Sturbridge Village, Sturbridge, Massachusetts.

Colonial Population about 1750

one-half feet (198 cm) in diameter. To make the wheel work, the spinner, usually a woman, had to pace back and forth, back and forth. In a single day, she would walk a distance equal to at least four miles (6.4 km). Even experienced spinners could produce only four skeins of thread in a long working day. That is only enough thread to weave two or three yards (2 or 3 m) of cloth.

If settlers wanted colored cloth, they had to make their own dyes. They hunted for roots, berries, and flowers which could be used as dyes. Often children were sent into the woods to collect materials for dyes. To get yellow, they picked goldenrod or stripped bark from birch trees. For red, they gathered berries. For browns, they chose nuts. Purple dyes were made from iris flowers or wild grapes.

The flowers, nuts, or berries were boiled in a big pot of water until the right color was obtained. Then the pot was hung on a hook in the fireplace and the cloth put in it. Someone had to keep stirring the pot with a long stick while it boiled. Very often the hot job of stirring boiling dye pots was done by children.

1. Why were clothes often handed down from generation to generation in colonial families?

2. What roles did women and children play in producing clothes?

How important were newspapers in colonial America?

In colonial times there was no television or radio, of course. But there were a few newspapers. They were an important means of communication among the colonists. People used them to advertise their goods and services. They also used them to express their opinions on many subjects, including their growing discontent with British rule.

The first regular newspaper was started in 1704 by John Campbell, a Boston postmaster. Not long after that several other newspapers were founded. Most of them were printed in the Middle Colonies.

Some newspapers from the Middle Colonies became famous. One was *The Pennsylvania Gazette* published by Benjamin Franklin. (See pages 103, 113, and 123 for more about Franklin.)

Focus on Skills

Reading charts and graphs is a skill important to the study of history. By observing details in a pictograph such as the one shown below, you can form a general idea of the kinds of peoples who lived in the British colonies in 1763. Study the graph carefully. Then show that you understand it by answering the questions which follow.

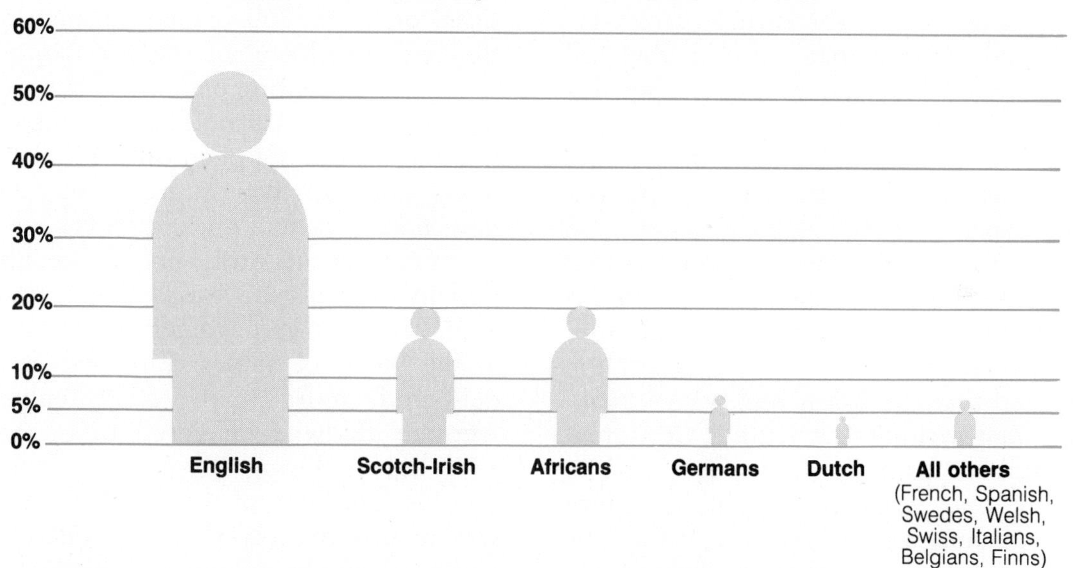

1. What question do the figures in this graph answer?
2. Which group of people made up the largest part of the population of the colonies in 1763? About what percentage of the population did they represent?
3. Which two groups of people represented equal numbers in the population?
4. What percentage of the population was German? Dutch?
5. If all other Europeans were grouped together, what percentage of the population would they represent?
6. Why do you think that no figures are given for the Indian population in the colonies in 1763?

Another well-known paper was the *New York Journal*. For thirty years John and Elizabeth Holt published it together. John died in 1784. Elizabeth Holt carried on the business. In fact, she took on an added job: she became state printer for New York.

Two other newspapers were founded by members of the Holt family. Their son moved to Norfolk, Virginia, where he began his own newspaper. Their daughter married and moved to Philadelphia. There she and her husband started the *Independent Gazetter*.

Their paper never rivaled Benjamin Franklin's, but it was an important force for independence.

Perhaps the colonial newspaper best known today is *The New York Weekly Journal.* Its fame rests on the story of its editor, John Peter Zenger.

Zenger was a German immigrant. He criticized New York's governor, William Cosby, in *The Journal.*

Angered, Cosby struck back. He ordered Zenger arrested for libel, or "telling lies." For ten months Zenger was kept in jail awaiting trial. During that time his wife showed both her ability and her courage by continuing to publish the paper.

At last Zenger was brought to trial in 1735. He was defended by a famous Philadelphia lawyer, Andrew Hamilton. In presenting Zenger's case, Hamilton argued that the editor had been "speaking and writing the truth." Certainly, Hamilton insisted, it was no crime to speak and write the truth! The jury agreed and set Zenger free, while the onlookers in the courtroom cheered.

Zenger's trial is important in history for two reasons. First, it showed that while people can be punished for libel, they cannot be punished for telling or printing the truth. Second, it marked a big step toward establishing freedom of the press in America.

3. Why were colonial newspapers an important means of communication?

4. What were two important outcomes of John Peter Zenger's trial?

Who provided health services in colonial America?

When people got sick during colonial times, there was little use sending for a doctor. Doctors were scarce. And most people who served as doctors had little or no training.

If you wanted to be a doctor, you just called yourself one. Barbers, preachers, and old people often took the title. Blacksmiths often served as dentists. They had one sure cure for aching teeth. Pull them out!

What little doctors knew of medicine they learned from others as apprentices, or on-the-job helpers. Sometimes they just read one of the few popular books about treating patients. There was no other way to learn. The first hospital in America did not open until 1751. But it did not train doctors or nurses. The first medical school opened in 1765.

One special and honored occupation in the early days was that of midwife. *Midwives* were women who assisted at the births of babies. Elizabeth King delivered more than 1000 babies. Another midwife delivered more than 1300 babies during 30 years of service. She lost only two of those babies. That was an amazing record because deaths in childbirth in those days were high.

Every family had its own "home remedies." When someone got sick, parents treated the illness according to "recipes" passed down through the family.

Serious illnesses often were treated by bleeding the patient. Sometimes a vein in the arm was cut to let out the "bad blood." At other times, leeches or blood-sucking worms were attached to the ailing part. George Washington was treated by bleeding.

Colonists and Indians feared the disease called smallpox. It was often fatal. Even if people survived the disease, they were left with scars, or "pock marks." Before settlers brought the disease from Europe, smallpox was unknown in America. Indians had no built-up defenses against the disease. Whole tribes of Indians died of smallpox. Although vaccination was known in colonial times, most people thought the process was too dangerous. So they refused to be vaccinated.

5. Who served as doctors in colonial times?

6. Why did people rely on home remedies?

7. Why did people in colonial times fear smallpox? Why did people refuse to be vaccinated?

Part Five

The French and Indian War

Which countries had claims to North America?

In 1750, three European countries claimed parts of the North American continent. They were Great Britain, (England), France, and Spain.

Great Britain owned northern Canada and the thirteen colonies along the Atlantic coast. The Appalachian (ap′ə lā′ chən) Mountains bordered the colonies on the west.

Spain had colonies in Florida and Mexico. The Spanish also had settlements in Texas and Mexico. Although the Spanish claimed California, the first permanent settlements there were not made until the late 1760s.

The French settled in southern Canada. From there, they pushed south of the Great Lakes in search of more territory.

French explorers sailed on the Great Lakes. They discovered a highway of rivers connecting Canada with the Gulf of Mexico. An explorer named La Salle made daring trips down the Ohio and Mississippi rivers. La Salle claimed the Mississippi River basin for France in 1682.

The French called their newly found territory *Louisiana* in honor of King Louis of France. Louisiana reached from the British colonies in the east to the Rocky Mountains in the west. It stretched from the Great Lakes in the north to the Gulf of Mexico in the south. Through the heart of this land flowed the Ohio and Mississippi rivers.

1. Name the three countries which laid claim to North America.

2. How far did French Louisiana stretch?

Why did Great Britain and France go to war?

The king of England had promised the land west of the Appalachian Mountains to Virginia and several other colonies. The colonists planned to move west over the mountains into the Ohio River Valley. Virginia sent a 21-year-old soldier named George Washington to warn the French against building forts there. The French did not heed Washington's warnings.

By 1750, both England and France were ready to fight for ownership of the western lands. But the prize was to be even bigger than that. The winner was to take all of the loser's colonies in North America.

Finally, England and France went to war to decide which would become the

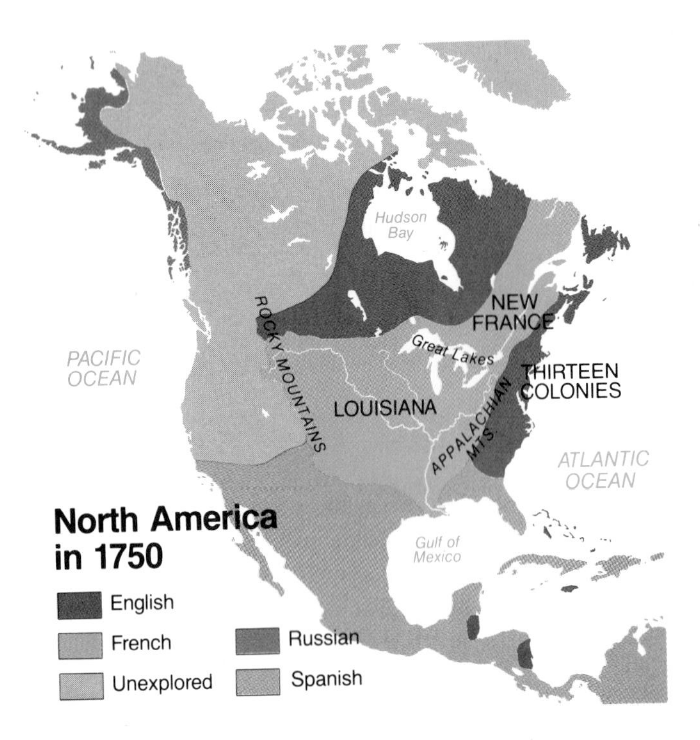

North America in 1750

world's leading nation. Battles raged around the globe—in North America, Asia, and Africa. French and English sailors clashed on the high seas.

In Europe, the worldwide contest between the British and French was called the Seven Years' War. It lasted from 1756 to 1763. In North America it was called the *French and Indian War*. This struggle was named for the French and for the many Indians who helped them.

3. Why and where did France and England fight during the Seven Years' War?

4. How did the French and Indian War get its name?

Why did most Indians side with the French?

For the most part, American Indians sided with France during the French and Indian War. The French treated the Indians better than the English did. Only the Indians of upper New York helped England. The French had once attacked those tribes, and the Indians had never forgiven them.

The rest of the Indians hated the English because they were destroyers. The English were farmers who chopped down trees in the forests. They cleared the land, built homes for their families, and drove the Indians away. The French did not live like the English. The French were trappers, not farmers. They left the forests intact because they wanted to trap beaver and other animals there. Nor did the French bring their families with them to America. Instead, the trappers married Indian women and raised families in the wilderness.

Thus the French and Indians mixed, while the English kept to their

North America in 1763

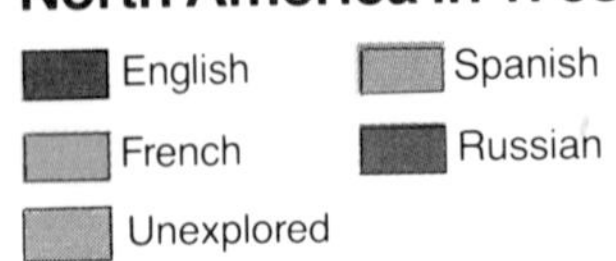

The French fought in the New World like their Indian allies. In this painting, British troops make easy targets for hidden French and Indian snipers. General Braddock (center) died from his wound.

own ways. It is easy to see why the Indians sided with the French in the French and Indian War.

5. For what three reasons did the Indians side with the French?

How and why did the British finally win the war?

At first the French were successful because they knew how to fight in the forests. In battle, the French and Indians hid behind trees and could scarcely be seen. The British, on the other hand, fought out in the open and charged shoulder to shoulder at the enemy.

George Washington warned the British general, Edward Braddock, to scatter his men behind trees in battle. But Braddock was stubborn and would not listen to the young American from Virginia. Braddock led the British and colonial troops across the mountains into western Pennsylvania. There he met the French and Indians near what is now Pittsburgh.

Wearing bright red coats, the British made perfect targets for their enemies. The men huddled together and were mowed down like grass. General Braddock was killed. George Washington, now a colonel, led about 500 soldiers in retreat.

It took years for the British "redcoats" to recover from this loss. They should have listened to George Washington's wise advice to take cover in battle. But the British soldiers looked down on the Americans as "farmers."

Finally the British pulled themselves together. Now it was their turn to win battles. Well-trained troops drove the French back into Canada. Then the British surprised the French at Quebec (kwi bek′) and captured the big fort there. A few years later, in 1763, the French surrendered.

All over the world the British were victorious. In North America, they took over all of the land east of the Mississippi River and all of Canada as well. The British Empire became the most powerful in the world. The English and the American colonists were delighted over their great success against France.

6. Why were the British forced to change their fighting style?

7. When and how did the war come to an end?

Building Your Vocabulary

Select the word(s) which best completes each of the following sentences.

1. Goods are (a) valuable things. (b) products which can be seen and touched. (c) tasks which people perform for one another.
2. When people teach, cut hair, deliver mail, or prepare meals, they are providing (a) services. (b) favors. (c) goods.
3. Soil, water, forests, minerals, and harbors are examples of (a) manufacturing. (b) services. (c) natural resources.
4. A frontier is (a) a crowded urban area. (b) on the edge of the wilderness. (c) a forest.
5. A person who learns by on-the-job training is called (a) a skilled worker. (b) an unskilled worker. (c) an apprentice.
6. —?— is telling or printing lies about another person. (a) Publishing (b) Protesting (c) Libel
7. The French and Indians were —?— in the war against England. (a) allies (b) foes (c) neutral

Recalling What You Have Learned

Match each item in Column A with the correct item in Column B.

Column A	Column B
1. fishing	A. large southern estate
2. Triangular Trade	B. a major trade center in the Middle Colonies
3. breadbasket of America	C. newspaper publisher accused of libel
4. Philadelphia	D. an important source of jobs and income in New England
5. John Peter Zenger	E. name of lands claimed by France
6. Paul Cuffe	F. part of world-wide struggle between France and England
7. Louisiana	G. the Middle Colonies
8. French and Indian War	H. black sea captain and shipbuilder
9. plantation	I. trade in rum, molasses, and slaves
10. Quebec	J. important French city captured by British

Discussing the Important Ideas in This Chapter

1. How do land, climate, and natural resources help shape the way people live?
2. Compare and contrast the kinds of work done by blacks in New England and blacks in the Southern Colonies.
3. Why was clothing expensive in the colonies?
4. Why did the Middle Colonies prosper?
5. Although there were few newspapers in colonial America, they were important. Explain why.

6. How were health services provided in colonial America different from those available today?
7. Compare and contrast town and city life among the Northern, Middle, and Southern colonies.
8. What "lessons" did the colonists and the British learn from the French and Indian War?
9. What major changes took place in the English colonies between 1607, when the first settlement at Jamestown was begun, and the end of the French and Indian War in 1763?

Improving Your Map Skills

The map shown on page 80 is called a *population density map. Population*, as you know, means people. *Density* refers to thickness. A population density map, therefore, is one which shows how thickly, or how densely, areas are populated.

The first step in reading any map is to look at its key. The *key* explains what various colors, shades, or symbols used on that map mean. Study the map key and use it to answer the following questions.

1. Look at the key to the map on page 80. What does one red dot mean?
2. What does a heavy red area mean?
3. Why are some areas not dotted at all?
4. With your finger trace the western edges of the lightly shaded areas. Those western edges were the frontier, the outposts. Beyond the frontier was the wilderness.
5. Write one or two sentences summarizing the data on this map.

Improving Your Study Skills: *Writing*

Imagine that you were a man, woman, or child in one of the thirteen colonies.

Write a letter to someone in another country. You might want to choose the land from which some of your own ancestors came. In that letter describe your daily life. Tell about your work, your pleasures, your hopes, and your concerns.

Chapter 4

The Colonies Win Freedom

The North Bridge and minuteman statue, Concord, Massachusetts

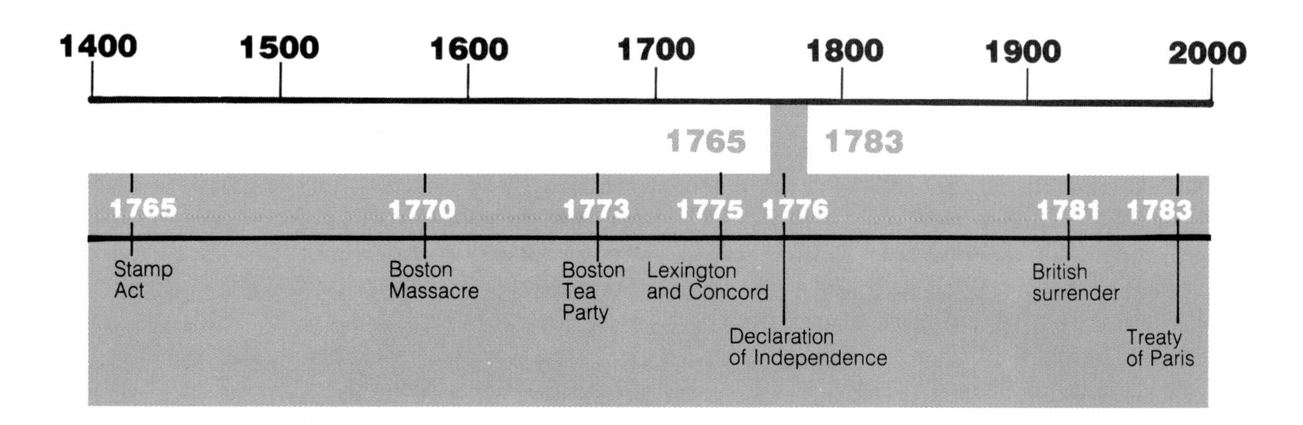

Part One

The British Empire and Its Colonies

Why were colonies both important and expensive to England?

For more than 150 years American colonists lived happily under British rule. From time to time there were disagreements, of course. But none were so serious that anyone even considered a break from England. From the beginning close ties had bound the peoples on each side of the Atlantic. They spoke the same language. They had similar ideas. Even the many non-English who went to the colonies shared the feeling that English protection was good.

With the end of the French and Indian War in 1763, however, some drastic changes began. Relations between England and the American colonies went from good to bad to worse. In thirteen years, the colonists would declare their independence and then fight a long, bitter war to obtain it.

To understand how and why those things happened, you need to know more about the British Empire. An *empire* is a group of colonies owned by one strong nation. In the 1700s a nation's empire showed its strength. Certainly

England's empire was the envy of other nations.

The English owned colonies in Ireland, North America, the West Indies, and Asia. Taken all together, England and its colonies made up the British Empire.

It is hard to say which of its colonies England treasured most. The thirteen American colonies were important, of course. But so were Ireland and India. The West Indies were small, but wealthy. The American colonies were only a part of the empire.

The colonies were valuable not only because they showed England's strength and power. The English traded with their colonies, always being sure to make a profit. The colonies supplied England with raw materials. In turn they bought English-made goods. The American colonies produced meat, grain, tobacco, and lumber for England. The West Indies were rich in sugar.

Having colonies was not all good, however. Sometimes they could be costly. When the British had to send troops to protect Americans from the French and the Indians, the costs were high. And when they had to fight, as they did in the far-flung Seven Years' War, the costs went even higher.

1. What is an empire? Why did England want one?

2. What were the advantages and disadvantages of having colonies?

Who ruled the British Empire in 1763?

In 1763 the British were ruled by a governing body called Parliament (pär′ lə mənt). Its members came from all parts of England, but none came from the colonies.

Parliament was supposed to represent all the British people. But in the 1700s many English people did not have the right to vote. In general, those who could vote were well-off. They elected members who also were well-to-do. Many were large landowners or merchants. They were the very people who had been taxed heavily to pay for the war in America and for the other costs of empire.

In addition to Parliament, the British had a king. In 1763 the king was a young man—then just 25 years old—named George III. George was a sincere, hard-working man. He loved sports, especially wrestling. He liked to hunt and fish, and he ran his own farm. George also loved his family, and he

George III posed for this portrait in an ermine mantle. Despite his royal clothes, George had trouble as a ruler.

spent much time with his children. He was, in short, a good man, and his subjects spoke kindly of him. They even called him "Farmer George." Unfortunately he was not a very good ruler. His mother wanted him to stand up to Parliament. "Be a king, George!" she told him time and again.

King George did try to rule Parliament. He spent a lot of his own money trying to get the "right" people elected to that important body. He even bribed some of the members to do what he thought was best for England and its empire. But Parliament was too strong for the king. It became the real force in running the empire. And the American colonists began to quarrel with Parliament.

3. What was Parliament?

4. Why did Parliament really rule the empire rather than the king?

Part Two

New Plans for the Colonies

Why was 1763 a turning point?

American colonists were proud and happy people in 1763. They had helped England win the French and Indian War. Foreign trade was bringing them wealth. Money jingled in their pockets. The colonists had all the rights the English enjoyed. Yet they governed themselves, for the most part.

By 1763 colonists had been in America for over 150 years. And England was a great distance away. Ships took weeks or months to cross the Atlantic Ocean.

It is not surprising then, that by 1763 the colonists had become different from people in England. The colonists liked to think for themselves. They dressed, ate, and even spoke differently from their British cousins across the sea. In short, the colonists had changed into Americans.

On the other side of the Atlantic, things did not look so bright. England was glad, of course, that it had won the long war against France. But the war had been very costly. The British treasury was empty.

The British also faced trouble with Indians in the western lands. An Ottawa chief named Pontiac led thousands of Indian braves. These Indians had fought on the French side. They mistrusted the English. Pontiac helped to wipe out all the English forts and settlements in the land just won from the French. For five months Pontiac laid seige to Detroit. During that long and difficult period, Parliament decided that something would have to be done to solve the "Indian problem" once and for all.

1. Why did the colonists feel proud and happy about themselves in 1763?

2. What two great worries troubled the British?

How did England try to solve its problems?

The first step England took was to bring peace to the western lands. Pioneers from the thirteen colonies were pouring across the mountains into the Ohio country. The Indians were fighting them desperately for the land. To stop this fighting, the English ordered all the settlers to return east across the mountains. Meanwhile, a large British army brought Pontiac under control.

The next step England took was to find a way to support its large army in America. Money was badly needed. Why not make the colonies pay? After all, the British army was protecting the colonists from the Indians. And the colonies were strong and prosperous.

Taking orders from England was something the colonists had never enjoyed. Usually England was very careful about laying down the law. But now Americans were being told that they could no longer settle in the West. England forbade them to move to the rich farm lands of the Ohio and Kentucky country.

On top of that, the British decided to send still more troops to America. Parliament made it clear that Americans were going to have to pay for those troops. It passed the first *Quartering Act.* (*Quartering* means providing housing, food, and other necessities.) The act said that the colonists would have to find rooms for the soldiers if regular army quarters were not available. The rooms could be in taverns, inns, houses, or barns. The colonists also had to give the soldiers food and furniture. All costs were to be met by the colonists. Their assemblies or governing bodies were expected to raise the necessary taxes.

3. Why did Parliament tell the Americans that they could not move west into Ohio and Kentucky?

4. What was the Quartering Act?

Why did England increase the taxes of the American colonists?

For many years, England had placed taxes on goods that were shipped into the colonies. For instance, there was a tax on molasses, which the colonists bought from the West Indies (page 70). These tax measures were called trade laws, because they controlled American foreign trade. In the early days, the British were not too strict about carrying out these laws. For instance, they pretended not to see shipments of molasses arriving at American docks. They let the molasses go through without taxing it.

But after 1763, the picture changed. The British needed money. They became more strict about the trade laws and also taxed the colonies in other ways. The Stamp Act taxed almost every kind of printed matter like calendars, newspapers—even playing cards. Legal forms were also taxed. Colonists had to buy stamped paper to prove that they had paid the tax. When this law was passed in 1765, Americans boiled over with anger. There was rioting in the streets.

5. What were trade laws?

6. Why did the British become more strict about the trade laws? Why did they increase taxes?

How did the colonists react to stricter trade laws and tax hikes?

No one likes to pay taxes, of course. But most of us are willing to help support the government. In the United States, if we do not like the way our tax money is used, we can vote against those in power. We can choose a new President and new representatives in Congress to serve us. In other words, the government represents the people and does what we tell it to do.

The colonists did not mind paying taxes to their own colonial governments. Americans served in these governments

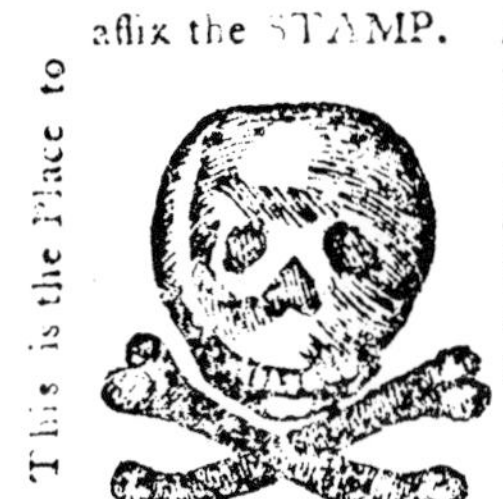

A stamp (above) showed that the tax called for by the hated Stamp Act of 1765 had been paid. The skull and crossbones (left) shows how some colonists felt about the tax. The broadside, or poster, calls for a boycott of a Boston importer.

WILLIAM JACKSON,

an *IMPORTER*; at the

BRAZEN HEAD,

North Side of the TOWN-HOUSE,

and *Oppoſite the Town-Pump,* in

Corn-hill, BOSTON.

It is deſired that the SONS and DAUGHTERS of *LIBERTY*, would not buy any one thing of him, for in ſo doing they will bring Diſgrace upon *themſelves*, and their *Poſterity*, for *ever* and *ever*, AMEN.

and controlled them. But the Stamp Act was different. This was the very first tax Parliament had ever placed directly on Americans. The colonists had no representatives in Parliament.

What difference did that make? "All the difference in the world," said the Americans. If the colonists had no representatives to speak for them in England, Parliament could tax them down to their last penny. There would be no way for the Americans to fight back.

Some of the colonists who were most angry about Parliament's actions joined secret clubs. Men joined the Sons of Liberty. They said they would use force, if necessary, to stop the British. Women joined the Daughters of Liberty. As early as 1766, women were active in tax-defying groups.

Most colonists did not join the Sons or Daughters of Liberty. But they did take part in another plan. They refused to buy goods from England until the taxes were removed. Such refusal to buy is called a *boycott*.

The American boycott on British goods worked so well that the loss of business hurt England more than the loss of taxes. Parliament canceled the Stamp Act.

Although Parliament backed down on the Stamp Act, its problems with the colonies were by no means solved. In a very short time there was more trouble.

7. Why were the colonists so angry about the Stamp Act?

8. In what ways did colonists react to the Stamp Act?

Part Three

Steps toward War

Why did violence break out at the "Boston Massacre"?

The peace between the colonies and Parliament was short-lived. Soon a series of events led to more anger on each side of the Atlantic. Those events finally resulted in the first outbreak of violence.

In 1767, Parliament put new taxes on the colonists. This time it taxed paint, glass, lead, tea, and paper. Once again the colonists reacted with a boycott. This angered Parliament. It ordered still more troops to America. Then the colonists set up a communications network. They called that network "Committees of Correspondence." In all but two of the colonies, the committees worked to keep the Americans stirred up. The network also kept committees in touch with one another. For the first time the colonies began to act as one.

Mercy Otis Warren was at the center of patriot activity before and during the Revolution.

One well-known member of the Committees of Correspondence was Mercy Otis Warren. She wrote poems and plays as well as letters. She had a keen mind and a sharp, biting wit. Her writings enraged the British, but they won many Americans to the patriots' cause.

In such a climate of mistrust and anger, it was only a matter of time before violence erupted. In Boston on March 5, 1770, some boys began throwing snowballs at a redcoat guarding the tax collector's office. The soldier called for help, which soon arrived. A crowd of colonists gathered. As they moved forward, the British opened fire. A few moments later, five Americans lay dead in the street.

American newspapers were quick to write horror stories about the "Boston Massacre" (mas′ ə kər: a bloody killing). The Sons of Liberty were eager to make the most of the event. One of them was Samuel Adams. He was a master of propaganda (prop′ ə gan′ də: the selection and use of those facts which support only one side of a story). Sam Adams wrote a very one-sided account. He called it "Innocent Blood Crying to God from the Streets of Boston." As he had hoped, it stirred up the people.

There was no photography in those days, of course. But artists drew pictures of the "cruel" redcoats killing "helpless" Americans. One of the artists was Paul Revere, a man we will read about later.

News of the Boston Massacre was spread throughout the colonies by engravings like this one. It was made and sold by Paul Revere, a Boston silversmith.

Looking at pictures of the Boston Massacre, Americans shook with anger. Whether or not what happened in Boston ought to be called a "massacre" is a matter of opinion. It was nonetheless a very important event. Sometimes it even is called the start of the American Revolution. If this is so, the men who died in the Massacre were the first patriots to shed their blood for American freedom.

One of the Americans who died in the Massacre was a black man named Crispus Attucks.

Not much is known about Attucks. He was born a slave in Massachusetts

This famous illustration of the Boston Tea Party was made in the 1800s. A gleeful crowd cheers as patriots dressed as Indians dump tea from the ship Dartmouth into Boston Harbor. How do you think the actual event differed from this drawing?

about 1723. Later he ran away and became a sailor. He was described as being tall and of light color.

At the Boston Massacre, Attucks stood in the front row of the Americans. His large size made him an easy target for British bullets.

Boston honored Attucks and the four other Americans who fell with him. Thousands turned out to parade in the streets. There was no mistake about the fact that anti-British feelings were growing.

After the massacre, British troops quietly left Boston. The soldiers who had fired at the Americans were tried in court. Strange to say, their lawyers were Americans who had no use for the British! Yet these Americans believed in justice and truth and fair play. They also believed that every person accused of a crime has the right to be defended. One of the lawyers was John Adams, who later became the second President of the United States.

The outcome of the trial was a surprise to many and a disappointment to people like Sam Adams. All but two of the British soldiers were freed. These two were given light punishment.

1. What series of events led to the first outbreak of violence in Boston?

2. Why was the Boston Massacre an important event?

What was the Boston Tea Party?

After the Boston Massacre, Parliament again backed down. It voted to repeal or withdraw all of the taxes it had put on the colonists except one small tax—on tea. The tax on tea made the colonists angry. Tea was a very popular drink. Many colonial merchants smuggled tea from Holland to avoid the tax. The boycott of English tea continued.

The British East India Company had tea stored in England. But the huge Company could not pay the customs duties on it. Without paying the duties, the Company could not sell the tea. The Company was important to England. It controlled the government in India as well as Indian trade. Rather than let the East India Company fail, the government decided to send the tea to the colonies. The Company would not have to pay duties, just the small colonial tax. The Company could still sell its tea for less than the price of smuggled tea. Ships carrying tea were sent to American seaports. Colonial merchants were furious. Their smuggling trade would be ruined. The cheaper price did not disguise the tax.

In December 1773, the tea ships began arriving. The Sons of Liberty were ready for them, however. In Charleston, the tea was unloaded. But the colonists kept it in a damp warehouse where it remained unsold. At Philadelphia and New York, the ship captains were "persuaded" to turn back to England without ever entering harbor. But in Boston trouble once again broke out.

Governor Thomas Hutchinson of Massachusetts had two sons who were tea merchants. Hutchinson ordered the colonists to unload the ships. For the colonists, who prized liberty so highly, this was just too much. At huge meetings they promised to disobey the governor.

On a night that will never be forgotten in the United States, the promise was carried out. Colonists dressed as Indians went aboard the tea ships in Boston Harbor. For three hours they ripped open hundreds of boxes of tea and poured the tea overboard into the water. What did it matter to them that the tea they destroyed was worth thousands of dollars? Americans gave their answer to England at the Boston Tea Party. English tax laws would not be obeyed.

3. Why did the government send the British East India Company tea to the colonies?

4. What happened to the tea ships in Boston's harbor? Why?

What was the reaction to the Boston Tea Party?

The English were furious over what the colonists had done. Parliament passed laws to punish the people of Massachusetts. It closed Boston Harbor to ships until the lost tea was paid for. It forbade town meetings. A general with a large army was sent to govern the Massachusetts colony. British soldiers were stationed in American homes.

Most colonists were proud of the Boston Tea Party. Others were shocked over the way the law had been broken. In Virginia, for example, most of the people sided with Massachusetts. This made Virginia's governor so angry that he would not let the House of Burgesses (page 45) meet. But the members met anyway, in secret.

Patrick Henry spoke up at one of these meetings. He told his fellow colonists not to hide their heads from the truth. War had come to America, and Americans must join together and fight. Pointing at his audience, Henry cried:

Why stand we here idle? What is it that the gentlemen wish? What would

they have? Is life so dear or peace so sweet as to be purchased at the price of chains and slavery? Forbid it, Almighty God. I know not what course others may take, but as for me, give me liberty, or give me death!

Meanwhile, in Massachusetts, farmers began training with guns. They called themselves *minutemen*, because they were ready to gather for a battle at a minute's notice.

Other colonies were quick to help Massachusetts. They sent wagonloads of food, so that no one would starve. Virginia held a day of prayer for its "Sister Colony of Massachusetts."

Finally, the colonies agreed to send representatives to a meeting at Philadelphia. This *Continental Congress*, as it was called, discussed the problems that all thirteen colonies faced with England. George Washington and Patrick Henry were among those present at the First Continental Congress.

5. What did Parliament do in response to the Boston Tea Party?

6. How did the other colonists react to what happened in Massachusetts?

Part Four

The American Revolution Begins

When and how did the Revolution begin?

The American Revolution did not happen suddenly. The idea of revolution had been growing "in the hearts and minds" of the colonists over a long period of time. But if one time is to be singled out as the actual beginning, it would be April 19, 1775. The place would be Lexington and Concord, near Boston.

During the spring of 1775, American minutemen were drilling and preparing for war. They had hidden gunpowder and supplies at Concord.

The British discovered the Americans' secret. One night hundreds of redcoats marched on Concord to capture the gunpowder. But the Americans learned of their plans. Paul Revere and William Dawes galloped on horseback ahead of the British. They warned the minutemen to get ready to fight.

Early the next morning, the British arrived at Lexington, near Concord. Minutemen were lined up on the village green to block their way. No one knows who fired the first shot. But when the smoke of battle cleared, eight minutemen lay dead in the grass. The victorious redcoats marched on to Concord.

Now the tide of battle turned. At Concord the British tried to cross a bridge over a river. American minutemen charged at the bridge, driving the enemy back. The redcoats turned around and started back to Boston.

The fight that followed was like the one that General Braddock lost in the French and Indian War. (See page 85.) American sharpshooters hid behind trees and stone fences. They fired at the British marching down the road. What perfect targets those redcoats made! Nearly 300 of them fell dead or wounded before the British got back to their main camp in Boston.

One British soldier wrote a letter to his family in England. Describing the

Amos Doolittle, a member of the Connecticut militia and an eyewitness to the start of the Revolution, made a series of engravings showing the battles of Lexington and Concord. Here the British retreat from Lexington, harrassed by minutemen who take cover behind a wall.

sniping that had taken such a heavy toll, he said, "Even the women had firelocks [guns]." On the road back from Lexington and Concord "One was seen to fire a Blunder Bus [a type of gun] between her father and husband, from their Windows. . . ."

1. When and where was the first battle in the American Revolution fought?

2. Why were the Americans able to win at Concord?

What happened at Bunker Hill?

Minutemen by the thousands surrounded Boston. They dug trenches on the hills overlooking the city. The British, who were cooped up inside Boston, decided to break out.

By now the British should have learned how to fight in America. They should have known enough to scatter their men in battle so that they would not make such perfect targets. But the lesson came hard. In Europe, armies fought each other with soldiers packed together in close ranks.

The British charged the Americans three times at the Battle of Bunker Hill in June 1775. Drums rolled and fifes whistled as the redcoats marched up the hill shoulder to shoulder. On and on they came in perfect order.

In the American trenches, the commander steadied his men. "Don't fire until you see the whites of their eyes," he told them. Twice the British marched all the way to the edge of the trenches before the Americans opened fire. And twice the Americans knocked the redcoats down like bowling pins. But on the third charge, the Americans ran out of gunpowder and had to fall back.

Disciplined British troops climb Bunker Hill in the face of fire from the patriots at the top. Although the patriots finally had to retreat after some of the bloodiest fighting of the entire war, they had proved that they could hold their own against crack British forces.

Bunker Hill was a British victory. Or was it? American farmers had shown they could stand up to British soldiers, the best in the world. Hearing of the battle, George Washington smiled and said, "The country is safe."

3. How did the Americans try to defend Bunker Hill?

4. Which side really won in the battle of Bunker Hill?

How did Americans react to the opening battles in the Revolution?

It is surprising how Americans felt about the war. At first, almost no one wanted to break from England. Americans demanded fair treatment from England, but not independence.

After several battles and the loss of many lives, Americans felt a little differently. They split into three groups about equal in size.

Out of every three Americans, perhaps one wanted freedom from England. Those who favored a complete break with England were called *patriots*.

The second American out of three still felt loyal to England. Those who sided with the British were called *loyalists*. Many of them were willing to fight against the patriots. Some loyalists just packed up and moved back to England. Others went to Canada to live.

The third American out of three did not really care which side won. Such people had their own worries or were too far removed from the events to be concerned.

5. In what three ways did the colonists feel about independence?

How were the thirteen colonies governed during the Revolution?

Americans had met at the First Continental Congress (page 98) to discuss their troubles with England. In 1775 the Second Continental Congress met to do the same thing. But this time there was much more to talk about. American and English soldiers were meeting each other in battle.

The Second Continental Congress took some very important steps. First, it announced that it was the *official* government of the thirteen colonies. Then Congress named the army of colonists around Boston the *official* American army. Picking a commander was easy.

He was, of course, George Washington of Virginia. Finally, Congress ordered the printing of *official* American money.

Still the colonists were not ready to break away from England. In their hearts they wanted peace and friendship with England. But they also wanted self-government. Congress wrote to King George, begging him not to let Parliament pass any more strict laws.

Meanwhile, Congress ordered war on England. By this time soldiers from all the colonies were taking part in the fighting. An army was sent to invade Canada. Other troops captured important British forts.

6. What important steps did the Second Continental Congress take?
7. What message did Congress send to King George III?

How did the English feel about the outbreak of war?

The British were very angry with their American cousins. King George refused to receive messages from the colonists. He said they were rebels. He promised to put down their rebellion and "bring the traitors to justice."

In Parliament reaction was divided. Most members agreed with the king that it was time to teach the colonists a lesson. Even so, they were not happy about the coming of war. They still were deeply in debt from their last war. Further, they could not work up much spirit for fighting against their fellow English.

A few members of Parliament openly supported the colonists. They spoke out against preparations for war. It was not too late, they said, for problems to be resolved. But in the face of the king's feelings and those of the majority, they were unable to bring about a peaceful solution.

8. How did the king and the majority in Parliament react to the colonists' actions?
9. Why were some members of Parliament opposed to war?

Part Five

The Declaration of Independence

Why did the Americans finally declare their independence?

The first shots in the Revolution were fired at Lexington and Concord in April 1775. After this battle, others followed. The colonists showed that they were willing to fight the British. Most were still not ready to declare their independence from England, however. But early in 1776 they began to realize that they could not remain colonies. The British were taking many steps to put down the American revolt. For example, the British navy took up positions off the Atlantic coast so that ships could neither enter nor leave the colonies. This move cut America off from the rest of the world.

Even worse, King George hired German soldiers from the state of Hesse to fight in America. These Germans were called Hessians (hesh′ ənz). They were well-trained soldiers who knew how to use the bayonet. Americans were bitter at King George for sending "hired killers" against them.

COMMON SENSE;

ADDRESSED TO THE

INHABITANTS

OF

AMERICA,

On the following intereſting

SUBJECTS.

I. Of the Origin and Deſign of Government in general, with conciſe Remarks on the Engliſh Conſtitution.

II. Of Monarchy and Hereditary Succeſſion.

III. Thoughts on the preſent State of American Affairs.

IV. Of the preſent Ability of America, with ſome miſcellaneous Reflections.

Man knows no Maſter ſave creating HEAVEN,
Or thoſe whom choice and common good ordain.

THOMSON.

PHILADELPHIA;
Printed, and Sold, by R. BELL, in Third-Street.
MDCCLXXVI.

Thomas Paine's 47-page pamphlet *Common Sense* aroused many colonists against the injustices of British rule.

In addition to British moves, something else happened to give the Americans a real push toward independence. In January 1776, Thomas Paine, a newcomer to America, published a small pamphlet. Paine was an English writer who came to America just before the Revolution. He hated King George and England. He wrote newspaper articles in favor of freedom and democracy. In one of his articles, Paine demanded that slaves in America be set free. Convinced that complete independence was the only answer for America, Paine wrote a pamphlet he called *Common Sense.* He told Americans that they would be better off if they broke away from England. The English were bleeding Americans of their freedom and their money. Paine laughed at King George, calling him a "royal brute."

Paine also presented some very sound arguments for independence. If Americans were free, he said, they could:

1. Trade with the whole world and profit from that trade.

2. Manufacture what they liked; England could no longer tell them what they could and could not produce.

3. Keep out of Europe's wars which were sure to come again and again.

Those arguments won over many people who had been unsure about independence. One of them was General George Washington. After he read *Common Sense*, Washington wrote to a friend saying he had decided separation was the only way. *Common Sense*, he said, contained "unanswerable reasoning."

1. What British actions helped push Americans toward independence?

2. How did *Common Sense* persuade many Americans that separation from England was necessary?

How and when was the Declaration of Independence written?

Ready at last to act, Congress named a committee to prepare a Declaration of Independence. A brilliant young Virginian, Thomas Jefferson, did most of the writing. He rented rooms in a comfortable brick house in Philadelphia. There he sat at a writing desk of his own design and wrote in his small, neat hand. When the first draft was ready, some others were asked to criticize it. Benjamin Franklin, old and wise, suggested a few changes, but he said he liked the Declaration. John Adams also made a few improvements. Then the representatives of all of the colonies signed their names at the bottom.

First to sign both the draft and the formal copy of the Declaration was John Hancock. He had served as President of the Continental Congress while the document was drafted. When it came time to sign the official copy, Hancock wrote his name in extra large letters. He did so, he explained, so that King George would not have to put his glasses on to read the name. Congress had the Declaration officially printed by Mary Goddard of Baltimore.

With the signing, the United States of America was officially born. Its birth date is July 4, 1776.

The Declaration is not a very long document. It is made up of three parts:

In the first part, the signers say *why* the thirteen colonies are breaking their connections with England. They demand to be treated as equals. But the British will not give them their rights.

The second part of the Declaration tells *what* the English have done wrong. It is a very long list! The Americans complain that England has taxed them without asking their consent. Also, England has cut off colonial trade. And there is no law and order left in the country. The Americans are at the mercy of their English masters. The king is "unfit to be the ruler of a free people."

The third part of the Declaration says that all connections between England and the former colonies are cut. The United States of America is an independent nation. Relying on the protection of God, Americans promise to help each other in the struggle that lies ahead. (For text of the Declaration of Independence, see pages 592-594.)

Americans celebrated their "birthday" in various ways. John Adams wrote to his wife, Abigail. He told her that in the future he thought Americans ought to celebrate every fourth of July. They should have "parades, shows, games, sports, guns, bells, bonfires, and illuminations [fireworks] from one end of the continent to the other."

New Yorkers held a public meeting on the common in New York City. After they listened to a reading of the Declaration, some of them pulled down a glittering statue of King George III. After they scraped off the gold leaf, they melted down the lead. Four thousand pounds of lead was made into cannon balls.

In Boston a huge crowd gathered at the State House. After the crowd heard the Declaration, some people took down the king's emblems from over the State House doors. They made a bonfire of them in King Street.

3. What did the three main parts of the Declaration say?

Part Six

The Fight for Freedom

How good were the chances for an American victory?

At the outset America's hopes for winning the Revolution were poor. In 1776 England was the most powerful empire on earth. Its population was small—about nine million. But America's was smaller—fewer than three million.

England, however, had some disadvantages. One of them was that many British were unwilling to take part in the Revolution. Some sided with the colonists. Others just refused to fight their relatives. They thought of all Americans as their "cousins," people who spoke their language and had similar customs and values.

Another of England's disadvantages was that soldiers had to be sent across the Atlantic to fight in America. It was hard to keep them supplied. When they moved inland, their supply lines grew very long. Sometimes the Americans were able to cut those lines.

Yet the British might well have won the war, except for two things:

First, America received help from foreigners. The assistance of the French was especially important.

Second, the colonists were struggling for their own freedom. They were fighting for an important cause. This made them hold on for eight long years through some very dark times.

1. What advantages did the British have in the Revolution? What disadvantages did the British have?

2. What two reasons probably account for the final American victory?

How successful was the American army in the early part of the war?

After the Battle of Bunker Hill, the Americans kept the British penned up in Boston. George Washington arrived to take command of the Continental (American) army. Washington finally drove the enemy out of Boston. But the British were far from beaten. Large forces of British and Hessian troops arrived at New York in August 1776. A much smaller American army was there to meet them. The Americans were beaten in a bloody battle at Long Island.

George Washington was calm and cool in defeat, however. He cleverly escaped with his army across a river at night. The British gave chase, and the Americans fell back 100 miles (160 km) across New Jersey into Pennsylvania.

Christmas, 1776, was a bad time for America. The country had declared itself free, but its army had been badly beaten. Freedom looked like a lost dream.

But George Washington was not ready to give up. He planned a Christmas surprise for the British and Hessians. While the enemy was enjoying the holiday, half-frozen Americans crossed the icy Delaware River from Pennsylvania to New Jersey in rowboats. Then they made a dawn attack at Trenton. As the surprised Hessians scrambled for safety, American soldiers cut them down. About 1000 were taken prisoner. For Washington and his army Trenton was a great victory.

3. What happened in the battle at Long Island?

4. Who won at Trenton?

George Washington's daring crossing of the Delaware River has inspired many American artists. This primitive painting was made by an unknown artist in the late 19th century.

Why did Americans spend a "winter of despair" at Valley Forge?

The British were furious over their defeat at Trenton. General Sir William Howe swore that he would "make the Rebels howl." Turning to General Cornwallis, he issued some very direct orders. It was Cornwallis's job to "run down that fox, Washington."

By January 1778, Cornwallis seemed to have succeeded in his mission. He defeated the Americans at Brandywine and Germantown. Cornwallis and his men were enjoying warm, comfortable quarters in Philadelphia. But he had pinned Washington's army down in a snowy camp called Valley Forge. There Americans endured their "winter of despair." They lived in unheated log huts chinked with mud and clay. They had no blankets, and their clothing was lice-infested. They suffered from frostbite and scurvy. (*Scurvy* is a disease caused by lack of vegetables and other essential foods.) More than 3000—or one soldier out of every four—died from starvation or disease. Those well enough to stand sentry duty often had to wrap their feet in rags to walk their posts. They had no shoes. It was easy to follow their trail by the bloody footprints left in the snow.

Washington did not permit the soldiers to huddle in their miserable cabins, however. He brought in Baron Frederick von Steuben, a tough German drillmaster, to weld them into a disciplined army. And Steuben did his job. When spring came and the Americans were able to break out of Valley Forge, they were a skilled fighting force.

Martha Washington also spent the winter at Valley Forge with her husband and his troops. In fact, she spent every winter of the war at the front. She organized camp and neighborhood women to roll bandages, knit socks, and mend shirts. She ministered to the sick and comforted the homesick. "I never knew a woman so busy from early morning to late at night," said one person who regularly accompanied her on her rounds.

5. Why was Valley Forge called the Americans' "winter of despair"?

6. Who was Baron von Steuben? Why was he important to the American cause?

Why was Saratoga the turning point of the Revolution?

In 1777 the British began a big campaign that they hoped would win the war. The plan was to cut America into two pieces by capturing New York State. Armies would move from three directions on Albany. (See map, page 107.) If the British could take New York State, New England would be cut off from the rest of the country.

The British plan failed. The only army to get anywhere near Albany was the one marching south from Canada. American forces gradually slowed it down in the forests. Finally at Saratoga the British were beaten in a fierce battle.

The Battle of Saratoga was "the turning point of the Revolution." It convinced the French that the colonists could defeat the British with French help.

The French had been watching the American Revolution with great interest. They had never forgiven England for their defeat in the Seven Years' War. They wanted to aid America, but were afraid to do so until the American army proved its strength. The king of France did not want to lose still another war to the British on the North American continent.

Before Saratoga, Benjamin Franklin had gone to France. He tried hard to convince French leaders to help the Americans. Although Franklin was very popular with the French, they were unwilling to act. They gave some supplies and money, but not until the Saratoga victory did they take official action. Then France recognized the United States of America as an independent country. And the French said that their powerful navy and their armies would fight for the patriots.

France's entry did not mean an immediate end to the war, however. The Revolution was to drag on for another three years. Many battles were yet to be fought. Nonetheless the tide had begun to turn in the Americans' favor.

7. Why did the Battle of Saratoga mark the turning point of the war?

How was the war carried on in the South and the West?

The British were not ready to give up after Saratoga. They were still strong.

The English put a new plan into operation. They would carry the war to the Southern Colonies. Many loyalists (page 100) lived there. With the help of the loyalists, Britain might yet defeat the Americans.

For a while, the new British plan worked well. Their soldiers captured Savannah, Georgia, and Charleston, South Carolina. Along the coast, the British won victories. But inland, the story was different. American pioneers were more than a match for the king's soldiers. They made the enemy run at the battles of King's Mountain, in North Carolina, and Cowpens, in South Carolina.

During the Revolution, thousands of Americans moved across the rugged

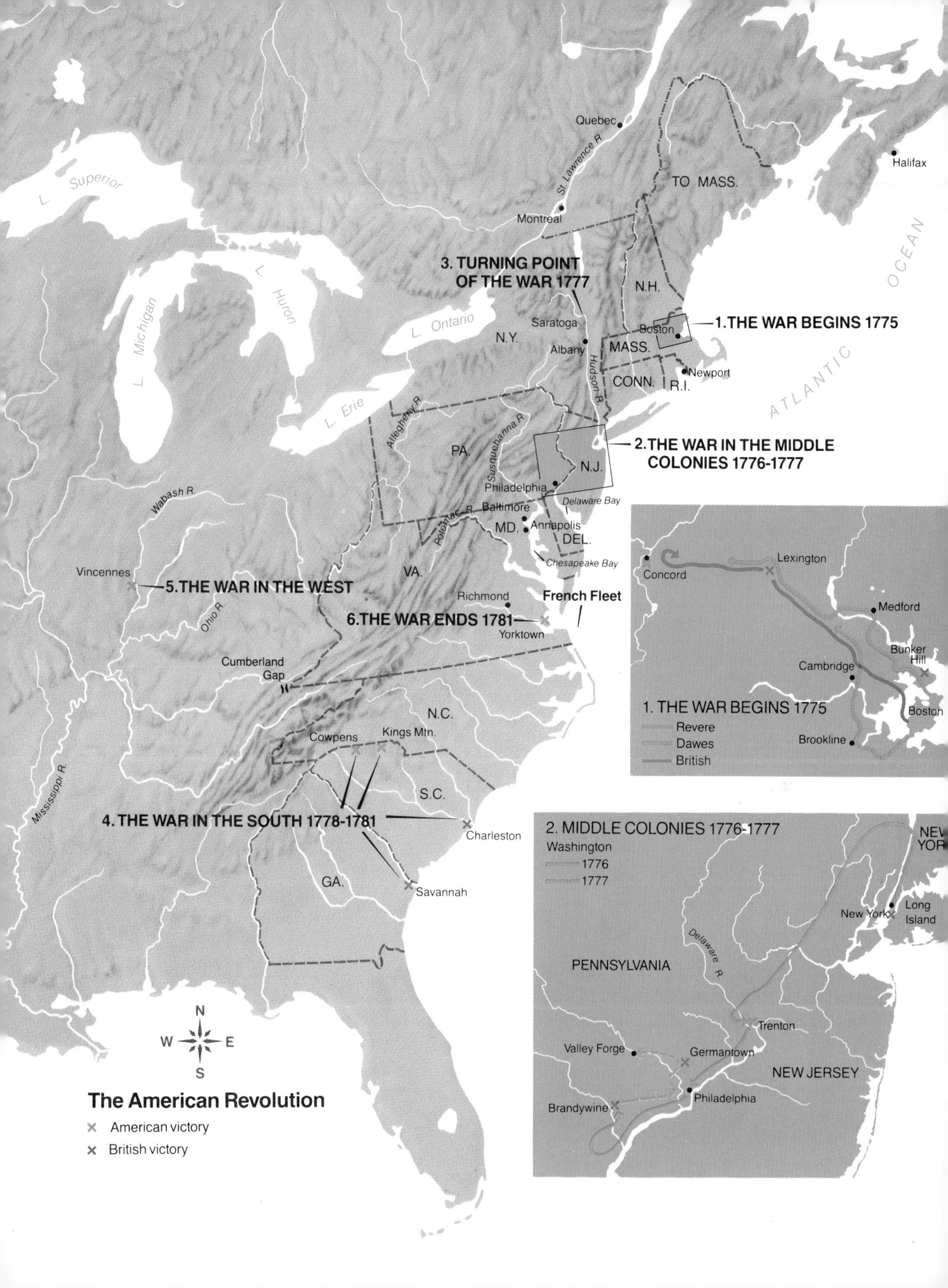

Quebec
Halifax
St. Lawrence R.
L. Superior
TO MASS.
Montreal
OCEAN
3. TURNING POINT OF THE WAR 1777
N.H.
L. Huron
L. Michigan
L. Ontario
Saratoga
N.Y.
Boston
1. THE WAR BEGINS 1775
Albany
MASS.
Hudson R.
Newport
CONN.
R.I.
ATLANTIC
L. Erie
Allegheny R.
Susquehanna R.
PA.
2. THE WAR IN THE MIDDLE COLONIES 1776-1777
N.J.
Philadelphia
Delaware Bay
Wabash R.
Potomac R.
Baltimore
MD.
Annapolis
DEL.
Chesapeake Bay
Vincennes
5. THE WAR IN THE WEST
VA.
Richmond
French Fleet
Ohio R.
6. THE WAR ENDS 1781
Yorktown
Cumberland Gap
N.C.
Cowpens
Kings Mtn.
Mississippi R.
S.C.
4. THE WAR IN THE SOUTH 1778-1781
Charleston
GA.
Savannah
N
W
E
S
The American Revolution
American victory
British victory
Concord
Lexington
Medford
Bunker Hill
Cambridge
1. THE WAR BEGINS 1775
Revere
Dawes
British
Boston
Brookline
2. MIDDLE COLONIES 1776-1777
Washington
1776
1777
NEW YOR
New York
Long Island
Delaware R.
PENNSYLVANIA
Trenton
Valley Forge
Germantown
NEW JERSEY
Philadelphia
Brandywine

The sides seem evenly matched in this painting of a cavalry skirmish after the Battle of Cowpens. The battle itself was a great American victory. Brigadier General Daniel Morgan lost only 12 men; the British lost 110.

Appalachian Mountains to western lands. They settled in the Ohio country and in the future states of Kentucky and Tennessee.

Daniel Boone was the most famous pioneer leader. He first went to Kentucky over the Wilderness Trail. This was an old Indian path that led through a mountain pass called the Cumberland Gap. Boone turned the trail into a road and built a fort at its western end. (See map, page 150.)

The British and Indians struck back at the settlers, and Boone was captured several times. But the tough pioneer was such a good woodsman and scout that he always managed to escape. Under his leadership, Kentucky managed to stay free.

Another American hero in the West was George Rogers Clark. With a very small army, Clark captured British forts on the Mississippi River. Then he took Vincennes (vin senz′), in what is now Indiana. Clark's victories forced England to give the western lands to America at the end of the Revolution. The British also promised to give up their forts in the Northwest.

8. Why did the British carry the war to the South?

9. Name two heroes who served on the frontier and tell what each did.

How did blacks serve in the American Revolution?

Five thousand blacks, slave and free, fought for American independence. Blacks were in the first battles at Lexington and Concord and Bunker Hill and in the last battle at Yorktown.

On the battlefronts and behind the lines, blacks helped the colonies win freedom. Some were with Francis Marion, the Swamp Fox, in South Carolina. Marion won his nickname because he and his men made daring raids on the British. Then they vanished into the swamps, only to return for another raid. Other blacks froze at Valley Forge with General Washington. Many were spies for the Continental army.

James Armistead of Virginia was the best known of the black spies. He knew his geography so well that he needed no maps to make his way. He waited around British camps and listened for information to take back to the Americans. His services proved so valuable to the patriots' cause that he was given his freedom. In October 1786, the Virginia legislature paid Armistead's master for him. Then the legislature voted Armistead a yearly pension.

Blacks served at sea as well as on land. They were in the Continental navy and on board privateers. Black pilots took boats through the waters of Chesapeake Bay.

There were no all-black units in the American Revolution. Black soldiers and sailors fought side by side with whites. Many states passed laws freeing all honorably discharged blacks.

Not all blacks in the Revolution fought for the Americans. In exchange for military service, the British offered freedom to slaves. In the South, the British used hundreds of runaways as combat troops.

It was as military laborers, however, that the British made the greatest use of blacks. Black carpenters, miners, and blacksmiths freed redcoats for service on the firing lines.

10. Where and how did blacks serve during the Revolution?

Colonel George Rogers Clark leads his weary frontier sharpshooters to the British fort at Vincennes. The last miles of the 17-day journey were through flooded rivers and icy marshes. Clark's successful assault on Vincennes destroyed any British claim to the Illinois country.

Historymaker

Pulaski

Kosciuszko

It is a common mistake to think that only Americans have played leading roles in our country's development. Many non-citizens also have affected the course of the history of the United States. Had it not been for foreign friends who believed in and fought for the patriots' cause, the outcome of the American Revolution might well have been very different.

A complete "honor roll" would be very long indeed. But, if we were to single out just a few non-Americans deserving of recognition, who would they be?

Perhaps two Poles ought to be mentioned first. Casimir Pulaski (pù las′ kē) is one. Liberty meant more to that young man than his own life. He died leading a cavalry charge in the Battle of Savannah. Before he came to volunteer his services to the United States, Pulaski had watched the Russians crush freedom in Poland. He made up his mind then that he would help other peoples keep their liberty, if he could.

Thaddeus Kosciuszko (kos′ ē us′ kō) is the other Pole. He was just 20 years old when he came to America in 1776. He constructed forts for the defense of the Delaware River. Later, as an officer in the Continental Corps of Engineers, he designed the first fortifications at West Point. Kosciuszko returned home after the Revolution. There he again took up the struggle for liberty. He became a Polish national hero in one of Poland's many wars against Russia.

Credit surely is due 545 black Haitian volunteers. They began arriving in 1778, after France had agreed to help the patriots. Haiti was then French territory.

Two of those volunteers later became important in Haiti's history. Henri Christophe was only twelve years old when he arrived to fight in the United States. He survived the bloody battle for Savannah. After the war, he returned home. There he helped his people unite and fight their own war of independence from France. Christophe then became the first king of Haiti.

Jean-Baptiste Belley's story is much like Christophe's. But instead of becoming a king, he became one of Haiti's diplomats, or representatives to other countries.

Most famous of all is a man with a very long name: Marie Joseph Paul Yves Roch Gilbert du Motier, Marquis de Lafayette. He is usually called by his last name alone,

Christophe

Belley

for obvious reasons. Lafayette has been called "the best foreign friend the United States ever had." Except for Winston Churchill, he is the only person ever named by Congress as an "honorary citizen of the United States."

Lafayette was the son of a rich, famous family in France. He was only eighteen years old—and already a captain in the French army—when he read the Declaration of Independence. He said, "At the first news of this quarrel, my heart was enrolled in it."

Still grieving over the loss of his father in the Seven Years' War, Lafayette went to see an American diplomat in Paris. He said he wanted to serve in Washington's army without pay. When his friends heard what he had done, they tried to discourage him. The king of France went even further. He forbade him to go. But Lafayette escaped. He made his way first to Georgetown, North Carolina, and then to Philadelphia where the Contintental Congress was meeting.

Congress was happy to accept Lafayette's offer of service. The next day he met with George Washington. The two became instant and lifelong friends.

Lafayette had come to fight in liberty's cause. And fight he did! He was wounded at Brandywine. He shared the trials at Valley Forge. He went South to help in the campaign there. He played an important part in the final victory at Yorktown.

When he came to America, Lafayette spoke little English. He learned more, but he never mastered its pronunciation. Even so, he knew how to communicate with his troops. He was very popular with Americans. They called him "the soldier's friend."

Besides risking his life, Lafayette gave half of his fortune to the American cause. The patriots, ever short of money, were delighted with his gift of $200,000. It bought a lot of clothing, food, and guns for the army.

Later Lafayette lost almost everything he had left. France had its own revolution. Because he had a title—he was a marquis—he was stripped of his wealth. When that happened, the United States Congress voted to send him $24,425. That was the exact amount of back pay due him for his services in the American army. Congress also gave him land in Louisiana.

More than 100 years after Lafayette's death, the United States entered World War I. You'll learn more about that in Chapter 17. But when the first American troops stepped ashore in France, their leader said, "Lafayette, we are here!"

Lafayette

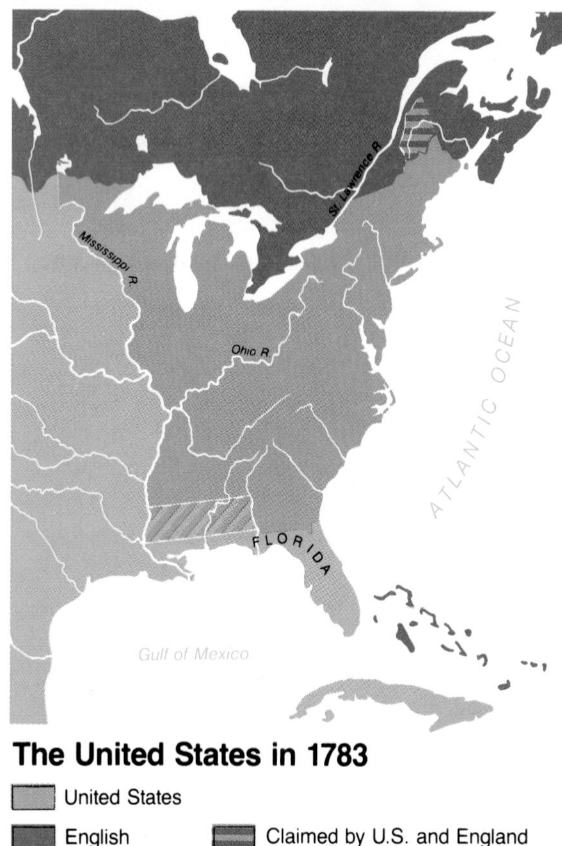

The United States in 1783

United States
English
Spanish
Claimed by U.S. and England
Claimed by U.S. and Spain

When and where did the American Revolution end?

The last act of the American Revolution took place at Yorktown, Virginia, in 1781. The British had fallen back to the coast, where they hoped to receive more troops and supplies.

By 1781, the French had many soldiers in America. A French fleet was ready to lend help offshore. General Washington formed a plan to surround the British at Yorktown and make them surrender.

Under Washington, American and French troops laid siege to Yorktown by land. At the same time, the French navy closed in on the British from the sea. Lord Cornwallis, the British commander, held out as long as he could. But the British were squeezed by the enemy like a nut in a nutcracker. Cornwallis finally gave up.

Focus on Skills

Under each of the main topics listed below you will find a list of events. Put those events in chronological order. Copy the list of events on a separate piece of paper. Put the number 1 by the event related to that topic which happened first. Put the number 2 by the one which came next and so on.

A. Topic: **England Angers the Colonists**
- American settlers ordered to leave Indian lands
- Pontiac leads Indians in seige of Detroit
- Parliament passes the Quartering Act
- Parliament passes the Stamp Act
- The Boston Tea Party

B. Topic: **The Revolution Begins**
- The Battle of Lexington and Concord
- The British blockade Boston Harbor
- The Boston Massacre
- Patrick Henry urges colonists to fight

C. Topic: **The American Revolution**
- Treaty of Paris
- Surrender at Yorktown
- Battle of Bunker Hill
- Winter at Valley Forge
- Battle of Saratoga

Benjamin West never completed this painting of the signing of the Treaty of Paris because the British representatives refused to pose. The Americans (from left to right) are John Jay, John Adams, Benjamin Franklin, Henry Laurens, and William Temple Franklin, a grandson of Benjamin Franklin.

The surrender at Yorktown brought an end to the American Revolution. The thirteen English colonies were now the thirteen free United States.

Two years of peace negotiations followed the surrender at Yorktown. During that time there was some scattered fighting. Finally, however, the Americans and the British signed the Treaty of Paris in 1783. England then officially recognized the United States as an independent nation. Its boundaries were fixed. (See map, page 112.) They extended from Canada on the north to the Mississippi River on the west. No longer were Americans to be confined to the Atlantic Coast. They now owned an area many times larger than England. And they were free to settle and develop it as they saw fit. Small wonder, then, that Americans were very happy with the terms of the peace treaty and with themselves.

11. How did the Americans force Cornwallis to surrender?

12. Why were Americans pleased with the Treaty of Paris?

Building Your Vocabulary

Copy and complete the following paragraph by filling in the blanks with the correct word chosen from the list below. Each word in the list is explained in the text.

In 1763 the American colonies were part of the British—?—. When—?—put a tax on glass, tea, lead, and other things, the colonists decided to—?— them. The colonists also objected when the British wanted them to—?—soldiers. Tensions increased until violence came in what was called the Boston —?—. Samuel Adams, a master of—?—, cried out that "Innocent Blood" had been spilled. He and others demanded that the Parliament—?—the taxes and let the colonists return to running their own affairs.

propaganda boycott Massacre
Empire repeal Parliament
quarter

Recalling What You Have Learned

Match the name of each person in Column A with the item in Column B for which she or he is remembered.

Column A	Column B
1. Benjamin Franklin	A. *Common Sense*
2. Martha Washington	B. surrender at Yorktown
3. Lord Cornwallis	C. Declaration of Independence
4. George Washington	D. spying for patriots
5. John Adams	E. training troops at Valley Forge
6. Thomas Jefferson	F. commander in chief of American forces
7. Daniel Boone	G. caring for soldiers during winter of 1777-1778
8. Thomas Paine	H. defending British soldiers who took part in Boston Massacre
9. James Armistead	I. helping to persuade the French to aid the patriots
10. Baron von Steuben	J. Wilderness Road

Discussing the Important Ideas in This Chapter

1. Even though the colonies were expensive and sometimes hard to manage, England wanted them to remain in the British Empire. Explain why.
2. Why was George III said to be a "good man" but a "poor ruler"?
3. Why did the year 1763 mark a great turning point in American history?
4. Do you think the Americans might have remained in the British Empire if they had been given representation in Parliament?

5. Why did John Adams believe it was important to defend the British soldiers accused of murder in the Boston Massacre, even though he personally was a patriot?
6. Why is *Common Sense* said to be one of the most important pamphlets ever written?
7. What are the main ideas set forth in the Declaration of Independence? Why are these ideas still important to all Americans?
8. Why were the Americans finally able to win the Revolution?
9. What role did blacks play in the Revolution?

Improving Your Map Skills

An *inset map* is a small map used with a larger map. The inset blows up an area on the large map to show greater detail.

The map on page 107 has two insets. Brown rectangles on the main map show the areas that are enlarged, or made bigger, in the insets. Look at the map and answer the following questions.

1. Find Boston on the large map. Find inset map #1—"The War Begins 1775." What towns are shown on the inset that are not labeled on the main map? What battle is shown on the inset map that is not marked on the main map? What can you tell about the geography of Boston in 1775 from the inset that you cannot tell from the main map?
2. Find Philadelphia on the large map. Find Philadelphia on inset map #2—"Middle Colonies 1776-1777." The inset enlarges parts of which three colonies? What battles are marked on the inset map that are not marked on the main map? Whose route does the inset map show in blue? What year does the solid blue line represent? What year does the dotted blue line represent?

Improving Your Study Skills: *Reading*

To find out what really happened in the past or how people felt about events, historians use what are called primary sources.

Primary means first. A primary source, therefore, is a firsthand source of information. It is what someone actually said or wrote rather than what someone else said they said or wrote.

An example of a primary source is shown on page 93. It is just one of the many posters which appeared in the colonies prior to the outbreak of the war.

Read the poster carefully. The only word in it with which you may not be familiar is posterity. *Posterity* means the people who come after you, or your descendants.

1. What does this poster ask people to do?
2. To whom is the poster directed?
3. What does the poster say will happen to those people who do not follow its advice?
4. Who is the merchant the readers are asked to boycott?
5. Where is that merchant's place of business?
6. Why do you think the poster ends with the words "for ever and ever, AMEN"?
7. Have you ever seen posters or bumper stickers printed today which remind you of this poster? If so, tell about those you have seen and the messages they carry.

Chapter 5

Establishing a New Government

Independence Hall, Philadelphia, Pennsylvania

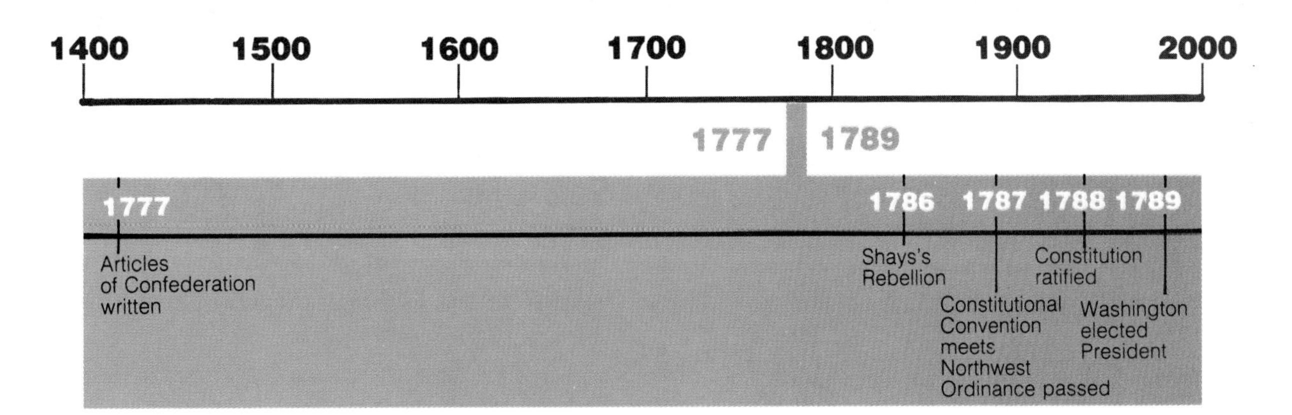

Part One

Our Country's First Government

Why was setting up a new government a hard task?

Americans were happy indeed when at last the Revolutionary War was over. For many patriots, the Peace of Paris marked the end of eight hard years of fighting. Americans looked to a future of peace and prosperity. But independence alone did not turn thirteen small states into a strong, unified nation. Five years after the battle of Yorktown, a remarkable group of Americans met in Philadelphia. There they helped form the government of the United States.

Forming a new government proved to be a harder task than anyone had imagined. There were no models or blueprints to follow. A new plan which could safeguard freedom and provide justice had to be worked out. Making that plan took a lot of debate and hard work. But at last, in 1787, a new plan, or *constitution*, was completed. It has proved to be the most successful constitution in history. It worked for the United States when there were just thirteen states and fewer than four million people. It still works today. What is more, the United

States Constitution has become a model for many other nations. They have followed the blueprint designed in 1787 and *adapted*, or changed, it only slightly to meet their own special needs.

1. How has the U.S. Constitution influenced other nations?

What were the Articles of Confederation?

During the Revolution, the Second Continental Congress ran the government. The Congress wrote the Articles of Confederation. Those Articles were the first plan of government for the United States. They set up a loose union of equal states, or a *confederation*.

Little power was given to the Confederation. The states had fought the Revolution to get rid of a strong British government. They did not wish to build another strong government of their own. The Congress met in Philadelphia. It was made up of representatives from the thirteen independent states. There was no President, as such. There was no way to raise tax money, except by asking the states to help.

The states printed their own money. They taxed goods sent in from other states. No national courts protected the rights of citizens. The Congress could declare war, but it could not raise an army.

Weak as they were, the Articles did keep the nation alive. The new states gave the central government a few powers. The Congress could set units of weights and measures, organize post offices, and handle Indian affairs.

2. Why were the states more powerful than the national government under the Articles of Confederation?

Why was the Northwest Ordinance important?

The most important act of the government under the Articles was the writing of the Northwest Ordinance. An *ordinance* is a law.

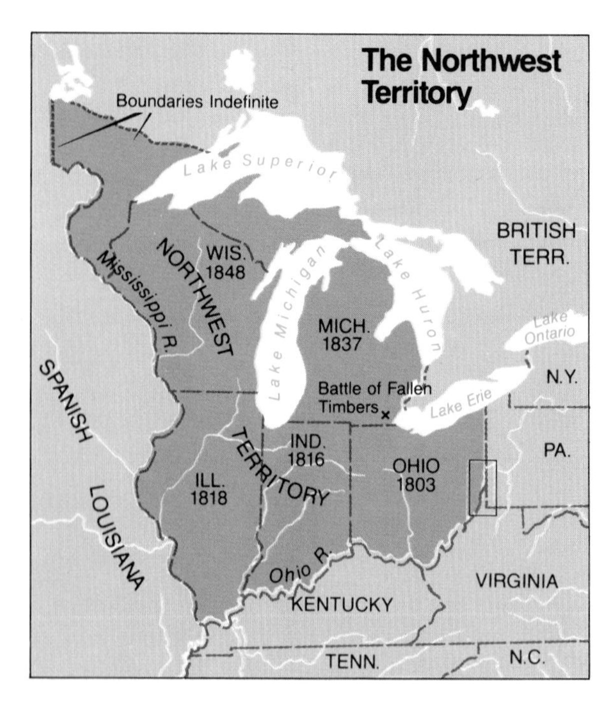

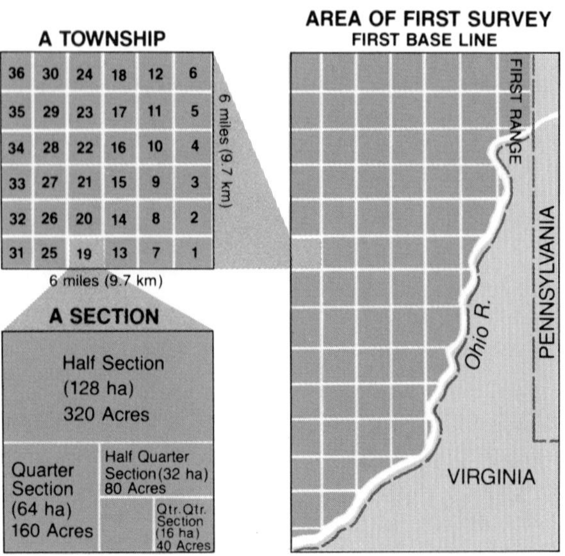

Indian tribes of the Old Northwest ceded their lands to the United States after the Battle of Fallen Timbers. (See page 148.)

Between 1782 and 1786, New York, Massachusetts, Virginia, and Connecticut gave up some land they claimed was theirs to the new national government. This land lay west of the Allegheny Mountains and north of the Ohio River. It was known as the Northwest Territory. (See map, page 118.)

Congress ordered the land divided into townships six miles square (15.6 km^2). Each township was further divided into 36 smaller squares, or sections, to be sold to settlers. Part of the money that came from the sale of land had to go for education.

Slavery was forbidden in the Territory. Freedom of religion, trial by jury, and other rights were promised to the people there. At first, Congress chose a governor and judges for the Northwest Territory. After enough settlers arrived, they could elect their own officials.

Later, five states were created from the Northwest Territory. They were Ohio, Indiana, Illinois, Michigan, and Wisconsin.

The great importance of the Northwest Ordinance was that it showed how to organize and govern new land. What is more, new states were to enter the Union as equal partners with the old states.

3. What rights and freedoms were guaranteed to citizens who settled in the Northwest Territory?

Part Two

Troubles at Home and Abroad

How did Europeans look upon the new United States?

Limping along under the weak Articles of Confederation, the United States government faced troubles at home and abroad.

Europeans tended to look down on the infant nation. It had no head of government. It had no permanent building as a capitol. To Europeans who were used to kings and palaces such things were very important. When the Dutch sent an official to the United States in 1783, he said he "couldn't even find" the government. It took him ten days, he complained, just to locate a member of Congress.

For eight years the British would not even send a representative to what they called the "backwoods" capital of the United States. If they sent one, they said, they would have to send thirteen—one to each state. That statement made Americans angry. But the British did more than make insults. They continued to occupy posts on American soil near the Canadian border. From those posts they controlled the North American fur trade. They also stirred up the Indians against American settlers flooding west.

Spain did not like England, but was not friendly toward the United States either. Spain's attitude was important because Spain now owned Louisiana. France had given that territory and the Mississippi River to Spain as part of the settlement of a dispute between the two countries. American pioneers in Tennessee and Kentucky needed to float their products down the Mississippi to New Orleans. (See map, page 150.) Spain threatened to stop American

When this watercolor was made in 1794, Fort Detroit was still occupied by the British.

travel and shipping on the Mississippi. The weak American government seemed unable to stand up against Spain.

Even the French, who had helped the patriots during the Revolution, were no longer friendly. They pressed the United States to pay back money it had borrowed to fight the war. The French also cut back on American trade in the French West Indies.

1. Describe the attitude of Europeans toward the new United States.

2. Why was control of the Mississippi River important?

Why did the Barbary pirates attack American ships?

Perhaps the worst insult to the new United States came from the Barbary States of North Africa. (See map, page 121.) Pirates from Morocco, Algiers, Tripoli, and Tunis demanded "protection money." If American ships were to sail the Mediterranean Sea, they would have to pay the pirates not to attack them. While the thirteen states still were colonies, the British had paid their protection money. Now the United States was both too poor to buy protection and too weak to fight. So pirates took sailors from American ships and made them slaves. They also helped themselves to the goods those ships were carrying. At the time there was nothing that the American government could do to stop them.

3. Where were the Barbary States?

4. Why couldn't the United States halt the pirate attacks?

How good was American money?

Before the end of the Revolution, paper money was almost worthless. A Continental (dollar) was worth less than three cents. It took $100 to buy a pair of shoes. A pound of tea cost $90, and a bushel of corn sold for $40, using Continental currency.

Under the Articles of Confederation, money problems continued. Congress had no power to tax, and it needed money. The United States owed about $8 million to foreign countries. About $32 million were owed to its own people. If the government could not pay its debts, no foreign country and no American citizen would ever again be willing to lend it money. The credit rating of the United States was very low.

5. Why didn't the United States use taxes to pay its debts?

6. Why were its unpaid debts a serious problem for the United States?

How did leaders try to solve the government's economic problems?

In 1786, a group of the nation's leaders called a meeting to resolve some trade problems between the states. But only five states sent delegates. Alexander

Hamilton, one of the meeting's leaders, called for a new convention. It would discuss not just trade problems, but all the problems of the government. Congress approved the new convention, but no action was taken on it until after Shays's Rebellion.

7. Who called for a convention?

What was Shays's Rebellion?

Many people were in debt following the Revolution. Some who could not pay their debts were put in prison or had their property taken away.

A few people had become rich selling war supplies during the Revolution. Those made poor by the war were angry at those who had become rich. Rioting started in New England. Daniel Shays, who had been a captain in the Revolution, led the rioters. They were farmers who were unable to pay their debts.

In January 1787, Shays and 1500 men attacked the U.S. arsenal (storage place for arms and ammunition) at Springfield, Massachusetts. State troops were called, and they defeated Shays's "army" in a blinding snowstorm.

Shays's Rebellion proved how bad conditions were in the young country. Law and order had to be restored, along with fair play for people in need.

8. Why did Daniel Shays and other debtors attack a U.S. arsenal?

9. What did Shays's Rebellion prove?

Why did Americans decide to call a new convention?

Although Shays's Rebellion upset American leaders, it was not the only

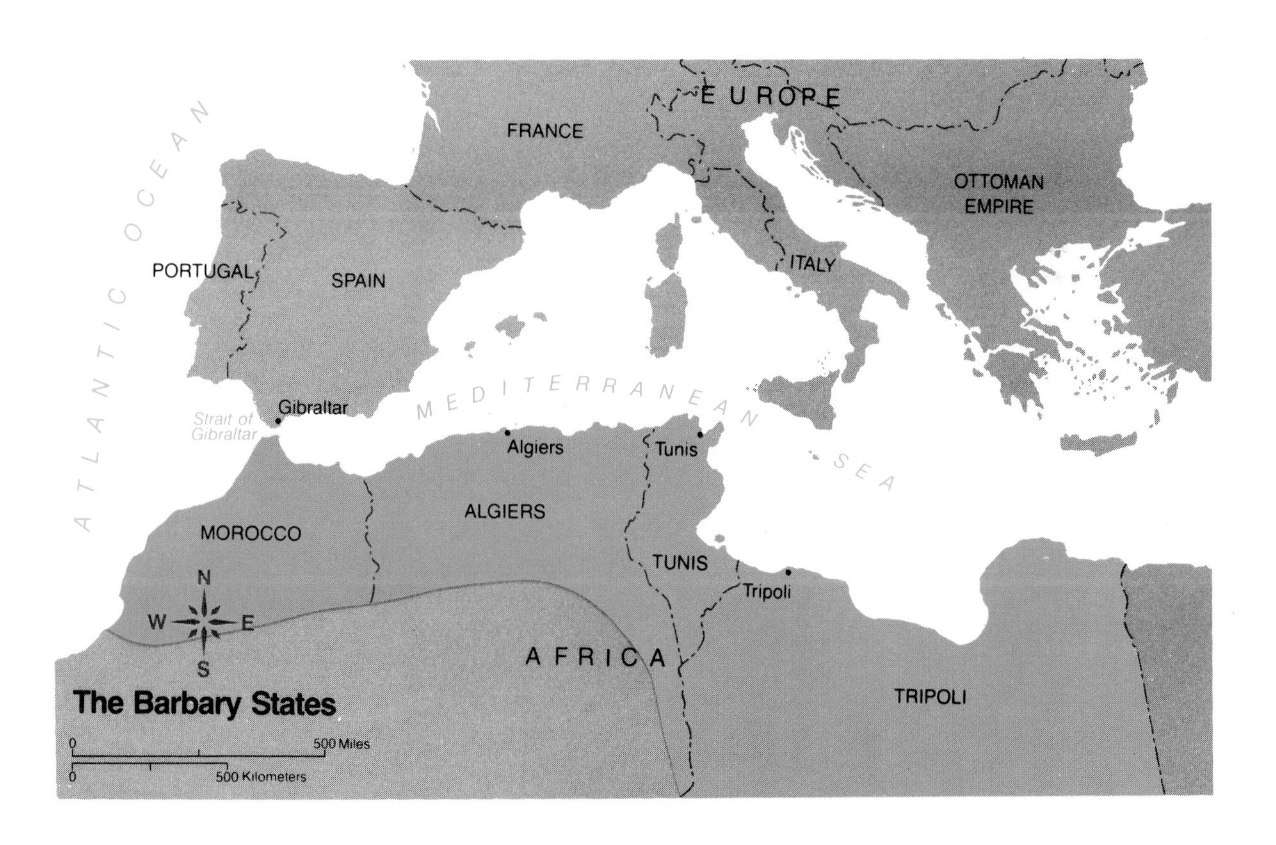

The Barbary States

event which convinced them that something had to be done. By 1787, five years had passed since the end of the Revolution. During that time it became clear that the Articles of Confederation were just not strong enough to give good government to the United States. The Articles were weak because:

1. The United States had no head or chief executive.

2. Congress had no power to make the states obey the laws it passed.

3. Congress had no power to levy (order to be paid) and collect taxes.

4. Congress could not regulate trade between the states.

5. Foreign governments did not respect the new nation.

6. The Articles could not be changed unless every one of the thirteen states agreed.

Leaders of the nation agreed something had to be done. Plans were made to call a convention, or meeting. The convention would try to solve the country's problems. As Ben Franklin put it, it was time for thirteen clocks to strike as one.

10. In what ways were the Articles weak?

11. What did the nation's leaders decide to do?

Part Three

The Gathering at Philadelphia

When and where was the convention held?

In February 1787, Congress invited each of the states to send *delegates*, or representatives, to a convention at Philadelphia in May. The delegates were to suggest changes which would improve the Articles of Confederation.

All of the states except Rhode Island accepted the invitation. New York named the smallest number of delegates, three. Pennsylvania named the largest, eight. The states chose 74 men in all, but only 55 came at one time or another.

The delegates arrived one by one over a period of several weeks. Most of them were bone-weary, dusty, or mud-spattered by the time they got to Philadelphia. The roads were unpaved and full of ruts. (See map, page 150.) Sometimes travelers had to ford streams or cross over dangerous bridges. They never could be sure that the ferries or stagecoaches would be on time. The trip from New York to Philadelphia took about one day if there were no mishaps. The trip from Virginia took at least four days.

In 1787, Philadelphia was the most exciting, attractive city in the United States. It boasted a population of 40,000 and ten newspapers. It had street lamps, fire companies, museums, and many large brick homes. Most of the delegates, however, stayed in small hotels or rooming houses. To reduce living costs, some stayed two to a room. The delegates served at the convention without pay. They did not even get money to pay their expenses.

When at last the convention began, it met in Independence Hall. The Declaration of Independence had been signed in that same building eleven years before. (See photo, page 116.)

Fording rivers was one peril of travel in the late 1700s.

1. What were the delegates to the convention in Philadelphia expected to do?

2. Describe travel conditions in 1787.

Who were the delegates to the convention at Philadelphia?

The 55 delegates worked in Philadelphia through the hot, muggy summer. They were remarkable people. It is doubtful that there ever has been a more able group. These delegates are sometimes called the "Founding Fathers." They are also called the "Framers of the Constitution." Not all of them could be on hand for the entire convention. But 29 did attend all, or nearly all, of the sessions. When at last their work was finished, 39 were there to sign the final plan of government which they had written.

Who were these delegates? Looking at them as a group, certain likenesses stand out. For the most part, the delegates were talented and well educated. About half of them had attended college. Several of them had studied in Europe. A surprising number had been educated privately. A few were self-taught.

Almost all of the delegates had a record of service to their country. Four out of five had been members of the Continental Congress. Most had backed the Revolution. About half had fought in the Continental army. Eight had signed the Declaration of Independence. All but a few were active in their state and local governments.

More than half of the delegates were lawyers. Others were merchants, planters, and large-scale farmers. Only two owned small farms. Three were doctors.

One of the most striking things about the delegates was their youth. The average age was 43. The youngest delegate was Jonathan Dayton, then just 26. Charles Pinckney and Alexander Hamilton were two of the more important young delegates. The oldest delegate was 81-year-old Benjamin Franklin.

The best known and most respected delegates were George Washington and Benjamin Franklin. Both lent great dignity to the convention. From time to time they reassured the others about the importance of the convention's work. Both men were calm under pressure. Many times during the long, hot summer they cooled the tempers of the other delegates.

3. What names are sometimes used to describe the delegates?

4. In what ways were most of the delegates alike?

Why were the meetings of the convention closed to the public?

Meetings were held in secret, and guards stood at the doors. That may seem strange to us today when important meetings are televised all over the world. In 1787, however, the delegates felt the convention should finish its work without a lot of publicity. "No Constitution would ever have been adopted . . . if the debates had been public." James Madison said that years after the convention. Most historians agree. By holding the debates in private, delegates were free to speak and change their minds if they wanted to. Debate was more open.

Since the meetings were secret, how do we know what went on? No official transcript was kept. There was an official record, or journal, but it told only the barest details.

Thanks to James Madison, we know what took place. As a delegate, he took a seat right in front of Chairman Washington. He could see and hear everything. At the end of each day, he wrote out his notes. He did not miss a single day, nor, as he put it, "more than a casual [small] fraction of an hour in any day . . . I could not have lost a single speech unless a very short one." Madison's record is one of the great treasures of our country.

5. Why were the meetings held behind closed doors?

6. Whose notes tell us what went on in the convention?

Why did the delegates decide to write a new Constitution?

Congress had asked the states to send delegates to Philadelphia to improve the Articles of Confederation. Once the delegates got there, however, they realized they could not just patch up the Articles. It would be better to write a new constitution. So without real authority to do so, they plunged into a job never before attempted.

That was not an easy task. People from the West, or "backwoods," felt that people on the East Coast had too much power. There were differences between the South and the North. There were differences between the rich and the poor. There were differences between large and small states. The delegates at Philadelphia had to find ways to keep those lines of difference from becoming battle lines.

Sometimes the quarrels and debates got so hot that it seemed the convention would go to pieces. The weather did not help. A heat wave hit Philadelphia in the middle of the convention. Tempers flared in the meeting room.

The delegates worked long hours. Nothing made the writing easy, but they kept on working six days a week and sometimes even on Sundays. They felt the nation was in great danger unless the government was made stronger.

7. Why did the delegates decide that they could not save the Articles of Confederation?

8. What were some lines of difference in the United States?

What compromises were made in the convention?

In a democracy there are many different ideas of what should be done. People have interests that are different. The Framers of the Constitution understood that to reach agreement, there must often be *compromise* (kom′ prə mīz), or "give and take." They had to make a number of compromises in the course of their work. The most important of them is called the "Great Compromise." It concerned how states should be represented in the Congress of the new government.

Large states wanted members of Congress elected according to population. The large states would have more power that way. Small states wanted each state to have the same number of members so that the large states couldn't outvote them. Large and small states argued bitterly.

Finally the delegates decided that Congress should have two houses, or parts. In the upper house, or Senate, every state, large or small, would have two senators. In the lower house, the House of Representatives, states would be represented according to population. The "Great Compromise" solved the hardest problem the convention had.

Today members of the House of Representatives are still elected on the basis of population. The states with the largest populations have the most members. Each state, however, has just two senators.

No group got exactly what it wanted in the Constitution when it was finally finished. But at last the delegates signed their final version. Then the Constitution had to be approved by the people.

9. What is a compromise?
10. What problem was settled by the Great Compromise?

Why didn't the Founders do away with slavery?

It is hard to imagine how it was to live in another time. To people today it might seem as though the convention missed a golden opportunity to end slavery.

Records of the debates show what a big problem slavery was for the Founders. Delegates had to deal with the facts and feelings of the time. If they had dealt any blow to slavery, the South might have turned down the entire Constitution. Many Southerners were opposed to slavery, but they said that it was a "necessary evil." The plantation system could not exist without it.

On the other hand, Northerners had strong opinions, too. Some Northerners called slavery "the curse of heaven" and "an evil thing." In time the whole country would have to make a decision about slavery.

Whether the makers of the Constitution could have done their job and done away with slavery, too, is a question which will long be argued. Remember, however, that slavery was forbidden in the new Northwest Territory. And the bringing of slaves to the United States was to stop in 1808.

11. How do we know that slavery was a big problem for the convention?
12. What attitudes toward slavery did Southerners and Northerners express?

Part Four

The New Constitution

On what basic ideas is the Constitution built?

If you examine the Constitution on pages 595-615, you will notice that it is not very long. The average reader can read it all in less than twenty minutes. Compared to the constitutions of various states and other countries, it really is quite short. And that is the way the Framers intended it to be. They did not want to spell out every detail. If they had, the Constitution soon would have been out of date. Instead they hoped to provide a framework on which to build. The Constitution, therefore, just sets forth the most basic ideas for government. Among the most important of those ideas are these:

1. The government of the United States has limited power. All power belongs to the people. The government has only those powers which the people give to it. It can do only those things which the people say it can do.

2. The United States has a republican form of government. That means that the people choose their leaders. No queen, or king, or persons with other titles are to have power simply because of their birth.

3. The United States has a federal system of government. Power is divided between the national government and the states. Some powers belong to the national government alone. For example, only the national government can declare war, coin money, or set up post offices. Powers not given to the national government belong to the states. For example, the states are in charge of voting and schools.

1. Why did those who wrote the Constitution want it to be a framework for government?

2. What are three basic ideas on which the Constitution is built?

What are the three branches of the federal government?

The delegates built a federal government consisting of three branches. First there is the *legislative* (lej′ ə slā′ tiv) branch, called Congress. Its duty is to make the laws for the country, such as raising money and providing for

The new Constitution gave the federal government power to print money. States and cities would no longer be able to print their own money.

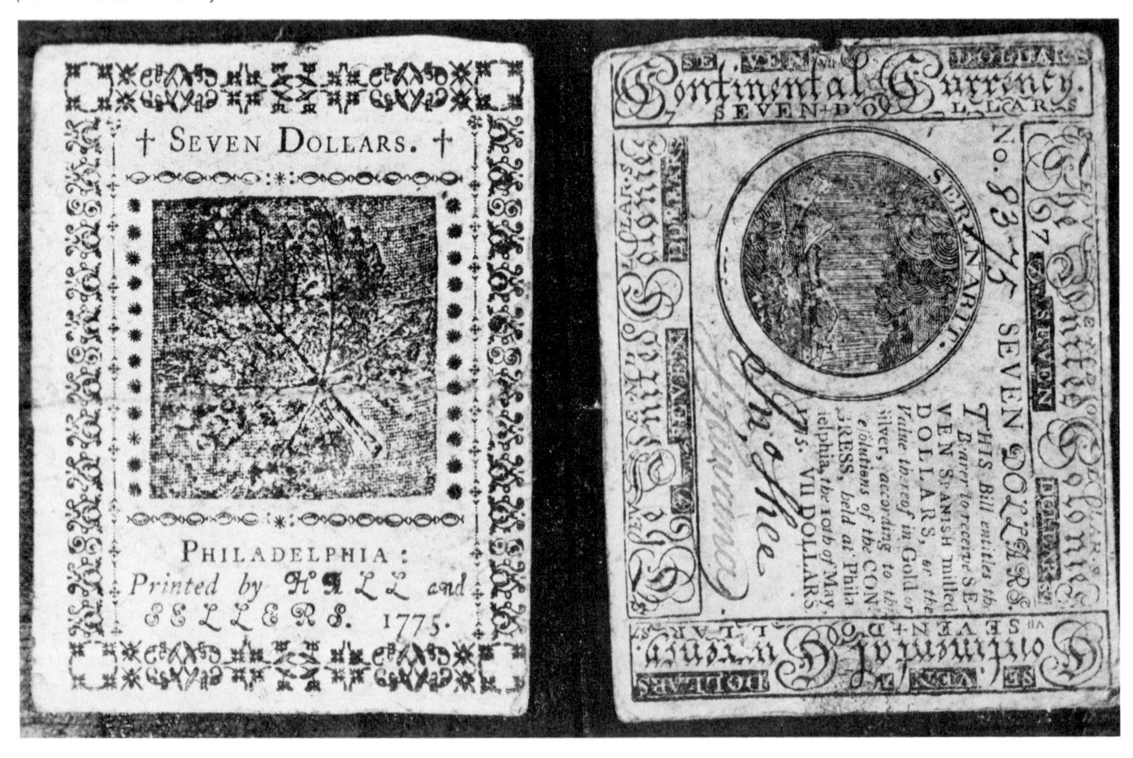

The Separation of Powers

The President and other executive officers carry out the aws

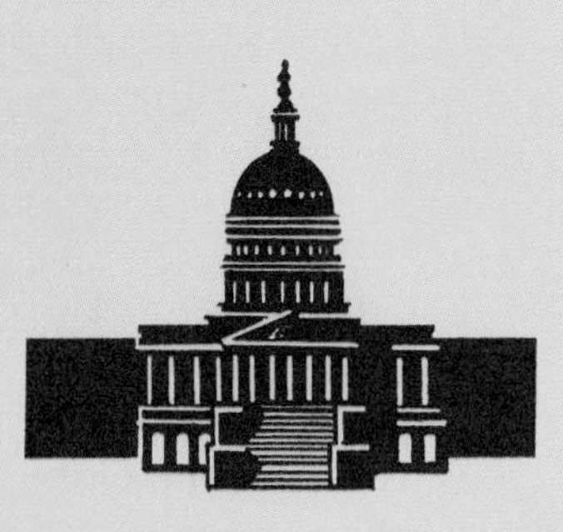

Congress enacts the laws

Federal courts apply and interpret the laws

defense. Second, there is the *executive* (eg zek′ yə tiv) branch, headed by the President of the United States. The executive branch carries out the laws that Congress passes. For example, if Congress passes a law providing for a larger army, it is up to the President, as head of the executive branch, to see that more soldiers are recruited.

The third part of the federal government is called the *judicial* (jü dish′ əl) branch. The judicial branch consists of the United States Supreme Court and other lower federal courts. The lower courts punish those who break federal laws. They also settle lawsuits between citizens of different states. The Supreme Court interprets, or judges the meaning of, the law. It decides whether or not the laws passed by Congress agree with the Constitution. If the Supreme Court decides that a law does not agree with the Constitution, that law is no longer in force. It is said to be *unconstitutional*.

3. Name the three branches of the federal government and tell what each one does.

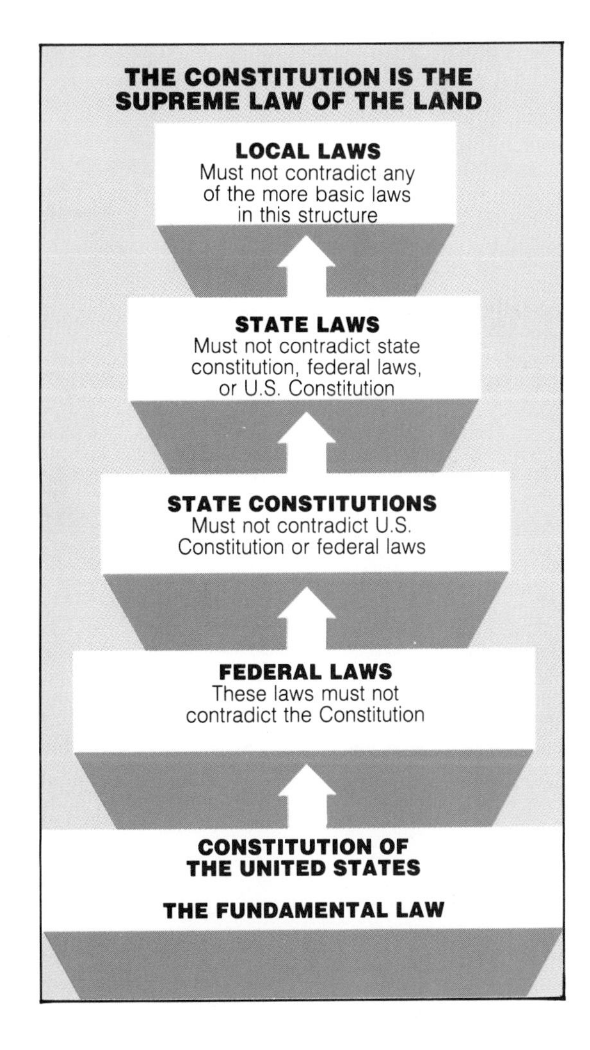

How do the branches of government check and balance each other?

Each branch of government checks and balances the others under the Constitution. For example, the President may *veto*, or refuse to sign, a law passed by Congress. The Senate may refuse to agree with, or *confirm* an appointment to the Supreme Court which the President makes. The Supreme Court may declare a law passed by Congress and signed by the President to be unconstitutional. Because each branch has different powers, the branches check and balance each other.

The Constitution on pages 595-615 and the chart below show more clearly how the check-and-balance system works. Without checks and balances, one branch of the government might become too powerful or might use its powers wrongly.

4. Why is a system of checks and balances important?

5. Explain how the President and the Congress may check or balance each other. How does the Supreme Court check or balance the President and Congress?

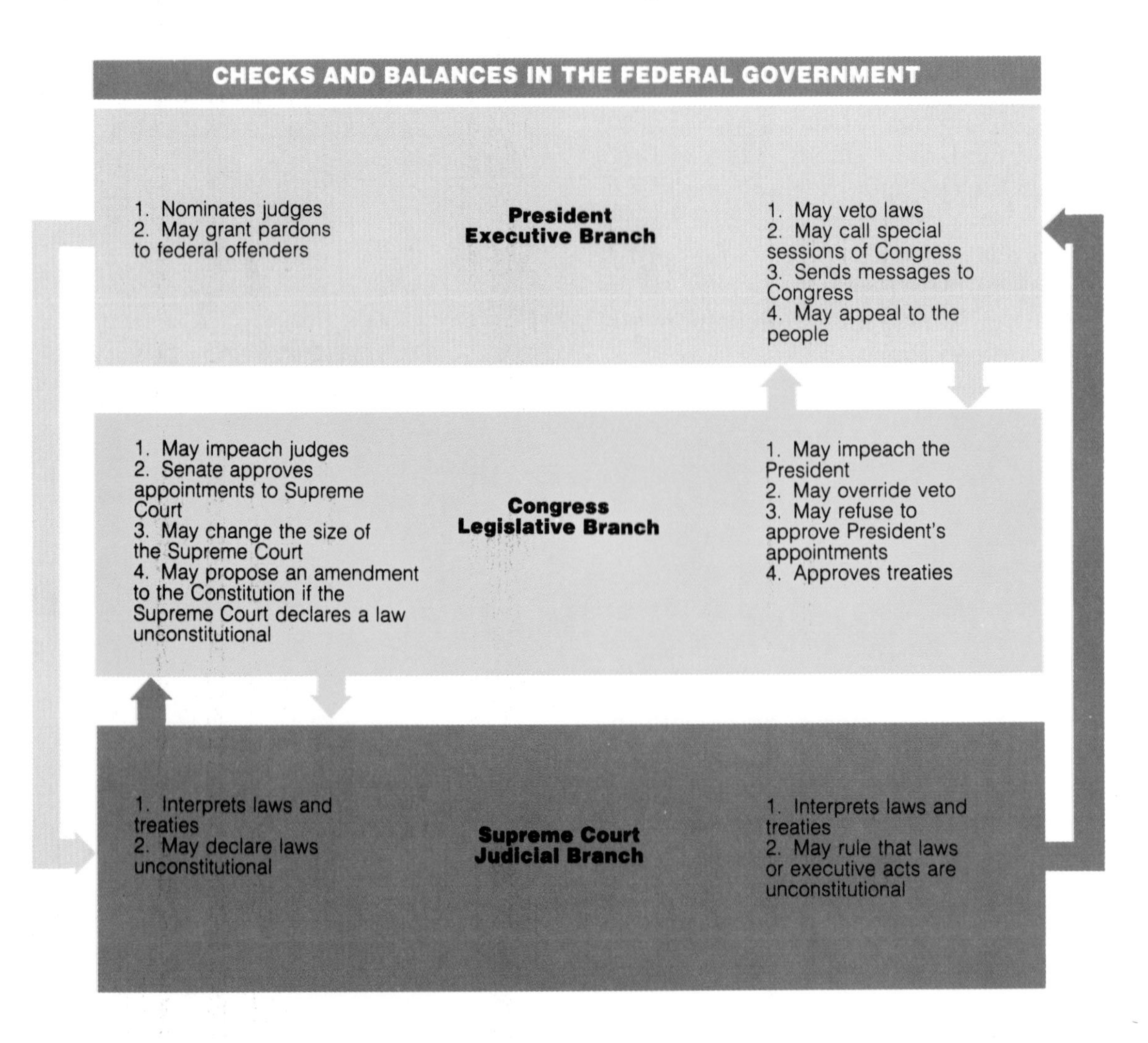

The work of the convention done, the delegates gather for the formal signing of the Constitution.

Part Five

Americans Adopt the Constitution

How did the people react to the new Constitution?

When the new Constitution was made public, some people said they were against it. They gave two reasons for objecting. First, they said they were afraid of giving any power to government, especially to a national government. They feared that any powerful government would be a bad government. They did not want to be trampled on, as the British government had trampled on them before.

Second, they pointed out that there was a very important part missing from the new Constitution—a Bill of Rights. Such a bill would protect citizens from their government by guaranteeing them rights such as freedom of speech and fair trial in court. Without such guarantees, opponents felt there was no sense in supporting the Constitution.

Other Americans realized that if the United States was to grow and prosper as a united country, a strong government was needed. Many people understood right away that a good Constitution had been written. Thomas Jefferson wrote that the Constitution was "unquestionably the wisest ever yet presented. . . ." He added, "The example of changing a Constitution by assembling the wise men of the state instead of assembling armies will be worth . . . much in the world."

1. For what two reasons did some Americans object to the new Constitution?

2. Why were many Americans in favor of the new Constitution?

When and why was the Constitution approved?

Each state, except Rhode Island which had refused to send delegates to Philadelphia, called a special convention to vote on the new Constitution. When nine of the states *ratified*, or approved, the new plan for government, it was to go into effect. It then would become the supreme law of the land.

Many Americans worked hard to get the states to ratify the Constitution. George Washington talked to the people, especially those in his home state of Virginia. John Jay, James Madison, and

Alexander Hamilton wrote articles called *The Federalist Papers* explaining the new Constitution. Jay, who later became the nation's first Chief Justice, tried to persuade others that they need not fear the power of the new government. "The people who own the country ought to govern it," he said again and again. And under the new Constitution the people would do just that. Madison and others promised that the first Congress would add a Bill of Rights. The first ten amendments to the Constitution that make up the Bill of Rights were adopted by the states in 1791.

Those who favored the new Constitution finally convinced a majority. One after another, the states ratified the new plan for government. Delaware was first. By June 1788, nine states had given their approval, and this was enough to start the new government. The problem, however, was that two big, key states, Virginia and New York, had not yet ratified. Without their approval, chances for success were not good. But at last, in the summer of 1788 after hot debate, they, too, agreed. Only North Carolina and Rhode Island held out until after the first President was elected.

3. Who were some of the Americans who worked to get the Constitution ratified?

4. When had enough states ratified the Constitution for it to go into effect?

Who was the people's choice for President?

Once the Constitution was approved, a President and members of Congress had to be elected. The people

As Washington traveled from Virginia to New York City for his first inauguration, he was greeted with cheers and celebrations. Here sailors row him across the harbor from New Jersey to Manhattan in a gaily decorated barge.

Focus on Skills

Using a separate sheet of paper, fill in the chart below by noting in Column 3 how the Constitution corrects the weaknesses of the Articles of Confederation described in Column 2. Find the place in the Constitution (pages 595-615) where the topic is discussed. Give the article and section number of the topic in Column 4.

Topic	*Articles of Confederation*	*Constitution*	*Article and Section*
1. Executive Branch	No President. When Congress was not in session, a committee ran the government.		
2. Interstate Commerce	Each state could tax goods coming across its borders from other states.		
3. Courts	No court system to resolve problems between citizens of different states.		
4. Money System	Each state issued its own money.		
5. Legislature	One house; one vote per state.		

wanted George Washington to be their first President. They would not even consider anyone else. Washington himself did not really want the job. He had served his country for many years. The Revolution had been hard on him, and he had suffered with his soldiers. Once the war was over, he wanted only to live a quiet life at Mount Vernon, his home.

But the people would not let Washington do that. They called him to be chairman of the Constitutional Convention and then elected him as their first President. John Adams was elected Vice-President.

George Washington was "battle-tested" and trusted. People knew he had laid down his military powers at the end of the Revolution. He had not tried to make himself a king or a dictator. When he was asked to be the first President, he agreed. Washington put serving his country above his own feelings and wishes.

Many, many problems faced the new nation. Even as Washington traveled the muddy roads to New York City to be *inaugurated* (in ô′gyə rāt əd: sworn into office), he must have worried about these problems.

5. Why did the people want Washington to serve as their first President?

6. How did Washington feel about becoming President?

Historymaker

In every group some members seem to be the ones who really make things happen. That was true also among those gathered at Philadelphia. All told there were 55 delegates to the convention. Of that number seventeen were the real movers and shakers. You've already met some of those who played key roles. Among them were Benjamin Franklin and George Washington, who was the chairman.

Here we cannot consider all who were especially outstanding. Instead, we'll look at just three members.

One of them signed what may be the three most important documents in United States history: the Declaration of Independence, the Articles of Confederation, and the Constitution. That person was Roger Sherman of Connecticut.

Another was the small, shy, but brilliant "Father of the Constitution," James Madison of Virginia.

The third was the convention's gadfly and its conscience. At the very last minute he decided he could not sign the document he had worked so hard to help produce. That nonsigner was George Mason, also of Virginia.

Roger Sherman. That Roger Sherman ever would play an important role in history seemed unlikely early in his life. He had to learn to read and write in the little spare time he had. Not only did he work long hours on his father's small farm, he also was busy learning the shoemaker's trade. There was neither time nor money for him to attend grade school, let alone college.

Sherman had a keen mind, however, and he used it. He had many interests: astronomy, finance, poetry, and politics. But he also had to make a living to support his family, which finally numbered fifteen children. He was in turn a surveyor, store owner, lawyer, and judge. By the time he went to Philadelphia, Sherman was 66 years old. He was the second-oldest delegate. Only Benjamin Franklin was older.

Sherman had an almost perfect attendance record at the convention. But he is best remembered for breaking the deadlock between the large and small states. When it appeared neither would give in on the question of representation in Congress, Sherman proposed the Great Compromise. The small states agreed to it because every state was to have the same number of votes in the Senate. The large states accepted it because membership in the House of Representatives would be according to the population of each state.

James Madison. If anyone can be said to have done his homework prior to the convention, it was James Madison. He was one of the world's most informed students of government. Even so, he arrived ahead of all

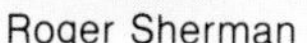
Roger Sherman

James Madison

George Mason

the other delegates to go over his notes. He also prepared materials for others which he thought would be helpful to them.

Despite his achievements, Madison was very modest—actually shy. His disposition was sunny, even though he always dressed in black and was very serious about the work at hand. Madison never missed a session. What is more, he kept a record of all that was said and done. That carefully guarded record was not published until after his death in 1840. It is the best account of the convention.

For his careful preparation, record-keeping, thoughtful speeches, encouragement of others, and his hard work in getting the Constitution ratified, Madison is honored with a title. He is called the "Father of the Constitution."

At the time of the convention, Madison was a 36-year-old bachelor. Later in life, he married a happy, outgoing young widow named Dolley Todd. He also became the third President of the United States. We'll read more about the Madisons later.

George Mason. Even if George Mason had never gone to Philadelphia, Americans would owe him a great debt. Earlier he had written the Virginia Declaration of Rights. It is one of the world's great documents of liberty. Thomas Jefferson used it as a model for the Declaration of Independence. The French borrowed from it for their Declaration of the Rights of Man. So, too, did the United Nations when it adopted the Universal Declaration of Human Rights in 1948.

Not one to mince words, Mason opened the Virginia Declaration with these words: "All men are by nature equally free and independent and have certain inherent rights. . . ."

It is not surprising, therefore, that Mason kept insisting that the United States Constitution needed a Bill of Rights. Others at the convention, Roger Sherman among them, said that was not necessary. The state constitutions had bills of rights.

"That's not enough!" Mason protested. "The national government whose laws will be above the states must guarantee human rights as well."

Although he thundered and pleaded, he could not convince enough delegates. Therefore, on September 15, 1787, when the others stepped up to sign the Constitution, George Mason said that his conscience would not let him do so.

Mason's conscience was bothered by another matter as well—slavery. Although he himself owned slaves, he worried that it was morally wrong. Speaking as much to himself as the other delegates, Mason warned:

Slavery discourages arts and manufactures. The poor despise labor when performed by slaves. . . . Every master is born a petty tyrant [dictator]. They bring the judgment of Heaven on a Country. . . . By a . . . chain of causes and effects, Providence punishes national sins by national calamities. . . .

Building Your Vocabulary

Match each item in Column A with the correct item in Column B.

Column A	Column B
1. ordinance	A. give and take to reach agreement
2. chief executive	B. changed slightly to meet special needs
3. delegate	C. a law
4. unconstitutional	D. approved
5. republican form of government	E. a loose union of equals
6. ratified	F. President of the United States
7. adapted	G. a representative
8. federal system	H. against the Constitution
9. confederation	I. power is shared by states and national government
10. compromise	J. a system under which the people choose their own officials

Recalling What You Have Learned

On a separate piece of paper copy and complete each sentence by selecting the correct word from those listed below.

1. In the summer of 1787, the Constitutional Convention met in—?—.
2. —?—served as chairman of that convention.
3. Before the Constitution was completed, the United States was governed under the—?—.
4. In the Senate, each state has—?—members regardless of its size.
5. The part of the United States Constitution which guarantees rights such as trial by jury and free speech is called—?—.
6. —?—is the supreme law of the land.

two
Philadelphia
the Bill of Rights
Articles of Confederation
the Constitution
George Washington

Discussing the Important Ideas in This Chapter

1. Why has the United States Constitution been called the most successful in history?
2. Do you think closing the Constitutional Convention to the public was a good idea? Why?

3. How do branches of the federal government check and balance one another? Why are those checks and balances important?
4. Why did the people want George Washington as their first President?
5. Could slavery have been outlawed when the Constitution was being written? What might have happened if it had been?
6. As a new nation, the United States was looked down upon by foreign countries because it was too weak and poor. Today some foreign countries do not like the United States because they think it is too strong and rich. How important are the feelings of other nations about the United States?

Improving Your Map Skills

Study the map on page 121 and use the direction finder to help you answer the questions below.

1. What is the title or name of the map?
2. Name the four Barbary States shown on the map.
3. On what continent are those states located?
4. What continent is directly north of the Barbary States?
5. Name the body of water which lies to the west of Portugal. What body of water lies to the northeast of Morocco?
6. Notice the very narrow entrance to the Mediterranean Sea which lies between Spain and Morocco. What is the name of that passageway?
7. Name the large city shown on the coast of Algeria.
8. What other city is shown which lies southeast of Algeria?
9. In what direction from Morocco does the United States lie?

Improving Your Study Skills: *Reading*

Use your textbook to help you find two reasons for each of the events listed below. Write the reasons on a separate piece of paper.

1. The delegates to the convention in Philadelphia decided to write a new Constitution because:
   A. ____________
   B. ____________
2. The new United States had serious money problems because:
   A. ____________
   B. ____________
3. The delegates to the Constitutional Convention closed their meetings to the public because:
   A. ____________
   B. ____________
4. Americans decided to approve, or ratify, the new Constitution because:
   A. ____________
   B. ____________
5. Americans wanted Washington to be their first President because:
   A. ____________
   B. ____________

Unit Two

Challenges

6 Setting the Course

7 A New Nation Grows in Size and Strength

8 Changing Times

9

for the New Nation

Chapter 6

Setting the Course

Monticello, Charlottesville, Virginia

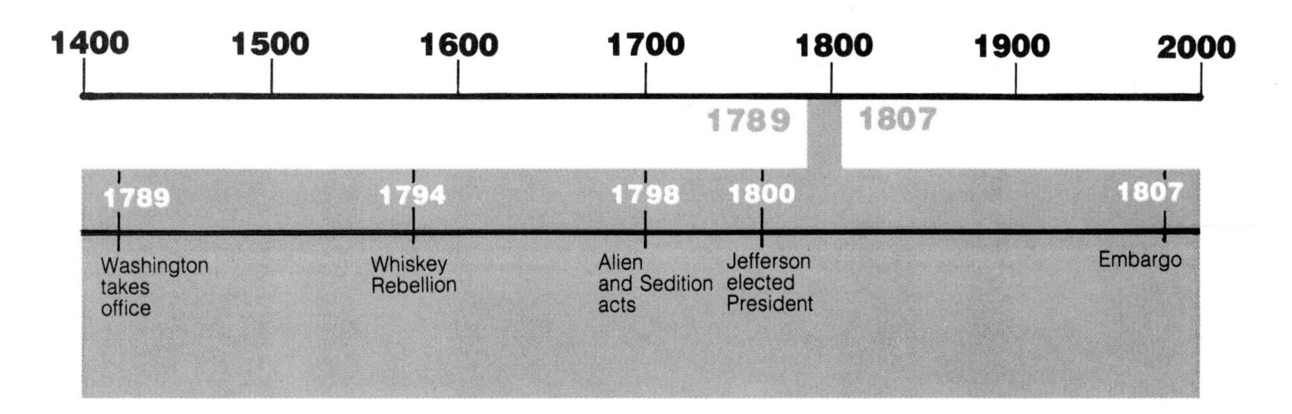

Part One

Making the New Government Work

What challenges faced the new nation?

Being President of the United States has been called the "toughest job in the world." George Washington's job was especially hard. As the first President, he could not benefit from the experience of those before him. He did have the new Constitution as a guide. It set the nation's goals. It was a good blueprint. But it did not spell out details for operating the government. Those details had to be worked out. No other country had ever set up a government quite like that of the United States. So Washington could not look to other countries for examples of what to do. Even so, much needed to be done and done quickly. Five major challenges faced the new nation:

1. Able people with good ideas were needed for many government jobs. These workers would have no one to show them how things had been done before. Where and how were skilled persons to be found to work in the postal service, the courts, and the offices of Congress? Who should organize the

army, design and coin the money, or set up a system of weights and measures? Which Americans should be chosen as judges and representatives to other countries?

2. The new nation needed money. Ways had to be found to pay the nation's debts. The new government had to find sources of income. Unless it had money it could not offer services or pay its employees.

3. Frontier settlers wanted protection against Indian and Spanish attacks. Settlers also wanted to be sure they could get their products to market.

4. The new government had to gain the respect of other nations. It also had to avoid new wars.

5. Americans needed to learn how to work together as Americans. Until 1776 they had been British subjects. Now they were citizens of a new nation. But many still thought of themselves as citizens of a state or a section of the country. As yet they did not put the United States first.

1. Why was Washington's job as first President especially hard?

2. What were the five great challenges which the new government faced?

Why did Washington establish a cabinet?

The President is head of the executive branch of government (page 127). As Chief Executive, the President must carry out the laws. That is a big job. Washington knew that he would need help. He asked several people to work closely with him. Each one was to be in charge of one department. The departments were set up by Congress. Those chosen made up the *cabinet*. The Constitution does not say there should be a cabinet. But every President since Washington has named one and looked to it for advice.

Washington took his time selecting the first cabinet. Almost a year passed before it was complete. He named just four persons to the first cabinet. Washington did not care if those he chose thought exactly as he did. Nor did he care whether they agreed with each other. He wanted to hear different points of view before making up his mind about a problem. He wanted advisers with plenty of good ideas, the skill to carry them out, and the courage to stand up for their ideas.

Two of those he named certainly did not agree with each other. They did have good ideas, however. They also had the skill to carry them out and the courage to fight hard for them. Those men were Alexander Hamilton and Thomas Jefferson.

3. What is the President's cabinet?

Who served in Washington's cabinet?

Hamilton was only 34 years old when Washington asked him to become head, or *Secretary*, of the Treasury. The ambitious Hamilton was born in the West Indies. He came to New York to attend King's College (later Columbia University). During the Revolution he had served as Washington's aide. Hamilton became a brilliant lawyer and helped write the Constitution (page 123). He was an outspoken opponent of slavery. He was short, scrappy, and something of a dandy. Although he had a lot of faith in himself, he had little faith in the common people. Washington chose him because of his talent for handling money. Hamil-

The Washingtons meet their guests at a formal reception. The President is in the center; Martha Washington stands on a platform. Some people called her "Lady Washington."

ton was known as a "money genius." He put that genius to work for the nation. In time Hamilton became the most important member of the cabinet.

Thomas Jefferson differed from Hamilton in almost every way. He was tall, slender, and sometimes almost careless about his clothes. Jefferson had been born to wealth. Although he held slaves, he was unhappy and uneasy about slavery. He believed in the common people, especially in small farmers.

When Washington asked him to become the first Secretary of State, Jefferson begged to be excused. He explained that he really wanted to stay at his home, Monticello, and be a farmer. Jefferson was, in fact, a good deal more than just a farmer. He wrote the Declaration of Independence (page 103). What is more, he had experience representing Americans in other nations. That, of course, is exactly why Washington refused to take "no" for an answer. So at last Jefferson agreed to head the State Department. He took charge of the nation's foreign affairs.

Washington was worried—for good reason—about the new nation's defenses. There were just 840 men in the whole United States Army when he took office. The twelve clerks who were its only employees had not been paid for some time. They were threatening to quit. So the President turned to the ablest and most dependable of all his generals during the Revolution. He asked Henry Knox, a Boston bookseller turned soldier, to be the first Secretary of War.

Knox was remarkable in many ways. Cool under pressure, he was known for his good nature and concern for others. He also was known for his size. He weighed about 300 pounds (135 kg).

As Secretary of War, Knox was to have three major duties. He was to be in charge of the army, the navy, and Indian affairs. Knox was especially concerned about the Indians. Even before he became Secretary of War, he showed that concern. He wrote a hard-hitting report to the Continental Congress in

1788. In it he charged that "the white inhabitants on the frontiers of North Carolina . . . have frequently committed the most unprovoked and direct outrages against the Cherokee Indians." Those outrages, he said, amounted to "an actual although informal war." After he took office, Knox pressed for just treatment of the Indians. He said, "The Indians being the prior occupants, possess the right of the soil. It cannot be taken from them unless by their free consent. . . ." Needless to say, his ideas were not very popular with settlers on the frontier.

To round out the cabinet, Edmund Randolph was picked to be Attorney General, or the nation's chief lawyer. Hailing from Virginia, Randolph had played an important role in the Constitutional Convention. He had also served in his state's legislature and as governor.

4. Name the four members of the first cabinet.

What actions did the first Congress take?

Because transportation was difficult, members of the first Congress were slow to arrive. Business did not begin until March 30, 1789. Congress met in a room in the New York City Hall, which was renamed Federal Hall.

The first Congress took three important actions:

1. It passed a *tariff*, or tax, on goods brought in from other countries. This tariff on imports was the major source of income for the federal government for more than fifty years.

2. It passed twelve amendments to the Constitution. The states ratified ten of those amendments, which became the Bill of Rights. Madison and others had promised the people that if they would ratify the Constitution, a Bill of Rights would be added.

3. It began the committee system. Congress quickly created a system to handle the many matters which came before it. The matters were first examined by small groups in each house. Then these groups reported back to all of the members. To this day, that is the way all of the bills introduced in Congress are treated. They are assigned to the proper committee. Its members discuss the bills. They then select those bills which they believe the whole Congress should consider.

The first Congress also took some other steps. First it concerned itself with the proper titles for elected officials. John Adams, the nation's first Vice-President, was especially worried about the President's title. He liked "His Highness the President of the United States and the Protector of the Rights of the Same." When others suggested just plain "Mr. President," Adams sputtered. If the Chief Executive had no better title, people "would despise him to all eternity." Finally a member of Congress from Pennsylvania put an end to the debate. He reminded those present that the Constitution says "No title of nobility shall be granted by the United States." (See Article I, Section 9, page 601.) Ever since, the Chief Executive has been addressed very simply as "Mr. President."

Naturally, members of Congress also got around to thinking about their own salaries. They argued for a time about whether senators ought to get more pay than representatives. Some felt that senators ought to get eight dollars a day, and members of the House five. In the end, pay was set at six dollars for all.

5. What were three important actions taken by the first Congress?

6. What title was finally agreed upon for the Chief Executive of the United States?

How were the federal courts organized?

The Constitution said there should be one Supreme Court and other lesser courts as Congress decides. It did not, however, say how many courts there should be in all. Nor did it say how many judges should serve in each court. Congress had to work out those details.

Congress lost no time in setting up the federal court system. It passed the Judiciary Act in 1789. The courts that were set up by that law still serve our nation today.

Congress provided for a Supreme Court with one Chief Justice, or judge, and five associate justices. It set up three circuit courts. It also set up thirteen district courts. Later the number of justices in the Supreme Court was fixed at nine. Other courts have been added. However, the framework of the nation's court system has stayed the same for almost 200 years.

7. What was the Judiciary Act of 1789?

8. Why is that law still important?

Part Two

Money Troubles

Why was money the new nation's greatest problem?

Money—or rather the lack of it—was the new country's number one headache. The federal government was in debt. It owed more than 54 million dollars. That was a huge sum of money in the 1700s. Because of the size of its debt, the government could not borrow any more money from other countries or its own citizens until it "established its credit." In other words, the government had to show that it could pay *old* debts before anyone would lend it more money. If the United States wanted to become strong and respected, it had to solve its money troubles.

How did the United States get so deeply into debt? During the Revolution the American government needed money. To borrow this money, the government sold certificates called *bonds*. A bond is a promise to pay back a certain amount of money plus interest.

After the Revolution, the government was very weak. It looked as if the people who had bought its bonds would never get their money back. By 1789 the value of these bonds was very low.

Poor people as well as rich people were "stuck" with these almost worthless bonds. In despair, poor people sold their bonds for any price they could get.

1. How did the United States get so deeply into debt?

2. Why was it important that the United States pay its debts?

How did Alexander Hamilton want to solve the money problems?

Secretary of the Treasury Hamilton thought four things should be done to solve the country's money problems:

1. All federal debts should be paid. Bondholders should be given back every cent of their money, plus interest. People, he said, must have faith in the government.

2. The federal government should pay state debts, too. Many states had fallen into debt during the Revolution. The war was fought for all Americans, Hamilton said. So all Americans should help pay those debts.

3. The government should begin collecting two new kinds of taxes. First, it should collect tariffs. Tariffs would help build American business and industry, Hamilton said. If foreign goods cost more than those made in the United States, people would buy American products. The United States could then become an industrial nation with many factories, offices, and banks. Second, Hamilton said some goods made in the United States should be taxed. This kind of tax is called an *excise tax*. This was a new idea, and it led to trouble, as we soon shall see.

4. The government should authorize a national bank. Income from taxes could be put in the Bank of the United States for safekeeping. The Bank could issue money. It could make loans, and the government could collect interest on them. In time, Hamilton argued, such a Bank could make the United States strong just as the Bank of England had helped make that nation strong.

Alexander Hamilton was young, ambitious, and handsome when he was selected as Secretary of the Treasury.

3. Why did Hamilton say the United States government should pay both the federal debts and those owed by the states?

4. What were the four suggestions Hamilton made for solving the new nation's money problems?

How did people feel about Hamilton's plans?

Some people were in favor of Hamilton's plans. Those who owned government bonds supported his plans. So, too, did those who hoped that business and industry would grow in the United States. They said Hamilton's ideas would put the country on its feet. It would gain respect. Poor people and those in debt were not happy about Hamilton's ideas, however. They said:

1. By paying old debts, the government would help speculators. *Speculators* try to get rich quick by taking risks in buying and selling. They are like gamblers. Ex-soldiers, widows, and farmers who needed cash had sold their bonds to speculators for a few cents on the dollar after the Revolution. Now the government would reward the speculators by paying them 100 cents on the dollar.

2. Some states had already paid their war debts. Why should they be taxed again to pay for other states?

3. Tariffs make foreign goods more expensive. Poor people argued that tariffs were unfair. They said that all

goods should be sold at the lowest possible prices.

4. A Bank of the United States would help the rich, but not the poor. Rich people would lend money to the Bank and make big profits. But poor people could not afford to lend money to the Bank.

In the end, all of Hamilton's plans were adopted. The federal government paid all state and federal government debts. Tariffs and excise taxes were collected. And the Bank of the United States was set up.

5. Why were some people in favor of Hamilton's plans?

6. Who opposed Hamilton's plans and why?

What did money problems have to do with the new national capital?

The first capital of the United States was at New York City. Then it was moved to Philadelphia. But the government wanted to build a brand-new city for itself, with beautiful buildings and wide streets. Where should this new city be built?

The state of Virginia did not want the federal government to pay state debts. But Virginians did want the new capital to be on the Potomac (pə tō′ mək) River. The Potomac was Virginia's northern border. Virginians believed that having the capital on their border would bring them honor and create jobs and trade.

Hamilton saw a chance to make a bargain with Thomas Jefferson. He promised Jefferson that the new capital would be built on the banks of the Potomac River. In return, Jefferson must support the payment of state debts by the federal government.

Jefferson, a proud Virginian, agreed to the bargain. A ten mile square area (26 km^2) on the Potomac was set aside as the new capital. This area was named Washington, District of Columbia. It was not a part of any state. Washington, D.C., became the capital of the United States in 1800.

7. When and where was the permanent capital of the United States built?

8. Why was that site chosen?

Who planned the nation's capital?

The new nation had a dream. That dream was a beautiful new capital to which all Americans could look with pride. Although he never was to live there, President Washington named a team of the best engineers and surveyors in the world to plan Washington, D.C.

A French engineer, Major Pierre L'Enfant, was asked to make the plans for the new city. L'Enfant had come to America with Lafayette. He had fond memories of Paris, the capital of his native country. So he drew plans for Washington, D.C., with Paris in mind. He laid out the city so that it resembled a wheel. At the hub, or center, were important government buildings. Streets spread out from the center like spokes in a wheel. (See illustrations, page 147).

The chief surveyor was Benjamin Banneker, a talented freeborn black. Banneker had great ability in mathematics. He invented the first clock in America that struck the hours. He was also interested in astronomy, or the study of the stars and the universe. Banneker became skillful enough to predict an eclipse of the sun. He wrote an almanac each year.

The streets of the nation's capital are wide, beautiful avenues. Those

This engraving of Banneker appeared in his almanac.

streets are reminders of the people who surveyed and helped plan them.

9. How did L'Enfant lay out the city of Washington, D.C.?
10. Who was Benjamin Banneker?

Why did money problems trigger the "Whiskey Rebellion"?

Farmers in western Pennsylvania raised corn and other grain. Shipping these goods to market over rough mountain roads was difficult. It was easier to turn the corn into whiskey and ship it in jugs. It took many bushels of grain to make a small amount of whiskey.

Whiskey became a very valuable product on the frontier. In many places it was as good as money. Farmers traded it for things they needed.

When the government of the United States placed an excise tax on whiskey, the farmers rebelled. Angry citizens attacked federal tax collectors in what is called the Whiskey Rebellion.

Washington and Hamilton saw the *Whiskey Rebellion* as a test of strength for the new national government. When the governor of Pennsylvania refused to call out state troops, Washington turned to the Supreme Court. The justices found the farmers in violation of federal law. So Washington ordered 15,000 soldiers to march into Pennsylvania. The governor of that state then decided to lead the troops himself. But he was slow about the march. Finally Washington and Hamilton went to see for themselves what was going on. When they appeared, the farmers ran away and the rebellion ended.

The Whiskey Rebellion was an important event in American history. The federal government showed that people had to obey the laws, even laws they did not like.

11. Why did farmers in the West make whiskey instead of selling corn?
12. Why was Washington's action toward the farmers important?

Part Three

Frontier Problems

How did the United States try to handle problems with the Indians?

President Washington had good reasons for worrying about the frontier. Thousands of pioneers poured through the mountain passes to make new homes in the western lands. Many Indian tribes lived there, including the Shawnee,

Focus on Skills

Although a good plan had been drawn for it, Washington, D.C., was unfinished in 1800. The streets of the new capital city were muddy. A swamp lay between the Capitol building, not yet completed, and the White House. Even the President's home was not ready, and its roof leaked when heavy rain fell.

For a time, Jefferson continued to live in a simple boardinghouse in the city. He was lucky. Many other officials had a hard time finding any place to stay. In 1800, Washington was really little more than a good-sized clearing in the wilderness. One European sent to represent his country moaned, "What have I done to be condemned to such a place?"

Today, Washington is said to be one of the most beautiful capitals in the world. It is a far cry from the "clearing in the wilderness" in which Jefferson took office. To appreciate the many changes which have taken place, compare the drawing (bottom left) with the aerial photograph (right). On a separate sheet of paper list at least three important changes which have taken place in the nation's capital since 1800.

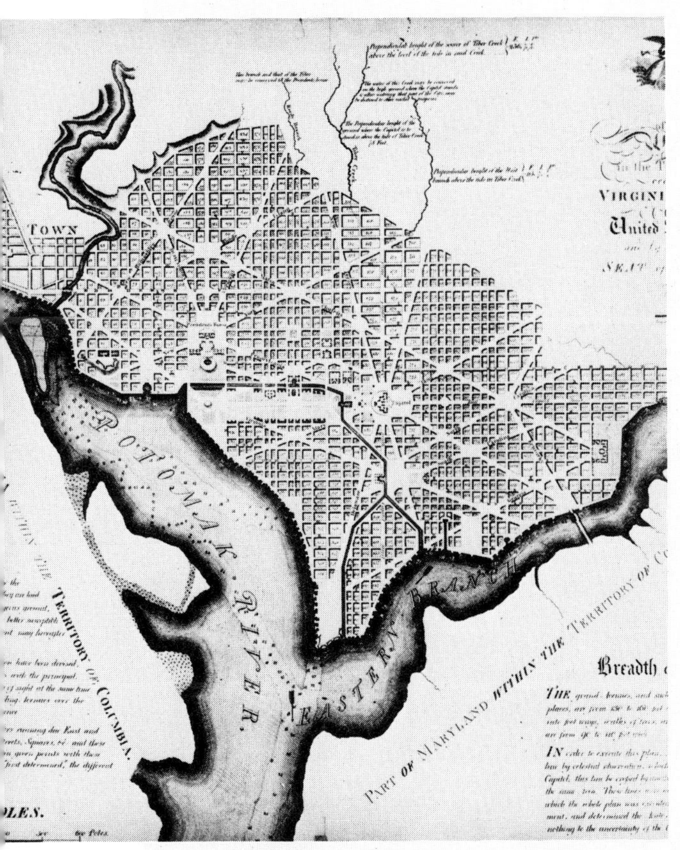

Washington, D.C., in 1800

Washington, D.C., today

Wyandot, and Miami. There were also members of the Delaware tribe who had come from the East. Of course, the Indians were not happy to see so many Americans moving into their lands.

The British encouraged the Indians to fight the new settlers. There were many raids and massacres. Westerners demanded protection. Some of them even talked of leaving a government that could not or would not protect them.

Washington sent troops to the Northwest. General Arthur St. Clair led 1400 soldiers against the Indians. St. Clair was caught off guard on the Wabash River and badly beaten. Only 600 Americans lived to tell the tale.

Treaties were another way the government tried to keep law and order. But the settlers and Indians did not trust each other. Treaties were often broken.

Discouraged, Washington turned to General "Mad Anthony" Wayne for help. Wayne had won his nickname during the Revolution. Anyone as daring as Wayne had to be "mad," the soldiers said.

But Wayne did not rush into battle or take risks this time. He prepared very carefully. For two years he drilled 2500 soldiers. Only then did he march to face the northwest Indian tribes.

Wayne and his men set up winter camp at Fort Greenville in western Ohio. (See map, page 118.) There 1600 seasoned frontier fighters from Kentucky joined them. Wayne pushed his troops hard. He made them drill and exercise.

After the Battle of Fallen Timbers, General Anthony Wayne negotiated the Treaty of Greenville. By that treaty, Indian tribes of the Northwest Territory ceded their lands to the United States. A member of Wayne's staff painted this picture which shows Wayne meeting with a group of Indian leaders.

He toughened them by sending them on scouting parties through the surrounding forests. When the snow melted, the troops were ready.

The Indians chose to make their stand in an area which had been hit by a tornado. Thousands of trees had been blown down. So the battle is called the "Battle of Fallen Timbers."

The battle site should have been ideally suited to the Indians and their style of fighting. But Wayne had a clever plan. His troops forced their way in. They jumped their horses over the fallen trees. In less than an hour, the battle was over. The Indians were forced to flee.

Little Turtle, who had led the winning attack against St. Clair, was again in command at Fallen Timbers. He was a long-time war chief for the Miamis. Short, well-built, brave, and extremely intelligent, Little Turtle had seldom known defeat. In this case, however, he was wise enough to see that the odds were against his people. They were no match for the well-equipped, well-led, disciplined Americans. So Little Turtle urged the other tribes to join him in getting the best terms they could from Wayne. They called him the "General-Who-Never-Sleeps."

The next summer warriors and chiefs from the many tribes of the Northwest gathered at Fort Greenville. Negotiations began. They lasted several weeks. At one point Little Turtle told the Americans: "[The Indians] are of the opinion that you take too much of their lands away and confine the hunting of our young men within limits too contracted."

But Little Turtle did not think peace was impossible. "Let us both own this place and enjoy in common the advantages it affords."

The Americans, however, did not want both sides to "own this place." They forced the Indians to surrender 25,000 acres (10,000 ha) of their best land. In return they gave the Indians about $20,000 in presents. They promised $10,000 a year to tribes which accepted the Treaty of Greenville and kept its terms.

At the end of the meeting, General Wayne spoke.

> **Brothers, I pray to the Great Spirit that the peace now established may be permanent, and that it will hold us together in the bonds of friendship until time shall be no more.**

As news spread that the Indian power in the Northwest was broken settlers flooded in. Problems with the Indians soon began again.

1. How did the government attempt to protect settlers in the West?

2. Who were the leaders in the Battle of Fallen Timbers? Why was that battle important?

How did the government reopen the port of New Orleans?

Westerners used the Mississippi River as a "highway" for floating their grain, lumber, and animal skins to market. In New Orleans, the Americans stored their goods on the docks until they could be loaded on ocean-going cargo ships. Storing goods without paying taxes was called the *right of deposit.*

Spain owned New Orleans and the Louisiana territory. The Spanish were not friendly toward the new United States. Suddenly, in 1784, Spain closed the port to Americans. Angry settlers threatened to reopen New Orleans with guns.

Major Roads in 1790
Roads
Paths
300 Miles
300 Kilometers
Lake Superior
Lake Michigan
Lake Huron
Lake Ontario
Lake Erie
BRITISH NORTH AMERICA
NORTHWEST TERRITORY
SPANISH LOUISIANA
WEST FLORIDA
SPANISH FLORIDA
GULF OF MEXICO
ATLANTIC OCEAN
APPALACHIAN MTS
Montreal
Portland
Portsmouth
Norwich
Boston
Albany
Providence
Hartford
New Haven
New York
Philadelphia
Lancaster
Baltimore
Fredricksburg
Richmond
Williamsburg
Norfolk
Raleigh
Charlotte
Wilmington
Charleston
Augusta
Savannah
St. Augustine
Pensacola
New Orleans
Natchez
Arkansas Post
St. Louis
Nashville
Cumberland Gap
Harrod's Town
Chillicothe
Cumberland
Ft. Duquesne (Pittsburgh)
Ft. Sandusky
Ft. Detroit
Ft. Niagara
Mohawk Trail
Boston Post Rd.
Forbes Rd.
Fort Cumberland Rd.
Braddock's Rd.
Great Valley Rd.
Great Trail
Zane's Trace
Scioto Trail
Warrior's Path
Wilderness Rd.
Great Trading Path
Avery's Trace
Nickajack Trace
Chickasaw Trail
(Natchez Trace)
Trader's Path
Virginia Rd.
Western
Cape Fear Rd.
Post Rd.
Charleston Path
Main
Surveyed Trail
Ohio R.
Cumberland R.
Tennessee R.
Mississippi R.
Savannah R.
N
S
E
W

Settlers float down the Ohio River in a flatboat. Notice how they feed their livestock during the trip.

The English saw a way to take back part of America. They asked the Westerners to leave the United States and rejoin England. Spanish officials also tried to take over the West. They promised free use of the Mississippi, if the people on the frontier would join Spain. There was real danger that the West would pull away from the Union unless the government ended transportation problems.

Washington saw serious trouble ahead. For ten years the United States tried to get a trade treaty with Spain. Westerners' tempers were growing hotter. "What is the good of paying taxes to a government that cannot solve your problems?" they asked.

Finally, in 1795, President Washington sent Thomas Pinckney of South Carolina to make a treaty with the Spanish. Pinckney was able to get back the right of deposit at New Orleans because the Spanish were afraid the angry settlers might take the port by force.

3. Why were the Mississippi River and the Port of New Orleans especially important to settlers in the West?

4. How did the United States win back the right of deposit?

Part Four

Political Parties Begin

Why and how did political parties get started?

When George Washington was elected President in 1789, there were no political parties. Washington was against them. He was afraid that the parties would quarrel with each other and divide the new nation.

Soon Washington's fears began to come true. Hamilton and Jefferson could not agree on how the country should be run. Their followers quarrelled with

THE FIRST POLITICAL PARTIES: HOW THEY DIFFERED

JEFFERSON AND THE REPUBLICANS	HAMILTON AND THE FEDERALISTS
Who joined them?	
Owners of small farms, skilled workers, shopkeepers, frontier settlers	Merchants, bankers, wealthy farmers, manufacturers, and some southern planters.
What sections of the country favored them?	
South and West.	New England and the Atlantic Seaboard.
What kind of government did they want?	
A democracy run by small property owners.	People of wealth and property should run the country.
Lower requirements for voting, so more common people could vote.	High requirements for voting, so only those who understood issues and had a stake in the government could vote.
A fairly weak federal or national government. Follow the Constitution word for word (strict construction).	A strong federal or national government. Use the Constitution to make the federal government stronger (loose construction).
More rights for the states.	More rights for the federal government.
Cut the number of people on the federal payroll.	Increase the number of people on the federal payroll.
How they felt about money matters	
Farmers were the most important citizens.	Industry was more important than farming.
No special favors for manufacturers.	Government should help manufacturers—especially by putting tariffs on goods coming into this country.
No national bank wanted.	National bank wanted and needed.
Nation should get out of debt and not borrow money.	Nation should borrow money to built up its strength.
Which foreign country they favored	
France.	England.

each other. Jefferson's supporters were called Republicans. Hamilton's followers were called Federalists.

Republicans said that Federalists wanted to help only the wealthy or business people. They also claimed that the Federalists wanted a strong federal government and weak state governments. In reply, the Federalists said that the Republicans would wreck the new government by turning it over to the "mob." Finally these two groups organized themselves into political parties. (See chart above.)

1. Why was Washington against forming political parties?

2. Which two groups organized themselves into the first political parties?

Why did the political parties disagree about the Constitution?

The Constitution, as you know, sets out the basic rules for running the federal government. Those rules give Congress the right to pass laws on certain subjects. For example, Congress can levy taxes, borrow money, set up post offices, and keep an army and navy.

John Adams became our second President in 1797.

The Republicans wanted the federal government "kept in its place." They wanted Congress to pass laws only on the matters named in the Constitution. "If it doesn't say you can do something, you can't do it," the Republicans argued.

The Federalists wanted a strong national government. They said that Congress could pass laws on some subjects not named directly in the Constitution.

Republicans and Federalists looked at the Constitution in different ways. The Federalists, for example, wanted to start the national Bank (page 144). The Constitution says that Congress may "borrow money on the credit of the United States." The Federalists declared that, loosely speaking, these words gave them power to start the Bank. The Republicans, on the other hand, said that, strictly speaking, these words said absolutely nothing about starting a bank. The Federalists wanted a loose construction of the Constitution. The Republicans wanted a strict construction.

Americans are still divided over strict construction and loose construction of the Constitution. Strict construction favors less federal government, while loose construction adds to federal power.

3. What was the difference in the way the Republicans and the Federalists looked at the Constitution?

4. Why did the Federalists say Congress could establish a national Bank, even though the Constitution did not provide for it in so many words?

Why have political parties proved helpful?

Today it is hard to imagine how our government would work without political parties. Since they began in the 1790s, political parties have helped our country in many ways:

1. They choose candidates.
2. They give voters a choice of parties and ideas.
3. They keep voters informed.
4. Parties act as "watchdogs" when they are out of office. They try to make the elected party run the government properly.

Most important of all, political parties see that our government is changed by ballots, not bullets. If Americans don't like the way their country is being run, they can vote a new party into office at the next election.

5. How have political parties helped our nation?

6. What can Americans do if they dislike the party in office?

Who was chosen to be the second President?

Washington did not want to serve a second term as President. But he agreed to do so because his country needed him badly. As his second term drew to a close, he made it very clear that under no circumstances would he continue in office. He was very tired. His health was failing, and he had been away from home for many years. In a letter to a friend Washington wrote, "I now compare myself to the wearied traveler who seeks a resting place."

Knowing that Washington was going to step down, the Republicans and the Federalists began to compete harder than ever. Both parties hoped to win the number one prize in American politics, the presidency. The Federalists chose Vice-President John Adams as their candidate. They said it was only right that the Vice-President should move up to the top office. What is more, they argued, Washington was a Southerner. It was only right that he be followed by a Northerner. For their candidate, the Republicans turned to Thomas Jefferson. He was younger, they pointed out, than Adams. Adams then was 61. Jefferson was, they said, a better leader. People followed him willingly, while Adams was not well-liked.

Adams just barely defeated Jefferson in the election. He did not have a very happy time in office, however. From the day he took over as President he had trouble. No one would have found it easy to fill Washington's shoes. But for Adams, the job was very hard. He was a man of experience and had a good mind. But he did not get along well with people. Even his appearance was against him. Washington was tall and handsome. Adams was short and pudgy. Washington wanted to hear all sides of a question before he made important decisions. Adams did not often consult others. He was likely to be cranky if their ideas did not agree with his.

7. Whom did Adams defeat for the presidency?

8. Why did he have trouble in office?

Part Five

Problems with Foreign Countries

Why was the French Revolution important to Americans?

The French Revolution began in 1789, the same year Washington became President. This upheaval lasted for many years.

For centuries France had been ruled by nobles who had lived in luxury while many common people went hungry or were shut up in prisons. Finally French men and women attacked public buildings and palaces in Paris. Soon a "Reign of Terror" began. The king and queen were imprisoned. In time they were beheaded. Thousands of their followers were beheaded in public in the same way. Months and years went by, and still the flow of blood did not stop. The French people said they had been inspired by the American Revolution. They, too, wanted to become democratic. But their leaders, unlike those of the American Revolution, fought among themselves and killed each other.

Other European countries watched events in France carefully. They were frightened by what was happening. Kings and queens were worried about the safety of their own thrones. They agreed that what they called "this democratic madness" in France must be stopped before it spread any further. So England and several other countries went to war with France.

Although Europe was far away, Americans were deeply interested in the French Revolution. France had been our ally against England only a few years before. And now the French were asking us to pay back our debt by siding with them against England.

Americans were divided over which country they wanted to back. The Federalist party believed in strong government and in law and order. Federalists sided with England. The Republican party believed in not-so-strong government and rule by the people. Republicans sided with France.

President Washington knew that our country was too young and weak to get mixed up in European wars. Washington declared that the United States would not take sides. Instead, we would remain neutral. That should have solved the problem, except for one important thing. Neither England nor France paid any attention to our neutrality.

1. Why did other European countries get involved in the French Revolution?

2. Why did Washington want the United States to stay neutral?

Why did Americans become angry with both England and France?

Because they had decided to be neutral, Americans believed they should be able to carry on trade with both England and France. So they became angry when both England and France interfered with that trade.

The American representatives refuse to give even a sixpence to the multiheaded pirate symbolizing the French government.

The British navy stopped American ships on the high seas to prevent goods and supplies from reaching France. The British also took sailors off ships by force and made them serve in the British navy.

The French also interfered with American shipping. They did not want goods and supplies to reach England. They captured more than 300 United States ships on the high seas.

When John Adams became President, he sent representatives to France to discuss the problem. Three French officials known as "X, Y, and Z" said they would talk—but only if we first paid them a huge sum of money. This insult to our country really stirred up a hornet's nest. Adams answered the demand for bribes with a loud, flat "No!" For once the nation lined up solidly behind him. Some hotter heads demanded we go to war against France. Adams kept cool and kept the peace.

3. What did the British and the French do to American ships?

4. Who were X, Y, and Z? Why did their actions anger Americans?

At That Time

The mission San Carlos Borromeo in Carmel, California, was built in 1770. It was made of *adobe*, or sun-dried bricks.

While Americans won their freedom from Britain and set about forming a new government, the Spanish were trying to settle California. Present-day California has the largest population of any state in the Union. It is known throughout the world for its fertile farmland. But in the 1700s, Spain had a hard time finding settlers for California. The government promised settlers cows, sheep, goats, land, clothing, farm tools, and seeds. In addition, families were paid ten dollars a month for the first two years of residence in California. Then that was a considerable sum of money. Settlers were also excused from paying taxes for five years. Still there were not enough takers.

Finally the Spanish developed a plan to speed up the settlement of California. It was similar to the one they had used successfully on the frontier in Mexico. The plan can be compared to a table with four legs. Each "leg" was an institution with a special purpose.

1. The first "leg" was the military one, or the presido. *Presidios* were forts or garrisons. They were set up at the entrances to California's best harbors: Monterey, Santa Barbara, San Diego, and San Francisco. Their purpose was to defend California from foreign invaders. But as it turned out, the soldiers' biggest enemy was boredom. The guns in the presidio in San Francisco to this day have never been fired in anger.

2. The second "leg" was the mission. Between 1769 and 1821, the missions were the most important institutions in California. Franciscan priests, or *padres*, set up 21 missions.

The primary purpose of the missions was religious. The missionaries wanted to convert the Indians to Christianity. They did succeed in converting about 55,000 Indians. Most missionaries were devout men who believed they were doing good. But at times their methods were cruel. Indians who ran away were tracked down and returned to the missions. Indians were punished for breaking Christian rules. Although the missionaries taught the Indians new skills, the old Indian ways were lost.

The missions had other purposes as well as being religious centers. They were educational centers where Indians could learn new skills such as soapmaking and bricklaying. The missions produced enough for the needs of all the people who lived in them. But they also produced a surplus. Missions were the storehouses, or granaries, for the whole area.

The missions were to maintain "law and order" for the Spanish. So the missions had jails as well as chapels and vineyards and shops.

The missions were also the centers of social and cultural life for the area around them. All of life's important ceremonies took place at the missions. Babies were baptized, couples were married, and the dead were buried at the missions. On feast days there was singing and dancing. The missions were located about one day's travel apart. So travelers used the missions as wayside inns. Travelers were always welcome, no matter where they came from. No one was ever turned away.

3. The third "leg" of the settlement plan was the *pueblo*, or town. The purpose of the pueblos was to attract settlers. Each pueblo had four leagues of land, about 17,600 acres (7040 ha). In the center of each pueblo was a plaza, or square. Public buildings such as the council house, church, storerooms, and jail all faced onto the plaza. Settlers built their homes on the remaining lots facing the plaza. Community life revolved around this central square. People met there to do business, young people exchanged glances under the watchful eyes of their chaperones, and fiestas were celebrated. Even bull and bear fights were held in the plazas.

California's first two pueblos were San Jose, founded during the American Revolution on November 29, 1777, and Los Angeles. When it was founded on September 4, 1781, Los Angeles had a much longer name. It was *Nuestra Señora la Reina de los Ángeles de Porciúncula.* Small wonder that the eleven settlers and their families who founded the pueblo soon shortened the name to Los Angeles. The first group of settlers included Indians, blacks, Spaniards, and people of mixed Spanish and Indian ancestry.

4. The last "leg" of the development plan was the rancho. *Ranchos* were large estates, or ranches. The people who owned them were called *rancheros*. While Spain owned California, only a few families were given huge grants of land for ranchos. After the Mexicans threw off Spanish rule, many more families were given ranchos. Any Mexican of good character or any foreigner willing to become a Mexican citizen and join the Roman Catholic Church could ask for eleven square leagues of land. A square league was about 4438 acres (1775 ha).

Cattle raised on the ranchos were the mainstay of the California economy. Beef was the principal item of food. But hides and tallow (animal fat) were also important. Hides were turned into leather. Tallow was used to make candles.

Ranchos needed Indian workers to be successful. Indians were hired to herd cattle, plant and harvest crops, and do other chores. Some ranchos employed more than 100 Indians.

The Spanish settlers in California used paints invented by the Indians to decorate their furniture. This cupboard may have been used to store dishes.

In California almost everyone rode and loved horses—children, women, and men. Horses were used for transportation and for the cattle roundups, or rodeos. Rancheros had to be good riders. At that time grizzly bears roamed throughout California. A rider who surprised a grizzly needed skill to escape.

Life on the ranchos was simple. It revolved around the family. Sometimes families had as many as twenty members. They included in-laws and orphans. It was considered an honor to care for orphans.

The father of the house was the unquestioned ruler of the family. He could punish his children even when they were 60 years old. Children asked their father's permission to be seated. They spoke to him only when spoken to. Even so, the ties of affection were strong in most rancho families. Mothers were not only respected, they enjoyed rights which other American women did not even dream of. After marriage, California women kept their own names and passed them along to their children. They could own property in their own names. And their opinions were sought and respected in important matters.

What were the Alien and Sedition acts?

An *alien* (ā′ lyən) is a noncitizen. She or he is a person who has moved to a new country, but has not become a citizen of it.

Sedition (si dish′ ən) means being disloyal to the nation. Some people said that criticism of high government officials was sedition.

The Alien and Sedition acts were passed by the Federalist Congress in 1798.

These laws were meant to crush the Republican party. In speeches and newspaper articles, Republicans objected to the way the Federalists were running the country. The Federalists were afraid they would lose the election of 1800.

The Sedition Act was designed to stop criticism of the Federalists. Anyone who criticized the President or the government could be fined or sent to jail.

The Alien Act was designed to weaken the Republican party. It was aimed at aliens who were thought to be disloyal to the United States. Many of these immigrants were French. They planned to join the Republican party when they became citizens. The Alien Act made it much harder for these people to gain citizenship. Also, the President was given the power to *deport* aliens (send them out of the country).

5. Who is an alien? What is sedition?

6. What was the main purpose of the Alien Act? The Sedition Act?

Why were the Alien and Sedition acts important?

Actually, very few people were punished for disobeying the Alien and Sedition acts. But the laws made Thomas Jefferson and the Republican party very angry. The Republicans said that these laws were against the Constitution and the Bill of Rights. Freedom of speech and of the press were in danger.

Jefferson and James Madison (pages 132-133) wrote protests which the legislatures of Kentucky and Virginia passed. The protests became known as the *Kentucky and Virginia Resolutions.* They said that a state could declare a federal law unconstitutional, or "null and void." For the first time in the nation's history, states claimed that they did not have to obey federal laws which they did not like. The issue of nullification would return to haunt the country several times before the Civil War.

In passing the Alien and Sedition acts, the Federalists went too far. They endangered precious American freedoms, among them freedom of speech and freedom of the press.

But the Federalists had launched the new nation well. They had avoided war with England and France. Thanks to Alexander Hamilton, the United States was prosperous. When the people went to the polls in 1800, however, they turned Adams and the Federalists out of office. Thomas Jefferson and the Republicans took over the government.

The Alien and Sedition acts helped defeat the Federalists. So did the heavy taxes they passed for defense against possible attacks by England or France.

7. Why did the Alien and Sedition acts lead to the Kentucky and Virginia Resolutions?

8. Why did the Alien and Sedition acts lead to the defeat of the Federalists?

Part Six

Thomas Jefferson Guides the Nation

Why was Jefferson's election important?

Thomas Jefferson was no stranger to the American political scene. Earlier in his life he had played many important roles. (See pages 103, 141, and 145.) Jefferson was a genius. But he was also a very modest and plain man. When he became President in 1801, he was 57 years old. Six feet tall, red-haired, and freckle-faced, Jefferson had done enough in those 57 years to fill the lives of several people. He was a scientist, inventor, musician, and lawyer. He designed his own home, Monticello, in the Virginia countryside. Because he believed in education, he helped start the University of Virginia. And he wrote the Declaration of Independence.

Jefferson was known and admired all over the world. But fame did not turn his head. He was a man of simple habits who believed in democracy with all his heart. When he became President, he was living in a boardinghouse in Washington, D.C. Instead of riding to his inauguration, Jefferson walked through the muddy streets of the new capital to take office as the nation's leader.

Thomas Jefferson became our third President in 1801.

When Jefferson was elected, political power passed peacefully from one party to another. There was no violent revolution. His election showed that peaceful changes in government could take place in a democracy. The Constitution had planned for such peaceful changes.

As we know, the Federalists and the Republicans had fought each other for a long time. They had fought hard. But after Jefferson's election, he made an important statement. "We are all Republicans—We are all Federalists," he said. Jefferson thus called on Americans to remember that they were all part of the United States. Sharp political differences did not and should not divide Americans, he said. And Jefferson added, "I believe this is the strongest government on earth—the world's best hope."

1. What were some of the great accomplishments of Thomas Jefferson?

2. What did the Jefferson election show to all?

What dreams did Jefferson have for the United States?

Jefferson wanted the United States to remain an agricultural country. He thought small, independent farmers were the nation's best citizens. He distrusted cities and the people who lived in them.

Jefferson also thought the federal government should interfere as little as possible in people's lives. Certainly government should never get mixed up in business matters! Most important of all, Jefferson wanted government kept as close to the people as possible. The people's wishes should be all-important to government, he said. But Jefferson was no fool! He knew that uneducated people could not make wise choices. For that reason he said, "Let the nation be supplied with good newspapers and sound schoolmasters." Then the nation could truly be ruled by the people.

When it came to education, Jefferson was ahead of his time. He believed that women as well as men should be educated. And he personally put into practice what he believed. He saw that his daughter, Martha, also known as "Patsy," had a good education. She became an accomplished musician, a good speaker, and an avid student of history, much to her father's delight. After Jefferson became President, she served with credit as his official hostess at the White House.

Jefferson also was interested in the education of all young people. After he retired from the presidency, he devoted most of the last ten years of his life to his pet project, the founding of the University of Virginia.

3. Who were the nation's best citizens according to Jefferson?

4. Why did he want Americans to be educated?

How did Jefferson respond to new troubles with England and France?

Troubles with England and France which had begun during Washington's term and continued through John Adams's term did not disappear. They became even worse while Jefferson was in office. These two nations were still at war in 1803.

American merchants made money delivering goods to both countries. Shipping grew by leaps and bounds.

Then the British said they would no longer allow American ships to trade with the French. The French answered that Americans could no longer trade with the British. The British continued to stop American ships at sea and to kidnap sailors. (See page 155.)

President Jefferson was alarmed. To keep peace, he put an embargo on all American ships. An *embargo* means that ships cannot leave home for foreign ports. Jefferson thought the French and British needed American goods. So he thought France and Britain would agree to leave American ships alone if the United States would trade with them again.

The embargo did not work out as Jefferson hoped it would. Neither England or France changed its mind. In one year's time, American exports fell from $108 million to $22 million. People's incomes dropped. Shipyard workers lost their jobs. Shipowners, especially in New England, saw their ships rotting at the wharves. Warehouses were filled with goods that could not be sold. Merchants and farmers had no buyers for their products. Of course, the blame fell on Jefferson. As we shall see in the next chapter, problems with England and France were not solved until after Jefferson had left office.

5. What is an embargo?

6. What was the embargo supposed to accomplish?

7. Who was hurt by the embargo?

Historymaker

This is the drawing that Eli Whitney submitted of his cotton gin when he applied for a patent on his invention.

How different the history of the United States might have been had it not been for the chance meeting of two people on a coach in the fall of 1792.

A 27-year-old man who had just graduated from college was en route to South Carolina. He had been promised a job as a teacher. Shy and uncertain about what he really wanted to do in life, Eli Whitney did not dream he could make a living doing what he most liked to do—invent things. As a small boy he had found a way to make nails faster and better than by the hand method then in use. Then he went on to make walking canes, pins for women's hats, toys for children, and countless other things. But as he rode on the coach, he thought he would have to spend his life teaching or practicing law. As it turned out, he did neither.

Also on board the coach was Catherine Littlefield Greene, a 37-year-old widow with five small children, a small unprofitable cotton plantation, and many debts. She had married Nathanael Greene when she was just 19 years old. Two years later her husband had been named one of Washington's generals. Where Greene went, she went, sharing in all the hardships of the Revolution. At the end of the war the state of Georgia gave Greene Mulberry Grove, a long-neglected plantation, in appreciation of his services. Greene died just nine months later. Catherine was left to carry on alone. She asked Phineas Miller, whom she married some years later, to help manage the plantation.

At the end of the coach journey, Whitney learned that his teaching job had been given to someone else. But Catherine Greene invited him to stay on at Mulberry Grove. Whitney repaired several things on the plantation. Recognizing his mechanical talents, Mrs. Greene encouraged him. "Why don't you see if you can find a way to remove seeds from our cotton?" she asked. Cotton grew well. But it was not a profitable crop, because of its stubborn seeds. It took a slave a whole day to pick the seeds out of one pound (.45 kg) of cotton.

Whitney worked for six months behind locked doors in a basement room of the plantation house. At last he produced a "gin," a machine that removed cotton seeds. It was so simple a machine it was surprising that it had not been invented before.

Whitney, like many an inventor, hoped that his fortune had been made. But that is not the way things turned out. News of the gin leaked out. Other people built cotton gins which they claimed to have invented. Meanwhile, Whitney was scrambling to get a *patent*, or legal protection, for his brainchild. Finally he went to Philadelphia, then the capital of the United States. He appealed to Secretary of State Thomas Jefferson, who was also in charge of the Patent Office. An inventor himself, Jefferson was helpful. At last President Washington issued the patent on March 14, 1794. By then Whitney was knee-deep in lawsuits. Catherine Greene offered all she had to help. The expensive lawsuits—there were 60 in all—forced her to sell Mulberry Grove.

Whitney moved back to New England. He opened an arms factory near New Haven, Connecticut. He began making muskets, or guns. Each musket was to be made exactly like every other one. Each part, therefore, could be *interchanged*, or slipped from one musket to another. All of the muskets were to be made in a special way. Each worker would perform only one or two simple operations. Then the musket would be passed to the next worker who would do one or two more things to it and pass it on. So it went, until the musket was finally assembled. In other words, the labor necessary to produce a single product was divided among a number of workers. The parts were to be interchangeable. The work was to be done assembly-line fashion.

Whitney's two new ideas—interchangeable parts and the assembly-line method of production—were further proof of his genius. They are ideas which now are used throughout American industry and all over the world. Whitney hoped his ideas would make him rich. But once again they embroiled him in bitter struggles.

Catherine Greene died of fever in 1814. Eli Whitney, embittered and in poor health, lived until 1825. But the cotton gin lived on. It set the United States on a new course. One machine could gin 1000 pounds (450 kg) of cotton a day—the output of 1000 people toiling by hand. So the once unprofitable crop suddenly became a money-maker. In the South planters rushed for lands on which to grow it. And in the North manufacturers built factories to turn that cotton into cloth. They clamored for workers, particularly for young women, to tend their machines. Life in the United States was never the same after that.

An American fleet attacks Tripoli, stronghold of the Barbary pirates, in August 1804. The success of the American navy against the Barbary pirates surprised Europe.

What did Jefferson accomplish during his terms as President?

During Jefferson's first term of office, Americans were more prosperous than ever before. Even though Jefferson did not like Hamilton, he used many of his ideas for running the country. As a result, foreign trade grew year after year. The United States debt was cut by $25 million. Jefferson removed the excise tax on whiskey. The Alien and Sedition acts were also dropped from the law books.

Abroad, Jefferson won respect for the young United States. The troublesome Barbary pirates of North Africa continued to raid ships of all nations in the Mediterranean Sea. (See page 120.) Jefferson sent a fleet of warships to North Africa and defeated the pirates.

One poor decision that Jefferson made was to start the practice of rewarding his followers by giving them government jobs. Good people in other parties could not serve their country in these jobs. This practice later became known as the "spoils system" (See page 214.) Not until 1883 would the spoils system finally be ended. (See page 341.)

Jefferson's second term as President was not as happy as his first. He was glad to retire to Monticello in 1809. People blamed him for the bad times that resulted from the embargo. Newspaper articles and cartoons blasted him for his failure to stand up against the British and French. Yet even though he was stung by newspaper attacks, he defended freedom of the press.

Jefferson's purchase of Louisiana was his most important accomplishment. We shall read more about that great real estate bargain in the next chapter.

8. What were three good things which Jefferson accomplished in his first term as President?

9. Why was Jefferson happy to leave the presidency?

Building Your Vocabulary

Which word or phrase shown on the right best explains the meaning of the word in italics on the left?

1. *neutral*	taking sides in a quarrel	not taking sides
2. *cabinet*	members of Congress	advisers to a President
3. *speculator*	gambler	settler
4. *tariff*	tax on goods leaving country	tax on goods coming into country
5. *alien*	citizen	noncitizen
6. *sedition*	being loyal	being disloyal
7. *embargo*	goods cannot be shipped	goods can be shipped
8. *bond*	certificate of debt	tax payment

Recalling What You Have Learned

Match each item in Column A with the correct item in Column B.

Column A	Column B
1. Alexander Hamilton	A. second President of the United States
2. Battle of Fallen Timbers	B. chief surveyor of nation's capital
3. First Secretary of War	C. set framework for court system
4. excise tax	D. wanted a bribe for discussing problems
5. Judiciary Act of 1789	E. storing goods in a port
6. right of deposit	F. protest against an unpopular tax
7. Whiskey Rebellion	G. first Secretary of the Treasury
8. Benjamin Banneker	H. broke the power of the Northwest Indian tribes
9. John Adams	I. tax on certain goods made in a country
10. X, Y, and Z	J. Henry Knox

Discussing the Important Ideas in This Chapter

1. Why did Washington establish a cabinet?
2. Why did critics say that Hamilton's financial plans favored the rich? Do you agree or disagree with them?
3. Why was building a beautiful capital important to Americans?
4. Why are political parties important to voters?
5. How did the way Federalists understood the Constitution differ from the way Republicans understood it?
6. Compare the Whiskey Rebellion to Shays's Rebellion (page 121). What power did Washington use to deal with the Whiskey Rebellion that the government did not have under the Articles of Confederation?
7. How did frontier problems threaten our nation's unity?
8. Why did the X Y Z Affair increase feelings of patriotism in America?

Improving Your Map Skills

The map on page 150 shows the major roads and paths in the United States in 1790. Look at the map and answer the following questions.

1. The Main Post Road and the Boston Post Road followed the east coast. What city was at the southern end of the Main Post Road? What city was at the northern end of the Boston Post Road?
2. What is another name that was used for paths and trails? In what part of the country was this term used?
3. Find Natchez on the map. Which roads or paths would you have taken to get from Natchez to Philadelphia in 1790?
4. Find Ft. Duquesne (which later became Pittsburgh). Name the two roads and two paths that met at Ft. Duquesne.

Improving Your Study Skills: *Research*

George Washington established the first cabinet. How many members are there in the cabinet today? What departments do they represent? Who is Secretary of State today?

You may find this information in an almanac. Because almanacs are published every year, they are good sources for some kinds of current information.

Almanacs have changed since the days of Franklin and Banneker. Popular general almanacs like *The World Almanac* and *Information Please* are full of statistical, historical, and general information. Some still predict the weather. Other almanacs are published by various organizations and contain specialized information. Ask your librarian to show you the general almanacs in your library.

Chapter 7 A New Nation Grows in Size and Strength

Pikes Peak, Colorado

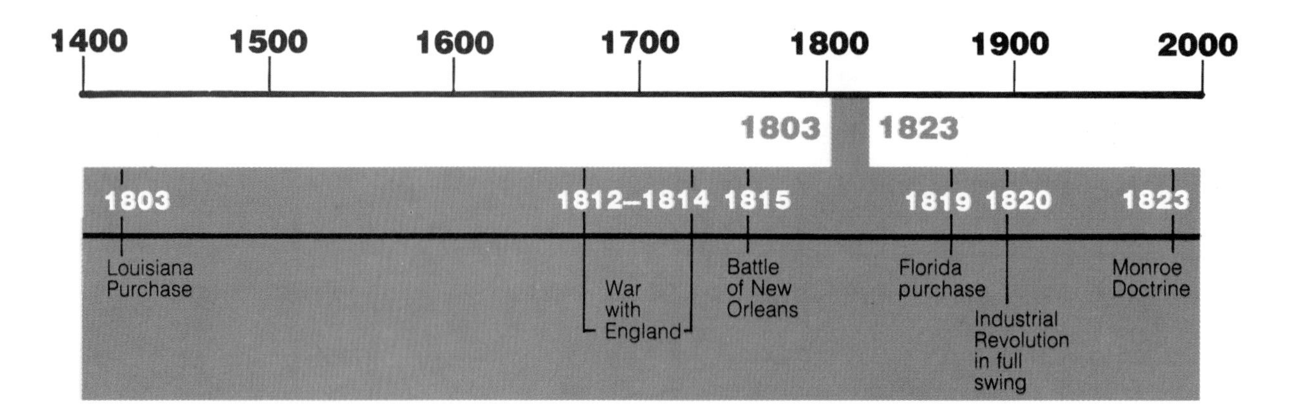

Part One

The United States Doubles in Size

Why were Americans especially concerned about Louisiana?

In 1800 the United States was already larger than any country in Europe, except Russia. Considering its small population, no more land was needed.

But President Jefferson and others were looking beyond their own time. In 1801, Jefferson wrote, "It is impossible not to look forward to distant times when our rapid multiplication will cover the whole Northern, if not the Southern continent." John Quincy Adams, who later became President, thought the same as Jefferson. He said that the country would one day take in all of North America. Many Americans agreed.

Such grand dreams could be put off for the future. But in the opening years of the 1800s, Americans had some urgent concerns. These concerns centered on the land lying between the Mississippi River and the Rocky Mountains. It was called Louisiana. (See map, page 172.) This area was much larger than the present state of Louisiana. It was very fertile, and it was very sparsely settled. Louisiana had been claimed by France, but was later taken over by Spain. As we have seen, the United States made a treaty with Spain in 1795. This treaty permitted Americans to use the Mississippi River and New Orleans for shipping.

At this time the French Revolution was in full swing. France was at war with most of Europe, including Spain. The French were led by a great general named Napoleon Bonaparte. Napoleon forced Spain to return control of Louisiana to France.

Americans worried over the return of the French to North America. Weak Spain had not been a threat. But France was very strong. There was no telling what Napoleon might do if he sent troops to Louisiana. He might even try to conquer the United States.

In 1802 New Orleans was closed to American trade. Americans could no longer do business there. Panic hit the country. Western farmers and traders urged President Jefferson not to lose America's right to ship goods down the Mississippi River. They reminded the President that they had helped elect him to office.

1. How large did some Americans expect the United States to become?
2. Why did Americans become worried about Louisiana?

Why was the United States able to purchase Louisiana?

Jefferson made a plan. He knew that France had spent a huge amount of money fighting its enemies. Perhaps Napoleon could use some more money for his war chest. Jefferson decided to offer him $2 million in exchange for the city of New Orleans.

Robert Livingston and James Monroe made the offer for New Orleans. Jefferson's hunch had been right. The French were anxious to raise money. They also had reasons to doubt the wisdom of holding on to territory in North America. A revolution against the French in the West Indies had greatly disturbed them. France owned Haiti, a colony on the island of Hispaniola. When the French Revolution started, the black slaves in Haiti demanded freedom. Napoleon sent an army of 20,000 soldiers to crush Haiti. But 400,000 slaves fought back, and the French army melted away. And Haiti became an independent black republic. (See map, page 187.)

The French defeat in Haiti helped to make up Napoleon's mind about selling Louisiana. He decided that he did not have enough soldiers and money to carry on a war in America. His losses in Haiti had been so great that he could no longer hold Louisiana.

Touissant L'Ouverture led the rebellion of Haitian slaves.

The artist who painted this 1803 view of New Orleans felt that the city would prosper as a part of the United States. American representatives went to France with the idea of purchasing New Orleans. Instead, they bought all of Louisiana.

Of course, the Americans in Paris did not know of Napoleon's decision. So they were surprised in a meeting with France's foreign minister, Talleyrand. Suddenly he turned and asked them an amazing question. "What will you give for the *whole* of Louisiana?" Unprepared for such a question, Robert Livingston gasped. "Well," he hesitated for a moment, "I suppose the United States would not object to paying $4 million." "Too low!" Talleyrand growled. "Think it over and see me tomorrow." There were no fast means of communication in those days. The Americans did not have time to check back with Congress or the President on what they should do. But our representatives were wise. They could recognize a bargain when they saw one. They returned the next day with a new offer. Finally they agreed on a purchase price of roughly $15 million. Eleven million dollars was to be the down payment. The rest was to be paid in installments over twenty years. The necessary papers were signed on April 30, 1803. Thus, with the stroke of a pen, the United States doubled in size.

3. Why was Napoleon willing to sell all of Louisiana to the United States?

4. How much did the United States pay for Louisiana?

How did Americans react to news of the Louisiana Purchase?

When Jefferson heard what his representatives had done, he was both glad and worried. He was glad because the United States had made a wonderful bargain. But he was worried because he had done things that he was not sure were right. Jefferson and his Republican party had said:

1. Good government should not spend much money—and yet he had just spent $15 million without even getting the approval of Congress.

2. The Constitution should be "strictly interpreted," or followed word for word. And yet there is not one word in the Constitution saying that the President has the power to buy land.

At first Jefferson thought he would ask for an amendment to the Constitution to approve what he had already done. Friends in Congress persuaded him not to do that. They were afraid that in the meantime the French would change their minds and the United States would lose its great bargain. They said Jefferson had the authority to buy land under the treaty-making powers granted the President by the Constitution. So Jefferson simply said he knew that the "good sense" of Americans would tell them he had acted for the good of the people. Most Americans agreed that he had.

Of course, there were some people who did not agree. They expressed their displeasure in the Federalist newspapers. Fifteen million dollars was a great deal of money, they said again and again. If that much money were stacked up in silver dollars, it would make a pile three miles (4.8 km) high. It would take 25 ships to carry that much money to France. But no one paid much attention to their complaints.

5. How did Jefferson react to news of the Louisiana Purchase?

6. How did most Americans feel about it?

How important was the purchase of Louisiana?

The Louisiana Purchase was one of the most important events in American history. The Mississippi became an American river. Frontier farmers were now free to use the Mississippi as a highway. Westerners no longer felt they had to leave the Union.

Most Americans, including Jefferson, did not realize how important the Louisiana Purchase was. Almost one million square miles (2.6 million km^2) of territory were added to the country.

Today more than thirty million people live in the thirteen states made from the Louisiana Territory. (See map, page 267.) The cost has been repaid more than a thousand times in farm values alone. The territory has supported a great cattle industry and provided pasture lands for sheep. Rich forests were in its boundaries. Copper, zinc, lead, and silver were under the ground. No wonder this purchase has been called the greatest real estate bargain in history!

7. What wealth has come from the territory?

8. How many states have been made from the area?

Why were Lewis and Clark sent to explore the West?

No one really knew very much about Louisiana and the Far West. The only information came from trappers likely to tell tall tales. Jefferson wanted facts! He knew that an American sea captain named Robert Gray had sailed up the Columbia River in 1792 and had seen the edge of the Oregon country. Now Jefferson wanted an overland party to explore the Louisiana Territory—and

Lewis and Clark and Pike Explore the West

beyond—to the Pacific. The President himself wrote the instructions. Twenty-nine-year-old Meriwether Lewis and his red-haired partner, William Clark, were to:

1. Look for an all-water route from the Mississippi River to the Pacific coast. There was no such route, of course.

2. Collect information about climate and wildlife, and to fill in every possible blank space on the map.

3. Learn more about the Indians. Tell the Indians that the United States now owned Louisiana and expected them to be loyal.

4. Strengthen American claims to the Oregon country. Prepare the way for trading in the future.

Lewis and Clark's party of about fifty soldiers and hunters left St. Louis in the spring of 1804. Captain Clark took along his slave, York.

The Lewis and Clark expedition meets a group of Chinook Indians who speak with Sacajawea in sign language.

For 1600 miles (2560 km) the men rowed north and west against the current of the Missouri River. Ice stopped them, so they built a log fort and spent the winter in what is North Dakota. Their camp was close to villages of the Mandan and Gros Ventre Indians.

Lewis and Clark needed an interpreter. Luckily they met an especially capable young woman named Sacajawea (sak′ə jə wē′ə) who had been brought up in the West. Sacajawea was married to a French trapper and had a baby son. She and her family joined the expedition.

After crossing the Rockies, the expedition found the mighty Columbia River. Then they floated down the river to the Pacific Ocean, arriving in November 1805. The first leg of their journey was complete. The continent had been crossed.

Lewis and Clark returned to St. Louis the following year. They had explored mountains and rivers in unknown country. Their maps and reports on the great American West delighted Jefferson and Americans everywhere. Soon pioneers would follow the trails that Lewis and Clark had taken from St. Louis all the way to the Oregon country. (See pages 174-175 for more about the expedition.)

9. For what four reasons were Lewis and Clark asked to lead an exploring party to the West?

10. What two rivers did they follow to reach the Pacific Ocean?

Why were Pike's journeys important?

Lewis and Clark were not the only explorers sent out to learn more about the Louisiana Territory. Lieutenant Zebulon Pike led several expeditions. Pike never attracted as much attention

Historymaker

Sacajawea

They called themselves the "Corps of Discovery." They are better known as members of the Lewis and Clark expedition. But the words "corps" and "expedition" make the group sound large. It was anything but that. The Corps was just a handful of hopefuls who set out on one of the longest, most dangerous journeys ever undertaken.

Just 44 men and one dog set out from St. Louis on May 14, 1804. They were to explore the territory of the Louisiana Purchase. A few months later their number increased by three. A teenaged mother, her baby boy, and his grumpy father joined the expedition. Together the members of the Lewis and Clark expedition walked into history.

For years Thomas Jefferson had dreamed about an exploring party which would make its way overland to the Pacific Ocean. He wanted to be a part of it, but that was not to be. So, after he became President and had purchased Louisiana, Jefferson decided the time had come to send others. He turned first to Meriwether Lewis, his trusted private secretary. Lewis, a captain in the army, knew a lot about the West. Jefferson told Lewis to pick his own partner, someone to share the responsibilities of leadership.

Lewis chose an army friend to be his co-captain. William ("Billy") Clark had the knowledge, experience, and personality needed. Not only was he an expert woodsman and mapmaker, he was a capable, self-taught "doctor." When the expedition camped with the Nez Percé Indians, Clark treated as many as forty patients a day. As his fame for setting broken bones and treating other ailments spread, Indians from miles around sought out "Doctor Billy."

Lewis and Clark made a good team. During their long trip they had only two minor disagreements. They differed on the taste of dog meat, and the need for salt.

In addition to Lewis and Clark four other key people stand out from the records of the expedition. Their efforts helped spell the difference between success and failure.

First there was **George Drouillard**. The Americans called him "Drewyer," because they found his French name difficult to pronounce. "Drewyer" was an expert in sign language. He was able to communicate to some degree with every one of the many Indian tribes the expedition met on its 3555 mile (5688 km) journey from St. Louis to the mouth of the Columbia River and back again.

Next there was young **Private Peter Cruzat**. A good musician, he took along his beloved violin. His music delighted the Indians. Never before had they heard such an instrument. Sometimes Indian groups and the explorers danced to Cruzat's violin all night.

Then there was **York**. He was a hard man to ignore. York was Clark's slave. Over six feet tall (182.8 cm) and weighing more than 200 pounds (90 kg), he was the main attraction for many of the Indians. From miles around they came to see him. Not only did they marvel at his stories and his dancing, they were even more amazed by the color of his skin. He was the first black man they had ever seen.

York was a good storyteller and a great dancer. And he used these talents to entertain Indian visitors. He was also skilled in hunting, fishing, and swimming. At the end of the journey, Clark gave York his freedom. It is said that he set out for the West again and became chief of an Indian tribe.

Finally there was the young mother whose own people, the Shoshones, knew as **Sacajawea**, or "Bird Woman." Her traveling companions called her "Janey." Today some historians number Sacajawea among America's six most important women. More statues have been erected to her than to any other woman in the United States.

Sacajawea was kidnapped from her own people by the feared Minnetarees when she was about ten or eleven years old. She was only sixteen or seventeen years old and awaiting the birth of her first child when she met Lewis and Clark. Two months later she strapped her baby to her back and went along with them when they hired her cross and cruel husband, Charbonneau. He was a French trapper.

So many stories have been told about Sacajawea that she has become a legend. She was not a guide or pathfinder, as has been incorrectly said. But she was extremely important to the expedition in other ways:

She was its interpreter, or translator. She was the only member of the expedition who could speak four languages: Shoshone, Minnetaree, French, and English.

Having wandered over much of the countryside with the Shoshones and the Minnetarees, she recognized many landmarks.

She knew which roots, berries, and grasses were good to eat and to use as medicines. Her knowledge was important to the survival and health of the party.

Most important, her presence with the expedition was a sign of peace to various Indian groups. The mere sight of a woman traveling with the Corps was enough to prevent armed conflict.

Sacajawea was brave, cheerful, and cool under pressure. She did not even get out of sorts with Charbonneau, and that was difficult. By the end of the trip, Charbonneau was unpopular with everyone. Lewis hated to pay him the $500 he had promised him in wages. Sacajawea had earned the money, but her husband collected. Sacajawea had earned the admiration and affection of all. And her baby, Jean Baptiste, nicknamed "Pomp," had stolen everyone's hearts. Clark called him "a beautiful, promising child." He offered to adopt him and rear "Pomp" as his own son. Sacajawea, however, said that he was "too young" for her to consider the offer. But, in time, she, Pomp, and a daughter born later did go to St. Louis to live under Clark's protection.

Zebulon Pike mistook the fertile Great Plains for wasteland.

as Lewis and Clark, however. He felt keenly about what he described as "a lack of appreciation."

Pike's first journey began in August 1805. His orders were "to explore the source of the Mississippi making a general survey of the river and its boundaries." He also was asked to find out about natural resources. Finally, he was directed to make observations of the Indians living along the Mississippi.

Pike was very interested in the Indians. In his journals he described their daily lives and their peace ceremonies, dances, and feasts. Pike was fascinated by the many Indian games. Once he and his companions stopped on the Racine River so that they could watch several hundred Sioux warriors play a game called *Le Cross*. They used sticks with leather webbing at their ends to catch a small ball. Today a version of that game is known as "lacrosse."

The search for the source of the Mississippi was not all feasts and games, however. Pike and his men were glad to return to St. Louis after some eight months of exploring.

Pike hardly had time to get his notes and personal affairs in order before he was sent to look for the sources of the Arkansas and the Red rivers. Some chiefs of the Pawnee and Osage tribes and their families went with him for a part of the trip.

In the course of this journey, Pike discovered the mountain peak now named for him. His party also explored Colorado and New Mexico. Those lands then belonged to Spain. The Spanish were not happy about having Americans roaming through their territory. Soldiers seized the explorers and put them into prison. When they finally were released, they made their way back down the Red River to Natchitoches.

On his return, Pike wrote a report which contained much useful information. But he made a mistake in describing the Great Plains as the "Great American Desert." He said:

> **In that vast country of which I speak, we found the soil generally dry and sandy. . . . These vast plains of the western hemisphere may become in time as celebrated as the sandy deserts of Africa. . . .**

On the basis of Pike's report, maps were printed showing desert instead of rich, fertile land. People believed those maps, and Pike's error delayed settlers from moving to the Great Plains.

11. Where was Zebulon Pike sent to explore?

12. What error did Pike make about the Great Plains?

How did Florida become part of the United States?

No one really knew where the correct boundaries of Florida were. This

Spanish colony bordered the southern United States. It was divided into two parts, East and West Florida.

The United States wanted West Florida because of its nearness to New Orleans and the Mississippi River. President Jefferson declared that it was part of the Louisiana Purchase and was therefore American. In 1810, the government took part of West Florida away from Spain by force.

The Spanish realized that they were not strong enough to keep Americans out of Florida. Spain could see that losing Florida was just a matter of time. Why not sell it? Spain did just that in 1819. For $5 million, Florida—East and West—became part of the United States.

13. Why did Spain sell Florida?
14. What was the purchase price?

Part Two

The War of 1812

Why was Madison unable to keep the nation out of war?

Fewer than forty years had passed since the United States had fought England in the Revolution. But in 1812 it was ready to do so for a second time. The struggle which lasted from 1812 to 1815 is known officially as the War of 1812. It also has been called "America's strangest war" and the Second War for Independence. We shall soon see why it was a strange war and how it made our nation more independent.

War with England did not come on suddenly. For twenty years the United States had been struggling with England and France for the right to send American ships overseas in safety. But those two nations were locked in a bitter war with one another. Neither wanted the United States to deliver supplies to the other. So they stopped American ships or fired on them. (See page 155.) The British were especially bold because they had the world's strongest navy. British ships continued to stop American ships and impress, or kidnap, the sailors. (See page 161.)

Presidents Adams and Jefferson had difficulty keeping the country from going to war. President James Madison was unable to do so.

"Little Jemmy" Madison became the fourth President of the United States in 1809. Madison was a brilliant man. As you have seen (pages 132-133), he was an outstanding delegate to the Constitutional Convention. But he was not a practical politician or a forceful leader. Madison was a small, shy man whose health never was very good.

President Madison did not want his nation to go to war. Neither did the people of New England. New Englanders needed trade. They were happy that the embargo was lifted when Jefferson left the presidency. They wanted to increase their trade with the British. But Americans from the South and West wanted war. And Madison finally could not stand against the pressures their members of Congress brought to bear.

1. Why had trouble with England been brewing for more than twenty years?

Who were the "War Hawks"?

The "War Hawks" were members of Congress who wanted war with England. Most of them were from the South and West. They had their own special reason for being angry with England. It was the British in Canada, they said, who kept stirring up the Indians on the frontier. Until the British were driven out of Canada, they insisted, no American frontier family would be safe.

Two of the War Hawks deserve special mention. Elected to Congress for the first time in 1811, these young men went on to become leaders in the nation for the next forty years. Both hoped one day to be elected President. But neither was. One of those War Hawks was Henry Clay of Kentucky; the other was John C. Calhoun of South Carolina.

Henry Clay began a long and brilliant career in politics as a "War Hawk."

Henry Clay enjoyed people. He was always at ease with them. He listened to their problems, and he knew how to speak to them. Clay's speeches could move people to laughter or to tears. Small wonder then that he was elected Speaker of the House of Representatives as soon as he arrived in Washington, D.C. With the exception of one year, he held that post through 1825. Then he became Secretary of State and finally a United States senator.

A tall, commanding figure, with a heavy shock of hair and piercing eyes, John C. Calhoun had a brilliant mind. Calhoun became a plantation owner after his marriage. In time he became a leading defender of slavery. Like Clay, Calhoun was a good speaker. But where Clay moved audiences by his wit and charm, Calhoun did so by his force and brilliance.

Clay, Calhoun, and their followers quickly gained control of the most important committees in Congress. They needled the President, moving him and the nation ever closer to war.

2. Who were the "War Hawks" and what did they want?

3. Name two "War Hawks."

What was the Tecumseh Confederation?

As pioneers poured across the Appalachian Mountains into the Northwest Territory, they met resistance from the Indians who lived there. (See map, page 180.) Those Indians had already sold much of their land to the government. Now they no longer wished to sell land. But settlers helped themselves to Indian land. Then they attacked the Indians.

Tecumseh was a brilliant Shawnee leader. He and his brother tried to unite all the Indian tribes from the Great Lakes to Florida in a confederation. They would sell no more land. They would fight settlers who took their land by force.

William Henry Harrison was governor of Indiana Territory. He made a treaty with some other Indians that took away three million acres (1.2 million ha) from Tecumseh's people. Tecumseh went to Vincennes, the capital of Indiana Territory. He demanded his people's land. He said that if the United States gave back the land, he would work against the British.

Harrison waited until Tecumseh went south to recruit other tribes for the confederation in 1811. Then Harrison took 900 men to the Tippecanoe River, close to Tecumseh's village. The Indians, fearing attack, struck first. But Harrison defeated them and burned their village.

After the Battle of Tippecanoe, Indians attacked and killed many settlers. The West became a battleground.

In a sense the Battle of Tippecanoe became the first battle in the War of 1812. It inflamed the West. The War Hawks cried for battle. We must take Canada, they said. Then the British would no longer stir up the Indians.

4. Who was Tecumseh?

5. Why was the Battle of Tippecanoe really the first battle in the War of 1812?

Tecumseh tried to stop the loss of Indian lands.

When and why did Madison ask Congress to declare war?

Finally, on June 1, 1812, President Madison sent a message to Congress asking that body to declare war on England. His timing was a surprise to many. Relations between the countries actually were getting better. The British were considering lifting their ban on American trade with Europe. In fact they did, just two days before the debate on going to war ended in the Congress. But in those times there were no trans-Atlantic cables, radios, or satellites. Congress did not learn that one of their major reasons for going to war no longer existed until it was too late. Madison's message said there were four important reasons why war should be declared. He said the British were:

1. continuing to impress, or kidnap, American sailors.
2. invading American territorial waters to seize ships, cargoes, and sailors.
3. interfering with the shipping of American products to Europe.
4. stirring up the Indians on the western frontier.

Area of the Tecumseh Confederation

Present State Boundaries

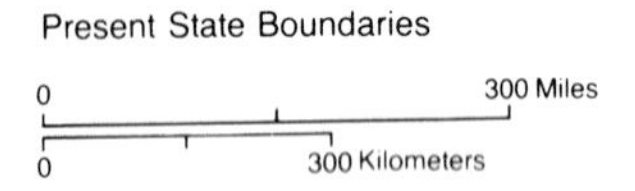

With the War Hawks in control of the House, the measure passed quickly. But in the Senate, it was a different matter. That branch of Congress debated for several weeks. The Senate finally called for war by a narrow vote, nineteen to thirteen, on June 17, 1812.

Despite the clamor for war, the United States was not at all prepared. Both the army and the navy were small. Most of the officers, who had fought in the Revolution, were now old men. And neither the Congress nor the President had thought about how to raise the money necessary for waging a war.

6. What were the four reasons Madison gave for a declaration of war?

7. When did Congress finally approve the declaration of war?

How and where was the war fought?

The War of 1812 was fought in three widely scattered areas:

1. the Great Lakes region.
2. Washington, D.C., and Baltimore.
3. New Orleans and the deep South. (See map, page 182.)

The British navy blockaded the coast and controlled the Atlantic Ocean. But the smaller American navy did well on the Great Lakes and on Lake Champlain.

One of the brightest spots for Americans in the War of 1812 was the Battle of Lake Erie. Captain Oliver H. Perry built a fleet of ten ships at Erie, Pennsylvania, in 1813. He loaded the vessels with soldiers, black laborers, and frontier scouts. Then Perry challenged the proud British to a fight.

In this unusual battle at the western end of Lake Erie, the two fleets could not move about. There was no wind. The ships drifted close to each other and fired away with everything they had. Because the Americans had more weapons, they destroyed the British. "We have met the enemy, and they are ours," Perry reported.

The Battle of Lake Erie forced the British to give up Detroit. It led to several American victories in Canada. Perry was promoted and hailed as a hero.

Farther south, the British landed an army near Washington, D.C. After winning victories in Maryland, they marched on the nation's capital. The poorly trained American troops retreated. President Madison was forced to flee into Virginia. But his wife, Dolley Madison, was not willing to leave the White House until she had tended to some important details. What she did

When Perry's flagship was damaged during the Battle of Lake Erie, he rowed to a fresh ship under heavy enemy fire.

made her a national hero. In a letter to her sister she described how she waited "within the sound of the cannon." She had a wagon loaded with the greatest treasures in the White House. Among them was Gilbert Stuart's famous portrait of Washington. She asked two men to cut it out of its frame and take it with them to New York for safekeeping. She ended her short letter with these words:

And now, dear sister, I must leave this house or the retreating army will make me a prisoner in it, by filling up the road I am directed to take.

Dolley Madison fled the capital not a moment too soon. The British entered the city and put it to the torch. The White House was completely destroyed except for the blackened walls which remained standing. The Capitol building was burned. So too were most of the other public buildings.

The physical destruction of the nation's capital was bad enough. But the psychological impact was even greater. Americans were shocked and angry about the ruin of their beautiful new city. Nor did the reaction of the British press make them feel any better. English writers gloated over what had happened. One of them said maybe the "young upstart country" would be more careful in the future about "twisting the lion's [England's] tail."

From Washington, the British turned to Baltimore and launched an attack on that city. An American named Francis Scott Key watched through the night as Fort McHenry was bombarded by British warships. The next morning, when he saw the American flag still waving, Key wrote a poem. That poem, "The Star Spangled Banner," was set to music and became our national anthem.

8. In what three scattered areas was the War of 1812 fought?

9. Why did Oliver Perry and Dolley Madison become war heroes?

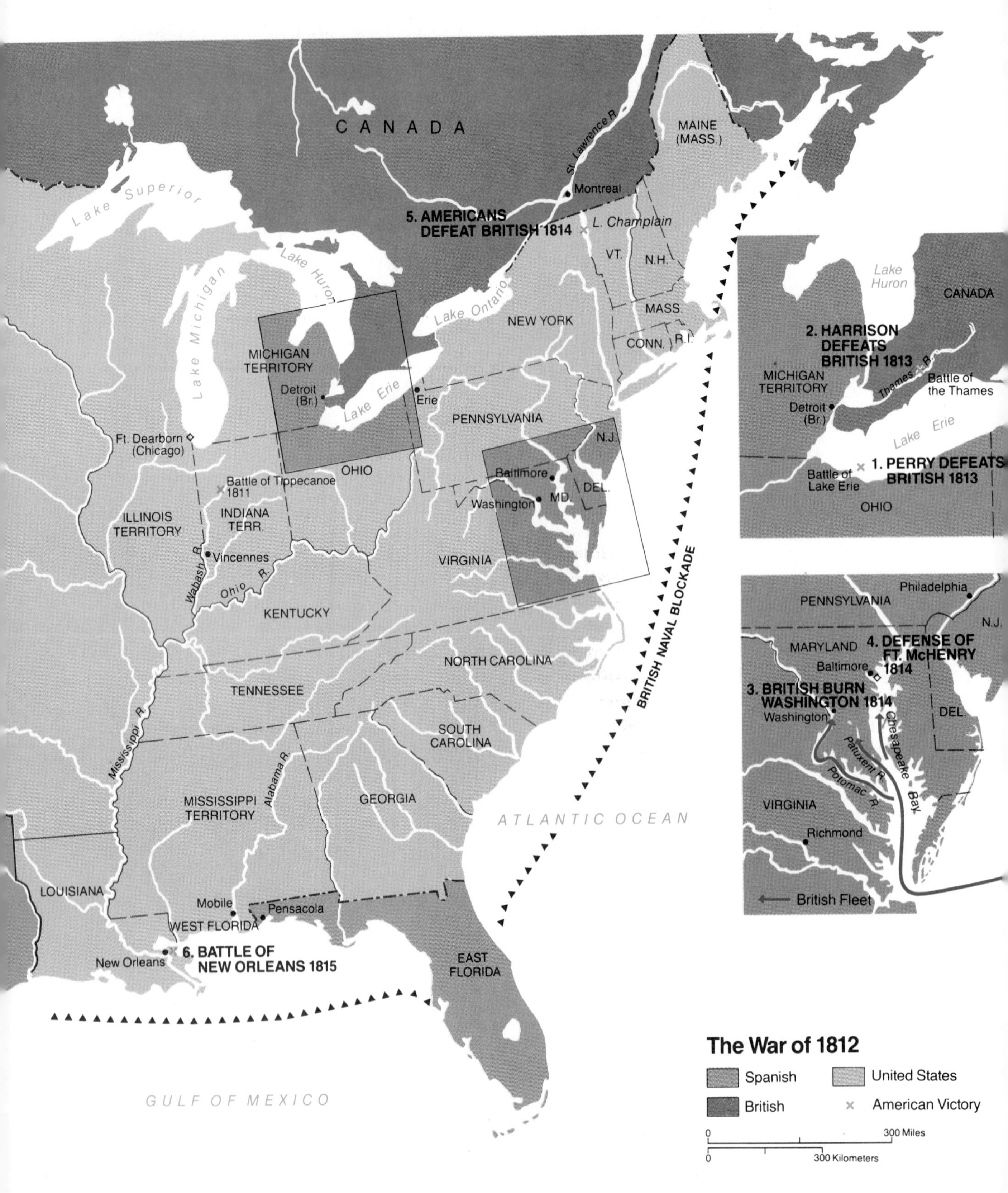
CANADA
Lake Superior
Lake Michigan
Lake Huron
Lake Ontario
Lake Erie
St. Lawrence R.
Montreal
MAINE (MASS.)
5. AMERICANS DEFEAT BRITISH 1814
L. Champlain
VT.
N.H.
MASS.
CONN.
R.I.
NEW YORK
MICHIGAN TERRITORY
Detroit (Br.)
Erie
PENNSYLVANIA
N.J.
Ft. Dearborn (Chicago)
OHIO
Baltimore
DEL.
MD.
Washington
Battle of Tippecanoe 1811
ILLINOIS TERRITORY
INDIANA TERR.
Vincennes
Wabash R.
Ohio R.
VIRGINIA
KENTUCKY
BRITISH NAVAL BLOCKADE
NORTH CAROLINA
TENNESSEE
SOUTH CAROLINA
Mississippi R.
Alabama R.
MISSISSIPPI TERRITORY
GEORGIA
ATLANTIC OCEAN
LOUISIANA
Mobile
Pensacola
WEST FLORIDA
New Orleans
6. BATTLE OF NEW ORLEANS 1815
EAST FLORIDA
GULF OF MEXICO
Lake Huron
CANADA
2. HARRISON DEFEATS BRITISH 1813
MICHIGAN TERRITORY
Thames R.
Battle of the Thames
Detroit (Br.)
Lake Erie
1. PERRY DEFEATS BRITISH 1813
Battle of Lake Erie
OHIO
Philadelphia
PENNSYLVANIA
N.J.
MARYLAND
4. DEFENSE OF FT. McHENRY 1814
Baltimore
3. BRITISH BURN WASHINGTON 1814
Washington
DEL.
Chesapeake Bay
Patuxent R.
Potomac R.
VIRGINIA
Richmond
British Fleet
The War of 1812
Spanish
United States
British
American Victory
0
300 Miles
0
300 Kilometers

Dolley Madison

What great battle was fought after the War of 1812 was over?

The Battle of New Orleans was one of the greatest victories in United States history. General Andrew Jackson of Tennessee led a force of frontier sharpshooters against the British. Among Jackson's soldiers were two battalions of blacks.

The British who attacked New Orleans were proud and sure of themselves. They had just defeated Napoleon's great French army in Europe. Now they would show these American farmers how to fight like real soldiers!

The redcoats came forward in their usual way, packed close together in straight lines. The American pioneers crouched in trenches. They squinted down their rifle barrels at the perfect targets in front of them. What followed was slaughter. Two thousand British were mowed down before their ranks broke and they retreated in defeat. Only thirteen Americans lost their lives in the battle.

New Orleans was a great victory for the United States. Americans were so proud of it that they later elected Andrew Jackson President. But important as the battle was, it need never have been fought. A peace treaty which ended the War of 1812 had been signed weeks earlier in Europe. But news that the war had ended did not reach the United States in time. And so the Battle of New Orleans was fought to its bloody conclusion.

10. What made Jackson a hero?

11. Why was the Battle of New Orleans fought needlessly?

Why was the War of 1812 called the Second War for Independence?

One of the strangest peace treaties ever written ended the War of 1812. It said only that the war was to stop. It did not even mention the kidnapping of American sailors. Not an inch of land was gained or lost. There appeared to be neither a winner nor a loser.

But the War of 1812 had some good results. The United States proved to itself and to the world that it could protect its own interests. For that reason the War of 1812 is called the Second War for Independence. Americans' pride in their country increased as a result of the war. Shipping and industry grew and helped bring prosperity. Just three years after the war, the United States agreed with Britain that no warships would ever again be stationed on the Great Lakes.

12. Why was the peace treaty one of the strangest ever written?

13. What were the four good results of the War of 1812?

What was the Hartford Convention?

As you know, the people of New England were strongly against the War of 1812. They had tried to prevent the United States from entering that war. As

This view of the Battle of New Orleans was painted by an engineer with the American army.

the war dragged on, their opposition grew. Ministers thundered against the war in their churches. State governments kept soldiers from leaving New England. Merchants traded secretly with the enemy. Even the beginning of peace negotiations in the summer of 1814 did not cool their anger.

Representatives of the New England states decided to get together to draw up a formal protest against the war. Their meeting began on December 15, 1814, just nine days before the United States and England signed a treaty bringing the war to a close. At Hartford, Connecticut, where the protest meeting was held, there was a lot of talk against the war and the federal government. The New Englanders did not threaten to leave the United States, but their unhappiness was plain.

The Hartford Convention sent "ambassadors" to Washington, D.C., to deliver their complaints. But by the time they arrived in the nation's capital, the war was over. There was nothing they could do but turn around and go home. People in the West and the South were angry at the New Englanders. They said that New England was unpatriotic and that it had failed to carry its share of the burdens of the war. But in later years other states would take much stronger action against the federal government, as we shall see later on in this chapter.

14. How did the people of New England express their opposition to the War of 1812?

15. How did people in the West and South feel about the way New England had behaved?

Part Three

The Nation Grows Stronger

What was the Era of Good Feelings?

An *era* is a period of time. For a period of several years after the War of 1812, the United States was a *happy* country. Americans were proud of the way they had fought the British to a standstill. Trade with foreign countries brought prosperity. This made New Englanders so happy that they loudly cheered President James Monroe when he paid them a visit. Monroe, another Virginian, followed Madison as President in 1817. All this pride, patriotism, and friendly goodwill was called the Era of Good Feelings. During this time the nation grew richer and stronger in many ways.

1. Why were Americans happy following the War of 1812?

How did John Marshall help strengthen the United States?

John Marshall helped the nation grow stronger by serving as Chief Justice of the Supreme Court for 34 years (1801-1835). During that time the Court decided more than fifty major cases about the Constitution.

Alexander Hamilton had said that the judicial branch would be the weakest part of our government. But Hamilton did not live long enough to see what a giant like Marshall could and would do as Chief Justice.

John Marshall was a giant in every way. He was a tall, strong man with simple tastes. He was brought up in a log cabin on the Virginia frontier. He fought in the Revolution and froze with Washington at Valley Forge.

Marshall was a giant as a judge, too. In his first decision he ruled that the Supreme Court was to have the final say about what is and is not the law of the land. Over the years, in case after case, Marshall declared that the federal government had more power than the state governments.

2. What important office did Marshall hold? For how long?

3. Did Marshall favor a strong federal government or strong state governments?

What European plans upset Americans?

European countries had discovered the New World continents of North America and South America. They had built many colonies there. About three hundred years later, some of these colonies began to break away from their parent countries. First to revolt were England's thirteen American colonies in 1776. Then French, Spanish, and Portuguese colonies followed the example of the United States. They declared their independence. (See map, page 187.) They took advantage of the fact that their parent countries were too busy with wars in Europe to stop them. But these wars ended in 1815. Then the European countries plotted together to get back the lost colonies of Spain.

The United States did not like to see Europe interfering in New World affairs. Americans were pleased that neighboring nations had won independence. These new, free countries would be friends. The United States did not want

José de San Martín led the fight against Spanish rule in southern South America.

Simón Bolívar led the revolution against Spain in northern South America. Bolivia was named for him.

powerful European countries as its neighbors.

Russia had planted a colony in Alaska in 1741. From there the Russians pushed south along the Pacific coast. In 1821 Russia laid claim to the Oregon country and told the United States to keep out.

To some Americans it seemed all too plain that Europe was planning to take over as much of the Americas as it could. The United States would be surrounded by enemies, and it would be in great danger.

The United States had just fought a second war for its independence. It was determined to show its ability to hold its own in the world. To do so meant taking a stand against the efforts of European nations to regain their lost colonies.

4. Why did European nations think the time was right for regaining their lost colonies in the Americas?

5. How did the United States feel about European plans?

What was the Monroe Doctrine?

In 1823, President James Monroe sent an important message to Congress. It is known as the Monroe Doctrine. (A *doctrine* is a statement of beliefs.) Monroe made clear to Europe how the United States planned to handle world affairs.

The Monroe Doctrine said:

1. The United States will not permit any foreign nation to plant new colonies in the western hemisphere. Colonies still held by Europe will not be disturbed, however.

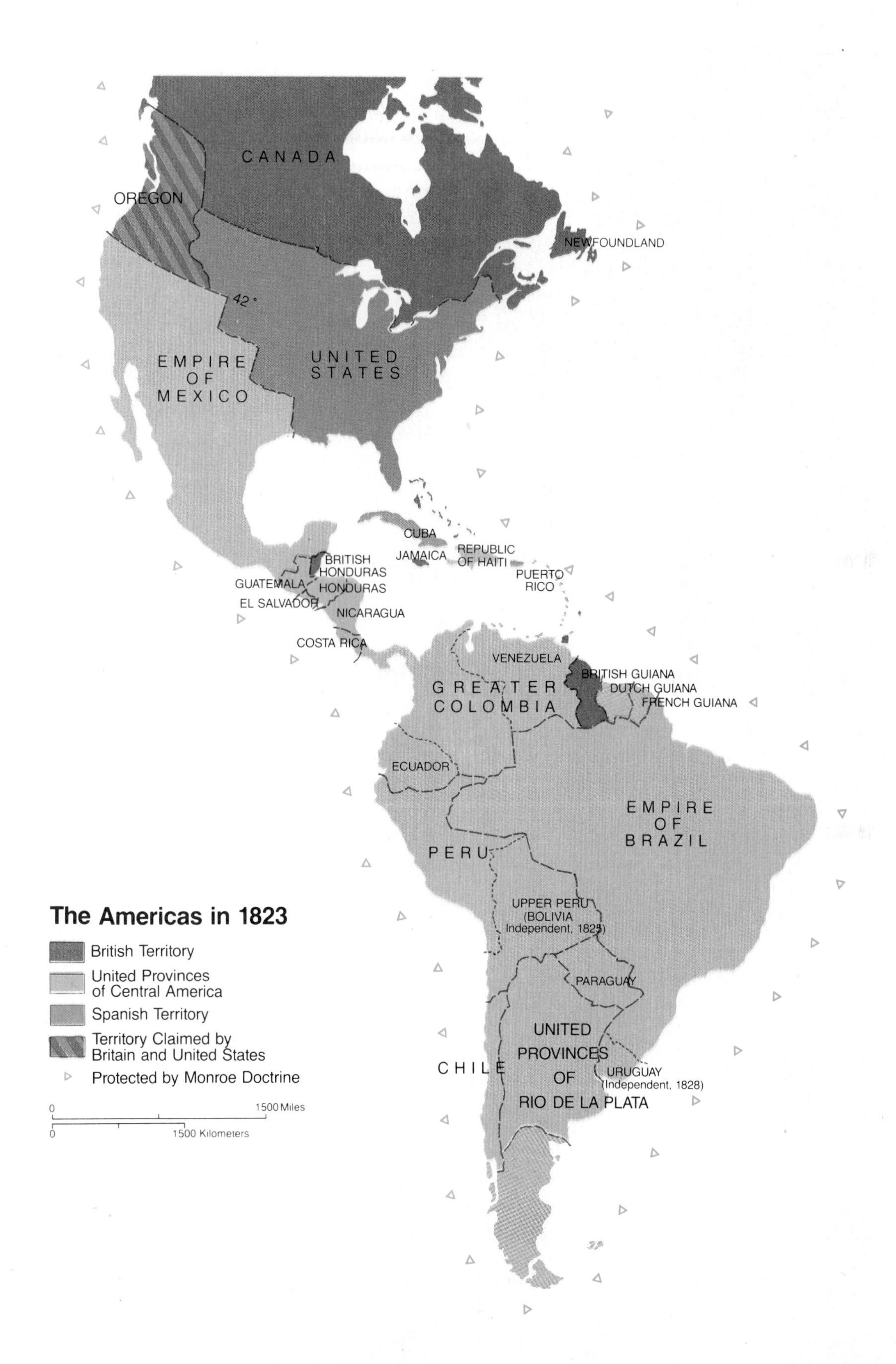
CANADA
OREGON
NEWFOUNDLAND
42°
EMPIRE OF MEXICO
UNITED STATES
CUBA
JAMAICA
REPUBLIC OF HAITI
PUERTO RICO
BRITISH HONDURAS
GUATEMALA
HONDURAS
EL SALVADOR
NICARAGUA
COSTA RICA
VENEZUELA
GREATER COLOMBIA
BRITISH GUIANA
DUTCH GUIANA
FRENCH GUIANA
ECUADOR
EMPIRE OF BRAZIL
PERU
UPPER PERU (BOLIVIA Independent, 1825)
PARAGUAY
UNITED PROVINCES OF RIO DE LA PLATA
URUGUAY (Independent, 1828)
CHILE
The Americas in 1823
British Territory
United Provinces of Central America
Spanish Territory
Territory Claimed by Britain and United States
Protected by Monroe Doctrine
0
1500 Miles
0
1500 Kilometers

2. The United States will not permit any foreign nation to attack any former colony in the western hemisphere.

3. The United States will not interfere in European affairs.

When the Monroe Doctrine was announced, the world's leading nations took a long, hard look at the United States. Was this young country strong enough to back up what it said? When Britain announced its support of the Doctrine, the answer became "yes."

The British supported the Doctrine because they wanted to trade with the new free countries in the Americas. Britain's powerful navy warned other countries not to try to regain their colonies in the western hemisphere. Through the years, the United States has called the Monroe Doctrine into play many times. "Hands off the western hemisphere!" has been an order to be obeyed.

6. What were the three most important declarations made by the United States in the Monroe Doctrine?

7. Why was British support for the Monroe Doctrine important?

Part Four

New Transportation Systems Strengthen the Country

How did turnpikes improve transportation?

As more people moved west, they demanded better transportation. In 1800 the only transportation, except by water, was by wagon or pack train over dirt roads. It cost the same amount of money to ship a product all the way from England to the United States as it did to move it thirty miles (48 km) overland after it arrived. It cost three times more than a bushel of wheat was worth to take it from Buffalo to New York City in 1817—and six times what corn was worth! It is easy to see why Westerners needed cheaper and faster transportation.

In 1796 a private company in Pennsylvania opened the first major turnpike (toll road). It was not like today's superhighways. That first turnpike between Philadelphia and Lancaster was just a graded road paved with stone. If farmers wanted to use the road, they had to pay a toll. Then the pike, or stick, blocking the road was turned. At the next pike, they paid another toll, and so

Travelers of all sorts meet at the Fairview Inn near Baltimore. Some have wagons, some drive coaches, and some plod along on foot.

Major Roads about 1851

As horses pull a boat toward the locks of the Erie Canal at Lockport, New York, travelers on the roof enjoy the scenery.

on. By 1820 about 4000 miles (6400 km) of improved roads had been built. They made travel easier and faster.

Congress agreed to build the National Road to help settlers move to the Northwest and Louisiana territories. The first section began at Cumberland, Maryland, and went to Wheeling, West Virginia. By 1833 the section to Ohio was opened. The road finally extended to Vandalia, Illinois. (See map, page 189.)

Big Conestoga (kon′ ə stō′ gə) wagons, covered by canvas tops, could travel almost 600 miles (960 km) on the National Road. Some of them were painted bright colors. Pulled by four to six horses, the wagons went at the breakneck speed of twenty miles per hour (32 km/h) under good conditions.

1. What is a turnpike?

2. Where did Congress build the National Road?

Why did Americans build a system of canals?

Water travel was faster and cheaper than overland travel. To go from one part of the country to another, Americans used lakes and rivers. But these are natural waterways that wind and bend as they were formed by nature. They do not always connect great cities with each other.

In the 1800s, Americans found the answer to this problem. They built waterways called canals. Like roads and turnpikes, canals were built to connect cities hundreds of miles apart.

The most important canal stretched from Buffalo to Albany. There, it joined the Hudson River to connect New York City with the Great Lakes. The Erie Canal, as it was called, was started in 1817 and completed in 1825. This canal linked the eastern part of the United States with the growing West.

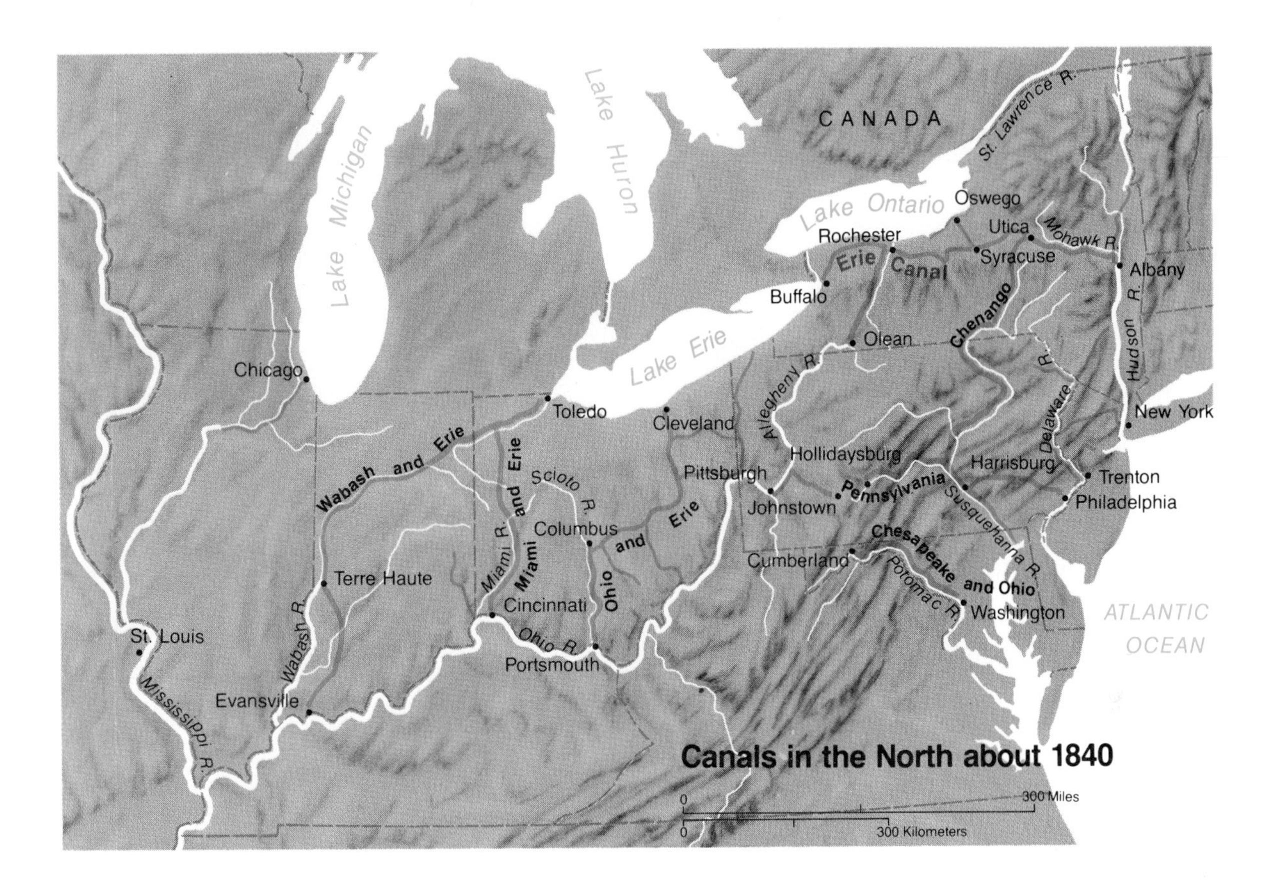

There was so much travel on the Erie Canal that it was paid for by tolls in fewer than ten years. The cost of shipping a ton of grain from Buffalo to New York City was cut from $100 to $5! The price of potatoes in New York City was cut in half almost overnight. Land values along the 364-mile (582.4 km) canal skyrocketed. New cities like Rochester and Syracuse sprang up.

The Erie Canal made it easier to go west and to ship products where they could be sold. Thousands of settlers moved to the Great Lakes area.

3. What special purpose did the system of canals serve?

4. What was the most important canal ever built in the United States? How did it affect western settlement?

How did steamboats change transportation on the rivers?

Steamboats were not invented until about 1790. Up to that time, all ships and boats were driven by oars or sails.

John Fitch and others experimented with steamboats before 1800. But the first useful steamboat was invented by Robert Fulton in 1807. Fulton's ship, the *Clermont*, sailed 150 miles (240 km) up the Hudson River from New York City to Albany at a speed of five miles per hour (8 km/h).

Steamboats solved some of the West's biggest travel problems. Before steamboats, people went down the Ohio and Mississippi rivers to New Orleans in flatboats, which were very slow. To come upriver, they had to use oar-driven keelboats or pole against the current.

Ornate steamboats round a bend in the Mississippi. Despite their elegant looks, steamboats were inexpensive to build.

That was backbreaking and slow work. The average speed a boat could be poled up the Mississippi was less than one mile per hour. Often people preferred to sell their boats for lumber at New Orleans and walk back up the river. The road they took was the Natchez Trace.

Steamboats, of course, had no problem bucking river currents. On the Mississippi, for instance, they could sail back and forth between St. Louis and New Orleans, carrying goods either way.

With their shallow wheels, steamboats could go far up the rivers that ran into the Mississippi. Westerners could then live far inland and still be able to get their goods to market without any trouble.

After the War of 1812, steamboating came to the West in a rush. By 1820 there were twenty steamboats on the Mississippi. Forty years later there were more than a thousand. Shipping costs were cut greatly, sometimes as much as 95 percent.

Besides cutting the costs of getting goods to market, steamboats brought entertainment to travelers on western rivers. Some of the boats were really "floating palaces," or "showboats," painted in bright colors. Singers, dancers, and gamblers on board livened up the trips. The boats also carried cotton and other kinds of freight.

Many a race was run between steamboats. Excited passengers would urge captains to pile on more wood at the risk of bursting the boilers. All too often the boilers did explode, with sad results. But people still came to the riverbank to make bets and cheer on their favorite steamboats.

5. Why were steamboats superior to flatboats for transporting goods and people?

6. Besides cutting the costs of transportation, what other functions did steamboats serve?

Why and how did Americans develop railroads?

Railroads were first used in England. This was another way to speed up and lower the cost of moving goods to market. American inventors worked hard at trying to build railroads. The first ones had tracks, but no steam locomotives to pull the cars. Horses and even sails were used for power instead.

America's first famous steam locomotive, the "Tom Thumb," was built by Peter Cooper in 1829. One day near Baltimore, Maryland, Cooper was trying out the engine. A horse and carriage drew up alongside the track. The horse and train ran a race.

It was a close contest. The horse and carriage took the lead, but the locomotive began to catch up. Smoke and flame poured from its chimney. Then, to Cooper's disgust, one of the engine belts slipped out of place. The locomotive came to a stop, while the horse and carriage kept going. The horse had won the contest.

7. With what sources of power to pull the cars on railroads did inventors first experiment?

How did railroads help the nation grow?

Early railroads were dangerous. Boilers often blew up. Trains slipped off the tracks. At first those tracks were nothing more than thin strips of cast iron nailed to wooden ties. In cold weather the strips often gave way. They would snap up and puncture the bottoms of the cars. Sometimes passengers were injured.

Even if no mishaps occurred, passengers faced many delays. One reason was that rival railroad companies wanted to prevent one another from using their tracks. So they built them of different *gauges*, or widths. For example, the New York and Erie Railroad had a six-foot (1.83 m) gauge. In the South most railroads used a five-foot (1.52 m) gauge. Still another gauge was used in the West. Many cities would not let railroads connect physically with other lines inside their limits. This caused more delays.

While there were disadvantages to early railroading, there also were advantages. The cost of shipping goods fell greatly. To ship a ton (.9 t) one mile (1.6 km) by turnpike cost about 15 cents. To ship a ton by rail cost about 3 cents. In

The first American railway train ran from Albany to Schenectady. Here it is ready to start.

1817 a passenger traveling by road between Cincinnati and New York City could expect the journey to take 52 days. But by rail the trip could be made in seven days. Even though passenger trains rattled along at only 15 to 20 miles per hour (24-32 km/h), that speed was dizzying to Americans of the time. They couldn't stop talking about how fast they traveled and how much time they saved.

Railroad "fever" caught on quickly, especially in the West. Inland cities wanted "iron horses" to provide them with better transportation. So, too, did river and lake cities. People believed their business would increase if a railroad stopped in their town. And that is just what did happen in the case of some lakefront and riverfront cities. Cleveland, Cincinnati, Louisville, St. Louis, and Chicago soon became thriving centers of commerce, thanks to the coming of railroads. Chicago, for example, had only forty families in 1830. Thirty years later it was the largest railroad center in the West. It boasted that 15 railroad companies served the city and that 100 trains a day came into Chicago. In the ten years between 1850 and 1860, railroad "fever" was most intense. Over 20,000 miles (32,000 km) of track were laid in that time. (See map, page 194.)

8. What were some advantages of railroads?

Part Five

The United States Begins to Industrialize

What is the Industrial Revolution?

Any great change is a *revolution*. Sometimes revolutions involve guns and the use of force. But revolutions can also be peaceful, as those in science, medicine, and industry usually have been. One of the greatest revolutions the world has seen is called the *Industrial Revolution*. It began in England. Then it spread to Western Europe. And in the late 1790s and the early 1800s it came to the United States. That revolution was triggered by the invention of new machines and ways of working.

The Industrial Revolution in the United States did not begin with a single invention or event. It was instead a combination of many changes, one following closely on the heels of another. You already have read about the invention of the cotton gin and interchangeable parts. (See pages 162-163.) You also have read about the invention of the steamboat and the coming of railroads. (See pages 190-191, 193-194.) But there were other changes as well. Three of the most important of them are these:

1. With the invention of new machines, factories were built. People then began to use the products produced in those factories, instead of making things they needed by hand.

2. Building a factory took more money than any one person was likely to have. For that reason, people began to pool their money.

3. Because factories were built in towns and cities, people began leaving their farm homes to go where the jobs were.

Factories needed laborers. They employed young unmarried women and children, as well as men. Some factories even hired whole families. Father, mother, and children as young as eight years old worked side by side. And, as all of those people left the farms and drifted into towns and cities, another movement began that was as important as the movement west.

These changes will be explored in more detail later.

1. How and when did the Industrial Revolution get started in the United States?

2. What three important changes were part of the Industrial Revolution?

Samuel Slater built the complicated machinery for the Almy, Brown mill in Pawtucket, Rhode Island.

When and where was America's first successful factory built?

At one time there were no factories in the United States. But England, the first country to industrialize, had many of them. Other countries, including the United States, sent their raw materials to Britain. There, they were turned into finished goods. Then those goods were sold back to the very countries which had supplied the raw materials, at a handsome profit. Take cotton, for example. It was grown in the United States. Then it was loaded onto ships bound for England. There it was turned into cloth in the textile mills. Then it was shipped back to the United States for sale. Many Americans, Alexander Hamilton among them, believed that was unnecessary. "Why couldn't the United States build factories of its own?" he asked. Then cotton and other raw materials produced here could be turned into finished products in our growing cities and towns. Factories here would mean jobs and lower prices for Americans.

To encourage the growth of industry in the United States, Hamilton persuaded Congress to pass laws favorable to would-be manufacturers. Hearing about those laws, a 21-year-old Englishman named Samuel Slater set off for the United States just four days before Christmas in 1791. With him he brought some important secrets. They were not the kind that spies or detectives hide. They were business secrets. And Slater carried them in his head.

In those days it was against the law for skilled workers to leave England. The British were determined to prevent the loss of their trade secrets. For eight years Slater had worked in an English textile factory. He was only thirteen years old when he started to work, but he had an amazing memory. He quickly learned how each machine in the factory was made. Then, dressed like a farmer, he slipped out of his country.

No sooner had Slater arrived in New York than he heard that a Rhode Island Quaker, Moses Brown, had started a cotton mill. Brown had put a lot of money into the mill, but it was not doing very well. Slater wrote Brown a letter. He told him that he could build machines just like those used in England. Brown replied at once, inviting Slater to come to Rhode Island.

When Slater arrived, he said Brown's mill was hopeless. To build a proper one they would have to begin from scratch. So Slater began to build from memory the complicated machines that were needed. He worked hard for eleven months. But at last Almy, Brown, and Slater Company was ready to begin operating. Seventy-two waterpowered spinning machines started turning out cloth faster and cheaper than it could be done by hand or brought to the United States from England.

Moses Brown, who lived to be 98 years old, grew rich from manufacturing textiles. Among other things, he used his wealth to found the university in Rhode Island which bears his name.

The success of Almy, Brown, and Slater Company encouraged others to go into the business of manufacturing textiles. By 1800 there were seven mills in New England with 2000 spinning machines in operation. More were built later, but the United States textile industry had been established.

3. Who was Samuel Slater and what important secrets did he bring to America?

4. When and where was the first of New England's textile mills built?

Why were most factories built in the Northeast?

Today there are factories in all parts of the United States. But most of the early factories were built in the Northeast, for good reasons. Water was needed to power the machines, and there were many rivers and streams in that region. Later when coal became important, it was found close by, especially in Pennsylvania. The Northeast also had good harbors with many ships ready to take factory products all over the world. These same ships could bring back millions of immigrants to work in the new factories. Poor Europeans looking for a chance to improve their lives were glad to come to America.

While the Northeast was becoming industrialized, the Southern states were turning more and more to farming. Southerners saw little reason to build factories. There was plenty of land in the South in the early 1800s. The climate was perfect for growing cotton. Thanks to the invention of the cotton gin, it had become the main money-making crop. Within 30 years after Whitney invented that machine, the South was producing 75 times as much cotton as it had before.

5. For what reasons were most factories built in the Northeast?

6. Why were Southerners less interested in building factories?

What were working conditions like in the mills?

Many workers were needed to tend the machines in the textile mills of the Northeast. Early employers were especially eager to hire young women. Already factory products were freeing young women from farm chores. They could earn money by working in a mill for a few years. Then the girls could return home. So the factory owners built boardinghouses connected to the mills. They printed handbills describing the advantages of working in mills. They sent people out to villages and farms to spread the news of jobs. One recruiter cruised the New England countryside in a long, black wagon. He talked to young farm women and painted a glowing picture of mill life. "You'll earn enough to dress in silk. You'll live in pleasant surroundings and be able to enjoy the company of other young women. You'll be able to spend half of your time reading or taking part in other interesting activities." His offer sounded good. Farm work was dull, hard, and lonesome. There were no wages for young people who worked on the family farm. But when the young women got to the mills, was life really like that for them?

There is a lot of disagreement about how good or bad life was for the early "mill girls." Certainly they did not earn enough to dress in silk. Nor did they spend most of their time educating or entertaining themselves. But some people who visited the first mills and the boardinghouses praised the conditions they found. They described the clean housing and well-lighted rooms. They were pleased with how well the young women were supervised. They pointed to the articles some of the "mill girls" wrote and the singing and art work others did. They insisted that the mills themselves were "attractive" and working in them was "healthful."

Workers in the first mills in Lowell, Massachusetts, put out a magazine.

Focus On Skills

No single event or invention caused the Industrial Revolution. It came about as a result of many changes, one following closely on another. In other words, one change or cause triggered other changes or results. All of them taken together make up the Industrial Revolution.

To help you understand how one change results in another, or how cause and effect are related, do the following exercise. On a separate sheet of paper write the changes, or causes, listed below. Then decide what results or effects each had. Put the numbers of those effects next to the correct cause. (A cause may have more than one effect.)

Causes

A. New machines were invented.
B. Factories in cities and towns needed workers.
C. Transportation became faster and easier.

Effects

1. Children were employed as workers.
2. People left farms and moved to towns.
3. Products could be turned out faster and cheaper than by hand.
4. Recruiters tried to persuade farm women to take factory jobs.
5. It became easier to ship goods to distant points.
6. People in one section of the country became more aware of how people in other sections lived and worked.
7. Factories were built.
8. No longer were the markets for products limited to one's immediate neighborhood.
9. Workers began to demand better working conditions.
10. People were less isolated from one another.

Other observers saw a different picture. The editor of the *Boston Daily Times* wrote in July 1839:

The young girls are compelled to work in unhealthy confinement for too many hours every day. . . . Their food is both unhealthy and scanty. . . . They are allowed insufficient time to eat. . . . They are crowded in ill-ventilated apartments . . . and in consequence they become pale, feeble, and finally broken in constitution [body].

Which observers were right? Perhaps both were. The truth about life in the early mills may lie somewhere between the contradictory reports. As industry grew, however, life in the mills became more uncomfortable. And as time went on, and as many thousands of workers joined the labor force, conditions in the factories grew worse.

7. In what ways did the reports of those who found conditions good differ from those who found them bad?

8. Why is it possible that all of the observers were partly right and partly wrong?

How did workers try to improve their conditions?

Work in the mills grew hard. Take Hannah Borden's case for an example.

Men, women, and even small children worked in the mills. Despite the long hours they worked, mill hands had to be quick and alert at all times.

Hannah learned to weave on a hand loom at home when she was eight years old. At fourteen she went to work at a textile mill in Fall River, Massachusetts. Hannah Borden became a superior worker and ran two looms at once. Like the others, she worked 75 hours a week, in winter often by candlelight. She lived in a boardinghouse where as many as six or eight young women were squeezed into a single room. She usually was up by 4:00 A.M. By 5:00 A.M. she had the looms going in a cold, unplastered room heated by a single stove. She ended her work at 7:30 P.M.

There was not much that workers like Hannah Borden could do to improve their working conditions. Labor unions then were forbidden by law. Strikers were put in jail. For that reason there were only 24 strikes in the United States before 1835. One of them was organized and carried out in 1834 by women who worked in the mills in Lowell, Massachusetts. Protesting a cut in their pay, they marched together singing:

> **Oh, isn't it a pity,**
> **Such a pretty girl as I,**
> **Should be sent to a factory,**
> **To pine away and die.**

The women lost in that strike. But factory workers did not give up. They went on to demand higher wages, shorter hours, free public education, and better, safer working conditions. It took time before improvements were made. Gradually, however, things began to change. Reporters called attention to the needs of workers. As more and more men were allowed to vote, they began to demand action from the leaders they helped elect. (Women were not permitted to vote until 1919, when the 19th Amendment was added to the Constitution.) One big breakthrough came in 1840. That year the President put federal workers on a ten-hour day. Slowly private businesses and industries began to set ten hours as their regular workday.

9. Describe factory conditions in the early 1800s.

10. How did workers go about trying to win sympathy and support for their demands?

How did the growth of industry begin to divide the country?

For the most part, good feelings among Americans had been the rule in the first part of the 1800s. The country was not divided by serious problems. It was a period of rapid growth. Settlers moved west in large numbers. In the East, factories began humming.

When the War of 1812 ended, the United States began a century such as no other western nation has ever seen. During the next 100 years, no foreign nation threatened the United States in any way. What did threaten peace and goodwill were the increasing differences between the northern and southern sections of the country. Those differences became more pronounced as the 1800s wore on. Northerners began to feel that their wealth was tied to industry. Southerners thought farming held the key to their wealth. And as for the people who pushed west, how they felt depended upon whether they settled north or south of the Ohio River. Those who moved north of the Ohio River could not hold slaves. The Northwest Ordinance said that area should be forever free. Like New England, the states north of the Ohio began to develop industry. Farming became less important.

South of the Ohio, however, things were different. As land wore out from growing crop after crop of cotton, Southerners moved west, too. They took their slaves with them to work on the new land. Farming, not industry, was the way Southerners chose to earn their living.

Thus it was that two strong sections were beginning to take shape in the United States. The North and the South had different ideas about slavery, and about industry and farming.

11. On what did the North and the South come to believe their wealth was based?

12. With which section of the country did those who moved west tend to agree? Why?

Building Your Vocabulary

Words which mean the same are called *synonyms*. Match each word in Column A with its synonym or definition in Column B.

Column A	Column B
1. era	A. width of railroad track
2. doctrine	B. written record or diary
3. turnpike	C. an exploring party
4. expedition	D. statement of belief
5. journal	E. toll road
6. gauge	F. kidnap or force into service
7. impress	G. a period of time
8. interpreter	H. translator

Recalling What You Have Learned

Select the correct word or phrase for each of the following questions.

1. Which of the following was not a War Hawk? (a) John C. Calhoun (b) Henry Clay (c) James Monroe
2. Which of these men was President when the United States purchased Louisiana? (a) Thomas Jefferson (b) James Monroe (c) John Quincy Adams
3. Which of these explorers has a mountain in Colorado named in his honor? (a) William Clark (b) Zebulon Pike (c) Meriwether Lewis
4. Which section of the country expressed its opposition to the War of 1812 in the Hartford Convention? (a) the South (b) New England (c) the West
5. Who wrote "The Star Spangled Banner"? (a) Oliver Perry (b) Francis Scott Key (c) Robert Fulton
6. "Iron Horse" is the nickname for which of the following things? (a) Conestoga wagon (b) steamboat (c) locomotive
7. In which of these countries did the Industrial Revolution begin? (a) Germany (b) the United States (c) England
8. Which of the following were not employed in the textile mills of New England? (a) children (b) young women (c) slaves
9. Which section of the country believed that its wealth depended mainly on farming, or agriculture? (a) the South (b) the West (c) New England

Discussing the Important Ideas in This Chapter

1. Why was Thomas Jefferson both glad and worried when he heard that his representatives had purchased Louisiana?
2. Why were the journeys of Lewis and Clark and Zebulon Pike important?
3. Why did Westerners want the War of 1812? Why did New Englanders oppose the war?
4. How did settlers violate the rights of Tecumseh's people?

5. Why did Oliver Perry and Dolley Madison become heroes?
6. Why is the War of 1812 called "The Second War for Independence"?
7. What important beliefs did the United States express in the Monroe Doctrine?
8. Why did new transportation systems help the United States grow stronger?
9. What was the Industrial Revolution? What changes did it bring to the United States?
10. Why did the North, South, and West begin to think more about their own interests and less about the nation as a whole?

Improving Your Study Skills: *Writing*

Imagine that you were a newspaper reporter living at the time each of the events listed below took place. Write a short article describing one of the events.

Include in your article the information newspapers call the five "w's." What happened? Where? When? Who was involved? Why did the event happen? Start your article with a sentence that gives brief answers to what, when, where, and who. Then tell why.

1. The race between the first steam locomotive, "Tom Thumb," and a horse and carriage. (See page 193 of text for help.)
2. The British burn Washington, D.C., during the War of 1812. (See pages 180-181 of text for help.)
3. The girls and women who worked in the mills of Lowell, Massachusetts, in 1834 go on strike. (See page 201 of text for help.)
4. Harrison burns Tecumseh's village after the Battle of Tippecanoe. (See page 179 of text for help.)

Improving Your Map Skills

As you know, Americans were moving west even during the Revolution. After the nation officially began, in 1790, pioneers poured across the Appalachian Mountains. New states were carved out of the wilderness and added to the Union. Study the map below and answer the questions which follow.

1. How many new states were added by 1819?
2. One of the new states was not in the West. Which state was that?
3. List all the new states in the order in which they joined the Union.
4. What territories were part of the United States in 1819?

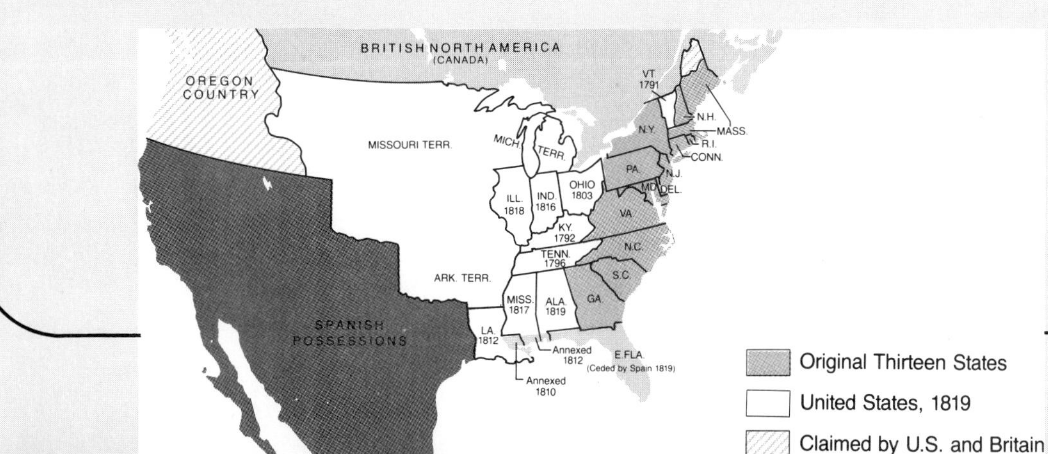

Chapter 8

Changing Times

The Hermitage, Andrew Jackson's home, near Nashville, Tennessee

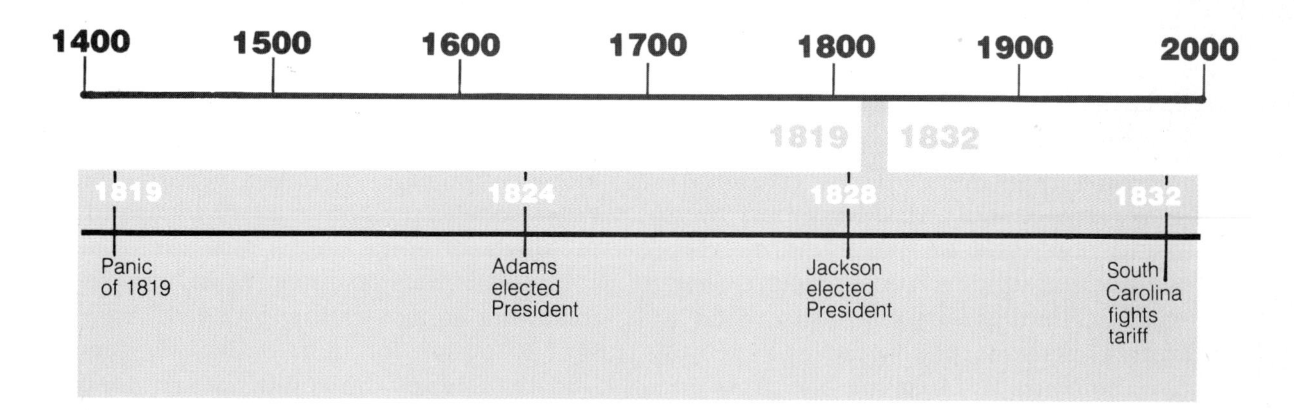

Part One

Hard Times Hit the Nation

When did "good feelings" come to an end?

We have read how "good feelings" grew in the nation as a result of the War of 1812. Americans' pride in their country hit a new high. As a whole, the country was well off.

Americans thought good times would continue. They borrowed more and more money to open new businesses and factories. More and more land was planted with cotton. People hoped that prices for the goods they produced would keep on rising. With the profits they made, they could easily pay back the money they had borrowed.

But Americans were in for an unpleasant surprise. There were signs of trouble by 1818. Then what is called the "Panic of 1819" hit. People *panicked*, or became very fearful. They were afraid of losing their businesses or their savings.

During good times, banks had made many loans to people who wanted to buy land, build factories, or open new shops. Often the banks were not as careful as they should have been about granting credit. So the banks began to worry about those loans and to demand immediate repayment. They refused to make any new loans. Many borrowers could not repay on short notice. Merchants and traders could declare *bankruptcy*. Here is what happens when a person declares bankruptcy. A debtor goes to court and explains the problem. The court then appoints someone to sell most things of value which the debtor still owns. Perhaps it is horses, wagons, furniture, land, or a house. Whatever money is raised through those sales is divided among the *creditors*, or persons to whom money is owed. Then the bankrupt person has to start over again.

Most Americans were farmers in 1819, and farmers were hard hit. Sales of cotton and wheat dropped. Within a few months, the price paid to farmers for their cotton fell from 32 cents per pound to just 15 cents. The price of wheat tumbled from $2 a bushel to just $1.05. In other words, in a matter of months, farmers' incomes were cut in half!

People in cities and towns were also hit by the hard times, or *depression*. The depression lasted through the next decade (ten years). What happened in Philadelphia, for example, was repeated in other places. In that city 30 businesses employing 10,000 persons in 1816 had been forced to lay off all but 2500 of their workers by 1818. Naturally the stores which depended on those workers as customers were affected. At one time there were 89 stores along Market Street. But by 1819 more than half of them had shut down. Some of their owners were bankrupt. The employees lost their jobs.

Numbers do not tell the human side of the story, however. People suffered in many ways from the depression. Some, especially those who lived in large cities, were hungry. They lined up at "soup kitchens." There, religious groups and other relief bands gave away thousands of bowls of soup daily. Not everyone could declare bankruptcy. Many people, including some "leading citizens," were sent to prison for their debts. The law said that those who could not pay their bills were to be kept in jail until they or their friends and relatives paid the debts. Until the late 1830s most states imprisoned people when they could not repay their debts.

For the next decade, Americans had to cope with hard times. Some people, even if they did not suffer from hunger or jailing, had their self-confidence shaken. And so the "good feelings" which had resulted from the War of 1812 disappeared.

1. Why did Americans borrow money after the War of 1812?

2. Why did good times change to bad?

Why was the Panic of 1819 important?

The Panic of 1819 did not start the longest or the most serious depression in the United States. You will read of others more severe, especially the "Great Depression" of the 1930s. (See pages 466-469.) But the Panic of 1819 was the first time a depression had hit *all* Americans at once.

Before, when one or two sections of the country had hard times, other sections did not suffer as much. But in the 1820s, Americans in every part of the country had to face the cold, hard facts of hunger and bad times.

The depression had important effects. People forgot about the welfare of the nation as a whole. More and more they asked, "What can we do to help our city or our section of the country? Never mind the rest of the country. Let's worry about ourselves."

Thus the depression of the 1820s divided Americans. New England worried about its own special problems. The South became most concerned about its troubles. The West accused both New England and the South of forgetting about pressing western problems. Mistrust and rivalry among the sections began to grow and fester. In time that rivalry was given a special name: *sectionalism.* It proved to be very harmful to the country, as we shall see. The bonds forged in good times which held Americans together were beginning to come loose as those good times changed to bad.

3. Why did the depression of the 1820s divide Americans?

4. What is sectionalism?

Part Two

The Common People Take More Interest in Politics

Why did people become more interested in politics?

During the 1820s the "common people," or "average" Americans, began to take a new interest in politics. That interest came in part from the hard times they were going through. But there were other reasons as well. Briefly, the common people's concern about politics increased because:

1. More people became eligible to vote and hold office, so they felt they had a greater stake in politics.

2. Elections became more exciting. They became a great source of entertainment.

3. Voting became easier and more private.

4. People wanted to elect leaders who understood and would try to solve the problems of everyday life.

5. People from the Northeast, South, and West wanted to make sure that their region's interests were protected in Congress and the White House.

Each of these reasons will be explored in this chapter.

1. For what reasons did the common people become more interested in politics?

How did more people become eligible to vote and hold office?

In 1800 a greater percentage of people could vote in the United States than in any country in Europe. Americans, however, were not satisfied. There were certain limits. The chief limit, other than that the voter had to be a male, was that he had to own property. Poor people in the West and workers in cities and towns who were not allowed to vote were unhappy. "We are citizens, too," they said. "We pay taxes. We serve in the army and navy. We help build this nation. Why shouldn't we be able to vote?" they asked. They decided to do something about their *suffrage*, or right to vote.

Under the Constitution the states decide who among their citizens may vote. To widen suffrage, people had to bring pressure on their state legislatures. And they did! Pressure was brought first in the frontier states. One by one those states struck down the property-owning requirements for voting. Vermont, then a frontier state, was first. Next came Ohio, followed by Illinois, Indiana, Alabama, and the new eastern state of Maine. Maine was part of Massachusetts until 1820. Then one by one the thirteen original states began to widen the suffrage until all adult white males could vote and hold office.

Did men really use their newly won right to vote? Indeed they did! Only 27 percent of those who could vote for President voted in 1824. But 56 percent of those able to vote did so in 1828. When the time came to choose a President in 1840, Americans really turned out at the polls. A big 78 percent of those who could vote cast ballots.

2. What were the two chief restrictions on voting?

3. Why was it necessary to bring pressure on state legislatures to widen the suffrage?

Whose voting rights were denied?

While more white males were getting the right to vote, suffrage was being withdrawn from black males. Slaves never had the right to vote, but free blacks did. New York dropped the property-owning requirements for white male voters in 1821. But it did not drop them for black men. Three southern states, North Carolina, Maryland, and Virginia, declared that free persons of color could no longer vote.

Women were not permitted to vote. They had enjoyed limited voting rights in the English colonies. They could vote in some local elections. But their suffrage disappeared after the Revolution, except in New Jersey. Even that state withdrew women's right to vote in 1807. Until 1834 women voted in no state. But in that year Kentucky took the lead in changing the law. It gave widows with children the right to vote in school district elections. The other states, however, were very slow to follow suit.

This picture from a 19th century magazine shows women voting in a New Jersey election before 1807. New Jersey discontinued female suffrage after an election scandal.

Of course, women were unhappy about their treatment. They did much to protest. But it was not until 1920 that women won the right to vote in all states. Later we shall read more about how they finally achieved victory.

4. How was suffrage for black males cut back?

5. What voting rights did women have?

Why did elections become more exciting?

Before 1820 there were not many elections, and they were not very exciting. Candidates did not make speeches. They did not go out among the people to ask for their support. Many thought such practices were undignified. But then things began to change. Fewer offices were filled by appointment. So there were more elections. More men could vote. Candidates had to find ways to win those voters and to get them to the polls on election day.

To attract the common people, candidates put on campaigns that were like circuses. They held great torchlight parades through city streets. They also held picnics and barbecues. Everyone was invited. There was plenty to eat and drink, and the price was right. Everything was free!

When the time for speeches came, new-style politicians provided a lot of entertainment. They got up on gaily decorated platforms, sometimes called "the stump." After telling a few jokes and stories, they began to flatter their listeners and downgrade their opponents. At the same time they boasted of their own talents. They loved to tell how they had been born poor. They paid tribute to their mothers. And they promised that, if elected, they would not forget their roots. Their speeches lasted several hours. Sometimes hecklers rose in the audience. But that only added to the excitement and gave the candidates a chance to show off their wit.

Before and after the speeches, candidates went through the audience. They shook hands with everyone. They kissed babies, patted little children on the head, slapped men on the back, and gave away campaign buttons. Politics was well on its way to becoming one of the nation's most popular pastimes.

6. How did candidates try to persuade the common people to vote for them?

7. Why did people enjoy the new-style campaigns?

How did the method of choosing candidates change?

The Constitution does not say how candidates for President or Vice-President should be chosen. As you know, political parties did not begin until Washington's second term. Washington was elected unanimously. He was the only President ever so chosen. But with the growth of political parties (pages 151-153) came changes in the selection of candidates for President and Vice-President.

At first, candidates were nominated at closed meetings held in Congress and in state legislatures. Those meetings were called caucuses. A *caucus* (kô′kəs) is a closed meeting of political party leaders or members called to get unified support for an issue or a candidate. But people became unhappy with the caucus.

A more open method of nomination, called the *convention*, caught on. It is still used today.

An 1836 campaign piece shows Martin Van Buren encircled by a star-studded horseshoe.

As political campaigns became livelier, banners and posters became part of the election process. The banner above was used in the successful 1844 campaign of James K. Polk and George M. Dallas. On the right is a banner showing the frontier hospitality of William Henry Harrison. He was elected President in 1840.

The first national nominating convention took place for the election of 1832. At that time the two political parties held their conventions in Baltimore, Maryland. Delegates "fresh from the people" gathered to cheer and parade for their favorite candidates. Conventions were exciting events and very noisy ones, too. Political conventions today are not much different from those first two.

8. How were conventions different from caucuses?

9. When and where were the first nominating conventions held?

What changes made voting easier and more private?

When the colonists came from England they brought with them the way of voting known there. And they continued to use it until long into the 1800s. It was called *voice voting* and it worked something like this:

On election day, the voters went to the center of town. There a small crowd was sure to be gathered. The candidates were on hand, too. Each voter then stepped up and announced his choice aloud. His decision was greeted by cheers or jeers. The candidate of his choice then would rise, bow, and express his thanks. "Ah, Mr. Winchester," he would say, "I appreciate your vote. I will never forget what you have done here."

In time people began objecting to voice voting. It was anything but private. "How I vote is no one else's business," said many a voter. And they began to demand paper ballots. But there were problems with them, too. The first ballots were just blank pieces of paper. It took time to write the names of all the people running for office.

Then, printed ballots came into use. At first they were printed by the political parties. Each party chose a different color ballot. So it was easy to tell what choice a voter made. Sometimes people were paid to vote for one party. The color of the ballot they chose showed if they kept their bargain. This system made it hard on the voter. He never knew who was watching. He might lose his job or suffer in other ways for his vote. Not until 1888 did all states require the use of truly secret ballots.

10. What was voice voting?

11. Why did written ballots give way to printed ballots?

What was the "favorite son" election?

As you know, rivalry among the three sections of the United States had been growing. So perhaps it was to be expected that the North, South, and West each would choose its own candidate for President in 1824. The North ran John Quincy Adams. The South ran Secretary of the Treasury William H. Crawford of Georgia. The West had two candidates, Henry Clay of Kentucky and General Andrew Jackson of Tennessee.

Each section voted for its own favorite son. As a result, no one candidate got a majority, or over half the total vote. By law, the election then went to the House of Representatives.

Andrew Jackson had made the best showing of the four candidates. But Henry Clay was not his friend. Clay gave his support to John Quincy Adams, and the House made Adams President.

If ever a man was qualified by intelligence and character to be President, it was John Quincy Adams. Son of two remarkable people, John and Abigail Adams, he had been well educated and trained by them throughout his life. He had served the nation in a number of ways, so he had a lot of experience. Yet he was one of the least successful Presidents. It is doubtful whether anyone ever was as miserable while in the White House. In Washington he was a lonely figure. He worked long hours, often until after midnight. He went swimming alone in the Potomac River. His personal life was haunted by tragedy. His wife, Louisa, imagined that she had one sickness after another. She spent most of her time in bed, refusing to see anyone. Adams even lost his children. His two sons died.

Jackson and his supporters were angry when the House chose John Quincy Adams. During the next four years, they never let Adams have a moment's peace. They accused him of "stealing the election." They raised the cry of "bargain and corruption." Again and again they reminded Americans that Andrew Jackson, the hero of the Battle of New Orleans, had received more votes from the people than anyone else. But he was not chosen to be President. What kind of democracy was that? they asked.

Jackson and his supporters worked tirelessly. When the election of 1828 rolled around, Jackson won a stunning victory. John Quincy Adams was turned out of office after serving just one term. But he continued to serve the nation in another way. Not too proud to be a member of Congress after having been President, he ran for the House in 1831. For the next seventeen years he played a key role there. He was violently opposed to the extension of slavery. In the midst of a debate on slavery Adams slumped over and died on the floor of Congress.

12. Who were the favorite sons chosen as candidates in 1824?

13. Why was John Quincy Adams unsuccessful as President?

Part Three

Andrew Jackson and Democracy

Why was Jackson's election a victory for the common people?

Jackson's election was proof of the new interest in government of the "plain people." Workers in the cities, people on the frontiers, and small farmers all believed that he would represent them. So from all over the country they went to the polls in 1828 and again in 1832 to vote for Jackson. As one newswriter put it, "It was a proud day for the people. Jackson was *their own* President."

Before Jackson, only men from the East had been elected President. Usually Presidents came from important families. They were well educated and often wealthy.

Jackson's background was different. His family had neither money nor power. As an orphan, he grew up in South Carolina without parents to set any rules. Fighting and dueling interested him more than education.

Tall, thin, red-haired Jackson moved to Tennessee, part of the West in those days. He made a reputation as a tough fighter. He became a national hero after winning the spectacular Battle

Happy citizens flock to the White House to celebrate Andrew Jackson's inauguration as the seventh President.

of New Orleans in the War of 1812. (See page 183.) His troops nicknamed him "Old Hickory," because he was as tough as hickory wood.

Jackson also did some fighting *without* a gun that brought him fame. As a hard-hitting lawyer and judge, he brought law and order to the rough Tennessee frontier.

When "Old Hickory" was finally elected President, he was the first American from the West in the White House.

Jackson, however, was probably the saddest man to live in the President's mansion. Just a few weeks before he took office, his beloved wife, Rachel, had died. Jackson thought the lies of his political enemies killed her. He never forgave them. A tired, grief-stricken, childless man of 62, Jackson took up living alone in the White House.

While Jackson himself may have been sad, his followers were wildly happy. Friends from all over poured into Washington. They slept on hotel floors or in hallways. On Inauguration Day, they rushed into the White House and nearly took it apart. Crowds were so great that people fainted. Clothes were torn. Glasses and china were broken. People wearing muddy boots climbed on top of $150 chairs to get a better look at their hero. The mob got so wild that Jackson had to escape out the back door to Gadsby's Hotel. Then the word was passed that the big punch bowls had been moved outside on the lawns. The White House quickly emptied.

Some Americans were shocked. They shook their heads sadly and said "King Mob" had taken over. In spite of muddied chairs and broken dishes and furniture, Andrew Jackson had shown on his first day as President that he believed what he had said. One person was as good as another.

1. How was Jackson different from the Presidents who served before him?

2. What part did the common people play in his election and in his inauguration?

Why was Jackson a strong President?

The United States has known two kinds of Presidents. The first kind believes in leading the people with a strong hand. The second kind lets Congress take the lead.

Jackson was the strong kind of President. He said the President is the leader of all the people because he is chosen in a national election every four years. Members of Congress, on the other hand, represent only their own states and districts.

So when President Jackson found himself blocked by Congress he took his case directly to the people. He told them what he wanted. The people then warned Congress to do what the President said, or else be voted out at the next election. The support of the people made Jackson a strong President.

Jackson believed that the duties of government officials should be made plain and simple. Then any intelligent person could hold office. Jackson also thought that one person should not hold an office for long. The job should be passed around. Then officials would never get too much power. They would do what the people wanted. But Jackson also believed that jobs should be passed among his own followers. One of them named the system of rewarding followers by giving them jobs or other advantages. It became known as the *spoils system* from the old saying "To the victors belong the spoils."

Jackson's foes criticized him for using the spoils system. But Jackson really replaced no more officials than Jefferson had. Jackson did make the spoils system an accepted part of national government, however. It was too easily abused, as we shall see later.

Jackson became the single most important, or *dominant*, person in the United States. Because he was such a dominant figure, few Americans were neutral about Andrew Jackson. Some people loved him. He was their hero. Others hated him. They said he was a "trigger-happy" tyrant. They called him "King Andrew" and predicted he would ruin the country.

3. Why was Jackson a strong President?

4. What is the spoils system?

Why did tariffs become a major issue?

Tariffs took on new importance in Jackson's time. As you know, tariffs are taxes placed on goods coming in from foreign countries. These taxes furnish money for the government. They sometimes protect makers of American goods, because they add to the price of foreign goods. As a result, products made in the United States can be sold at lower prices than those made abroad.

The northern states depended on manufacturing. Naturally, people who lived in the North liked high tariffs. Those tariffs guaranteed their jobs and their profits.

The southern states were more interested in raising cotton than in building factories. Southerners sold their cotton to both Northerners and Europeans. In return, they bought manufactured goods.

Focus on Skills

The two drawings shown here picture the same man. That man was Andrew Jackson, seventh President of the United States.

Jackson was a very controversial figure. Some people loved him and admired him. Others hated and laughed at him. Compare these two drawings. Why do you think the same man looks different in each drawing? Which one of them do you think was drawn by his friends? Which by his enemies? Which do you think is the "truest" picture of Jackson as he really was?

1. In the cartoon on the left, how are we told that the men Jackson is driving from the Temple are evil men?
2. Why is the "common man" happy and patting Jackson on the back?
3. Why are Jackson and the "common man" shown in large size?
4. In the cartoon on the right, what does the artist tell us has happened to the people since Jackson became President?
5. Why would showing Jackson in robes like those worn by the king of England have made Americans of those times especially angry?
6. What is being crushed beneath Jackson's feet? Why is this a threat to democracy?

Can you find some modern examples of cartoons or pictures showing the good and bad sides of the same person? Analyze those examples in class.

Historymaker

Andrew Jackson helped to write one of the saddest chapters in American history. It concerns the Cherokee. They were one of the largest and most important Indian tribes in the Southeast. President Washington recognized the Cherokee as a separate nation. He signed a treaty with them in 1791. It said the Cherokee were entitled to their lands and to make their own laws. But in Jackson's time that treaty was torn up. The Cherokee not only lost their lands and their independence, but one-fourth of the people of that nation lost their lives.

Unlike many other Indian tribes who lived by hunting and fishing, the Cherokee were a settled people. They owned prosperous farms and businesses. Some even held slaves. Most of them wore "European style" clothes. Their land was mainly in Georgia, but some parts were in Tennessee and Alabama. (See map, page 217.) This land was criss-crossed by roads and dotted with houses and churches. The Cherokee had a constitution patterned after that of the United States. They had courts in which disputes were settled peacefully. They elected representatives to their own legislature.

Despite the fact that the United States had said the Cherokee were a separate nation, the state of Georgia kept nibbling away at their lands. When gold was discovered on Cherokee land in 1828, Georgians' appetites knew no limits. Gold-seekers rushed into the Cherokee nation.

Of course the Cherokee were upset. Led by John Ross, a brilliant man who later became their principal chief, they took their case all the way to the United States Supreme Court. John Marshall, who was still serving as Chief Justice, said he was very sympathetic. In 1832, Marshall and the Court ruled that the Cherokee nation was a real political community. The laws of Georgia had no force there. Only federal law governed Cherokee territory.

Andrew Jackson refused to protect the Cherokee. He said of the ruling of the Supreme Court: "John Marshall has made his decision; now let him enforce it."

Earlier, Andrew Jackson had asked Congress to pass an Indian Removal Act. Not only did he want the Cherokee to move west of the Mississippi River, he wanted the Creeks, Chickasaw, Seminoles, and Choctaw to go, too. (See map, page 217.) It would be best if they went "voluntarily." But, if they chose to remain in their homelands, they would have to accept without question the authority of federal and state governments.

Jackson's ideas were unacceptable to the Cherokee. It was unthinkable to them to give up their homes, farms, and businesses,

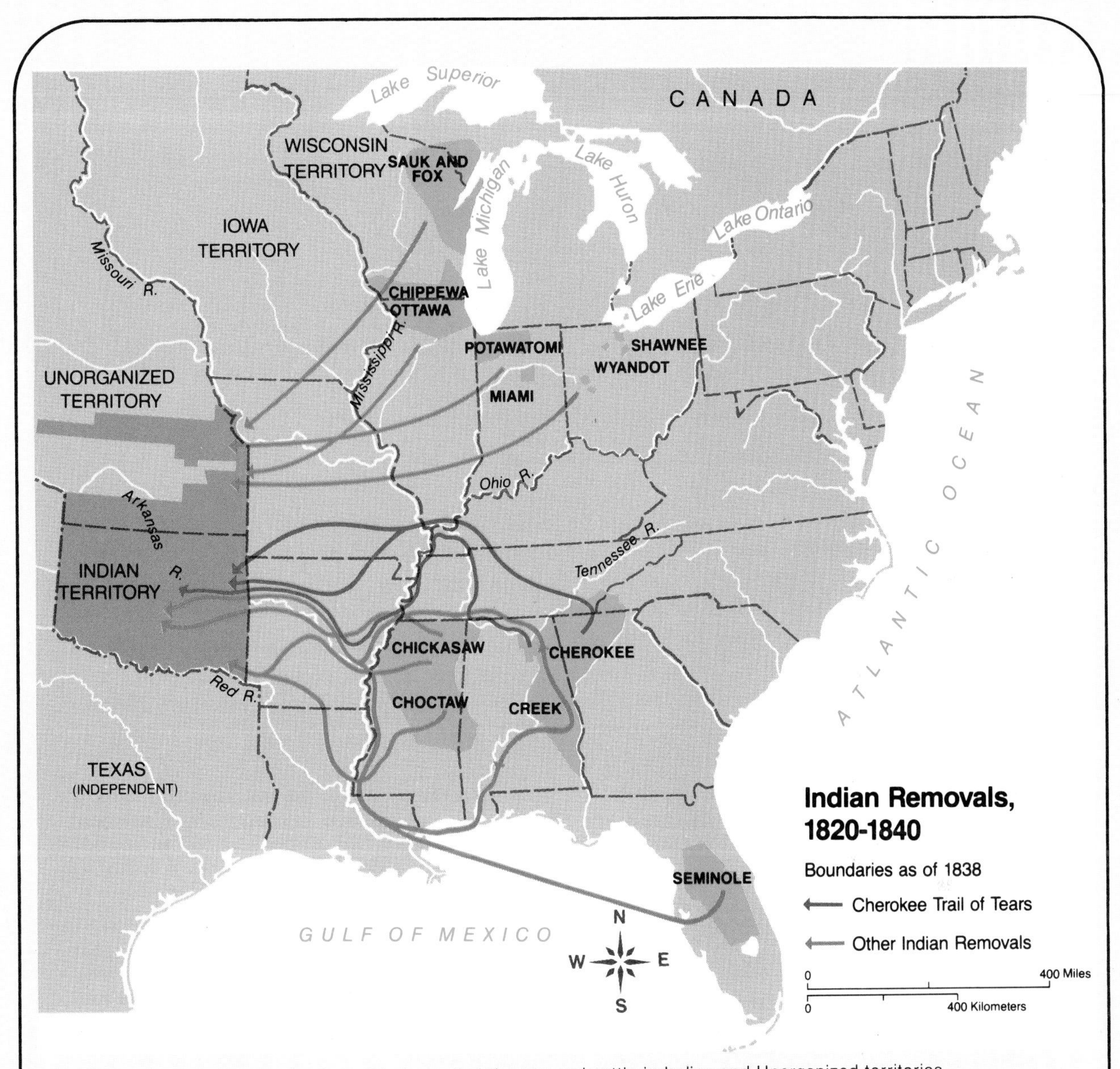

Other Indian tribes were also forced to leave their homes and settle in Indian and Unorganized territories.

let alone for them to abandon the graves of their ancestors.

Few voices were raised in Congress on behalf of the Indians. But one man, seldom mentioned in history, did have the courage to speak out. He was Senator Theodore Frelinghuysen of New Jersey. His listeners did not like what he had to say:

How can we ever dispute the right of the Cherokees to remain east of the Mississippi, when we . . . promised them that very location? How can we drive the Indian from his home? . . . Let conscience answer. . . . Yes, sir, we have acquired and now own more land than we shall dispose of at the present rate to settlers in two hundred years . . . and yet, we crave more. . . . Where the Indian has always been, he enjoys an absolute right still

This famous painting of the Cherokee on the "Trail of Tears" gives some idea of the suffering they endured on the journey.

to be, in the free exercise of his own thought, government, and conduct. . . .

Later, Henry Clay of Kentucky also rose in the Senate to "denounce the shabby and dishonorable proceedings." His action, like that of the senator from New Jersey, took a lot of courage. Indians had no votes. Kentucky voters were unlikely to agree with Clay. Even so he appealed to America's sense of justice and decency. His speech drew tears from the eyes of some of the senators, but they did nothing to stop the forced removal.

When the Cherokee refused to go "voluntarily" as some of the other tribes did, Jackson sent the army to round them up. They then began a long, forced march to lands "reserved" for them in what is now Oklahoma. On the way 4000 Cherokee died of disease and other hardships. Small wonder that they called their 1000 mile journey the "Trail of Tears."

Did the Cherokee just give up in despair? No, they did not. They asked John Ross, often and rightly called "the bright star of the Cherokee," to serve as their principal chief. As soon as they arrived in Indian Territory, Ross called a great meeting for all the tribes which had been removed from their homelands. More than seventeen different tribes attended. Many of those tribes had been enemies in the past, so Ross asked them first to smoke the pipe of peace and "shake the right hand of friendship." Then he spoke to them saying:

Brothers: When we see that our people have been compelled to remove to a new and distant country, we cannot but feel sorry; but we should not despair of once more enjoying the blessing of peace in our new homes.

Brothers: by this removal, tribes that were once separated by distance have become neighbors. . . . Let us then act that peace and friendship may be forever preserved and that we may always live as brothers of the same family.

Ross's dream was never realized. The tribes never united to present a single strong front. Even so, John Ross never ceased to press for the best interests of all of them. During the next forty years he made many trips to Washington, D.C., to plead the Indians' cause. He died there while still in the service of his people on August 1, 1866.

Tariffs protected the North, but they hurt the South. Southerners wanted to trade their cotton for low-priced goods. That way they could earn a profit. But tariffs made the price of foreign goods, and even northern goods, more expensive. As tariffs went up, so did the price of manufactured goods. These high prices angered Southerners. They ruined many plantation owners.

While Jackson was President, the North and South collided head on. This happened when Congress raised tariffs in 1828 and again in 1832.

In South Carolina, people said flatly that they would not pay the new tariffs. John C. Calhoun of South Carolina was so angry that he resigned as Vice-President of the United States. In the Senate, he said the new tariff laws were "null, void, and no law." Throughout the South there were mass meetings to protest the unpopular taxes. Some newspapers talked of striking back at the North.

5. Why did the North favor and the South oppose tariffs?

6. How did the South respond to new, higher tariffs?

How did Jackson handle the South's threat to disobey a federal law?

Hot-tempered Jackson was furious! In private he threatened to "hang the nullifiers," or people who said they would not obey the federal law. Jackson said those who put themselves above the law were guilty of treason. Then the President declared, "The law of the United States must be executed [carried out]. . . . My duty is in the Constitution."

To show that he really meant business, Jackson prepared to use military force. "I will meet treason at the threshold," the President thundered. "In forty days I will have fifty thousand men in South Carolina to enforce the law."

To avoid a war over tariffs, one or both sides had to back down. Senator Henry Clay of Kentucky wrote a compromise bill. It was bitterly debated in the Senate. Finally the North gave in enough so that Jackson would not have to use troops. The North agreed to lower tariffs. South Carolina took back what it said about not obeying a federal law.

Like all compromises, this one meant that neither side won a clear-cut victory. South Carolinians did not get all they wanted. But tariffs were reduced. On the other hand, Northerners had avoided war.

7. Who were "the nullifiers"? Why was Jackson so angry with them?

8. How did the North and the South finally solve their tariff problems?

Why did Jackson destroy the Bank of the United States?

The Bank of the United States was something about which Americans long had disagreed. As you will recall, Hamilton and Jefferson had some bitter arguments over whether or not such a Bank was needed. Nor did those arguments die down after the Bank was founded. They continued right up to Andrew Jackson's time.

Some people insisted the Bank was a good idea. It provided a safe place for the United States government to keep its money. And the Bank was very careful about those to whom it gave credit. It did not take many risks.

But it was exactly because the Bank was so particular about making loans that others objected. The Bank, they said, was not designed to help the poor

A bleak shopper examines his bill. Many people were unable to pay their debts after the Panic of 1837.

or the "common folk." It was a tool of the rich and run for their benefit. What is more, they charged, the Bank and its advisers acted as though they were more powerful than the government itself.

Andrew Jackson hated the Bank with a passion. He called it "The Monster." He announced "I will kill the Bank." And he did. When Congress passed a bill to extend the Bank's life, Jackson vetoed the bill. He said the Bank was unconstitutional, undemocratic, and un-American. But the Bank had four years to go before its charter ran out. So Jackson made another blistering attack on it. He removed all government deposits from the bank. He put them in state banks which his opponents quickly began to call "pet banks." Jackson had a little trouble switching the funds, however. He had to fire two Secretaries of the Treasury before he found one willing to do as he told him.

Trouble followed on the heels of Jackson's actions. The state banks loaned money recklessly. They gave credit to almost anyone. In 1837 panic hit. It was similar to, but even more serious than, the Panic of 1819. But by that time, Jackson had finished his second term as President. So the blame was put on Martin Van Buren, who followed Jackson as President. "Old Hickory" himself had no regrets over what he had done.

Jackson made mistakes as President, but he greatly strengthened democracy. He was, above all, the "plain man of the people." The voters had sent him to Washington, D.C., to govern for them. And he did not disappoint them.

Jackson also made the office of President much stronger. He firmly believed that the President represented the people better than any other elected official. As President, Jackson thought it was his duty to put the people's will into action.

9. How did Jackson bring down the Bank of the United States?

10. Why did Jackson think the office of President was most important?

Building Your Vocabulary

Complete the sentences below by selecting the correct word(s) from those listed below. All of the words listed have been used in Chapter 8.

1. A—?—is a meeting of political party leaders which is not open to the public.
2. Rewarding friends and supporters by giving them jobs or other benefits is called the—?—.
3. During the—?—, or hard times, which followed the Panic of 1819, many people lost their jobs.
4. The right to vote is called—?—.
5. A—?—is a period of ten years.
6. When people are hopelessly in debt, they may declare—?—.
7. Andrew Jackson was so powerful that he was the—?—figure of his time.
8. When people are afraid of losing their savings and businesses because credit is tight, they set off a—?—.

bankruptcy	depression	decade
suffrage	dominant	spoils system
panic	caucus	

Recalling What You've Learned

Match each item in Column A with the correct description in Column B.

Column A	Column B
1. Andrew Jackson	A. wanted tariffs
2. John Ross	B. served in the House after being President
3. voice voting	C. opposed tariffs
4. John Quincy Adams	D. said he would "kill" the Bank of the United States
5. convention	E. without legal or binding force
6. "the stump"	F. oral ballot
7. sectionalism	G. method of selecting a political nominee
8. null and void	H. a platform from which candidates speak
9. Northerners	I. principal chief of the Cherokee
10. Southerners	J. putting one's part of the country ahead of the nation as a whole

---

Discussing the Important Ideas in This Chapter

1. Why did the Panic of 1819 and the depression which followed it change the way Americans felt about their country?
2. Why did the common people become more interested in politics?
3. In what ways did voting practices and elections become more democratic during the 1820s and 1830s? What undemocratic practices were allowed to continue?

4. How are political campaigns of today like those in the 1820s and 1830s? How are today's campaigns different?
5. Describe three actions taken by President Jackson which show that he was interested in the common people.
6. Why did Jackson favor the spoils system? How could the spoils system lead to corruption?
7. Why did Jackson's interest in the common people not extend to the Indians?
8. Why was state nullification of federal laws a serious threat to the Union?

Improving Your Map Skills

Any map is, of course, much smaller than the area of the world it represents. One map of the United States may cover a whole wall. Another map of the same area may fit on an index card. That is why mapmakers use a scale to tell you the relation between the size of their map and the real size of the mapped area. (Not all maps have scales. Sometimes a mapmaker distorts the areas on a map in order to illustrate an important concept.)

Study the map on page 217. Find the scale in the lower right. Notice that one scale is given for miles and another for kilometers.

How many miles (or kilometers) does the whole scale represent? Half of the scale represents how many miles (or kilometers)?

To find the distance between two points on the map, place the edge of a piece of paper between the two points. Mark the paper at each point. Then measure the paper along the scale to find the distance in miles (or kilometers). Use the scale to answer the following questions.

1. How long is the northern boundary of the Indian Territory?
2. About how far did the Sauk and Fox Indians have to travel from their homes in Wisconsin to the Unorganized Territory?
3. About how far did the Seminole Indians have to travel from their homes in Florida to the Indian Territory?

Improving Your Study Skills: *Reading*

For each of the paragraphs below, find the sentence that contains the main idea. Remember that the main idea is not always found in the first sentence. Write the main idea in your own words.

1. Americans thought good times would continue. They borrowed more and more money to open new businesses and factories. More and more land was planted with cotton. People hoped that prices for the goods they produced would keep on rising. With the profits they made, they could easily pay back the money they had borrowed.
2. Numbers do not tell the human side of the story, however. People suffered in many ways from the depression. Some, especially those who lived in large cities, were hungry. They lined up at "soup kitchens." There, religious groups and other relief bands gave away thousands of bowls of soup daily. Not everyone could declare bankruptcy. Many people, including some "leading citizens," were sent to prison for their debts. The laws said that those who could not pay their bills were to be kept in prison until they or their friends and relatives paid the debts. Until the late

1830s most states imprisoned people when they could not repay their debts. Some people, even if they did not suffer from hunger or jailing, had their self-confidence shaken.

3. The Constitution does not say how candidates for President or Vice-President should be chosen. As you know, political parties did not begin until Washington's second term. Washington was elected unanimously. He was the only President ever so chosen. But with the growth of political parties (pages 151-153) came changes in the selection of candidates for President and Vice-President.

4. Before 1820 there were not many elections, and they were not very exciting. Candidates did not make speeches. They did not go out among the people to ask for their support. Many thought such practices were undignified. But then things began to change. Fewer offices were filled by appointment. So there were more elections. More men could vote. Candidates had to find ways to win those voters and to get them to the polls on election day.

5. Tariffs protected the North, but they hurt the South. Southerners wanted to trade their cotton for low-priced goods. That way they could earn a profit. But tariffs made the price of foreign goods, and even northern goods, more expensive. As tariffs went up, so did the price of manufactured goods. These high prices angered Southerners. They ruined many plantation owners.

Chapter 9

Reform in America

Staircase in trustee's office, Shaker village, Pleasant Hill, Kentucky

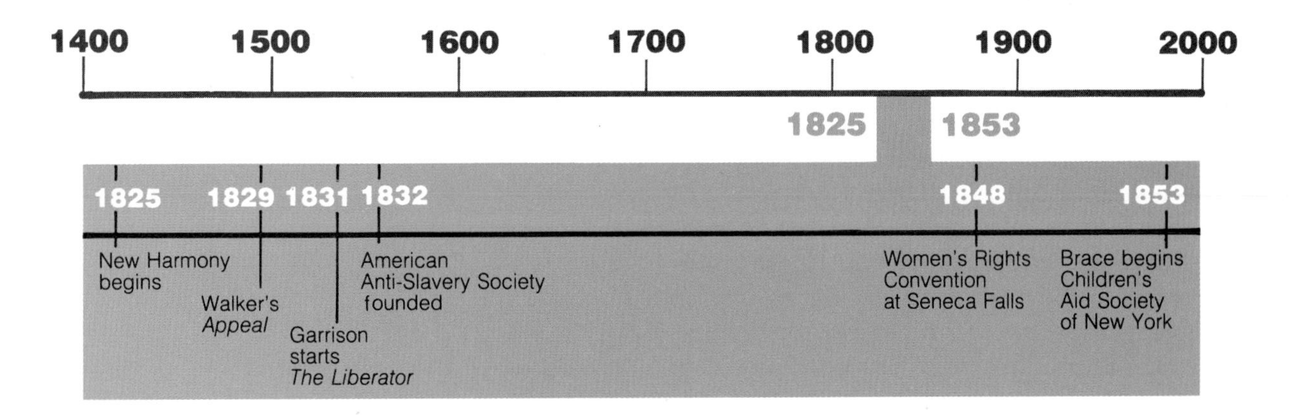

Part One

Reform and Reformers, 1815–1860

Why did some Americans think reforms were needed?

Americans have always looked for better tomorrows. If Americans have had one thing in common, it is probably their belief that life can and should be better. That belief is expressed in the Declaration of Independence and the Constitution.

After the War of 1812, some Americans began to take a long, hard look at their country. What did they see? They saw people whose very lives were in danger because of poor health or poverty. They saw many who were denied liberty. They saw others who were not able to "pursue happiness." Who were those people? First and most obvious were the thousands of black slaves. Then there were women. Women could not vote, hold office, or attend college. Other Americans were limited because they lacked education. Those with physical or mental handicaps often lived hard lives.

Certainly none of those conditions was new. Slavery had existed in America since at least 1700. Women had never enjoyed the freedoms men knew. Schools were rarely free, and not everyone was allowed to attend them. The poor and the handicapped had long been ignored. Why, then, did some Americans suddenly become excited about those problems? Why did they decide to try to bring about *reform*, or change for the better? Those are not easy questions to answer. Each person had his or her own reasons for becoming a *reformer.* But there are some general reasons:

1. After the War of 1812, the United States enjoyed a long period of peace. So people were able to think about conditions at home. They had time and energy to work on those which they felt were not good.

2. Thanks to improvements in transportation, it was easier for reformers to travel and meet one another.

3. All reformers were deeply troubled by the "evils" or "shortcomings" they thought existed in their country. They wanted to make the United States a perfect society. They each felt an urgent sense of mission.

1. What conditions did some Americans find troubling?

2. How might the sudden, great interest in reform be explained?

Who were the reformers?

One reform movement after another was born in the United States between 1815 and 1860. In this chapter we are going to learn about the most important of them. We also are going to meet many of the colorful people who worked in them. But before we do that, let's try to form a general idea about the kinds of people who became reformers.

No two reformers were exactly alike, of course. But most of them did have certain things in common.

Most of them came from middle-class families. Many had strong religious beliefs. Most were Protestants. The majority came from the Northeast.

Well-dressed slaves dance at a kitchen ball. Slavery supporters tried to claim that scenes like this were common. Abolitionists claimed that most slaves were treated cruelly. They also said that slavery was evil in itself.

Reformers tended to think they were "special." Some believed that a higher power had chosen them to right certain wrongs. Others said their consciences drove them to act.

Reformers could stand up to fierce opposition. In fact, the more hardships they suffered, the more convinced they became of the rightness of their causes.

Reformers tended to be involved in more than one cause. They might begin by wanting to do away with slavery. Then they would become interested in the rights of women or of Indians. They often knew and worked with one another because they were interested in more than one reform.

There were many exceptions to that general picture of reformers, however. Some were old; others were young. Men, women, and sometimes even children played active roles in the various movements. So, too, did blacks, whites, and Indians. Certain reformers were well educated. Others had never been to school a day in their lives. A number of reformers came from families who supported their work. But the families of others bitterly opposed what their daughters and sons were trying to do. Sometimes reformers married one another and became husband-wife teams. But others said they were far too busy righting wrongs to have home and family ties.

3. In what ways were most reformers alike?

4. In what ways were reformers different from one another?

Part Two

The Antislavery Movement

Why did the American Anti-Slavery Society become important?

The first antislavery organization was set up in New England in 1832. The next year 60 delegates, blacks and whites, from ten states met in Philadelphia. They founded the American Anti-Slavery Society. The crusade against slavery became the most significant reform movement of the time. It also was one of the few movements which won its goal, the outlawing of slavery in the United States.

Opposition to slavery did not begin in the 1830s, of course. You already have read about people and groups who were against slavery in colonial times. You also know that there were bitter debates about slavery at the Constitutional Convention. And you are aware that many slaves had shown their feelings ever since slavery began. They ran away. They resisted daily in many ways. They slowed down their work and broke tools, for example. Sometimes slaves took part in violent uprisings. But until the founding of the Anti-Slavery Society, there was no one important center for people who wanted to stop slavery. The society grew very quickly. By 1838, just five years after the meeting in Philadelphia, it had more than a quarter of a million members and about 1300 local chapters.

The members of this new society were more than just opposed to slavery. They demanded that it be totally wiped out, or *abolished*. For that reason they were given the name *abolitionists.* Although abolitionists were few in number compared to the total population of the United States, they had a huge effect on American life.

1. When and where was the American Anti-Slavery Society born?

2. Who were the abolitionists?

What did abolitionists believe?

All abolitionists agreed that slavery must end. But they did not agree about when or how it should be stopped. Some said that slavery should end slowly for the sake of both slaves and owners. Everyone in the South would need time to adjust to new ways of living and working together. But other reformers would not hear of a gradual approach. They demanded an end to slavery at once. If plantation owners were ruined and life in the South totally changed, so be it. Those reformers were called "radicals." *Radical* means drastic or extreme. *Radical abolitionists* were willing to use any means to end slavery.

When people pointed out that slavery was protected by the laws of the United States, some radicals became very angry. They began to attack the Constitution. It was a "wicked" document, they said, because it permitted slavery. There was another law, a "higher law," than the Constitution, those abolitionists insisted. It was this "higher law" they would obey.

The attitude of radicals toward the Constitution and other laws cost the antislavery movement a lot of support. Most Americans in both the North and the South upheld the Constitution. They believed that everyone ought to obey the laws of the land. "If our laws are wrong," said most Americans, "we have ways of changing them. No one has the right to break the law."

3. Why did abolitionists disagree about when and how slavery should be ended?

4. How did some radicals feel about the Constitution and obeying the law?

William Lloyd Garrison was a radical abolitionist.

This banner celebrates the founding of *The Liberator*.

Garrison's paper *The Liberator* was an important force in the abolitionist movement.

Who were some of the leading abolitionists?

Blacks and whites, men and women, Northerners and Southerners—all were to be found among the leaders of the abolition movement.

One of the first of those reformers to win fame was William Lloyd Garrison. He was a founder of the Anti-Slavery Society. In 1831 he began publishing an antislavery newspaper in Boston. He called it *The Liberator*, a name taken from the word liberty. He set the tone of that paper with its very first issue. In it he wrote these words:

> **I am in earnest. . . . I will not excuse—I will not retreat a single inch—AND I WILL BE HEARD!**

For the next thirty years Garrison's words were heard, but they did not make most people happy. As early as 1841, he began calling for the breakup of the Union. His own words tell us how he felt:

> **I do not wish to think, or speak or write with moderation [calmness]. . . . No! Tell a man whose house is on fire to give a moderate alarm. Tell him to moderately rescue his wife . . . tell the mother to gradually extricate [remove] her child from the fire . . . but urge me not to use moderation in [this] cause. . . .**

The longer Garrison worked against slavery, the more violent he became. He publicly burned a copy of the Constitution because it upheld slavery.

Garrison's followers loved him. They admired his courage. But the general public did not. Most Americans thought Garrison was too radical. He wanted to destroy the Constitution, the Union, and state laws.

The state of Georgia at one time offered $5000 for Garrison's arrest and conviction. An angry mob in Boston grabbed him, slipped a rope around his neck, and led him through the streets of the city. Time and again he was hooted and booed when he tried to make speeches. But nothing stopped him. His interest in other causes grew. He began to work for women's rights, Indian rights, and *temperance.* (Those who urged *temperance* wanted people to give up drinking. We will read more about the temperance movement later in this chapter.)

In time Garrison became too radical even for most members of the Anti-Slavery Society. Others then began to become leaders in that group. Theodore Dwight Weld was one of them. He was one of the best of the abolitionist

Sarah (left) and Angelina Grimké attracted large crowds when they spoke about the evils of slavery.

speakers. Again and again he pounded home his themes. Slavery was inhuman, he said. It corrupted all Americans, not just those who owned slaves. It must be stamped out. Weld wrote one of the great antislavery pamphlets. It was called *American Slavery as It Is.* The pamphlet contained eyewitness accounts by runaway slaves and articles taken from southern newspapers.

Weld's wife, Angelina Grimké, helped him write that pamphlet. She was called "Devilina" by those who disliked her work. Her brother, Thomas, and her sister, Sarah, also defied their family to work against slavery. Their father was a wealthy South Carolina state judge. They grew up on a plantation. They saw the horrors of slavery firsthand. When any of the Grimkés spoke, they drew large crowds. People were eager to hear their accounts of life in the South. The audience usually heard pleas for women's rights as well. The Grimkés were also deeply involved in that reform.

Needless to say, supporters of slavery hated the Grimkés. When Angelina mailed antislavery pamphlets to Charleston, the postmaster publicly burned them. She was warned that she would be jailed if she dared set foot in Charleston. Plantation owners denounced all three Grimkés. They were called traitors—and worse. Some people said they would tar and feather the Grimkés, if ever they could catch them.

5. Why was William Lloyd Garrison considered a radical abolitionist?

6. How did Theodore Weld and the Grimkés work against slavery?

How did black abolitionists work?

Blacks showed their hatred of slavery long before there were any special groups to oppose it, as you know. But when antislavery groups began to form, black men and women took active roles. Six black men helped found the American Anti-Slavery Society. Other blacks served in different ways. Among the most famous were Frederick Douglass, Sojourner Truth, Henry Highland Garnet, and David Walker.

Douglass was born a slave. Because laws in the South forbade teaching slaves to read or write, he had to learn in secret. Later Douglass ran away from his Maryland owner and made his way north. He became a famous speaker. A tall man with a mass of silver-gray hair, Douglass had a deep musical voice. Large crowds in England as well as the United States came to hear him speak.

Douglass was a fine writer as well as an exciting speaker. In 1845 he wrote the story of his own life, or his *autobiography*. It is still popular with readers today. He also started his own newspaper. He called it the *North Star*. He chose that name because runaway slaves usually traveled by night. They used the North Star as their guide to freedom.

In time Douglass also worked for women's rights. Later, when the Civil War began, he used his talents to recruit black soldiers for the armies of the North.

Isabella was Sojourner Truth's real name. She never knew her last name. She was torn from her parents when she was only nine years old and sold on the auction block. She grew up speaking Dutch, the language of her first owners. Later, after she had married another slave and borne five children, she ran away. It was then that she changed her name to Sojourner (traveler) Truth.

For years she lived up to her name. She traveled far and wide. She carried a white satin banner that became her hallmark. On it were the words: "Proclaim liberty throughout all the land. . . ."

Sojourner Truth not only proclaimed liberty for slaves. With the same vigor she worked for the rights of women.

Just as some white reformers were more radical than others, so, too, were some black abolitionists. They urged blacks, free and slave, to break laws they thought were unjust. Sometimes they urged slaves to rise up in arms and overthrow slavery. Many other reformers were opposed to these calls for violence. One of the most famous radical black abolitionists was Henry Highland Garnet. David Walker was another.

Frederick Douglass was a black abolitionist.

When Garnet spoke to a meeting of blacks in Buffalo, he shocked many reformers by saying:

Brethern, arise! Arise! Strike for your lives and liberties! Now is the day and hour. Rather die freemen than live to be slaves!

David Walker's call to slaves was contained in a pamphlet called *Walker's Appeal*. It also contained a warning to whites:

Remember, Americans, that we must and shall be free and enlightened as you are. Will you wait until we shall, under God, obtain our liberty by the crushing arm of power? Will it not be dreadful for you?

Sojourner Truth electrified her audiences when she spoke against slavery and for women's rights.

Walker's Appeal was published in 1829. Before the year was out, three editions of it had rolled off the press. Southerners were terrified. Georgia offered $10,000 for Walker taken alive and $1000 for him dead. Southern states made it a crime to pass on copies of the *Appeal*. Then suddenly Walker disappeared. Some said he was murdered. But his death did not stop his words. His *Appeal* was passed from hand to hand in spite of the laws of the southern states.

7. Who was editor of the *North Star*? What causes did he work for?

8. In what ways were Garnet and Walker more radical than other black abolitionists?

Part Three

Women's Rights

How did the Women's Rights Movement get started in America?

Women did not suddenly become aware that they had fewer rights and less freedom than men. They had known that for a long time. Earlier in history some women had complained bitterly about their unjust treatment. You will recall the protests of Abigail Adams, the "she-merchants" of New York City, and the "mill girls" who went on strike in New England. But the efforts to secure rights for women took a new turn in the mid-1800s. In part those efforts grew out of the antislavery crusade. It was through their work against slavery that men and women, white and black, met one another and began to work together. As Angelina Grimké put it, "The investigation of the rights of the slave has led me to a better understanding of my own." Understanding those rights, she and hundreds of others set about trying to obtain them.

Women went about trying to get better treatment in many ways. For example, Emma Willard opened a "female seminary," or school for young women, in 1821. Elizabeth Blackwell demanded and finally won the right to attend medical school. Put down at every turn, she was told that "the only degree you need is the MRS." But she persisted and was given a chance in a small college in Geneva, New York. She graduated and became the first woman doctor in the United States. Then she began helping other young women, including some Indian women, to become doctors. But the real turning point for women's rights came in July 1848, when a convention met at Seneca Falls, New York.

A group of American women had gone to an antislavery meeting in London in 1840. Lucretia Mott and Elizabeth Cady Stanton were among them. But the women were denied admission. Women could watch the meeting, said the English leaders. But they would have to keep silent and sit behind a curtain. Such treatment angered the women. It was time, the women agreed, to go back home and do something about rights for women. They would call a convention. They would draw up their own "declaration of independence," just as the colonies had done.

It took longer than the leaders hoped it would to organize the convention. But at last it met in the little town of Seneca Falls, New York, in July 1848. An unexpectedly large crowd of about 300 appeared, including about 40 men. Frederick Douglass and James Mott, Lucretia's husband and fellow reformer, were among them.

The local newspaper called the meeting "shocking and unnatural." But that barb and others like it did not stop the delegates. They drew up what they called their *Declaration of Sentiments*. It was patterned after the Declaration of Independence. They began by declaring the causes for their actions:

We hold these truths to be self-evident: that all men and women are created equal; that they are endowed by their Creator with certain inalienable rights; that among these are life, liberty, and the pursuit of happiness. . . .

Then they went on to point out that women had never been treated equally. "The history of mankind is a history of repeated injuries . . . on the part of man toward woman," they declared.

They said women were denied the vote, the right to participate in government, the right to hold property. Then they said how they intended to change

Susan B. Anthony and Elizabeth Cady Stanton (seated, second and fourth from left) meet other workers for women's rights in 1888.

Historymaker

Lucretia Mott

Lucretia Mott is sometimes hailed as the "Dean of American Women," because the women's rights movement really began with her. She devoted her own life to working for the causes of women's rights and abolition. But she was also both teacher and inspiration for the generation of women leaders who came after her. One of them, the dynamo Elizabeth Cady Stanton, once was asked to describe her greatest experience. Without hesitation she answered, "Lucretia Mott."

Mott began influencing others early in life. Born a Quaker, she never hesitated to speak in their meetings, even as a child. She began teaching school while she was still a teenager herself. In fact she met and married a fellow teacher, James Mott, when she was just eighteen years old. For almost half a century they worked happily side by side as business partners, parents, and reformers. James was quiet, hard-working, thoughtful. Lucretia was quite different, although her looks belied her real nature. Small, almost frail-looking, she always dressed in somber, starched Quaker-style clothes with a dainty bonnet that tied under her chin. To look at her one would think that she was a kindly, thrifty, timid woman.

She was kindly. Nothing was too much effort for family, friends, or those in need. For them she cooked, washed, ironed, and cleaned. When they were ill, she nursed them back to health. When runaway slaves appeared at her door, she took them in and hid them. When they or other reformers needed a friend in court, Lucretia Mott was there.

She was also thrifty. The Motts were not poor. Together they built a thriving business in cotton. Then, feeling that the sale of cotton helped support slavery, they gave up that business. They started another in wool, and they did well in it. But neither James nor Lucretia used their money to make life more comfortable for themselves. They preferred to use it to support the causes in which they believed. Lucretia wove rags into carpets. Sometimes she even wrote her letters on old scraps of paper.

Was she timid? Let's let three incidents in Lucretia Mott's life speak to that question.

1833. Sixty delegates, both blacks and whites from ten states, have come to Philadelphia to form the American Anti-Slavery Society. The delegates—all men—are busy on the floor. In the balcony are four women who have been invited to be "listeners and spectators." Lucretia Mott is one of them. She is knitting as she listens. But then it begins to appear that the first session of this convention also is apt to be its last session. Some delegates are upset and angry over various words used by William Lloyd Garrison. A leading citizen of Philadelphia has refused to give the opening speech. Delegates suggest that the convention be postponed. At that point, Mrs. Mott puts down her knitting. She rises and from the balcony asks for the floor. All eyes turn to her.

"Gentlemen," she begins. "Right principles are stronger than names. If our principles are right, why should we be cowards?"

There is a burst of applause. The meeting begins without further argument.

During the meeting, Mrs. Mott speaks twice more. As it draws to a close, the delegates are asked to come forward to sign their names to a "Declaration of Sentiments and Purposes." James Mott hesitates. Someone has warned him that he might hurt his business by signing. Lucretia leans over the balcony. She smiles warmly at her husband. Then she urges, "James, put down thy name."

1838. A meeting of the Philadelphia Female Anti-Slavery Society is about to start at the new Philadelphia Hall. Angelina Grimké and Maria Weston Chapman are there. So, too, is Lucretia Mott. In fact, she is presiding as President of the society. The new hall replaces one burned down by a proslavery mob. Some say the city's mayor was involved. The new hall was paid for by contributions.

The meeting begins. Then suddenly the sound of breaking glass is heard. A hooting, howling mob streams through the doors. Some of the intruders rush to the platform and try to drown out the speaker. Others begin to mark up the walls and break the remaining windows. Still others open small bottles of acid and begin splashing it on the audience. Mrs. Mott urges those present to remain calm and in their seats. She continues to lead the meeting. When it becomes clear to the mob that no one is going to flee, the intruders leave and the meeting is completed as planned.

1842. Lucretia and James Mott have just completed a trip through Maryland and Virginia. There they spoke to many audiences about the rights of slaves and women. On the way home, Lucretia decides to stop in Washington, D.C. She says she wants to "speak her mind" not only to some members of Congress, but to President Tyler as well. The President receives her kindly. Soon, however, they get into an argument about slavery. Tyler, a slaveowner himself, says that he favors "colonization." The thing to do, he says, is to ship slaves back to Africa. In fact, Tyler says, the Quakers of Baltimore have just made a similar suggestion. He asks Mrs. Mott if she agrees.

"Indeed, I do not, Mr. President," she responds.

"And why do you object?" asks the President.

"Because," says Mrs. Mott, looking the President straight in the eye, "talk of colonization is just a way of putting the slaveholder's conscience at ease."

things. They would write pamphlets. They would send petitions to lawmakers. They would try to get ministers and newspapers to support them. They would hold more conventions across the country. They said they knew they would be subject to "no small amount" of misunderstanding and ridicule. Time was to prove how right they were. No reform movement ever aroused so much anger. Few reformers ever were subject to the kind of abuse given those who worked for the rights of women.

1. What were some of the injuries to women listed in the Declaration of Sentiments?
2. What means did the Seneca Falls delegates say they would use to obtain women's rights?

How successful was the early movement for women's rights?

Those who worked against slavery saw a final victory for their cause in 1863. In that year slaves were set free. Amendments outlawing slavery were then added to the Constitution. But women did not win such a quick or complete victory. They made some gains, to be sure. More schools were opened to them. Some states revised their divorce laws so that women got better treatment. In 1860, New York gave women the right to sue as well as to control their own wages and property. Women did not win the right to vote until much later. Nor were they able to hold office, serve on juries, or enjoy many other rights. Later in this book we shall learn how and when they did obtain those rights.

Women may not have achieved all they hoped for as quickly as they wished. But the early women's rights movement proved to be an important training ground for future leaders. Lucy Stone, Catherine Beecher, Susan B. Anthony, and many others carried on the work. What they did inspired still another generation of crusaders for equal rights.

3. What gains did the early women's rights movement make?
4. Who were some of the leaders of the women's rights movement?

Part Four

The Temperance Movement

How widespread was interest in the Temperance Movement?

The antislavery movement was not very popular with the general public. Neither was the work for women's rights. But that was not the case with the temperance movement. It was popular in both the South and the North. It had more followers than any reform movement. The efforts of temperance workers won praise from the pulpit and press.

In colonial days alcohol was usually treated as a part of life. Rum was a staple of New England trade, as you know. Soldiers in the American Revolution were given rum, beer, and other spirits as part of their pay. Farmers in the West, you will recall, turned their grain into whiskey. That made it easier to haul to market. Alcohol was used instead of money to buy other goods. Even frontier preachers sometimes were paid with jugs of spirits. Not everyone approved of those uses for alcohol, of course. Some religious groups, the Quakers and the Methodists, for example, did not approve. But the general public did not begin to think about temperance until after the War of 1812. People then began to blame drinking for poverty, crime, disease, and insanity.

In 1813 two organizations were formed to "stamp out" drinking. One was in Massachusetts. The other was in Connecticut. From then on temperance groups began to mushroom. By 1834 there were 5000 or more state and local groups working for that cause. More than a million members, including many children, had taken some sort of a pledge to avoid alcohol.

1. When and how did Americans' attitudes toward alcohol begin to change?

2. How many temperance societies were there? Where were they to be found?

Why did temperance groups become popular?

Many reformers from other causes also worked for temperance. Good speakers such as Frederick Douglass, William Lloyd Garrison, and Susan B. Anthony drew large crowds for temperance meetings. But there was another reason why people flocked to temperance meetings. Leaders in that movement had learned a lot from watching how political parties drew crowds. The temperance leaders used the same means. They put on great picnics and parades. They trained their speakers to use the words of the common people. People who had drinking problems themselves spoke to the crowds about their own battles with alcohol. The meeting would end with a plea for everyone to come forward and sign a pledge. The pledge was to stop drinking—or never to start.

The biggest temperance "hit" was a play. It was called *Ten Nights in a Bar Room and What I Saw There.* In theater after theater it played to packed houses. It was published in 1854 and by 1880 more than 100,000 copies had been sold.

By 1855 thirteen states passed prohibition laws. These laws were called *prohibition* laws because they *prohibited*, or forbade, the making or sale of alcoholic beverages. Later in our history an amendment to the Constitution was passed that prohibited alcohol. We shall read more about that amendment later.

3. What ways of attracting followers did temperance leaders borrow from political parties?

4. What is prohibition?

Children who joined the Cold Water Army pledged never to drink alcoholic beverages.

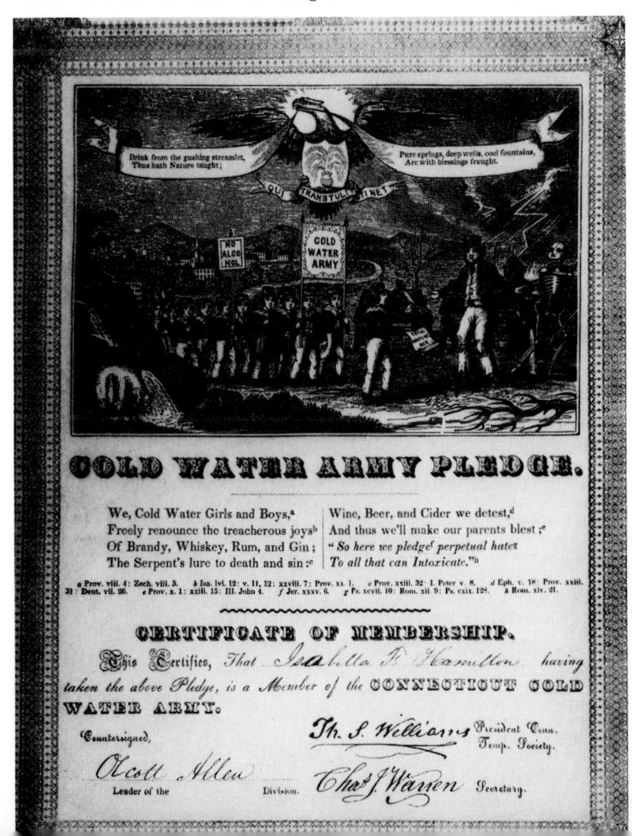

COLD WATER ARMY PLEDGE.

We, Cold Water Girls and Boys,[a]
Freely renounce the treacherous joys[b]
Of Brandy, Whiskey, Rum, and Gin;
The Serpent's lure to death and sin:[c]

Wine, Beer, and Cider we detest,[d]
And thus we'll make our parents blest;[e]
"*So here we pledge[f] perpetual hate[g]*
To all that can Intoxicate."[h]

a Prov. viii. 4: Zech. viii. 5. b Isa. lvi. 12: v. 11, 12: xxviii. 7: Prov. xx. 1. c Prov. xxiii. 32: 1. Peter v. 8. d Eph. v. 18: Prov. xxiii. 31: Deut. vii. 26. e Prov. x. 1: xxiii. 15: III. John 4. f Jer. xxxv. 6. g Ps. xcvii. 10: Rom. xii. 9: Ps. cxix. 128. h Rom. xiv. 21.

CERTIFICATE OF MEMBERSHIP.

This Certifies, That Isabella F. Hamilton having taken the above Pledge, is a Member of the CONNECTICUT COLD WATER ARMY.

Countersigned,

Th. S. Williams President Conn. Temp. Society.

Alcott Allen
Leader of the Division.

Chas. J. Warren Secretary.

Part Five

"Heavens on Earth"

Why did reformers try to build ideal communities?

Some reformers, as you have learned, tried to improve life for people in their communities. But others thought they had a better plan. "Why not leave the troubles and evils of cities behind us? Why not move into the country and build our own society?" they asked.

During the 1800s many did just that. No one knows exactly how many ideal communities were built, but there were at least 100 or more. Despite the high hopes of their founders, none of the groups succeeded for very long.

Some of the first and most successful attempts were those made by a religious group called the "Shakers." They were given that name because of the dances they did as a part of their worship service.

"Mother" Ann Lee founded the Shakers in 1787. It was she who spelled out the rules for Shaker communities. No one could own property; it was to belong to all. Men and women were to be treated as equals and live together as "brothers and sisters." Marriage was not permitted. All had to promise to work hard and to live by the highest moral standards.

The Shakers reached their height in the 1830s. They had about 6000 members. There were eighteen communities. Those settlements were scattered across New York, New England, and the states of the Ohio River Valley.

Another attempt to build "heaven on earth" was made by Robert Owen and his son. In 1825 they founded New Harmony in the woods of Indiana. Owen thought that people's characters are formed by the kind of environment in which they live. So he tried to provide an ideal climate. He insisted that all should have the right of free speech and equal opportunity to work. Like the Shakers, Owen did not believe in private ownership of property.

New Harmony had troubles right from the start. When it opened it had over 800 members, but housing for only 700. Some who came to the community were bright, hard-working people who were willing to share and to work with others. But most were not. Owen was not equal to the task of running his "model community." Two years after it began, New Harmony had to be disbanded.

Perhaps the best known of the would-be "heavens on earth" was Brook Farm. It, too, had a short life span. Brook Farm never had more than 100 members. They lived on 200 acres (80 ha) in Massachusetts. They pledged to work with both their heads and their hands. The members were artists, writers, musicians, and teachers. But they were also supposed to be farmers. And that is where the trouble came. The newspaper they wrote and the schools they set up did well. So, too, did the weeds. But their crops failed. Just five years after Brook Farm opened its doors, it had to close them. Nathaniel Hawthorne, a famous writer, was one of the first members. His novel, *The Blithedale Romance*, is based on Brook Farm.

1. Why did New Harmony and Brook Farm fail quickly?

The Shakers believed in a life of simplicity and order. Their arts and crafts, architecture, and labor-saving inventions are unique. Above left is an inspirational drawing. Drawings like these were given as gifts by Shakers. Above right Shaker women use a pile driver to build a bridge. Below is a hall in a Shaker dwelling. Chairs, like clothes, were hung on pegs when not in use. Shakers used so many pegs that they developed ways to mass-produce them.

Part Six

Concern for Life's Forgotten People

Who were the "forgotten people" of the 1800s?

While some reform movements were drawing crowds and getting headlines, others were quietly making great strides. The quiet movements helped life's forgotten people. They worked for the mentally ill, the blind, the deaf, and the orphans.

Almost singlehandedly Dorothea Dix changed the attitudes of Americans about the mentally ill. A small, frail woman who seldom raised her voice, she volunteered to teach a Sunday school class in a Massachusetts jail. The conditions she saw there shocked her. People who had committed no crimes, but who were mentally ill, were locked in a cold, crowded room. No attempts to cure their illnesses were being made. Dix decided to see if mentally ill people were as badly treated in other jails and institutions. So she began a tour of inspection on her own that lasted for eighteen months. She visited every single prison, workhouse, poorhouse, and insane "asylum" in Massachusetts. When she was through, she wrote out her findings and presented them to the state legislature. Her report was a blockbuster. She described people locked "in cages, closets, cellars, stalls, . . . beaten with rods, and lashed into obedience!" Some legislators refused to believe that things could be that bad, particularly in the insane asylums. They went to see for themselves. They learned that Dix had not exaggerated. So the legislature voted funds to build hospitals for the mentally ill.

Dorothea Dix worked to improve life for the mentally ill.

Not content, Dorothea Dix went into other states. She worked for fifty years, never drawing so much as a dollar for her work. She never accepted a single public honor. Her work was her reward. In 1840 there were just thirteen institutions for the mentally ill in the United States. There, patients were chained to beds and chairs, or bound in handcuffs. No effort was made to cure them. By 1880, there were more than 123 hospitals for the mentally ill. No longer were they just locked away. Efforts were being made to help them recover and return to their homes and communities.

While Dorothea Dix worked for the mentally ill, Thomas Gallaudet (gal ō dā′) devoted his life to helping the deaf. He went to Europe to study the methods used there to teach the handicapped. When he returned, he set up the first American free school for the deaf in Hartford, Connecticut. It became a model for the nation. His son, Edward, followed in his footsteps. Edward went to

Focus on Skills

Select one of the reformers below. Prepare a short illustrated talk that will answer these questions: (1) How did he/she become interested in the cause? (2) How did the person try to win others to the cause? (3) Who were the friends and enemies of the reform? (4) How and why is this person remembered today? Illustrate each question with a comic-strip-style sketch (stick figures will do). For example, the first drawing should show why or how the reformer became interested in the cause. Ask your teacher or librarian if you need help in finding reading material for your research.

Topics for Research

Reformer	*Cause or Causes for Which He or She Worked*
Susan B. Anthony	Women's rights, temperance, abolition
Henry Barnard	Education
Catherine E. Beecher	Education for women/girls
Henry Ward Beecher	Abolition
Lyman Beecher	Temperance
Elizabeth Blackwell	Education for women, women's rights
Charles Loring Brace	Child welfare
Lydia Maria Child	Abolition
Dorothea Dix	Mentally ill, prison reform
Frederick Douglass	Abolition, women's rights, temperance
Thomas Gallaudet	Education for deaf
Edward M. Gallaudet	Education for deaf
William Lloyd Garrison	Abolition, women's rights, Indian rights
The Grimkés: Angelina, Sarah, and Thomas	Abolition, women's rights
Frances E. W. Harper	Abolition, women's rights
Thomas Gridley Howe	Education for the blind
Elijah Lovejoy	Abolition
Edward Livingstone	Prison reform
Horace Mann	Education, mentally ill
Lucretia Coffin Mott	Abolition, women's rights
Robert and Robert Dale Owen (father/son)	Model community
Elizabeth Cady Stanton	Women's rights, abolition
Lucy Stone	Women's rights, abolition
Sojourner Truth	Abolition, women's rights
Harriet Tubman	Abolition
David Walker	Abolition
Theodore Weld	Abolition, women's rights
Emma Willard	Education for women

Two famous students at the Perkins Institute were Helen Keller (left) and her teacher Anne Sullivan Macy.

Washington, D.C., as head of a school for the deaf. Later its name was changed to Gallaudet College in honor of the father-son reformer team. Today it is the world's only institution offering higher education for the deaf.

"Every creature in human shape should command our respect," wrote Samuel Gridley Howe. "The strong should help the weak. . . ." Howe did more than write those words. He lived them. For 44 years Howe directed the Perkins Institute in Boston. There he trained teachers of the blind in new methods which he had developed. His methods drew high praise from Charles Dickens, the great English writer. Although he found little to admire in the United States, Dickens did say that he thought Howe's system should be copied all over the world.

1. How did Dorothea Dix help the mentally ill?

2. In what ways did the Gallaudets and Samuel Gridley Howe help the deaf and the blind?

What efforts were made to help orphans and homeless children?

There were many orphans and homeless children in the United States in the 1800s. President Andrew Jackson had spent some years in an orphanage. But he was more fortunate than many orphans. They often had no place to go. Charles Loring Brace described their lives:

> **For the most part, [they] grow up utterly by themselves. No one cares for them, and they care for no one. Some live by betting, by petty pilferings [shoplifting], by bold robbery. Some earn an honest support by peddling matches, or apples, or newspapers. . . . They sleep on steps, in cellars, in old barns, and in markets. . . . They cannot read. They do not go to school or attend a church. . . .**

Charles Loring Brace, "First Circular of the Children's Aid Society," in *The Life of Charles Loring Brace*, Edited by His Daughter (New York, 1894), pp. 489-92. Quoted in Henry Steele Commager, *The Era of Reform, 1830-1860* (Princeton, N.J.: D. Van Nostrand Company, 1960), p. 163.

Brace had trained for the ministry. But when he saw the lives of New York City orphans, he decided to devote his life to working with homeless children. He interested others in his project. They founded the Children's Aid Society of New York in 1853. The Society established rooming houses and summer camps, and it worked in other ways to protect homeless young people. It became a model for similar societies which sprang up elsewhere.

3. How did the Children's Aid Society help homeless young people?

Building Your Vocabulary

Which word or phrase shown on the right best explains the meaning of the word in italics on the left?

1. *reform*	to bring about peaceful change	to overthrow
2. *abolish*	do away with	preserve
3. *autobiography*	life story written by one's self	life story written by someone else
4. *prohibition*	forbids completely	allows
5. *asylum*	meetinghouse	a shelter or place for the sick
6. *radical*	wants complete change	wants no change

Recalling What You Have Learned

Select the correct word or phrase for each of the following questions.

1. Which of the following things did most reformers have in common? (a) They came from the middle class. (b) They believed they had a special calling. (c) They were interested in more than one cause. (d) All of the above.
2. Which of the following was not an abolitionist? (a) William Lloyd Garrison (b) Frederick Douglass (c) Angelina Grimké (d) Andrew Jackson
3. Where was the first women's rights convention held in America? (a) New York City (b) Seneca Falls, New York (c) New Orleans (d) Boston
4. After which of these American documents did women pattern their Declaration of Sentiments? (a) The Constitution (b) The Bill of Rights (c) "The Star Spangled Banner" (d) The Declaration of Independence
5. The temperance movement became the most popular reform movement of the middle 1800s because (a) many people were convinced that drinking had become a problem. (b) churches favored temperance. (c) temperance leaders borrowed crowd-pleasing ideas from political campaigns. (d) all of the above.
6. Which of the following was not a model community? (a) New Harmony (b) New Hampshire (c) Brook Farm
7. Who is remembered for work on behalf of the mentally ill? (a) David Walker (b) Edward Livingstone (c) Sojourner Truth (d) Dorothea Dix
8. Who was the leader in founding the Children's Aid Society of New York in 1853? (a) William Wells Brown (b) Charles Loring Brace (c) Elizabeth Cady Stanton (d) Emma Willard

Discussing the Important Ideas in This Chapter

1. Reformers usually thought of themselves as "special people" called upon to right certain wrongs. Do you agree?
2. Why do you think that reformers often worked for several causes?
3. What are three possible explanations for the great interest in reform in the United States between 1815 and 1860?
4. Why do you think more people opposed the women's rights movement than any other reform proposed during the 1800s?

5. Why do you think the temperance movement was more popular than any other reform?
6. None of the 100 or more model communities established during the 1800s lasted for very long. What possible explanations might there be for their failure?
7. Compare the problems which some children face today with those described in this chapter which some children of the 1800s had to face.

Improving Your Graph Skills

The graph here is a circle graph. Circle graphs are used to show how the parts of something relate to the whole. Circle graphs are most often used to show percentages. The whole circle represents 100 percent. Study the graph and answer the following questions:

1. What does the whole circle represent?
2. What type of work did over half of all the workers in the United States do in 1850?
3. What percentage of American workers were employed in agriculture and manufacturing in 1850?
4. Was the transportation industry very large in 1850?
5. Another way to look at the labor force in 1850 is to compare the number of free workers to the number of slaves. In 1850, 78 percent of American workers were free. Slaves made up 22 percent of the work force. Draw a circle graph showing this information.

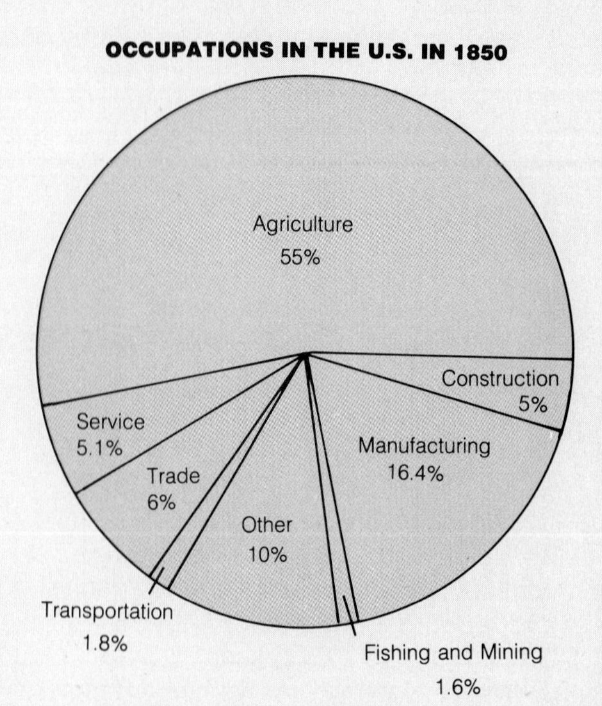

Improving Your Study Skills: *Writing*

Imagine that you were living while all of the reform movements described in this chapter were taking place. Write a letter to the editor of your hometown newspaper. In it explain why you support or oppose a particular reform. In your letter you might:

1. Offer additional facts.
2. Point out why the reform would save—or cost—the taxpayers money.
3. Discuss why the reform would make your community a better—or a worse—place in which to live.

Your letter should not be more than two or three paragraphs long.

Chapter 10

The United States Reaches the Pacific

The Alamo, San Antonio, Texas

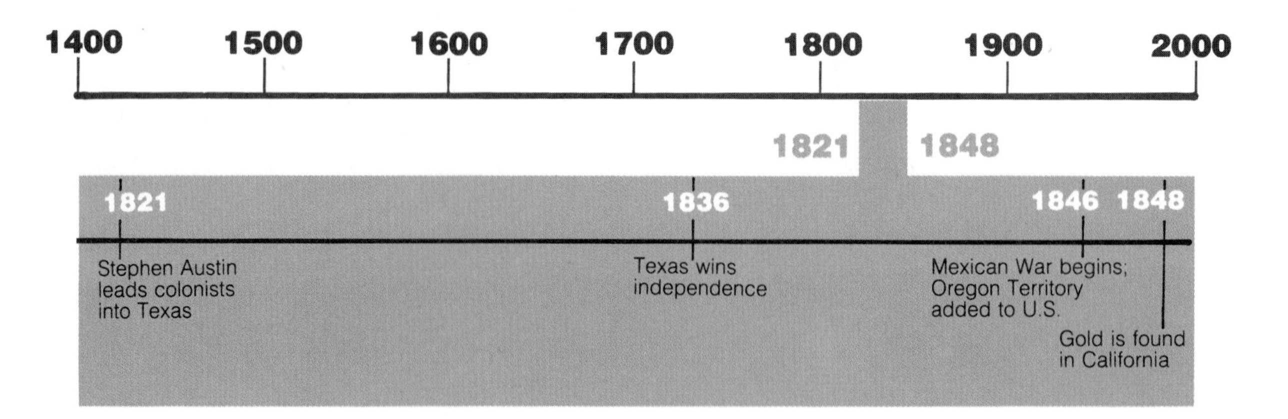

Part One

Americans Keep Moving West

Why did people keep moving west?

In the 1800s many forces pushed and pulled Americans west. But not everyone wanted to pioneer. Many Americans were content in the places which they first called home. They watched their farms prosper and their businesses grow. They took pride in the schools and churches which dotted the landscape. They enjoyed the new transportation systems which were springing up. Why give up all of those things?

Other Americans were more restless. They were eager to move west. They were willing to give up all the comforts of a settled life. They wanted to make a new start. Sometimes they moved west not just once, but two or three times. Just why they did is not always easy to understand. Moving west was anything but easy. The diaries and letters of pioneers show that. Look at these fairly typical reports.

Wolves and panthers were destructive to our stock [cattle and sheep]. I have carried a gun on more than one occasion to assist the killing of wolves that were after our stock. I was chased by a panther

nearly a mile, taking refuge in an old cabin. When just having closed the door, it sprang upon the roof, and I had to remain there all night.

From an 11-year-old girl's letter, 1822.

Elizabeth Clemmon Smith (at age 11 she migrated with her parents from North Carolina to Pike County, Ill.) in folio "Stories of the Pioneer Mothers of Illinois," Illinois State Historical Library, Springfield, Ill. Quoted in William Forrest Sprague, *Women and the West: A Short Social History* (Boston: Christopher Publishing House, 1940), p. 43.

Our ignorance of the route was complete. We knew that California lay west, and that was the extent of our knowledge. . . .When we killed our last ox, we shot and ate crows or anything we could kill. One man shot a wildcat. We could eat anything. . . . Of course sleep was impossible, for I had neither blanket nor coat, and burned or froze alternately as I turned from one side to the other before the small fire which I had built. . . .

From the writings of John Bidwell en route to California, 1841.

John Bidwell, *Echoes of the Past about California* (Chicago: R.R. Donnelley, 1928).

The first [person] I conversed with was from Jersey, out 32 days. She was sitting upon a log which served for the double purpose of a seat and a fire. Their wagon had broken down the day before. Her husband was with it at a distant blacksmith's. She had been seated there all night. Her last words went to my heart. "Ah, Sir, I wish to God we had never left home!"

From the diary of a British traveler in the region east of Pittsburgh, 1817.

H. B. Fearon, *Sketches of America* (London, 1818), pp. 189-195. Quoted in Sprague, *Women and the West*, pp. 33-34.

Despite hardships such as those just described, few pioneers went back home. They kept moving west. And, as the century wore on, more and more people followed in their footsteps. Some crossed the continent hoping to "get rich quick." They took wild risks trying to make their fortunes. But most pioneers dreamed of land which they could call their own. They dreamed of better lives, especially for their children. To those people the frontier meant promise.

In this chapter we will meet many pioneers. Their lives are a part of the story of how the United States finally reached the Pacific.

1. Why were many Americans content to remain in the communities they first called home?

2. What were people looking for in the West?

In what ways were those who moved west alike?

It is difficult to generalize about the kinds of people who migrated, or moved, west. But the records do point to some likenesses.

Many pioneers had not done well in older communities, often through no fault of their own. Some could not farm the poor soil of New England. Others were crowded out of the South as huge slave plantations spread farther inland. Still others were immigrants from overpopulated countries in Europe and Asia. So the pioneers were usually poor. Most were farmers. More moved west in good times than in times of depression.

You probably have heard the old slogan, "Go West, young man, go West!" Research shows that young men took the advice. Pioneers were very likely to be young and male, especially if they moved to the Northwest. More women moved to the Southwest. Men outnumbered women in both sections.

A pioneer family stops for rest. They are dirty and tired, but their faces show the courage and determination needed to make the hard trip west.

But pioneers to both sections tended to be young.

Although fewer elderly people moved west, more made the trip than most people realize. They were more likely to travel with groups than alone.

Diaries kept by people trekking to Oregon note the presence of a number of elderly people. There was "one old man, with silver hair" who walked beside a covered wagon. He and the others in the party "were all clean and evidently [dressed] in their best Sunday gear." Another older pioneer, Alexander McClellan, died a hero's death. The small boat in which he, two young men, and three boys were traveling overturned in the rapids. Seventy-year-old McClellan dove into the swirling waters in a vain effort to save one of the boys.

The pioneers came from many different ethnic groups. Most of them were white, but many blacks also went west. Those blacks who moved into the northern back country usually were free. Those who moved into the southern backwoods more often were slaves. They were marched into the wilderness to clear land and set up new plantations.

3. In what ways were those who moved west alike?

Where is the "moving frontier"?

Where the known meets the unknown—where a settled way of life touches the wilderness—that is where the frontier is. Throughout the history of the United States there have been many frontiers. As Americans moved, so did the frontier. (See chart, page 249.) Even today, the United States has frontiers. Pioneers are forging new ways of life on the frozen slopes in northern Alaska. The known and the unknown meet in space and under the oceans. Tomorrow's citizens will map, explore, mine, and live on the new frontiers. Uncharted skies and oceans call to Americans just the way the West did.

4. Where is the frontier?

5. Why does the frontier "move" or keep changing?

WHERE WAS THE AMERICAN FRONTIER?
(See also map on page 267.)

FRONTIER AND DATE OF SETTLEMENT	LOCATION OF FRONTIER	HOW THE FRONTIER WAS SETTLED
First or Colonial 1607–1763	Land between the Appalachians and Atlantic from Maine to Florida.	Settlers moved inland, fighting Indians for land; settlers moved into the back country and river and mountain valleys.
Appalachian 1763–1812	Headwaters of coastal rivers and just over Appalachian Mountains.	Just before and right after the American Revolution, settlers poured through the Mountains into Tennessee, Kentucky, Ohio, and Illinois. Settlers fought with Indians and the English.
Mississippi and Ohio Valleys 1812–1840	Lands watered by two great rivers—Ohio and Mississippi. (In the north, Ohio, Indiana, Illinois, Michigan, Wisconsin. In the south, Alabama, Mississippi, Louisiana, Missouri, Kentucky, Tennessee, and Arkansas.)	Pioneering here began to bring about two different ways of life: A northern way based on free labor, and a southern way that included slave labor. Trouble between the two ways of life grew.
Far Western 1825–1865	Texas, California, Oregon, and other far western lands.	Added to United States during time of Manifest Destiny. War with Mexico added thousands of square miles of territory.
"Last" Frontier 1865–1900	Great Plains and Rocky Mountain regions.	Few settlers here until after Civil War. Many thought these treeless plains and mountains were "The Great American Desert." Coming of the railroads and farm machinery and end of wars with Indians made settlements possible.

What patterns did people follow as they went west?

Not every frontier was settled in the same way. But usually people went west in "waves," or patterns something like this:

1. First came hunters and trappers. They spied out the riches on the frontier and brought back news of their findings. To survive, hunters and trappers had to be good with ax, rifle, snare, and fishing line. Mainly, they were rough, strong, unmarried men who blazed trails for the next wave to follow.

Jedediah Smith was one of the most famous trappers. He was one of the so-called "mountain men." Smith was the first person known to reach California by an overland route. But not many of us would want that honor if we had to do

A large caravan of trappers heads West. Why do you think they are traveling together?

A town, a valley, a mountain peak, and the pass he discovered all are named for James Beckwourth.

what Smith did. In 1826 he tackled the unexplored deserts of present-day Nevada and Arizona. He blazed a trail to southern California.

For practice, Smith had already explored and trapped in northern Utah and around the Great Salt Lake. Once a grizzly bear attacked him. The bear got Smith's head inside its giant jaws. An ear and part of Smith's scalp were left hanging from his bleeding skull. One of Smith's men pulled out needle and thread. He stitched up the battered trapper, and they were off again.

Even though Smith was an expert scout, the trip across the deserts of the Southwest to California was not easy. Food and water were in short supply. But Indian attacks, heat, and rattlesnakes were plentiful.

The Mexicans who owned California were not glad to see the 28-year-old trapper and his party. When Smith asked permission to trap, he was thrown in jail as a spy. Some Boston shipmasters visiting California helped free him.

Smith went to northern California and continued to trap. In the spring of 1827, he and two other men made the first crossing of the great Sierra Nevada, a mountain range.

Nothing kept Jedediah Smith from crossing and recrossing the mountains he loved. The trails he blazed opened the way for thousands to get to California. Smith opened more new paths and made

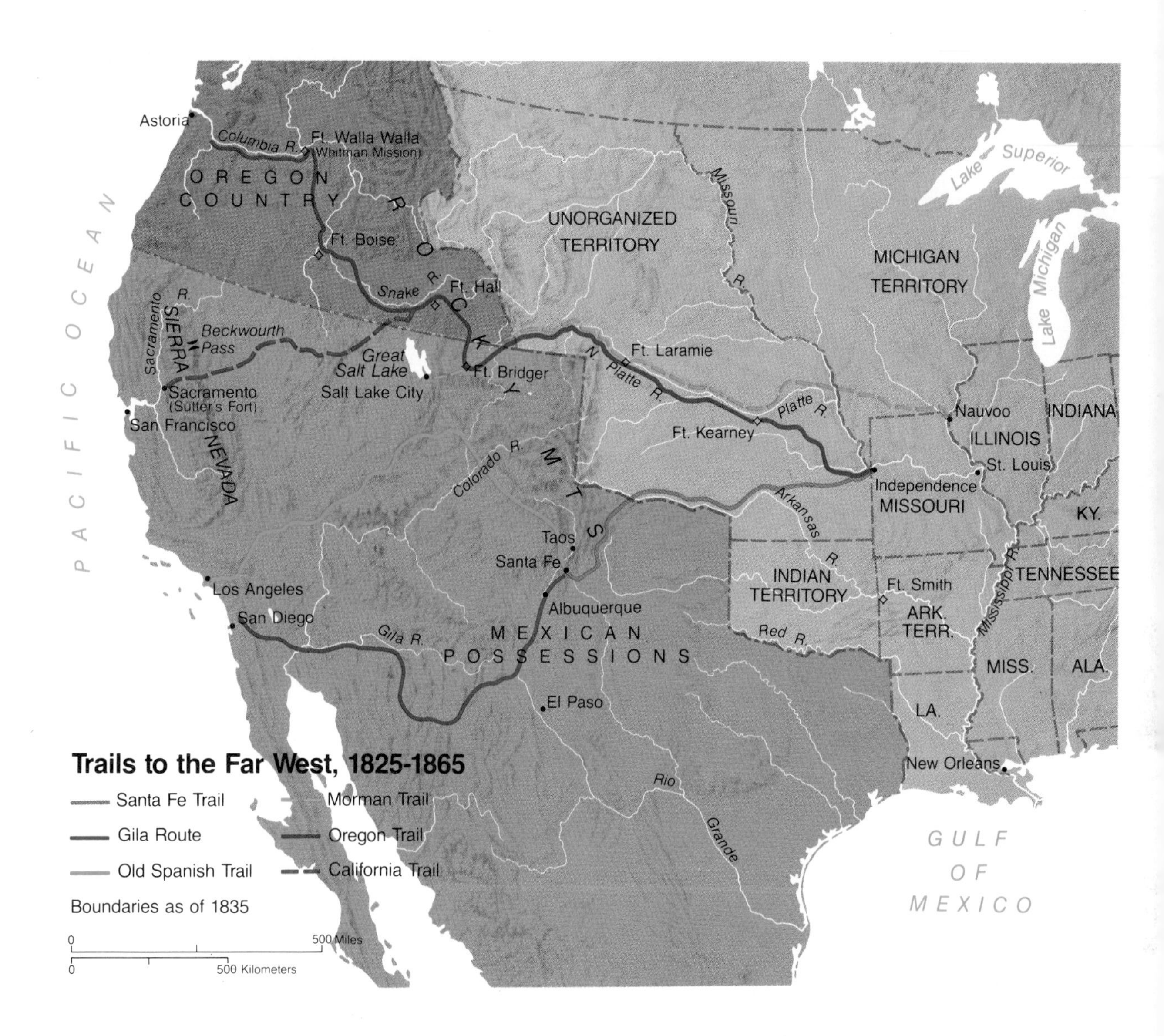

longer journeys of western exploration than anyone since Lewis and Clark.

Another famous "mountain man" was James Beckwourth. At age 19, he ran away from slavery in St. Louis. He headed west and learned to live by his wits and his courage. With his bowie knife, hatchet, and gun, Beckwourth became one of the most famous fighters of his time. He was named chief by the Crow Indian nation. The Crow gave him a new name, "Morning Star."

In April 1850, Beckwourth found a pass through the Sierra Nevada. The pass—named for him—became an important gateway into California during the Gold Rush.

2. Miners came on the heels of the trappers. They searched for gold and other precious metals, just as people had been doing ever since Columbus arrived.

Most miners were men, although a few women also set out to "make a

Trappers unload their pelts at a compound near present-day Council Bluffs, Iowa.

strike." Miners went to an area to take out everything of value as quickly as they could. Then when all of the lead, gold, or silver was gone, they moved on. Behind them they often left "ghostly" reminders of once lively towns.

3. Next came those who raised cattle and sheep. Modern television has made people think that there was open range only in the Far West. That is not true. Cattle raisers have always looked for open grasslands unfenced by farmers. Before the American Revolution, cattle raisers fattened their animals on the frontiers of Virginia, the Carolinas, and Massachusetts. Later they drove their stock onto the prairies of Illinois. Each time civilization pushed west, ranchers had to move on.

The first three groups to come onto the frontier seldom had much effect on the wilderness. They moved west to "skim off" surface wealth, be it furs, minerals, or grasslands. Then they, too, moved on. Permanent settlers came in the last "waves" to reach the frontier.

6. What three groups usually moved onto the frontier first?

7. Why did those groups have little lasting effect on the wilderness?

Who became the permanent settlers?

Soon, others followed trails marked by trappers, miners, and cattle raisers.

Usually the "pioneer farmer," or "squatter," came first. Squatters did not bother to buy land. They built rough cabins and made small clearings where they chose. Life was hard for these people, but they had the kind of toughness it took to tame the wilderness. These pioneer farmers refused to be beaten by the forces of nature or other humans.

Along with the "squatters" came "equipped farmers." These people had the necessary tools and equipment to settle down and make a living.

In the Southeast, rich families who moved west sometimes sent out an advance party. When workers, slaves, and overseers got a comfortable home set up, the family followed.

In the Northwest, "equipped farmers" moved onto land they had bought. They cleared forests, pulled out tree stumps, built frame houses, and fenced their lands. Then they set about building roads. Lawyers, doctors, preachers, and merchants followed as soon as they saw settlements growing. With the services these people provided, the frontier became a settled area.

8. How was the "squatter" different from the "equipped farmer"?

9. When did the frontier become a settled area?

Part Two

Americans and the War for Texas Independence

Why were Americans encouraged to come to Texas?

What is now the state of Texas once was a part of the Spanish Empire. So, too, was Mexico. But in 1821, Mexico won its independence from Spain.

In the northeastern part of Mexico lay a vast, rich, unpopulated area, known as Texas. (See map, page 254.) The Mexican government wanted settlers to develop that territory, so it invited some carefully chosen Americans to move in. Moses Austin, a pioneer miner in Missouri, agreed to select 300 hard-working families who would make their permanent homes in Texas. The Mexican government promised them some of the richest land in Texas. Moses died before the contract was carried out. His son, Stephen, was left to fill it.

The Americans who moved to Texas loved it. They could not hide the good news about what a wonderful place it was. For example, here is a part of a letter which a certain Dr. Hoxey wrote to a friend in Georgia:

Cole's Settlement, Texas
April 2, 1834

Dear Sir:

It affords me great pleasure to be able to inform you that all my . . . notions about Texas are . . . far exceeded. . . . I have receive[d]. . . $30,000 dollars profit on my investments. . . . The weeds grow 20 feet

When this lithograph was made in 1840, Austin had been the capital of the Republic of Texas for four years. The white house on the hill belonged to President of Texas Mirabeau Lamar. The capital building (center left) was stockaded for defense.

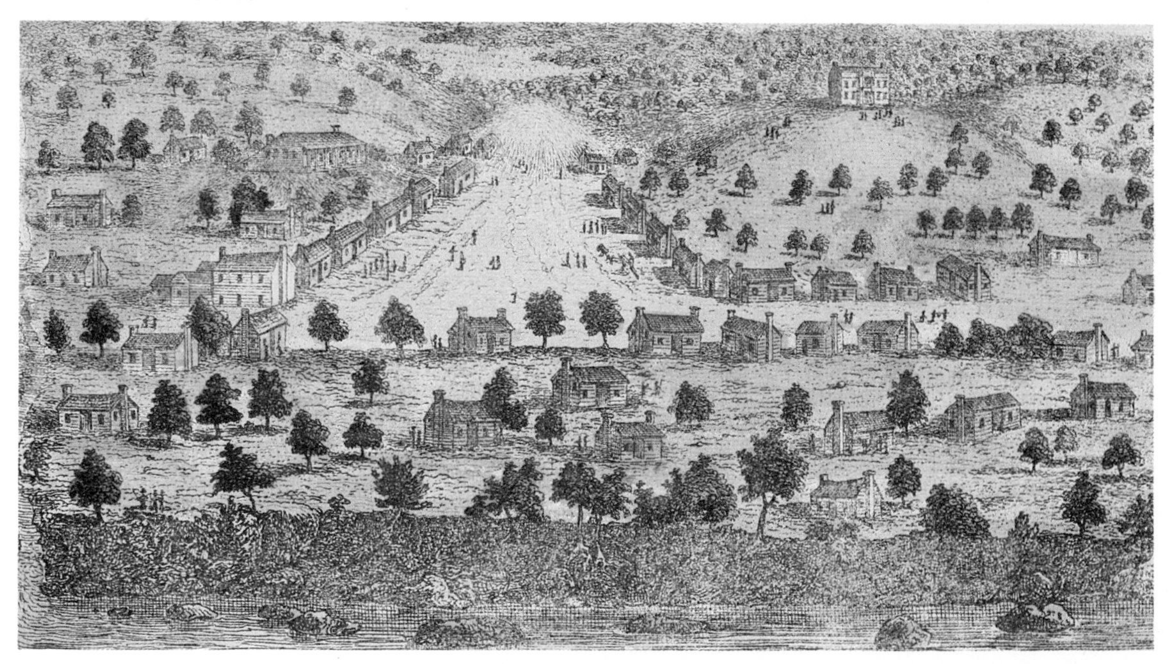

[6.1 m] high, but there is no trouble to clear the land. . . . The soil of this land is at least 50 feet [15.2 m] thick. . . . Texas is the easiest country in the World for a farmer to live in. . . . My mules and horses, although they have worked hard all the winter and spring, are very fat. . . . We have no taxes or any duties to pay, and hence want no better government.

As the news about Texas spread, more and more Americans poured in. In a few years time there were 20,000 of them, including several thousand slaves.

Then the Mexican government decided to close its gates to new settlers. It was angry that many of the newcomers refused to live up to the terms Mexico had set. For one thing, some Americans brought slaves with them, even though slavery was forbidden. Although the settlers had promised to become Catholics, few settlers actually did so. Finally, and most galling to the Mexicans, many of the Texas settlers seemed to look down upon the newly independent, proud Mexican nation. The settlers still considered themselves Americans.

Things came to a head in 1835. Mexico's President General Antonio López de Santa Anna swept away the freedoms guaranteed Texans by the Mexican Constitution.

1. Who were Moses and Stephen Austin?

2. Why did Mexicans and settlers become angry with one another?

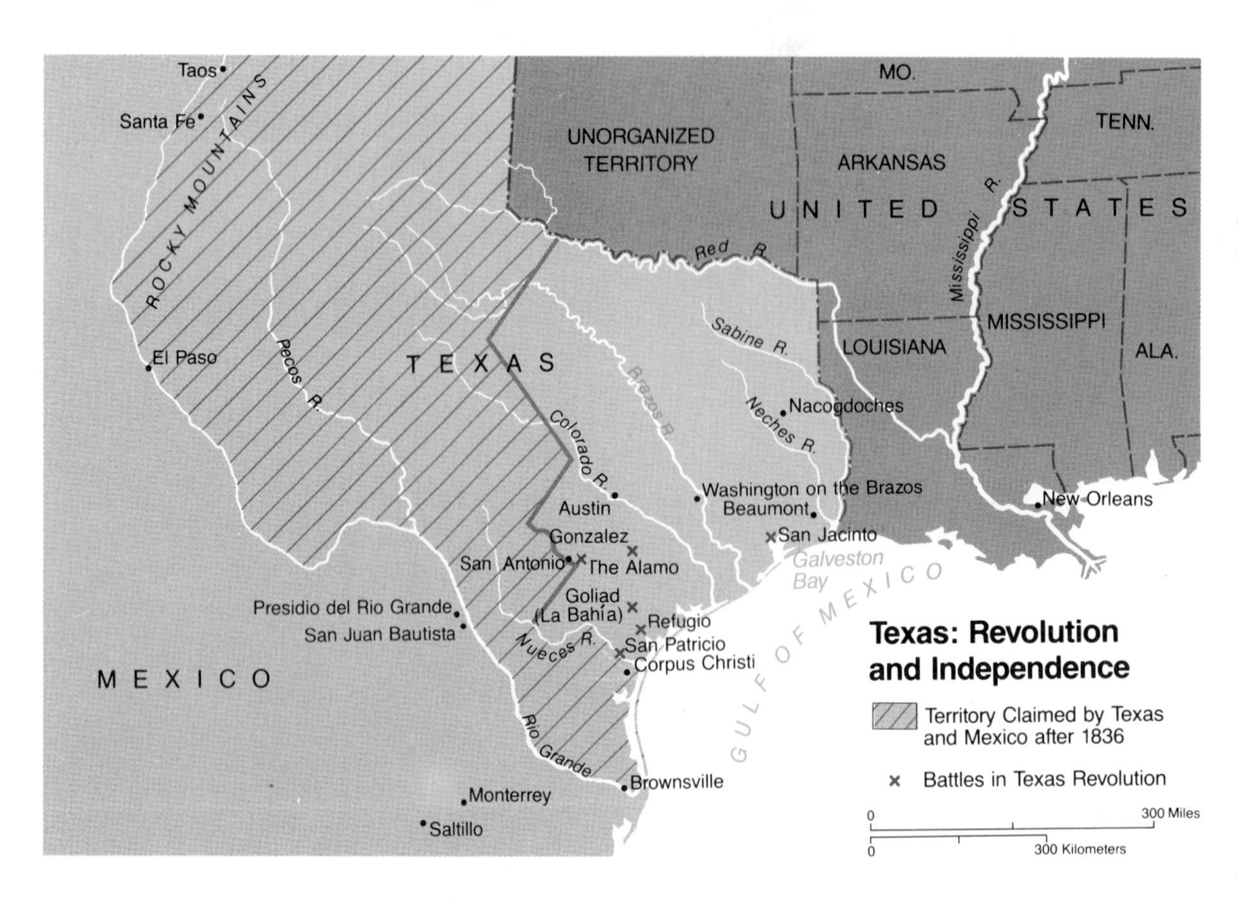

Texas: Revolution and Independence

James (Jim) Bowie fought in several skirmishes for Texas independence before he died at the Alamo.

Houston learned of the disaster at the Alamo from Susanna Dickinson, who survived the siege.

How did Texas become independent?

For some time the Texans had been threatening to set up a government of their own. They carried out that threat in 1836. Proclaiming themselves the independent Republic of Texas, they elected David Burnet as President and Lorenzo de Zavala as Vice-President. They unfurled the Lone Star flag.

Santa Anna led a Mexican army of several thousand men north to San Antonio. There he laid siege to the Alamo, an old mission building held by 187 Americans. William B. Travis was the senior officer at the Alamo. He sent a message to the people of Texas and all Americans saying, "I shall never surrender or retreat." Santa Anna stormed the Alamo and killed every defender. One of the victims was Davy Crockett, the American frontier hero. Another was James Bowie, inventor of the long and deadly bowie knife.

Then Santa Anna, who liked to think of himself as the "Napoleon of the West," turned and swept eastward. The whole American population fled before him toward the Sabine River, which then marked the border between the United States and Mexico. But in April 1836, on the San Jacinto River near the present city of Houston, the defenders of the Lone Star Republic turned the tide. They were led by Sam Houston, an experienced soldier who had served with Andrew Jackson. Houston caught the Mexicans off guard. Yelling "Remember the Alamo!" the Texans won a smashing victory.

Santa Anna was found in the tall grass near the San Jacinto battlefield. With bowie knives (sometimes called Arkansas toothpicks) held over his head, Santa Anna signed treaties giving Texas independence. Later he said the treaties were no good since he had been forced to sign them. But Texas was free. Texans then asked to join the United States.

3. When did the Texans declare independence?

4. What happened at the Alamo? At San Jacinto?

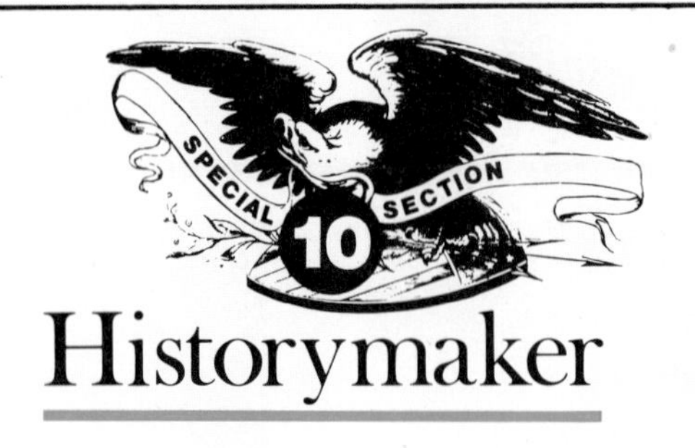

Historymaker

Member of Congress
Governor of Tennessee
Commander of a victorious army
President of the Republic of Texas
United States Senator
Governor of Texas

Sam Houston

Sam Houston won that grand list of titles in his time. One might think his life was nothing but honors, one heaped upon another. But that was not the case. He was a complex, colorful man. He led a stormy life. He failed in the two things he most wanted—to secure better treatment for the Indians and to prevent the Civil War. His great courage was not understood until after he died.

Houston was born in Virginia. His father did not manage money very well. When he died, he left his family poor. Luckily, Sam's mother was equal to the task of rearing nine children. She packed them up and moved to the east Tennessee frontier. There she bought 400 acres (160 ha). She built a home, and put the children to work clearing and planting the new farm.

Sam did not like farm work. Nor did he like clerking in the local store. He tried that for a year. He envied the life of the Cherokee who lived in the forest nearby. One day, when he was just 15 years old, he ran away to join them. His worried mother and brothers searched everywhere for him.

Three years later he returned home. His mother hardly recognized him. The Cherokees had given him a new name. They called him "The Raven." He had adopted their clothes and lifestyle. For the rest of his life, Sam Houston was a rarity on the frontier. He was a true friend of the Indians. He respected them and worked for their rights.

Sam was 24 years old when the War of 1812 came along. He served in the Tennessee militia under Andrew Jackson. He became Jackson's friend and loyal follower. After the war, everything seemed to go right for Houston. He studied law, completing an eighteen-month course in just six. Then one after another, he became a district attorney, member of the United States Congress, and governor of Tennessee. Just before taking over as governor, he married the daughter of one of the richest and best known families in the state. There was talk of "Houston for President." But as quickly as things had gone up for Houston, they came crashing down. His bride left him. He resigned as governor. He went back to live among the Cherokee.

For the next six years Houston remained with the Cherokee; out of touch with all his old political friends. But he did act as the Cherokee's lawyer. Once a year he made a trip on their behalf to Washington, D.C. The Cherokee had formally made him a member of their tribe. He dressed in Indian clothes and resumed the name "The Raven."

In 1832 his old friend, now President Andrew Jackson, asked Houston to go to Texas for him. Jackson said he needed someone to make a treaty with the Comanches. He knew "The Raven" was the man for the job. Houston not only went to Texas. He decided to stay there. From then on his life was bound up in Texas.

When the Texans revolted against Mexico, Houston was chosen as head of the army. Then the army was just 743 raw recruits. They were no match for the 3000 Mexican soldiers led by Santa Anna. Santa Anna's men crushed the Texans defending the Alamo. Three weeks later the Mexican army wiped out an entire garrison at Goliad. Then the Mexicans pushed on to Galveston Bay. It seemed that the war for independence was lost. But Houston did not give up! He launched a surprise attack at San Jacinto. Fifteen minutes later the battle was over. The Texans were victorious. Santa Anna was their captive.

Once again honors were piled on Houston. Grateful Texans made him their first President. And they re-elected him. When Texas became part of the United States, they chose Houston as one of their senators. Then they asked him to come back to Texas and serve as governor. But once again, things went wrong.

The North and South were pulling apart, as you know. There was talk of the slave states leaving the Union, and Texas was a slave state. But Houston did not, would not, and could not agree to break up the Union.

When people said that as a Southerner Houston should stand by the South, Houston responded, "I know neither North nor South: I know only the Union."

Texas did decide to withdraw from the Union. Houston then was 70 years old and serving once again as governor. Because he refused to support that decision, he was forced to resign. As he did, he wrote these, his last words as governor: "I love Texas too well to bring civil strife and bloodshed upon her. . . ."

Not long after he wrote these words, Houston died. But today his memory lives in honor throughout the state and the nation he loved and served so well.

Sarah Childress Polk carried this fan at her husband's inauguration. It has portraits of all the Presidents who preceded Polk, the eleventh President of the United States.

Why did the United States hesitate to admit Texas as a state?

Texans and Southerners wanted the Lone Star Republic welcomed into the Union. But antislavery people in the North were opposed. Texas was big, and it permitted slavery. Northerners were against any further spread of slavery in the United States.

Meanwhile, Britain encouraged Texas to remain independent. The British loaned Texas money, and trade between the two countries was brisk. British abolitionists tried to get Texas to forbid slavery. These moves by Britain made the southern states demand that Texas be brought into the Union. The southern states were afraid that Britain might take over Texas.

But Andrew Jackson and the Presidents who followed him were still afraid to take the step. President Santa Anna of Mexico warned that if Texas joined the Union, his country would go to war with the United States.

For almost ten years, Texas remained a republic. Americans simply could not make up their minds what to do about the problem. Then almost by accident the country elected a President who was determined to bring Texas into the Union. President James K. Polk was a man of action from Tennessee.

5. Why did the North oppose adding Texas to the Union?
6. What was Santa Anna's warning?

Part Three

The American Flag Waves over Texas and Oregon

Why was James K. Polk's election as President important?

In 1844, Henry Clay and former President Van Buren were the leading candidates for President. But neither of these well-known American leaders dared to speak out in favor of admitting Texas to the Union. The man who did dare to speak was a "dark horse," a person given little or no chance to win. His name was James K. Polk, and he won the election.

The surprising dark horse winner was called "Young Hickory," because he was a follower of "Old Hickory," Andrew Jackson. Polk was one of our hardest working Presidents. In fact, he took life so seriously and drove himself so hard that he died when he was only 54.

Polk had a stubborn streak. He knew what he wanted, and he went after it. A friend wrote, "What he went for, he fetched." The friend was right. Polk promised Americans that he would get them Texas and Oregon. He did not break that promise.

As soon as Polk was elected, the United States government carried out the wishes of the American people. Before Polk could take office in 1845, Congress invited Texas to join the Union. Texans, who wanted to be with "their own people" in the United States, gladly voted to accept the invitation. And so the Lone Star Republic became the Lone Star State.

1. What did Polk promise to do if he were elected President?

2. When and how was Texas brought into the Union?

What did Americans believe was their "manifest destiny"?

In President Polk's time Americans were interested in more than just Texas. They had great dreams about the size and importance of their country. What is more they were sure that fate, or the "stars," had already determined what it was to be. One day, they insisted, the United States would reach from the Gulf of Mexico to the Far North. Its boundaries would go from the Atlantic Ocean on the east to the Pacific Ocean on the west. This was the manifest destiny, or fate, of the nation.

Four nations claimed the land stretching from Alaska to California and from the Rockies to the Pacific. The vast territory of the Pacific Northwest was called the Oregon Country. (See map, page 262.) In time two nations, Spain and Russia, withdrew their claims. That left Britain and the United States in the race for Oregon.

The United States rested its claim on visits made by Americans in 1792 and 1805. Captain Robert Gray made the first visit. He sailed his ship, *The Columbia*, into the mouth of the river which now bears his vessel's name. The second visit was made by the Lewis and Clark Expedition. It aroused great interest, as you know. Quickly trappers followed the trail Lewis and Clark had blazed into the rich Oregon Country. The British also sent trappers into the region. They hunted for beaver and other valuable fur-bearing animals.

As long as Oregon had few settlers, the fact that two countries said they ruled it did not matter. Really there was very little "rule." The few settlers and the rough traders made their own rules. But things were to change in the late 1830s and the early 1840s. First a trickle and then a flood of Americans headed for Oregon. Arguments then began to boil up between the United States and Britain about control of that rich area.

3. How large and powerful did Americans think their country was destined to become?

4. What nations claimed the Oregon Country?

Why were settlers encouraged to move to Oregon?

Some Americans thought they knew how to win the argument with Britain

St. Ignatius Mission in Montana Territory was painted in this 1845 watercolor by Peter Peterson Toftt, a Danish immigrant.

about control of Oregon. Peter Burnett, who later became the first governor of the state of California, said:

> **. . . the most ready and peaceable way to settle the conflicting and doubtful claims . . . was to fill the country with American citizens. If we could only show, by a *practical* test, that American emigrants could safely make their way across the continent to Oregon with their wagons, teams, cattle, and families, then the solution of the question of title [ownership] to the country was discovered. Of course, Great Britain would not covet [try to take over] a colony settled by American citizens.**

Peter Hardeman Burnett, *Recollections and Opinions of an Old Pioneer* (New York, 1880).

It was Dr. Marcus Whitman who planned and carried out that "practical test" in 1843. His plan was to move several hundred families overland in a great wagon train.

Whitman played a key role in the history of Oregon. He was a doctor. He also was a very religious man, eager to persuade others to believe as he did. Whitman heard about the request of four Nez Percé who accompanied an American Fur Company caravan to St. Louis. The Nez Percé said that they wanted to know more about the "Book of Heaven," the Bible. When newspapers reported the Indians' request, church groups got very excited. They began to raise money and organize volunteers to start missions for the Indians.

Many missionaries responded to the Nez Percé request. Among them were Dr. Whitman and his 20-year-old bride, Narcissa. They left St. Louis in the spring of 1836 along with another husband-wife team, Henry Spaulding and his wife, Eliza. Those two women became the first white women to travel overland to Oregon. The trip took five months. En route the missionaries had to discard first one and then another of the articles packed into their hand-drawn carts.

When the Whitmans reached Fort Walla Walla in what is now the eastern part of Washington State, they set up a mission. Dr. Whitman treated many Indians from various tribes who came to him with their illnesses. Narcissa Whitman taught in the school they started. Any Americans who made their way to Oregon Country were welcome to stay at the mission until they could get settled.

Six years after the Whitmans arrived in Oregon, the doctor returned to Washington, D.C. He met with government leaders. He urged them to keep claims to the Oregon Country "at all costs." Then he led a large party of settlers back to Oregon. This wagon train was the practical test of American settlement in Oregon.

5. How did Americans think they could win the argument with England about ownership of Oregon?

6. Who were Marcus and Narcissa Whitman?

How did Dr. Whitman's wagon train travel?

Whitman estimated that 200 families, or 1000 persons, took part in that great journey to Oregon. Driving oxteams, the settlers made about two miles an hour (3.2 km/hr). The journey from Independence, Missouri, to Fort Walla Walla covered 1691 miles (2705 km).

When the settlers gathered at Independence in May 1843, their first order of business was to elect leaders. The candidates stood in a row in front of all those ready to make the trip. Only men were allowed to vote. At a signal each man ran to stand behind the leader of his choice. Those who had the most people lined up behind them were declared winners. They became the "Council of Ten" and drew up the rules for the trip. The council was called on to solve many problems during the six-month trip.

During the day on the trail the leaders headed the long lines of covered wagons. At night the wagons made a circle. Sentries slept outside the circle.

At first some worried about a rule Dr. Whitman made. If someone became ill, all those in that person's wagon had to be left behind. Dr. Whitman would stay with the wagon and tend the sick. The

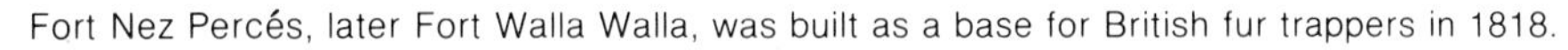

Fort Nez Percés, later Fort Walla Walla, was built as a base for British fur trappers in 1818.

others could not wait. They had to go on. Dr. Whitman told his followers:

Travel, travel, travel! Nothing else will take you to the end of your journey. Nothing is wise that does not help you along. Nothing is good for you that causes you a moment's delay.

The Whitman journey of 1843 proved that wagon trains could travel overland to Oregon. It was possible for families to move to the Northwest and settle there. Those who made that trip usually did well in their new homes. So more people followed them along the Oregon Trail. During the very wet spring of 1844 three parties set out for Oregon, each with between 700 and 1500 people. Wagon trains in 1845 took about 3000 persons into Oregon. By 1846 the British realized that Americans would not give up their claims to Oregon. The stage was set for a compromise.

7. Describe the way Dr. Whitman's wagon train traveled.

8. What did that wagon train prove?

What part of the Oregon Country went to the United States?

When James K. Polk ran for President in 1844, he promised to get Oregon for the United States. Believers in manifest destiny shouted, "All of Oregon or None!" and "54-40 or Fight!" The 54° 40' line would have pushed the border of the United States all the way to Alaska (which was then owned by Russia). The British replied that Oregon was theirs all the way south to the Columbia River.

The truth was that neither Britain nor the United States really wanted war over Oregon. President Polk knew two things well:

Oregon Boundary Settlement

1. We were about to fight a war with Mexico over Texas. We could not fight Britain at the same time.

2. Our claims up to 54° 40' were about as good as our claims to China!

On the British side there was no wish for war either. Many Britains asked, "Why fight a war over a few square miles of wilderness so far from home?"

In 1846, Britain and the United States finally reached a happy compromise. Land north of the 49th parallel became British. All the rich, green Pacific Northwest below the 49th parallel became American soil.

9. What boundaries did the British and Americans claim?

10. What compromise did the two sides reach?

Part Four

The Mexican War

What other western lands did the United States want?

Besides Texas and Oregon, Americans had eyes on other areas of the West. In fact, they wanted all of the West from the Rocky Mountains to the Pacific Ocean. To stretch the nation's western border to the Pacific was the goal, the manifest destiny of the United States.

Lying between the Oregon Country and Texas was some rich, almost unpopulated land. Much of it was mountains and desert. This area had once been claimed by Spain, but now it belonged to Mexico. It included land that is today in the states of California, Nevada, Utah, Colorado, Arizona, and New Mexico.

For many years Americans had known what a wonderful, fertile land California was. Overland travel to California did not begin until 1826. But Americans were able to get there before that time. They sailed on ships around the tip of South America and into the Pacific Ocean.

Sailors who had seen California brought back reports of sunny skies, good food, and wonderful harbors. One of them said that San Francisco Bay was big enough to hold "the navies of all the world."

Americans not only knew about California, they tried to buy it. But the newly independent Mexican government was not selling.

Even though Mexico owned California, Americans began settling there. They hoped that in time California would drop like ripe fruit into the outstretched hands of the United States. And there were good reasons for such

Southwesterners of Spanish, Mexican, and Indian descent watch a herd of cattle.

hopes. Californians were unhappy with the poor government Mexico provided. Many of them wanted to join the United States. Everything added up to a good chance that California could be had without paying a penny or firing a shot.

Finally some Americans in California tried to revolt and set up a "Bear Flag Republic" independent of Mexico. Their leader was an American army officer named John C. Frémont. But by the time the revolt got underway, war between the United States and Mexico had begun. Frémont's troops then joined American forces pushing into California. United States naval forces arrived at Monterey. Six months later, troops led by Stephen Kearney marched in from Fort Leavenworth, Kansas. In seven months the conquest of California was complete.

1. How did the United States try to get California?

2. What was the Bear Flag Republic?

Why did the United States and Mexico go to war?

When the United States finally took Texas into the Union, the Mexicans were furious. They said the United States had no business adding Texas as a state. In their eyes, Texas had never even been independent.

As soon as President Polk entered the White House, he ordered troops to Texas. He also sent a representative to Mexico City to make one more try at buying California and the Southwest. General Herrera of Mexico talked politely with the American representative. He said that Mexico wanted to solve the Texas problem, but it did not want to sell any part of it.

American and Mexican soldiers glared at each other across the Rio Grande. This river was the southern boundary of Texas, Polk claimed. (See map, page 265.) The Mexicans had a different view, of course. They said the boundary was farther north and that the American troops were on Mexican soil.

In April 1846, Mexican troops crossed the Rio Grande and killed a number of Americans. Polk had his chance. He declared that Mexicans had "shed American blood upon American soil." War with Mexico followed.

3. Why were the Mexicans angry about the United States taking Texas into the Union?

4. What event touched off the war with Mexico?

Why was the Mexican War unpopular?

Many Americans, especially in the North, were against the war with Mexico. Abolitionists did not want the United States to get any new territory which might be opened to slavery.

In Congress, many spoke against "Mr. Polk's War." Some said the United States was a "big bully" to push Mexico around and take away its land. A young member of Congress from Illinois, Abe Lincoln, demanded that Polk point out the exact spot where American blood had been shed. Lincoln said that the President had forced the war on the people.

While debate about the war was going on, American forces struck quickly and deeply into Mexican territory. Success came rapidly. California and the Southwest were conquered. Generals Zachary Taylor and Winfield Scott drove into Mexico itself.

The Mexican War, 1846-1848

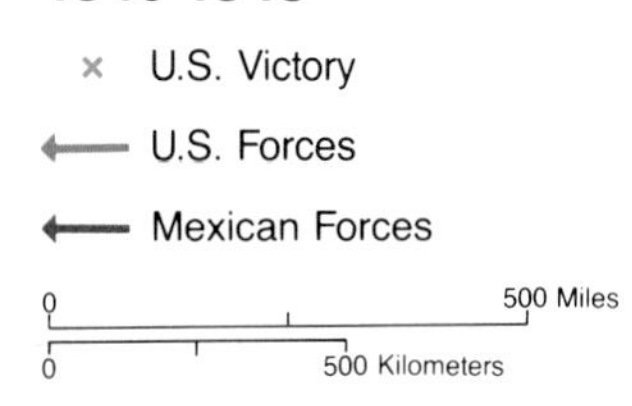

Santa Anna was still the dictator of Mexico. He tried to stop General Taylor at the Battle of Buena Vista. The Mexicans outnumbered the Americans three to one, but Taylor won the battle.

Then Santa Anna tried to hold the capital at Mexico City against the attacks of General Scott. Again the Americans were victorious. Scott marched into Mexico City in 1847, and the fighting was over.

5. Why did some Americans oppose the war?

6. When did the war come to an end?

What were the results of the Mexican War?

Unpopular as it was, the Mexican War had important results. A peace treaty signed in 1848 had these terms:

1. More than half a million square miles (1.3 million km^2) of land were added to the United States. California and the Southwest were brought under the American flag. This was called the Mexican Cession. (See map, page 267.)

United States forces storm the Mexican fortress of Chapultepec, three miles (4.8 km) southwest of Mexico City.

2. The United States paid Mexico $15 million for the land added to our territory. The United States also said that it did not intend to press for payment of $3 million which our government claimed that Mexico owed for damages to American property.

3. The Rio Grande became the boundary between Texas and Mexico.

Five years after the peace treaty was signed, the United States bought a small strip of land from Mexico for $10 million. It was called the Gadsden Purchase in honor of James Gadsden, then ambassador to Mexico. With the addition of that small area, the southern boundary of the United States was fixed.

There also were some long term results of the Mexican War which cannot be expressed in miles or in dollars and cents.

First, the war left the North and the South even more divided. Northerners charged the war had provided "bigger pens to cram with slaves." Southerners insisted they had the right to open new lands to plantations if they wanted to. What the southern states did, they insisted, was none of the North's business.

Second, the war damaged relations between Mexico and the United States. To this day some Mexicans insist that their country was forced to yield land rightly its own. They also believe that the payment received was very small considering the value of the lands they had to give up.

7. What territory did the United States gain under the Mexican Cession? Under the Gadsden Purchase?

8. Why did the Mexican War deepen the division between the North and the South?

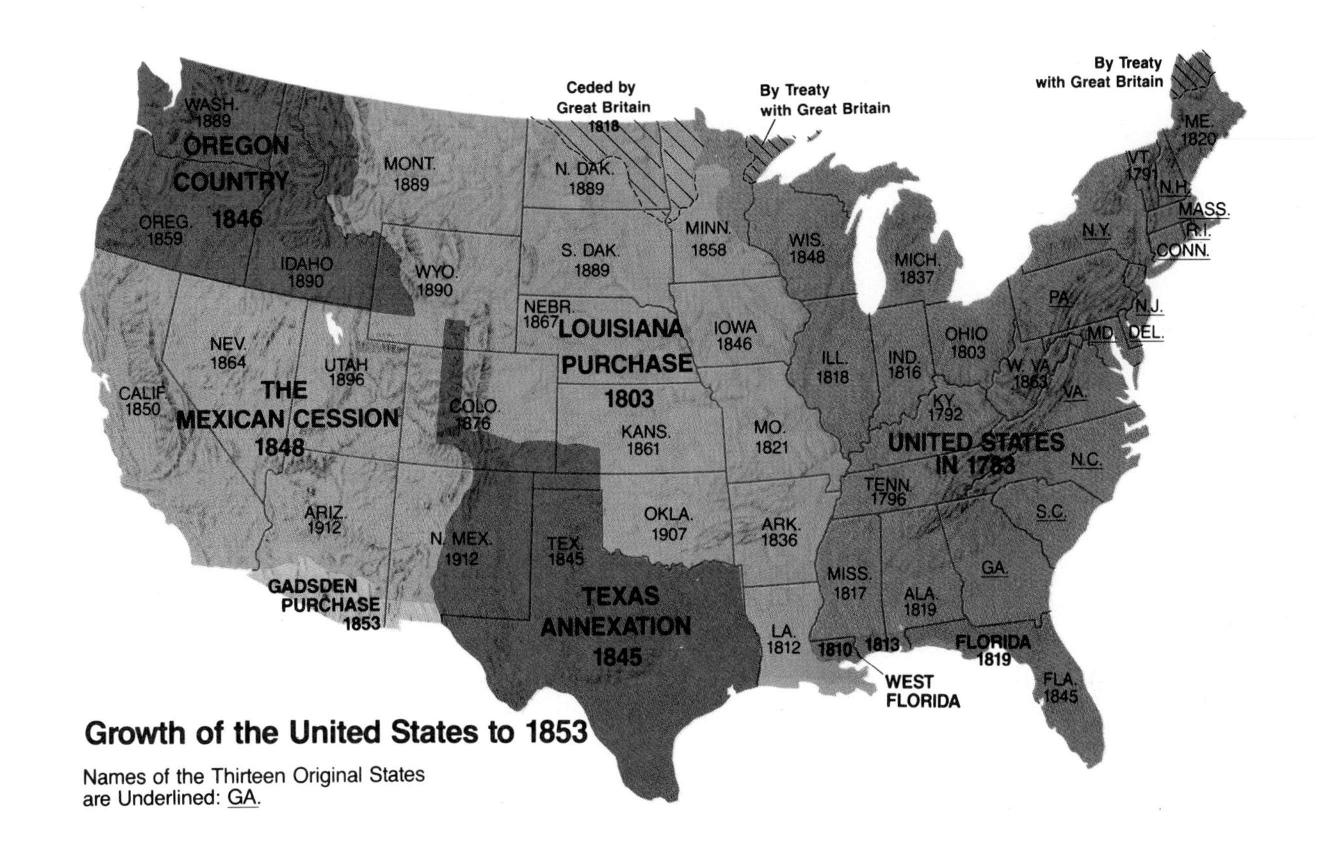

Growth of the United States to 1853

Names of the Thirteen Original States are Underlined: GA.

Part Five

The California Gold Rush

When and where was gold discovered in California?

Captain John Sutter was a pioneer who settled in California in 1839. He was given a large piece of land by the Mexican government where the city of Sacramento stands today.

There was fine timber on Sutter's 100,000 acres (40,000 ha) of land. He wanted to turn it into lumber and sell it. So he hired a mechanic named James Marshall to build a sawmill on the American River.

One day in January 1848, Marshall was working on the bank of the river. Suddenly he saw a sparkling yellow pebble in the water. When Marshall picked it up, he noticed how heavy it was. Heavy and shiny pebbles sometimes turn out to be gold.

Marshall found some more of these pebbles and took them to Sutter. The two men tested them in a number of ways. Finally they were sure that Marshall had discovered precious gold.

News of the great find soon leaked out. From all over California, people swarmed to Sutter's ranch to prospect (hunt) for gold. It did Sutter no good to ask them to get off his property. The

Sutter's Fort already flew the United States flag in 1847.

prospectors had gold fever, and they tore his place to pieces with their picks and shovels. Poor Captain Sutter. His great good luck turned out to be bad luck. He died a poor and discouraged man.

Meanwhile, President Polk himself announced proudly in a speech that gold had been discovered in California. The speech was printed in newspapers all over the world. As a result, thousands of gold hunters packed their bags and headed for California in 1849. These gold seekers are called the "forty-niners."

1. Where and how did James Marshall discover gold?
2. Who were the "forty-niners"?

How did the "forty-niners" get to California?

There were three ways to get to California from the eastern part of the United States.

1. Go by ship around the tip of South America into the Pacific Ocean. Then sail north to California. This long, expensive trip took at least three months. (There was no Panama Canal in those days.)

2. Take a ship to Mexico or Panama. From there hike overland to the Pacific coast. Then board another ship and sail to California. This route was also expensive, and a person could not take much baggage.

3. The most popular route was to go all the way to California by land. Many "forty-niners" rode across the western trails in covered wagons.

Mountains and deserts barred the way of those who traveled overland. Many died of hunger, thirst, or disease. Some were trapped in heavy snows in the mountains and froze to death. But on and on came the gold seekers. Of course, their coming alarmed the Indian tribes. On the way, the gold seekers killed much game and scared away still more. They muddied the streams and ruined the fishing. When they got to California, the miners chopped down trees to build cabins, dams, and mine shafts. The miners, in short, upset the ways in which Indians on the Great Plains and in California had lived for hundreds of years. And, as they might have been expected to do, the Indians fought back.

Sarah Royce, who traveled west with her husband and two-year-old daughter, told how one group of Indians tried to stem the tide of people flowing west:

. . . [There were] Indians by the hundreds. Soon they had arranged themselves on each side of the way. A group came forward, and at the Captain's command our company halted, while he with several others went to meet the Indians and hold a parley [talk]. It turned out that they had gathered to demand the payment of a certain sum per head for every emigrant passing through this part of the country, which they claimed as their own. The men of our company after consultation, resolved that the demand was

unreasonable! The country we were traveling through belonged to the United States . . . [the men said] if the Indians attempted to stop us [from going on], they would open fire with all their rifles and revolvers.

Sarah Eleanor Royce, *A Frontier Lady: Recollections of the Gold Rush and Early California* (New Haven: Yale University Press, 1932).

The Royce party did go on. Later it was attacked by Indians angry about the way they had been treated. What happened to the Royce party was not unusual. It was something which happened again and again as relations between Indians and migrants grew worse.

3. What were the three main ways "forty-niners" used to get to California?
4. Why did relations between Indians and migrants become strained?

Hardworking prospectors pose for a photograph in 1852. Their digs are on the American River in California.

Why did Salt Lake City become a popular stopping place?

On the long way west there were few comfortable stopping-off places. Salt Lake City was an exception. That city was built by members of the Church of Jesus Christ of the Latter Day Saints. Members of that church were later nicknamed the "Mormons." Sometimes they were called the "Saints."

The Mormons had come to what is now the state of Utah in 1846. They called their new home "Deseret." Salt Lake City was its capital. It was a neat, well-planned community which the Mormons kept very clean. The Mormons also kept it stocked with all kinds of provisions. Travelers were welcome to trade there. The sick were cared for. Many pioneers stayed through the winter. They praised the Mormons for their hospitality.

Perhaps the Mormons were kind to weary travelers because they knew only too well what it was like to travel overland. The Mormon Church began in New York State. The Mormons had lived in Ohio. Then they were forced to move to Missouri. When they were driven out of Missouri they went to Illinois.

Wherever they went, Mormons met hatred for their beliefs. They believed in living, working, and sharing as a group. Later, another of their beliefs really angered people. Mormons felt that men could legally have more than one wife at a time. (They no longer hold that belief.)

When a mob in Illinois murdered the Mormon leader Joseph Smith and his brother in 1844, the Saints decided they would have to move farther west. They would have to live by themselves in order to live as they thought right. Brigham Young was chosen to be their new leader. He led his people out of

Travelers headed west could stop in Deseret (later Salt Lake City) for provisions and a rest.

Illinois to Deseret. There the Mormons made the desert bloom. And they prospered from the brisk business they did with those going to the gold fields.

5. Why did travelers like to stop in Salt Lake City?

6. Who were the Mormons?

How did the Gold Rush change life in California?

When Sam Brannan, a San Francisco shop owner, heard news of Marshall's discovery, he burst onto the streets. "Gold! Gold! Gold from the American River!" he shouted. It seemed as if the whole world heard his cry. People came from everywhere. There were direct sailings from European ports. So many Chinese came that in time one miner in every five was from China. People surged up from South America and Mexico. Still more poured in from Australia. There were 6000 people in California when gold was discovered. By the end of 1849 there were 65,000! Three years later, in the boom year of 1852, the population reached a quarter of a million. In that year gold worth $81 million was mined from California's earth.

Those who mined "in the diggings" lived a very rough life. They tried to spend every possible moment looking for gold. They cooked over open fires and ate on the run, unless they were lucky enough to find a hotel or boardinghouse. But even if they did find a hotel, they couldn't expect to get a room to

Focus on Skills

On a separate sheet of paper draw a circle, or "pie," graph like the one shown here. You can complete the graph by using the information in the table. Consult the figures. Then enter the proper figure for each occupation in the correct "slice" of the pie. A sample has been done to help you get started.

OCCUPATIONS OF HEADS OF FAMILIES MOVING WEST

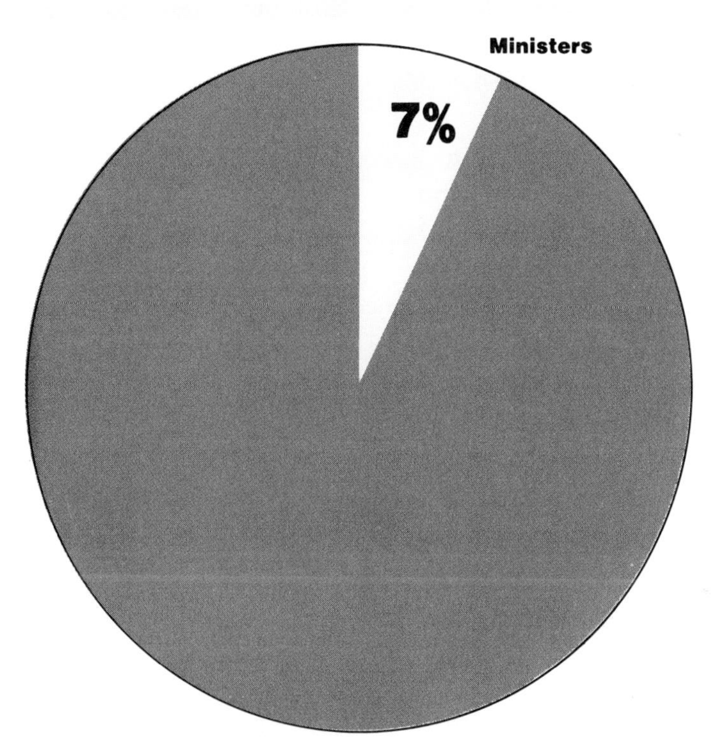

Occupation	Percentage
Farmers	61%
Professionals (doctors, lawyers, editors, teachers)	12%
Skilled workers (carpenters, blacksmiths, mechanics)	10%
Small merchants	9%
Ministers	7%
	100%

themselves. One miner told of paying a dollar—then a considerable sum of money—not for a room. Not even for a bed. His dollar entitled him to space on the dining room floor where he could roll up in his own blanket. During the night he said he was so disturbed by the "loud snorings and terrible smells" of the other miners that he moved outside and slept on the ground.

Why miners "smelled" is understandable. Mining was dirty work and washing facilities were few. One miner said:

Have two shirts. Wear one until it is dirty. Hang on a limb, exposed to wind, rain, and sun. Put on second shirt. Wear until dirty. Then change to clean one.

All those who worked in the diggings endured hardship. But not all found their fortunes. A few did get rich, mainly those who arrived early. Those who came later often found no gold at all. Or, if they did find some, it was stolen by thieves.

In the long run those who gained most from the Gold Rush did not seek gold. Instead they provided the services miners needed. Some became farmers and raised food crops. Others served as doctors, lawyers, bankers, and storekeepers. Still others ran sawmills, saloons, and hotels.

All of the newcomers brought changes to California. Not only did they swell the population. They made California "home" for peoples from all continents and of all ethnic groups.

7. Why did California become "home" for many different ethnic groups?

8. Why did those who provided services often prosper more than miners?

When and where did California form a government?

Forming an orderly government was difficult during the Gold Rush. People poured into California at a tremendous rate. New towns sprang up overnight. Many had very unusual names, such as Red Dog, You Bet, Poker Flat, Poverty Flat, Rich Bar, and Humbug. Few of those towns had city councils, mayors, police, or judges to see that law and order were respected. So citizens formed their own groups called vigilance committees, or *vigilantes*. These were groups of citizens who banded together and took the law into their own hands. They seized people accused of crimes and tried them, as in court. Those found guilty—men and women alike—were often whipped or hanged. Some of the trials were fair; some were not.

Clearly Californians needed better government. Late in 1849 a group of Californians held a meeting at Monterey and wrote a constitution. It was printed in both Spanish and English. Under the constitution, a governor was elected. Slavery was forbidden. The people then asked to join the Union.

The slavery problem made admission of California difficult. Northerners, of course, were in favor of gaining another free state. Southerners were unhappy, and said so. There the matter had to stand until some sort of compromise could be worked out. We will learn more about that compromise in the next chapter.

9. Why did citizens form vigilance committees?

10. Why did the federal government hesitate to admit California to the Union?

Building Your Vocabulary

Match each item in Column A with the correct item in Column B.

Column A	Column B
1. pioneer	A. mines
2. frontier	B. fate
3. vigilantes	C. one who moves onto frontier
4. squatters	D. where settled life touches wilderness
5. manifest destiny	E. citizens who take law and order into their own hands
6. the diggings	F. people who settle on land they don't own

Recalling What You Have Learned

Complete each of these sentences by selecting the correct word or phrase from those listed below.

1. Another name for Texas is—?—.
2. —?—was elected President because he favored taking Texas and Oregon into the Union.
3. —?—led the first American settlers into Texas.
4. Those who rushed to California in search of gold were called—?—.
5. The—?—was established as the boundary between Texas and Mexico by the treaty the two nations signed in 1848.
6. Americans believed it was their—?—to become a large, powerful nation stretching from the Atlantic to the Pacific.
7. The—?—built Salt Lake City.
8. The man who led the first wagon train into Oregon was—?—.
9. —?—opened more new paths and made longer journeys of exploration in the West than anyone since Lewis and Clark.
10. —?—was one of the Americans who died at the Alamo.

the Lone Star State
Dr. Marcus Whitman
James K. Polk
forty-niners
Mormons
Jedediah Smith
Stephen Austin
Rio Grande
manifest destiny
Davy Crockett

Discussing the Important Ideas in This Chapter

1. Why were some Americans willing to leave the comforts of a settled life and move onto the frontier?
2. How were those who moved onto the frontier alike? Different?
3. What is the meaning of the term "the moving frontier"?
4. What contributions to the opening of the West did the "mountain men" make?
5. What is the difference between "squatters" and "equipped farmers"?

6. Why did the United States government hesitate to admit Texas and California into the Union?
7. Why did the United States government encourage settlers to move to the Oregon Country?
8. Why did the Indians on the Great Plains and in California become very upset about the numbers of settlers who moved west?
9. How and why did the Gold Rush change life in California?

Improving Your Map Skills

Study the map on page 267 and answer the following questions:
1. List all the states which include territory acquired by the Louisiana Purchase.
2. What was the last state in the Louisiana Purchase to join the Union?
3. Which two states include territory acquired through the Gadsden Purchase? In what year did these two states join the Union?
4. What four states were admitted to the Union in 1889?
5. Which state includes territory gained from the Louisiana Purchase, Texas Annexation, Mexican Cession, and the Oregon Country?
6. Which other states were carved from the Oregon Country?

Improving Your Study Skills: *Reading*

The "theme song" of the California Gold Rush was "Oh, Susanna." Miners used the music written by Stephen Foster. They set their own words to it, composing endless verses. Here are the first and last stanzas and the chorus as sung by entertainers popular in San Francisco, Sacramento, and other "boom towns" of the time. Read the words, then answer the questions.

I came from Salem City,
With my wash bowl on my knee,
I'm going to California
The gold dust for to see.
It seemed all night, the day I left,
The weather it was dry,
The sun so hot I froze to death,
Oh! brothers, don't you cry.

Chorus
Oh! California,
That's the land for me,
I'm going to Sacramento
With my wash bowl on my knee. . . .

I soon shall be in Francisco,
And then I'll look around,
And when I see the gold lumps there,
I'll pick them off the ground.
I'll scrape the mountains clean,
I'll drain the rivers dry,
A pocket full of rocks bring home,
So, brothers, don't you cry.

From Octavius Thorndike Howe, *Argonauts of '49* (Cambridge: Harvard University Press, 1923), pp. 78-79. Reprinted by permission.

1. What evidence is there in this song that forty-niners expected to get rich quickly and easily?
2. What evidence is there that the miners did not intend to stay in California after they had "struck it rich"?
3. How did the singers feel about skimming off surface wealth in California?

Chapter 11 The Nation Divided

Battlefield, Gettysburg, Pennsylvania

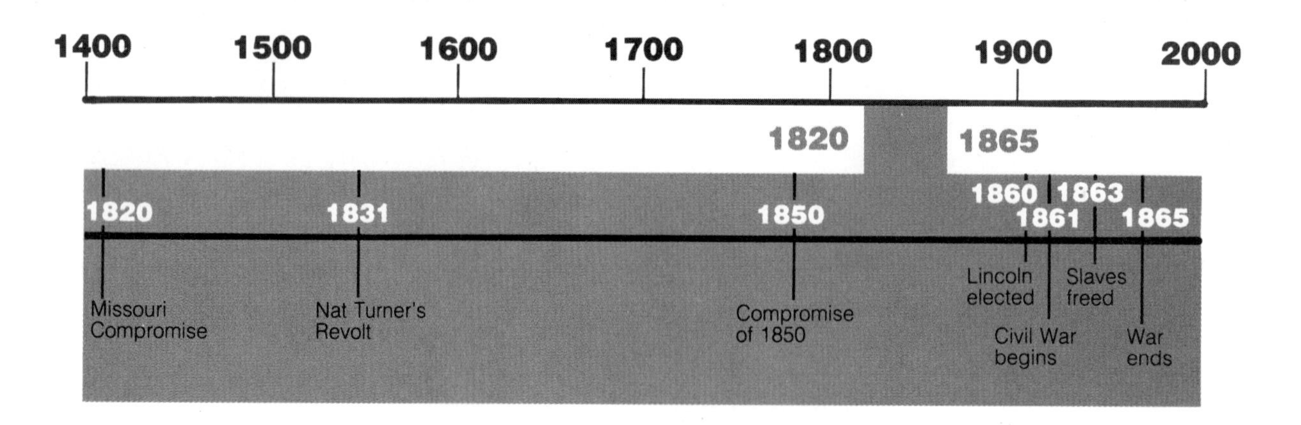

Part One

Slavery Splits the Country

Why did the North and South become different sections?

People can grow to be very different, even though they come from the same family. Two sections of our country grew to be very different, even though they had the same roots. Before the Civil War, the North and South had come to be different in almost every way. The chart on page 277 shows just how different they had become.

Yet, as important as these differences were, they alone would not have caused South to turn against North. There was one great problem that seemed impossible to solve. As Thomas Jefferson put it, the South "had a wolf by the ears." It could not hold the "wolf," and it could not let it go. The "wolf," of course, was the problem of slavery.

In the early years of our country, many people, including Jefferson, were sure that slavery would disappear by itself in time. They thought all Americans would become free without the government taking any action.

Some Americans went ahead and freed their slaves. Others gave slaves the

GREAT DIFFERENCES BETWEEN NORTH AND SOUTH	
NORTH	**SOUTH**
Becoming urban. Many large cities. New York City had almost one million people.	Mostly rural. Only one large city—New Orleans.
Much manufacturing. Iron, textiles, shoes, watches, farm machinery, shipbuilding, meat packing, milling flour.	Little manufacturing. One Northern town—Lowell, Massachusetts—handled more textiles than all the mills in the South put together.
Heavy immigration from Europe starting. Irish settled in cities. Germans and Scandinavians went to farms. British scattered everywhere.	Very little immigration from Europe. South wanted immigrants, but immigrants did not want to go there to compete with slave labor.
Railroad construction increasing. Connecting lines built over and around Appalachians.	Little railroad building.
Favored tariffs.	Opposed tariffs.
Wanted free land for small farmers.	Wanted public lands sold for good prices.
Wanted a national banking system.	Opposed a national banking system.
More democratic. More people voted and took part in government.	Political power and wealth held by a small group.

chance to buy their freedom, and many of them did. Many slaves ran away. Most people believed that slavery would become so expensive that it would die out.

Before the 1830s, Southerners said that slavery was necessary to keep the South alive. However, they felt sorry about this "peculiar institution." Making human beings into slaves was not right.

About 1830, however, the feeling of most Southerners changed. They defended slavery. They insisted it was "good." In the end, they were even willing to give their lives in defense of the slave system.

1. What "wolf" did the South have by its ears?

2. How did most Southerners feel about slavery before the 1830s?

Why did the South's attitude toward slavery change?

In the 1830s, Southerners became more determined to keep the slave system. They thought slavery should continue for three main reasons:

1. New lands, good for growing cotton, were opening up in the Southwest. Planters thought they would do well to move west onto those fresh, new lands and plant them with cotton. They would need slaves to clear new plantations and grow cotton.

2. Southerners became more and more fearful of slave revolts. Even Jefferson had been afraid that the two races could not live side by side in peace. He thought there had to be some plan to free blacks or remove them from the United States. The more frightened Southerners became of their slaves, the more they

defended slavery as a way to control a "dangerous population."

3. The words and deeds of abolitionists angered many Southerners. Abolitionists, those Southerners said, were "wild-eyed radicals." They did not understand the South's problems. What is more, abolitionists wanted to take away "property," which is how slaves were thought of, without payment to the owners. To do that would be against the Constitution, Southerners argued. (See Amendment V.)

3. What were three reasons Southerners believed that slavery should continue?

Why did nonslaveholding Southerners support slavery?

Only about 25 percent of the families in the South owned slaves. Half of the slaveowners had fewer than twenty slaves.

Why did most Southerners favor slavery if they owned no slaves themselves? That is a good question. Most Southerners were sure the prosperity of the South depended on the slave system. Many were afraid of what would happen to them if the slaves were freed. The poorest whites "looked down" on slaves.

Southern leaders like John C. Calhoun tried to convince themselves and others that slavery was a "positive good." The majority of Southerners agreed—at least outwardly.

Finally, the more the Northerners pointed the finger of guilt at the South, the greater the South's anger became. Southerners asked what business it was of the North to meddle in their affairs. Each time an attack on slavery blew down from the North, Southerners drew closer to defend the slave system.

4. What percentage of Southern families owned slaves?

5. Who said slavery was a "positive good"?

How serious were slave revolts?

While no single slave revolt succeeded, records show that slaves were most unhappy. Between 1663 and 1865, more than 100 slave revolts took place on land. At sea there were 55 revolts.

Three big slave revolts shook the South in the early 1800s. On September 1, 1800, 1100 slaves set out to destroy Richmond, Virginia. Rain delayed the planned attack. Two slaves told about the plot. The leaders and 33 others were caught and put to death.

The second big revolt was led by Denmark Vesey. After buying his own freedom for $600, Vesey worked as a carpenter and studied in his spare time. For 22 years he read everything he could about the French Revolution and slave revolts in Haiti. Then he planned an armed attack on Charleston, South Carolina. Vesey was betrayed by a slave. A total of 139 blacks were arrested and 47 were executed, including Vesey. Whites who had encouraged Vesey were fined and put in prison.

One of the most violent slave revolts was led by Nat Turner in 1831. Turner thought God had chosen him to lead slaves against their white owners. Voices from heaven told him what to do.

On the night of August 21, 1831, Turner started a slave revolt in Southampton County, Virginia. The first victims were Turner's master and four members of his family. All were murdered in their beds.

Then Turner and a well-armed band of seventy slaves marched toward

Nat Turner (with outstretched arm) plans his revolt with some of his followers. Before troops stopped the rebellion, 59 white people and more than 100 slaves were killed.

the county seat. Their targets were slaveholders and their families. In a few hours, the slaves killed ten men, fourteen women, and thirty-five children.

After that, Nat Turner disappeared. The entire South was in an uproar. Everyone expected a full-scale revolution.

Three thousand troops hunted for two months before they tracked down Turner. He and sixteen of his men were hanged. But even his death did not end the South's fears. Nat Turner's revolt showed that many slaves were willing to kill and die for freedom.

6. How many slave revolts took place on land between 1630 and 1865? How many took place at sea?

7. Who were Denmark Vesey and Nat Turner? What happened to them?

In what other ways did slaves protest?

Taking up arms against their owners was not the only way blacks rebelled. Slaves used every way to resist they could think of.

Sometimes the slaves made farm animals lame, or set fire to barns. In some cases, mothers smothered their newborn children rather than let them grow up slaves. Records of plantation owners show that slaves used every possible way to protest, including running away.

Slaves who ran away often traveled north to freedom via the underground railroad. Of course, it was not a real railroad, but a trail of escape to Canada. Free blacks and whites opposed to slavery helped slaves escape from the South. But even in the North the slaves were not safe. Federal laws said that slaves had to be returned to their owners. So the underground railroad was kept secret.

People on the underground railroad used railroad language. That way they hoped they would not be found out. Runaways were called "passengers." Hiding places were "stations." Men and women who guided slaves northward were "conductors" or "agents." Usually slaves moved at night and were hidden in "stations" during the day.

No one knows for sure how many slaves made their way to freedom in Canada on the underground railroad. One estimate is that from 1830 to 1860 about 2000 slaves a year escaped.

Escaping slaves arrive at Levi Coffin's farm in Newport, Indiana. Coffin's house was a station on the underground railroad.

8. What were some of the means slaves used to protest?

9. What was the underground railroad?

Who was a famous "conductor" on the underground railroad?

Only five feet tall, Harriet Tubman was probably the most famous conductor on the underground railroad. Known as the "Moses" of her people, in ten years she made nineteen trips south. She led more than 300 slaves to freedom. Never once did she lose a passenger. Many times, however, she had to frighten some of them into continuing their trips. She packed a loaded revolver. She threatened to use it on those who lost their nerve on the journey north. At one time a $40,000 reward was offered for the capture of Harriet Tubman.

Harriet Tubman knew how to disguise herself and how to throw people off her track when necessary. She gave sleeping medicine to babies whose coughing or crying in the night might give away their hiding places.

Many famous Americans were proud to call Harriet Tubman their friend. Ralph Waldo Emerson, the writer, and Senator William Seward, who later became Secretary of State, helped hide her and gave her money.

When the Civil War came, Harriet Tubman served as a nurse and later as a spy behind the Southern lines. Despite her dangerous life, she lived to be 93 years old.

10. Who was Harriet Tubman?

11. Why was she a successful "conductor" on the underground railroad?

Part Two

Compromise: Tried and Found Wanting

Why did Americans try to solve the slavery issue by compromise?

Compromise is the way that people who disagree on something solve their differences. Each side gives a little. American history is filled with compromises. The Constitution was put together by a series of compromises.

Slavery brought strong disagreements to the country. Few blacks lived in the North, and slavery was never practiced there to any great extent. The South, of course, had many slaves.

Americans tried to keep an even number of slave and free states, so that there would be a balance in the Senate. This system worked until 1819, when there were eleven free and eleven slave states. Then Missouri asked to join the Union as a slave state. That would upset the balance. The slave states would have more senators than the free states.

A storm broke out in Congress and among the people. To solve the problem, Americans once again turned to compromise.

The first important effort at compromise was made in 1820. Henry Clay suggested a plan to the Congress. It was accepted. As a result, Missouri came into the Union as a slave state. Maine was cut loose from Massachusetts and came in as a free state. The rest of the land bought in the Louisiana Purchase was divided. (See map, bottom right.) A line was drawn across the map of that territory. Slavery could never go north of that line.

Compromise had saved the day. However, farsighted people knew and said that the problem of slavery had not been solved by compromise. It had only been postponed.

1. What is a compromise?
2. What were the results of the Missouri Compromise?

What did the Compromise of 1850 provide?

After the Mexican War, Congress again faced the question of allowing slavery in new territories. Southerners argued that they had helped fight the war and win the new territories. Why shouldn't they be allowed to move anywhere they wanted with their slaves? Northerners shouted back. Slavery should not be allowed to go one inch farther! In the midst of the hot debates in Congress, Henry Clay again suggested compromise. His suggestion was passed by Congress. It was called the Compromise of 1850. It declared:

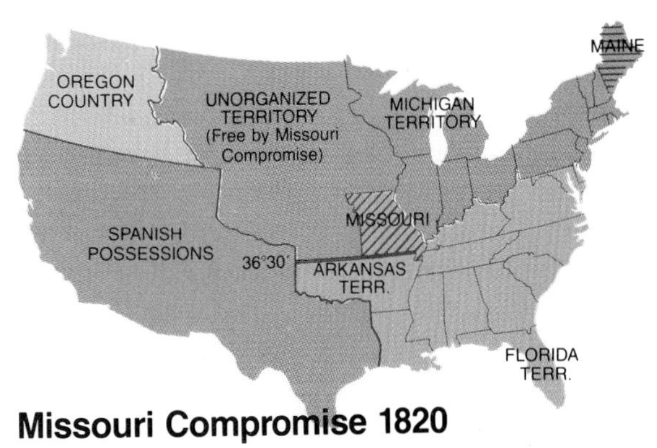

Missouri Compromise 1820

Free States and Territories

Slave States and Territories

Maine. Admitted as a Free State, 1820

Missouri. Admitted as a Slave State, 1821

Compromise of 1850

1. California was to come into the Union as a free state.

2. New Mexico and Utah territories were to decide about slavery for themselves.

3. Slave trade—but not slavery—was to be forbidden in Washington, D.C.

4. Runaway slaves in the North were to be promptly returned south without a trial. This was the Fugitive Slave Act.

The trouble with the Compromise of 1850 was that it didn't really solve the problem of slavery. Northerners would not cooperate in enforcing the Fugitive Slave Act. Southerners in Washington, D.C., could easily buy slaves in nearby Virginia. Again the problem of what to do about the growth of slavery in the United States was just postponed. Abolitionists and supporters of slavery continued their bitter debates.

3. What state was admitted as a free state in 1850?

4. Why did the Fugitive Slave Act need cooperation from Northerners?

Why did Senator Douglas propose the Kansas-Nebraska Act?

In less than four years, the old problem of slavery in the territories was opened again. This time trouble came in the Kansas and Nebraska territories. Kansas was getting ready to become a state.

Henry Clay was no longer in Congress to offer another compromise. However, Stephen A. Douglas, the "Little Giant," tried to take his place. Senator Douglas of Illinois was a very short man. But as a speaker and a leader, he was considered a giant.

Douglas was very ambitious. He wanted to become President. One way this Northerner hoped to gain support was to please people in the South. If he

Stephen A. Douglas tried to please both North and South so he would be elected President.

played his cards right, he might get the whole nation behind him.

In the Missouri Compromise, Congress had drawn a line across the West. Slavery was allowed south of the line. Because Kansas and Nebraska were north of the line, they could not have slaves.

Senator Douglas said this was unfair. Kansans and Nebraskans should have the right to decide for *themselves* whether they wanted slavery or not. So Douglas pushed the Kansas-Nebraska Act through Congress. This law said that the Missouri Compromise was no longer in force. The people of Kansas and Nebraska could vote for or against slavery as they pleased.

The South was pleased with the Kansas-Nebraska Act. There was a good chance that Kansas would now become a slave state. For this very same reason, the North was alarmed. Slavery was on the march into western territories that had once been free.

5. Who proposed the Kansas-Nebraska Act? Why?

6. Why did the South like the Kansas-Nebraska Act? Why didn't the North like it?

Kansas-Nebraska Act 1854

Why did Americans take the slavery issue to the Supreme Court?

If the people of Kansas were going to vote on slavery, each side wanted its people there to cast ballots. Poor Kansas! It became a battleground. It was called "Bleeding Kansas." New England abolitionists sent guns, money, and settlers to vote in the coming elections. Proslavery border roughnecks crossed the river from neighboring Missouri. They brought illegal ballots, more guns, and still more settlers to vote.

No peaceful election was held in Kansas. Each passing year saw more fighting and bloodshed. Senator Douglas's idea of letting the people decide for themselves had become a complete failure.

Finally, Americans decided they would take their tough question to the Supreme Court. Did the Constitution allow Congress to forbid or control slavery in territories? To find out if slavery could be controlled by Congress, the Supreme Court heard the Dred Scott case in 1857.

Dred Scott was a slave who said he should be free because he had been taken into free territory in Minnesota by his owner. Chief Justice Roger Taney and the majority of the Court ruled that "slaves were property." People could take their property where they pleased in the United States. Slavery could go *anywhere*, the Court said.

In the South there was joy over the Supreme Court's decision. In the North, there was great anger. The writer William Cullen Bryant wrote that the

Abolitionists and proslavery forces (with cannon) clash at Hickory Point, Kansas, about 23 miles (37 km) north of Lawrence.

flag should have the light of the stars and the streaks of morning red erased from it; it should be dyed black. . . . Are we to accept, without question, these new readings of the Constitution? . . . Never! Never!

7. Why didn't the plan for letting settlers themselves vote on slavery work out?

8. Who was Dred Scott? What was the Supreme Court's ruling in the Dred Scott case?

What did the South demand as the price for staying in the Union?

Southern leaders were sure that the North needed the South. But, they said, the North gave little to the South. If things got too bad, the South could get along very well by itself. Cotton was King! Cotton would support Southerners. What the South really was demanding as the "price" for staying in the Union was:

1. The right for slavery to spread. Southerners insisted that slavery be allowed in new states and territories. Some Southerners wanted the United States to take over Cuba or other lands in warm climates where cotton and slavery could go.

2. No interference with the "property rights" of Southerners. Slaves were property. Every time Northerners helped slaves escape, they were really stealing property.

3. An end to attacks on slavery. The North had to recognize the South's right to own slaves.

9. What were the three conditions which the South said must be met for it to stay in the Union?

Part Three

The Build-up to War

How did a book feed the fire?

In 1852, a New England woman named Harriet Beecher Stowe wrote a powerful book called *Uncle Tom's Cabin.* Although she had never lived in the South, she described slavery as being very cruel. She had, of course, heard and read about slavery.

Hundreds of thousands of people read and cried over the story. They believed the book was the truth about slavery.

Stowe's book was made into a play. *Uncle Tom's Cabin* was a great hit on the stage. Many Northerners who had not listened to the abolitionists turned strongly against slavery after seeing or reading *Uncle Tom's Cabin.*

Southerners were very angry about *Uncle Tom's Cabin.* They also were worried about its popularity. It was widely read not only in the United States, but in Europe as well.

Several Southern writers tried to produce books which would reply to Harriet Beecher Stowe. One even entitled his book *Uncle Tom's Cabin as It Is.* But none of those books drew many readers.

1. Who wrote *Uncle Tom's Cabin*?

2. Why were Southerners angry about that book?

When and why was the Republican party organized?

Death comes to political parties just as it does to people. In the mid-1850s, a political group called the Whig party died because it tried to avoid taking sides on slavery.

But for every death there is a birth. The Republican party was born in 1854 after the Kansas-Nebraska Act was passed. The Republicans took a strong stand on the slavery issue. Eastern business people and western farmers liked the party's number one demand—that slavery be kept out of all the territories.

The first Republican candidate for President was the famous John C. Frémont. (See page 264.) Frémont had led five exploring trips to the Far West. Using the campaign slogan of "Free Soil, Free Speech, Free Men, and Frémont!" the Republicans almost won the election of 1856.

3. When was the Republican party founded?

4. What was its position on slavery?

Why were the Lincoln-Douglas debates important?

Two men ran for election to the Senate from Illinois in 1858. But it was no ordinary election. As the two candidates debated, the whole nation listened.

Abraham Lincoln was the Republican candidate. He did not make a very good appearance. Lincoln stood six feet four inches tall (183 cm). His long arms and big hands hung down from a coat that looked as though it had been made for his opponent. That opponent was Stephen Douglas, the "Little Giant." Douglas was only about five feet tall (152 cm). But he was a "giant" as a speaker.

In the debates Lincoln argued that slavery was "a moral, a social, and a political wrong." Douglas replied that it was up to the people to decide this question. Lincoln said he would let slavery continue where it was already established—but it could not go any further. Again, Douglas said it was up to the people in the territories to decide whether they wanted slavery to spread or not.

Douglas won the election to the Senate at the end of the debates. But Lincoln had gained many followers and was known from coast to coast. As a leader of the Republican party, he looked forward to being a candidate for President in 1860.

John Brown pauses for a farewell on his way to the scaffold. This romantic painting was made in 1884.

5. Why was the race between Lincoln and Douglas no ordinary election?

6. What was Lincoln's stand on slavery in the debates?

Was John Brown a hero or a murderer?

John Brown was a Northern abolitionist who believed that God had given him the task of freeing the slaves.

Brown went to Kansas and took part in the fighting there. Then in 1859 he tried to start a slave uprising at Harpers Ferry, Virginia. Brown and a band of eighteen men, including his sons and five blacks, seized a government weapons storehouse. They killed several citizens and waited for slaves to rise up and join them. None came. However, the United States Marines arrived. Brown and his men were quickly trapped in the storehouse. Silver-haired, wild-eyed old Brown was captured.

John Brown was given a speedy, but fair trial. Friends asked for mercy, saying he was insane. Brown said he was not.

Eight days after the raid, Brown was hanged as a traitor and a murderer. He marched bravely to the scaffold. He said he was proud to die for slaves.

Brown's courage made many Northerners say he was a hero or a saint. In his memory, the song "John Brown's body lies a'mouldering in the grave" was written.

Brown may have been a hero to Northerners. To the South he was a murderer! There was no way to bring back the innocent lives he had taken in his wild rebellion. Southerners said, "There! You see? That is exactly what the North wants to do to us." Murderer or hero, John Brown was a man Americans will never forget. His raid marked a big step towards the Civil War.

7. What happened to John Brown?

8. How was he regarded by the North and South?

Who were the candidates in the election of 1860?

The election of 1860 was a four-way race. The Democratic party split over the slavery question and put up two candidates. Stephen A. Douglas, the "Little Giant," was chosen by the Northern wing of the party. Southern Democrats backed a strong proslavery man, John C. Breckinridge of Kentucky.

The up-and-coming Republican party held an exciting convention in Chicago. It named Abraham Lincoln as its candidate.

The border states were torn between the North and the South. They ran John Bell of Tennessee for President.

The Northern Democrats wanted to save the Union by keeping things as they were. Douglas warned that if Lincoln was elected, the South would leave the Union.

The Republicans promised that, if elected, they would not permit slavery to expand into the western territories. They also favored a high tariff. With money raised from the tariff, they would encourage settlement of the West. A railroad would be built to the Pacific Ocean.

The Southern Democrats demanded the right to expand slavery into the western territories. They also said it was the government's duty to protect slavery there. The Southerners were against high tariffs. (See page 219.) Tariffs cost them money and ruined their trade.

The border states were eager to keep peace. They did not take sides between North and South, and offered no program.

9. How many candidates ran for President in 1860? Who were they?

10. What did the Republicans say they believed in? The Southern Democrats?

Why was the election of 1860 important?

The year 1860 has been called the most dangerous and terrible year the United States has ever known. North and South were on a collision course.

Southerners made no secret of their dislike of Lincoln. They called him a "Black Republican" who talked too much about human rights. The governor of Georgia said that if the Republicans won, he would ask the Georgia legislature for one million dollars for "defense."

Lincoln did win the election in 1860. He received 40 percent of the popular vote. Douglas received 30 percent. Breckinridge and Bell ran far behind. But Lincoln received 180 electoral votes. Douglas got only 12. He carried only Missouri and part of New Jersey. (See maps, page 289.)

Lincoln did not get a single electoral vote in the South. States of the lower South had threatened to leave the Union if Lincoln was elected. Now they began to go.

South Carolina was the first to leave the Union on December 20, 1860. By February, six more states followed. They were Mississippi, Florida, Alabama, Georgia, Louisiana, and Texas. Eight other Southern states waited and thought the matter over. Finally Virginia, Arkansas, North Carolina, and Tennessee voted to leave the Union. This made a total of eleven states.

11. Why did Southern states begin to leave the Union?

12. Which state was first to go? When did it leave?

How did Northerners feel about the breakup of the Union?

The states that left the Union called themselves the Confederate States of America. They were also called the Confederacy. Their first capital was at Montgomery, Alabama, but it was soon moved to Richmond, Virginia. Jefferson Davis of Mississippi was elected president of the Confederacy.

Many Northerners found what was happening hard to believe. In the past,

A young Lincoln splits logs in this 1858 painting. His frontier background appealed to voters.

Lincoln's stovepipe hat became his trademark. "Honest Abe" won the election of 1860.

Southern politicians often had threatened to leave, or *secede* from, the Union. Few people believed those threats were real. In the North, Senator William Seward of New York said, "They did not humbug [fool] me with their secession. And I do not think they will humbug you." Seward also told Americans, "If we keep entirely cool and entirely calm and entirely kind," the South would forget about secession.

Lincoln, too, asked the people to stay calm. He told them, "If the great American people will only keep their temper on both sides of the line, the troubles will come to an end."

In March 1861, Abraham Lincoln took the oath of office as President. His inauguration address was directed to the South. In it, Lincoln said plainly that no state had the right to leave the Union. He begged the South not to go, saying:

In your hands, my dissatisfied countrymen, and not in *mine* is the momentous [big] issue of civil war. . . . We are not enemies, but friends. We must not be enemies.

However, Lincoln warned the South that he had an oath to obey. He had sworn before God to "preserve, protect, and defend" the government of the United States against any attack.

13. Why did Lincoln and Seward urge Americans to "keep cool"?

14. What oath did Lincoln say he had to obey?

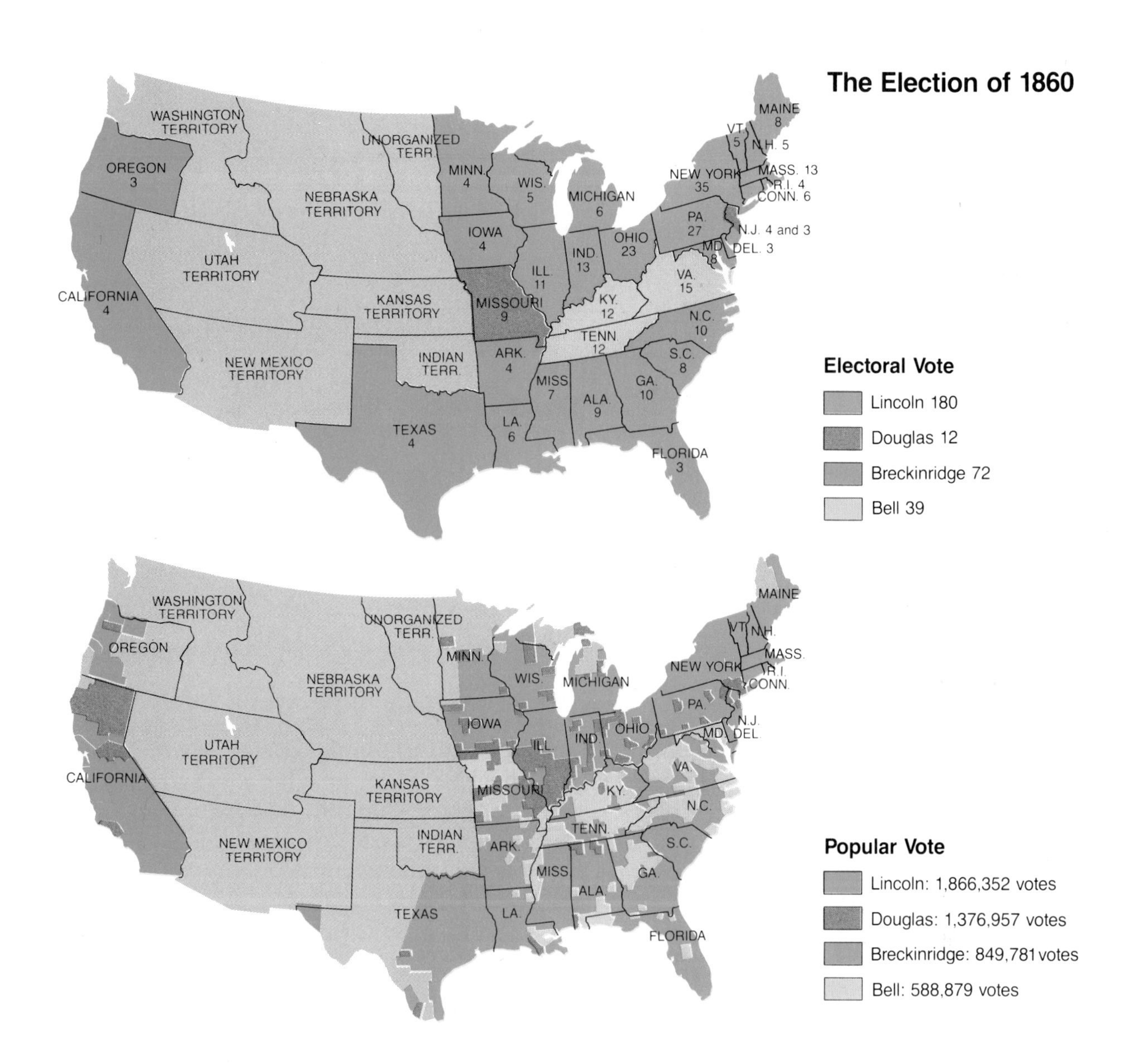

When and where did fighting begin?

Fighting between the North and South began at Fort Sumter. The fort lay on a small island in Charleston Harbor, South Carolina. It was held by United States troops. Their supplies were running low. Lincoln told the South that he was sending provisions to the fort.

The Confederate government demanded the surrender of Fort Sumter. The soldiers of the United States refused. On April 12, 1861, the cannons of Charleston opened fire on the fort. Admiring crowds watched, cheered, and waved handkerchiefs as the guns roared.

Fort Sumter was a sitting duck for the guns ringing Charleston Harbor. The fort was badly pounded and set on fire. There was nothing its defenders could do except surrender and lower the American flag. Southerners rejoiced over their victory.

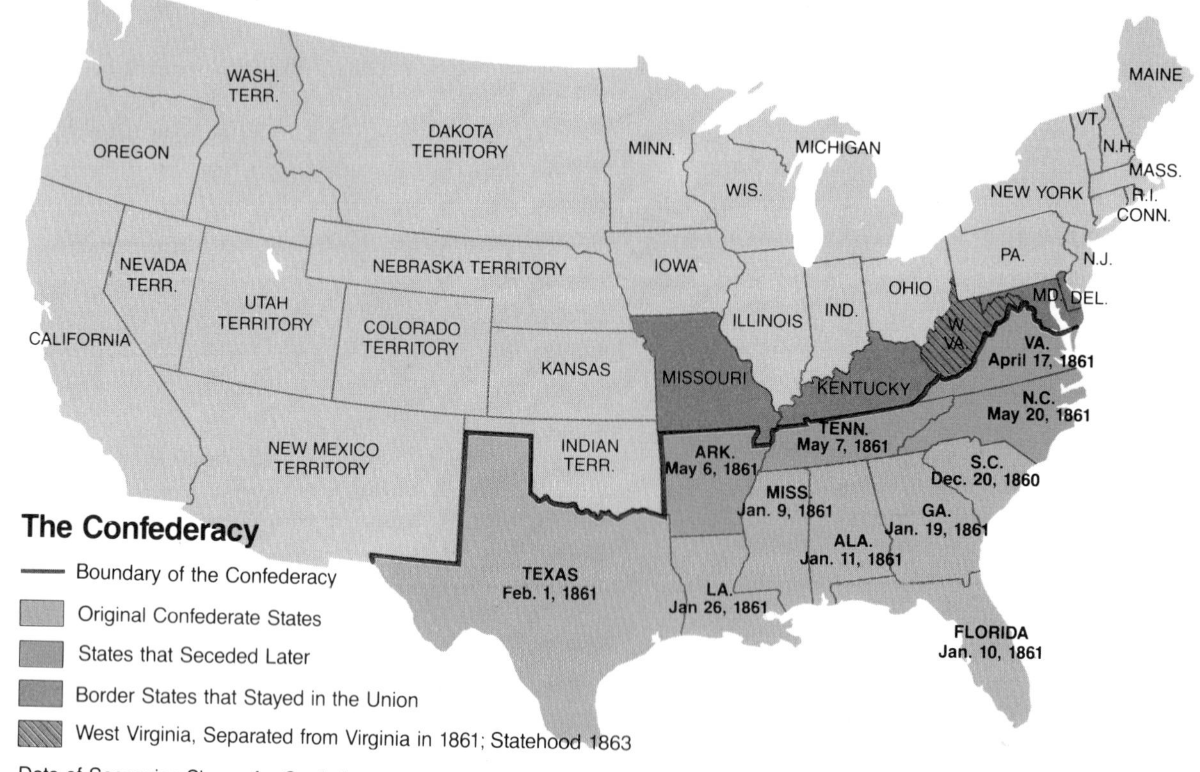

When the American flag was fired upon, the people of the North were shocked. Many Northerners had felt that the South should be allowed to leave the Union in peace. But the fall of Fort Sumter changed their minds. Almost every Northerner demanded that the South be punished and not permitted to leave the Union.

President Lincoln asked for an army of 75,000 volunteers. Many more answered his call. The years of cold war were over. Suddenly the hot war had come.

15. Why did the South attack Fort Sumter?

16. How did the North's feelings change after Fort Sumter fell?

This optimistic 1860 cartoon shows President Lincoln rejoining North and South with "Union glue." But Lincoln was unable to stop the secession of the Southern states.

Part Four

The Nation at War

What surprises lay in store for both sides in the war?

When the war began, both sides expected that it would be short, easy, and that they would win. They also thought that the war would be fought mainly along the border between the Union and the Confederacy. But time was to prove them wrong on all those counts.

First, the war was not short. It lasted almost exactly four years, from April 1861 to April 1865.

Second, it was anything but easy. It was hard and bitterly fought. Some 600,000 persons died as a result of the war.

Third, the area over which battles raged was far wider than anyone had dreamed possible. That area stretched from the Atlantic Ocean in the east all the way to the Mississippi River (and even beyond) in the west. (See map, page 294.)

Even the first big battle of the war turned out to be a surprise, at least as far as the North was concerned. The Battle of Bull Run, in Virginia, opened the Civil War. The North had great confidence in its armies. "On to Richmond!" was the battle cry. In July 1861 a Union army marched from Washington, D.C., into Virginia. Northerners thought this was going to be exciting fun! Members of Congress and their families took picnic lunches along to watch the battle.

If there was any picnic at the Battle of Bull Run, it was a Southern picnic. After a bad start, the Confederates rallied and defeated the North. The untrained Union troops fled back to Washington in confusion.

Bull Run taught the North a lesson. This was not going to be an easy war. Northern soldiers would have to be well trained. They would have to fight hard if they ever expected to conquer the South.

1. What expectations about the war did both sides have as it began?

2. What "lesson" did the North learn at Bull Run?

How was the war fought in the West and in the East?

The Union did well in the West. Its greatest general, Ulysses (yü lis′ ēz) S. Grant, was in command there.

Grant moved south into Tennessee. Then he pushed down the Mississippi River. His aim was to cut off Arkansas, Louisiana, and Texas from the other Confederate states.

While Grant drove south, Union warships and troops captured New Orleans. Then they moved north. Finally, in 1863, Grant captured Vicksburg, the South's last fort on the Mississippi. The North then controlled the whole river.

Having succeeded in the West, Grant now turned to the East. His help was badly needed there.

The South fought very well in the East. Every time that Northern forces moved on Richmond, the South threw them back. Southerners were fighting on their own soil to protect their homes and families. This made them fierce and brave. And they had truly great leaders. General Robert E. Lee, their commander, showed great skill in battle after battle of the long Civil War.

Historymaker

He was 55 years old and at the peak of his physical and mental powers when the offer came to him. All his life he had been a soldier. He had served his nation well and gladly. Now the nation was on the eve of a war it had hoped would never come. It invited him to become field commander of the United States Army. The offer was tempting. It was a "crown" for any military career. But, after agonizing for many hours, he not only turned it down, he resigned from the army.

Who was that man? He was Robert E. Lee, who still is regarded as the most capable general in the history of the United States. As a strategist, or battle-planner, he is second to almost no one in the history of the world.

Robert E. Lee

Why did Lee spurn the offer to become field commander of the United States Army? Perhaps the best explanation is found in a letter he wrote to his sister, Anne Lee Marshall, just two days after he said "no."

Arlington, Virginia
April 20, 1861

My dear sister:

I am grieved at my inability to see you. . . . Now we are in a state of war which yields to nothing. The whole South is in a state of revolution. . . .

With all my devotion to the Union and the feeling of loyalty and duty of an American citizen, I have not been able to make up my mind to raise my hand against my relatives, my children, and my home. I have therefore resigned my commission in the Army. . . . I hope I may never be called upon to draw my sword. I know you will blame me; but you must think as kindly of me as you can, and believe that I have endeavored [tried] to do what I thought right.

Your devoted brother,
R. E. Lee

What did Lee think was "right"? He believed that his duty lay in serving his native state, Virginia, even though he did not agree with everything it did. Lee did not believe in secession. He told his son, "Secession is nothing but revolution." Lee did not believe in slavery. Although he had owned a few slaves at one time, he had set them free. He thought slavery was morally wrong. Yet he chose to stay with Virginia when it seceded. He explained his feeling this way to his son:

A Union that can only be maintained by swords and bayonets . . . has no charm for me . . . I shall return to my native state and share the miseries of my people. Save [except] in defense I will draw my sword on none.

Lee did return to his native state, and was asked to head its forces. He accepted the post. For the next 34 months he did his best to "defend" the state of his birth. Then he was named General-in-Chief of all the Confederate armies.

During the long course of the Civil War, Lee never had a force which compared in numbers, guns, or equipment to his opponents. The odds were always against him. Even so, Lee almost always outfought and outfoxed the armies sent against him. Two key battles went against Lee, however, and they turned the tide. Lee's first big loss came at Gettysburg, when he tried in vain to move the battleground into the North. Although that loss was not his fault, he took responsibility for it. He even offered to resign as general, but Jefferson Davis would not hear of such a thing. Lee's second and final loss came in April 1865. He faced General Ulysses S. Grant and his thousands outside Petersburg, Virginia. By then Lee had fewer than 8000 soldiers with guns. His men had only enough ammunition for two more hours. His ragged troops had not been fed for six days. Even their horses were hungry. They munched on what spring grass they could find, their ribs clearly visible. There was no way Lee could carry on. He was forced to surrender. The end of the long, bloody Civil War had come at last.

Lee met Grant in a small farmhouse. There Lee signed the surrender. Then slowly and sadly he rode over the rolling hills back to his waiting troops. As they saw him coming, they pulled off their hats and waved them in salute. Tears streamed down their dirty, weather-beaten faces. Some of the soldiers surged forward to grasp Lee's hand. Others reached out to touch his famous and faithful horse, Traveller. Lee was overcome at the demonstration of affection and respect. Struggling to control his emotions, Lee spoke these few words: ". . . we have fought through the war together. I have done my best for you; my heart is too full to say more."

The war was over, but like many Southerners, Lee had no home to which to return. Once "The Arlington," a spacious house overlooking the Potomac River had been his home. It was part of his wife's inheritance. But in 1863 it was sold for nonpayment of taxes. So Lee went to live in Richmond for a time. He was treated kindly by federal officers, but he was a paroled prisoner. Like others who had borne arms against the United States, Lee had been charged with treason. He never was brought to trial, however.

In June 1865, Lee applied for a pardon. It was not granted.

In the midst of his gloom, a new opportunity came to him. He was asked to be president of Washington College in Lexington, Virginia. He gladly accepted the invitation. So well did he serve the school that on his death its name was changed to Washington and Lee University.

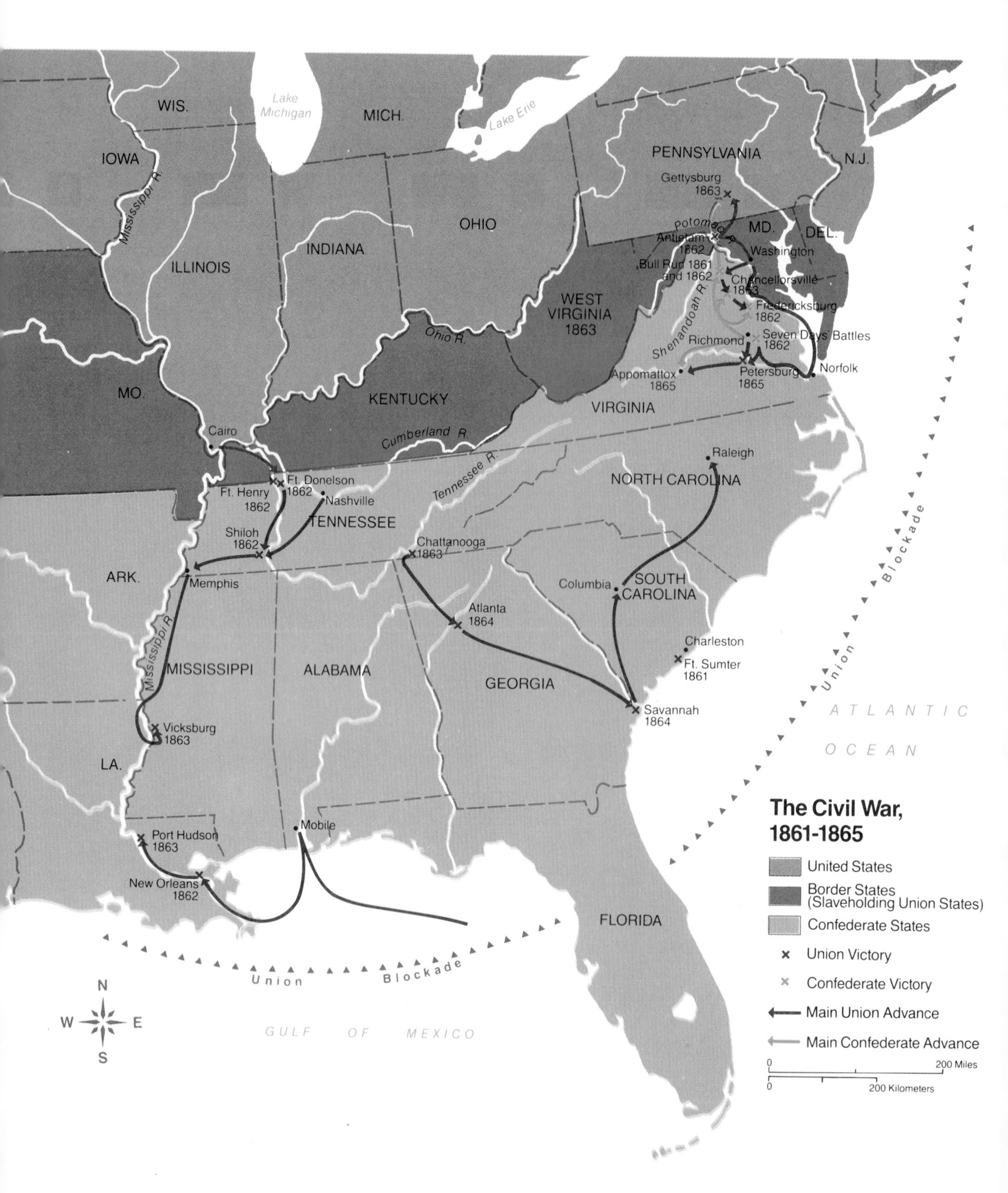

The Civil War, 1861-1865
United States
Border States (Slaveholding Union States)
Confederate States
Union Victory
Confederate Victory
Main Union Advance
Main Confederate Advance
0
200 Miles
0
200 Kilometers
WIS.
Lake Michigan
MICH.
Lake Erie
PENNSYLVANIA
N.J.
IOWA
Mississippi R.
OHIO
INDIANA
ILLINOIS
Gettysburg 1863
Potomac R.
Antietam 1862
MD.
DEL.
Washington
Bull Run 1861 and 1862
Chancellorsville 1863
Fredericksburg 1862
WEST VIRGINIA 1863
Shenandoah R.
Richmond
Seven Days' Battles 1862
Petersburg 1865
Norfolk
Appomattox 1865
Ohio R.
MO.
KENTUCKY
VIRGINIA
Cairo
Cumberland R.
Tennessee R.
Raleigh
NORTH CAROLINA
Ft. Henry 1862
Ft. Donelson 1862
Nashville
TENNESSEE
Shiloh 1862
Chattanooga 1863
ARK.
Memphis
Columbia
SOUTH CAROLINA
Atlanta 1864
Charleston
Ft. Sumter 1861
MISSISSIPPI
ALABAMA
GEORGIA
Savannah 1864
Vicksburg 1863
LA.
Port Hudson 1863
Mobile
New Orleans 1862
FLORIDA
ATLANTIC OCEAN
Union Blockade
Union Blockade
GULF OF MEXICO
N
W
E
S

3. In what section of the country did the North do well? Who was in command there?

4. In what section did the South do well? Who was in command there?

Why did Lincoln decide to free the slaves?

In 1862 the war was going badly for the North. The war in the West had not yet been won. The South was strong in the East. Northerners knew at last that the war would not be short. They were losing heart. Abolitionists said, "Stop this useless war and let the South go its own way."

The North faced another danger. Britain was friendly with the South. Britain threatened to help the South against the big Northern "bully." The war was going badly enough for the North without having to worry about Britain, too.

Abraham Lincoln thought about the problems of the North. Something needed to be done to rally the people. The war must be made worth fighting and dying for if the North was to win it.

President Lincoln was not an abolitionist like William Lloyd Garrison or John Brown. Lincoln believed slavery was wrong, but that was not why he had gone to war against the South.

At the start of the war, Lincoln had just one goal in mind. That goal was to defeat the South and bring it back into the Union. The war was *not* being fought to free the slaves. It was being fought to keep the United States from splitting in two.

But in 1862, Lincoln changed his mind about slavery and the Civil War. He still wanted to save the Union. But he also decided to free the slaves and end slavery in the United States forever.

U. S. Grant was a clerk in a hardware store at the start of the Civil War. He became the Union's greatest general.

There was a cause worth fighting for! From now on, the North would fight for the mighty cause of freedom.

5. Why did people in the North begin to lose heart about the war?

6. For what new cause did Lincoln decide the war should be fought?

What was the Emancipation Proclamation?

Emancipation (i man′ sə pā′ shən) means "to be set free." *Proclamation* means "announcement." President Lincoln announced to the world that on January 1, 1863, all slaves held in the Confederate states were to be considered free. Northern armies would fight to bring them freedom. And all slaves freed by the North were invited to help their own

Soldiers in trenches wait near Petersburg, Virginia in 1864. Trench warfare started during the Civil War.

cause by joining the Union armies. Nearly 200,000 of them did just that.

The Emancipation Proclamation greatly lifted the spirits of the North. Abolitionists who had been against the war were now very much in favor of it. Northerners became more determined to see the war through to victory.

Lincoln's announcement also removed the threat of Britain's helping the South. The British could not help in a fight against a country that was trying to get rid of slavery. The British themselves had abolished slavery in 1833.

The Emancipation Proclamation changed the course of the Civil War. It gave new life to the discouraged North. It took away the South's hope of getting help from Britain. And it added many thousands of black soldiers to the Union armies.

7. What does Emancipation Proclamation mean?

8. How did the Proclamation help the North?

When and where was the turning point of the war?

Early in 1863, Lee's Southerners made their last gallant try to win the war. Lee outfoxed and outfought several Northern generals in Virginia. Then he marched his army north all the way into Pennsylvania. The South was fighting on Northern soil.

The Union and Confederate armies met in battle at the little town of Gettysburg on July 1, 1863. For three days the two sides slugged it out. The North was pushed back onto a row of hilltops. But not even the fiercest Southern charges could break through the troops in blue. The Yankees held, and General Lee had to take his brave Rebels back to Virginia. Never again did the South seriously threaten the North.

News of Union victories at both Gettysburg and Vicksburg reached the North on the nation's birthday, July 4, 1863. It was the beginning of the end for the South.

9. What happened at the Battle of Gettysburg?

10. Why was the Battle of Gettysburg important?

How did the Civil War end?

Almost two more years of hard fighting remained in the war. Time after time General Lee won battles against much larger Union forces. But the North was strong, and its commander was General Grant, who was determined and capable. Northern forces attacked the South time and time again from all directions. General William Sherman burned Atlanta and marched through the South from Georgia to South Carolina. Sherman's mission was to make it impossible for the South to continue fighting. His troops burned crops and houses. They destroyed cotton, machines, and bridges. They left a scar

Focus on Skills

The bar graph below compares the economic resources of the North and South before the Civil War. Bar graphs show the relation of one part of something to other parts of the same thing. Use the graph to complete the following exercises.

1. Write one sentence that summarizes the information shown on the bar graph.
2. Make two bar graphs showing the following information: The North had 71 percent of all railroad track in the country. The South had 29 percent. The North had 92 percent of all the industrial workers. The South had 8 percent.
3. Select any one of the bars in the graph. Use the information it contains to make a pie graph.

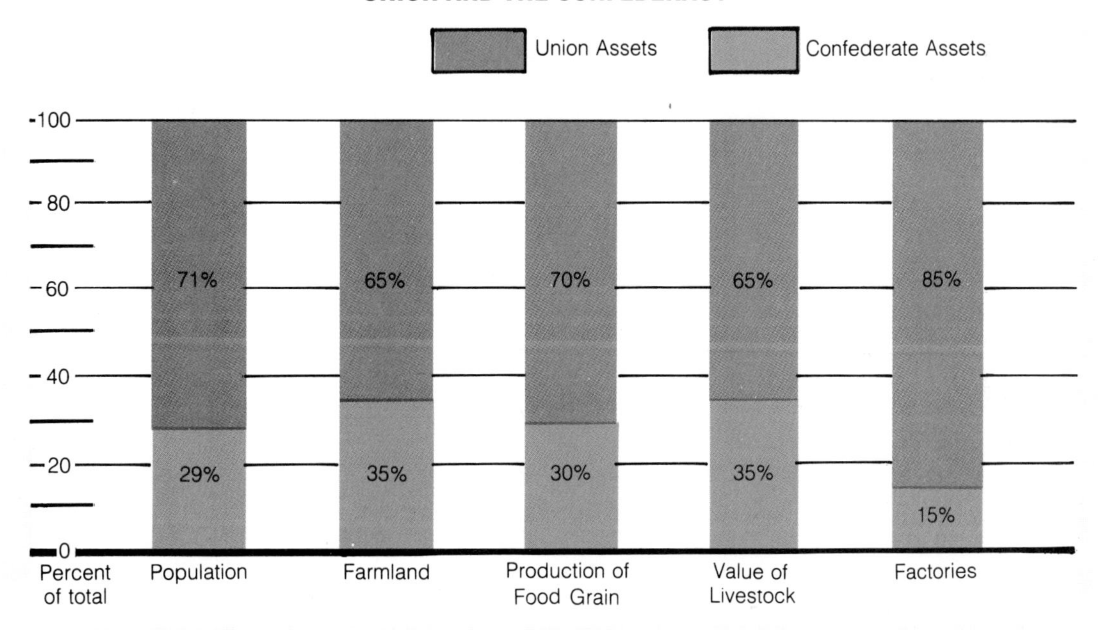

60 miles (96 km) wide through the South. Finally in 1865, Lee had to surrender to Grant at Appomattox (ap′ ə mat′ əks) Court House, Virginia.

The terms of surrender were generous. Southern soldiers were treated with respect. They were allowed to go home to their farms to get ready for spring planting. General Grant allowed the Confederates to keep their horses and mules to help with the farming.

11. When and where did the Civil War end?

Building Your Vocabulary

Complete each of the following sentences by selecting the correct word from those listed below.

1. Lincoln challenged Douglas to—?—in the election of 1858.
2. Although the South threatened many times to—?—from the Union, most Northerners did not think that would ever happen.
3. To avoid bloodshed and the breakup of the Union both North and South tried to—?—.
4. John Brown tried to lead a slave—?—at Harpers Ferry.
5. The states that left the Union were known as the—?—.
6. The—?—Proclamation changed the course of the Civil War.

compromise	debate
Confederacy	secede
uprising	Emancipation

Recalling What You Have Learned

Match the name of each person in Column A with the item with which he or she is identified in Column B.

Column A	Column B
1. John Brown	A. Emancipation Proclamation
2. Stephen A. Douglas	B. The Confederate States of America
3. Harriet Tubman	C. Harpers Ferry
4. Robert E. Lee	D. "Free Soil, Free Speech, Free Men"
5. Ulysses S. Grant	E. underground railroad
6. Dred Scott	F. Kansas-Nebraska Act
7. Harriet Beecher Stowe	G. Confederate army
8. John C. Frémont	H. Union army
9. Jefferson Davis	I. Supreme Court case on slavery
10. Abraham Lincoln	J. *Uncle Tom's Cabin*

Discussing the Important Ideas in This Chapter

1. How and why did the attitude of Southerners toward slavery change in the 1830s?
2. What were the major differences between the North and South?
3. About 75 percent of the white population of the South did not own slaves. Why did they support slavery?
4. How did slaves protest? How did Southerners respond to these protests?
5. Why weren't Americans able to work out a compromise to prevent war?

6. What were the major arguments for and against slavery?
7. Americans often settle important questions by voting. Why then couldn't settlers in Kansas settle the question of slavery by voting?
8. Why did the Emancipation Proclamation change the course of the Civil War?

Improving Your Map Skills

Use the map shown on page 294. It will help you answer these questions.

1. Which city served as the "permanent capital" of the Confederacy?
2. Locate Washington, D.C., the capital of the United States. Estimate the distance between the two capital cities.
3. Name the four states which bordered the Confederacy in the North.
4. Which state was divided in two during the course of the Civil War? Which part sided with the Union?
5. In what general direction did Sherman march from Atlanta to Savannah? How long a march was it?

Improving Your Study Skills: *Reading*

Thomas Rutling was only 9 years old when Lincoln issued the Emancipation Proclamation. Later, when Rutling was a student at Fisk University, he recalled that important event. Read the account. Then show that you understand the details by answering the questions.

About this time [early 1863] the old slaves told me that something was going on. I must listen sharp up at the house and come and tell them what the white folks said. . . .

I was a table waiter then, and after talking over the news at table, missus [the planter's wife] would say, "Now, Tom, you mustn't repeat a word of this." I would look mighty obedient, but—well—in less than half an hour some way every slave on the plantation would know what had been said up at massa's house.

By and by the Rebels [Confederate soldiers] kept getting beaten. Then it was sing, sing all through the slave quarters. Old missus asked what they were singing for. But they would only say, because we feel so happy. One night the report of Lincoln's Proclamation came. Now, master had a son who was a young doctor. I always thought him the best man going. He used to give me money. He didn't believe much in slavery. Next morning I was sitting over in the slave quarters waiting for breakfast, when the young doctor came along and spoke to my brother and sister at the front door. I supposed it was about work. But they jumped up and down and shouted and sang, and then told me I was free. I thought that was very nice, for I supposed I should have everything like the doctor and decided in a moment what kind of horse I would ride.

Interview of Thomas Rutling, 1872, in Gustavus P. Pike, *The Jubilee Singers and Their Campaign for Twenty Thousand Dollars* (Boston, 1873). Quoted in John W. Blassingame, ed., *Slave Testimony* (Baton Rouge: Louisiana State University Press, 1977), pp. 616-617.

1. Who told Tom that he must listen carefully to the conversations in the plantation house?
2. What was Tom's job?
3. How long did Tom say it took for every slave on the plantation to know what had been said at the big house?
4. When the slaves learned the Confederate soldiers kept losing battles, what did they do?
5. Who brought the news of freedom to Tom and the other slaves?
6. How did Tom feel about his master's son?
7. How did Tom's brother and sister react to news that they were free?

Chapter 12

Restoring the Union

Presidential box, Ford's Theater, Washington D. C.

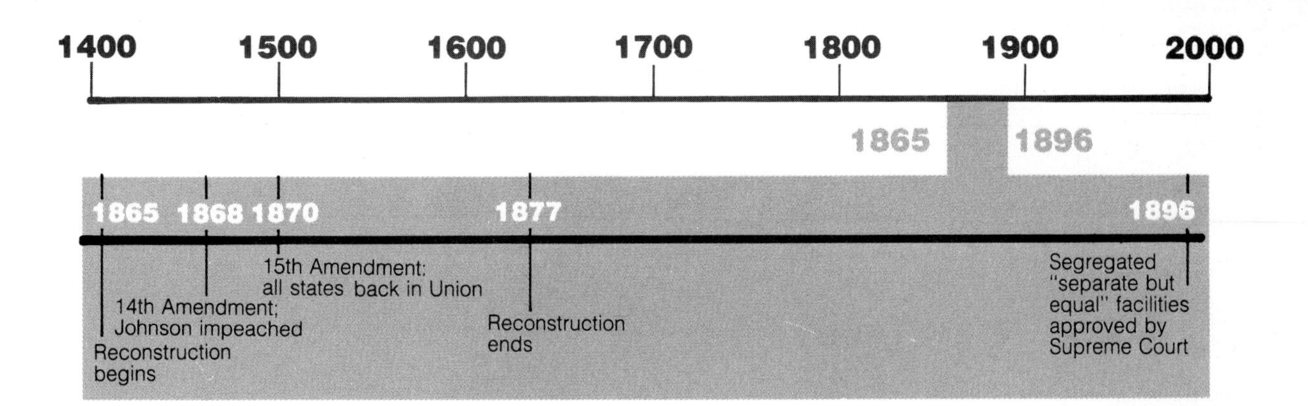

Part One

After the War Was Over

What event stunned the nation in April 1865?

On the evening of April 14, 1865, President Lincoln and his wife went to Ford's Theater in Washington to see a play. The whole North was celebrating its final victory over the South.

A mad actor named John Wilkes Booth hated the President. Booth, pistol in hand, managed to slink up behind the seat where Lincoln was sitting. Suddenly the actor raised his pistol and shot the President in the head. Then Booth jumped to the stage and escaped.

President Lincoln died the next morning. The nation was filled with grief. Booth was finally tracked down, trapped in a barn, and killed.

There was sorrow not only in the North, but in the South. Wise Southerners knew that Lincoln was a kind man. He had planned to "bind up the nation's wounds," as he put it, and to help the South. But now he was dead, and fear and hate walked across the land. With Abraham Lincoln gone, healing the terrible wounds of war would not be an easy task.

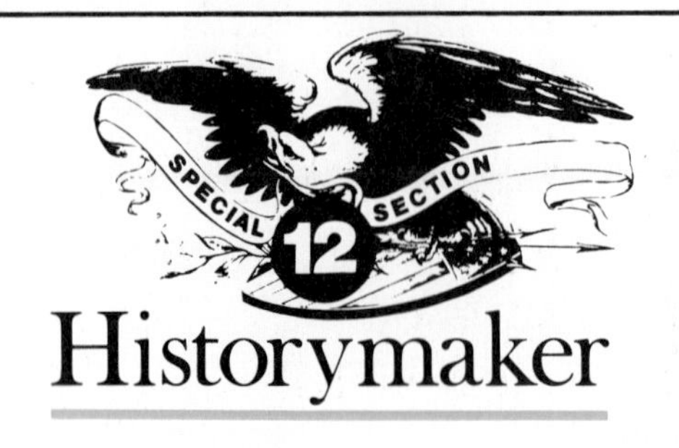

Historymaker

It has been said that if George Washington was the father of the country, Abraham Lincoln kept it from becoming twins. Lincoln holds an equal place with Washington in the country's history.

Born in a log cabin in Kentucky, Lincoln was a son of the frontier. He grew up in the forests of Indiana and Illinois where "the panther's screams filled the night with fear." Young Abe spent much of his youth chopping down trees to clear the woods for farm land. He seldom had time to go to school. According to Lincoln, the whole of his schooling was less than a year.

But Lincoln was ambitious. He loved to write and to read. He had many favorite books which he read time and again. First among his favorites was the Bible. He memorized hundreds of passages from it, and he knew in detail the contents of every book of the Bible. He also liked Shakespeare, *Aesop's Fables,* and *Robinson Crusoe.*

After working as a clerk in a country store, Lincoln became a lawyer. Later he said that he "fell in love with the law," and that "love affair" lasted a lifetime. Looking at his account books, one might think that he took cases for love instead of money. Sometimes he charged his clients nothing at all. At other times he made charges like these:

Trial of J.F. Davis case	$5.00
Trial—Dickinson	$10.00
Centre Case	$2.50

Lincoln enjoyed politics. He served first in the Illinois legislature, then in the United States Congress. When he ran for the Senate, Stephen Douglas defeated him. But Lincoln won a greater prize. He was elected President of the United States in 1860 and reelected in 1864.

As President, Lincoln faced the staggering problem of the Civil War. Probably no President has ever served under more trying circumstances. For more than three years, the North missed chance after chance to defeat its smaller rival, the South. Northerners grew weary of the war. There were riots when young men were asked to sign for the draft. Newspaper editors openly called for an end to the conflict. "Let the South go! Good riddance!" they wrote. They also suggested that it would be a good idea to let Mr. Lincoln go, too. In fact, few people have ever been so harshly and bitterly attacked in the press as Lincoln was. Cartoons pictured him as a gorilla, a bearded ruffian, an ugly beast, and an idiot. Yet Lincoln never responded in kind. He ignored his tormentors. Patiently and firmly he guided the country to final victory.

During the grueling war years, Lincoln worked long hours. He slept so little that there were permanent dark circles under his eyes. He often had his meals carried to his office on a tray. They would be left untouched for hours. He took no regular exercise, and he rarely enjoyed any recreation.

Lincoln and his son Tad

But Lincoln did enjoy people, and he found time for all kinds of visitors.

Lincoln loved to have old friends from the West drop in at the White House. Once an old friend with whom he used to ride in a lumber wagon over the prairies of Illinois came to see him. "Call me Lincoln," he told his friend. "Mr. President is entirely too formal for us."

Lincoln did not wait for soldiers to come to the White House. He went to them. He visited them on the battlefields and in hospitals. A man who accompanied him on one of his visits had this to say:

The President went through the hospital tents . . . and insisted upon stopping and speaking to nearly every man, shaking hands with many of them, asking a question or two here and there, and leaving a kind word as he moved from cot to cot. More than once, as I followed the President through the long lines of weary sufferers, I noticed tears of gladness stealing down their pale faces; for they were made happy by looking into Lincoln's sympathetic countenance [face], touching his hand, and hearing his gentle voice; and when we rode away from the camp, . . . tremendous cheers rent the air from the soldiers, who stood in groups, eager to see the good President.

Noah Brooks, *Washington in Lincoln's Time* (New York: Century Company, 1894), pp. 43-53. Quoted in Paul M. Angle, ed., *The Lincoln Reader* (New Brunswick, N.J.: Rutgers University Press, 1947), p. 395.

On March 4, 1865, Lincoln was inaugurated as President for a second time. It was a gloomy, rainy day. The crowds making their way to the Capitol Building to watch the noonday ceremonies had to make their way through the mud. Victory was not yet in the North's grasp, but by now it was clear that it would not be too long in coming. So when he delivered his inaugural address, Lincoln looked beyond the victory that soon was to belong to the Union. He looked to the future of the nation and to what should be done to make it whole again. Not a word of his own achievements did he speak. Instead he delivered a short speech that has been hailed as one of the greatest in American history. He concluded it with these words:

With malice toward none, with charity for all, with firmness in the right, as God gives us to see the right, let us strive to finish the work we are in, to bind up the nation's wounds, to care for him who shall have borne the battle, and for his widow, and his orphan, to do all which may achieve and cherish a just and lasting peace among ourselves and with all nations.

Lincoln did not live to help "finish the work we are in." Events after his inauguration moved with terrible swiftness. Just about a month later—on April 9, 1865—Lee surrendered to Grant. The long, terrible war was over. Five days after the surrender, Mr. Lincoln did something unusual. He took a night off to go to the theater to relax, never to return. An assassins's bullet claimed his life.

This haunting photograph of the ruins of Richmond, Virginia, shows some of the terrible cost of the Civil War.

1. Who killed Abraham Lincoln?

2. Why were many Southerners sorry about Lincoln's death?

What questions did the Civil War answer and leave unanswered?

Lincoln's death left a great void. But fortunately, the Civil War did answer two questions which had troubled the nation for many years.

First, the war meant that no American could ever again own another person as a slave. The 13th Amendment to the Constitution was ratified in 1865. This amendment abolished slavery everywhere in the United States.

Second, the war showed that the federal government had more power than the state governments. No state could leave the Union. The United States would continue to be one country with one Constitution and one flag.

But those were not the only issues which faced the nation. Wars often create more problems than they solve. The Civil War was no different. It raised many hard questions that still have not been answered—even today. Some problems had to be answered immediately. They were:

1. How to bring the states that had seceded back into the Union. Should they be punished for trying to leave?

2. How to help the South rebuild its cities, farms, railroads, and schools.

3. How to help Southerners learn to live without slavery.

4. How to help newly freed blacks gain their rightful place in society.

Americans had to find ways to solve those problems. They tried to do that during the years between 1865 and 1877. That period in American history is called Reconstruction. Reconstruction means rebuilding. Reconstruction was a time when former slaves were given citizenship. It was a time of great change and much confusion. For the defeated Confederates, it was also a time of bitterness.

3. What two questions did the Civil War answer?

4. What was Reconstruction?

Focus on Skills

Americans first learned that Lincoln had been shot by reading the newspapers. At that time there were no radios or television. When important happenings took place, newspapers were printed hurriedly. They were sold on street corners as "extras." People rushed to buy them so they could find out the latest news. How much of what they were told was fact? How much was opinion? You be the judge in this case. Examine this front-page story taken from *The New York Herald*, April 15, 1865. Read the story line by line. Decide which statements are facts, or matters which could be proved by evidence. An example of a fact is: "President Lincoln and wife, with other friends, this evening visited Ford's Theatre." Determine which are opinions, or what someone thinks about an event. An example of an opinion is: ". . . all seemed delighted with the scene before them." Then compare your decisions with those of your classmates.

THE PRESIDENT SHOT!

Washington, April 15-1:30 a.m.

President Lincoln and wife, with other friends, this evening visited Ford's Theatre, for the purpose of witnessing the performance of the *American Cousin*. . . .

The theatre was densely crowded, and all seemed delighted with the scene before them. During the third act, while there was a temporary pause for one of the actors to enter, a sharp report of a pistol was heard, which merely attracted attention, but suggested nothing serious, until a man rushed to the front of the President's box, waving a long dagger in his right hand and exclaiming 'Sic Semper Tyrannis!' [thus ever to tyrants] and immediately leaped from the box, which was in the second tier to the stage beneath, and ran across the opposite side, making his escape, amid the bewilderment of the audience, from the rear of the theatre, and mounting a horse, fled.

The screams of Mrs. Lincoln first disclosed the fact to the audience that the President had been shot, when all present rose to their feet, rushing towards the stage, many exclaiming 'Hang him! Hang him!'

The excitement was of the wildest possible description, and of course there was an abrupt termination [end] of the theatrical performance.

There was a rush towards the President's box, when cries were heard: 'Stand back and give him air.' 'Has any one stimulants?'

On a hasty examination it was found that the President had been shot through the head, above the back of the temporal bone. . . .

He was removed to a private house opposite to the theatre, and the Surgeon General of the Army sent for to attend to his condition. . . .

A military guard was placed in front of the private residence to which the President had been conveyed. An immense crowd was in front of it, and deeply anxious to learn the condition of the President. It had been previously announced that the wound was mortal [fatal], but all hoped otherwise. The shock to the community was terrible. . . .

What was homecoming like for the soldiers of the South and the North?

Southern soldiers came home to see the terrible cost of the war. Many cities were in ruins. Looters had run off with everything they could get their hands on. Stores, warehouses, docks, bridges, and houses needed to be rebuilt.

In the country, farm animals were gone. Crops had been destroyed. Someone said that even a crow would have to carry its own food if it wanted to fly over Georgia.

Returning Union soldiers found busy cities and towns. More factories had been built and more people employed.

Because the war was fought in the South, property in the North was not destroyed. Even so, there was great sorrow for returning Union soldiers. Many of their friends and relatives had been killed or wounded.

5. How had the war affected the South? The North?

What was life like for the freed slaves?

Freed slaves found that some of their biggest problems were still ahead of them. Thousands wandered about homeless and hungry. Many were confused. Some thought the "day of jubilee" had come. They had been told that the government was going to give them "forty acres and a mule." Some ex-slaves even paid money to fast-talking, phony salesmen for red, white, and blue markers to put at the corners of the land they were to get.

Freed slaves were happy to be their own masters at last. Suddenly, however, they discovered they had no food, no work, no shelter. Their old familiar way of life was gone. They had no land to plant crops and no tools to work at other jobs. Instead, there was great need and suffering.

6. How well off were the freed slaves?

7. What did the expression "forty acres and a mule" mean?

How did Lincoln want to solve the problem of Reconstruction?

Lincoln began his plans for Reconstruction before the war was over. He was a forgiving man. He said, "Blood cannot restore blood. Government should not act for revenge." He wanted the nation to be reunited as quickly as possible. Lincoln said he would pardon all but the most important leaders in the Confederacy.

Lincoln argued that since a state cannot leave the Union, the South had never really withdrawn. Southerners needed to do only a few things to take back their full places in the Union. When 10 percent of the voters in a state swore allegiance, they could set up a new constitution. They had to do away with slavery. Then their state could rejoin the Union.

8. How did Lincoln feel toward the South?

9. What were Lincoln's terms for rejoining the Union?

What were Johnson's Reconstruction plans?

After Abraham Lincoln was assassinated, Andrew Johnson became President of the United States. If ever a man ran into trouble, it was Johnson.

To begin with, Johnson was a Southerner from Tennessee. He was the

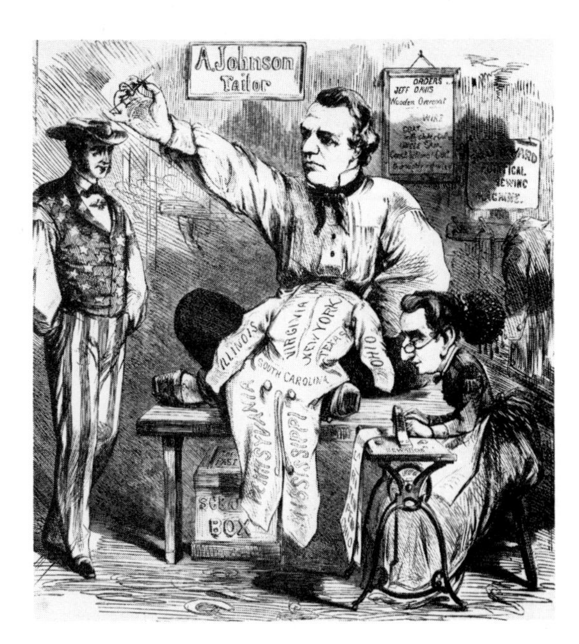

An 1865 cartoon shows Andrew Johnson, who once was a tailor, sewing up Uncle Sam's Union coat.

only Southern senator to remain loyal to the Union when the Civil War broke out. Lincoln picked him to be Vice-President in 1864. Many people in Washington were very unhappy over Lincoln's choice of a Southerner as his running mate.

To make matters worse, Johnson had a bad temper. He was not good at getting along with people. Soon he had strong enemies in the government.

President Johnson went ahead with much the same plan that Lincoln had made. The Southern states were told to form new governments. They were to abolish slavery by ratifying (approving) the 13th Amendment. Most of the Southern leaders were pardoned by Johnson. The door stood open for the South to return home to the Union.

Most Southern states were quick to meet Johnson's terms for rejoining the Union. They abolished slavery and elected members to Congress to represent them in Washington. It looked as if the trouble between North and South was over.

But when the Southerners went to take their seats in Congress, they were not permitted to do so. Northern members of Congress would not allow it. These Northern leaders disagreed with Lincoln and Johnson. They argued that the Southern states had left the Union completely. Bringing them back in was *not* the job of the President. Only Congress had the power to bring the states back.

The American people were bewildered by this problem. Who should be in charge of Reconstruction, Congress or the President?

10. How different were Johnson's plans for Reconstruction from those which Lincoln had made?

11. What happened when the South sent its representatives to Congress?

Part Two

The Fight between the President and Congress

Who were the Radical Republicans?

A *radical* is a person who believes in making sweeping changes. The Radical Republicans were Northern members of Congress who wanted to make sweeping changes in the South. They said that President Johnson was treating the beaten enemy much too well.

Radical Republicans wanted to keep Confederate leaders from regaining power. These were the people who had started the war in the first place, the Radicals said. Another goal of the Radicals was to insure that former slaves received full citizenship and voting rights. The Radicals held this goal because they felt that blacks were entitled to full equality with whites. But there was another reason as well. Blacks would vote Republican, because the Republicans had freed them. With the black vote, the Republicans would be able to control the South and the whole of the nation.

1. What is a radical?

2. What were the goals of the Radical Republicans?

Frederick Douglass (center), and six prominent ex-slaves are honored in this poster.

What were Black Codes?

When the legislatures of the Southern states met for the first time, they adopted "Black Codes." These laws were supposed to control the former slaves. Some of these laws would not let blacks gather in groups. Others said that blacks who quit their jobs before their contracts ended could be put in jail. In South Carolina laws said that blacks could do only farm or domestic work. Still other laws said that black children could be made to work without their parents' consent. Blacks and Radical Republicans hated the Black Codes.

Americans had different reactions to the Black Codes. Blacks held mass meetings to protest them. Former slaveholders said these laws were needed. They worried about possible race riots. They said that the newly freed slaves needed rules to make them responsible. In Congress, the Radical Republicans said that the Black Codes were putting blacks back into slavery. "Was the Civil War fought for this?" they asked.

3. What restrictions did the Black Codes put on blacks?

4. How did former slaveholders feel about the Black Codes? How did Radical Republicans feel about them?

What suggestions were offered to help ex-slaves?

The great black leader Frederick Douglass was very critical of the way freedom was given to slaves. He said that when the Russians freed their serfs (slaves) "they were given three acres of ground upon which they could . . . make a living." But in this country, he said, slaves

were sent away empty-handed, without money, without friends, and without a foot of land. Old and young, sick and well, were turned loose to the open sky, naked to their enemies.

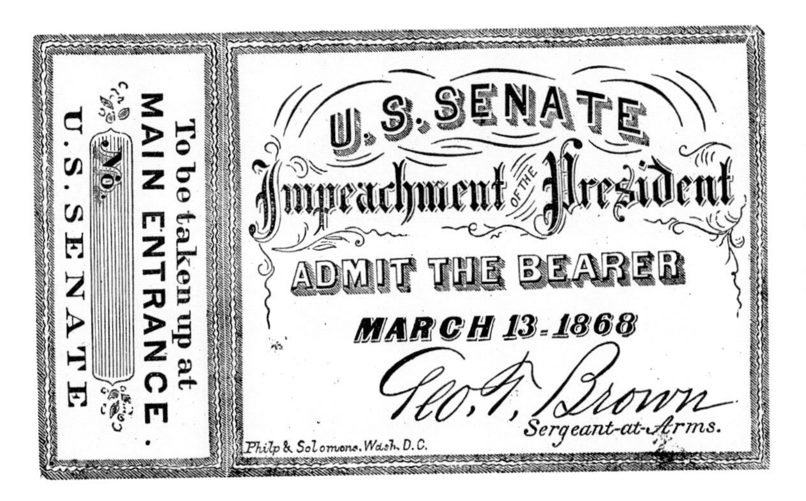

Tickets were issued for Andrew Johnson's trial by the Senate. As the nation held its breath, the Senate voted on the impeachment brought by the House. Johnson remained President by one vote.

A number of suggestions for solving the blacks' problems were made during the Reconstruction period. Some suggestions were:

1. Establish a new territory of "Lincoln" somewhere in the West. Allow only ex-slaves to move to Lincoln. Give them all free land. Have the federal government supply help and education until statehood was granted.

2. Seize the land of all those who had fought against the United States. Distribute that land to ex-slaves.

3. Colonize blacks in foreign countries. Abraham Lincoln himself was interested in this plan. As it turned out, Haiti and Liberia were the only countries willing to take refugee blacks. Most blacks did not want to leave the United States.

4. Move blacks to the North and West. Some blacks did take up homesteads. Others went to live among the Indians. Many went to Kansas. A former slave, "Pap" Singleton, said he was the Moses of his people. He led 300 blacks to Kansas in 1873. Then he returned south and persuaded many more to go. By 1879 between sixty and eighty thousand had gone to Kansas. The bitter climate of the state, with its extremes of hot and cold, was too much for many. They returned home disappointed.

5. Why was Douglass critical of the way freedom was given to slaves?

6. What four suggestions were made for solving the problems blacks faced during Reconstruction?

How did Congress handle the problems of Reconstruction?

Radical Republicans gained control of Congress. They made war on President Johnson by passing laws over his veto. Johnson fought back by traveling around the country making fiery speeches. But almost everyone, at least in the North, was against the President.

In 1867, Congress passed a law that wiped out the governments of the Southern states. Federal troops were sent into the South to help organize new state governments. Black men began to vote and to hold office in the new governments. Some Southern white leaders were not allowed to take part. In several states, black voters outnumbered white voters.

To get back into the Union, the Southern states had to ratify the 14th Amendment. This gave citizenship to blacks. And it protected them from having their rights taken away by the states. All the Southern states ratified the 14th Amendment. All of them were back in the Union by 1870.

The Radicals were determined to protect the blacks' right to vote. So they passed the 15th Amendment. It was ratified by the states in 1870. It says that neither the federal government nor any state government can take away anyone's right to vote because of race or color.

7. Who gained control of Congress?
8. What do the 14th and 15th amendments say?

Why was President Johnson impeached?

Anger between President Johnson and the Radical Republicans reached a white heat. Johnson made wild speeches against the Radicals. Sometimes he swore. Such conduct only hurt the President in his desperate fight.

Then Congress passed the Tenure of Office Act. That law said that Johnson could not fire anyone without the permission of Congress. Johnson vetoed the law. He did even more than that. He fired the Secretary of War, Edwin M. Stanton. Johnson said Stanton was a Radical "spy" in his cabinet.

Johnson's move was just what the Radicals in Congress had been waiting for. They impeached the President and ordered him tried for "high crimes."

Impeach means to accuse an official of bad behavior. The impeached official is then put on trial to see if he or she should be put out of office.

The trial was a very important event. Our whole system of government was being challenged. If Congress could get rid of a President because it didn't agree with him, future Presidents would have very little power. Our system of checks and balances would be upset. (See page 128.) The President would be controlled by Congress.

Presiding as judge at Johnson's trial was the Chief Justice of the Supreme Court. Members of the Senate were the jury.

The trial lasted for two months. Crowds watched from the Senate galleries. Newspapers were filled with stories of what happened each day.

Johnson had four good lawyers. They made the charges brought against him by Congress look foolish. Even so, the President barely won his case. A two-thirds majority was needed to defeat him. He was saved by exactly one vote.

Andrew Johnson finished out a miserable term as President and did not run for reelection.

9. Why was Johnson's trial a very important event?
10. What happened to Andrew Johnson after the trial?

Why did Southerners object to Reconstruction governments?

For years historians have argued about how bad Reconstruction really was. Some say Reconstruction was a "tragic time" when there was a "blackout of honest government." Other historians argue there has been too much talk about bad government. The many good things done during Reconstruction have been overlooked. In Part Three of this chapter, we shall look at both the good and the bad of this time.

Most Southerners who lived during Reconstruction saw it as a very difficult period. They especially resented all Northerners who went to the South during that time. They called them *carpetbaggers*. Carpetbaggers were supposed to be able to pack everything they owned into one cheap bag made of carpet material. Southerners said carpetbaggers

Carpetbaggers got their name from the cheap luggage shown in this cartoon by Thomas Nast.

came only to get rich. Even missionaries and schoolteachers who went South to help were called carpetbaggers.

Scalawags (rascals) were also hated. They were white Southerners who had been against secession. After the war, the scalawags cooperated with the Reconstruction governments.

Southerners did not like the fact that federal troops were stationed in the South to see that peace was kept. In some cases, white Southerners were not allowed to vote or hold office.

Southerners complained bitterly. They said the people with the most experience in government could not take part when they were most needed. They said Southerners faced "taxation without representation." They were angry about carpetbaggers and scalawags making laws. They said these get-rich-quick artists were using poor, uneducated blacks as "fronts."

11. Why did Southerners dislike carpetbaggers and scalawags?
12. How did Southerners feel about federal troops stationed in the South?

Part Three

Good and Bad in Reconstruction

What bad and what good did the Reconstruction governments do?

There is no doubt that graft and theft took place in the South during Reconstruction. The worst of the Reconstruction legislatures bought hams, perfume, champagne, and even coffins with public money. The public debt doubled and tripled in the Southern states. All of those things obviously were evils for which the Reconstruction governments were responsible.

On the other hand, Reconstruction governments did do many good things.

Each Confederate state had to write a new constitution. Delegates, blacks and whites, wrote constitutions which provided free public schools for all children for the first time in the South. The new constitutions made it easier for citizens to vote and hold offices. Men no longer had to be property owners to vote or serve on juries. Cruel punishments for crimes were forbidden.

In some states better tax systems were set up. Public works were started. Women gained additional rights. For the first time in its history, South Carolina passed a divorce law.

1. What were some of the bad things which Reconstruction governments did?

2. What were some of the good things which they achieved?

What did the Freedmen's Bureau accomplish?

Just before the Civil War ended, Congress set up the Freedmen's Bureau. "Freedmen" was the term used for ex-slaves. The bureau was to run for one year to give "provisions, clothing, and fuel" to blacks and whites driven from their lands. Helping Southerners start their lives again was such a hard job that the Freedmen's Bureau lasted for seven years.

The Bureau did more than just keep people alive and well. Many teachers went south with the American Missionary Association to help. The Bureau set up 4000 new schools. In just three years time, more than 200,000 freed slaves learned to read.

Blacks were very eager for education. In one school in North Carolina, four generations of the same family attended class together. A 75-year-old great-grandmother learned to read along with her 6-year-old great-grandson.

Besides helping blacks get an education, the Freedmen's Bureau offered job training. Health service and legal advice were also given.

Students of many ages attend a school for freedmen.

Some of the most famous black schools in the United States were started by the Freedmen's Bureau. Fisk University at Nashville, Tennessee, began as a primary school in 1865.

Hampton Institute at Hampton, Virginia, began in 1868. General Samuel Armstrong, a white commander of black troops during the Civil War, was its first president. He was interested in helping blacks. His own words tell about his dream. He said:

I will found a school to educate teachers for this race [black] . . . I will begin . . . a more patriotic, more difficult work than fighting for my country. I will open the door for the people whom I dearly love.

Today Hampton is still educating men and women for many professions.

Howard University in Washington, D.C., began in 1867 with the help of the Freedmen's Bureau. Students of all races, men and women from all over the nation, have studied there since then. Howard's medical and law schools are especially famous. Thurgood Marshall, the first black Supreme Court justice, was both a student and a teacher at Howard.

3. When and why was the Freedmen's Bureau set up?

4. Besides helping blacks get an education, what other services did the Freedmen's Bureau provide?

Why were secret societies started in the South?

White Southerners wanted to end the Reconstruction state governments. They said that these governments were run by blacks and carpetbaggers. Some white Southerners organized secret societies to do illegally what they could not do openly. They used fear and violence to try to regain power in the South.

The most famous and feared of the secret societies was the Ku Klux Klan. Night riders wore sheets and covered their faces with hoods. They patrolled the South with guns, whips, and clubs.

Blacks were warned not to vote. The Klan beat and murdered blacks and carpetbaggers to drive them out of public life.

Fair-minded Southerners were upset by the lawlessness of the Klan. They tried unsuccessfully to break up the terror groups. But the Klan was too strong. It continued to terrorize blacks and Northerners. Later the Klan turned its hatred toward Catholics and Jews as well.

5. What was the Ku Klux Klan?

6. How did it operate? What were its goals?

Was the South badly treated after the Civil War?

Being the loser in a war or revolution is never pleasant. In recent years, the world has seen many losers treated badly. People on "the wrong side" of the Russian, Chinese, Cuban, and Iranian revolutions know only too well what defeat can mean. Many of these countries had bloodbaths like that which followed the French Revolution.

Compared to the way other defeated sides have been treated in history, the South did well. There were no wholesale executions. The only people put to death were Lincoln's murderers and one Confederate who was cruel to Northern prisoners of war. Jefferson Davis, the Confederate president, spent two years in prison. Officers of the Confederate army were paroled and sent home with their troops. General Lee said goodbye to his troops and rode home to live in peace. Bloodshed really stopped with the surrender at Appomattox.

Reconstruction officially ended in 1877. At that time federal troops were withdrawn from the South. Even before then, however, the number of troops had been gradually reduced.

Contrary to what many people think, withdrawal of troops did not mean an immediate end to blacks' rights as citizens. Throughout the 1870s and 1880s there were few attempts to weaken their freedom.

In the 1890s, however, the picture started to change. Poor whites began to get political power. Many were anti-black. Laws and customs began which pushed blacks back and took away their rights. We shall read how that happened in the next section.

7. Compared to other defeated sides in wars or revolutions, how was the South treated?

8. When did the Reconstruction officially end?

Part Four

The New South

What was meant by the "New South"?

A Southern writer named Henry Grady first used the term the "New South." He wrote articles and made speeches urging Northerners to set up businesses in the South. He said that a "New South" was rising from the ashes of the Civil War.

Grady wanted friendship with the North. He believed that blacks were entitled to the same rights as whites. No one could blame Grady for trying to get help for the South. The war-torn, devastated South needed help to recover.

In time, the South did get back on its feet. Slowly the ruined cities of the South were rebuilt. Cotton mills and tobacco and furniture factories started.

One important new city suddenly sprang up on the site of a small, sleepy village. This was Birmingham, Alabama, where coal and iron were found in large amounts. Birmingham became a great manufacturing center, the "Pittsburgh of the South."

For a while it looked as though the drive to get industry to the "New South" would succeed. But by 1900 the drive had slowed. Most of the profits of the industries that did develop flowed out to other sections of the country. Prosperity did not return to the South until World War II.

1. Who was Henry Grady? What did he believe in?

2. What new industries sprang up in the South?

Why did the sharecropping system get started in the South?

When the Civil War ended, there was plenty of land and plenty of labor in the South. There was not plenty of money, however. That was the problem. Plantation owners needed workers, but they had no money to pay them. Former slaves and other workers needed jobs badly.

It was clear that landowners and workers needed to cooperate in some way to produce crops. Then they could share the profits they made.

The planters, therefore, divided their land into small farms. Then they turned over these pieces of land to ex-slaves and poor white farmers. The planters provided cabins, seed, and tools for the farmers, but no wages. The farmers lived on the land, but paid no rent. Instead, landowners and farmers produced a crop together—usually cotton.

When the crop was in, the farmers turned over half or one-third of what they had raised to the landowner. In other words, the farmers shared part of

Sharecroppers often found themselves in an endless cycle of poverty.

their crop with the planters as payment for use of the land. For this reason the farmers were called *sharecroppers*.

Sharecropping led to many new problems in the South. Sharecropper families had to be fed and clothed while they waited for their crops to grow. These poor families were forced to borrow money. Owners of country stores charged the borrowers extra high prices.

Soon the sharecroppers were hopelessly in debt. Before their crops were in, they had already spent what little they might have earned.

The system of sharecropping was not slavery. Sharecroppers could not be bought and sold. However, they were forever in debt. Even their children had to work instead of going to school. Sharecroppers were often trapped on their little pieces of land all their lives.

Besides causing many people to fall deeply in debt, sharecropping damaged the South's farmland. Cotton is a plant that wears out the soil. It uses up the soil's minerals. Unlike fruit or grain crops, cotton returns little or nothing to the soil.

The people who loaned the sharecroppers money ordered them to plant cotton—and nothing else. Cotton was in demand and brought higher prices than other crops. So instead of planting fruit and grain that they could have eaten, the sharecroppers did as they were told. They planted cotton until the soil wore out.

3. What is sharecropping? Why did it begin in the South?

4. What problems did sharecropping lead to?

How was freedom for blacks limited?

In the 1890s, Southern legislatures passed laws, and customs began which limited black freedom. Here are some of the ways freedom for blacks was limited:

1. Before a man could vote, he had to pay a poll tax. Those who could not pay were not allowed to vote. Poor blacks and whites were kept from voting in this way. Today the 24th Amendment to the Constitution makes poll taxes illegal for federal elections.

2. Before people could vote, they had to pass a literacy test. *Literacy* means being able to read and write. In many cases, blacks were given harder tests than whites. The white people in control decided who passed the test. The Voting Rights Act of 1965 stopped the use of literacy tests for a time. Use of literacy tests was completely ended by Congress in 1975.

3. "Grandfather clauses" were added to some state voting laws. Under these laws, only men whose father or grandfather had voted on January 1, 1867, were able to cast ballots. Of course, very few blacks had voted in 1867. In 1915 the Supreme Court ruled such clauses unconstitutional.

4. "Jim Crow" laws were passed to separate the races. Trains had separate cars for black and white passengers in the North as well as in the South. Schools, parks, hospitals, and libraries were segregated by law. Custom separated "colored" and white swimming pools, hotels, drinking fountains, and rest rooms. The Supreme Court has declared all such segregation illegal today.

5. How were blacks and poor whites kept from voting?

6. What were the Jim Crow laws?

What happened to dreams of a "New South"?

When Henry Grady called for creation of a "New South," he had two ideas:

1. a "New South" filled with business, industry, and prosperous farms.

2. a "New South" where white people would treat blacks with fairness and justice.

Dreams of a "New South" were good. But they did not come true. As time passed, fewer and fewer Northerners were willing to work for the good things started during Reconstruction. Northerners closed their eyes. They refused to see that the blacks were no longer being protected by the 14th and 15th amendments. They remained silent while blacks were turned into "second class citizens." Jim Crow laws took hold in the North, too. In 1896 the Supreme Court said segregated but "equal" facilities were legal.

While the dreams of a "New South" were fading, a new political trend was growing in the South. White Southerners began to vote only for Democrats. They blamed the Republicans for what had happened to their section of the country during Reconstruction. So when they went to the polls they voted solidly for Democrats for national, state, and local offices. Because of that practice, the term the "Solid South" came into use. The "Solid South" meant that no Republican candidate had a chance to get elected. For fifty years after federal troops left, no Republican presidential candidate won any electoral votes in the South.

7. Why did dreams of a "New South" fade?

8. What was the "Solid South"? Why did it develop?

Building Your Vocabulary

Which word or phrase on the right best explains the meaning of the word in italics on the left?

1. *Reconstruction*	rebuilding	designing
2. *ratifying*	approving	disapproving
3. *radical*	believes in sweeping changes	wants no changes
4. *codes*	laws	voluntary agreements
5. *impeach*	to accuse an official of bad behavior	to approve
6. *sharecropper*	lives and grows crops on another's land	lives and grows crops on own land

Recalling What You Have Learned

Select the correct word or phrase for each of the following items.

1. Lincoln was assassinated by (a) Henry Grady. (b) Andrew Johnson. (c) John Wilkes Booth.
2. Newly freed slaves were called (a) freedmen. (b) sharecroppers. (c) scalawags.
3. Which amendment to the U.S. Constitution outlaws slavery? (a) the 21st Amendment (b) the 13th Amendment (c) the 15th Amendment
4. The purpose of Black Codes was to (a) allow women to vote. (b) control ex-slaves. (c) encourage industry to come to the South.
5. The black leader who was critical of the way freedom was given to slaves was (a) Andrew Johnson. (b) William Tecumseh Sherman. (c) Frederick Douglass.
6. Northerners who went south during Reconstruction were called (a) carpetbaggers. (b) Radical Republicans. (c) scalawags.
7. President Johnson was impeached because (a) Southerners turned against him. (b) he could not get along with Congress. (c) he misused federal money.
8. Which of the following things did the Freedmen's Bureau accomplish? (a) It gave food, clothing and fuel to the needy. (b) It established schools and colleges. (c) If offered job training and legal advice. (d) It did all of the above.
9. The most feared secret society established in the South was the (a) Sons of the South. (b) Ku Klux Klan. (c) Civil War Veterans Association.
10. The term the "New South" was used to describe (a) the rebuilding, industrializing South. (b) the war-scarred South. (c) the prewar South.

Discussing the Important Ideas in This Chapter

1. Why did Lincoln's assassination change the course of history? How might Reconstruction have been different if he had lived?
2. Why did Congress and President Andrew Johnson fight about Reconstruction?
3. What problems did the Civil War solve? What problems did the Civil

War leave unsolved?

4. Many people criticized the way newly freed slaves were treated after the war. How fairly do you think they were treated?

5. How good and how bad was Reconstruction in your opinion?

6. What is sharecropping? Why did it create new problems for the South?

7. Why did some Southerners dream of a "New South"? Why didn't that dream come true?

Improving Your Chart Skills

Below you will find information about the economic growth of the New South. The information is presented in a table. A *table* presents numerical information in rows or columns. A table can present a large amount of data in a convenient form. But, unlike a graph, a table does not translate the data into visual form.

Study the table and answer the following questions.

1. What years does the table cover?
2. About how many items does the table give data?
3. How many more bales of cotton were produced in 1910 than had been produced in 1870?
4. In what year did the amount of land used for farms decline from the amount used ten years before?
5. Look at the numbers of people employed in industry. Which of the

GROWTH OF THE NEW SOUTH, 1870–1910

	1870	1880	1890	1900	1910
Production of raw cotton (in bales*)	3,011,996	5,755,359	7,472,511	9,645,974	10,594,360
Tobacco production (pounds)	178,418,922	199,281,213	348,107,607	604,918,720	802,618,483
(kg)	80,288,514	89,676,545	156,648,423	272,213,424	361,178,317
Farmers and farm workers	-----------	4,611,751	5,735,948	7,331,025	7,048,650
Farmland (acres)	189,556,302	234,919,786	256,605,867	362,036,351	354,452,860
(ha)	75,822,520	93,967,914	102,642,346	144,814,540	141,781,144
Cotton manufacture (by spindle)**	328,551	542,048	1,554,100	4,298,188	10,376,888
Steel production	-----------	3,883	163,599	377,144	543,916
		3,497	147,239	339,430	489,524
Persons employed in industry	-----------	500,342	827,177	1,114,570	1,292,197
Factories	38,759	36,938	46,455	84,257	92,184

*1 bale of cotton = 500 pounds (225 kg) of cotton.
**A spindle is the shaft on which thread is wound. One spinning machine would have several hundred spindles.

following sentences is true? (a) The number of people employed in industry more than doubled between 1880 and 1910. (b) The number of people employed in industry declined by one-third between 1880 and 1910. (c) The number of people employed in industry increased by only a small percentage between 1880 and 1910.

6. Make a bar graph that displays the data shown in the table about the number of factories.

Improving Your Study Skills: *Writing*

Choose one:

Imagine that you were a Southern soldier who returned to find your farm destroyed, your animals gone, your crops burned. Write a letter or diary telling what has happened to you and what you expect to do next.

Imagine that you were a slave in the South. Suddenly you received the good news that you were free at last. But you have no money, no property, no home, no job, no idea where your relatives are. Write a letter or diary telling what has happened to you and what you expect to do next.

Unit Three The Nation's

13 The United States Becomes an Industrial Giant

14 The Disappearing Frontier

15

Growth

Urban America in the Making

16 Politics, Protests, and Progressives

17 Rise to World Power

Chapter 13 The United States Becomes an Industrial Giant

Glenmont, home of Thomas Edison, Edison National Historic Site, West Orange, New Jersey

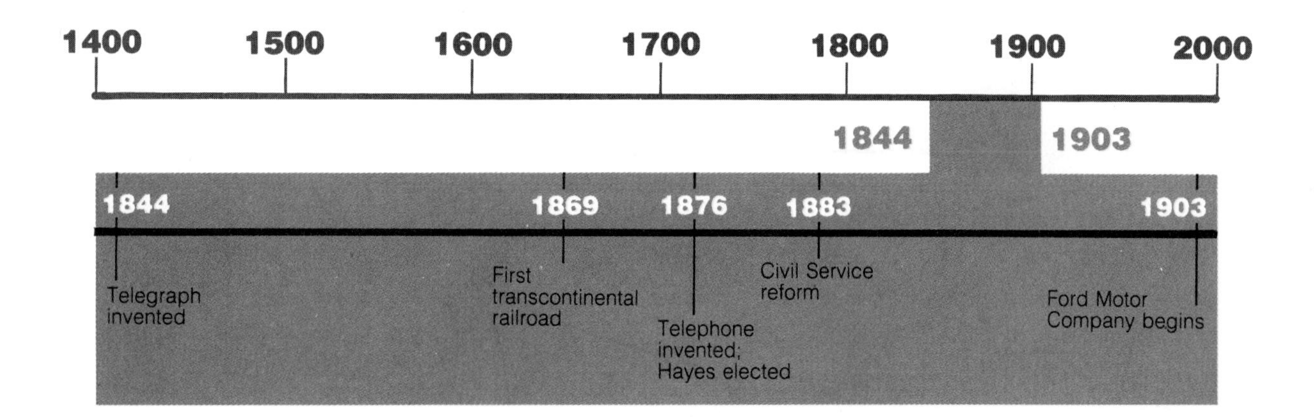

Part One

Railroading Becomes the Nation's Biggest Business

How large was the railroad boom after the Civil War?

Loud whistles and the clacking of railroad wheels rolled the United States into the "Age of Big Business" after the Civil War period. Between 1830 and 1860 Americans had built canals, steamboats, and stagecoaches. Railroads grew rapidly between 1850 and 1860.

When the Civil War ended in 1865 there were 35,000 miles (56,000 km) of track in all of the United States. Most of them were in the eastern third of the nation. Just 35 years later, in 1900, there were almost 200,000 miles (320,000 km) of railroads. That was an increase of more than five times! The United States had more railroads than all of Europe. No section of the country was without train service. One historian describes that amazing growth as the time when "the iron colt became an iron horse."

Railroading did "grow up" in many ways in the 35 years following the Civil War. Inventions made train travel safer. The safety coupler linked cars more securely to one another. The air brake and automatic signaling devices that

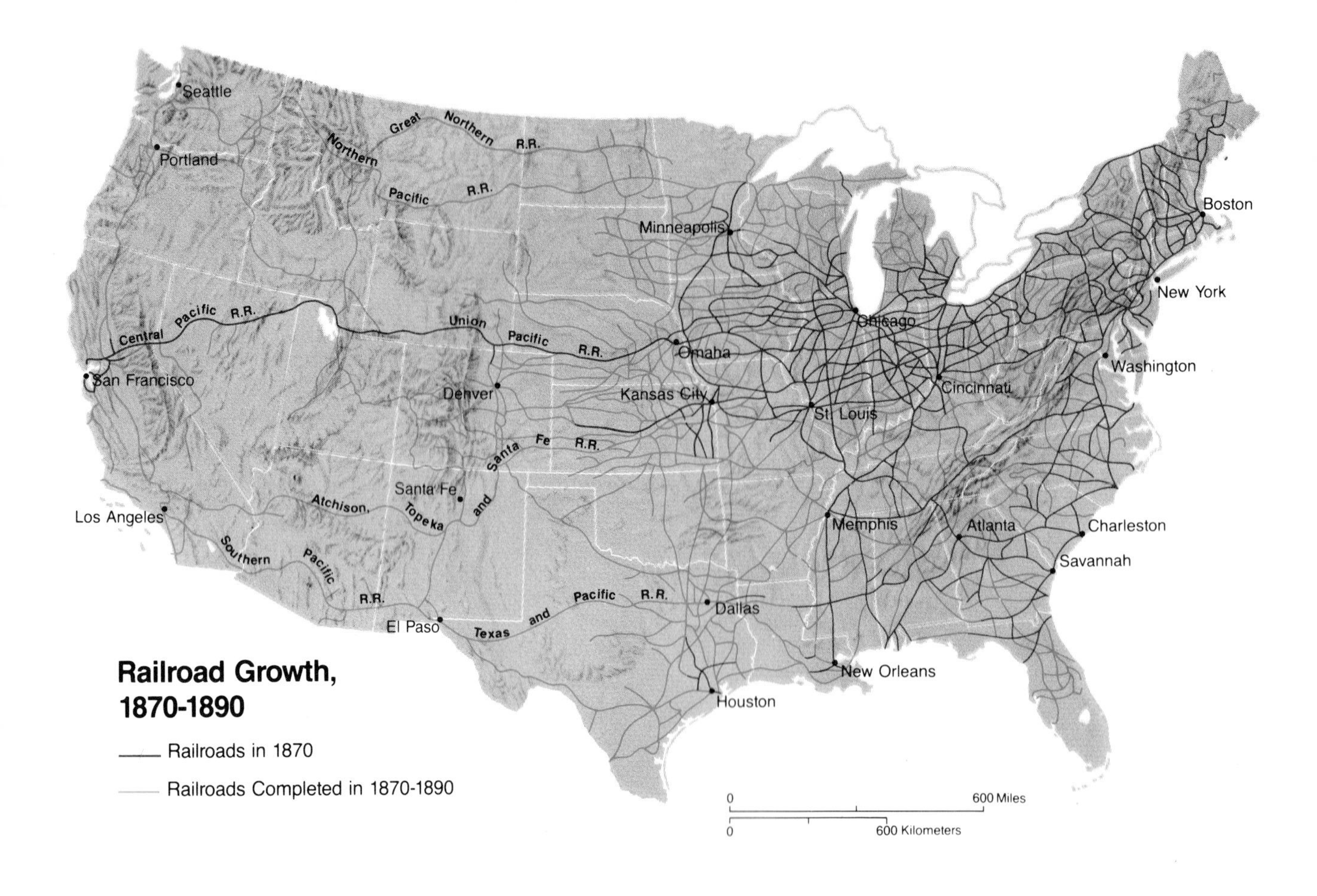

George Westinghouse invented helped to prevent accidents. Inventions also made train travel more comfortable. George M. Pullman built sleeping cars. Passengers could climb into berths and sleep as they traveled. They also could enjoy the comforts of so-called "parlor cars." In the dining cars they could have delicious meals at tables covered with white linen. Prices for such service were high, of course. But the United States was entering a "Gilded Age." And as that age wore on, there were many who not only could afford, but who also demanded such luxuries. And the railroads were happy to provide them.

1. Between 1865 and 1900 how many additional miles or kilometers of railroad track were laid in the United States?

2. What inventions made railroad travel safer? More comfortable?

Why did governments help with railroad building?

Building railroads was expensive. The average cost per mile was $40,000. Clearly no one person could afford much railroad building at that price. Even several people working as partners could hardly afford to build more than just a few miles.

Congress realized that help was needed. Railroads would make the nation strong and rich. To help get them built, the federal government gave large amounts of money and land to private companies willing to do the job. The government gave those companies more than 156 million acres (62 million ha) of land along the railroad routes. Western states gave another 49 million acres (20 million ha). Altogether, the railroad companies were given more land than there is in the whole state of Texas.

State and local governments also were eager to give every privilege they could to the railroads. Bypassed towns often became "ghost" towns. Towns along railroad routes were bound to grow.

More business came to railroad towns. Travelers going through slept in the hotels. They ate in the restaurants and bought goods at the stores.

Settlers moving west wanted land near the railroad tracks so that they could get their products to market easily. More people and more business meant more money pouring into state treasuries from taxes.

3. Why did Congress help the companies willing to build railroads?

4. Why were state and local governments eager to help railroad builders?

How and when was the first transcontinental railroad built?

Americans were pleased as railroads began to connect towns and cities in the eastern half of the country. But they dreamed of something grander. They dreamed of binding the Atlantic and Pacific coasts with ribbons of steel. They dreamed of a transcontinental railroad. To build one would be a costly and difficult undertaking. Some people argued that it could not be done. Still Americans wanted to try.

Congress gave the go-ahead signal for a transcontinental railroad in 1862.

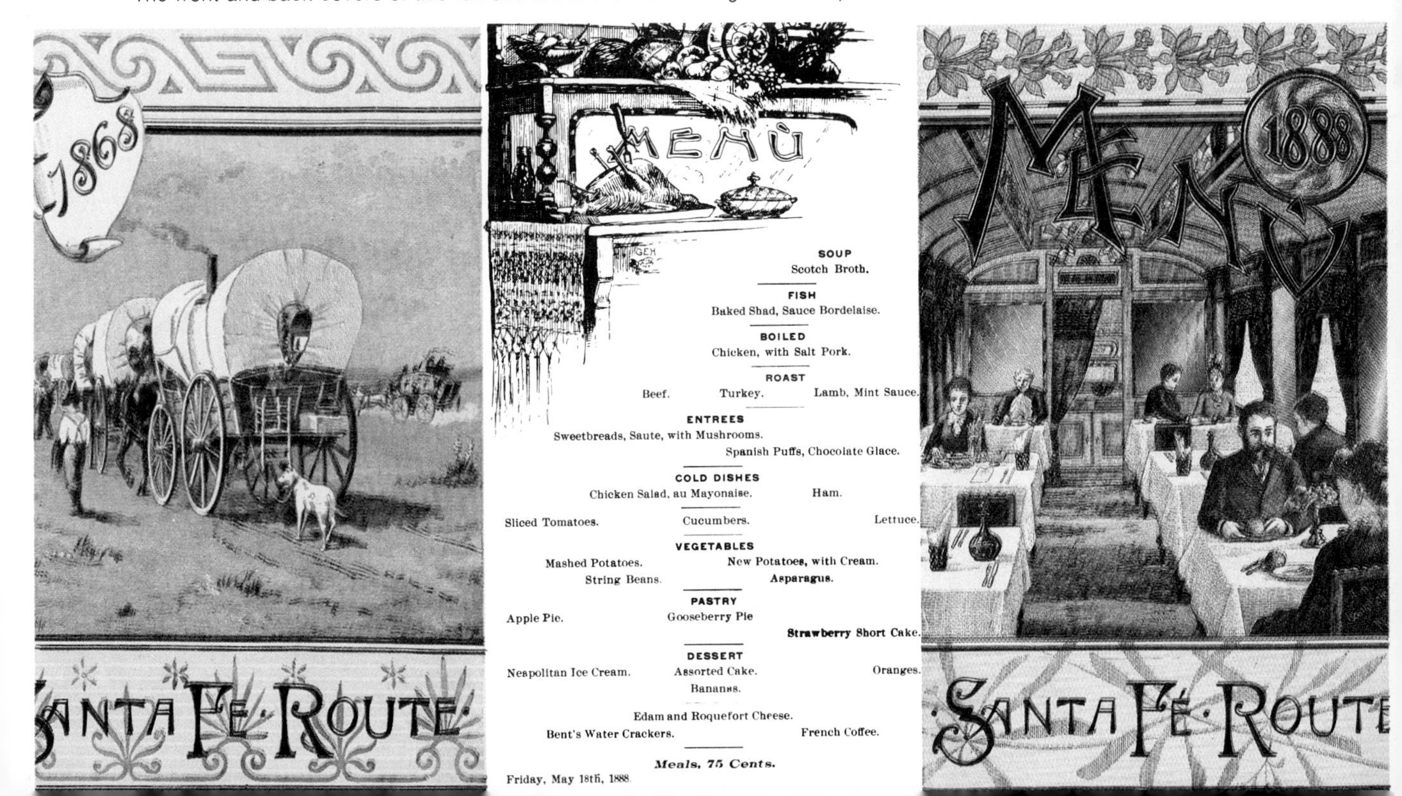

The front and back covers of this railroad menu show the changes in transportation between 1868 and 1888.

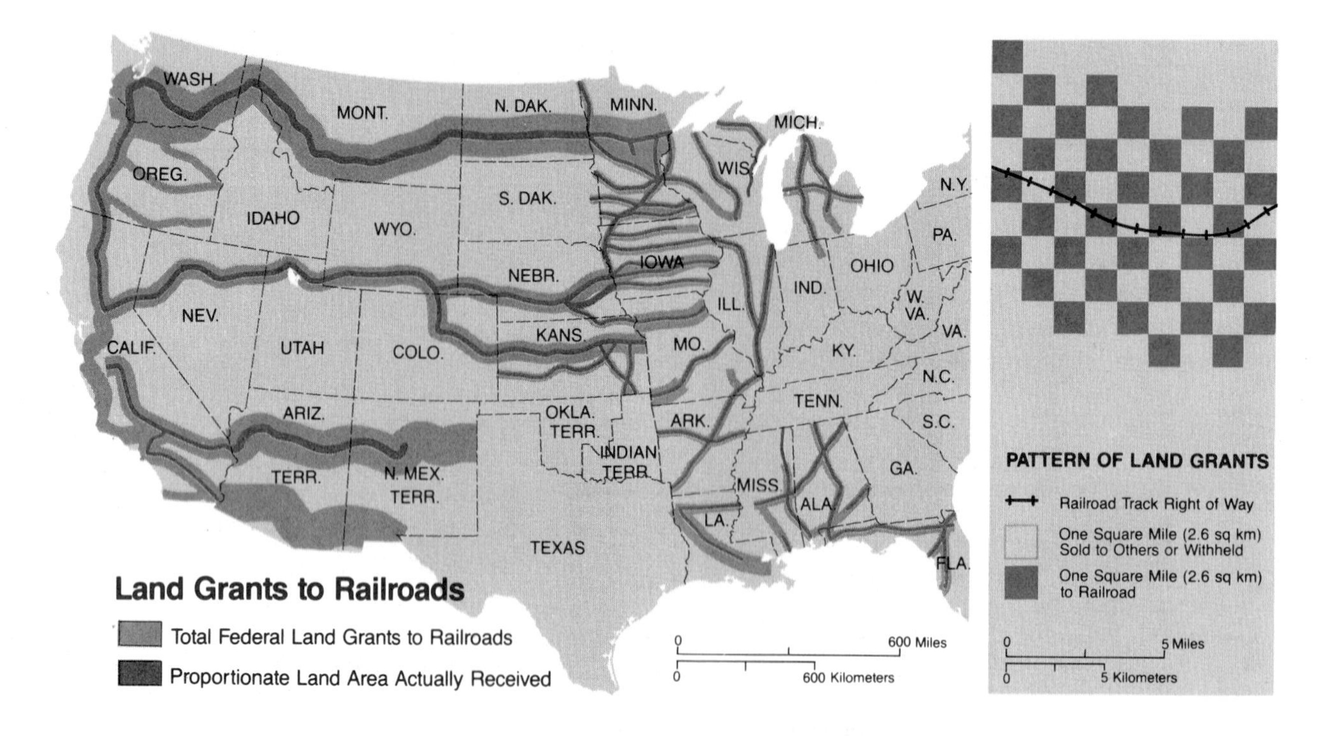

The Union Pacific was to begin in Omaha, Nebraska, and lay track west as fast as possible. Meanwhile, the Central Pacific was to begin laying track in Sacramento, California, and push eastward.

The Central Pacific had the more difficult job. Its owners and engineers wondered, "How could tracks be laid across the towering, mighty, rock-bound Sierra Nevadas?" They also asked themselves where they would find workers to tackle one of the toughest jobs in the world.

The Central Pacific called on the Chinese for help. More than 15,000 Chinese immigrants came to tackle the dangerous task. These fearless workers chipped at the sides of the high Sierra cliffs. They were tied together by ropes around their middles. With hand axes, picks, and shovels, they chiseled out crude footings on steep canyon walls. Then other Chinese used these toeholds to climb up and blast out roadway for track. For such risky work, the Chinese made less than two dollars a day.

While the Central Pacific used the Chinese, the Union Pacific relied mainly on Irish immigrants. The two immigrant groups raced each other.

One day the Irish of the Union Pacific laid six miles (9.6 km) of track. The next day the Chinese laid seven. And so it went. Finally, the Chinese set a record of 10 miles and 56 feet (16 km) in just under 12 hours.

Feverishly the two railroads built toward each other. At last they met near Ogden, Utah, on May 10, 1869, for a "wedding of the rails."

When the two lines were joined on that day, there was a great ceremony. Locomotives from east and west drew together. A golden spike was driven to hold the last rails in place.

It was a popular slogan to say the Irish built the Union Pacific and the

Chinese the Central Pacific. However, many other Americans worked on the railroads as well. Swedes, Germans, Blacks, Mexicans, Scots, and many others all helped in one of the nation's giant adventures.

The importance of the first transcontinental railroad can hardly be overstated. In Philadelphia, citizens were so excited that they again rang the cracked Liberty Bell in Independence Hall. More recently the achievement of building the first transcontinental railroad has been compared to putting Americans on the moon.

5. What two railroads built toward each other? When did they meet?

6. To what other achievement in history has the first transcontinental railroad been compared?

Trains of the Union Pacific and Central Pacific meet at Promontory Point, Utah, near Ogden.

What other transcontinental lines connected the country?

Once the first transcontinental line was built, four other transcontinental lines were completed before the end of the century. Congress gave money to the Union and Central Pacific's builders. But it did not give money to those who followed. All of them, except James J. Hill, who built the Great Northern, did get generous grants of land, however.

By 1893 four more transcontinental railroads were in operation—the Southern Pacific; the Atchinson, Topeka and Santa Fe; the Northern Pacific; and the Great Northern.

The last of the transcontinental lines was the Great Northern, finished in 1893. It was the work of far-sighted James J. Hill. He has been hailed as "the greatest railroad builder of them all." Although Hill made large profits from his railroad, he was concerned about service as well as money. Hill believed that no railroad or any other business could do well unless the people it served did well also. So Hill helped his customers in many ways. He sent demonstration trains along the route. Farmers were invited to visit them and learn better ways to raise crops and cattle. Hill brought five bulls from England and gave them to families served by the Great Northern. He used much of his wealth to build "Hill Schools" for frontier children.

7. What were the five transcontinental railroads completed by 1893?

8. Who was James J. Hill? What did he believe about his customers?

In what ways did railroads change American life?

The steel rails which stretched across the United States had a powerful effect on American life. Railroads came

At That Time

First they came by the hundreds, then by the thousands, and finally by the tens of thousands. Between 1850 and 1882 more than 200,000 Chinese left their homeland bound for *Gum Shan*, land of the Golden Mountains. We know that land better by another name, the United States.

Almost all of the Chinese who came were men. That is because the jobs open to them were chiefly in the mines and on the railroads. The builders of the Central Pacific were especially eager for Chinese workers. They were known for their willingness to tackle any job, no matter how difficult.

The demand for Chinese workers always exceeded the supply. So Americans offered a bounty to Chinese recruiters. Those recruiters went through China giving out handbills. Those handbills were advertisements for the United States. Here is one example:

1862

There are laborers wanted in the land of Oregon, in the United States, in America. There [are many reasons] to go to this new country, as they have many great works there which are not in our own country. They will supply good houses and plenty of food. They will pay you $28 a month after your arrival and treat you considerately when you arrive. There is no fear of slavery. . . . The ship is now going and will take all who can pay their passage. The money required is $54. Persons having property can have it sold for them . . . or borrow money of me upon security. I cannot take security on your children or your wife. Come to me in Hong-Kong and I will care for you until you start. The ship is substantial and convenient.

Au Chan

Russell E. Conwell, *Why the Chinese Emigrate and the Means They Adopt for the Purpose of Reaching America* (Boston: Lee and Shepard, 1871). Quoted in Rhoda Hoff, ed., *America's Immigrants: Adventures in Eyewitness History* (New York: Henry Z. Walck, 1968), pp. 74-75.

Chinese workers cheer as a Central Pacific train passes. The train has just gone through a snowshed built by the workers to protect the train from heavy snow in the high Sierras.

to be thought of both as friend and as foe. Railroading became the single greatest business in the United States. It touched the lives of almost everyone. We shall learn later why some people became angry at the railroads.

After the main lines and the five great transcontinental lines were completed, branch lines were built to connect them. (See map, page 324.) Those branch lines linked the continent from north to south. New England was joined by rail with Florida and Georgia. Other lines tied Louisiana to Illinois. As the 19th century drew to a close, the United States was crisscrossed by more rails than any nation in the world.

Thanks to those miles and miles of railroad track, Americans began to feel a new sense of unity. It was as though the rails were metal arms reaching out to link the giant, sprawling nation.

Exchanging goods became easier. Products made or mined in one part of the country could be loaded onto freight cars and whisked to another part. Freshly slaughtered beef could be shipped from Chicago to eastern cities. California growers could get their fruits and vegetables to eastern markets.

People everywhere enjoyed a new sense of freedom. Railroads could take them from the outskirts of civilization to the great cities. Immigrants who were pouring into great cities could escape those crowded centers. Railroads would carry them to the most distant parts of the United States and sell them land at bargain prices.

New railroads sprang up to meet demand.

9. What other railroad building took place in addition to the main and transcontinental lines?

10. In what ways did railroads change American life?

Part Two

Inventions Change the American Way of Life

How did inventions change life for the average person?

Americans have probably invented more things than any other people in history. Not only have American inventors come up with new machines and products, they have also found new and different ways to produce them.

During the 1800s, railroads and other inventions made the United States into the world's richest nation. We have already read a little about the beginnings of this huge outpouring of inventions. It was called the Industrial Revolution.

After the Civil War, inventing became almost a national pastime. So many things were invented that a "Second Industrial Revolution" took place between the Civil War and 1900. Three-quarters of a million patents for new inventions were granted during those years.

All these new inventions resulted in thousands of new products. Life became better and easier for the American people. The business of making and selling new goods provided Americans with jobs and money.

Of course, there were poor people in the 1800s, just as there are today. But the average person living in 1900 was much better off than the average person who lived 100 years before. In 1800 most people lived on farms. They had no electric light, no running water, no furnaces, and no transportation, except for horses and sailing ships. In 1900 many people had electric light, good heating in their homes, running water, and even telephones. Trains ran everywhere. There were even a few automobiles.

Inventions made life richer and better. Americans wanted more and more of them. Inventions did not "just happen." Inventors and scientists worked long hours in laboratories to create new methods and products.

The industrial and scientific revolutions that took place after the Civil War have never stopped. Today both industry and the United States government spend billions of dollars yearly on inventions and research.

1. Why was the period between the Civil War and 1900 called the "Second Industrial Revolution"? When did that revolution end?

2. Why was the average person better off in 1900 than in 1800?

Why did industry need electricity?

Water and steam supplied power for early factories, railroad locomotives, and ships. But waterfalls and steam engines did not provide enough power to handle industry's growing needs. A much stronger form of energy was needed to run the new machines.

Electricity was a powerful and mysterious force that scientists had studied for centuries. Benjamin Franklin and others experimented with electricity in the 1700s. But it was more a plaything than a source of energy.

Gradually, scientists learned how to store and control this form of energy in batteries, magnets, and coils of wire. When scientists finally put electricity to work, the Industrial Revolution took a giant step forward.

The first important electric invention was the telegraph. It was developed by an American, Samuel F. B. Morse. The federal government gave Morse $30,000 to work on his mysterious "talking wires."

Morse used a magnet wrapped in wire. He sent waves of electric current to the magnet, which caused a piece of metal to knock against it. Long and short knocks made a special kind of code. The code was made up of letters and numbers which could be translated into messages.

In 1844, Morse sent a telegraph message forty miles (64 km), from Washington, D.C., to Baltimore, Maryland. The operator in Baltimore received the message and tapped it back. The message read: "What hath God wrought?" meaning "What has God made?"

3. Why was electricity important to the growth of industry?
4. What was the first important electric invention?

What did the telegraph and the railroads have in common?

The telegraph grew up side by side with the railroads. Telegraph offices were located in railroad stations. Telegraph wires followed railroad lines all across the country.

Railroads provided fast *transportation* for people and goods. The telegraph provided rapid *communication* of news and messages. Together, the telegraph and the railroads knit Americans together.

The telegraph was also the "eyes and ears" of the railroads. A talented black inventor, Granville T. Woods, improved on the telegraph system. He worked out a way to send messages to moving trains. Danger warnings sent this way helped reduce train accidents.

At first telegraph wires were strung only over land. Then better ways of coating wires were invented so that cable could be laid under the Atlantic Ocean.

5. How did railroads and the telegraph grow up together?

Who was Thomas Edison?

Thomas A. Edison and his assistants made the first successful light bulb. In 1879 electric light bulbs began to replace oil lamps in the nation's homes.

Edison and his assistants invented many other things, including the first phonograph, film and projectors for motion pictures, and batteries.

But Edison's greatest achievement was the art of inventing itself. Edison set up the world's first research and development laboratory in Menlo Park, New Jersey. There he and his associates worked day after day for the sole purpose of inventing new machines and processes.

6. Who invented the light bulb?
7. How did Edison change the art of inventing?

How was the telephone invented?

A young Scot named Alexander Graham Bell invented the telephone. Bell came to the United States in the 1870s and made a living as a teacher of the deaf. Naturally he was interested in sound and the human voice. One of his pet projects was to invent a machine that would carry voices by electric current.

One day in 1876, Bell and his assistant, Thomas A. Watson, were experimenting on their equipment. Bell was in one room, Watson in another. Suddenly Bell spilled some acid on his clothes. He called, "Mr. Watson, come here. I want you." The words went through the wire and were heard clearly by Watson in the other room. This was the first telephone message in history.

Within a few years, telephone companies were started. Networks of wires began to crisscross the country. Another great invention and another change in people's ways of living had come to the United States.

8. When and how did Bell invent the telephone?

What new machine was important to the sugar industry?

A former slave invented a machine as important to the sugar industry as the gin was to cotton. Norbert Rillieux (ril′ yu) was an intelligent young man. His master sent him to France to become an engineer. When Rillieux returned to New Orleans, he was a freedman. A large sugar refining plant asked the young college graduate to reorganize its company.

Rillieux invented a machine to speed up evaporation and cut the cost of getting sugar from cane. Before Rillieux's machine was used, sugar was coarse and brown. His new method made fine, white sugar. Rillieux's process of evaporation is still used today to make such products as condensed milk, soap, and glue.

9. Who invented the "sugar machine"? How did it change the production of sugar?

Why did business machines change American life?

The term "blue-collar" workers often is used to describe workers on farms and in factories. Blue-collar workers once made up the majority of the nation's labor force. But after the Civil War more and more new kinds of workers began to appear. They were called "white-collar" workers, because their jobs did not require them to get dirty. As more and more business machines were invented, jobs for white-collar workers opened up in stores and offices. Many women took those jobs.

Probably no invention made more white-collar jobs possible than the typewriter. Many Americans had ideas for typewriters. More than fifty designs were produced before Christopher Sholes of Milwaukee came up with his in 1867. He called it a "literary piano" because keys punched out words instead of music. Sholes's typewriter was the first to be marketed. His keyboard is still in use, almost unchanged. Sholes was proud of his "brainchild." He taught his daughter, Lillian Sholes, to use his keyboard. She is said to have been the first woman typist in the United States.

Not long after the typewriter appeared, the first successful adding machine was ready for use. Cash registers were not long in coming. In time machines folded, sealed, and addressed advertisements and political postcards by the thousands.

All these new business machines meant new jobs and great changes in American life. Women began to go outside the home to work in ever greater numbers. The speed with which office work could be done increased.

10. What is the difference between blue- and white-collar workers?

11. What new business machines were invented? Why did they change American life?

When was the automobile invented?

Many inventors from many different countries developed the automobile. Cars run by steam engines were built as long ago as 1770. Electric cars ran in the 1890s.

Gasoline, or internal combustion, engines were first built about a hundred years ago in Europe. But it was Americans who made the automobile a part of everyday life.

In 1903, Henry Ford started the Ford Motor Company. Ford used Eli Whitney's ideas of mass production and the assembly line. (See page 163.) Sturdy, low-priced Model-T cars poured out of Ford's factories by the thousands, and then the millions. Americans were put on wheels. The huge parade of automobiles along the streets and highways had begun. (See page 461 for more about Ford and the Model-T.)

12. Who used mass production to turn out automobiles?

How did science and invention change farm life?

No real changes in farm machinery were needed as long as farmers grew food just for themselves. In 1800 farming methods were still almost the same as they had been for 3000 years.

As cities began to grow, the situation changed. And it changed in a hurry! Thousands of city stomachs depended on farm products to fill them. New methods were needed to produce more food for city workers who could not grow their own products.

As a result, one farm machine was invented after another. Steel plows replaced wooden ones. With a hand sickle, a farmer in 1800 could cut one-half an acre (0.2 ha) of wheat a day. Then Obed Hussey and Cyrus McCormick invented a reaping machine in the 1830s that cut five or six acres (2 or 2.4 ha) in a day. By the 1880s the "combine" had been invented. It reaped, threshed, cleaned, and bagged grain in one operation. Seventy or eighty acres (28 or 36 ha) could be harvested in one day.

Farming became a big business, too. Just as improvements in industry depended on scientists and inventors, so did improvements in farming.

George Washington Carver was a great farm scientist. He probably did more to help southern farmers than any other single human being. Carver was born a slave. A sickly boy, he was once traded for a horse. In time, Dr. Carver

Thomas Edison said "Genius is 2 percent inspiration and 98 percent perspiration."

George Washington Carver works in his laboratory. His research changed farming in the South.

became world famous for his scientific research at Tuskegee Institute.

Dr. Carver found over three hundred different products which could be made from the peanut. Some of them were paper, ink, coffee, shaving cream, cheese, soap, milk, and linoleum. He found many new uses for the sweet potato, also. Because of Dr. Carver's discoveries, new industries and more jobs were opened to southern workers. Cotton no longer ruled the South.

13. Who invented the reaper? How did it change farm life?

14. Who was Dr. George Washington Carver? Why did his work bring about changes in farm life?

Part Three

Great New Industries Are Born

What mineral resources helped industry to grow?

Look at the map on page 335. You will see that nature gave Americans more important mineral resources than any other nation in the world. Coal, oil, and natural gas were there waiting to be used. Iron ore and copper were plentiful.

But a nation will not become great and strong just because it has mineral resources. These resources have to be used properly. In this section you will learn how Americans used their resources to create new industries.

You have seen how railroads changed transportation after the Civil War. Then came a whole series of inventions. Suddenly Americans could communicate with each other instantly through the telephone and telegraph. They could travel or send things to each other faster and cheaper than ever before. The stage was set for the growth of really big industries.

Between 1865 and 1900, many important businesses began. We cannot look at all of them. However, in this chapter we will look at two examples. First we will study iron and steel. Then we will study the oil industry.

1. What important mineral resources did Americans have?

What natural resources are needed to make iron and steel?

Three materials are needed to make iron and steel. First there is the iron itself. Iron is not found in pure form. Rather, it is mixed with rock, sand, or dirt, and looks like lumpy red earth. This mixture is called iron ore. When this ore is made pure by a cooking and mixing process, it becomes iron or steel.

The second material needed is coal. Coal is baked and treated until it becomes a fuel called coke. Coke is used to "cook" and purify iron ore.

Finally, limestone is needed to make iron and steel. This rock is cooked with the iron ore.

Most iron ore has been found near Lake Superior. The Mesabi (mə sä′ˋbē) range in Minnesota yielded the richest iron deposits ever found.

Coal is found in the eastern United States in a band stretching all the way from Pennsylvania to Alabama.

Limestone is found in many parts of the United States. Pennsylvania and Indiana have rich deposits.

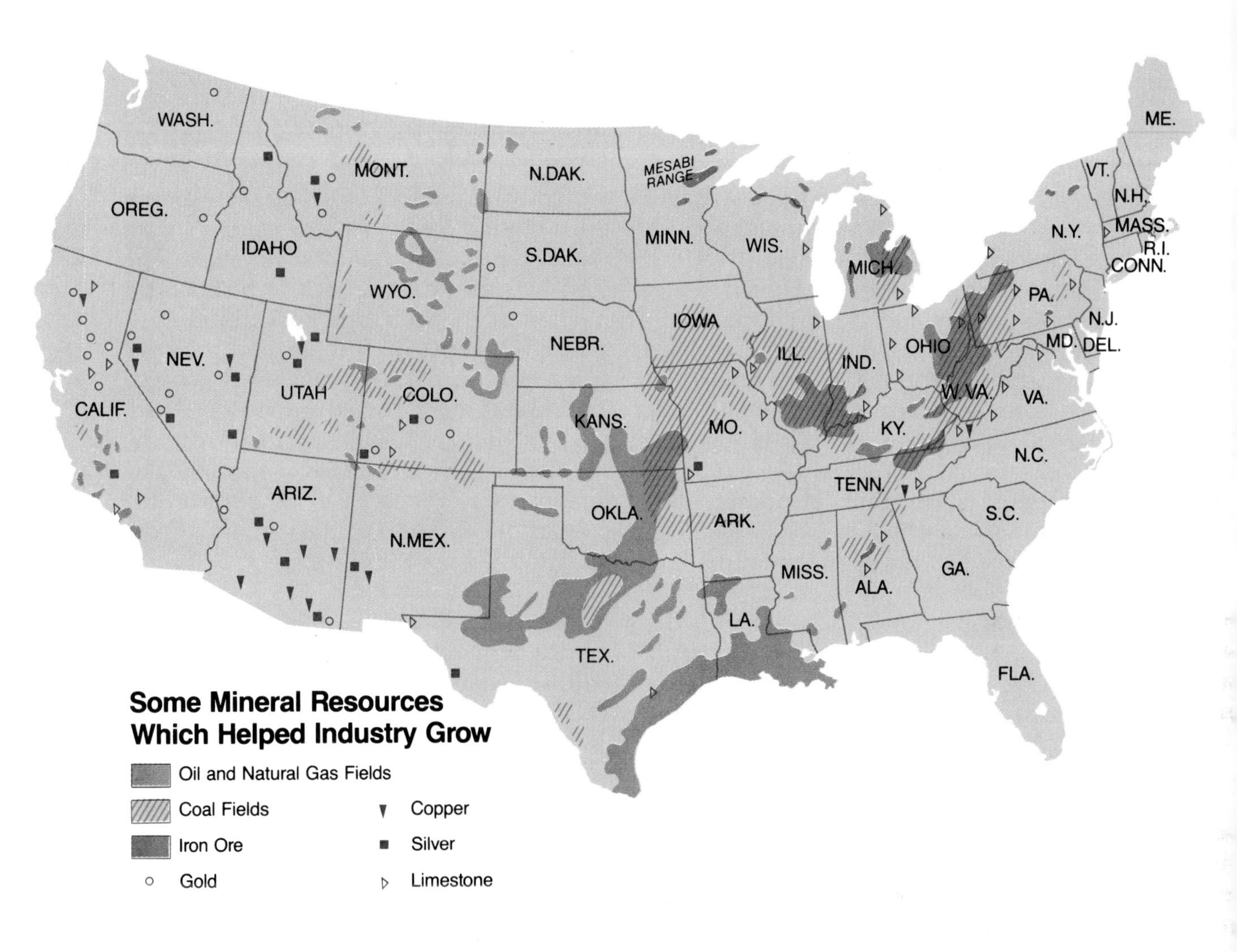

The Great Lakes provided a way of bringing iron ore, coal, and limestone together. Iron ore from Minnesota was loaded onto barges. Then it was shipped at low cost to the coal fields of Pennsylvania, Ohio, and Illinois. Limestone was ready and waiting nearby.

Big blast furnaces at Pittsburgh, Cleveland, Detroit, and Chicago cooked iron ore and limestone with coke. Out of the furnaces came bars of iron to be made into various products. To make steel, more cooking and purifying of the iron was needed. Steel costs more than iron to make. It is stronger and more flexible.

2. How were iron ore, coal, and limestone brought together?

3. Which costs more to make, iron or steel? Which is stronger?

How did the United States become the world's leading steel producer?

Before the Civil War, locomotives, train tracks, and farm machinery were made of wood or iron. Neither material worked very well. Iron was brittle and broke too easily. Wood burned. Less expensive steel was needed.

The next step was to find a leader who would build the new industry. Such a man was Andrew Carnegie. By 1900, Carnegie had made the United States the world's leading steel producer.

Carnegie was no stranger to hard work. He came to the United States as a poor immigrant from Scotland. At the age of 12, he went to work in a cotton factory for $1.20 per week. Later he worked as a telegraph operator. Then he was secretary to a railroad executive. He worked his way up in the railroad industry before turning to steel.

Carnegie worked hard and demanded that everyone around him do the same. That was part of his secret of success. But what really put him ahead was the way he took control of everything needed to make steel. For example, he gained control of the rich Mesabi iron ore. He owned a fleet of ships to carry the ore to his steel plants. And he controlled enough coal mines to cook all the iron ore he could put in his furnaces.

With this kind of organization, Carnegie did not have to pay high prices to other people for iron ore or coke. He owned them himself, so he could charge lower prices than his competition. This was what made Andrew Carnegie the king of the steel industry. When he sold his company, it was worth almost $1.5 billion dollars. That was more money than all the wealth of all the people in the United States one hundred years earlier!

4. How did Carnegie organize his steel business?

5. Why was he able to sell steel at lower prices than his competitors?

Where and how was the oil industry born?

Titusville, a little town in western Pennsylvania, was the birthplace of the mighty oil industry. Oil had seeped from the ground there for many years. No one paid much attention to it, however. The sticky stuff was supposed to be good for falling hair, colds, and snake bites.

In the 1850s people thought of a new use for oil. Why not use it to light lamps? A man named Edwin L. Drake was sent to Titusville to look over the situation. Drake decided it was too slow to wait for oil to seep to the surface. Instead, he drilled into the ground for the oil and pumped it out.

Drake's operation was a great success. And almost at once there was a great demand for oil. Everywhere people drilled wells, hoping to "strike it rich."

6. Who was Edwin L. Drake?

7. Why did people drill for oil?

What big problem faced the oil industry?

Running an oil business is expensive. Crude oil pumped from the ground has to be refined, or specially treated, before it can be used as kerosene or fuel. Refining oil requires large plants costing millions of dollars to operate.

Transporting oil costs money, too. Oil is bulky. Cheap transportation had to be found for the oil industry.

The main problem facing the oil business, then, was money. Profits—big profits—were waiting for the person who could raise enough money to refine and transport oil. The man who was able to do this was John D. Rockefeller.

8. What was the major problem facing the oil business? Why?

How did Rockefeller gain control of the oil industry?

In 1862, John D. Rockefeller was an unknown, hardworking young man in Cleveland, Ohio. He set up an oil refinery and managed it well. With his profits, Rockefeller bought another refinery. In 1870 he started the Standard Oil Company and continued buying refineries.

Suddenly Rockefeller was far bigger than his competitors. He was out to get control of the whole oil industry. Such control, where one company owns all the others in its field, is called a *monopoly.* Monopolies hurt the public because they can charge high prices for their services. There is no one to undersell them.

Rockefeller moved toward a monopoly by making deals with the railroads. The railroads needed Rockefeller's business because it was so large. Rockefeller made the railroads charge him lower rates than his competitors. If the rail lines refused, he would ship his oil by pipeline or by canal barges.

The railroads lowered their rates for Rockefeller. This ruined most of the other oil companies, who could no longer compete. Rockefeller bought them out and formed his holdings into a giant organization called the Standard Oil Trust. A *trust* is a form of monopoly.

In 1892 the Supreme Court of Ohio ruled that the Standard Oil Trust was illegal. Rockefeller was ordered to break it up, which he did. Even so, Rockefeller remained in control of much of the oil industry.

Rockefeller and others grew rich making kerosene and lubricating oils. They worried, however, about how to get rid of a "waste product," gasoline, that came from the refining process. Rockefeller himself wrote about the

In this famous cartoon, giant trusts loom over the Senate floor. The door for the people is closed.

trouble he had trying to "get rid" of gasoline in the early days of his Cleveland refinery.

By the end of the 1890s more and more homes and factories began to use electricity instead of kerosene for lighting. It looked as though trouble lay ahead for the oil industry. However, some Americans had been experimenting with automobiles. When their experiments succeeded, a new demand for gasoline suddenly appeared. A "waste product," gasoline, became the means of making a big business even bigger. Gasoline made Rockefeller even wealthier. He became the richest man in the United States, with a fortune of more than one billion dollars.

9. What is a monopoly? How did Rockefeller create one?

10. What "waste product" made the oil business even more profitable?

How well did "Big Business" serve America?

Andrew Carnegie and John D. Rockefeller were two outstanding men in the Age of Big Business. There were many other "captains of industry" who piled up great fortunes.

These business people did a great deal of good—and also some harm. They did produce large quantities of goods and services for the American people. They changed the United States from a small nation of farmers into the greatest, most powerful country the world has ever seen. The American people have better jobs and more comfortable homes than any other people on earth. That is one reason why so many immigrants have come to the United States over the years.

The "captains of industry" had one idea in mind. That was to get to the top of their fields as quickly as possible. Workers had to work long hours for low pay. Competitors had to be stamped out. There were many other trusts besides the Standard Oil Trust we have just read about. There was a sugar trust, a copper trust, a tobacco trust, and a beef trust, to name just a few.

To some extent, the public suffered at the hands of Big Business, and this is where the harm came in. Workers lived in slums. Prices often went too high. Small businesses were forced to close their doors. Big Business did not care about the public.

In time, the American people worked through the federal government to make Big Business act fairly in its dealings. Trusts and monopolies were broken up. Then the great good that industry had done for our country carried us forward to better times for everybody.

11. How much good did Big Business do for America? How much harm?

12. What was done to get rid of the harm?

Part Four

Politics Takes a Back Seat to Business

Why did politics take a back seat to business?

American history up to 1865 is an exciting story of exploration, wars, and other struggles. From the end of the Civil War until about 1895, the picture is different. The most important events in history were the changes made in people's lives resulting from inventions and the growth of industry.

The reasons why history changed after 1865 are fairly complicated. For one thing, many of the nation's brightest young people went into industry instead of politics. There were greater opportunities in industry than in government.

As for politics, there was a letdown in good behavior after the Civil War. Some government leaders were more interested in serving their own selfish goals than that of the public. Many of them proved to be dishonest.

Probably no American President was more troubled by dishonest officials than Ulysses S. Grant.

Grant was elected President in 1868 on the Republican ticket. General Grant had led the North to victory in the Civil

After a presidency marred by corrupt officials and scandals, Ulysses S. Grant set off on a trip around the world. Here he poses with Li Hung Chang, the Viceroy of China in 1879.

War. He was the hero of the American people. His followers were sure that Grant would be the kind of President that General Washington had been. In that hope they were sorely disappointed.

Grant was not interested in politics. Inexperienced and shy, he was a poor choice for the White House. He was a poor judge of character. As a result, he appointed many swindlers to office.

One scandal followed another. Members of Congress took money dishonestly from the Union Pacific Railroad. Crooked treasury officials were bribed by the whiskey trust. In exchange for bribes, they did not collect taxes.

Ambassadors, cabinet members, and even Grant's private secretary were mixed up in dishonest deals. Grant himself was innocent of wrongdoing. However, he was blamed for allowing such things to happen.

1. Why were many bright young people more interested in industry than in government after the Civil War?

2. Why was Ulysses S. Grant a great disappointment to the American people?

Why was the election of 1876 hotly disputed?

Americans were disgusted with scandals and corruption by the end of Grant's second term. In addition, a depression hit the country. Thousands of businesses failed. Many workers were without jobs.

The Republicans worried about the upcoming election in 1876. They had to live down Grant's poor record. So they picked a very honest and religious man, Governor Rutherford B. Hayes of Ohio.

The Democrats saw a chance to win an election for the first time since before the Civil War. They put up Governor Samuel Tilden of New York. Tilden was known as a fine man and a reformer.

When the ballots were counted, it looked as if Tilden had won. More people voted for him than for Hayes. But remember that elections for President are won by electoral, not popular, votes. The result of the electoral vote was in doubt. Some southern states had sent in two separate sets of returns. One set was approved by the Republicans. The other set was approved by the Democrats.

While the Constitution says electoral votes shall be counted in Congress, it does not say *who* shall do the counting. Never before in the country's history had a question like that had to be answered.

The Republicans controlled the Senate. If the Senate counted the votes, Hayes would win. But the Democrats controlled the House. If the House counted the votes, Tilden would win.

The nation was in an uproar. Violence was threatened. Of course the United States could not have two Presidents. Some answer had to be found.

3. Who were the candidates for President in 1876?

4. Why did the question of who in Congress should count the electoral votes become important?

How was the election of 1876 settled?

A committee of fifteen was set up to count the votes. Five senators, five representatives, and five Supreme Court members would do the counting. As it turned out, there were seven Democrats and eight Republicans on the counting committee. It looked as if Hayes would win.

But the trouble was not yet over. Both the Senate and House had to approve the committee's decision. The election of Hayes could still be prevented.

At this point a "deal" was made between the North and the South. Southern Democrats agreed to let Republican Hayes become President. In return, the last federal troops occupying the South were withdrawn. Reconstruction came to an end. Control of the South returned firmly to the hands of white Southerners.

5. How was the problem of the election of 1876 finally solved?

Why did Americans demand a system of civil service?

People who hold government jobs are called "civil servants." For years people were given government jobs through the "spoils system." (See page 164.) Each time a different party won an election there was great turnover among civil servants. Out went many of the workers—even very good ones—who belonged to the losing party.

While the United States was still a small nation, civil service was not very important. But as the country grew, the government faced bigger tasks at home and abroad. Expert civil servants were needed to run the government.

At last a tragedy brought home the need for an end to the spoils system. James A. Garfield was elected President after Hayes. But less than four months

Governor Samuel Tilden of New York was the Democratic candidate in 1876.

Governor Rutherford B. Hayes of Ohio was the Republican candidate.

after he took office, Garfield was shot. A disappointed office seeker shot him at point-blank range.

During the months that Garfield lay suffering, Americans searched their consciences. When he died, they made up their minds. It was time to act. Civil service *must* be reformed.

Congress responded to the public's demand for reform by passing the Pendleton Act in 1883. It put 14,000 government jobs under civil service rules. No longer were those jobs to be handed out as political favors. People wanting jobs would have to take examinations. Those with the highest scores on the tests would get and keep their jobs. It did not matter which political party was in office. This way of selecting government employees is called the "merit" system.

6. What is civil service?

7. What was the Pendleton Act? Why was it important?

Why did Americans delay in making other reforms?

Often after wars, people want to relax. They avoid facing new problems. This is what happened in the United States after the Civil War.

Americans were proud of all their new inventions and discoveries. They were dazzled by the "rags to riches" stories of people in business. They concentrated on business and neglected politics. In a democracy that is dangerous.

But the time was coming when Americans would have to face growing problems. Unpleasant facts of life do not just go away. Industry had built the nation, but it had produced poverty along with wealth. Poor people were living in the midst of plenty. Big Business had to serve the people, not be their master. Later we shall learn when and how reforms were brought about.

8. Why do people often want to ignore problems after a war?

Focus on Skills

Below is a table showing the numbers of patents applied for and issued in selected years. (A *patent* is a grant by the government to an inventor which excludes others from making or selling the patented invention.) Use the data in the table to create a bar graph. See page 297 for a sample bar graph. Before you begin your graph, study the table and answer the following questions.

1. A bar graph begins as two lines at right angles to each other like this:

Each of the two lines is called an axis. Each axis is divided to show dates or other *increments*, or parts, of the graph. Your bar graph will show the number of applications and patents issued by years. What years does the table cover? Where will you put the years on your graph? If "years" is one axis, the second axis should show even divisions of the numbers you will need to plot your bars.
2. What is the largest number of patent applications you have to show on your graph? How will you divide the second axis so that the largest number will fit? In other words, how many thousands should the second axis show?

PATENTS APPLIED FOR AND ISSUED FOR INVENTIONS AND DESIGNS

Date	Patent Applications	Patents Issued
1865	10,664	6,490
1870	19,171	13,518
1875	21,638	14,742
1880	21,761	12,903
1885	34,697	23,285
1890	39,884	25,313
1895	39,145	20,856
1900	39,673	24,644
1905	54,034	29,775
1910	63,293	35,141
1915	67,138	43,118

Building Your Vocabulary

Complete the following sentences by selecting the correct word or phrase from those listed below.

1. A—?—is a form of monopoly.
2. With the invention of business machines, more—?—jobs were available.
3. —?—workers are chosen because of merit rather than because of their political connections.
4. Railroads which span the country are called—?—lines.
5. A—?—is a machine which can reap, thresh, clean, and bag grain in one operation.
6. The United States became the world's leader in the steel—?—.
7. When one company owns all the others in its field, it is called a—?—.
8. Oil must be—?—before it can be used as fuel.

monopoly	combine
white-collar	transcontinental
Civil service	refined
industry	trust

Recalling What You Have Learned

Match the name of each person shown in Column A with the event, invention, or industry for which that person is best known in Column B.

Column A	Column B
1. Alexander Graham Bell	A. civil service reform
2. John D. Rockefeller	B. automobile
3. Andrew Carnegie	C. typewriter
4. James J. Hill	D. contested election of 1876
5. Cyrus McCormick	E. scientific farming
6. Samuel F. B. Morse	F. telegraph
7. Norbert Rillieux	G. railroading
8. Christopher Sholes	H. oil
9. Henry Ford	I. steel
10. George Washington Carver	J. reaper
11. James Garfield	K. sugar
12. Rutherford B. Hayes	L. telephone

Discussing the Important Ideas in This Chapter

1. Why did railroads play a major role in the Age of Big Business?
2. What contributions did the Chinese and the Irish make during the great age of railroading?
3. How did the many inventions of the post-Civil War years help to improve life for the average American?
4. What mineral resources made great new industries possible? How did those industries benefit America?

5. What changes did business machines bring about in American life?
6. How well did "Big Business" serve America?
7. Why is the civil service system better than the "spoils system"?
8. Why did Americans neglect politics for business after the Civil War? What great price did they pay for that neglect?

Improving Your Map Skills

Examine the key to the map on page 335. Notice that important mineral resources are shown on the map using the symbols in the key. Show that you understand the symbols and know how to use a map key by answering these questions.

1. What mineral resources of your state are shown on this map?
2. Name the mineral resources to be found in any one state which borders your state.
3. Which three southwestern states have the largest oil and natural gas fields?
4. Name five states in which coal fields can be found.
5. Describe the symbol used for copper in the key to this map.
6. Name three midwestern states in which limestone is available.
7. Name three western states which contain silver.
8. In what state is the Mesabi Range located?

Improving Your Study Skills: *Reading*

General Grenville M. Dodge was the chief engineer for the Union Pacific Railroad while that transcontinental line was being built. In the passage which follows he describes what happened on that day in May 1869 when the Union Pacific and Central Pacific met at Promontory Point in Utah. Read his words carefully, then show that you understand the details of his account by answering the questions which follow it. The answers to some of the questions are *implied*, that is, not stated directly.

. . . The two trains pulled up facing each other, each crowded with workmen. . . . Prayer was offered; a number of spikes were driven in the two adjoining rails, each one of the prominent persons present taking a hand, but very few hitting the spikes, to the great amusement of the crowd. . . . The engineers ran up their locomotives until they touched, the engineer upon each engine breaking a bottle of champagne upon the other, and thus the two roads were wedded into one great trunk line from the Atlantic to the Pacific. . . It was a bright but cold day. . . .

G. M. Dodge, "How We Built the Union Pacific Railway, and Other Railway Papers and Addresses." Quoted in Henry Steele Commager and Allan Nevins, *The Heritage of America* (Boston: Little, Brown and Co., 1939), p. 837.

1. From which two directions did the trains approach each other?
2. Who were crowded onto each of the trains?
3. What was offered at the start of the ceremonies?
4. Who drove the spikes in the adjoining rails? With what success?
5. What did each engineer do to the other's engine when they met?
6. What two oceans were "wedded," or joined, by one great trunk line?
7. What was the weather like on the day the Union Pacific and the Central Pacific met to become the first transcontinental railroad?

Chapter 14 The Disappearing Frontier

Mount Rushmore National Memorial, South Dakota

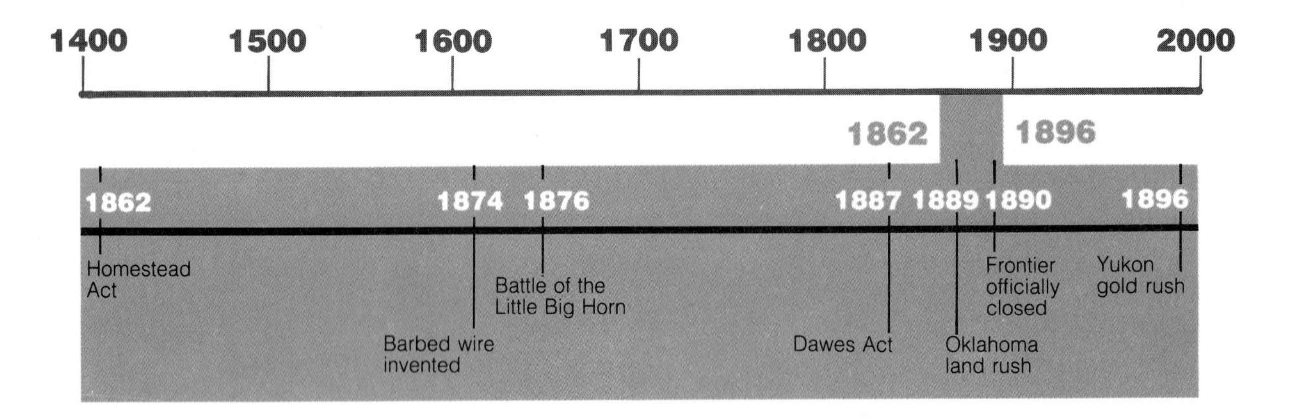

Part One

Mining and Cattle Kingdoms in the Last West

Where was the Last West?

Americans did not settle the country in an orderly march from east to west across the continent. They "leapfrogged" across it. On their way to California and Oregon in the late 1840s and 1850s, settlers just skipped over a large part of the West. Not until after the Civil War were many Americans willing to make their homes in the Rocky Mountain region and the Great Plains. This area was called the "Last West."

The Last West was a huge stretch of land. (See map, page 347.) It contained towering mountains, trackless deserts, and treeless plains. Its climate was severe. The summers were hot, the winters were cold, and rainfall was scanty. For centuries the area had been home to Indian tribes who made no secret of the fact that they did not want settlers. It also was home for wild buffalo, horses, and long-horned cattle, as well as wolves, prairie dogs, coyotes, and rattlesnakes. Small wonder, then, that it was not settlers' first choice.

At first just a few Americans ventured into the Last West. They were miners and cattle drovers. But on their heels, in the pattern of settlement described in Chapter 10, came farmers and city dwellers. Once they started coming, they came quickly.

1. Why did settlers bypass a large portion of western America?
2. Where was the Last West?

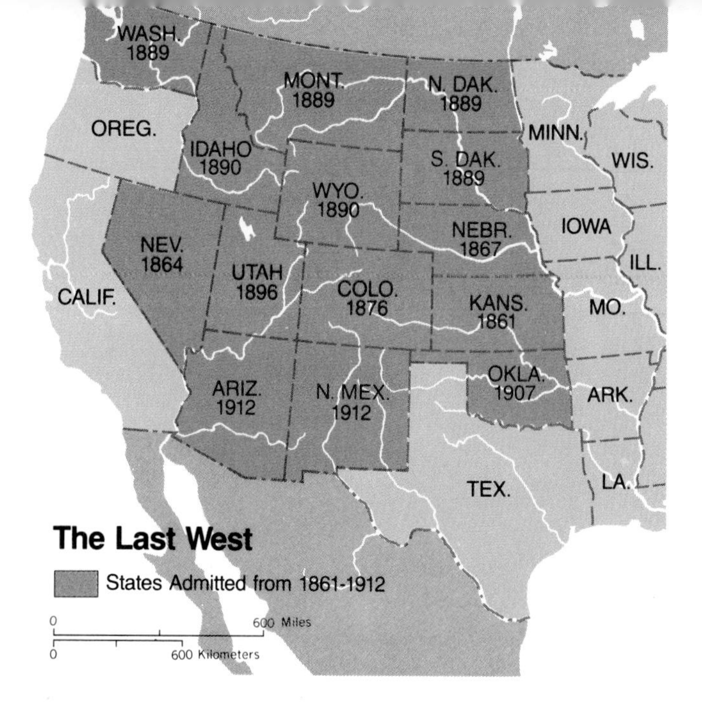

The Last West

Where was the mining frontier?

Miners were the first settlers of the Last West. They moved into the Rockies in search of silver and gold. Wagons painted with the words "Pikes Peak or Bust!" crawled up the Colorado mountainsides. In 1870, Colorado had a population of almost 40,000. By 1880 the population had jumped to 119,565. Colorado became a state in 1876.

The mining frontier spread from Arizona to Alaska and from South Dakota to Washington. Waves of miners rolled westward looking for copper, lead, and zinc, as well as gold and silver.

Tombstone was the best known of the Arizona mining boom towns. Through its streets walked Wyatt Earp, Billy the Kid, and others. Modern television has made their adventures known to all.

A wild rush for gold made the Black Hills of South Dakota lively in the 1870s. Twice each month, Wells Fargo and Company wagons rolled into Deadwood, the mining center there. When the wagons left town, they often carried as much as $350,000 in gold.

Even the cold of the North did not stop miners. The last of the gold rushes came in 1896 in the Yukon region of Canada. Dawson, a tiny town, grew to more than 40,000 within one year's time.

3. What minerals were the western miners looking for?

4. Where did the last gold rush take place?

What happened to the mining kingdoms?

Life and death came quickly to most of the mining towns, or "kingdoms," as the largest ones were called. Nature put just so much gold or silver in a particular place. When it was gone, there was no more mining to do.

Miners had to work hard to extract what minerals they found. Their work was difficult and dangerous. Temperatures deep in the mines were either too hot or too cold. In the Nevada silver mines temperatures climbed as high as 150°F (65°C)! Miners could work in such heat only a short time. Then they had to be hauled to the surface and rubbed with ice.

Ice became almost as valuable as the silver the miners took from the earth. To supply ice to the mines, ponds were dammed on the eastern slopes of the Sierras. Blocks of ice were cut from these ponds and loaded onto wagons pulled by mules. So great was the demand for ice

Prospectors headed west could buy supplies at this Omaha, Nebraska, store.

that one mine had a standing order for $1700 worth of ice per day.

In the days of the mining kingdoms there were no elevators. Miners had to climb down slippery ladders. They worked in semidarkness. The only light they had was from candles or oil lamps. Air was in short supply. There were no blowers to force air to the farthest ends of the tunnels as there are today.

When the minerals were all gone, the miners had several choices. They could go prospecting elsewhere. Or they could stay and take up farming or cattle raising. Some found work on the railroads which were pushing in from the East.

One thing was sure. In the long run, the real wealth of Montana, Colorado, Wyoming, Idaho, and even California was not in mining. The real treasure of the Last West lay in its grass and soil and in its fish and fruit. When the miners moved out, cattle ranchers and farmers moved in.

5. Why did life and death come quickly to the mining kingdoms?

6. Describe the working conditions in the mines.

Why did Texas become the home of the cattle kingdom?

Long-horned cattle were at home on the ranges of Texas even before there was a United States. When the Spanish first came to Mexico in 1521, they brought along some of their prized longhorns. Descendants of these cattle were driven north and west by Spanish explorers and missionaries. The longhorns found the plains of Texas to their liking. Their numbers multiplied. It is estimated that by the time the first Americans came to Texas there were

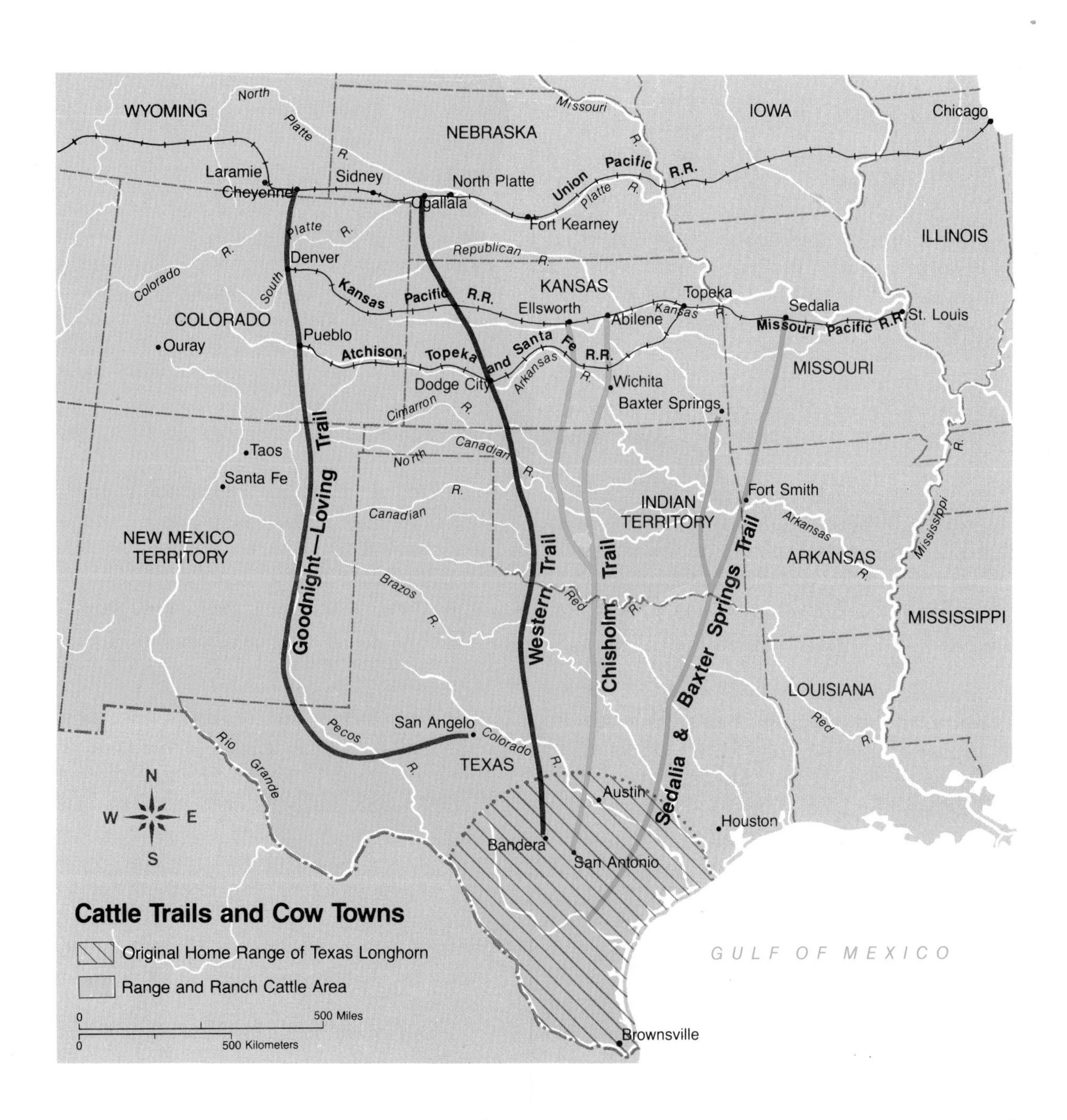

several million head of cattle grazing there. By then Mexico was independent. It was the Mexicans who taught the Americans how to be cowboys. Mexicans showed Americans how to brand, rope, and round up cattle. The cowboys learned Mexican words such as *sombrero*, *lariat*, and *rodeo*. But it took more than cattle and cowboys to make the cattle industry. That industry might never have grown up without the railroads.

Before the Civil War, western cattle were raised more for their hides and tallow (fat) than for their beef. Hides and tallow could be shipped more easily than live cattle or fresh meat. It wasn't that people in cities did not want fresh beef from the West. They did. The problem was moving cattle all the way from Texas to New York or San Francisco. The railroads provided the answer. In the 1870s and 1880s, several railroads crossed the western plains from coast to coast.

Every year Texas cowboys rounded up their herds and drove them north. The trip was called the *Long Drive*. Thousands of cattle were strung out in long lines, following the trails marked out for them. (See map, page 349.)

The goal of the cowboys was to reach the railroads in Kansas, Missouri, and other western states. Along the railroads were "cow towns," such as Abilene, Cheyenne, Dodge City, Wichita, and Sedalia. The cowboys sold their cattle in these towns. Then the animals were shipped to large cities to be slaughtered and sold to stores.

From Texas, the cattle business spread north to the Great Plains. It was found that Texas cattle did well on the plains. The animals lived through the cold winters and grew fat on the rich summer grasses. Soon there were large ranches in Colorado, Wyoming, and Montana.

Until the 1880s, western ranches were unfenced. Cattle roamed freely on the open range. A special mark, or brand, was burned into each animal to show who owned it.

7. How and why did the cattle industry get started in Texas?

8. What role did railroads play in the cattle industry?

What was cowboy life like?

Modern television shows cowboy life as more comfortable and glamorous than it really was. Being a cowboy was a lonesome, dirty, uncomfortable, and often dangerous job. Cowboys wore special clothes from necessity. They needed large hats as protection from the hot sun. Chaps protected their legs, and neckerchiefs covered noses and mouths against wind and dust.

On the trail each cowboy was allowed to take a pair of blankets and a sack of extra clothes. That was all. Cowboys had no tents or shelter other than their blankets. Food was cooked over open fires. Anyone who got sick or injured was really in trouble. Medical aid was miles away.

Danger was the cowboys' constant companion on the Long Drive. Cattle thieves, or rustlers, lay in wait to steal cattle. Many animals were lost to cattle fever or in stampedes, but even so the Long Drive was profitable.

Cowboys came from many different ethnic groups. There were Mexicans, Indians, and Americans of all backgrounds. There were about 5000 black cowboys.

One of the most famous of the black cowboys was long, lean Bill Pickett. He

A cowboy's life could be uncomfortable and dangerous, as Frederic Remington's painting "The Stampede" illustrates. Born in New York State, Remington took the American West as the subject for many paintings and statues.

and his horse, Spradley, toured the rodeo circuit for years with their famous "bulldogging" act. Pickett would ride out on Spradley. Then he would jump out of the saddle and onto the head of a running steer. Sometimes he had to jump as far as six feet (1.8 m). Pickett would grab a horn in each hand. Then he would fall to one side of the steer, dragging along beside it until the beast fell down exhausted. Pickett's daredevil bulldogging brought him invitations to perform before the crowned heads of Europe.

9. Why was the life of a cowboy uncomfortable and often dangerous?
10. From what ethnic groups did cowboys come?

What troubles brought an end to the cattle kingdom?

Profits could be made raising cattle. For that reason eastern and foreign business people invested money in herds. Cattle became "Big Business." More and more cattle were raised. Of course, with more beef on the market, prices fell.

Further trouble came when terrible droughts (dry spells) and blizzards hit the Great Plains in the mid-1880s. Many ranchers lost their herds.

Finally, range wars broke out. They spelled the end of the golden age of the cowboy. In the early days of unfenced ranges there was trouble between rival ranchers. Each tried to get the best water and grazing area. Rustlers moved into range country and stole grazing herds.

Later some very tough wars broke out between cowboys and sheepherders. Like cattle, sheep were first brought west by the Spanish. Colorado, Wyoming, and Nevada became sheep country.

Sheep and cattle cannot graze in the same place. Sheep eat the grass down so close to the ground that cattle can't feed. Also, the sharp hooves of sheep pack the

When a rancher fenced off public water, these Nebraska farmers took matters into their own hands.

soil. They make it hard for grass to grow back. Cattle ranchers said their herds would not eat or drink on land where sheep had been.

As a result, sheep wars broke out on the range. Ranchers destroyed thousands of sheep. Many cowboys and sheepherders lost their lives fighting.

The worst war of all was between ranchers and farmers, or "nesters." Nesters fenced off their land to protect their crops from animals.

One of the nesters, Joseph Glidden, worried about how to fence in his farm. He experimented with wire, putting points, or "barbs," every few inches. In 1874, Glidden patented his invention and called it "barbed wire." He rented a small factory in DeKalb, Illinois. He hired young boys to string the barbs.

Within months, Glidden's fencing sold so well that he put in steam machinery. The Barbed Fence Company sold barbed wire for 18 cents a pound. At that price there was a long waiting list of customers.

A simple invention of twisted and barbed wire spelled the end of the days of the open range. The cowboys finally fenced in their own cattle on private ranches. Law and order came to the West.

11. Why did the price of beef begin to fall?

12. What were sheep wars? Why did they break out?

Part Two

Farmers Settle on the Great Plains

Why did people begin to farm the prairies?

Many weary Civil War veterans decided to seek a new, better life in the West. The lands open to them were on the Great Plains. Just the name, "Great Plains," tells a lot about what those lands were like.

On the Great Plains there was little rainfall, a harsh climate, tough grass, and few trees. Except for a few rolling hills, the land was flat. Americans had first settled in the forests of the eastern and western United States. To them the treeless plains, or prairies, were grim.

Of course there were a few people who loved the prairies right from the start. For example, Orpha McNitt was a young, newly married woman when she moved to the Colorado Territory. In a letter to her family in Wisconsin she wrote: "I wish you could see the prairie. It is beautiful but as different as anything could be from the moss-covered rocks and the ferns you know."

But most people had to be coaxed to move to the prairies. And they were coaxed by Congress, by railroads, and by promoters hired by the states.

Congress passed a series of laws which made it easy for settlers to get land of their own on the Great Plains. In 1862, Congress passed the Homestead Act. Under that law any head of a family who for 5 years lived on and cultivated land owned by the government could get 160 acres (64 ha) free. People who took advantage of the Homestead Act were called *homesteaders*.

But 160 acres was not enough on the Great Plains for a good farm. Because of the climate, a farmer needed far more land in order to survive. Many homesteaders gave up. Others found ways to buy more land. In 1873, Congress passed the Timber Culture Act. Homesteaders could get another 160 acres free. All they had to do was plant at least a quarter of that land in trees. Later, still other laws were passed which offered more free land.

The laws allowed women as well as men to homestead, provided they were the head of a family. Many women took advantage of that opportunity. A young black girl described how her mother moved her family onto the eastern plains of Colorado.

My mother came out this way and she met some people who told her about land in Colorado. . . . My mother said, 'Well, I'm going to go and see. . . .' And that's how it turned out that we came to where we have been, with a free range to expand to have things that we wanted. . . .

Sarah Jacobus, "Exploring the Past through Diaries and Journals," *Mills Quarterly*, vol. 30, no. 3 (1978), p. 17.

Railroads probably did the most coaxing. As you know, they received large grants of land along their rights of way. (See map, page 326.) Railroads were eager to sell that land to settlers. Their main interest was not in the money they could get for the land itself. Railroads wanted more customers for their services. If farmers moved onto the Great Plains, in time they would need to send their crops to market. They also would want to buy goods made in the East or Far West. And that, of course, is where the railroads would come in. They would make money hauling things back and forth.

To get families to move onto the prairies, railroads did a lot of advertising. They offered free inspection trips so people could see the land and look over the farms. They allowed people to pay for land over time at low interest.

States and territories hired promoters. Their job was to attract more settlers. Often promoters went to Europe to urge people there to come to the states or territories the promoters worked for. Promoters were very eager to recruit German farmers. They were thought

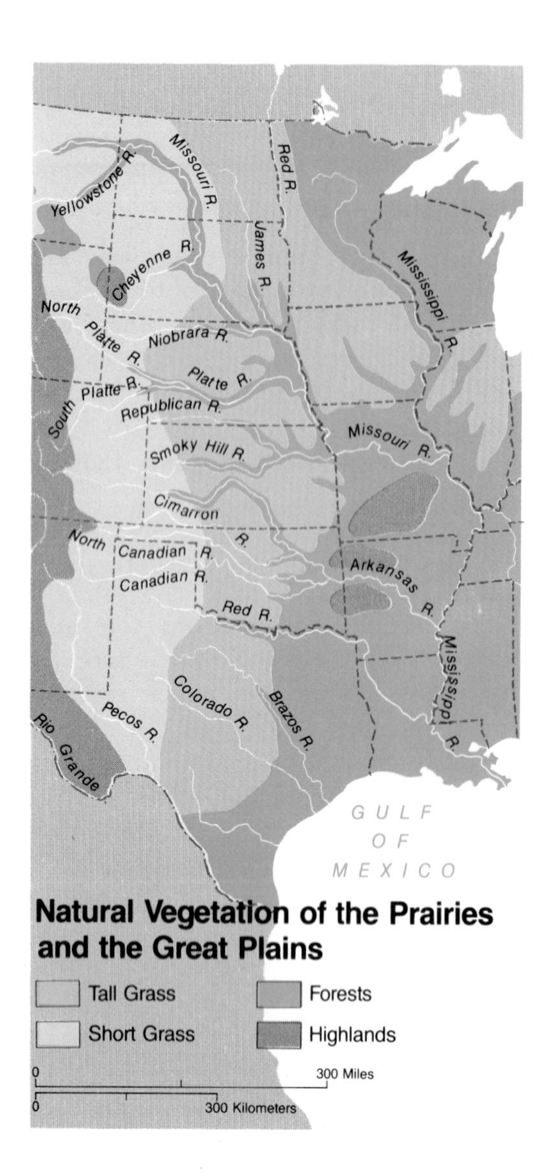

Natural Vegetation of the Prairies and the Great Plains

Average Annual Precipitation of the Prairies and the Great Plains

to be the best farmers in the world. Recruiters also put out the "welcome mat" for English, Welsh, Scots, and Scandinavians. (Danes, Swedes, Finns, and Norwegians are Scandinavians.) In 1882 almost half a million Germans and Scandinavians moved onto the Great Plains.

Blacks were recruited as well as immigrants. And blacks responded by the thousands. Many of them poured into Kansas. Others pushed farther west to become pioneers in Nebraska, Colorado, and Wyoming.

1. Why did people have to be "coaxed" to move onto the Great Plains?
2. Who did the coaxing? How?

How did pioneers learn to live on the Great Plains?

If people were going to survive on the plains, they had to learn to live there. Because there were no trees, there was

A Montana homesteader begins the grueling task of breaking the sod on his land.

no lumber for houses. Settlers had to learn to build homes of sod. Sod is the top part of the ground. On the plains the ground was very hard and held together tightly by sagebrush roots. Homesteaders cut sod into bricks. Then the bricks were used to build houses and barns. The bricks were held together with a mixture of straw, dirt, and water.

To keep wandering cattle out of their water holes and fields, the settlers strung barbed wire fences. To get water, they dug wells and used windmills to pump the water. To cultivate the tough soil, they used sharp steel plows.

Life on the plains was hard. Winters were cold; summers were hot. Winds whipped through the great open spaces and lashed at the settlers. Dust stung their eyes and filled their homes. Only courage and the ability to learn to live under difficult conditions made it possible for the farmers to hang on. Weaker settlers simply packed up and went back home.

3. What kind of homes were built on the plains?

4. Why was life on the plains so difficult?

Part Three

Indian Problems

Who were the Plains Indians?

The Plains Indians had learned how to live on the prairies long before the settlers arrived. And those Indians did not intend to let their homes be destroyed without a fight.

A few of the tribes such as the Mandan and Hidatsa lived in permanent earthen lodges. But most of the Plains Indians were nomads, or always on the move. Tribes such as the Arapaho, Crow, Cheyenne, Apache,

Proud homesteaders pose outside their Nebraska sod house.

Geoge Catlin made this painting of a buffalo hunt in 1832.

Kiowa, Blackfoot, Sioux, and Comanche rarely stayed put for long. They were hunters. They followed the buffalo for hundreds of miles, taking their belongings with them.

The Plains Indians depended on the buffalo for much of what they needed. They ate buffalo meat. They dried some of the meat for later use. They used buffalo hides for their tents, or tepees. They used other parts of the buffalo for clothes, shoes, rope, and tools.

Horses were also important to the Plains Indians. As mounted warriors they had no equals. They could raid and ride away. When they were pursued, they were such expert riders that they could hang by a heel on one side of a horse running at full speed. At the same time they could rapidly fire their bows and arrows.

The Plains Indians were such brave fighters that killing an enemy was not their highest battle honor. Taking a living enemy's weapon was the highest honor. Touching an enemy, or *counting a coup*, was also an honored feat.

Long before they began trading with white fur trappers, the Plains Indians were traders. Trading for horses was especially important.

1. How did the Plains Indians live?
2. Why would settlers fear the Plains Indians?

Why were settlers a serious threat to the Plains Indians?

Signs of the times were plain enough. Many Indians read the danger signals correctly. The Great Plains was the last line of defense for the Indians.

Settlers were coming in huge numbers. Promises made by the United States government that certain lands should be "forever Indian" were broken. Buffalo, the Indians' source of food, clothing, and shelter, were being slaughtered. First the railroads cut across the buffalo's grazing land. Then shooting buffalo became a sport for city slickers. Sometimes tourists shot buffalo from train windows. Millions of the animals were killed, then left to rot on the prairies. By 1889 there were only about 1000 buffalo left.

Indians had ideas about how to live and use the land which were different from the ideas of settlers. Free wandering, hunting, and fighting prized by Indians did not fit with life in towns through which trains whistled. It is little wonder that violent wars broke out between settlers and Indians.

One of the most famous battles in the long series of Indian wars was fought at the Little Big Horn River. In 1874 gold was discovered in the Black Hills of the Dakotas. This land belonged to the Sioux Indians. But as was so often the case, little attention was paid to the Indians' rights. Gold hunters swarmed into the Sioux country.

The story of the Indian wars was nearly always the same. The settlers wanted the Indians' land and took it away from them after fierce fighting. But the Battle of the Little Big Horn in Montana was different. This was one fight that the Indians did not lose.

At the Little Big Horn, the Sioux were led by Chief Sitting Bull. Opposing the Indians was Colonel George A. Custer and his crack 7th Cavalry. On that fatal day in 1876, Custer split his forces at noon. He sent Major Reno and three companies in one direction. In the opposite direction he sent Captain Benteen with three more companies. Custer himself kept five companies.

Reno's men met the Indians first. The Indians drove them back. About three o'clock, Reno was forced to retreat across the Little Big Horn River.

Then suddenly the Indians were gone. They moved up to take Custer by surprise. One by one, the Indians picked off the 265 encircled American troopers. Custer fell, fighting to the last. All of the soldiers were killed.

3. Why did the Sioux go on the warpath?

4. Who won the Battle of the Little Big Horn?

Why was Custer's Last Stand the turning point in the Indian wars?

News of the Custer defeat shocked Americans. Newspapers were full of articles about "Custer's Last Stand." More troops were sent west. Indians were hunted down until there was no place left for them to go.

One by one the great Indian chiefs had to admit defeat. The year after Custer's death, Chief Crazy Horse gave up. He led his people onto a reservation.

Sitting Bull, who had defeated Custer, escaped to Canada. Later he returned to the United States and lived on a reservation. In a final Sioux uprising in 1890, Sitting Bull was killed at Wounded Knee, South Dakota. More than 200 unarmed Indians were also killed. The Indian wars were over.

5. How did Americans respond to Custer's defeat?

6. What happened to the great Indian chiefs?

Who spoke up for the Indians?

Quite a few people in the United States were angry about the way the First Americans were being treated. But these people had waited too long. Their protests came after the Indians were defeated and most of their lands were taken away.

William T. Sherman, commander of the United States Army, sympathized with the Indians. He said:

Historymaker

The old chief knew he was dying. He called his son, Joseph, and said:

My son, . . . When I am gone, think of your country. You are the chief of these people. They look to you to guide them. Always remember that your father never sold this country. You must stop your ears whenever you are asked to sign a treaty selling our home. A few years more, and white men will be all around you. They have their eyes on this land. My son, never forget my dying words. This country holds your father's body. Never sell the bones of your father and your mother.

Chief Joseph pressed his father's hand. He promised never to sell the beautiful "land of the winding water." That land was nestled among the high, grassy hills where Washington, Oregon, and Idaho come together.

No sooner had the old chief died than representatives of the United States government appeared. They told Chief Joseph, then 31 years old, tall and straight, that he and his people had just 30 days left to live in the land of the winding water. "If you let the time run over one day, the soldiers will be there to drive you onto the reservation. Then all your cattle and horses outside the reservation at that time will fall into the hands of the white men," General Oliver O. Howard warned.

General Howard's words stung Chief Joseph. They seemed especially cruel in view of the way the Nez Percé had treated whites. The Nez Percé had befriended whites ever since Lewis and Clark first came to their country. Chief Joseph said his people had admired Lewis and Clark.

All the Nez Percé made friends with Lewis and Clark, and agreed to let them pass through their country and never to make war on white men. This promise the Nez Percé have never broken.

Chief Joseph was a realist, however. As he put it,

We were like deer. They were like grizzly bears. We had a small country. Their country was large. We were contented to let things remain as the Great Spirit Chief made them. They were not, and would change the rivers and mountains, if they did not suit them.

Chief Joseph decided on a bold course of action. He ordered his tribe to assemble quickly. He told them that they must try to escape to Canada. Old people, young people, newborn babies, and sick people—everyone was to go.

So it was that the Nez Percé began the long, difficult journey north at the beginning of June 1877. It was a poor year to be traveling in the Northwest. Spring was late. The rivers were swollen with melting snow waters. Many were at flood stage. The meadows were soggy, the firewood wet.

Chief Joseph

When General Howard learned of the Nez Percé's departure, he ordered his army to pursue them. His orders were to capture the tribe. Those orders, however, proved hard to carry out. Day after day telegraphers sent news to the waiting public of still another defeat by the Indians.

For 115 days the Nez Percé kept going in spite of the cold weather and rough country. Many of the soldiers were upset. How could that small band keep on outwitting and outfighting them? Why were they unable to capture them?

On the 116th day the army was camped on a ridge across from the Nez Percé. General Howard stood talking with his aides. "What possible choices does Chief Joseph have now?" he demanded of them.

"He could leave the sick, the old and the children behind," suggested General Nelson Miles. "They've really slowed him down. Without them Joseph and his warriors could easily make it to Canada. They're only thirty miles [48 km] from the border."

"I disagree," said another officer. "Joseph could use everything he's got left for a surprise attack. He could risk it all in one last battle. Who knows? He might win. Joseph certainly has shown himself to be quite a general."

Then a third officer gave his opinion. "Joseph could surrender. I think he will. His people must be suffering terribly. They must be short of food. It's bitter cold. Still almost no smoke curls up from their campfires."

While the officers stood talking, Chief Joseph came out of his lodge. He mounted his horse. All alone he rode toward the soldiers. The generals and their aides watched in silence as he came toward them.

Wearily Chief Joseph dismounted. He unwrapped the ragged blanket that hung about his shoulders. From it he took his rifle. Without a word he handed it over to General Howard. Then he spoke these words which are counted as among the most beautiful ever uttered in American history. Chief Joseph said:

I am tired of fighting. . . . My people ask me for food, and I have none to give. It is cold, and we have no blankets, no wood. My people are starving to death. Where is my little daughter? I do not know. Perhaps even now, she is freezing to death.

Hear me, my chiefs. I am tired; my heart is sick and sad. From where the sun now stands, I will fight no more forever.

"Hear Me, My Chiefs" from "Chief Joseph's Surrender Speech." Quoted in Walter Lowenfels, *The Writing on the Wall* (Doubleday & Co., 1969).

Chief Joseph did lay down his arms. He and his people were herded into railroad cars. They were transported to Bismarck, North Dakota. Then they were taken to Baxter Springs, Kansas. Later they were moved to still another reservation. But never were they allowed to return to their beloved land of the winding water. It would be wrong, however, to say that Chief Joseph fought "no more forever." True, he never again used a gun or a bow and arrow. But he did use his energy and his words to fight for the rights and dignity of his people. He appeared before Congress. He spoke to the President's cabinet. He appealed to the consciences of Americans time and again.

Focus on Skills

These two pictures are proof again that no two people ever see an event in quite the same way. Each picture gives the artist's view of what "really" happened at the Little Big Horn. (See page 357.)

The picture(page 361, below) is a famous print company's view of what happened on the day when Custer and all 264 soldiers serving with him were killed. Examine it carefully.

The picture (page 361, top) was drawn by Kicking Bear, one of the Indian survivors of the battle.

Twenty-two years after the Battle of the Little Big Horn, Kicking Bear was persuaded to draw his version of what had happened. He worked all of one winter to draw this pictograph on a piece of cloth. Today Kicking Bear's picture is one of the most valued art treasures in the United States. It hangs in the Southwest Museum in Los Angeles.

You will need to examine this pictograph very carefully because it is quite different from the kind of art most people are used to seeing. If you know these things about Sioux art, you can better appreciate Kicking Bear's masterpiece:

a. The main point of the picture is to show how great and complete the Indian victory was.

b. Sioux pictures do not show mountains, trees, or other landmarks, so you cannot get an idea of the lay of the land or the distance one spot is from another.

c. The Indian village in the lower right was more than two miles (3.2 km) from the battleground. Although the women, children, and dogs appear to be in the thick of the battle, they really were not.

d. The cavalry did not carry knives in the Battle of the Little Big Horn. However, the Indians called the soldiers "Long Knives," so swords are shown beside the dead soldiers.

e. Custer appears in faint outline at the left center of the picture near the four Indian chiefs. Can you find him?

Now compare the two illustrations.

We took away their country and their means of support, broke up their mode [way] of living, their habits of life. We introduced disease and decay among them. And it was for this and against this that they made war. Could anyone expect less?

Another strong protest was the book, *A Century of Dishonor*. Helen Hunt Jackson wrote this book in 1881. She told of wrongs she thought the government had done to the Indians. Finally, aroused by the book, President Cleveland suggested a law to improve life for the Indians. On the reservations life was hard and poor. But there, Indians lived in tribes and governed themselves.

1. According to the print company's version, who would you say were the heroes? Who were the heroes in the Sioux version?
2. Can you find a woman who is holding an American flag? Why do you suppose she is holding it?
3. How many ways can you list in which these two pictures are different?
4. If you saw only one picture—either one—and had no other information, how would you feel about the battle?
5. Do you think either picture is a true or accurate portrayal of what really happened? Explain.
6. Do you think the artists intended their pictures to be "accurate"? If not, why do you think they made them?

Cleveland's plan to get the Indians off the reservations was the Dawes Act. It was passed by Congress in 1887.

Under the Dawes Act, the reservations were broken up into farms. Any head of an Indian family could claim 160 acres (64 ha) of land. Members of the family could claim smaller amounts. Indians willing to give up tribal life were given this land, plus American citizenship.

The Dawes Act was not very successful. As you have learned, 160 acres was not enough land for successful farming on the Great Plains. And somehow others ended up with the best land which had been set aside for the Indians. To break up the tribes was to destroy Indian culture. Many Indians, therefore, preferred to stay on the reservations.

7. How did Helen Hunt Jackson help the Indians?

8. What was the Dawes Act? How successful was it?

Part Four

The Frontier Disappears

When and how was Oklahoma opened to settlers?

Oklahoma means "red people" in Choctaw. Oklahoma has long been home for many thousands of Indians. Many were living there at the time that the Spanish under Coronado first explored Oklahoma in 1541. Still more came in the 1830s when the United States government forced 22 tribes to march along a "Trail of Tears" to new homes. (See pages 217-218.)

Oklahoma proved to be rich land. It had good soil for farming and plenty of oil underground. Once again, whites looked at the Indians' lands with longing eyes.

Several parts of Oklahoma were still unsettled by the Indians. Pioneers urged the government in Washington to let them settle in these unused lands. Congress bought up the land bit by bit from the Indians and opened it for settlement. Each time this happened, pioneers rushed in as fast as they could to claim valuable land.

The most famous land rush took place on April 22, 1889. At exactly noon, soldiers on the border fired shots. Settlers could enter central Oklahoma. The great race was on!

Thousands of people had been lined up for hours ready to go. On the "run" they used trains, horses, carriages, and even bicycles. About 50,000 adventurers rushed in on the first day to stake out their claims. At the end of that first day, Oklahoma City had a population of 10,000 tenters. Guthrie was a city of 15,000 by nightfall.

Within weeks, land was being planted and homes were being built. By 1900—just 11 years later—Oklahoma had a population of 800,000. In 1907 it became a state.

Of course, some people sneaked into the territory before it was officially opened. These people were called "Sooners," because they arrived sooner than anyone else. Oklahoma's nickname as the "Sooner State" comes from these early birds.

1. What does the name "Oklahoma" mean? Why was Oklahoma nicknamed the Sooner State?

2. Why did Congress declare land in Oklahoma open to settlers?

When was the frontier officially closed?

In 1890, just a year after the great land rush into Oklahoma, the United States Census Bureau officially announced that the frontier was closed. In one sense, the Bureau was correct. By 1890 only four western states were not yet in the Union. They were Utah, Oklahoma, New Mexico, and Arizona. But, in another sense, the Bureau was

At the starter's gun, eager settlers race for land in the great Oklahoma land rush of April 22, 1889.

wrong. Four times as much land was homesteaded after 1890 as before. Even today there are still millions of acres of unoccupied land.

Americans have never been rooted to their soil as European farmers have been. Americans still have the urge to "get up and go." Many modern pioneers are moving to the frontiers in Alaska. Other Americans are eyeing new frontiers under the sea and in space.

3. Why was the Census Bureau both right and wrong in saying the frontier was closed in 1890?

How did the last frontier help democracy grow?

Like earlier frontiers, the Last West helped our country to become more democratic. Most of the new towns allowed women to vote. Wyoming led all the states in giving suffrage, or the right to vote, to women in 1869.

Some of the new state constitutions gave people a more direct voice in their government. For instance, laws passed by state legislatures had to be voted on by the people before the laws could be final. Also, the people could demand special elections to remove unpopular officials.

In the Last West, there were almost no private schools. Everybody's children went to public schools together. Western states set up state-supported colleges and universities. .Students paid little or no money to attend.

All ethnic groups contributed to the building of the Last West. Coming from an "old family" had little meaning. Many democratic practices started on the frontier.

4. In what ways did democracy grow on the last frontier?

5. Which state was first to give suffrage to women?

Building Your Vocabulary

Match each word in Column A with its definition in Column B.

Column A	Column B
1. nomad	A. to live on and farm an area for a certain length of time
2. longhorn	B. someone who is continually moving
3. range	C. a name for cattle
4. homestead	D. unfenced grasslands
5. count coup	E. cattle thief
6. rustler	F. touch an enemy

Recalling What You Have Learned

Complete each of these sentences by selecting the correct word or phrase from those listed below.

1. The final portion of the United States to be settled was called the—?—.
2. The largest mining towns were called—?—.
3. —?—was the home of the cattle kingdom.
4. Cowboys rounded up cattle and drove them north on the—?—.
5. Joseph Glidden invented—?—.
6. —?—coaxed settlers to the Great Plains because they wanted customers.
7. —?—was the turning point in the Indian wars.
8. —?—was the first state to grant women suffrage.

Texas	mining kingdoms
barbed wire	Railroads
Wyoming	Last West
Custer's Last Stand	Long Drive

Discussing the Important Ideas in This Chapter

1. Why were the Great Plains and Rocky Mountains the last areas to be settled?
2. Why did the mining and cattle kingdoms come to an end?
3. How realistic or historically accurate is the picture of cowboy life shown on today's television programs?
4. Why did a simple invention like barbed wire have an important effect on the history of the Last West?
5. Who was responsible for coaxing people to settle on the prairies?
6. In order to survive on the Great Plains, what adjustments did settlers have to make?
7. Would you say that the Plains Indians were a greater threat to settlers or were settlers a greater threat to the Plains Indians? Why?
8. Why did the Battle of the Little Big Horn mark a great turning point?
9. What impact did the frontier have on American life?

Improving Your Map Skills

J. G. McCoy first got the idea of connecting the cattle drives with the railroads. In time four major trails led north from Texas. They ended in cow towns along the railroad rights of way. You can learn more about those famous trails and cow towns by looking at the map on page 349. Study the map and answer the following questions.

1. What river in the southwest bounded the original home of the Texas longhorns? What body of water formed a boundary on the east?
2. Locate the Goodnight-Loving Trail.
   a. Where in Texas did it begin?
   b. To which three cow towns did it connect in the north?
   c. Along which river did the trail run for part of the way?
   d. Note the scale in the lower left corner of the map. Use the scale to find the approximate length of the trail.
3. Locate the Chisholm Trail.
   a. Where did it begin?
   b. In what cow towns did it end?
   c. How long was the drive from San Antonio to Abilene?
4. What were the names of the other two major trails?
   a. Which of those trails lay farther west?
   b. Which trail went to Dodge City?

Improving Your Study Skills: *Reading*

Read the short selection below. Decide which sentence contains the main idea. Show that you understand the details which support the main idea by answering the questions at the end of the selection.

The Neglected History of Sheep Drives

The high drama of the great cattle drives has overshadowed the accomplishments of the drivers who brought sheep to the West. It is time they got a better break from history.

Take "Uncle Dick" Wootton, for example. In the spring of 1852 he started with 9000 head of sheep from Taos, New Mexico. With him were eight New Mexican shepherds, eight armed guards, eight goats to take the lead, and one dog to herd. They struck off northwest up the Rio Grande. They crossed the Continental Divide south of where Ouray, Colorado, now stands. There a band of Ute Indians charged out of the forest. They were shooting and whooping to stampede the sheep. When this failed, the chief of the Utes rode into the sheepherders' camp. He demanded part of the flock. But Uncle Dick persuaded him to take some tobacco and flour instead.

From Ouray, the herders took off across Colorado, Utah, and northern Nevada. They hurried their sheep to get them across the mighty Sierras before the snow flew. Then they brought them safely down the western slopes and onto their winter range near Sacramento, California. The next spring Uncle Dick sold the flock for better than $50,000.

1. What is the main idea in this selection?
2. When did "Uncle Dick" Wootton leave New Mexico?
3. How many people went with him?
4. How many head of sheep started the trip? What other animals went along?
5. Where did the party cross the Continental Divide?
6. Where did the sheep spend the winter?
7. For what price was the flock sold?

Chapter 15

Urban America in the Making

The Statue of Liberty, New York City, New York

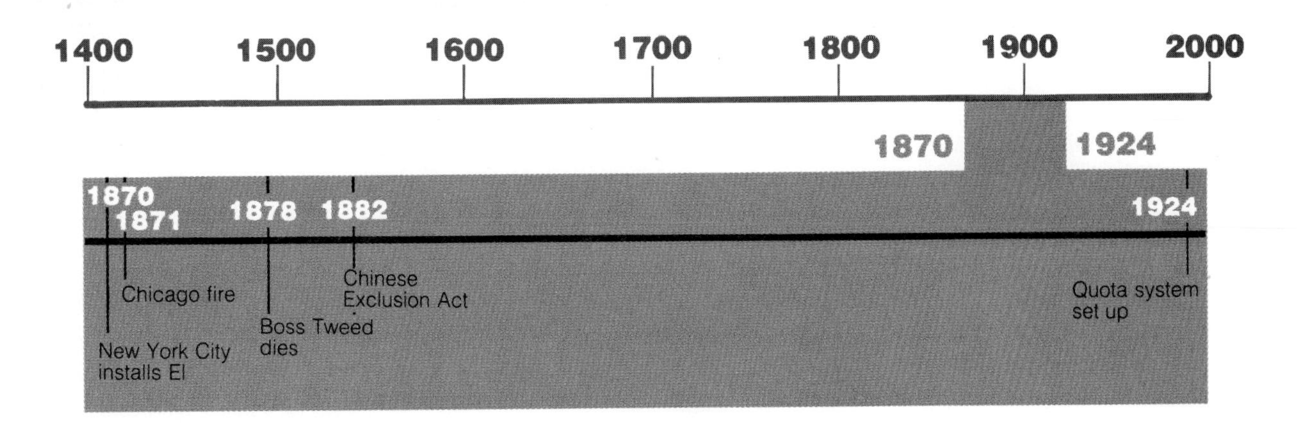

Part One

Rapidly Growing Cities and Their Problems

When and why did people begin moving to cities?

When the Civil War began, in 1860, only one American in five lived in a city. No American city held as many as a million people. But forty years later, three of every ten Americans were city dwellers. New York City, Chicago, and Philadelphia each had passed the million mark. In 1900, New York City boasted five million people. Only London, England, was larger.

Many who crowded into the cities were immigrants. You will read of their coming later in this chapter. Large numbers of the city dwellers were farmers who decided to take jobs in the cities. They went to new office buildings and stores, where workers were needed.

To many people looking for excitement, city lights looked brighter than they really were. On the farm, there were too many cows to milk, hogs to feed, and acres to plow. The same chores had to be done over and over again. In a popular short story of the time one young woman summed up how many felt. She said,

By 1895, New York City had electric trolleys and elevated trains. Some brave people are even driving automobiles in this drawing of "The Bowery at Night."

I'm sick of farm life. . . . It's nothing but fret, fret [worry] and work the whole time, never going any place, never seeing anybody. . . . I spend my time fighting flies and washing dishes and churning. I'm sick of it all.

Life on the farm was hard. Newly invented comforts and conveniences had not yet reached the farms. Telephones, electric lights, and indoor plumbing were found only in cities—and not even in all cities.

But city life was not all excitement and comfort either. Urban areas had grown too fast. Many new problems had to be faced.

The cities were not prepared for all the people who crowded into them. Urban leaders had to do what they could, as fast as they could, to try to solve their problems. Meanwhile city dwellers had to live amid noise, dirt, disease, and traffic jams.

1. Name three cities which had over a million people by 1900.

2. Why did people move from farms into cities? How prepared were cities to receive them?

Why were improvements in transportation needed?

Imagine, if you can, what New York City must have been like when horses and wagons were the chief means of transportation. Yet that was the case until 1870.

New Yorkers began to experiment to find a better system of mass transportation. First they tried putting steam trains on stilts over city streets. They called their system the "el" because the tracks were elevated. The el could haul many people rapidly. But it was noisy. It created vibrations and danger to the traffic below. Other cities did not install els until after the electric train was invented.

In 1873, San Francisco started using cable cars to haul passengers up and down the city's steep streets. In 1888, Richmond, Virginia, became the

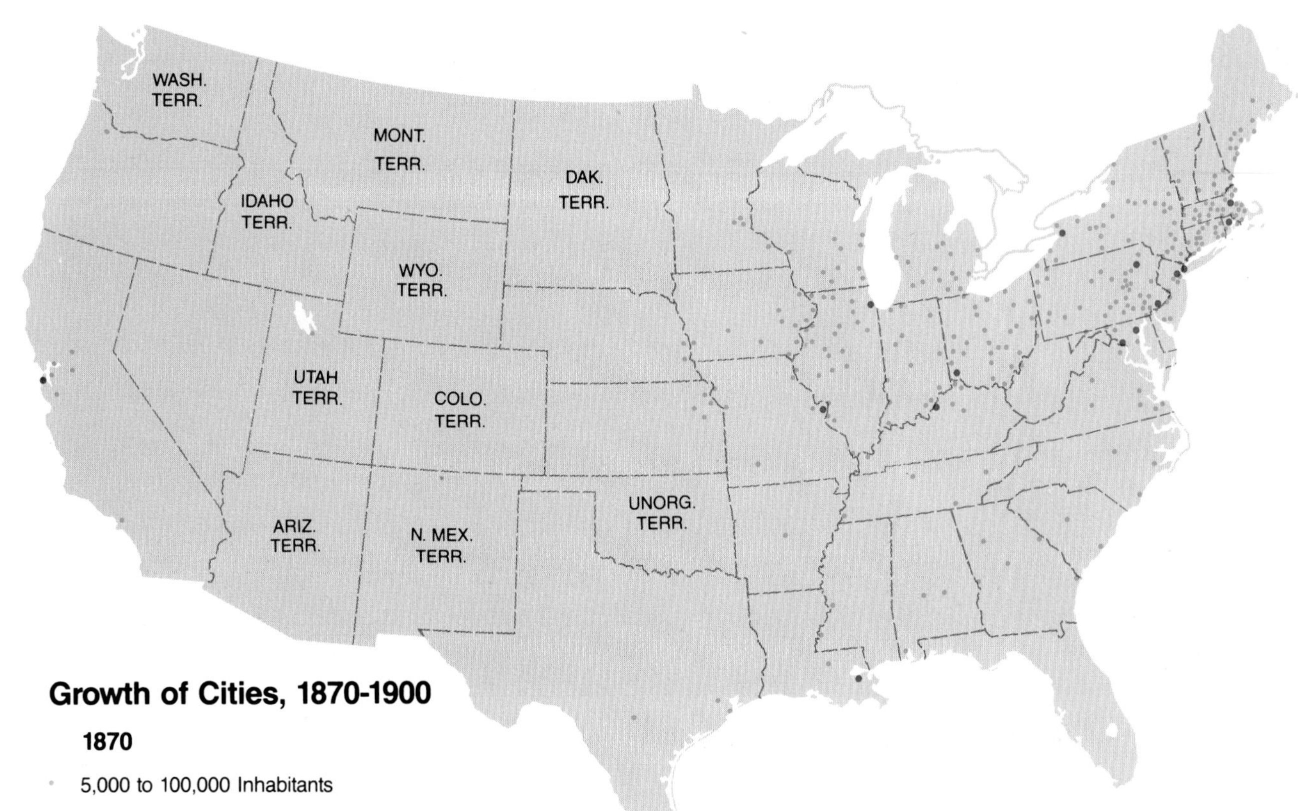

Growth of Cities, 1870-1900

1870

• 5,000 to 100,000 Inhabitants

• 100,000 Inhabitants and Over

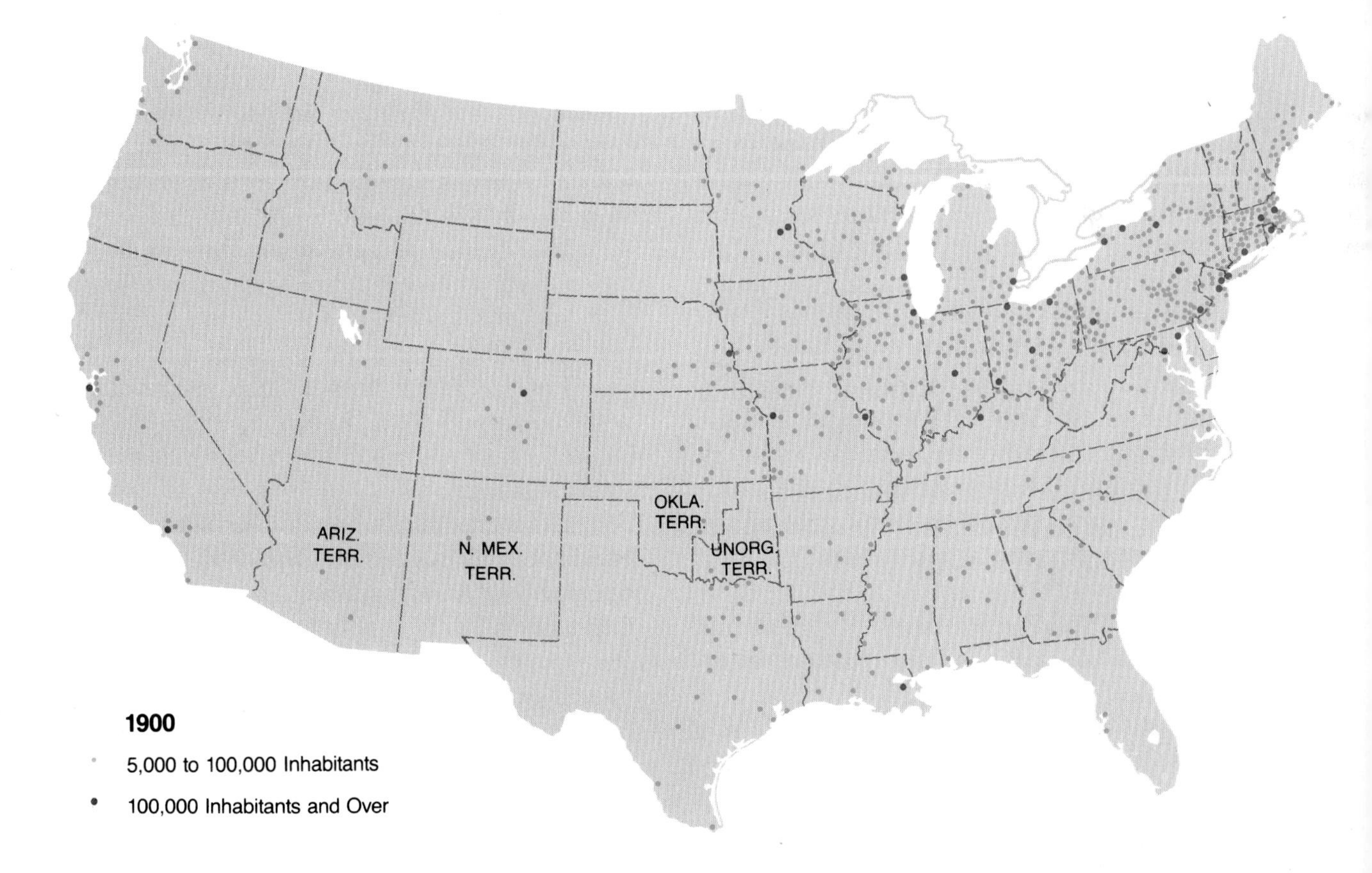

1900

• 5,000 to 100,000 Inhabitants

• 100,000 Inhabitants and Over

The terrible Boston Fire of 1872 was stopped before it reached the State House on Beacon Hill (center).

first city to use electric streetcars. Ten years later almost every other large city had streetcars. Boston built the nation's first subway system in 1895. It, too, was soon copied.

Although these new forms of mass transit solved some problems, they created others. Elevateds, streetcars, and subways made it possible for many families to move out of the cities. They could live in green and airy suburbs and still get to work on time. As those who could afford to moved to "streetcar suburbs," the inner city was left to the poor and the immigrants. However, some of the very richest families kept houses in the heart of the city. These rich homes stood out amid the poverty around them.

3. What were three of the means used to improve mass transportation in cities?

4. What new problem did improved mass transportation create?

How did cities try to cope with the problem of fire?

In closely packed cities fire has always been a danger. The oldest method of fire fighting was the "bucket brigade." When a fire broke out, people formed lines and passed buckets of water to pour on the flames.

In colonial times, most American cities had volunteer fire departments. The members were trained to use hand pumps and hoses to put out fires.

Later, horse-drawn fire engines were equipped with pumps operated by steam. These pumps could throw water a great distance.

Even so, many terrible fires blackened the nation's cities. One of the most disastrous and famous fires swept Chicago in 1871. It was set, according to the story, when Mrs. O'Leary's cow kicked over an oil lantern. No one is sure how the fire really started. But it did terrible damage. The heart of the city was destroyed and 17,000 buildings went up in flames. About 100,000 people were left homeless.

Chicago was not the only city hit by fire. Seattle, New York City, San Francisco, Boston—the list could go on and on. All suffered serious fires that almost destroyed them.

The time had come for cities to have professional fire departments. Full-time fire fighters were hired. Special equipment was built. High-pressure water mains and hydrants were set up. Buildings got new automatic sprinkling systems and electric fire alarms.

5. How did cities first try to fight fires?
6. What improvements were made in fire fighting?

How did cities tackle the problems of disease, water, and sewage?

Three troubles that seemed linked together worried growing cities. Those three were disease, water, and sewage.

Disease swept the growing cities. Tuberculosis and typhoid fever took many lives. New cures and vaccines were developed after the Civil War. But medicine alone could not end *epidemics*, or large-scale outbreaks of illness. Epidemics went along with the twin problems of sewage and water.

Making water safe to drink was a big step toward preventing disease. In the 1890s, New York City found a cheap method of making water pure. When a small amount of chlorine was added to water, wonderful things happened. Purified, or "chlorinated," water, along with better health practices, brought the death rate down 20 percent in 20 years!

City sewers were ridden with disease. In some places sewage ran through open gutters in the streets. In other places, sewage was dumped in nearby rivers or streams. But the public's health could not be protected as long as rats and insects fed on sewage in streets and streams. Cities had to do something. They put up large plants where sewage was treated by chemicals and made harmless.

7. What happened to the death rate when water was purified?
8. Why were health problems linked to sewage disposal?

Why did cities organize police forces?

As cities grew, so did crime within them. Gangs of criminals whose "regular work" was crime moved into the cities. They set up strongholds that were almost towns within cities. One of the most famous was New York City's "Bandit's Roost." Others were San Francisco's "Barbary Coast," Chicago's "Levee," and Bourbon Street in New Orleans.

As crime increased, cities realized that better methods for policing the streets were needed. Just before the Civil War, Boston replaced its watchmen with full-time uniformed police. Other cities soon did the same. Plainclothes detectives joined city police departments in the 1880s.

Police had a difficult time fighting crime in the cities. Some of their problems were of their own making. Sad but true, not all police were honest. Many of them worked secretly for big city bosses. You will read about them later in this chapter. Some police took bribes from criminals. In exchange, the police looked the other way instead of making arrests.

But hardworking, honest law enforcement officers were in the majority.

Jacob Riis took striking photographs of slum life in New York City at the turn of the century. Above left is a slum called "Bandit's Roost." Above right are tenement porches.

They used science and new inventions to help in the war on crime. Police urged people to use improved locks and safes. Call boxes and electric lights were placed on street corners. Unfortunately, criminals also put new tools and inventions to work. The battle against crime went on—as it still does today.

9. Why did crime increase in cities?

10. How did cities try to combat crime?

How did cities try to cope with the problem of slums?

The worst problems of the cities grew out of poverty. Within a short distance of one another lived the very rich and the very poor.

In New York City, the very rich built big, beautiful homes on Fifth Avenue. Many servants waited on the rich. Wealthy families tried to outdo each other in spending money.

Meanwhile, only a few blocks away from Fifth Avenue were long rows of shanties. Poor Irish immigrants lived there.

Even worse than shanties were the tenements. *Tenements* were substandard apartment houses. Sometimes they were old houses designed for a single family in which six or eight families lived. Some families lived in the cellar. Other families lived in the attic. Some families lived in only one room. There was no indoor plumbing. There were no kitchens and there was no heat. A wood-burning stove was the only appliance.

In an effort to do something about such poor living conditions, New York City held a contest. A prize was to be given to the designer who could offer the best plan for healthful, but inexpensive, housing. The winning design was called the *dumbbell tenement.* It called for multi-storied apartments with a window in every room. The stairway ran up the middle, so front and back rooms got light and air. The side rooms were also to get light and air from an air shaft between buildings. But the idea backfired.

One dumbbell tenement was crowded upon the next. The result was that the air shafts were too narrow for any air or light to get through. The air shafts became garbage heaps. They were breeding places for insects and ducts for fire.

Despite their disadvantages, dumbbells sprang up in many eastern cities. In 1900, half a million people lived in 40,000 buildings of this design in New York City.

As crowding in cities grew worse, some far-sighted Americans began to take action. They could see that unless something was done to preserve some open space, cities would become nothing more than concrete jungles and tumble-down back alleys.

New York City set aside 840 priceless acres (336 ha) to make Central Park in the 1850s. People today treasure those 51 blocks of greenery running down the middle of Manhattan Island.

Boston wisely kept its green Common where the Puritans' sheep and cattle once grazed. The Common, in the very heart of the city, was turned into a public park.

Chicago developed parks and beaches along the shores of Lake Michigan. Philadelphia opened Fairmont Park. San Francisco turned 1000 acres (400 ha) into Golden Gate Park, one of the most beautiful in the world. New Orleans named its lovely park for one of its most famous sons, James Audubon. Smaller cities also set aside some land for rest and recreation.

11. Why did the idea for improving slum dwellings by building dumbbell tenements backfire?

12. Why did some cities begin building parks?

THE DUMBBELL TENEMENT PLAN

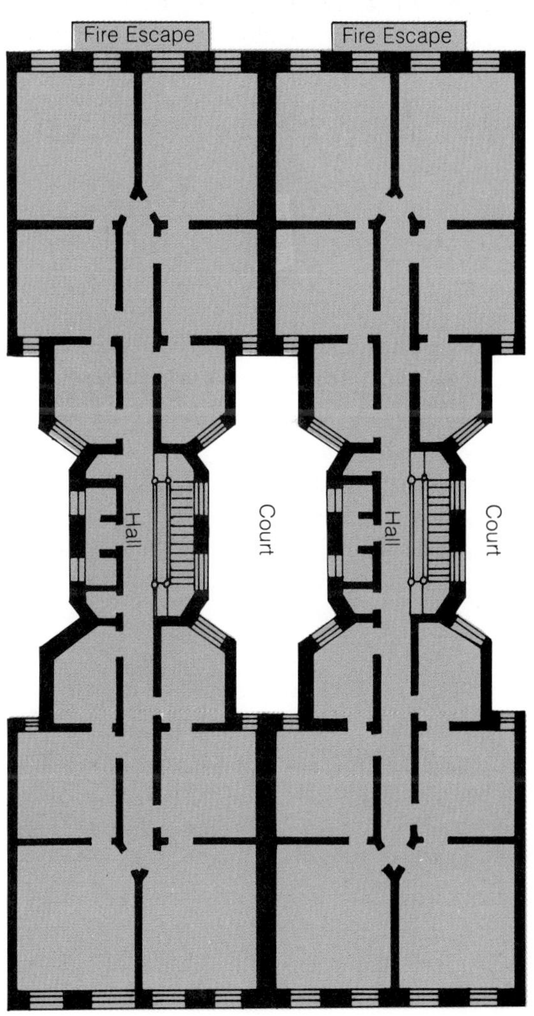

Part Two

Immigrants Crowd into the Cities

When and why did immigration increase?

"My brother, Michael, and I arrived two days ago. All we've had to eat since then is some bread and meat which a lady gave us today. We have no place to stay tonight."

Mary was not trying to make people feel sorry for her when she made those statements. She was simply telling the truth.

Mary was 16 years old; Michael was 15. They decided to come to the United States when their parents died. There was little for them to stay for in their native Ireland. Almost a million Irish people had died of starvation when the potato crop failed. Mary and Michael's parents were among them.

When Mary and Michael arrived in New York City, they carried no suitcases. They didn't have any. What few clothes they had were rolled into the bundles they carried under their arms. How did they expect to live in a strange, new country? Mary explained to a New York State committee. "I can read middling well. I can write my name middling, too. And Michael and I are willing to work."

Mary and Michael were not unusual. Millions of people with stories similar to theirs came to the United States between 1850 and 1914. Most of them came from Europe, but the other continents were represented as well. Almost all of the immigrants were poor. Many did not know another person in the United States. But the immigrants were full of hope. They believed life in the United States would be better than it was in the "old country." They were willing to work to make their hopes and dreams come true. And they knew that the United States needed many workers. It was a nation on the move. Its industries were booming. Men and women were needed to keep them growing.

The first great wave of immigrants came in the middle 1800s. But after the Civil War new industries and immigration both skyrocketed. The tide of immigration rose higher and higher. It reached flood stage between 1870 and 1914. In some years, as many as one million newcomers entered the United States.

1. Why did the growth of industries bring a flood of immigrants to the United States?

2. When did most immigrants come?

What was the Atlantic crossing like?

Most immigrants came in steerage class, the cheapest kind of space they could buy on a ship. Like cattle or "steers," they were herded together in the cargo hold. There they suffered from poor food, bad water, stale air, seasickness, darkness, and contagious diseases. Most immigrants wanted to forget their two or three weeks of travel as soon as possible. For example, here is what a 17-year-old who traveled steerage from Athens, Greece, to New York City wrote about his trip:

. . . The rooms had about 150 people in each one; sometimes more. . . . We had no place to put our bags, so we had to

Immigrants arriving in New York City in 1906 wait for a glimpse of the United States. What might they be thinking?

hold them on the mattress. . . . There was no fresh air and after about three days the smell was terrible. . . . I don't believe I have ever felt worse in my life. . . . We ate in our berths. The cooks came with big pots of soup and stew and filled our dishes, but most people did not even try to eat. We had to wash our dishes in the salt water in the same basin where we washed our faces and hands.

Story told by Teodor Matropoulus. Quoted on pp. 39-40 of *The Story of Ellis Island* by Willard A. Heaps. Copyright © 1967 by Willard A. Heaps. Published by Seabury Press. Used by permission of Willard A. Heaps.

The first sight for most immigrants when they landed in New York City was the Statue of Liberty. On its base is written, "Give me your tired, your poor, your huddled masses yearning to breathe free. . . ."

3. Why was crossing the Atlantic in steerage such a hard journey?

Why did immigrants settle in cities?

Most immigrants who came between the Civil War and World War I settled in the nation's cities. Some had spent all their money on the ocean voyage and could travel no farther. Others had lived in cities in the "old country." They had no desire to live on farms. Others stayed in cities because they wanted to be near people from their homelands. The big cities of the United States sprouted little cities of immigrants. An immigrant from almost any country in the world could find a neighborhood in the large cities of the United States that seemed like home. Germans, Italians, Poles, Hungarians, and people from many other countries could find a neighborhood where they felt at home.

4. Why did many immigrants settle in large cities?

New York City's Lower East Side was home to immigrants from many lands at the turn of the century. Italians, Poles, Chinese, and Jews from many countries gathered there.

What was the difference between "old" and "new" immigrants?

Foreigners who came before 1870 were called "old immigrants." They came mainly from northern Europe. Usually old immigrants could read and write. They spoke English or learned it quickly. Soon they lived much like their American neighbors.

"New immigrants" came from southern and eastern Europe after 1870. Often they were unskilled laborers who could neither read nor write. Many "old Americans"—who were either "old immigrants" or descended from "old immigrants"—looked down on the newcomers. Their huge numbers were frightening to "old Americans." Their languages and customs seemed strange.

Most of the new immigrants went to work in factories. They got the hardest jobs and the lowest wages. Hard pressed for money, they crowded into city tenements. Some who couldn't find steady jobs became peddlars. Life was anything but easy for the newcomers.

5. Name several ways in which "new immigrants" were different from "old immigrants"?

When did Asians come to the United States?

Not all immigrants sailed past the Statue of Liberty. Many got their first look at the United States in Seattle, San Francisco, or Hawaii. The Chinese came first. In the 1850s and 1860s, they worked in mining camps and on the railroads. By 1880 there were 75,000 Chinese in California alone. Most of them were men. They did not intend to stay in the United States, as most European immigrants did. The Chinese expected to work hard and get rich quick. Then they would go back home and rejoin their families in China. That was their plan. But the plan seldom worked out. Some Chinese did return to China with the money they had saved. If they could afford it, some sent for their families. A few did get rich. But most never got enough money either to return home or to bring over their families. They worked hard. They sent as much money as they could to their families in China. But hard feelings against the Chinese were building. Most of the men who came to the United States in the middle 1800s never were reunited with their families.

Japanese did not begin coming to the United States as early as the Chinese. Often the Japanese immigrants are called "latecomers." To understand why Japanese did not emigrate until after 1900, we must look briefly at Japan's history.

For about 250 years, Japan might as well have had a great wall around it. Few foreigners could enter that country. No Japanese could leave it. Japan was sealed off from the rest of the world. Its rulers did not want strangers to bring their religions or ways of living into the island kingdom.

The United States tried to persuade Japan to open its doors. At last, in 1854, the United States was successful. (See page 433.) Japan agreed to trade with the United States. And Japan said its people could leave, if they wanted to. But the Japanese were in no hurry to leave their homeland. Not until the beginning of this century did large numbers begin to emigrate. Then they went mainly to Hawaii, California, Oregon, and Washington.

There were three main reasons why the Japanese finally began coming to the United States.

1. Jobs were hard to find in Japan, especially for farm workers.

2. In 1882, Congress passed a law which stopped Chinese immigration. So employers who had depended upon the Chinese began to turn to the Japanese.

3. Many American companies sent recruiters to Japan. They were eager to hire Japanese because they had a good reputation as workers. Recruiters told stories of high wages and many job openings. Those jobs were for men only, however. As a result, most Japanese immigrants were men. For every 24 men, only one woman emigrated.

6. When did most of the Chinese come to America? The Japanese?

7. Why were most Chinese and Japanese immigrants men?

Why did demands for control of immigration grow?

As the number of immigrants grew, so did demands to limit the number of newcomers. Some Americans forgot that their ancestors were once immigrants, too. Some Americans thought the "new immigrants" were strange and perhaps even dangerous. They worried about the large number of immigrants. They were afraid that the newcomers might take away their jobs.

Asians were the first immigrants to have the door of opportunity slammed in their faces. In California a "Workingman's Party" was started by Dennis Kearney. His party promised to "rid the country of cheap Chinese labor . . . by all the means in our power." Kearney wrote and spoke against the Chinese. He led riots against Chinese immigrants. Amazingly, Kearney himself was an Irish immigrant.

In 1882, Kearney's words bore bitter fruit. Congress passed the Chinese Exclusion Act. It stopped immigration from China for ten years. Chinese already in the United States were not allowed to become citizens.

Needless to say, the rioting and the law passed against them frightened the Chinese. They huddled in ghettoes, afraid to leave their "Chinatowns."

The Japanese got much the same treatment. They were not allowed to own property. Some California cities made Asian children go to separate schools. Finally an agreement was worked out with the Japanese government. Japanese laborers were no longer

Well-to-do Americans stop the entry of an immigrant in this drawing by an Austrian-born cartoonist. The newcomer sees what the old Americans have forgotten—the shadows looming behind them of their own immigrant parents.

allowed to get passports to come to the United States.

8. Why were Americans afraid of unlimited immigration?

9. How was Chinese and Japanese immigration stopped?

When and how was European immigration limited?

Once Asian immigration had been shut off, there was increasing pressure on Congress to clamp down on Europeans coming into the country. Beginning in 1917, only immigrants who could read and write were admitted. Then in 1924, Congress said only 150,000 immigrants per year could come.

More laws limiting immigration from Europe followed. One law spelled out how many people from each country could enter. This was called the "quota" system. The new laws allowed few people from eastern and southern Europe to come to America.

Although Congress limited Asian and European immigration, there was no quota for Latin Americans or Canadians. Many immigrants came in from south of the border.

The quota system for immigration remained law until 1965. Then, President Lyndon B. Johnson, standing beneath the Statue of Liberty, reopened the nation's doors. Later you will learn more about the reopening of immigration and about the many people who currently are coming to the United States.

10. What was the "quota system"? When was it ended?

Focus on Skills

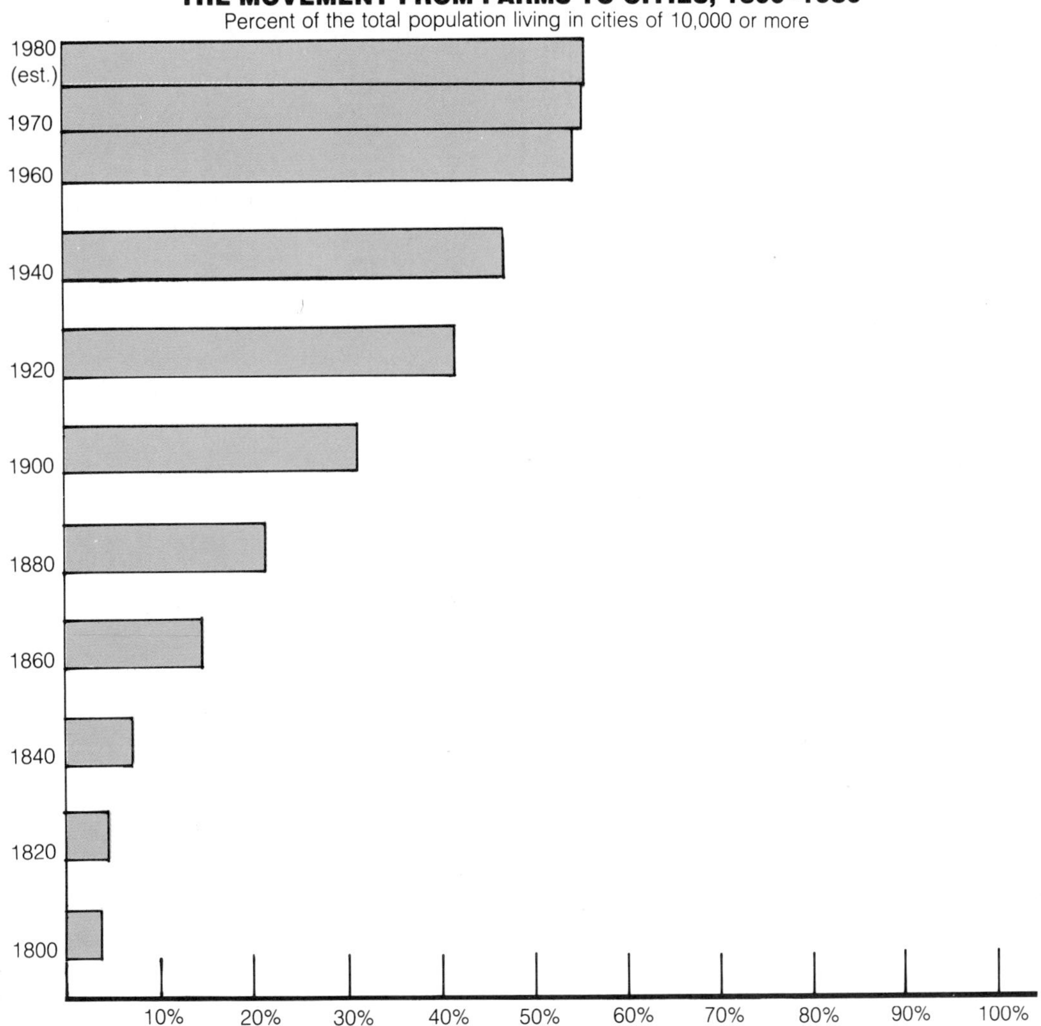

1. What is the title of this graph?
2. What information is it designed to give you?
3. How many people must live in a place for it to be counted as a "city" in this graph?
4. What percentage of Americans lived in cities in 1800?
5. What percentage of Americans lived in cities at the beginning of the Civil War (1860)?
6. In what year did most Americans first live in cities?
7. Look at the overall pattern or the long-term trend shown in this graph. How would you describe that trend?

Part Three

City Bosses Come to Power

Why did cities need better government?

As long as cities were small, there were no great problems in governing them. But as cities grew, the picture changed.

Cities grew out toward the farms. They grew upward with skyscrapers and tenements. They grew crowded with immigrants and people moving in from the country. No plans were made for orderly growth. Cities cried out for better government. But the kind of leaders they needed were often not found.

Most cities were run by a mayor and a council. The mayor was the chief executive, or "president." The council was the lawmaking body, or "congress."

As long as the mayor and council were honest, cities were well run. But in the larger cities, a new type of leader appeared on the scene. This leader was more interested in power and money than in running the city properly. This type of leader was the political "boss."

Bosses were professional politicians. They studied the cities they wanted to rule. They understood the people who lived in those cities and what their needs were. Then they built organizations, or "machines," to run the city, with the boss as head.

1. Why did cities need better government as they grew larger?

2. What is a political boss?

How did political machines manufacture votes?

Just as a machine can make shoes, so a political machine can "make votes." To run a political machine, the boss organized all the voting districts within the city. Those districts were called wards. A captain was put in charge of each ward. The captain's job was to "manufacture" votes for the boss.

Ward captains and their helpers were very friendly with voters in their districts. They did favors for everyone. If a family had trouble, someone from the political machine rushed to help.

Machine politicians played up to different ethnic groups. They promised certain things to Irish Catholics in exchange for votes. They made other promises to Italians or Poles. Each year the machine gave free dances, boat rides, and picnics for voters and their families. The machine got jobs for the unemployed. When election day came, the people voted for those who had helped them.

Sometimes bosses got themselves elected as mayors. At other times the boss stayed in the background. The boss picked the candidates for mayor and council. When they were elected, the boss controlled them from behind the scenes.

3. What was the ward captain's job?

4. Why did city people vote for political bosses?

Who was Boss Tweed?

William Tweed was the most famous boss in New York City's history. He took control of Tammany Hall, headquarters for the Democrats in New York City.

Tammany Hall woos voters at a barbecue on the New York waterfront about 1910.

For years this 240-pound (108 kg) giant of a man stole money in giant-sized ways.

Tweed and his machine, or Ring, stole about $200 million from the city of New York. Here is how they did it.

For instance, a bricklayer would be hired for a job that should have cost $10,000. However, before the contract was signed, the bricklayer had to agree to "pad," or add to, the bill. Instead of a bill for $10,000, the taxpayers of New York got a bill for $100,000! The bricklayer got $10,000 all right. But the Tweed Ring divided up the extra $90,000. Tweed's own books showed that a plasterer once got $138,000 for two days' work.

Taxpayers were cheated when political pals of Tweed were put on the public payroll for doing nothing.

5. How did Boss Tweed steal money from New York City?

How was the Tweed Ring smashed?

New York City's newspapers attacked Tweed and his political machine. *The New York Times* told its readers exactly what Tweed was doing.

At the same time Thomas Nast, one of the nation's most famous cartoonists, attacked Tweed in a series of brilliant cartoons. Nast was cartoonist for *Harper's Weekly*, one of the most popular magazines in those days. (See cartoons, page 382.)

Tweed tried to silence both the *Times* and Nast. He offered $5 million to the newspaper to keep quiet. But neither the *Times* nor Nast could be bought.

Tweed was brought to trial by lawyer Samuel Tilden, who later ran for President. (See page 340.) Tilden had no trouble in proving Tweed guilty. Boss Tweed died in jail in 1878.

6. Who was Thomas Nast?
7. What happened to Boss Tweed?

The Tweed Ring passes the blame in the Thomas Nast cartoon above. Tweed is on the left, wearing a huge diamond tiepin. Vulture Tweed waits out the storm of public wrath in the cartoon on the left.

When did political machines reach their peak?

In the late 1800s and early 1900s, political machines were at their peak. Some bosses were Democrats. Others were Republicans. They all had one thing in common. They were out to get and keep control of the cities.

Some of the most powerful bosses were "Doc" Ames of Minneapolis, "Big Bill" Thompson of Chicago, James and Tom Pendergast of Kansas City, James McManes of Philadelphia, and Abe Reuf of San Francisco. Most of these men used William Tweed as their "model."

Dishonest as they may have been, political bosses were leaders. They knew how to appeal to people. The bosses themselves had grown up in cities. They knew what it was like to be poor and feel the sting of prejudice. When they got power, the political bosses enjoyed making the rich pay.

Ordinary citizens were slow to see that boss rule hurt the entire city—including themselves.

8. In what cities did political bosses hold power?

9. What did political bosses have in common?

Which cities had good governments?

Not all cities were controlled by bosses. Some city mayors and councils gave honest service to the citizens who elected them. Mayor Hazen Pingree was Detroit's honest, faithful public servant in the 1890s. Later, he carried on his fight for good government as governor of Michigan.

"Golden Rule" (Samuel) Jones was mayor of Toledo, Ohio. For seven years Jones worked hard for his city. He put the police on civil service. He insisted on an eight-hour day and minimum wages for workers. Those were unheard-of things for the 1890s! Jones also opened kindergartens and put on free concerts.

Cleveland's mayor, Tom Johnson, was said to have been the best in the nation. He forced streetcar fares down to three cents. Johnson built recreation areas. He insisted on careful inspection of meat and milk. Instead of putting his friends into government jobs, Johnson searched for the best people he could find.

10. Who were three good mayors?

How did city reforms get started?

Newspapers, magazines, preachers, and women's groups all began calling for city reform. They told Americans that good citizens had to run the nation's city halls. If bosses and machines were left unchecked, cities would be poorly run. And the taxpayers would pay the bills.

Americans realized that if they wanted good, honest city government, they themselves would have to get out the scrub brushes. And, what is more, they would have to do the scrubbing. Democracy, as Americans have had to learn over and over, is really a "do-it-yourself" kind of government. The price of democracy is each citizen caring and taking responsibility for government.

Not only did Americans become concerned about city reforms, they became interested in many other improvements in life as well. You will learn more about those reforms in the next chapter.

11. What groups began calling for reform in the cities?

12. Why is democracy sometimes called a "do-it-yourself" kind of government?

Part Four

Life Changes for Urban Americans

How did family life change in the city?

Like a rock thrown into water, the growth of cities set off ripples of change. After the Civil War, life in the cities became far different from what it was in the country or in small towns. City families changed their ways of living. City churches and schools also changed to meet people's needs.

On the farm, families stayed close together. Sons and daughters worked side by side with their parents. The whole family sat down together for meals. Usually the family's children went to the same small school. One teacher taught all the grades and all the subjects.

When families moved into large cities, however, things were different. Parents and children often grew apart. Both parents often were gone all day at work. Streets and back alleys became "playgrounds" for untended children. Brothers and sisters went to different schools, depending on their ages. The number of children born to city families dropped greatly.

Another change was that divorce rates began to climb. Between 1870 and 1880, the population increased 30 percent, but the divorce rate rose 80 percent. This meant that more women became single parents and the heads of their families.

City life brought a great loss of privacy. People were jammed into close quarters. Paper-thin walls often were all that divided one family from another.

1. What major changes took place in the ways families lived?

2. What other changes did city life bring?

Why did churches change?

Churches, too, had to change to fit into the new, urban society. Like the nation, churches were unprepared for the sudden growth of cities. But in time they began to respond.

Many immigrants were Roman Catholics. The Roman Catholic church was probably the first to recognize that newcomers to cities had special needs. Some of its religious leaders decided to devote themselves to work in urban areas. Mother Frances Cabrini, an Italian nun and immigrant, is one example. She and six followers began their work among Italian immigrants in New York City in 1889. Mother Cabrini was a tiny woman with a frail body, but she was a dynamo nonetheless. In quick succession she established orphanages, schools, adult classes, and a hospital in New York City. Then she moved on to New Orleans, Chicago, Seattle, and other cities. By the time she died in 1917, Mother Cabrini had established 67 religious houses with more than 1500 nuns pledged to carry on her work. The Roman Catholic church recognized her contributions by declaring her a saint in 1946. She was the first citizen of the United States to be so honored.

Jewish leaders also were concerned about the special needs of city dwellers, so they did more than build places of worship. They provided for the practical needs of Jews as well. They established schools and hospitals. They formed credit unions from which immigrants could borrow money without interest. They built special homes for young working women and day nurseries where women who worked in factories could leave their babies. A Ladies Fuel and Aid Society even held a banquet each year to collect funds to provide coal for needy newcomers.

Mother Frances Cabrini started schools, orphanages, and hospitals for Italian immigrants.

Most immigrants were Roman Catholics or Jews, so at first Protestant churches were not very involved in city life. But as more people moved in from farms and failed to attend church, preachers got worried. Workers in the 1880s said that they did not attend church because it "seemed to be a place for the rich." Ministers worried about dropping attendance.

At last Protestant churches began to push activities right into the city itself. Volunteers went into the slums to help the poor. They started youth groups. A very new and different kind of church, the Salvation Army, tried to meet city needs.

With trumpet, tambourine, and drum, the uniformed "soldiers" of the Salvation Army turned street corners into churches. This new kind of religion was the largest Protestant group active in the city slums in the 1880s.

Started in England, the Salvation Army spread to the United States. The Army's first aim was to help the poor. Its second goal was to persuade people to become Christians. Before any preaching was done, the poor were fed and clothed. In summer the "Slum Angels" got ice for the poor. In winter the Army gave out warm clothes and food.

Many other, older churches looked down on this unusual Army. But Ballington Booth, head of the American Salvation Army and son of its founder, was not bothered. He said flatly, "The Salvation Army in no sense wants to be respectable. It only wants to help lighten the load of the poor and discouraged."

By the opening of the twentieth century, many who had looked down on the Army began to see how much good it had done in cities.

3. What changes did churches make to meet city needs? Why?

4. What was the Salvation Army? What role did it play in cities?

What changes came in education?

In cities, education spread both up and down the age scale. High schools, colleges, and adult classes grew. So did kindergartens.

The first American kindergarten opened in St. Louis in 1873. Within 25 years, more than one million children were in kindergartens throughout the nation.

Adult education got started about the same time with home reading and study courses. By 1900 more than 100,000 adults were enrolled in special courses.

Another major change in education came with the growth of public high schools. In 1870 there were only 500 public high schools in the whole nation. Many people thought that the states had no right to levy taxes for high schools. "Let those who want more than a grade school education pay for it," those people said.

People who favored public high schools asked the courts to decide. In 1874, the Michigan State Supreme Court heard the landmark Kalamazoo case. The Court decided that public money could be used for high schools. Of course, the decision was only good in Michigan, but it blazed the trail. Other states quickly followed. Twenty-five years later more than 6000 high schools had opened their doors.

In cities, the public school was *the* ladder to climb out of the ghetto. Many grabbed that ladder and climbed as fast as they could. Probably no Americans were more eager to take advantage of education than the immigrants.

Public schools helped children of immigrants become "Americanized." In school they were taught to speak English. They mixed with children of different backgrounds and religions. Immigrant children soon began to speak, dress, and act like other Americans.

Sometimes, however, great gulfs opened between parents and their

Historymaker

Jane Addams

Jane Addams's name appears on almost every list of great American women. She worked for cities, for immigrants, and for peace. In 1931 she received a Nobel Prize for her many achievements. Yet in her own time, Jane Addams was a very controversial person. At one and the same time she was the best loved and most hated woman in the United States. Some called her a saint. Others said she was a radical. But all agreed she had great influence.

Jane—or "Miss Addams," as she wished to be known even to her friends—got off to a halting start in life. She wanted to be a doctor. She enrolled in medical college. But her poor health forced her to quit. She had to have surgery for a spinal condition. She was in bed for months and troubled by that disability for the rest of her life.

In an effort to sort out what to do with her life, she went to Europe. She was deeply troubled. Her thirtieth birthday was approaching. Still she had not found work into which she could pour her energies. Then she happened to visit Toynbee House, a home in the East London slums open to city dwellers who needed help. While she was there, Miss Addams "invented" her own career. She said:

I became convinced that it would be a good thing to rent a house in a part of the city where many needs are found. Young women given too much to study could live there. They could help the needy of the city. And, more important, they could help themselves at the same time. They could restore a balance to their own lives by combining their bookish pursuits with practical, down-to-earth work.

As soon as Jane Addams returned to Chicago she and a woman friend rented the old, decaying Hull mansion. Once it had been a country home for a wealthy family. But in 1889 it was in the middle of the 19th Ward. Around Hull House lived some 5000 immigrants—Greeks, Russians, Germans, Italians, and others. The two women moved their own furniture into the house. They scrubbed and painted. They put white lace curtains on the windows. They told their immigrant neighbors that they were "at home." Any and all neighbors were welcome to visit Hull House and talk about their problems.

Did the neighbors come? Indeed they did—in ever increasing numbers. It was not long before 2000 people every week visited Hull House. They came for a variety of reasons. Some attended clubs. Others came to use the gymnasium or to leave their babies in the day nursery. Young working girls just moved in. They paid what they could in money and shared cleaning and cooking chores.

In time it became apparent that Hull House needed to do more than just respond to people's needs one by one. Something had to be done to prevent problems from occurring and to tackle head-on those which already existed.

Jane Addams proved to be an expert troubleshooter. Once when the immigrants told her that garbage was not being collected in their neighborhood, she got herself appointed as garbage inspector. For weeks she was up daily at dawn. She followed the garbage collector through the streets. She made him angry, but the trash was hauled away.

Miss Addams also put pressure on the state legislature. She and her Hull House helpers worked for the first Factory Inspection Act. It was passed by the legislature in 1893. They worked for child labor laws, protection for immigrants, and compulsory school attendance. The establishment of the nation's first juvenile court in 1899 was largely the result of Hull House efforts.

No friend of Chicago's political boss, Jane Addams worked against his election and that of his dishonest ward captains. She also worked for those whom she believed were good leaders. One to whom she was devoted was Theodore Roosevelt. When he was nominated for President in 1912 she made the seconding speech at the Progressive party convention. Then she stumped the country for him. (See page 409.) She did the same kind of work for Herbert Hoover in both 1928 and 1932. (Hoover was elected in 1928, but lost his bid for reelection in 1932.)

If Jane Addams did all those good things, why did some people come to hate her? They did so mainly because she very often stood for things which the majority of "old Americans" disapproved. For example, when most people called for quota systems and limits on immigration, she objected. She insisted that immigrants added spice and diversity to American life. Let all who wanted to come do so! When most Americans agreed that the United States should enter World War I, she opposed it. All wars were wrong, she said.

Jane Addams lived and worked at Hull House for 46 years. As her life was nearing its end, those she had served sought to honor her. Chicago named her its "leading citizen." Yale University awarded her the first honorary doctor's degree ever given to a woman. Six other universities quickly followed suit. She was guest of honor at a White House dinner. The Greek government gave her a Medal of Military Merit for her services to Greek Americans. She had the Nobel Peace medal slipped round her neck in Stockholm, Sweden.

Grateful as she was for all those honors, Jane Addams went back home, home to Hull House. There she remained at work until her death in 1935. One of the last tasks at which she labored was trying to answer the many letters she had from grade school children from all over the world who wrote to her to say they had been studying about her life and work in their history classes.

children. Immigrant parents often clung to the ways of the old country. Their children preferred new ideas and ways. In many cases, children and their parents became strangers.

5. In what ways did education spread both up and down the age scale?
6. How did public schools help "Americanize" newcomers?

When did public libraries start?

Public libraries, often called "the poor person's university," first opened in cities after the Civil War. Boston and New York City built good libraries.

When Andrew Carnegie opened his pocketbook, public libraries really began to spread. As a boy, Carnegie was book-starved and poor. When he became rich, Carnegie gave more than $60 million to build public libraries all across the nation.

7. When were the first public libraries opened in cities? How did Andrew Carnegie help libraries?

Why did newspapers grow and change?

In fast-moving cities, Americans wanted to know what was going on each

Jacob Riis, himself a Danish immigrant, took this picture of immigrant children saluting the flag in the early 1900s.

day. Quicker means of printing newspapers were invented. Newspapers grew in size and in numbers.

Big city newspapers printed both good stories and trash. Publishers drew readers by printing the most sensational news they could find. Gossip, scandals, murders—anything that would sell newspapers—was printed. These sensational stories were called "yellow journalism." Later we shall see the part "yellow journalism" played in bringing on the Spanish-American War.

At the same time, newspapers did much good. They educated their readers and called attention to problems Americans needed to face. Many features we now take for granted were started through newspaper competition in the late 1880s. Headlines, cartoons, editorials, sports, recipes, advertisements, and comics all began in the drive for readers.

8. What is "yellow journalism"?

9. What good did newspapers do? What features were added to newspapers in the late 1800s?

How did Americans spend their increased leisure time?

On farms, families worked from dawn to dark. Some city workers, especially unskilled immigrants, kept hours just as long. But other workers had more time for themselves. After the 1860s, people could buy canned and packaged foods in stores. This saved time in preparing meals. Smaller apartments did not take as much time to clean as big farm houses. New appliances made housework easier and faster.

In many cases, city people had more money to spend and more time to spend it. Professional sports became especially popular. Spectators turned out in large numbers, particularly for baseball games. Baseball became the national sport. The National League started in 1876, and the American League began in 1900. The first World Series was played in 1903.

Football, too, became popular. Huge crowds turned out to see college teams play. The first All-American team was chosen by sportswriters in 1880.

Basketball was invented by James Naismith in 1891. Naismith was a YMCA instructor in Springfield, Massachusetts. Basketball was originally played with a closed hoop, or basket. Every time a player scored, someone had to fish the ball out of the hoop.

Boxing was a rough sport. Fighters fought to the finish with bare fists. Matches had to be held in secret because they were against the law. When three-minute rounds and padded gloves were introduced, boxing became legal. Huge crowds turned out in the cities to see the fights.

All eyes were on the world's championship battle at New Orleans in 1892. "Gentleman Jim" Corbett, a "scientific fighter," took the crown from the "Boston Strong Boy," John L. Sullivan. Corbett scored a knockout in the 21st round.

Sports were not the only recreation on which city dwellers spent time and money. Concerts and shows of all kinds became big businesses. By 1920 one-fourth of the money spent in the United States went for recreation.

10. When was baseball organized? When was basketball invented?

11. Why did professional sports, concerts, and other shows become big businesses?

Building Your Vocabulary

Complete each of these sentences by choosing the correct word or phrase from those listed below.

1. The cheapest space immigrants could buy on the Atlantic Crossing was—?—.
2. Before the Civil War the United States was mainly rural; after the Civil War it became increasingly—?—.
3. Overhead steam and electric trains were called—?—.
4. Many poor immigrant families crowded into multi-storied buildings called—?—.
5. Bosses depended upon their—?—to get out the votes necessary to keep them in power.
6. Newspapers that printed sensational stories practiced—?—.
7. To halt the flow of immigrants a—?—was adopted.
8. Because sewage was not properly disposed of,—?—often broke out.

urban	political machines
steerage	quota system
elevateds	yellow journalism
epidemics	tenements

Recalling What You Have Learned

Match each item in Column A with the correct definition or phrase in Column B.

Column A	Column B
1. Chicago	A. public libraries
2. dumbbell	B. established public high schools in Michigan
3. "latecomers"	C. city which suffered disastrous fire
4. Dennis Kearney	D. good mayor of Toledo, Ohio
5. William Tweed	E. boss of Tammany Hall in New York City
6. "Golden Rule" (Samuel) Jones	F. Japanese immigrants
	G. a style for a tenement building
7. Salvation Army	H. turned streetcorners into churches
8. Kalamazoo case	I. organized the Workingman's Party to halt Chinese immigration
9. Andrew Carnegie	
10. Jane Addams	J. Hull House

Discussing the Important Ideas in This Chapter

1. Why weren't cities prepared to receive the many people who flooded into them after the Civil War?
2. How did cities combat crime?
3. Why was the dumbbell tenement an idea that backfired?
4. Why did immigrant groups live together in certain sections of cities?
5. Why were some "old Americans" opposed to "new immigrants"?

6. Why did more Asian men than women come to the United States?

7. Do you think the quota system was a fair means of controlling immigration? Why or why not?

8. Why did political bosses and machines thrive in the nation's cities?

9. In what major ways did life change as the United States became more urban?

Improving Your Map Skills

Study the two maps on page 369. Show that you understand the information they are intended to convey by answering the questions below:

1. What is the title of the top map? Of the bottom map?
2. In what section of the United States (the Northeast, Southeast, Northwest, Southwest) were most cities located between 1870-1900?
3. How many cities with more than 100,000 inhabitants were there between 1870-1900?
4. Find the state in which you live on the top map. How many cities with 50,000 to 100,000 inhabitants were there in your state in 1870? How many with 100,000 or more?
5. Compare the two maps. What changes in the numbers of cities in your state had taken place by 1900?
6. Use the map of the present-day United States which appears on page 588. Compare it with the bottom map on page 369. See how many of the cities which had 100,000 or more inhabitants in 1900 you can identify by name. For example, the two cities with 100,000 or more in California in 1900 were San Francisco and Los Angeles.

Improving Your Study Skills: *Reading*

Behind every immigrant there is an interesting story. Each of the statements you are about to read is true. Each was written by an immigrant. As you read them, prepare a chart like the one shown below. It is called a *retrieval chart* because it helps you retrieve, or "bring back," information contained in the case studies. Use a separate sheet of paper for your chart.

Immigrant's name		
Country he/she left		
Reasons for coming to U.S.		
What he/she liked about U.S.		

1. Boris Treschoff. *His father tried to explain to Boris, who was only 8, why they were leaving Russia. Life there was impossible for people who worshipped God as they did. Because they were Jews they could live only in certain places. They could not own land. Only certain jobs were open to them. Years later Boris wrote of his family's move.*

. . . We worked hard [in Russia] and received nothing except the bare necessities. . . . Our only happiness was the family, for like all Jews we were close together. We had been peasants [farmers] living on the same plot of land for generations. . . .

My father told us that he knew he could never change his low station [the way he was treated] and that he was discontented. Some of our fellow villagers had gone to America a few years before. Their letters, passed from hand to hand, made him think that here was his chance, and the more he thought about it the more determined he was that he would follow them.

. . . [He] sold everything [he] had. . . .

Now you see what coming here meant to us. Father wanted us to be individuals and was willing to gamble on the future. . . .

2. Dr. Marie E. Zakrszewska. *Marie graduated when she was only 22 from medical school in Berlin, Germany, with a "diploma of highest degree." Two years later, in 1853, Dr. Zakrszewska decided to leave Germany. She could not speak English. She knew she would have to attend medical school again in the United States before she could practice. Why, then, did she come? She explained many years later.*

I came here [to America] to carry out my plans. In Germany, the government would not let me practice medicine in my native city. I had to show those men who opposed me, because I was a woman, that I could be a doctor in this land of liberty.

Dr. Elizabeth Blackwell [the first woman doctor in the United States] invited me to come and help her. She, her sister, Dr. Emily Blackwell, and I opened the first true "Woman's Hospital" in the world in Philadelphia. Later [in 1862] we opened the New England Hospital for Women and Children. During our lives, we pioneer women doctors met a lot of prejudice. But the path now is open.

3. Anton Petrak. *When he was just 20 years old, Hungarian Anton Petrak decided to "follow the end of the rainbow."*

One day a man came to our village. He talked about how much miners were needed in America, and how much money was to be made. Well, some from our village had gone and I had started to save money for the trip. . . . He said there was a job waiting for me once I got to the town called Windber, Pennsylvania. . . . He did not offer to pay my fare, nor did he write down his promise. He just told me to look him up when I got there. He gave me his name on a card, but at that time I could not read.

When I [arrived in New York] I was afraid of the questions, because I did not have any piece of paper telling me I had the job promised. But I was young and strong and experienced. I knew I could get some other mining job, if this did not work out. Well, it didn't. . . . But I was lucky. Some others from the coal mines came to meet some of my people [other Hungarians]. They . . . promised to take care of me, so I went with them, and it turned out all right.

Chapter 16 Protests, Politics, and Progressives

Yosemite National Park, California

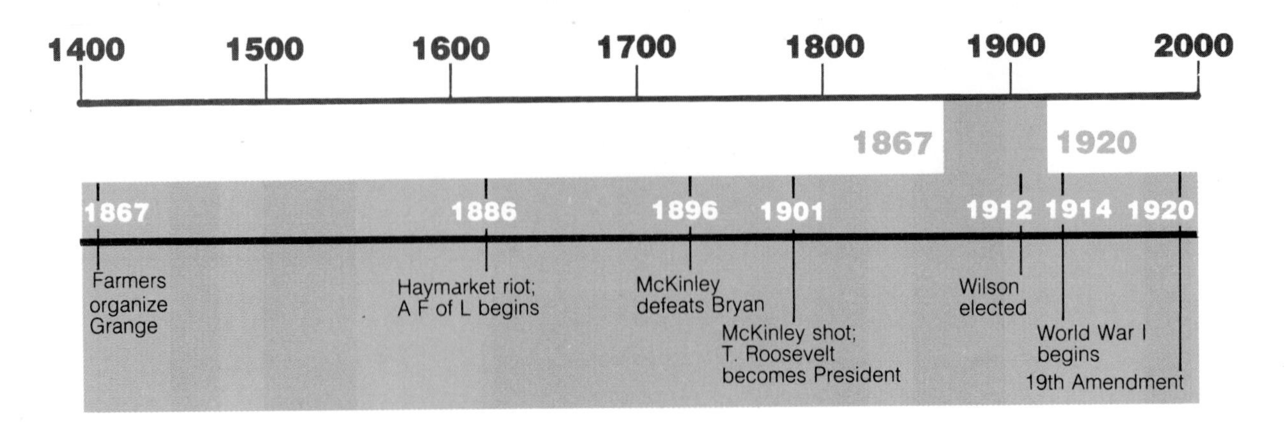

Part One

The Rise of Organized Labor

Why did workers become discontented?

"All that glitters is not gold," goes an old saying. After the Civil War, American workers began to see the truth of that saying. Immigrants from Europe, blacks moving to the North, and young people from farms—all of these people were attracted by the "glitter" of new jobs. Industries boomed as invention followed on the heels of invention. Employers hired men, women, and even children to keep factory wheels turning. But often the jobs did not turn out to be the "gold" that workers hoped they would be.

Many workers had good reasons for complaining about their jobs. Among the most important were these:

1. Wages were low and hours were long. In the steel mills, workers toiled twelve hours a day, six days a week. They earned about 15 cents an hour. In the new city department stores, people worked from 7:30 in the morning until 9:00 at night. Coal miners usually made about $1.50 a day. Most machine operators in the clothing industries earned between 10 and 20 cents an hour.

Prices between 1865 and 1900 were much lower than they are today, of course. But it was still impossible for workers to save money for illness, accidents, or old age. If they argued with their employers, or asked for better wages or working conditions, they were fired.

2. Jobs were not steady. When work was available, people put in long hours. But workers also had times of long idleness. Coal miners, for example, were usually laid off in winter. Between 1893 and 1898, Pennsylvania miners averaged no more than 178 working days per year. A spinning machine operator told a congressional committee that he and others like him had worked only 113 days in a year. His son, a sickly child, had to wear shoes which did not match. One shoe did not even have a heel on it. Because the spinner's family could not afford fuel, they had to collect driftwood from the seashore. The main source of food, week in and week out, was chowder made from clams dug on a beach.

3. Working conditions were poor. Many mines, factories, and offices did not have enough light and air. There were few safety devices, even on dangerous machinery operated by children. There was little or no protection from fire. When the Triangle Shirtwaist Factory caught fire in March 1911, Americans were shocked. The factory was on the eighth floor of a ten-story building. The factory doors were locked. Trying to escape death in the fire, employees leapt from the windows. That tragedy took the lives of 146 women workers.

4. Many more fortunate Americans did not understand workers' problems. They could not identify with the suffering of people like the spinner described above. Many wealthy people believed that people could always get jobs, if they were not too lazy to look for work. Many well-off Americans thought that if people were poor, it was because they had not saved for "rainy days." Many Americans also thought that workers had no right to bargain with employers about wages, hours, or working conditions. It was up to the employer to set such things.

Needless to say, such attitudes upset workers. They accused the more fortunate of being selfish and indifferent. Many workers began to resent the very rich industry owners. They lived like kings in great mansions. Meanwhile many workers, no matter how hard they tried, could not provide for their families.

1. What complaints did many workers have about their wages, hours, and working conditions after the Civil War?

2. Why did some workers and others who were more fortunate fail to understand one another?

Why was the Order of the Knights of Labor organized?

Given the problems they faced, workers realized they were going to have to stick together. Complaining one by one to their employers did no good. Employers fired workers who complained. But if all workers acted as a group, or a *union*, they might be able to improve their situation. Employers could not fire all their workers.

Even before the Civil War, there were attempts to organize labor unions. But none succeeded. Most unions were small and weak.

In 1866 several unions joined to form the National Labor Union. It tried

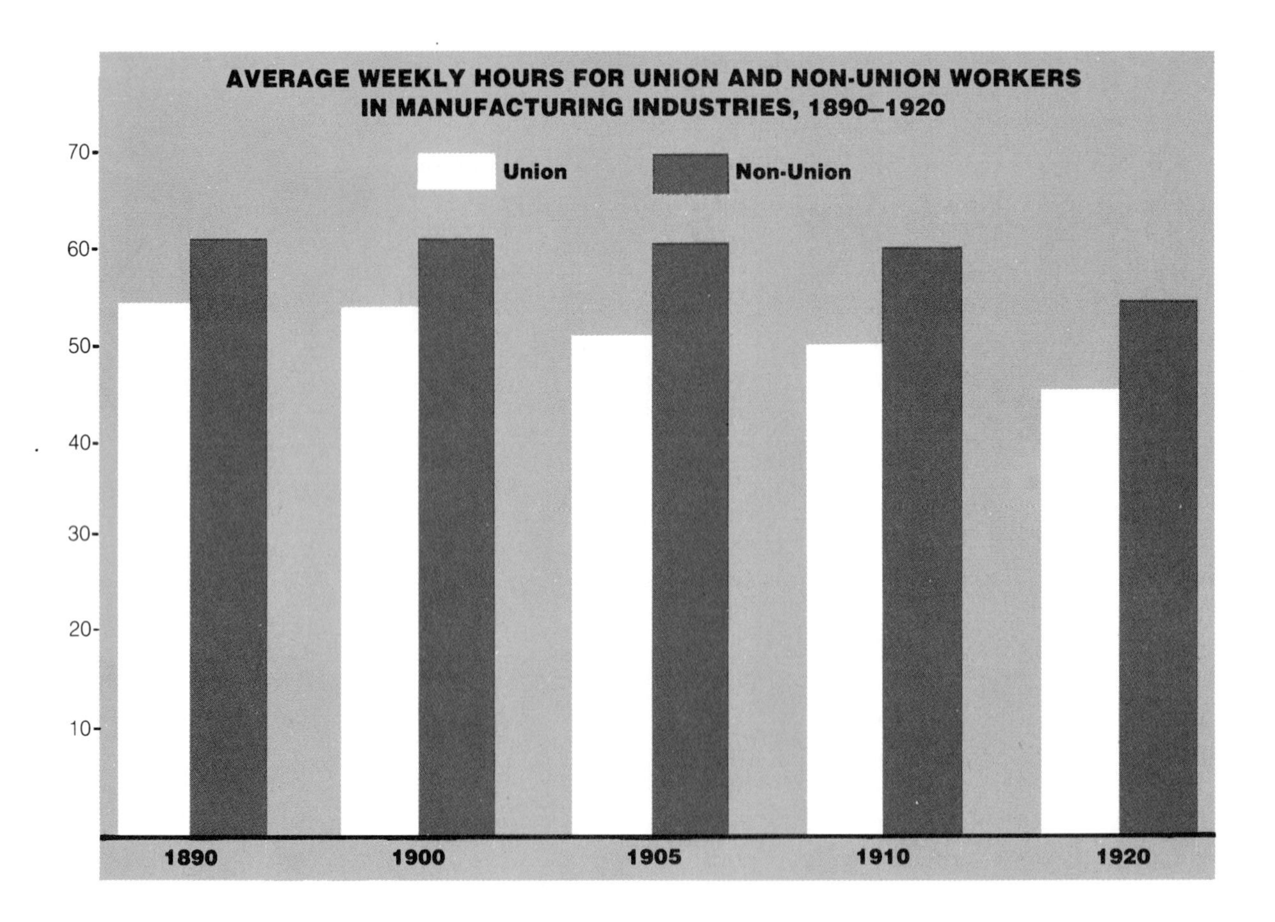

to get laws passed to help workers. The Union got little public support. It fell apart in a few years.

Another labor union rose to take its place. This one was called the Noble Order of the Knights of Labor. Its members demanded shorter hours and higher wages. They called for an end to child and convict labor. The Knights even tried to run their own cooperative stores, but these were not successful.

Many banks failed in 1873, and hard times hit the nation. Many workers lost their jobs. More than 16 percent of the total work force was unemployed. Other workers had their wages cut. Hoping to stop wage cuts, the Knights called a strike against the powerful Union Pacific Railroad.

The strike brought the giant railroad to a halt. The Union Pacific had to give in and restore wage cuts. Labor leaders were happy. They had won a great victory. Membership in the Knights soared. By 1886 the Knights had 700,000 members.

Then the Knights called a strike on all the transcontinental lines south of the Union Pacific. Traffic was stopped along miles of track.

But this time, the employers stuck together and would not give in. They hired strikebreakers who carried guns and clubs. Strikebreakers ran the trains right past the striking workers. Bloody clashes followed.

It took two months before the strike collapsed. The workers had lost. Those

Factory work could be dangerous. This photograph, taken about 1900, shows a lathe room with no safety devices.

who could got their old jobs back. Many dropped out of the Knights of Labor.

3. Why did the Knights of Labor strike the railroads?

4. How well did the strikes succeed?

Why did the Haymarket riot spell the end of the Knights of Labor?

In May 1886, the Knights of Labor encouraged members to demonstrate for an eight-hour day. Orderly marches were held in various parts of the nation. Union members paraded through the streets carrying signs calling for a shorter working day. But in Chicago, things turned out badly. A riot broke out in Haymarket Square, and it spelled the end of the Knights of Labor.

Anarchists (an′ ər kists)—not the Knights of Labor—mounted soapboxes. *Anarchists* are people who believe in no government at all. The anarchists said some ugly, threatening things about the government. Their angry talk frightened many people.

The police were called to break up the meeting. In the commotion, someone threw a bomb. It killed a police officer and wounded some bystanders. Fighting broke out, and ten more people were killed. Six were police.

It was not clear who threw the bomb. But twelve labor leaders were blamed. Eight of them were hanged. One committed suicide. The other three went to jail.

Seven years later, when things had calmed down, Governor John Peter Altgeld of Illinois ordered an investigation. It proved that none of the labor leaders had been guilty, and those still living were freed. But the harm had been done. Labor unions were linked in the public's mind with terrorists. Members dropped out by the thousands. By 1900 the Knights of Labor was dead.

The Knights of Labor did not have a long life. But it was an important trailblazing group. It marked paths which other unions were to follow. For example, the Knights were concerned about the welfare of all workers, unskilled as well as skilled. The union admitted blacks to full membership, and it showed special concern for the problems which women and children faced as workers.

Leonora Kearney Barry, an Irish immigrant and widowed mother of three, became head of the women's department of the union. She immediately launched a study of working conditions for women and children. It was the first systematic study of working conditions conducted by a labor union. Barry presented her findings to all who would listen. Her efforts led to the passage of the Pennsylvania factory inspection act in 1899. She was less successful in trying to end child labor.

5. What happened at the Haymarket riot? Why did it bring about the death of the Knights of Labor?

6. What did the Knights of Labor accomplish?

How did employers fight unions?

Although the Knights of Labor collapsed, other unions managed to survive. But they had a difficult time. Employers strongly opposed unions. They planted spies in the unions to find out who the members were. Union members were fired. Employers then made a "black list" that contained names of union workers. Those on a blacklist would not be hired by anyone.

If things got too bad, employers shut down their plants. Employees were "locked out" until they agreed to come back on the employers' terms.

Before hiring workers, many companies asked them to sign *yellow-dog contracts*. These were agreements in which workers promised not to join a union.

If workers finally did organize and call a strike, employers could get court orders to stop picketing and end the strike. Such court orders to stop an action are called *injunctions*.

In some cases, employers were able to persuade the federal government to send troops to stop strikes. This happened in the case of the Pullman strike in 1894. President Cleveland sent federal troops to break up a railroad strike that was tying up mail deliveries.

7. Name four methods used to discourage workers from joining unions.

How and why was the American Federation of Labor organized?

Even before the Knights of Labor died, the American Federation of Labor was struggling to be born. Its birth was due mainly to the work of Samuel Gompers. His tough wit and tireless work helped make it a strong organization which survives to this day.

Gompers was born to a Dutch-Jewish family in London in 1850. When he was just thirteen, he came to the United States. He went to work as a cigarmaker. While still in his teens, he was chosen as spokesperson for his union. In time he came to be head of the cigarmakers' union. But he dreamed of a bigger union, one which would include all skilled workers. He spent many years trying to organize such a union.

In 1886 he realized his dream. He became president of the new American Federation of Labor. The next year, he presided over a giant labor rally in New York's Union Square. He told fellow workers that they must learn from the mistakes of earlier unions. Then he presented some of his ideas for the American Federation of Labor (AF of L):

Samuel Gompers prepares to cast his vote in a labor election. Gompers began his union work as a young boy while working as a cigarmaker.

1. Labor's goals should be higher wages, shorter hours, better working conditions.

2. Bargain, or talk, with employers first. If talk fails, strike.

3. Build up strike funds ahead of time. Be sure that the workers have something to live on while on strike. Insist that each local union of the AF of L contribute regularly to a strike fund.

4. Don't line up with any one political party. Members should "defeat labor's enemies and reward its friends." Whether a candidate is a Republican or Democrat does not matter. Union members should apply just one test in voting. Is this candidate a friend of labor?

5. Pay special attention to public opinion. See that the workers' side of the story is told.

Workers did not belong to the AF of L directly. They joined a craft, or trade, union. Painters belonged to the painters' union. Plumbers joined the plumbers' union, and so on. The AF of L itself was made up of many national craft unions. Only members of a craft could belong to an AF of L union. There was no place for unskilled workers.

The AF of L grew at a tremendous rate. It started with 45,000 members. By 1920 its ranks had grown to four million.

8. Who was Samuel Gompers? What were some of his ideas?

9. What is a craft, or trade, union?

Why was the United Mine Workers union organized?

Life for coal miners was very hard. Most mines, of course, were off in isolated hills and mountains. Many families had to live in lonesome company towns. Miserable shacks passed for homes. Rents were high.

Miners themselves often never saw much daylight. They started work at dawn and came out of their tunnels at sunset. Even lunch was eaten in the dark mine tunnels.

Danger was a miner's constant companion. Death could come quickly in the mines. Tunnel walls caved in and snuffed out lives. Carelessly handled

This poster from the Locomotive Firemen's Union honors George Stephenson, the "father" of the locomotive.

dynamite crippled and killed. Gas often collected in tunnels. When miners entered with their lamps, explosions rocked mine shafts. Fires roared through the tunnels.

Death could also come slowly in the mines. Day after day coal dust built up in the lungs of the workers. Lack of sunshine, proper food, and exercise claimed many lives.

John Mitchell, a miner's son, led the fight for better conditions for miners. Although his United Mine Workers were part of the AF of L, Mitchell let anyone who worked in the mines join. They did not have to be skilled or craft workers. Such labor organizations are called industrial unions.

In his fight for better working conditions, Mitchell had the help of good friends. One was Samuel Gompers. The other was President Theodore Roosevelt. By 1902 the United Mine Workers had won a nine-hour day and a 10 percent wage increase.

10. What was the life of a miner like?

11. What is an industrial union?

How did public attitudes toward unions change?

When unions were first organized, the public generally did not support them. Nor was the public very happy with all the labor unrest between 1881 and 1900. During that time there were 23,000 strikes involving more than 6 million workers. Workers won their demands in less than half of those strikes. Even so, the public's attitude toward organized labor began to change slowly.

By 1900 it was clear that the public was much more favorable to organized labor. But that did not mean that people rushed out to join unions. At the turn of the century less than 3 percent of the total work force belonged to unions. Even so, most Americans had come to believe that workers had the right to organize. They said workers should be able to bargain collectively, or as a group, with their employers about wages, hours, and working conditions. And they even felt that workers should have the right to strike, if they could not solve their problems by other means. Americans generally had come to agree with Samuel Gompers. He said: "Show me a country in which there are no strikes, and I'll show you a country in which there is no liberty."

The changed attitude toward organized labor was shown in other ways. Many states began to pass laws for the benefit of workers. Some states forbade child labor. Several made employers pay for on-the-job accidents. Some required regular safety inspections in factories.

Focus on Skills

One way to gather information is to ask people questions. An organized question-asking session is called an *interview*. Interview at least three people on the topic of labor unions. Follow the steps listed below. If your class decides on the questions together, you can compare the results after the interview.

Before the Interview

1. Decide if you want to limit your choice of people to interview. You want to ask people questions that they can answer. If you decide to interview *only* members of labor unions, you can ask questions about how the union works.
2. Write out the questions you will ask before the interview. Your class might prepare a form to record responses. Write down the answers during the interview. Try to use the respondent's (person being interviewed) own words.
3. Ask simple, clear questions. For example, you might ask: (a) Do you belong to a labor union? (b) Do you think workers should be able to join unions? (c) Is there any group of workers you think should not be able to join unions? (d) What do you think is the single greatest advantage of union membership? (e) What do you think is the single greatest disadvantage of unions?

At the Interview

1. Introduce yourself. Tell the respondent (person being interviewed) why you are doing research and that you would like to interview him or her.
2. Announce a time limit for the interview and stick to it. Say, "May I please have ten or fifteen minutes of your time?" Do not wear out your welcome.
3. Be courteous, interested in what is being said, and really listen to the respondent. Be nonjudgmental, or neutral, about any beliefs or feelings the individual may express. Try to record the respondent's answers in his or her own words.
4. After the interview has been completed, read it over carefully to be sure you understand it clearly. See if you need to ask for any further information.
5. Ask the respondent if you may use his or her name in presenting the result or if the respondent wishes to remain anonymous.

Congress also took action. In 1882 it set eight hours as the official working day for federal workers. Many other employers then followed its lead. Congress also declared the first Monday in September a holiday, Labor Day. In that way Congress recognized the contributions of workers and showed its support for their organizations. Finally, in 1913, a Secretary of Labor was added to the President's cabinet.

All of those developments helped make life better for working people. But bigger strides forward for organized labor did not come until the 1930s.

12. What changes in the public's attitude toward unions had taken place by 1900?

13. In what ways did states show support for labor? How did Congress show its support?

Part Two

Farmers Demand a Fair Share

Why were farmers angry?

Farmers had many complaints in the late 19th century. They did not feel that they were getting their fair share of the riches of the newly industrialized nation.

Farmers could not sell their meat and grain at good prices. It took a lot of cash to buy land, machinery, and livestock. Naturally the farmers had to borrow money to get started. Sometimes they had to pay as much as 20 percent interest on loans. If they failed to make their payments, the banks took their property.

Taxes also made the farmers angry. In those days there were no income taxes. The main tax was on land. For that reason, farmers claimed that they paid higher taxes than businesses.

The unhappy farmers were angry at bankers, tax collectors, and big business. But they were most angry at the railroads.

The honeymoon between western farmers and the railroads was over. At one time western states had tried hard to get railroads to pass through their lands. Why did western farmers change their minds and turn against the railroads?

Farmers had only one way to get their products to market. They used the railroads. The railroads also owned most of the grain storehouses and stockyards. Farmers had no other place to put grain or livestock until it could be loaded on trains.

So farmers were at the mercy of the railroads. If the railroads charged high rates, the farmers lost money. The railroads had a monopoly. They charged the helpless farmer as much as they pleased.

Farmers battled bugs, floods, and dry spells to get their crops ready. They spent hours planting and harvesting and raising livestock. After struggling to get their products ready for market, they did not want the railroads to take away their hard-earned money. Farmers rolled up their sleeves. The time had come to show the Iron Horse who was boss.

1. Why were farmers angry at bankers, tax collectors, and big business?
2. Why were farmers angry at railroads?

When and why did farmers decide to organize?

Business and labor were both organized. Farmers realized that they must organize and press their demands, too. But doing this was not easy. Farmers worked for themselves. Yet they had to unite to hold their own against railroads, bankers, and monopolies.

In 1867, farmers started an organization called the Grange. It enrolled hundreds of thousands of members and was a huge success.

Through the Grange, farmers sold and shipped grain together to get better rates. Then the organization went to the state legislatures. Farmers, with fire in their eyes, demanded that laws be passed to control the railroads. The Grange was strong enough to vote the politicians in or out of office. So the lawmakers had to pay attention to its demands.

State after state passed laws regulating railroad rates. Other laws set fair prices for storing and shipping grain. These laws were known as *Granger laws*. The Grange was so powerful that many of its members were elected to political offices.

3. What was the Grange? Why was it organized?

4. How did the Grange get state laws that were helpful to farmers?

Why did the Granger laws become important to the whole nation?

Railroad officials were unhappy about the new Granger laws. They said that these new laws took away their right to make a profit. Railroads took their side of the story to the courts.

The courts upheld the Granger laws. In 1876, the Supreme Court even said that states could control railroad prices "for the common good." By then, many state legislatures were controlled by the farmers. They lowered railroad prices even more.

The lower the rates were pushed, the louder the railroads complained. Finally, the railroads got a new hearing before the Supreme Court. This time, the Court said two important things:

1. States could not cut rates to the point where the railroads were put out of business. Railroads must be able to make a reasonable profit.

2. States could only control railroad rates for business that was strictly in that state. Most railroads crossed state lines. The Constitution says that Congress alone has the right to regulate interstate commerce.

Granger laws were the first to regulate big companies for the benefit of all the people. Granger laws began a whole new course, or policy, in American government. The new laws said that the government has the right to regulate any business that is important to the people as a whole.

5. What did the Supreme Court say the first time Granger laws were tested? The second time?

6. How did Granger laws start a whole new policy about government regulation of business?

The Fred Judas family works at haymaking on their farm near Medford, Wisconsin, in 1895.

Fiery Mary Elizabeth Lease of Kansas was a Populist leader. She told farmers to fight for their rights.

Why was the Interstate Commerce Act important?

Farmers were not the only ones who had suffered from high and uneven railroad rates. Small businesses complained, too. Powerful businesses got low rates and special treatment from the railroads. For that reason, many small business people joined farmers in demanding that Congress control the railroads.

Congress responded by passing the Interstate Commerce Act in 1887. It proved to be one of the most important acts ever passed. The act said that railroad rates had to be the same for everyone. No more secret or unfair deals could be made by the railroads with their customers.

To be sure that this law was enforced, Congress wisely set up a "watchdog" committee. That was the Interstate Commerce Commission (ICC).

The ICC became a model. It was the first of many watchdog commissions Congress has set up to guard the public's interests. All new commissions have followed the pattern set by the ICC.

7. What were the main ideas in the Interstate Commerce Act?

8. What agency sees that the Interstate Commerce Act is obeyed?

When and why did farmers organize a third political party?

Farmers in the South and the West felt that neither major political party had helped them enough. For that reason, they formed a new political party of their own.

The Populist party, or the "People's party," was born in wild excitement in 1892. Populists demanded things which then were thought extreme.

The Populists wanted income taxes which hit the rich harder than the poor. They asked for secret ballots for voters at elections. They wanted United States senators chosen by the people, not by the state legislatures. And they wanted the federal government to own the railroads.

One other big demand by the Populists really frightened eastern bankers and business people. The western farmers wanted to use silver, as well as gold, for minting (making) dollars. A great deal of silver was being mined in the West.

Bankers were horrified at the idea of using silver for dollars. Silver is not as valuable as gold. A flood of silver money would cheapen the dollar. A rise in the supply of money tends to lift prices. If a great deal of silver were used, money would become practically worthless. This bothered the bankers, but not the farmers, who needed any kind of money they could get. Farmers thought that if the price of farm crops went up, their problems would be solved.

9. What did the Populists want?

How strong did the Populists become?

In 1892 a Democrat named Grover Cleveland was President. Cleveland was more sympathetic with eastern businesses than with the farmers of the South and West. He believed in sound, gold money, rather than silver. The Populists had no use for President Cleveland. They planned to take over the Democratic party at the next election.

In 1896 the Populists did just that. They found a champion among their own people. William Jennings Bryan of Nebraska, only 36 years old, was a great speaker. On July 8, 1896, he stepped before 20,000 hot, yelling delegates at the Democratic convention in Chicago. He was young, calm, smiling in the midst of confusion. As his voice carried to the farthest corner of the hall, deep silence fell. Then cheers followed every sentence. Bryan played on the delegates as a master musician might play an organ.

Bryan's speech was short. It was powerful. It was a speech no listener ever forgot.

Bryan's last words were a warning. To the rich, the powerful, and those demanding sound, gold money instead of silver, he thundered: "You shall not press down upon the brow of labor this crown of thorns. You shall not crucify mankind upon a Cross of Gold!"

The Populists and Democrats both nominated Bryan for President of the United States. His powerful, silver-toned voice matched the silver that he wanted Americans to use for money.

The election of 1896 was one of the most exciting in American history. The Republicans nominated William McKinley, a man who was against any great changes. McKinley and his supporters warned that the safety of the country was threatened by Bryan and the Populists. Republicans said they had no use for worthless money and a busybody government telling everybody what to do. Such conditions would ruin the country, the Republicans said.

The battle was between business in the East and farmers in the West and South. Worried business owners told their employees not to bother to come to work if McKinley lost the election. As it turned out, the workers kept their jobs. McKinley won by one million votes.

Big business had beaten the "common people." But the "common people" were not discouraged. After all, they had waged a good campaign. Their voice would be heard louder and louder in the years that lay ahead.

10. Who was William Jennings Bryan? Why was he nominated for President by two political parties?

11. How close was the election of 1896? Who won?

William Jennings Bryan was called the "Boy Orator of the Platte," after the river near his Nebraska home. Despite his great speaking skill, Bryan was never elected President.

Part Three

Theodore Roosevelt Offers a "Square Deal"

How did Americans get a reform-minded President?

All over the nation, voices called for reform. In the cities, citizens threw out the political bosses and elected reform-minded mayors. Labor organized into unions. Farmers put pressure on state legislatures to regulate the railroads.

In newspapers, books, and magazines, Americans were urged to take action. Voice after voice called to average citizens. Those voices seemed to say, "Come on, Americans. We can do better than this!"

What the nation needed was a leader in the White House who would speak for all. The nation needed a leader to pull together all the forces working for reform.

Americans did not get such a leader through an election. Instead, they got him by accident. In 1901 a madman assassinated President McKinley. Vice-President Theodore Roosevelt of New York became President.

1. In what ways were Americans attempting to bring about reforms themselves?

2. Why did they want a reform president in the White House? How did they get one?

What new ideas did Roosevelt have?

For years government had been the partner and helper of big business. Roosevelt, however, thought government should give everybody a "square deal," or fair treatment. He was no more for business than he was for labor or any other group. "TR," as Roosevelt was called, believed in and fought for good government, no matter what political job he happened to have.

As police commissioner of New York City, TR walked the beats at midnight. He checked up on the police to see they were doing their jobs. Heaven help those he caught in saloons or coffee shops during duty hours!

When Roosevelt became governor of New York State, he continued his battle for good government. And how he could battle!

Big business was afraid of Roosevelt and his ideas. The more its leaders

TR cracks his whip and the Wall Street lions bow low. How did the cartoonist feel about trusts?

watched him, the more worried they became. Republican bosses decided the safest thing to do with that ball of energy and reform ideas was put him in a "dead-end" job. For that reason they offered him the vice-presidency in 1900.

But even when Vice-President Roosevelt was presiding quietly over the Senate, the bosses still worried. As one of them put it, there was only a heartbeat "between that madman and the presidency." And when McKinley died and Roosevelt went to the White House, a boss named Mark Hanna moaned, "Now look! That . . . cowboy is President of the United States!"

3. What did Roosevelt mean when he said he thought everybody should get a "square deal"?

4. Why did Theodore Roosevelt become Vice-President?

What kind of President was Roosevelt?

"Teddy" Roosevelt was a dynamo. He had the push, roar, and energy of Niagara Falls. When he wanted something, he went and got it.

If Congress would not do what he wanted, Teddy appealed to the people for support. Usually, the people rushed to his side.

Sometimes Roosevelt went beyond what many people thought a President ought to do. If he thought he was right, TR went ahead and took any action he felt was necessary. Later he either explained to the people what he had done, or let them figure it out for themselves.

Because he was a super-charged, self-certain man, few people were neutral about him. Some loved him. They thought his fist-shaking insistence about his ideas was exciting. When Teddy wore cowboy boots and hats and charged about, they were delighted.

Other people could not stand TR. They found his high-pitched voice and roughshod methods annoying. They did not like what they called his "Sunday School" lectures. But people agreed that Roosevelt got things done.

For the first five months he was in office, Roosevelt was strangely quiet. Big business thought it had worried without cause about "that cowboy in the White House." And then it happened! The new President exploded his first bombshell. He took one of the nation's biggest trusts to court.

For more than ten years there had been a law saying monopolies were illegal. But that law, the Sherman Antitrust Act, had not been enforced. TR decided to put the Sherman Act to work for the good of the American people.

For his first trust-busting, or monopoly-breaking, case Roosevelt took on the giant of them all. This was a trust called the Northern Securities Company. It had a stranglehold on the railroads and was threatening to hurt the public by charging high freight rates. President Roosevelt filed suit in court against the Northern Securities Company. He wanted it broken up.

J. P. Morgan and other bankers who owned the company fought to keep it going. But the Supreme Court agreed with Roosevelt and broke the company's hold on the railroads. Teddy had "busted" his first trust.

5. Why did Roosevelt make enemies as well as friends?

6. Why did President Roosevelt take court action against the Northern Securities Company? What finally happened to the company?

Why was the Northern Securities Case important?

Roosevelt's action against the powerful Northern Securities Company showed that government would no longer be the servant of business. TR's action did not mean that government would break up *all* big businesses. But it did mean that the government would control monopolies that hurt the public.

"Trust-buster" was the nickname the common people gave Roosevelt. He was their champion. They saw him as a brave David standing up to Goliath, giant business.

During his nearly eight years as President, Roosevelt brought 44 lawsuits against the trusts. The two Presidents who followed him rolled up even better records. William Howard Taft took 90 monopolies to court. Woodrow Wilson busted even more trusts.

But it was Teddy Roosevelt who blazed the trail. He gave a "square deal" to all Americans.

7. Why was Roosevelt called a "trust-buster"?

How did Roosevelt handle the coal strike?

In 1902, John Mitchell led a strike by the United Mine Workers in the anthracite (an′ thrə sīt: hard coal) coal mines. (See pages 399-400.) The miners complained that the coal operators would not listen to their demands for decent wages and working conditions.

Winter was coming on, and coal was scarce. It looked as if millions of Americans would soon be shivering in unheated homes.

At this point, TR charged into the picture. The President asked the miners to go back to work at once. Meanwhile, he would appoint a board to arrive at a fair settlement of the strike. The miners agreed to the idea, but the owners would not give an inch.

Roosevelt soon solved the problem. He threatened to call out the army to break the strike. Soldiers would help run the mines.

This pressure forced the mineowners to give in, and an agreement was reached. The miners won most of their demands. The public got heat for the winter. And millions of Americans were grateful to Theodore Roosevelt for his prompt action. Once again he believed the public had been given a square deal.

8. Why was it necessary to settle the coal strike in a hurry?

9. How did President Roosevelt persuade the mineowners to come to terms?

Why did Roosevelt urge Americans to conserve their natural resources?

Americans had been careless about using their natural resources. Many thought the continent was a rich storehouse that could never be emptied. As a result, precious natural resources were wasted. Little thought was given to what unborn generations would do for wood, water, or minerals. Thousands of square miles of forests had been cut down. No thought had been given to replanting.

Roosevelt loved nature as probably no other President has. He called for action. Speaking to Congress, he said, "The forest and water problems are perhaps the most vital [important] problems inside the United States." He then set aside about 150 million acres (60 million ha) of forest land. He insisted that 85 million acres (34 million ha) that

Small children work in a mine in this photograph called "The Coal Breakers." Miners complained that mine owners did not care about workers' safety. Miners also said that owners cheated them of the wages due them by the amount of coal they dug.

were sources of minerals and water power be saved for the future.

Roosevelt was not one to leave things to chance. He set up "watchdog" conservation agencies. He wanted to be sure that the natural resources the nation had "banked" would not be withdrawn too soon.

Americans today are still benefiting from Roosevelt's conservation work. No other President ever worked so hard to preserve the beauty and resources of the United States.

10. What did Roosevelt do to save the nation's natural resources?

How did Taft continue Roosevelt's policies?

After nearly eight years, Roosevelt stepped out of office. William Howard Taft, Roosevelt's hand-picked successor, was elected President in 1908. Although Taft carried on Roosevelt's policies, he was not a colorful President. He could not excite people and get them to follow him.

Taft served only four years. In that time he broke up more trusts than Teddy did. But, like Roosevelt, Taft did not think that just because a company was big it had to be "bad." Both Presidents insisted that there were "good" and "bad" trusts. They only wanted to break up those trusts which hurt the American people.

Taft could not please most Americans. At the end of four years, two men ran against him for President.

Differences had grown up between TR and Taft. Just back from a safari in Africa, Roosevelt put his cowboy hat back into the ring. But TR did not get the Republican nomination. It went to Taft. To run again, Roosevelt had to form his own political party. It was called the "Progressive" party, but it soon got a nickname. Someone asked TR about his health. He said that he was as "strong as a bull moose." His party became known as the "Bull Moose" party. It split the Republicans for the election of 1912. As a result, the Democrats won the election. The Democratic candidate was Woodrow Wilson.

11. What kind of a President was Taft?

12. Why did Wilson win the election of 1912?

Historymaker

Theodore Roosevelt, like Jefferson, had a keen mind and many interests. Like Andrew Jackson, he was sure he represented the common people. Like John Kennedy, he took office in his early forties.

But those comparisons aside, there really never has been anyone quite like TR. He was a nonstop reader, thinker, talker, and doer. He was the only President who has ever complained that he didn't have enough to keep him busy while in office.

Teddy Roosevelt was a vigorous campaigner. Here he makes a point during a speech in 1900.

TR's early life gave little clue to the kind of man he became. He was almost blind in one eye. He suffered asthma attacks that left him gasping for breath. He had to sleep sitting up. But he was determined not to be a puny, sick, over-protected, rich boy.

Teddy persuaded his family to build a gym for him right in their house. Week after week and year after year he lifted weights to build muscles. He rode horseback, swam, climbed mountains, played tennis, and took up judo. In time he became a skilled boxer, fighter, and an expert shot.

When TR was President, others had trouble keeping up with him. Teddy was not one to sit in an armchair while discussing matters of state. Foreign nations had to recall ambassadors who could not keep up with Teddy. The British sent a representative who liked mountain climbing. The Germans chose one whose love of sports matched TR's. The French selected a man willing to tramp through the woods.

Roosevelt's mind was as active as his body. He graduated from Harvard with top honors. He became an expert in naval affairs and history. He wrote books, chiefly biography and history but also on big-game hunting and other subjects.

TR is best remembered for the things in which he believed: his country, peace, family life, and himself.

Teddy put service to his country first. He held many important jobs, and he gave his all to each of them. When the United States went to war against Spain, he organized a volunteer cavalry unit called the Rough Riders. (See pages 424-425.) He led the Rough Riders in a charge up San Juan Hill in Cuba and into the hearts of Americans. When TR returned from Cuba he was elected governor of New York and then Vice-President of the United States.

The only post about which Roosevelt ever had doubts was the vice-presidency. He was afraid it was too tame for him. He did not look forward to presiding over the Senate. So, soon after taking office, he went on vacation with his family in the Adirondack Mountains. While TR was out climbing, a messenger came searching for him. McKinley had been shot and was dying. TR must return at once. Teddy did not care that it was night or that rains had washed out the roads. He and a driver jumped into a buckboard. They half-rode and half-skidded down the muddy mountainside. It was 5:30 in the morning, September 14, 1901, when they reached the railroad station. There TR learned that McKinley had died. Roosevelt was President.

Roosevelt believed in a strong United States. He did not want it to be second to any nation. But neither did he want war. When France and Germany threatened one another, he helped them resolve their differences peacefully. He could not prevent Japan and Russia from going to war, however. But he did bring them to the peace table. He invited Russian and Japanese representatives to meet in Portsmouth, New Hampshire. At last an agreement was reached. Teddy later was given the Nobel Peace Prize for ending the dispute between Russia and Japan.

Teddy valued family life. The family was, he said, the single most important institution, the backbone of the nation. TR himself was a devoted husband and a doting father. He lost his first wife in childbirth. They had one daughter, Alice. Some years later he married Edith Kermit Carow. They had four sons and one daughter.

Even as President, TR was never too busy to spend time with his children. He read to them, talked with them, walked with them, played games with them. They enjoyed pillow fights in the White House. When they skated or walked on stilts in the halls, TR laughed. He shared his children's enthusiasm for all kinds of pets. The White House was home to parrots, dogs, a pony, even snakes. One time some members of Congress were waiting to see TR. He asked one of his sons to entertain them for a few minutes. The boy showed them his pet king snakes. The guests pretended to be interested and admired the snakes from a distance. But when the boy wanted to show how the snakes could travel up the sleeves of their suitcoats, the guests suddenly found urgent business elsewhere.

Along with his beliefs in country, peace, and family, Teddy believed in himself and his ideas. Like Benjamin Franklin, he had a way of putting his thoughts into short sayings. Here are a few for us to ponder:

"Keep your eyes on the stars and your feet on the ground."

"Book learning is very important, but it is by no means everything."

"Do what you can, where you are, with what you have."

"Speak softly and carry a big stick; you will go far."

"Far and away the best prize that life offers is the chance to work hard at work worth doing."

Part Four

Americans Work for Better Lives for All

Who were the muckrakers?

Muck is another name for mud or dirt. A group of writers looked at bad conditions in the United States and described them. These writers were nicknamed "muckrakers."

Muckrakers turned floodlights of publicity on needed reforms. Their articles and books made people look and think.

Some of the muckrakers wrote for magazines. The first inexpensive, popular magazine to be published in the United States was *McClure's*. It sold for five cents a copy and contained articles by famous muckrakers.

Ida Tarbell wrote a series of articles on "The History of the Standard Oil Company." She told of the unfair practices of that giant trust. The articles helped Americans to understand the problems that big business had brought.

Lincoln Steffens also wrote for *McClure's*. His series, later printed in a book called *The Shame of the Cities*, opened Americans' eyes to city bosses.

Other muckrakers turned to more stomach-turning subjects. In 1906, Upton Sinclair wrote a book about unhealthy conditions in meat-packing plants. It was so bloodcurdling that Americans joined President Roosevelt in demanding the Pure Food and Drug Act.

At that time there were no controls over the food and drug industries. Bottles and cans often had false labels. Meat and other foods could be prepared under unsanitary conditions. Sometimes drugs were sold which caused serious illnesses or even deaths.

Writers and reformers had long demanded protection for the public. They had made quite a case for action. But, in his usual fashion, President Roosevelt was not satisfied with second-hand information. He had bills introduced into Congress. While the laws were being debated, TR released his own report. He called conditions in the Chicago stockyards "revolting." The people joined Roosevelt in putting pressure on Congress to pass bills protecting their health.

Two important laws were passed in one year's time. The Pure Food and Drug Act required labels which listed exactly what was in a package. The Meat Inspection Bill said that only healthy animals could be shipped across state

Ida Tarbell exposed the Standard Oil Company.

Energetic Robert La Follette calls for reform in a speech at Cumberland, Wisconsin. He served as governor of Wisconsin, as a U.S. senator, and ran for President in 1924.

borders. Meat had to be prepared and packed under clean conditions.

1. What reforms did muckrakers want? How did they call public attention to those reforms?

2. What was the Pure Food and Drug Act? How did it become law?

Who was Robert La Follette?

Four great Americans stand out as reformers in this period of history. We have already read about William Jennings Bryan and Theodore Roosevelt. In the next chapter we shall read more about Woodrow Wilson. The fourth was Robert M. La Follette (lə fol′ it).

La Follette became a great reform governor of Wisconsin. He took on the political machine in his state and beat it. Then he led the citizens of Wisconsin in making progressive laws.

"Fighting Bob" was the nickname his friends gave him. In every speech he doubled his fists and pounded on tables. Short, stocky, with bushy hair, "Fighting Bob" not only looked like a lion but acted like one.

Under La Follette's leadership, the state passed laws to help the poor. It set safety standards in factories. More laws protected child workers. Ways to control the old enemy, railroads, were found. Wisconsin began working on conservation. Land was preserved for future generations. Water, wildlife, and forests were protected.

La Follette gave the citizens of Wisconsin greater voting power. He stopped the practice of having machine politicians nominate candidates for office. Instead, the right to nominate candidates went directly to the people. This more democratic way of picking candidates is called the *direct primary.*

3. What reforms did Robert La Follette bring about while he was governor of Wisconsin?

4. What is a direct primary?

What organizations were formed to help black Americans?

The first organization formed for the benefit of black Americans was called the Niagara Movement. It started as a protest against the views of Booker T. Washington, then the most influential black leader. He said that blacks should first train for jobs. Then they could work on social and political questions.

Dr. W. E. B. Du Bois (dü bois′), the first black to graduate from Harvard with a Ph.D. degree, led the Niagara Movement. He did not think that Booker T. Washington was moving fast enough. Du Bois and his followers demanded total equality with whites and an end to race discrimination.

The Niagara Movement did not last long. Most of its members, including Du Bois, left to become part of a new group formed in 1909. That group was the National Association for the Advancement of Colored People. For short, it is called by its initials, the NAACP.

The NAACP, which is still active today, decided to use two main methods. First, it would work through the courts. It would bring lawsuits whenever and wherever the NAACP thought the rights of blacks were being ignored. Second, the organization decided to carry on a publicity campaign. It would work constantly to bring blacks' needs to the attention of all Americans.

Another important group dedicated to serving blacks was formed in 1910. It was called "The Urban League" because it was, and still is, especially interested in helping black newcomers to cities.

5. Who led the Niagara Movement? What did it hope to accomplish?

6. What two methods did the NAACP decide to use?

How and when did women finally win the right to vote?

During the Progressive, or reform, period women stepped up their campaign for the right to vote. As you know, women had been demanding suffrage for a long time. (See pages 209 and 232-236). But despite all women had done, they had been unable to obtain full-fledged citizenship. They had won victories in some states. Their first big breakthrough came in 1869 in the territory of Wyoming. There they were granted the vote on the same terms with men. Twenty years later, when Wyoming became a state, its Constitution guaranteed women the right to vote. Wyoming thus became the first state in the Union to give women suffrage. Then other states followed: Colorado in 1893, Utah and Idaho in 1896. By 1914, women had won the right to vote in eleven states. All were in the western part of the United States. Then in 1917, New York fell into line.

To force all of the states to give them the vote, women made great efforts to bring their cause to the public eye. They paraded in the streets. They picketed public buildings. Some even handcuffed themselves to the White House fence to dramatize their cause. They gladly went to jail to enlist public sympathy for their demands.

Among the most active leaders in the suffragist movement during the Progressive years were Carrie Chapman Catt, Dr. Anna Howard Shaw, and Alice Paul. Catt and Shaw used quiet persuasion and education to reach the goal of woman suffrage. Paul was in favor of more dramatic action. Together they won the support of the Progressive party and finally of President Wilson.

Women appreciated the words of support. But words did not give them the

Suffragists campaign for their cause. Women who marched in parades and demonstrations for the right to vote suffered great ridicule. But public support for their cause grew, in part because of womens' work during World War I. The 19th Amendment was finally ratified in 1920.

vote. Only a constitutional amendment finally made it possible. Congress passed the 19th Amendment by a narrow margin. Nearly fifteen months later it was ratified by the last state needed, Tennessee, on August 26, 1920.

7. Which states were among the first to give women suffrage?

8. How did suffragists dramatize their cause during the Progressive era? How and when did they finally win the right to vote?

Who led the fight for protection of animals?

In the United States today it is a crime to be cruel to animals or to neglect them. Just over 100 years ago the New York State legislature passed the first law to protect animals. A most unlikely man was responsible for that first, historic law.

Henry Bergh was a rich young man who traveled to amuse himself. One trip took him to Russia. There he saw a driver beating his horse. The sight sickened Bergh. He ordered the driver to stop the savage beating.

When Bergh came home, he found horse beating was just as common in the United States. He decided to take action. He persuaded New York's lawmakers to declare cruelty to animals a crime. Then he made himself a one-person police force for animals. He watched horses working on New York City's streets. If loads were too heavy, he stopped wagons and horsecars right in the middle of traffic. He made the drivers change teams. If he found horsekickers or dogbeaters, he had them arrested on the spot.

Bergh also organized the New York Society for the Prevention of Cruelty to Children. He left that enforcement work to others. But he still carried on his own battle for animals.

Today, every state has laws against cruelty to animals. The American Society for the Prevention of Cruelty to Animals (ASPCA) inspects pet shops, zoos, and stables. It checks complaints about mistreatment of animals.

9. Who was Henry Bergh?

10. What organization did he help start?

Part Five

Woodrow Wilson and the Progressives

Why is Wilson called a Progressive?

Progressive was both the name of a party and the term used for reformers who believed that government should become stronger. Those reformers said it was the duty of public officials to help the weak and the poor. They also wanted to regulate big business. In the early 1900s, Progressives made reforms in business and government. Like Theodore Roosevelt and "Fighting Bob" La Follette, Woodrow Wilson was a Progressive. But unlike Roosevelt and La Follette, Democrat Wilson never ran on the Progressive ticket.

When he ran for election in 1912, Wilson had two opponents, Roosevelt and Taft. Roosevelt had made quite a hit with his "Square Deal." To show voters that he had even more progressive ideas than Roosevelt, Wilson called his program the "New Freedom."

New Freedom plans called for cutting tariffs and lowering prices. If elected, Wilson said he would give Americans a "New Freedom" from bankers and monopolies.

1. What did Progressives want?
2. Why did Wilson call his program the "New Freedom"?

How did Wilson operate as President?

Wilson was very different from the colorful, bouncy Roosevelt. The new President had been a teacher and college president. Very thin, tight-lipped, and intelligent, Wilson held himself back from people. He seemed cold and serious and aloof.

Born the son of a Presbyterian minister, Wilson was a very religious and strict young man. He grew up in the South. After graduating from Princeton University in New Jersey, he became first a lawyer and then a college professor. Princeton called him back, and he became its president.

Wilson's next step was to become governor of New Jersey. His record as governor made him the Democrat's choice for President in 1912.

Wilson had very definite ideas about the duties of the President. He believed that the President must lead Congress and tell it what laws to pass.

Wilson began his first term by calling a special session of Congress to lower the tariffs. Business people wanted a high tariff which would protect them from low-priced foreign competition. Big business put pressure on Congress to keep tariffs high.

Before Wilson's time, if a President wanted something from Congress, he sent a written message. No president had appeared in person before Congress in over 100 years. Wilson broke the custom by going directly to Congress with a speech urging tariff reform. He spoke briefly but forcefully, and won his audience over. Congress lowered the tariff.

Congress didn't always go along with Wilson's desires, of course. When it refused to follow him, Wilson believed the President should appeal directly to the people, the way Theodore Roosevelt did. The people will then put pressure on Congress to follow the President. Members of Congress who do not listen to the people may be voted out of office.

President Wilson makes a speech to representatives of foreign groups while standing in the shadow of the Washington Monument. On his right is his wife, Edith Bolling Galt Wilson.

As President, Wilson controlled the Democratic party. He kept his fellow Democrats in line by granting or withholding favors. While Wilson was in the White House, there was no doubt about who was in charge.

Those who liked Wilson said he was intelligent, firm, and fair. Like all Presidents, Wilson also had enemies. They said he was stubborn and would not listen to advice.

3. How did Wilson believe a President should handle Congress?
4. How did Wilson control the Democrats?

What new taxes did Wilson persuade Congress to levy?

When the Constitution was written, it forbade the governments to levy any direct tax except on the basis of population. (See page 601.) For many years, the courts argued about the direct tax. Did it mean that the government could not levy an income tax?

The question was finally settled just before Wilson became President. In 1913, the 16th Amendment to the Constitution was passed. It permitted the federal income tax.

Wilson quickly called for an income tax along with lower tariffs. Money raised from the tax would make up for the money lost by lowering the tariff.

Progressives were happy to have an income tax. They said it was fairer than other taxes.

Wilson also persuaded Congress to pass an inheritance tax. People inheriting money from friends or relatives had to give part of it to the government.

5. What two new taxes did Wilson favor?
6. What did he do about tariffs?

What was the Federal Reserve Banking System?

With the tariff problem settled, Wilson turned to the question of money and banking. All too often banks did not have enough money to lend when businesses and farmers needed to borrow. Also at times a big city bank would fail, and smaller banks having money in the big bank might then have to shut down. The trouble could spread to many banks.

What the nation needed was a system under which banks worked together. Steps had to be taken to keep banks from failing. They had to have money to lend. These were the aims of the Federal Reserve Banks planned by Wilson.

Under the Federal Reserve Act, which Congress passed in 1913, all national banks joined the Federal Reserve System. The country was divided into twelve districts. In each district there was a Federal Reserve Bank. The national banks contributed money to build up the capital of the Federal Reserve Banks. The Federal Reserve Banks were the central banks for their districts. All Federal Reserve Banks in the United States were run by a board of eight members in Washington. They were responsible to the President of the United States. The Board's job was to raise or lower credit rates at the banks in order to keep the American economy sound. And if banks in one part of the country needed help or support, assistance was promptly sent them from member banks elsewhere.

The Federal Reserve Act also created a new kind of money. They were called Federal Reserve notes. These notes could be issued according to the needs of businesses.

Today the Federal Reserve System is still in operation. It has been strengthened and changed. But it still helps to keep the banks strong and the money supply big enough to meet the nation's needs.

7. Why was a better banking system needed? How did the new system work?

What were President Wilson's other reforms?

Besides overhauling the banking system, Wilson had other programs for regulating big business. He was very much against trusts and other kinds of monopolies.

To control monopolies further, Congress passed two laws that Wilson wanted. One set up the watchdog Federal Trade Commission. That Commission has power to look into how businesses operate. If it finds them breaking laws, the Commission can take them to court.

The second law was the Clayton Antitrust Act. It made clear for the first time the difference between good and bad trusts. The law spelled out a number of things that companies could not do to hinder competition, such as giving some buyers a better price than others. It also helped labor unions by saying that the law was not to be applied against them.

During his first term, President Wilson spent most of his time on domestic problems. He was concerned about improvements at home. That was his main interest.

Unhappily for Wilson, he soon had other problems to face. In 1914, war broke out in Europe. Slowly the United States was drawn into the struggle. There were also problems in the western hemisphere with Mexico and countries in South America. You will read about all of these difficulties later.

President Wilson never lost his interest in reform. But after he was reelected in 1916, he had to give more and more time to foreign affairs. The problems of Europe finally became even greater than the problems of reform at home.

8. How did Wilson regulate trusts and monopolies?

9. What drew Wilson's attention away from problems at home?

Building Your Vocabulary

Which phrase on the right best explains the meaning of the word(s) in italics on the left?

1. *union*	employers' association	workers' organization
2. *yellow dog contract*	an agreement not to join a union	paying another's union dues
3. *injunction*	court order permitting an action	court order to end an action
4. *collective bargaining*	each employee bargains alone	all employees bargain as a unit
5. *monopoly*	no competition	much competition
6. *suffragists*	favored women's right to vote	opposed women's right to vote
7. *trust*	a bank set up by Populists	giant business
8. *grievance*	workers' complaint	a strike

Recalling What You Have Learned

Match each item in Column A with the correct item in Column B.

Column A	Column B
1. Samuel Gompers	A. farmers' organization
2. Ida Tarbell	B. leader of United Mine Workers
3. Populist	C. leader of Niagara Movement
4. Woodrow Wilson	D. reform governor of Wisconsin
5. William Jennings Bryan	E. candidate for President on both Populist and Democratic tickets
6. Robert La Follette	F. Vice-President who became President when McKinley was assassinated
7. The Grange	G. followed Taft as President
8. John Mitchell	H. wrote "The History of the Standard Oil Company"
9. W. E. B. Du Bois	I. American Federation of Labor
10. Theodore Roosevelt	J. a third political party, the "People's" party

Discussing the Important Ideas in This Chapter

1. What major complaints caused workers to organize labor unions?
2. Why and how did public attitudes toward labor unions change?
3. What made farmers believe they were not getting their fair share of the wealth being produced in the United States? How did they try to improve their situation?

4. In what ways did Granger laws benefit the entire nation?

5. What did Theodore Roosevelt mean when he offered a "square deal"?

6. In this chapter you have met three Presidents of the United States: Theodore Roosevelt, William Howard Taft, and Woodrow Wilson. In what ways were they alike? How were they different from one another?

7. Who were the muckrakers? How did they try to improve life in the United States?

8. Name two organizations formed to help black Americans in the early part of the 20th century. How did they try to help?

9. How and when did women finally win the right to vote? Why do you think they had such a long and difficult struggle?

10. What reforms made in the late 1800s and early 1900s still affect American life today? Which of those reforms has a direct effect on your life? How?

Improving Your Chart Skills

Use the data from the graph on page 396 to complete the table below. The first row has been done to help you get started. Use a separate sheet of paper for your table.

AVERAGE WEEKLY HOURS FOR UNION AND NON-UNION WORKERS IN MANUFACTURING INDUSTRIES, 1890–1920

YEAR	UNION WORKERS	NON-UNION WORKERS
1890	54	62
1900		
1910		
1920		

Improving Your Study Skills: *Writing*

Complete one of the following exercises.

1. Pretend you are a farmer living in Iowa in 1870. Write a letter in which you encourage a friend to join the Grange. Tell why you joined.
2. Pretend you are a woman voting for the first time in the presidential election of 1920. Write a letter to a woman friend in which you encourage her to vote. Tell why you are voting.
3. Pretend you have just joined the NAACP in 1910. Write a letter asking a friend to join. Tell why you joined.

Chapter 17

Rise to World Power

Sitka Harbor, Alaska

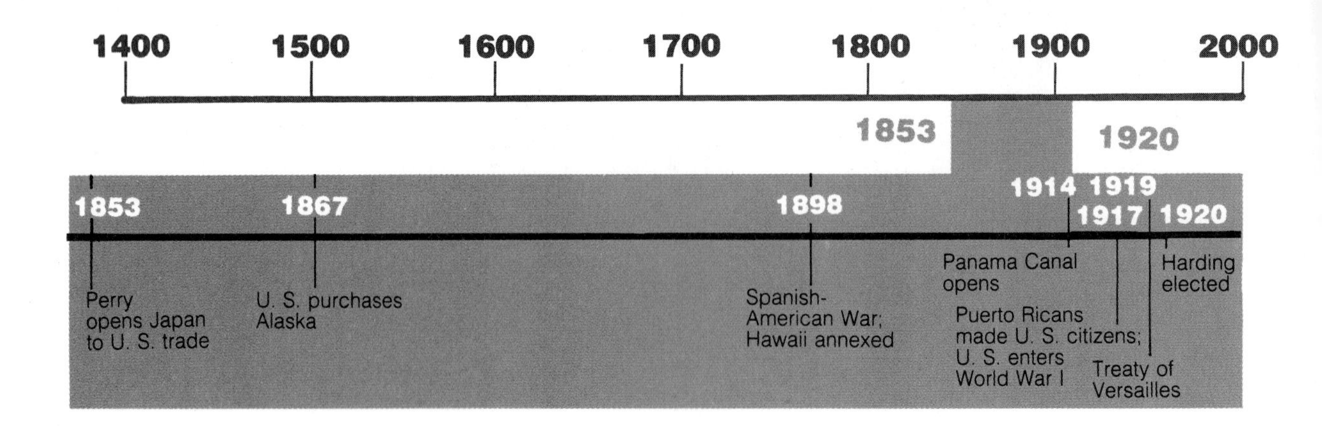

Part One

The Spanish-American War

Why did Americans become concerned about Cuba?

Spain once had the largest empire in the western hemisphere. (See pages 23-28.) But after several centuries, Spain became weak. Its colonies revolted, and many of them won freedom.

In 1898, Cuba and Puerto Rico in the Caribbean were still under Spanish control. Spain also owned Guam and the Philippine Islands in the Pacific.

In Cuba there was great unhappiness with Spanish rule. Cubans tried to revolt several times without success. Finally, the Spanish sent an army to put down the latest rebellion.

General Valeriano Weyler was in charge. In the Spanish army he was nicknamed "The Butcher." Weyler was not gentle with the Cubans. He burned their fields and farms and put the rebels in concentration camps. Food was scarce. There was sickness and suffering in the camps. Many Cubans died.

American feeling against Spain rose as newspapers reported the cruelties of General Weyler. The sensational newspapers headlined the troubles in Cuba in

AN AMERICAN PAPER FOR THE AMERICAN PEOPLE.

The Examiner.

GOVERNOR BUDD MAY GO TO WAR

He Is Ready to Lead California's Forty-One Hundred

SPANIARDS PLAN TO STRIKE FLEET

Desperate Attempt to Be Made to Blow Up Our Ships

CUT OFF FROM THE WORLD

THE BUGLE CALL: "TO ARMS!"

The *San Francisco Examiner* calls for war with Spain.

their "yellow journalism." (See page 389.) Some news stories of the yellow press were exaggerated. But Cubans clearly were suffering, and Americans felt sorry for them. As trouble grew, American volunteers and weapons poured into Cuba to help the rebels.

Of course, the Spanish government protested. It said that American citizens had no business interfering in the affairs of Spanish possessions. Relations grew worse between Spain and the United States. Riots broke out in Havana, Cuba's capital, in January 1898. To protect American citizens, President William McKinley ordered the battleship *Maine* to Havana Harbor.

1. Why did people in the United States become angry with Spain?

2. Why did McKinley order the battleship *Maine* to Havana Harbor?

How did Americans respond to the sinking of the *Maine*?

Quietly riding at anchor in Havana Harbor on the night of February 15, 1898, the *Maine* suddenly blew up. A column of fire spiraled into the sky. Ammunition in the hold of the ship exploded. Over 200 American sailors were killed.

American reaction was almost like a second explosion. The newspapers went wild. The yellow press called for war. Mass demonstrations started in American cities. Americans cried, "Remember the *Maine*!"

President McKinley, a veteran of the Civil War, did not want war. "I have been through one war," McKinley said. "I have seen the dead piled up, and I do not want to see another."

But while the President remained cool, Americans heated up. McKinley's picture was booed in theaters. Dummies dressed up to look like the President were hanged by the neck at war rallies.

Finally the pressure on McKinley became too great. He asked Congress to declare war even though he made it clear that no one knew what had happened to the *Maine*. There was no proof that the Spanish were responsible. To this day no one knows for sure why the *Maine* blew up.

Thousands of Americans answered their country's call as soon as war was declared. These included two former Confederate generals and more than 100 black commissioned officers. This was a war that was popular with everybody. One of our statesmen called it "a splendid little war."

3. What happened to the battleship *Maine*? Who was responsible for what happened to the *Maine*?

The Spanish-American War

U.S. Forces

Spanish Forces

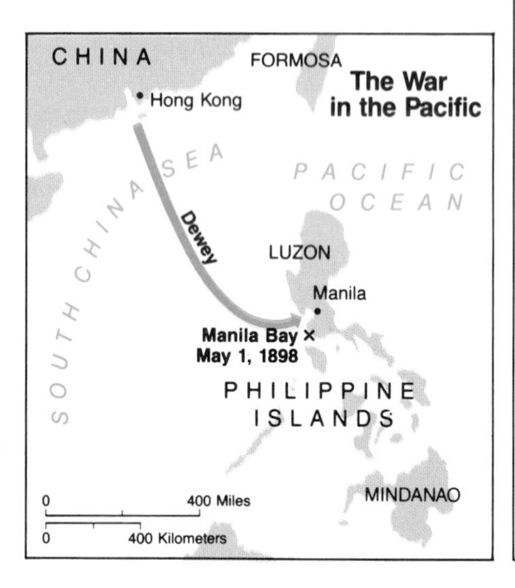

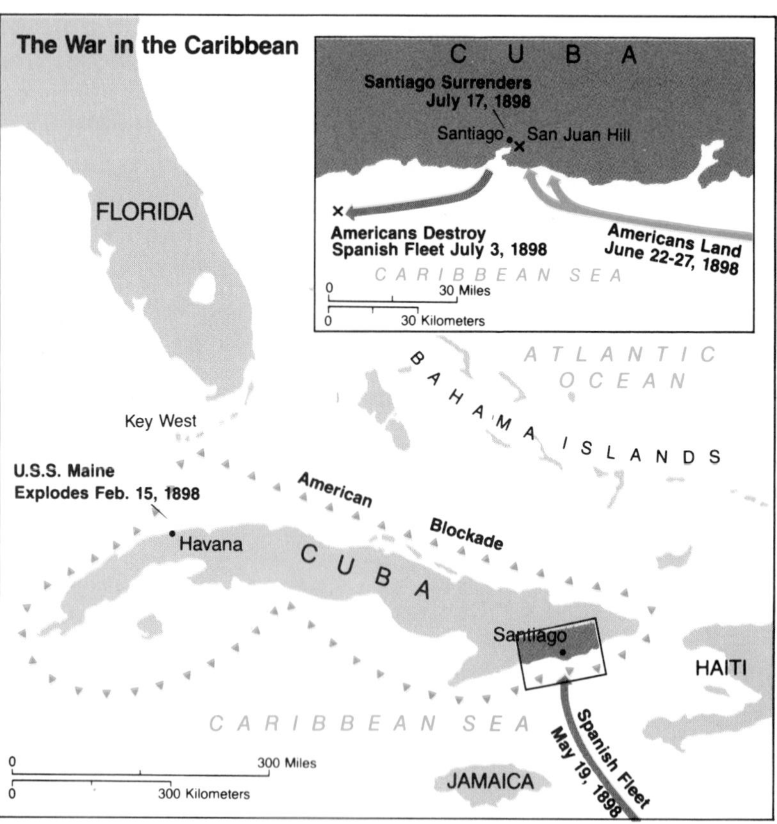

4. How did McKinley feel about going to war? How did the American people feel?

Why is the Spanish-American War called a "little war"?

The Spanish-American War was short and exciting. It lasted only 115 days. Most of the fighting was at sea. The United States won victories that filled the nation with pride. Few soldiers and sailors lost their lives.

The first battle of the war was in the Philippine Islands, far from where the *Maine* went to its watery grave. (See map, above.) Just six days after the war started, Commodore George Dewey sailed into Manila Bay and destroyed the Spanish fleet there. Not a single American life was lost. Manila, the capital of the Philippines, lay at the mercy of the American navy.

Another part of the American fleet moved to blockade Santiago Harbor in Cuba. Land forces captured the outer defenses of the city in what was the most colorful action of the war. That action took place at San Juan Hill.

Under cover of tropical bush, American soldiers waited. The hot July sun beat down on them. At the top of San Juan Hill, the Spaniards had dug trenches. Spanish bullets from the protection of the trenches took an increasing toll of the Americans below.

On the narrow trails of that Cuban hill were some of the most famous American troops ever assembled. Colonel Theodore Roosevelt's volunteer cavalry regiment of "Rough Riders"—cowboys and college students—was there. So were the famed Ninth and Tenth regiments of black troopers. The Tenth was commanded by John Pershing. Later, Pershing was commanding general in World War I.

All of a sudden, the Americans decided to break out of the trap. Shouting "Charge!" and leading the way was Teddy Roosevelt. Blue-shirted Americans fought up the hill. The Spaniards broke from their trenches and ran. Americans poured into the blockhouse at the top of the hill and captured the Spanish flag.

That day—July 1, 1898—Roosevelt made a reputation that later helped him win the presidency. TR was always proud of his Rough Riders' part in the battle for San Juan Hill and Santiago.

As General Pershing recalled that day, he said, "White regiments, black regiments, regulars and rough riders . . . fought shoulder to shoulder . . . mindful only of their common duty as Americans."

When Santiago fell, the Spaniards gave up hope. An American army moved quickly to take over Puerto Rico. Military action then ended.

5. How long did the war last?

6. Where did the military action of the war take place?

How did the war lead to the conquest of yellow fever?

It was the lowly mosquito rather than enemy bullets that took most American lives in the Spanish-American War. Strange as it may seem, it was easier to fight the Spanish than to conquer the mosquito. All told, the United States lost 5462 soldiers in the war, but only 379 died in combat. The rest died of typhoid and yellow fever.

For centuries, people in Cuba had been dying from yellow fever. No one

The Ninth and Tenth regiments of black troopers and Teddy Roosevelt's "Rough Riders" won fame in the battle for San Juan Hill.

really knew what caused the feared disease. After the war, the United States government asked three doctors to become medical detectives. They were to find the cause of yellow fever.

Month after month they worked without uncovering the right clues. Finally Dr. Walter Reed hit on the idea that it was the mosquito that carried the disease.

A human "guinea pig" was needed to test Reed's hunch. Dr. James Carroll volunteered. He let a suspect mosquito bite him. Sure enough, Dr. Carroll got the dread disease. He almost died.

It looked as though Dr. Reed's idea was correct. More Americans volunteered. They allowed themselves to be bitten by mosquitoes. Some of the volunteers died. But at last the cause of yellow fever was known for sure.

Cubans and Americans under Dr. Walter Reed's direction set out to clean up Cuba. Swamps were drained. Every wet place where mosquitoes could hatch was dried up or sprayed with oil. Soon yellow fever was almost wiped out on the island of Cuba.

7. Who was Dr. Walter Reed? What did he think caused yellow fever?

8. How was yellow fever wiped out in Cuba?

What were the terms of the peace treaty?

When the United States went to war against Spain, it declared that it did not want Cuba. Americans only wanted to halt the suffering there.

Late in 1898 the United States sent representatives to Paris to draw up a peace treaty with Spain. By the terms of the treaty, Cuba became independent. But the Americans reserved the right to intervene in Cuban affairs. This right remained in force until 1934. The United States also built a strong naval base at Guantanamo (gwän tä′ nə mō) Bay in Cuba. The base later became a sore point between the two countries.

The United States said that it did not want to own Cuba. But Americans had become interested in owning territory overseas. And now the Spanish-American War gave them the chance to acquire territory.

Spain gave the United States the Philippine Islands and Guam in the Pacific Ocean. (See map, page 435.) In return, Congress paid Spain $20 million. Spain also yielded Puerto Rico to the United States.

9. What happened to Cuba after the war?

10. What islands did Spain give the United States under the treaty?

How did Puerto Rico become a Commonwealth?

By the terms of the treaty, Spain turned over Puerto Rico to the United States. The Puerto Ricans, then numbering almost a million, willingly accepted American rule. In 1900 the Foraker Act set up the government of the island. The President of the United States would appoint a governor and a council. Of the eleven members of the council, five would be Puerto Ricans. The council was the upper house of the legislature, or senate. The Puerto Rican people would elect their own lower house of the legislature. A court system like that of the United States was set up. In 1901, Congress did away with customs duties between Puerto Rico and the United States. In 1917, Puerto Ricans won more self-government. They became

These Puerto Ricans work for a large drug company. Many United States businesses have plants in Puerto Rico.

United States citizens. They began to elect both houses of their legislature.

Since 1947, Puerto Ricans have elected their own governor. In 1952, Puerto Rico became a Commonwealth. This means that Puerto Rico governs itself, although it is still a possession of the United States. There is no restriction on migration from Puerto Rico to the fifty states.

11. Describe the government set up in Puerto Rico under the Foraker Act.

12. When did Puerto Rico become a Commonwealth?

Why were Americans deeply divided about taking the Philippines?

Americans were sharply divided about taking the Philippines. Those in favor said, "Our flag should continue to march." They wanted democracy and better government to go across the Pacific Ocean just as it had gone across the continent. Missionaries were interested in new fields. Business people looked at the profits that could be made in the Philippines.

Many Americans were strongly against taking the Philippines. They argued that the United States had plenty of work to do at home to improve democracy. These people were opposed to the idea of an American world empire.

President McKinley was not sure what to do. He thought about the question. Then he toured the Midwest to find out how the people felt.

Finally, McKinley recommended American rule of the islands until the Filipinos were ready to govern themselves. The Senate approved the treaty taking over the Philippines by a very narrow margin.

The Filipinos, however, were not ready to accept American rule. They

At That Time

One of the greatest detective stories of all time was written during the Spanish-American War. Scientists then matched their wits against a killer, yellow fever.

Each year that dread disease claimed the lives of thousands of men, women, and children. Yet no one in the world had been able to find its cause. Some scientists thought it was transferred from one infected person to another as many diseases are. They believed yellow fever germs were hidden in food, bedding, or clothing. Still others thought the disease was caused by filth. If only cities were cleaned up and kept clean, yellow fever would disappear. But kindly old Dr. Carlos J. Finlay of Cuba had another idea, a theory, about the true cause of yellow fever. He suspected it came from the bite of a particular mosquito—a variety called *stegomyia*.

One of those who listened to Dr. Finlay was an American doctor, Walter Reed. In June 1900, Dr. Reed had been appointed head of a four-person team to investigate the causes of yellow fever. He was ordered to Havana, Cuba, along with Drs. James Carroll, Jesse W. Lazear, and Aristides Agramonte. The United States Surgeon General told the team to find the cause of yellow fever—and do it quickly.

Before work started on the Panama Canal, the area had to be cleared of the mosquitoes which carried yellow fever, or "yellow jack."

At first Reed doubted Finlay. But on the last day of July 1900, Reed went to visit an army barracks where an epidemic of yellow fever had broken out. One case caught his attention. A soldier who was locked in the guardhouse became ill with yellow fever. Six days later he died.

"I began to puzzle over that case," said Dr. Reed. "How could the soldier have caught the disease?" I asked myself. "He couldn't have caught it from his fellow prisoners, because none of them had it. He did not get it from filth, because the guardhouse was very clean and he could not leave it."

Reed was baffled. Then he began to think again of what Finlay had said. Could it be that an insect—probably a particular kind of mosquito—caused yellow fever?

To answer that question Reed knew he would have to experiment with human beings. So he turned first to the doctors on his team. They knew the risks involved. Even so, they allowed themselves to be bitten by the suspected mosquitoes. Dr. Carroll was first. On August 27 a mosquito was applied to his arm. A few days later Carroll fell ill. He recovered, but his health had been damaged so severely that he died a few years later. Dr. Lazear was even less fortunate. Bitten on September 13, he, too, contracted yellow fever. Five days later he was dead.

Convinced at last that Finlay's theory was right, Reed needed to prove it. So he set up an experimental hospital just outside Havana. He named it Camp Lazear, in honor of the doctor who had given his life for science. Then he asked for two groups of volunteers.

For twenty days one group of volunteers lived in a small house on Camp Lazear under very unpleasant circumstances. They slept in the unwashed pajamas of yellow fever victims. They used the same sheets, pillowcases, blankets, and mattresses which those victims had used. But at the end of twenty days they were released with no disease.

The other group of volunteers lived in very pleasant circumstances—except for one. For company they had mosquitoes which were suspected of carrying yellow fever. Those bitten did contract the disease. But because they had been provided with special vaccinations, they recovered. Thus it was that the American Yellow Fever Commission proved the *stegomyia* mosquito caused the disease.

Once the cause of yellow fever was known, the American army launched a search and destroy mission. Under the direction of Major William Gorgas, soldiers searched for and destroyed the *stegomyia's* breeding places. Screens were put over small bodies of water such as water barrels and wells. A film of oil was spread on larger bodies of water. When the young mosquitoes surfaced, they were smothered. Gorgas was so successful that not a single case of yellow fever was recorded in Havana in 1901. The scourge of centuries had been wiped out.

Philippine leader Emilio Aguinaldo fought U. S. control.

demanded independence right away. Bloody clashes broke out. A fearless leader, Emilio Aguinaldo (ä′ gē näl′ dō), led Filipinos in guerrilla warfare against American troops. It took the United States troops three years to win control of the Philippines. More American soldiers died in those three years than had died in the Spanish-American War.

The United States controlled the Philippine Islands for the next 45 years. During that time much was done to improve life there. New schools, roads, and houses were built. Businesses got started. Filipinos were gradually given a larger share in governing themselves. Finally a time schedule for full independence was agreed upon. On July 4, 1946, the United States granted independence to the Philippine Islands, just as it had said it would. In doing so, the United States made history. It became the first great power ever to give up a colony of its own free will.

13. Why did some Americans favor taking the Philippine Islands? Why did some Americans and Filipinos object?

14. When and how did the Philippine Islands become independent?

Why was the war with Spain called a turning point in American history?

The war with Spain marked a real turning point in American history. At the end of that "little war," the United States became a world power. It was an empire with colonies in the West Indies and the Far East.

One lesson Americans learned from the war was that they needed a canal across Panama. When a battleship in the Philippines was ordered to rush to Cuba, it had to sail all the way around the tip of South America to reach the Atlantic Ocean. We will read about the building of the Panama Canal later in this chapter.

Before the Spanish-American War, American interests were mainly in the western hemisphere. After the war, the United States had worldwide interests and responsibilities. No longer could Americans concentrate only on their own problems. The United States was involved for better or worse in all the problems of the world.

15. Why did the war with Spain change the position of the United States in the world?

16. Why did the war show the need for a canal across Panama?

Part Two

New Interests in the Pacific

Why did American interest in the Far East develop slowly?

Before the Spanish-American War, there was little American interest in the Far East. To most Americans, China, Japan, and even Hawaii seemed very far away. There was plenty to do at home without worrying about such distant lands. Besides, the Monroe Doctrine (pages 186-188) pledged us to protect the western hemisphere and to stay out of foreign affairs.

Another reason for lack of interest in the Far East was that Europe and Africa were so much closer to America. Europe and Africa were closer in miles and also closer in blood ties. Most Americans traced their families back to either Europe or Africa. Only a small percentage of the population of the United States was Asian.

After a time, however, Americans began to realize that what happened in the lands across the Pacific Ocean was of great importance.

The first Asian nation in which Americans became interested was China. For hundreds of years, trade with China has been important to the world. (See page 16.) Columbus first came to America to find China and profit from its trade.

After the American Revolution, Britain cut down trade with its former colonies. Americans looked for new markets and found one in distant China. Oriental tea and silks brought high prices in the United States.

In the 1800s, the United States and many other nations tried to increase their trade with China. Merchants were anxious to sell manufactured products to millions of Chinese customers.

1. Why weren't Americans as interested in the Far East as they were in the western hemisphere? In Europe and Africa?

2. Why did Americans try to increase trade with China?

Why did the United States propose an "Open Door" policy for China?

China was a big country with rich natural resources. But it had a poor government and was too weak to defend itself.

Powerful European nations, and also Japan, eyed China greedily. What a fat prize it would make! Why not send in troops and slice up the helpless country? The only problem was that the strong countries were jealous of each other. Each was afraid that someone else would take too big a piece of the Chinese pie.

The nations that wanted to swallow up China tried to convince each other that they really meant no harm. They told each other that they were in China only to trade and to "help" the Chinese develop their country. At the same time those nations said they had no wish to take over Chinese territory. But Japan did take some territory, and England, Germany, France, and Russia prepared to do the same.

The United States Secretary of State, John Hay, did not believe for a moment that those Great Powers would keep their promises to leave China alone. England, France, and Germany had sliced up Africa. Africa had been

United States troops unfurl our flag in Peking. They were part of an international expedition against the Boxers.

conquered and divided up into colonies. China would be next.

Hay wanted to save China. He also wanted the United States to get its fair share of trade there. To gain both of these ends, Hay began the "Open Door" policy in 1899. He sent notes to each of the Great Powers telling them to treat the Chinese fairly and not to seize their land. He also called on the countries trading with China to work together instead of each country trying to seize all the business for itself. In other words, there should be an *open door* for everyone trading with China.

The Great Powers avoided answering Hay directly. But he announced that they had accepted the Open Door policy.

3. What countries wanted to carve up China? Why?

4. Who proposed the Open Door policy? What was its purpose?

How did the Chinese react to the Open Door policy?

Tired of foreigners meddling in their affairs, a group of Chinese tried to get revenge. They formed a patriotic society called the "Harmonious Fists." Europeans translated this strange name to "Boxers."

In 1900 the Boxers attacked and killed white foreigners in their midst. Foreign ambassadors and their families in the Chinese capital at Peking were in great danger. To save them, the United States sent 5000 troops to China. The other Great Powers also sent soldiers, and the Boxer Rebellion was soon crushed.

China was made to pay heavily. China's debt to the United States was put at almost $25 million. To show goodwill, the American government returned some of the money. It was then used to educate Chinese students in the United States in the hope of promoting understanding between the two countries.

5. What was the Boxer Rebellion? How did the United States react to that rebellion?

6. What gesture of goodwill did the United States make after the rebellion was put down?

How did the United States open Japan?

One of history's most amazing stories is how Japan was opened. The Japanese had shut their island kingdom off from the rest of the world. Japanese were forbidden to leave their country. Foreigners were not allowed to enter Japan. For hundreds of years Japan was sealed off from other nations.

The Japanese could hardly believe their eyes, therefore, when Commodore Matthew Perry of the United States Navy sailed into Tokyo Harbor in 1853. Perry carried a letter from President Millard Fillmore to the Emperor of Japan. It asked for permission to trade and for protection for shipwrecked American sailors.

Japan's rulers thought about the American request for trade for quite a while. They realized that they were far behind the West in science and industry. By trading with the West, they would be able to catch up. The Japanese ended their isolation and signed a treaty of friendship with the United States.

Commodore Perry then gave the Japanese emperor many gifts from the President. The gifts included pistols, rifles, and a miniature railroad. When the Japanese saw these things, they started learning how to make them for themselves.

Once the Japanese decided to enter the modern world, they did so in a rush. Scholars were sent all over the world to find the best of everything. They copied the best machines, military equipment, factories, and schools that they saw. At a breathtaking rate, Japan rushed into the modern world. In a matter of years, it became one of the leading industrial nations of the world.

7. Why was Perry able to persuade Japan to open its gates?

8. How did Japan become a leading industrial nation in such a short time?

How did Alaska become a part of the United States?

Shortly after the Civil War, the United States had a chance to buy Alaska. Its Russian owners were disappointed that it was not a money-making colony for them. In 1867 the czar of Russia needed money. So he sent an

A Japanese artist drew this portrait of Matthew Perry.

ambassador to discuss the sale of Alaska with the United States Secretary of State, William H. Seward.

Seward was happy to buy Alaska. He worked out a real estate deal almost as remarkable as the Louisiana Purchase. For less than two cents an acre (0.4 ha), an area larger than all of the thirteen original colonies was added to the United States. The sale also included Midway Island in the mid-Pacific, which became a coaling station for American ships.

Just thirty years after Seward bought Alaska, gold was discovered there. People rushed north by the thousands, hoping to get rich. In 1959 Alaska became a state.

Throughout history there have always been those who cannot see or think beyond the present moment. When Seward spent $7 million for Alaska, he became the butt of many jokes. Some laughed out loud at "Seward's Folly." Others called Alaska "Seward's Icebox" or "Icebergia." They shook their heads over the "waste" of money on a "land of ice and snow."

However, Alaska has proved to be rich beyond measure in fish, furs, minerals, oil, forests, and recreation lands. The purchase of Alaska was one of the best investments the United States has ever made.

9. Why were the Russians willing to sell Alaska to the United States?

10. What did Americans think about the purchase of Alaska? Why was Alaska a good investment?

How did Hawaii become part of the United States?

Long before Alaska was purchased, Americans were living in Hawaii. Traders and missionaries fell in love with the beautiful islands. More Americans poured in to buy pineapple and sugar plantations. Some started great cattle ranches. By 1890, Americans owned most of the farm lands in the independent country of Hawaii.

Just as Americans had revolted against the Mexicans in Texas, Americans revolted against Queen Liliuokalani (lə lē ə wō kə län′ ē) of Hawaii in 1893. Then they asked the United States to annex Hawaii or accept it as an independent republic.

Just as the United States had delayed about admitting Texas, it did not rush to accept Hawaii. For six years Americans debated about taking the islands. President Cleveland decided against annexation. One reason for his decision was that he found the American minister in Hawaii had helped start the rebellion against Queen Liliuokalani.

Queen Liliuokalani was the last monarch to reign in Hawaii. She fought U.S. annexation of her country.

United States Possessions 1899

Cleveland tried to help the queen regain her throne.

Finally, while the United States was at war with Spain in 1898, Hawaii was annexed by an act of Congress. Hawaii was a useful place for American ships to refuel and take on fresh supplies on their way from the West Coast to the Philippines.

Hawaii became a state in 1959. It lies 2100 miles (3360 km) southwest of San Francisco.

11. When and why did Americans begin moving to Hawaii?

12. When and how did Hawaii become an American territory? When did it become a state?

Part Three

New Interests in the Caribbean

Why did the Caribbean area become important?

It has been said that the Spanish-American War turned the Caribbean Sea into an American lake. There are three reasons why our interests in the Caribbean area grew in the twenty or so years after the war.

The Culebra Cut of the Panama Canal, shown in this painting, was a difficult section to complete.

1. The United States needed a canal to link the Atlantic and Pacific oceans. The nation had become a world power. As such, it had to be able to move ships quickly from one ocean to the other. Panama, in the Caribbean, was the place to dig a canal.

2. People from the United States began moving into the Caribbean area in greater numbers. They were owners and workers in new companies that started in Puerto Rico, Cuba, and other Caribbean lands.

3. For years the Monroe Doctrine had said that the United States would guard the western hemisphere against foreign powers. (See page 186.) Now the United States went a step further. It made itself responsible for keeping order in countries south of its border.

1. Why did the United States become more interested in the Caribbean area?

How did the United States get the Panama Canal?

During the Gold Rush to California, Americans realized that a canal across Panama would be helpful. But it was not until the United States got possessions in the Far East that the need for a canal really hit home. Such a canal could cut 10,000 miles (16,000 km) off the long trip around the tip of South America.

The idea of building a canal across Panama was not new. As early as 1850, the United States and Britain had agreed to work together to build one. But they never got around to it.

French engineers had succeeded in building the great Suez Canal in Egypt. Then they tried to cut one through Panama. However, the jungles and swamps of Panama were too much for them. Malaria and yellow fever killed thousands of workers. The French packed up and went home in 1889.

When Theodore Roosevelt became President, he was determined to cut a canal through Central America. He lost no time taking action.

Panama was a province of the South American nation of Colombia. The United States bought up the French interests in the canal. All that was needed was a lease for the land from Colombia. But Colombia held back, hoping to get a higher price for the canal.

Suddenly the people of Panama revolted against Colombia. President Roosevelt quickly sent marines and a warship to help them. His action meant that Colombia was powerless to stop the revolution in Panama.

Immediately, the United States recognized Panama as an independent nation. A treaty was worked out. The new country of Panama leased the

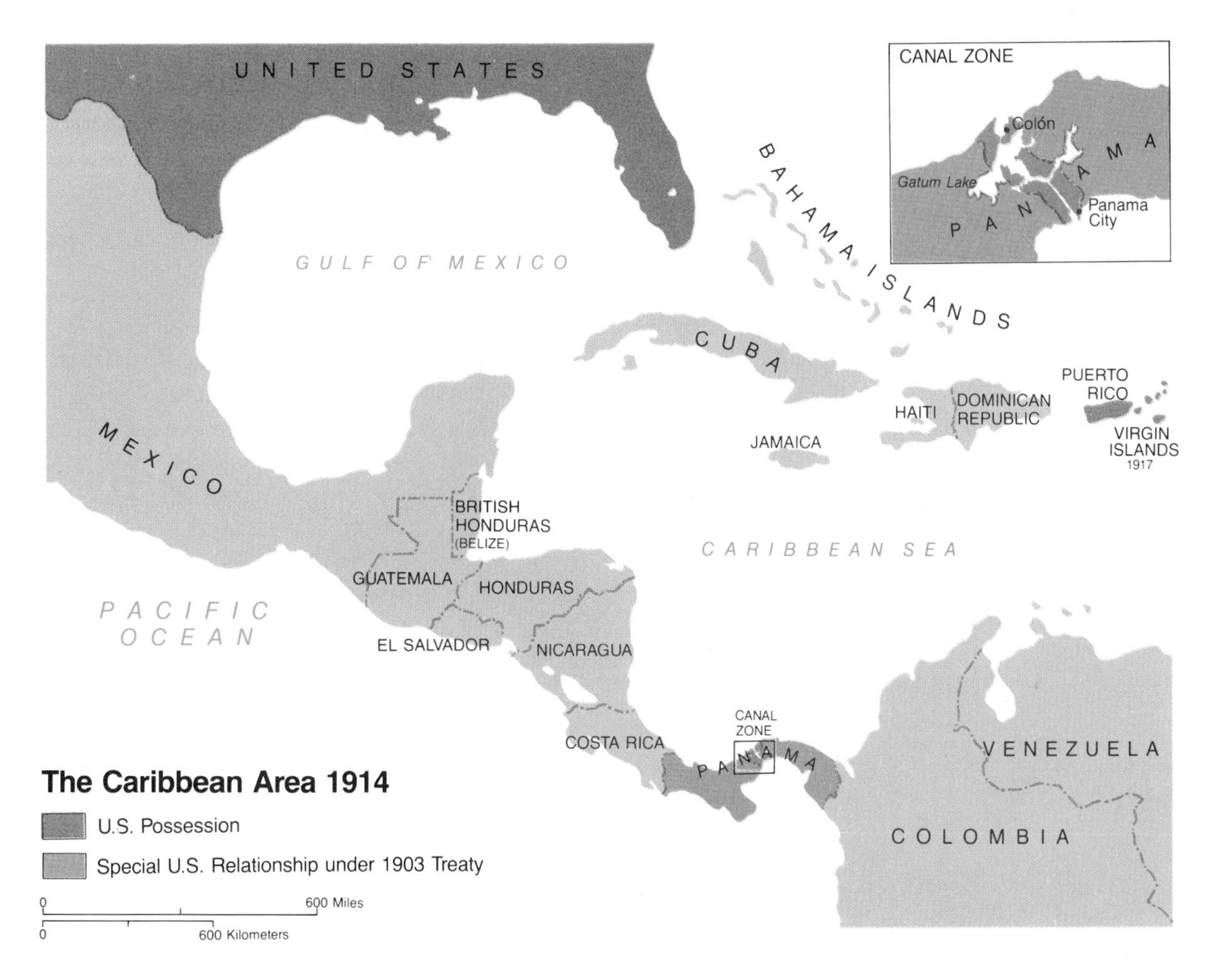

The Caribbean Area 1914

United States a strip of land ten miles (16 km) wide. For that strip of land, called the Canal Zone, Panama got $10 million. In addition, the United States agreed to pay rent for the Canal Zone each year. (See map, above.)

2. Which country tried first to build a canal across Panama? Why did the attempt fail?

3. How did the United States help Panama in its revolt?

Why is the Panama Canal one of the world's great engineering feats?

It took more than ten years and $380 million to build the Panama Canal.

Before work could start, Colonel William C. Gorgas, a United States army doctor, went to Panama to solve disease problems. Gorgas used methods that Walter Reed and others had used to stamp out yellow fever in Cuba. Swamps were drained. Windows and doors were screened.

Colonel George Goethals (gō′ thəlz), a West Point engineer, then moved down to start construction. He asked people from all over the world to join in the building. Workers came from Ireland, Jamaica, India, and many other countries. They worked side by side with Panamanians and Americans. One million cubic feet (28,300 m^3) of dirt per

Focus on Skills

Trace the outline map below of South America on a separate piece of paper. Fill in the names of each country on the map. Use an atlas to help you. Compare your completed map with the map on page 187. How many countries have changed their names or boundaries since 1823?

month had to be dug out. Rivers were dammed. Giant locks, or gates, had to be built to raise and lower ships as they made their way through the 50-mile (80 km) canal.

Theodore Roosevelt made a prediction about the "Big Ditch," as the canal was called. He said that it would benefit the whole world. History has proved him right.

4. What problems had to be solved before the canal could be built?

Why did the United States continue to interfere in Latin America?

The Panama Canal proved a benefit to Latin American countries. Even so they were not happy about the way the United States had obtained the land to build it. They said that a strong nation like the United States had no business interfering in their affairs.

In an attempt to soften Latin American anger, the United States paid Colombia $25 million for the loss of Panama. It also signed a friendship treaty with Colombia. But the United States did not halt its activities in the Caribbean. As time went on, the United States played an increasingly important role in Latin America.

The major reason for United States involvement in Latin America was that in the early 1900s Latin American countries had a great deal of political trouble. Dictators ruled many nations. Governments were changed by revolution rather than election. These turnovers in government caused some serious problems in the western hemisphere.

European bankers loaned money to Latin American countries and expected to be paid back, with interest. But Latin American governments often refused to pay those debts. They said they would not take responsibility for money owed by governments they had overthrown.

England, Germany, and other European countries took action to collect the debts. They threatened to invade Latin America and take by force what was owed them. Such interference was clearly against the Monroe Doctrine.

President Roosevelt was a man of force and energy. The way to solve the problem, as he saw it, was to send *United States* troops into Latin American countries that were in debt. Our own troops, not foreign troops, would collect the money and pay it back to the lenders. Such a policy would keep foreign nations out of Latin America and save the Monroe Doctrine. And it would improve conditions in Latin American countries.

Roosevelt had his way. United States troops were sent to Latin America a number of times during the next 25 years. As soon as the financial affairs of those countries were straightened out, the United States withdrew its troops.

Not only Roosevelt, but also Presidents Taft and Wilson sent troops into Latin America whenever they thought it necessary. Of course, the marines and soldiers were not welcomed in Latin America.

In recent years, the United States has worked hard to improve relations with Latin America. Instead of taking action on its own, the United States has worked with Latin American nations to solve problems and be a "good neighbor."

Later we shall learn about some of the actions the United States has taken.

5. Why did the United States believe it had the right to interfere in Latin American affairs?

6. How did the Latin Americans feel about the United States behavior?

Part Four

World War I

Why did Europe go to war in 1914?

Trouble in Europe had been building up for years. European nations were locked in a power struggle over colonies, control of the seas, trade, and leadership.

One group of nations called the *Allies* lined up against another group known as the *Central Powers*. The Allies were Britain, France, and Russia. Germany and Austria-Hungary were the Central Powers. Later, Italy joined with the Allies, while Turkey and Bulgaria sided with the Central Powers. (See map, page 440.)

Americans worried as the European nations built large armies and navies in the years before 1914. Presidents Roosevelt, Taft, and Wilson tried to head off the war they could see coming, but without success.

Europe's bonfires were built. Every country in Europe was tied by treaties and promises to other European nations. All it took was a spark to set them afire. In 1914 an Austrian archduke and his wife were assassinated by young nationalists from the tiny country of Serbia. And the flames of war roared up. Austria-Hungary went to war with Serbia. Russia rushed to Serbia's defense. France was allied to Russia. Germany came into play as an ally of Austria-Hungary. Because of the elaborate system of alliances, all Europe was suddenly at war.

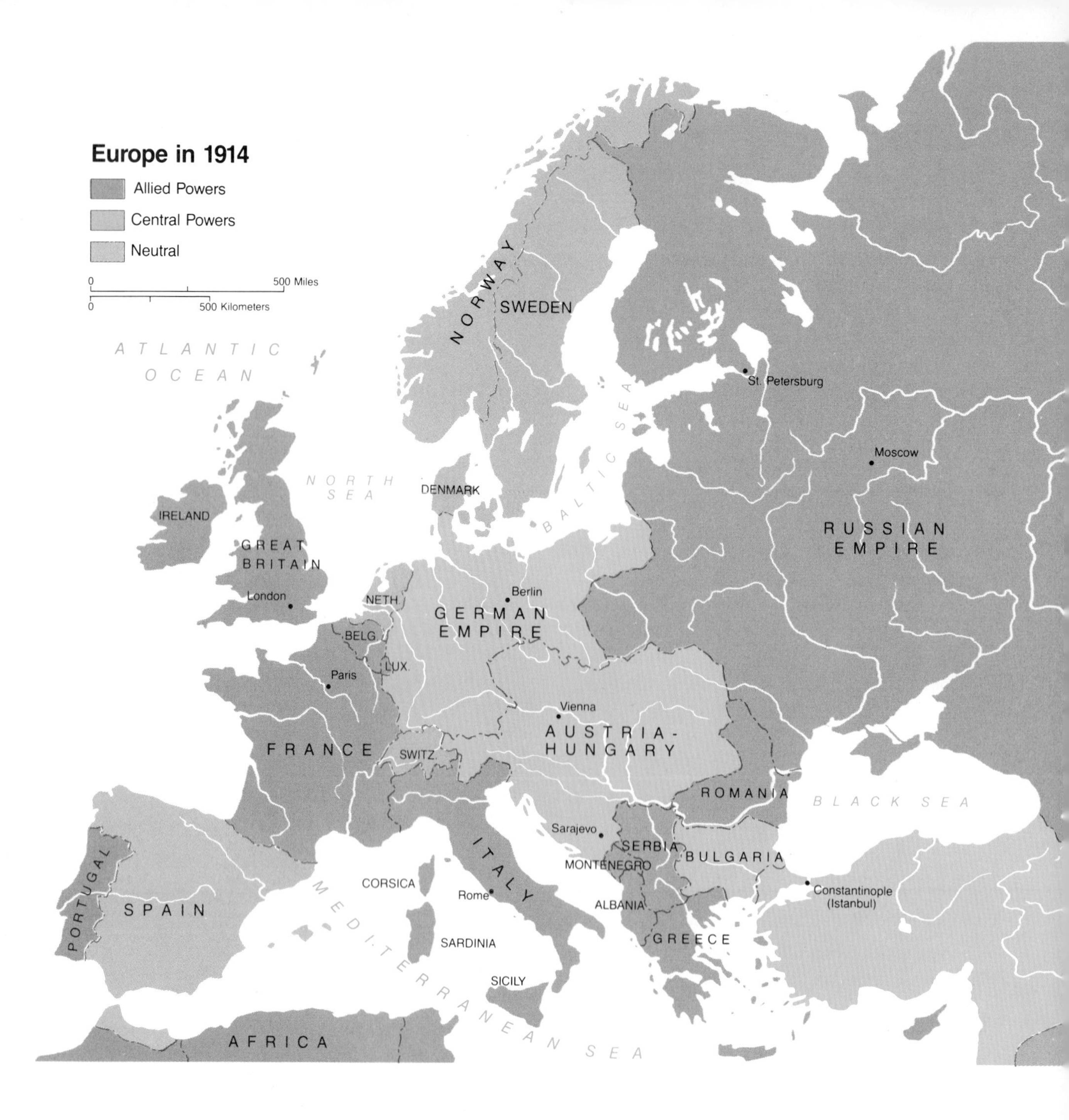

The German armies were well trained and ready to go. Quickly they raced across neutral Belgium toward France. Germany hoped for a quick knockout punch. But the French and British finally held their ground.

A new kind of fighting began. Trenches, or ditches, were dug across northern France. The Allies and the Central Powers dug in opposite each other for a long death struggle. Little ground was taken or lost.

The war extended far beyond France. There were battles in many other places as well. German armies marched eastward to fight the Russians.

The British sent troops into the Middle East and Africa. In time Japan joined the Allies and took Germany's colonies in the Pacific. Naval battles were fought on many seas. Because fighting was so widespread and because so many nations became involved, the conflict was called a *world war.*

1. Who were the Allies and the Central Powers? Why did they fight each other?

2. Why did the conflict come to be called a world war?

Why did Americans change their minds about remaining neutral?

Most Americans in 1914 felt that the war in Europe was none of their business. Many remembered and repeated George Washington's advice about staying out of foreign wars. But in 1914 it was not easy to stay neutral.

Americans had a large trade with Europe. That trade grew even larger once the war began. Europeans had no time to produce goods themselves. They were eager to buy all the American materials they could get. More sales meant greater prosperity for Americans. Because the British controlled the seas, American trade was almost entirely with the Allies. Soon the United States found that it had a great economic stake in an Allied victory.

At first Americans wanted to profit from trade with the Allies. Then they went a step further. They began to sympathize with the Allies. Many Americans were drawn to the British side. A shared language, customs, and history all linked the United States to Britain.

Another reason for this feeling of sympathy was the clever way that Britain and France spread stories about the war. Early in the war, the British cut the transatlantic cable that brought news from Germany directly to the United States. After that, all news from Europe had to go through England. The propaganda used by the Allies was very effective.

Along with sympathy for the Allies, Americans felt the need to try to stop the war. Trench warfare was a stalemate. Month after month and year after year, soldiers killed each other by the thousands. Yet the battle lines scarcely moved. Many Americans felt that by joining the Allies, they could turn the tide and end the long struggle. World War I would be "a war to end all wars."

3. Why did Americans at first hope to remain neutral?

4. Why did some Americans change their minds about staying out of the war?

Why did submarine warfare become important?

What really angered Americans most was Germany's conduct at sea. Britain's powerful navy hemmed in the Germans. American ships delivered boatloads of ammunition and food to the Allies. But Britain would not allow neutral ships to carry supplies to Germany. Nor would Britain allow supplies to go to neutral countries like the Netherlands and Denmark, which could resell the supplies to Germany. The only way the Germans could fight back was to use submarines. These underwater craft could sneak past British warships into the open sea. There they lay in wait. The submarines torpedoed and sank ships headed for Britain.

Submarines were something new. Hidden below the water's surface, they

German submarines were called U-boats (for *Untersee-boote.*) The German poster above urges U-boats to battle. Germans claimed that the notice below, which appeared in some American newspapers shortly before the *Lusitania* sailed, had warned travelers of the danger of submarine attack.

NOTICE!

TRAVELLERS intending to embark on the Atlantic voyage are reminded that a state of war exists between Germany and her allies and Great Britain and her allies; that the zone of war includes the waters adjacent to the British Isles; that, in accordance with formal notice given by the Imperial German Government, vessels flying the flag of Great Britain, or of any of her allies, are liable to destruction in those waters and that travellers sailing in the war zone on ships of Great Britain or her allies do so at their own risk.

IMPERIAL GERMAN EMBASSY
WASHINGTON, D. C., APRIL 22, 1915.

attacked without warning. Their torpedoes crashed suddenly into their targets, blowing them to pieces. But submarines were only safe below the surface of the ocean. If they came up, even one shot could destroy them.

So German submarines did not surface to warn vessels that they would be torpedoed. The survivors of submarine attacks were left to look after themselves in lifeboats or life preservers. No attempt was made to rescue them.

In May 1915, a German submarine sank the British liner *Lusitania.* More than 1100 passengers were killed, including 128 Americans. Though the Germans had warned Americans not to sail on British ships, many Americans called for war.

But in 1916, Germany promised the United States that it would not sink ships without warning them first and helping their passengers afterward. Americans breathed easier.

Early in 1917, Germany changed its policy again. The war was wearing Germany out. In desperation, the Germans turned again to their most powerful weapon, unrestricted (no-holds-barred) submarine warfare. Ships carrying supplies to the Allies were attacked. On one day, three American ships were sunk without warning.

German submarine warfare was the main reason why the United States finally entered World War I. As in the case of the War of 1812, freedom of the seas was at stake. Germany, fighting for its life, tried to deny the United States that freedom.

5. What does "unrestricted submarine warfare" mean?

6. What was the main reason the United States entered World War I?

Why did President Wilson finally ask Congress to declare war?

Powerful voices spoke out both for and against war with Germany. Some people argued that the United States should avoid the bloodiest, most costly struggle the world had ever seen. Secretary of State William Jennings Bryan begged President Wilson to prevent war by ordering Americans off the seas.

On the other side were the war hawks. Led by Theodore Roosevelt, the hawks argued that we must not put "peace above righteousness." They said "duty to humanity" and "self-respect" demanded that Americans fight.

In the midst of all the debate, something very dramatic happened. The British intercepted a secret message from German Foreign Secretary Arthur Zimmermann to the German minister in Mexico. The note contained an offer from the Germans to the Mexicans. If Mexico would help Germany fight the United States, Mexico would get back Texas, New Mexico, and Arizona. (Mexico had lost this land to the United States in the Mexican War.) In return, Mexico was to ask Japan to join in the war against the United States.

Britain wasted no time in publishing the Zimmermann note in the United States. It had the desired effect of heightening American feelings against Germany.

Finally and with much regret, President Wilson decided that it was a "moral duty" to fight. He said, "The world must be made safe for democracy." When the President asked Congress to declare war on April 2, 1917, only a few voted no. The United States was at war on April 6.

7. What were the arguments for and against war?

How did the United States prepare to fight?

To train and move armies and supplies thousands of miles from home takes a lot of organization. And that organization had to come quickly. The Allies were in desperate need. They were near the end of their food and other supplies. Russia was no longer with the Allies. The Russian armies had collapsed. Russia signed an armistice, or cease-fire, with Germany. Russia dropped out of the war and was about to undergo a Communist revolution.

Heavy loss of life was weakening the Allied armies. One of every three French males between 17 and 25 years of age had already been killed.

To help the tiring Allies, the whole United States economy was shifted to a war footing. Farmers were pushed to grow more food. Americans were urged to eat less so that more could be shipped to Europe. Railroads were taken over by the government. Factories were ordered to produce war goods.

Millions of Americans were drafted into the armed forces. Two million soldiers, or "doughboys," as they were called, served in France before the armistice. Two million more were ready to sail when peace came. Their commander was General John J. Pershing. (See page 425.)

Among those who served were almost 400,000 black Americans. Black soldiers made up more than 10 percent of the total American forces. Most served in laboring jobs, but a number of individuals and units won fame in battle against the Germans. American blacks fought especially well as parts of larger French units.

Women also played vital roles in World War I. Many went overseas to

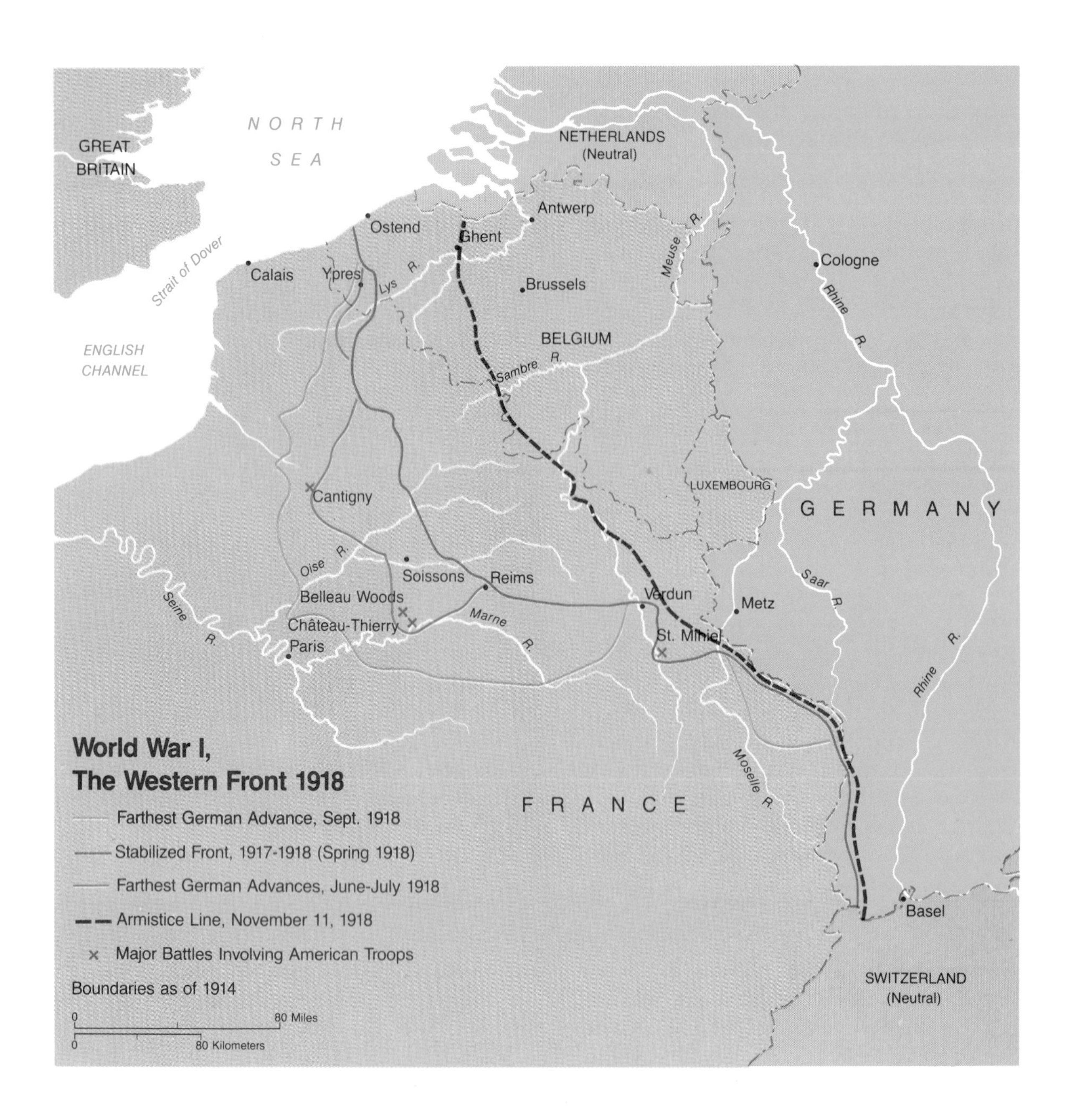

serve in the armed forces and Red Cross units. Still more women began to fill jobs in the United States which formerly had been closed to them. They swelled the labor force by more than one million. Women worked on assembly lines in factories. They made guns and built airplanes. Some stoked furnaces. Others laid railroad track and ran streetcar lines. Because it took twenty people working in industry to supply one soldier in combat, women's contributions to the war effort made a great difference.

8. In what condition were the Allies when we entered the war?

9. How did Americans shift to a war footing?

How and when was Germany finally defeated?

By March 1918, German leaders realized that their submarine warfare was failing. Steady streams of fresh Allied troops and supplies were pouring into France. Within Germany the will to fight was weakening.

The Germans made a final effort to capture Paris. But American troops moved quickly to fill up the holes in the British and French lines. During the summer of 1918, American fighting units won victories in fierce battles at Belleau (bel′ ō) Wood and Château-Thierry (shə to tye′ rē). In the autumn, the Americans turned the tide of battle at St. Mihiel (san mē yel′). Then they smashed through at the Argonne Forest. (See map, page 444.) By October, the German army was in full retreat along the entire line of battle.

Kaiser (Emperor) Wilhelm of Germany resigned and fled to the Netherlands. The German high command then asked for peace. A cease-fire, or armistice, was signed on November 11, 1918. The war was over, and the Allies had finally won.

10. What part did American troops play in ending the war?

11. When was the armistice, or cease-fire, signed?

In the photograph above, American soldiers crawl through a blasted forest. In the photograph below, soldiers leave the safety of the trenches to go "over the top."

Women served with our forces overseas in the Nurses Corps of the army and navy, and as yeomen office workers in the navy.

Part Five

War's Aftermath

How did President Wilson try to build a lasting peace?

It is easier to make war than to stay at peace. That is a lesson human beings have learned again and again throughout history. World War I was no exception.

Americans had sent their soldiers to Europe hoping that this would be "the war to end all wars." American soldiers had fought and died to "make the world safe for democracy." President Wilson wanted a peace treaty that would fulfill the high hopes of Americans in entering the war.

To build a just and lasting peace, Wilson made a peace plan even before the war was over. It was called the Fourteen Points.

The first five points aimed at improving relations among nations. Point number one said that nations must deal openly with each other and not make secret "deals." Nations should also enjoy freedom of the seas, trade with each other, and build fewer weapons.

The next eight points dealt with giving Europeans freedom. Many small countries in eastern and southern Europe had been conquered by their more powerful neighbors. Wilson said these people should be given the right to decide how and by whom they wished to be governed. This right of people to choose their own government is called *self-determination.*

The fourteenth and final point was the one closest to Wilson's heart. To prevent wars, he proposed a League of Nations. Members of the League would *discuss* their problems and differences, not go to war over them. And "great and small states alike" were to show respect for each other.

The Fourteen Points were announced early in 1918. Wilson hoped that all the European nations would agree to them when peace talks began. Late in 1918 the Germans asked for a cease-fire and a peace based on the Fourteen Points.

World reaction to Wilson's Fourteen Points was mixed. Some people hailed his plan for a "peace without victory." The defeated Germans were in favor of it, of course.

In the United States, the Fourteen Points ran into trouble. President Wilson asked the people to vote Democratic in the congressional election of 1918. By doing so, they would show their support for him and his program. But many people did not want the United States to become too deeply involved in world affairs. They went against Wilson's wishes and elected a Republican Congress.

Wilson soon found that the British, French, and Italian leaders did not like his plan of "peace without victory" at all. They thought it was too friendly and soft. The Allies had fought a long, bitter war. Now they wanted to get revenge on Germany and Austria.

1. What were the Fourteen Points? Who proposed them? Why?

2. Why did some people oppose the Fourteen Points?

Who went to the peace conference?

In 1919, the winning powers sent representatives to a peace conference in

The Treaty of Versailles was written in the beautiful French Palace of Versailles. Woodrow Wilson (seated, fourth from left) was disappointed in the harsh terms of the treaty.

Versailles (ver sī'), France. Germany and Austria-Hungary were not allowed to take part in making the treaty. Neither was Russia.

President Wilson himself headed the American delegation to the peace conference. This was the first time a President had traveled to Europe while in office. Many Americans thought it was wrong for the President to leave the United States. When Wilson arrived in Paris, he soon found himself disagreeing with the British, French, and Italian leaders.

3. Name three nations that were not allowed to attend the peace conference.

4. Who headed the American delegation at Versailles?

What was the Treaty of Versailles?

A harsh peace treaty was written at Versailles. President Wilson fought as hard as he could for his Fourteen Points and for fairness and mercy. But the Allied leaders were determined to punish Germany severely.

By the Treaty of Versailles, Germany was forced to surrender some of its own land and all of its colonies to the Allies. Its army and navy were reduced to almost nothing. The German people were made to pay impossibly large amounts of money for war damages. They were forced to admit that they and they alone had started the war. Finally, the Germans had to sign a treaty which they had no part in making.

To be forced to sign such a treaty seemed very unfair to Germany. Wilson's Fourteen Points had said that nations could not make secret "deals" with each other. But now it was plain that the Allies had made secret agreements with each other to carve up Germany.

Look at the map of Europe in 1914 on page 440. Then look at the map of Europe in 1926 on page 449. These maps show dramatically how Europe was almost "remade" by the Versailles Treaty. Several new nations were created.

One new nation was Poland. It was formed by combining parts of Russia, Germany, and Austria-Hungary.

Serbia was made larger and given a new name. Today it is still called by its new name, Yugoslavia.

Another new nation was Czechoslovakia. It was also carved from Germany and Austria-Hungary.

The new map of Europe meant that many Germans were put under Polish, French, and Czechoslovakian rule. Germany angrily pointed out that Wilson had called for self-determination for Europeans. This idea worked well for everybody except the Germans. Millions of them now had no homeland of their own.

5. Why was the Treaty of Versailles considered a harsh peace?

6. How did the treaty remake the map of Europe?

Why did the United States Senate reject the Treaty of Versailles?

Wilson was not happy with the Treaty of Versailles as a whole. But his League of Nations was written into the treaty.

The League of Nations provided a way for nations to work together. Decisions about peace and war would be made by a nine-member council. The United States was to be a member of the council. Countries holding German col-

onies would have to account to the League for how they ruled them.

Wilson returned home from France feeling that he had done the best he could. One more big hurdle lay before him. He had to win approval of the Treaty of Versailles from the United States Senate.

The United States Constitution allows Presidents to make treaties.

After World War I, the nation was troubled by strikes and violence. A series of bombs shook the country. Then, on April 16, 1920, a bomb exploded on busy Wall Street in New York City during lunchtime. Hundreds were injured; 38 were killed. Ordinary citizens were frightened and leery of "foreigners."

However, they do not become law until the Senate approves them by a two-thirds majority.

At first the Senate leaned toward approving the Treaty of Versailles. But a two-thirds majority is hard to get. Months passed, and the debate went on and on. In time many senators came to oppose the treaty. They feared that it would involve the United States too deeply in European affairs.

President Wilson could see that the League for which he had worked so hard was in danger. He decided to rally the American people behind him by making speeches across the country. Perhaps the people would put pressure on the Senate to ratify the treaty.

Wilson, never too strong, had worked at too fast a pace. He had taken part in the crushing debate at Versailles. Now he spoke in towns all over the nation. On his way home, he suffered a stroke. One side of his body was paralyzed.

For days Wilson was almost unconscious. His wife guarded him from pressures. Someone later said Edith Wilson was "the first woman President of the United States."

While Wilson lay helpless in bed, the Senate turned down the treaty and the League. In 1920, our country signed a separate peace treaty with Germany.

7. Why was Wilson willing to accept the Treaty of Versailles even though he did not like it as a whole?

8. Why did the United States turn down the treaty?

What was the mood of America after World War I?

After World War I, Americans were tired. "Was all the fighting and money worthwhile?" they asked. Europe was still full of hatred and bitterness. More trouble there seemed certain to come.

Many Americans thought that there would be great danger in joining the League of Nations. Suppose the United States were outvoted on certain questions and forced to take actions it did not approve of? The country would lose part of its precious independence. This was a frightening thought.

Certain changes to guarantee freedom of action by the United States were suggested. The Senate probably would have voted for the League if those changes had been made. But the ill and saddened Wilson would not accept changes in the League plan.

Americans were also upset by the Communist revolution in Russia. Communists talked of spreading their revolution around the world. Strikes and violence in the United States added to the fears. "Foreigners" of all kinds were suspected of being Communists.

In the presidential election of 1920, the Republicans campaigned on a slogan of "Back to Normalcy." This meant a return to the old days when the United States was not so involved with its world neighbors.

Americans voted for the candidate who promised to bring life back to normal. Republican Warren G. Harding was swept into the presidency.

9. How did Americans feel about world affairs after World War I?

10. Why were Americans upset with the Communist revolution in Russia?

Republican candidates Harding and Coolidge promised to bring the country back to normal. They appealed to voters who were frightened by strikes and violence at home and afraid of more wars abroad.

Building Your Vocabulary

Complete each of the sentences by selecting the correct word from those listed below.

1. The United States became an empire as a result of the Spanish-American War. It acquired—?—overseas.
2. The United States suggested the—?—policy so that all nations could trade with China.
3. Building the Panama Canal was one of the great engineering—?—of all time.
4. Latin Americans did not like United States—?—in their affairs.
5. When an Austrian archduke and his wife were—?—in 1914, World War I began.
6. The Allies used—?—to stir up Americans against the Germans in World War I.
7. President Wilson asked Congress to declare war to "make the world safe for—?—."
8. The cease-fire, or—?—, was signed on November 11, 1918.

colonies
achievements
armistice
interference
Open Door
propaganda
democracy
assassinated

Recalling What You Have Learned

Select the correct word or phrase to complete each of the following items.

1. American feeling against Spain rose because of (a) the cruelties of General Weyler in putting down the rebellion in Cuba. (b) newspaper accounts of the explosion of the *Maine*. (c) riots in Havana. (d) all of the above.
2. The Spanish-American War lasted (a) 115 days. (b) 4 years. (c) 6 years. (d) 24 months.
3. Who was the American doctor who believed correctly that it was the mosquito which caused yellow fever? (a) John Pershing (b) John Hay (c) Walter Reed (d) William Seward
4. Who was the American naval officer who "opened" Japan? (a) Theodore Roosevelt (b) William McKinley (c) Matthew Perry (d) Millard Fillmore
5. From which country did the United States purchase Alaska? (a) Russia (b) England (c) Colombia (d) Cuba
6. For which of the following reasons did the United States interfere in Latin American affairs? (a) because European nations threatened to invade Latin American countries to collect debts owed them (b) because there was great political unrest which brought many dictators to power (c) because the United States wanted to build a canal across Panama (d) all of the above
7. Who were the Americans who moved to Hawaii while it still was an independent nation? (a) missionaries (b) people who bought pineapple and sugar plantations (c) people who started great cattle ranches (d) all of the above
8. Woodrow Wilson's plan for bringing

peace was called (a) the Treaty of San Mihiel. (b) the Fourteen Points. (c) the Treaty of Guantanamo. (d) the Open Door policy.
9. The organization which Wilson wanted the United States to join was called (a) the Treaty of Versailles. (b) the Peace and Friendship Association. (c) the League of Nations. (d) the United Nations.

Discussing the Important Ideas in This Chapter

1. The Spanish-American War was a great turning point in American history. Explain why.
2. Why did American interest in the Pacific develop more slowly than interest in Europe?
3. How and why did the United States become involved in the Caribbean?
4. Are newspapers still as important in forming public opinion as they were during the Cuban Revolution?
5. Why did Presidents McKinley and Wilson oppose war? Why weren't they able to withstand public pressures for war?
6. Compare American feeling about annexing Hawaii with feeling about annexing Texas. (See page 258.)
7. In 1946, after 45 years of control, the United States set the Philippines free. It became the first great power in the world's history to give up a colony of its own free will. Why do you think the United States took that history-making action?
8. What plan did President Wilson propose for building a lasting peace? Why wasn't that plan accepted?
9. In just twenty years, 1898-1918, the United States came to be a world power. How and why did that rise to power occur?

Improving Your Map Skills

Compare the maps shown on page 440 and page 449. They will help you understand how World War I changed the map of Europe. Show that you understand the information contained in these maps by answering the questions which follow:

1. Which nations were members of the Allied Powers?
2. Which nations were members of the Central Powers?
3. Which nations did not fight, or were neutral, in World War I?
4. Nine new countries were formed in Europe after World War I. Name those nine nations.
5. Describe Great Britain's location in relation to Germany. Use the direction finder to help you.
6. Locate the northeastern part of Germany. Compare that section of Germany as it was in 1914 and in 1926. Describe an important change which took place in that section. Why do you think that change made the Germans very unhappy?
7. It is often said that World War I "remade the map of Europe." Do you agree with that statement? Explain why or why not.

Improving Your Study Skills: *Reading*

Read the following selection first for its main ideas. Show that you have understood the main ideas by answering the first set of questions which follow. Then reread the selection. Think about the meaning of those main ideas. Go beyond what the selection says in so many words. Answer the second set of questions. Compare your answers with those of your classmates.

Why Wars Bring Changes in the Way People Live

Wars bring many changes. They result in changes in maps and leaders of nations. They destroy some empires and create new ones. Wars also bring changes which sometimes are not written about in history books. Wars can bring changes in people's life-styles.

Take World War I, for example. It brought a need and a demand for American women on the front lines in Europe. There they served along with American men. They were nurses, stretcher-bearers, ambulance drivers, social service and recreation workers. Women were in demand in the United States, too. They were needed in ammunition plants, factories, and on the railroads. Suddenly they were called upon to fill jobs formerly reserved for men. Prior to World War I, some people thought women could not handle those jobs. But women showed themselves to be more than equal to them.

While women had no trouble with the jobs themselves, they did discover that certain styles were a handicap. Take long hair, for instance. Before World War I, most women did not cut their hair. They let it grow very long. Then they piled it on top of their heads, or they braided it and wound it row on row around their heads. Styling hair in those ways not only took time, it was dangerous. Sometimes hair got tangled in machinery. Women in ammunition factories worried because gunpowder settled into their long hair. If the gunpowder exploded, it caused serious burns. So women decided to do something about hair styles. And that something proved to be very shocking to old-fashioned people. American women began to cut, or "bob," their hair.

Bobbing hair became a very controversial matter. Sometimes preachers spoke against it from their pulpits. Cartoons and comic strips often made fun of women who cut their long tresses. Newspapers showed unflattering pictures of women with bobbed hair. They also showed unflattering pictures of women wearing short skirts, overalls, and "knickers," or knee-length pants that then were popular with men.

Did ridicule stop American women? No. As more women learned of the comfort and time saving that short hair could bring, they, too, bobbed their hair. They began wearing short skirts and pants, because that made getting on and off trucks, streetcars, and bicycles easier.

Reading for the Main Ideas in This Selection

1. What is the title of this selection?
2. What is the most important idea in this selection? (a) How wars change maps. (b) Why women went to work during World War I. (c) How and why wars can bring about changes in styles. (d) Why some people objected to bobbed hair.
3. The expression "bobbing hair" means (a) cutting it short. (b) letting it

grow long. (c) piling it atop the head.
4. A major reason women insisted on style changes was (a) because they wanted to make old-fashioned people angry. (b) because they were tired of the old styles. (c) because of the needs brought on by their new jobs.

Thinking about and Discussing the Main Ideas in This Selection

None of these questions can be answered in so many words. There are no "right" or "wrong" answers to them. To deal with these questions you must "read between the lines." You must draw on your own knowledge and understanding.

1. Why did World War I bring about a need and a demand for women workers at the front and at home?
2. Why did hair styles, skirt lengths, and wearing pants or overalls suddenly become very important to women?
3. Why do you think some people opposed changes in women's hair and dress styles?
4. Why might pictures of women with bobbed hair and short skirts which appeared in newspapers have encouraged the new styles, even though those pictures were unflattering?
5. What other changes in life-styles have been brought about by wars?

Unit Four Challenge and

18 Boom and Bust

19 World War II and Its Aftermath

Change

20 Years of Change, Years of Challenge

21 New Directions

Chapter 18 Boom and Bust

Norris Dam, near Oak Ridge, Tennessee

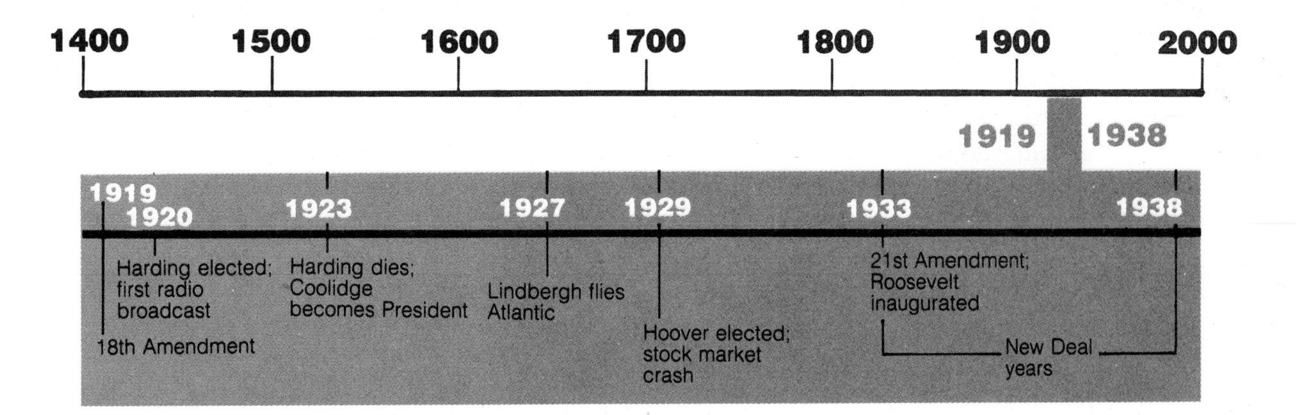

Part One

The Golden Twenties

Why were the 1920s called "golden"?

After the weary, sad years of World War I, Americans enjoyed a "golden" decade. The 1920s were years of prosperity and peace. They were also years of great change in daily life. New music, new dances, new styles, new machines, and new customs gave the decade its other name, "The Roaring Twenties."

Americans could scarcely believe how well off they were in the 1920s. Though not rich, the average person was much better off than in the past. Average Americans could support their families and even have a few luxuries.

People in many foreign lands found it hard to imagine a nation where the average family could have more than just the necessities of life.

During the 1920s, prices went down and incomes went up. Refrigerators, radios, electric stoves, and vacuum cleaners were priced low enough so that working people could afford them. Credit and installment buying started. Workers made down payments on homes and automobiles.

Not all Americans would have called the 1920s "golden," however. There were still many poor people in the United States. Coal mining regions in Pennsylvania, Ohio, and West Virginia were hard pressed. As factories began using electric power, there was less demand for coal.

As a group, farmers were probably the least well-off during the 1920s. All during World War I, they had received high prices. Europeans bought all that American farmers could produce. But when the war ended, European farmers went back to their own land. Demand for American products fell off.

Many American farmers found it hard to repay loans on their land and machinery. Few farm homes had running water or electric power. They did not have the fine new home appliances.

1. Why were most Americans much better off in the 1920s than at any time in the past?

2. Which groups did not share in the prosperity of the 1920s?

Who were the two Presidents during the 1920s?

During the 1920s two men served as President who were very different from Theodore Roosevelt and Woodrow Wilson. They also were very different from one another.

Warren G. Harding was elected in 1920. He succeeded Wilson. Harding came from a small town in Ohio. There he had owned a weekly newspaper. He was a friendly, out-going person who liked people. In return they responded to him. Americans were shocked and saddened by his sudden death in 1923.

When Harding died, Vice-President Calvin Coolidge moved into the nation's top office. In 1924 he won the presidency on his own. Coolidge was as reserved as Harding was outgoing. Coolidge seldom spoke. When he did, he used the fewest words possible. For that reason he earned the nickname "Silent Cal."

As different as Harding and Coolidge were in their personalities, they were alike in one important way. It was a way that the American people of the time approved. Neither man believed that a President should take much action. Both said the country was well off and should be left alone. They were convinced that government should not interfere with business. As Coolidge put it, "The business of the United States is business." He also said that "the man who builds a factory builds a temple."

Coolidge himself was a very thrifty man. He believed that government should not be a big spender either. So under Coolidge, taxes were cut. Part of the national debt was paid.

Most Americans felt that Harding and Coolidge were right to leave business alone. After years of reform and the strain of World War I, "normal" times were welcomed.

3. Who were the two Presidents who served during the 1920s?

4. What attitude toward business did they have? How did Americans feel about that attitude?

How did we become a "nation on wheels"?

There was one business Americans learned to love in the 1920s. It was the automobile business.

In 1900 there was not a single gas station in all of the United States. Only 4000 cars had been built by the turn of

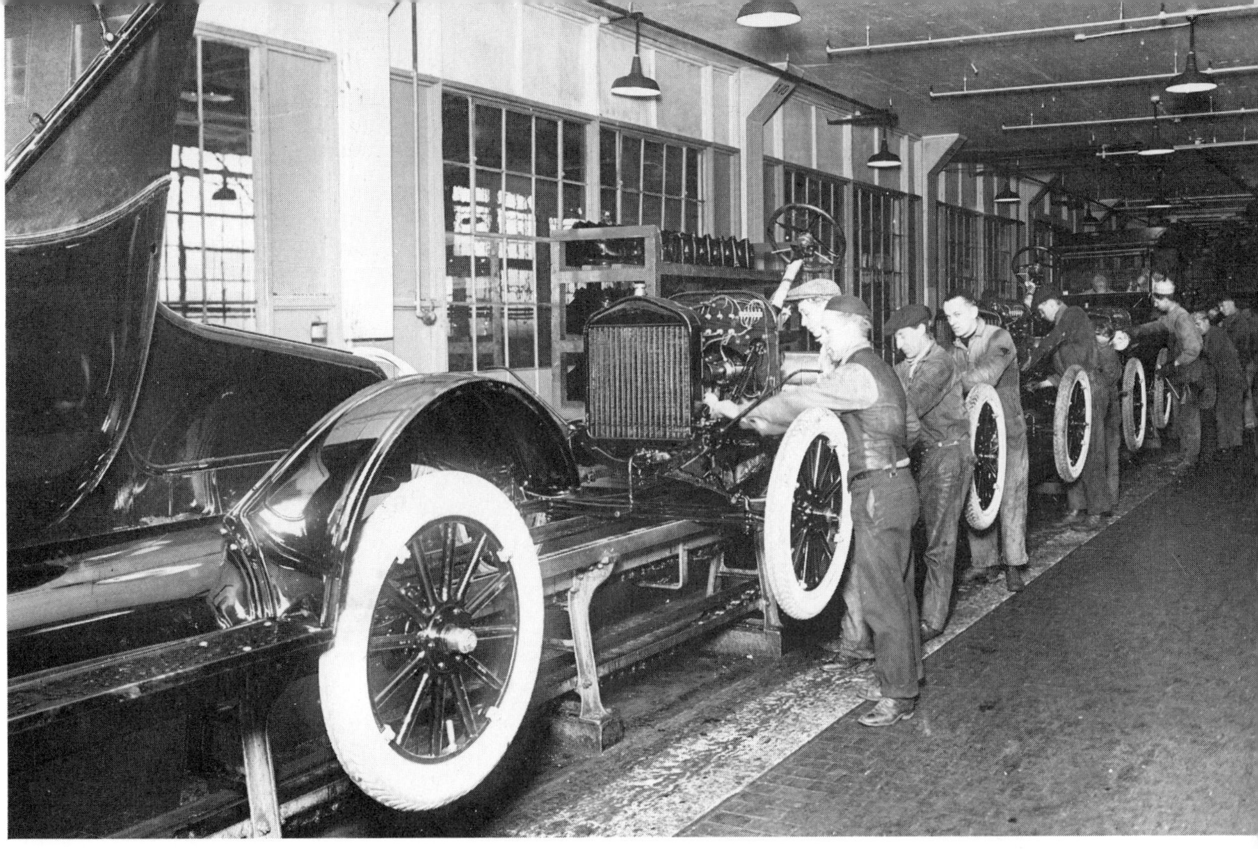

Ford's use of the assembly line increased efficiency and helped him lower the price of his automobiles.

the century. They were "toys" for the very wealthy. And then things began to change. By 1910 one American in twenty owned an automobile. By 1929 one out of five Americans owned a car. In some towns cars outnumbered bathtubs and homes with indoor plumbing.

The automobile industry did more than provide Americans with transportation. It provided them with jobs as well. More than four million workers were employed building cars. Others found jobs in related industries. For example, workers were needed in steel, paint, rubber, and glass plants. Workers were needed to manufacture fabrics for seats, to build highways, to pump gas, and to repair autos. They also were needed to build and staff roadside restaurants, hotels, and motels. The automobile industry, in short, provided a large base on which the prosperity of the 1920s was built.

The individual most responsible for putting America on wheels was Henry Ford. Ford had two ideas which were very important. First, he said the automobile industry had to "get the prices down to the buying power." In other words, the price of automobiles had to be low enough so that many people would be able to buy them. Second, Ford said the industry had to get wages up so that the ordinary person could afford a car.

Ford worked on those two ideas at the same time. First, he began to turn out the Model-T, or the "Tin Lizzie," as it was affectionately known. It was a simple, no-frills car. Ford said that a customer could have a Model-T in any color desired—as long as it was black.

The first Model-T sold for $850. By 1916, the price had dropped to $360. In 1924, a person could buy a "Tin Lizzie" for just $290. And people did. At one time there were 15 million Model-T's on

Charles Lindbergh flew the fragile *Spirit of St. Louis* on the first nonstop, solo flight from New York to Paris. His flight thrilled the world, and his modesty about his achievement made him even more admired.

the streets and highways of the United States.

Bringing down the price of automobiles was good, Ford said. But it was not enough. Wages had to come up at the same time. So, in 1914, Ford dumbfounded the business world. He offered the unheard of wage of $5 a day! The going rate was $3 a day. Naturally, workers flocked to Ford plants. Working on the assembly line may have been dull, but it paid well. Workers made enough so that they could buy the cars they produced. Workers were happy. So was Henry Ford. By the mid-1920s, he was sole owner of the Ford Motor Company, and it was earning $25,000 per day.

5. Why was the automobile industry a large base for the prosperity of the 1920s?

6. What were Henry Ford's two main ideas? How did he carry out those ideas?

What were the first steps taken toward the Air Age?

About the same time that Henry Ford was making his Model-T, other Americans were trying to fly.

Two brothers, Orville and Wilbur Wright, had done "the impossible." At Kitty Hawk, North Carolina, in 1903, they put a plane into the air. For 59 full seconds—almost one minute—it stayed aloft! Once the Wright brothers proved they could fly, other engineers and mechanics worked at building better flying machines. Airplanes were used in World War I.

In the 1920s, small airports and landing strips were laid out near cities. Stunt pilots put on Sunday afternoon air shows. They flew upside down and "looped the loop" while American families watched in wonder. A few brave souls began to hire pilots to fly them on intercity business trips.

But the most exciting flight and the loudest cheers were saved for Charles Lindbergh.

Alone, Lindbergh took off from New York City for Europe on May 20, 1927. He was trying to win $25,000 in prize money for being the first person to make a solo, nonstop flight from New York to Paris. Lindbergh named his plane *The Spirit of St. Louis*. In that way he honored the citizens of St. Louis who had bought the plane for him.

For 33 hours and 39 minutes, Lindbergh listened to the monotonous roar of the plane's motor. Desperately he fought against falling asleep at the controls. When his plane finally landed in Paris, a wildly excited crowd greeted the lanky, shy, and tired young aviator. One newspaper said that Lindbergh's flight was the greatest achievement by one person in the record of the human race.

When the "Lone Eagle," as Lindbergh became known, flew home, he found a hero's welcome waiting. A mountain of telegrams congratulating him was piled up at the airport. One telegram signed by 17,500 people was so long that it took ten messengers to carry it. Lindbergh was named a Colonel and given the Flying Cross and the Congressional Medal of Honor. City after city held parades in his honor.

Exactly five years after Lindbergh's pioneer flight, another American made aviation history. On May 20, 1932, Amelia Earhart also set out alone. She became the first woman in history to fly solo across the Atlantic. Earhart was not only an accomplished pilot, she was an engineer as well. Earhart was the first woman to fly nonstop across the United States. She was the first woman to cross the Pacific alone. In 1937, as she was attempting to fly around the world, she and her plane disappeared.

7. Who were the Wright brothers?

8. How did Charles Lindbergh become a hero? What records did Amelia Earhart set?

Record-setting aviator Amelia Earhart was the first woman to fly alone across the Atlantic and the Pacific.

When did radio broadcasting begin?

The few thousand Americans who owned radio sets put on their earphones on election night, 1920. They listened to the results of the Harding-Cox election over station KDKA in Pittsburgh. That was the first scheduled radio broadcast in the United States.

Then radio stations began springing up all across the nation. Listeners tuned in to music, sports events, and, of course, commercials. Use of loudspeakers instead of earphones made it possible for all the family to hear a program at the same time. Some favorite programs were *Amos 'n' Andy*, the *National Farm and Home Hour*, *Fibber McGee and Molly*, and *The Rise of the Goldbergs*. On New Year's Day, 1927, Americans were treated to their first sportscast from the Rose Bowl in Pasadena, California.

Many farm families had a radio that was powered by batteries.

Radio broadcasts made it possible to flash news from one place to another as soon as it happened. Americans became "witnesses" to important events all over the world.

9. What was the first scheduled radio broadcast in America?

10. When and from where was the first radio sportscast made?

How did motion pictures change American life?

Just as radio changed American life, so did the coming of motion pictures. A little-known, sleepy town in Southern California called Hollywood became famous because movies were made there.

At first movies were silent. Words were printed under the pictures so people could read what the actors "said." Thousands of Americans flocked to movie theaters, which sprang up all over the country. Many theaters were so large and ornate that they were almost like palaces.

By the end of the 1920s, talking pictures had replaced silent films. A hundred million Americans went to the movies every week during the 1920s.

Motion pictures brought a new figure to American life—the movie star. Clara Bow was a silent film star.

Newsreels were shown as "extras" in theaters. Americans who went to the movies for entertainment had their eyes opened. The miracle of motion pictures let people see and hear what life was like in the rest of the world. Movies helped educate Americans.

11. When did "talking pictures" replace silent films?

12. How did motion pictures help educate Americans?

What changes did the 1920s bring for blacks?

Between 1914 and 1920 about a million blacks moved into industrial centers in the North. Special labor agents toured the South. They recruited workers for the jobs created by World War I.

After the war, blacks stayed in the North. Talented authors, musicians, educators, artists, and entertainers became famous for their accomplishments. In fact, the 1920s are often called a time of "renaissance," or rebirth, for blacks because of their many outstanding contributions. Black artists, writers, and musicians were especially active in Harlem, a part of New York City. America's libraries, museums, and art galleries still proudly display their work.

Along with the good things which the 1920s brought came some bad developments. Most Americans had hoped that the Ku Klux Klan of Reconstruction days was dead. But in the 1920s, it suddenly came back to life.

The "new" Klan was something like the first one. But the new Klan was even more violent than it had been in the 1860s and 1870s. The Klan hated blacks, Catholics, Jews, and immigrants. Wear-

Black artist Jacob Lawrence painted "Moving North" in 1940 and 1941. It depicts the migration of blacks to the North during World War I.

ing white robes and hoods to cover their faces, Klan members attacked these groups. They tarred and feathered their victims and warned them to get out of town. Sometimes they tortured, beat, or even killed them.

During the 1920s, the Klan gained power in Indiana, Oregon, California, and throughout the South. However, decent Americans fought back and the Klan declined. It did not completely disappear, however.

13. Why did many blacks move North? What contributions did they make?

14. Where did the reborn Klan gain power? Who were its victims?

What was Prohibition?

As you know, reformers in the United States had long been concerned about temperance. (See pages 236-237.) Some wanted to forbid, or prohibit, the sale and use of all liquor. They pointed to the troubles alcohol caused. They argued that it should be outlawed in the public interest.

Finally, in 1919, the 18th Amendment to the Constitution was ratified. It was called the *Prohibition* amendment. It forbade the sale and use of alcoholic beverages. Support for the amendment was especially strong in rural states.

Most people obeyed the law, but many refused. Some made their own liquor. Others visited "speakeasies," or nightclubs where liquor was sold. People could buy their own liquor from "bootleggers." Bootleggers got their unusual name because they hid bottles of liquor in their boots or elsewhere in their clothes.

Bootleggers quickly learned they could get rich by selling liquor illegally. So rival groups began to fight one another. What were called "gangster wars" broke out among these groups. The most famous of all the gangsters was Al Capone of Chicago.

Americans became very disturbed about the gangster wars. Finally they decided that Prohibition was causing more problems than it was solving. Another amendment to the Constitution was ratified in 1933. The 21st Amendment repealed, or cancelled, the 18th Amendment. (See Constitution, pages 612 and 613.) People were free to buy and sell alcoholic beverages once more. However, sale and use were, and still are, regulated by state and city laws.

Many reformers were sorry that the 18th Amendment was repealed. They said it had been a "noble experiment." But once again the people had used their right to change the Constitution as the majority thought best.

15. When was the 18th Amendment passed? What did it provide?

16. When and why was the 18th Amendment repealed?

What signs appeared that prosperity was ending?

To those watching closely, there were signs as early as 1927 that prosperity might be slipping. But prices on the New York Stock Exchange kept rising anyway. (A *stock exchange* is a place where shares in business and industry are bought and sold.)

More and more people used their savings and borrowed money to buy stocks in the hope of getting rich.

Then, on October 24, 1929, prices suddenly started dropping . . . and dropping! The bottom fell out of the stock market. There were no more buyers. People who thought they were rich found they were poor. All that they had were worthless stocks.

A new President, Herbert Hoover, had just come into office in 1929. Like other Americans, he kept thinking and hoping that the "bust" was temporary. Hoover said, "Prosperity is just around the corner." But he was wrong. The Great Depression hit Americans with cyclone force.

17. What did the fall of the stock market mean?

Part Two

The Great Depression

What caused the Great Depression?

Why did a terrible depression hit the richest, most productive country in the world? Americans asked themselves that question in 1929 and throughout the next eleven years of hardship.

Hard times came for many reasons. Credit was easy to get, so Americans borrowed and spent too much money. Even with all the things bought by Americans, more goods were produced than could be sold.

Warehouses and storage bins were piled high with unsold goods. Europe was too poor to buy the products.

Factory owners with more goods than they could sell laid off workers all over the United States. Businesses began to fail. As a result, prices on the New York Stock Exchange crashed. Millions of people lost some or all of their money. People lost their faith in banks, too. Some banks failed. People feared that their banks, too, would fail. So they tried to get their money out. They started "runs" on banks. More banks failed because they could not pay out all the money their customers wanted. In 1929, 642 banks failed. In 1932, 2298 banks failed. People lost their life savings and soon found themselves with nothing.

Americans realized that the golden 1920s had vanished. Unemployment, hunger, and despair stalked the land.

1. Why did hard times come to the United States?

How did Hoover try to cure the Great Depression?

Herbert Hoover had been President for less than a year when the Great

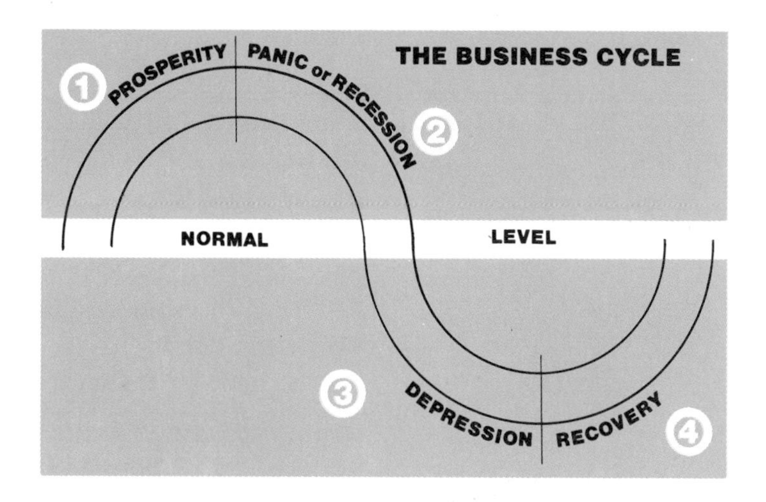

Depression hit with full force. Naturally he was troubled when he saw his fellow Americans sinking into poverty. But Hoover believed deeply that people should look after themselves. He said that people in need should be aided by private citizens or by charities, not by the government.

Hoover also thought that businesses were private affairs. He thought that government should not interfere much with business. Certainly, he said, governments should not own or operate businesses.

But Hoover did not simply sit back and wait for hard times to end. He took action. He called business leaders to meetings. Hoover urged them to keep on producing and to keep wages up. The President cut taxes and made credit easier to get.

To help long-suffering farmers, Hoover loaned them $500 million dollars for seed and livestock. But the loans did not help much. Farm prices continued to fall.

To create more jobs, Hoover asked for a new government agency. It was called the Reconstruction Finance Corporation (RFC). The RFC loaned money to insurance companies, railroads, banks, and even to state governments.

Hoping to help business, Hoover signed into law a new, higher tariff. But the tariff backfired. Foreign goods were kept out, as planned. However, Europeans bought even less from the United States, which hurt trade.

Finally, as the situation grew more and more serious, the President started building public works, such as dams and roads. More than $2 billion went into these projects. Workers were hired. Materials were purchased. But even these projects did not stem the depression tide.

2. What did President Hoover try to do to bring back good times?

How serious did the Great Depression become?

Nothing like the Great Depression had ever hit America before. In the past, business had often had its ups and downs. Americans had weathered depressions in 1819 and 1873. They had lived through a "panic" in 1893. But the Great Depression was in a class by itself. It began in 1929 and dragged on for twelve years. Not only did it last longer than any other depression, but it was more serious in every way.

Even those who did not lose their jobs were hurt. Wages dropped. Between 1929 and 1933, salaries fell 40 percent and factory wages went down 60

Many of the unemployed tried to earn money by selling apples as this man is doing near the nation's Capitol.

percent. More than 100,000 stores, banks, and factories closed their doors. Profits of the businesses that managed to stay open fell 57 percent.

The number of unemployed was almost unbelievable. From October 1929, when the stock market crashed, to October 1930, five million people lost their jobs. One year later, almost eleven million Americans were out of work. Then the figure climbed to nearly thirteen million. By January 1, 1933, a third of the nation's wage earners were jobless.

Blacks who had moved to cities complained they were the last hired and the first fired. They were probably right. As a group, blacks were especially hard hit by the depression.

As times grew worse, many jobs then thought of as "black" jobs were taken by whites. Ten years earlier, whites would not have considered those jobs. By mid-June 1934, more than half the blacks in northern cities were on relief rolls. Only about 13 percent of the whites were on relief.

3. Why was the Great Depression the most serious in United States history?

4. Why were blacks especially hard hit by the depression?

What was the "Bonus March"?

In 1932, about 14,000 unemployed veterans of World War I organized an "army." They walked and hitchhiked to the nation's capital to get immediate payment of a bonus, extra wartime pay. It was to have been paid in a few years, but the veterans wanted it now.

Just outside Washington, the veterans built a shantytown. However, the Senate refused to give them their bonuses. About half the marchers sadly went home. The other half stayed on and refused to take "no" for an answer.

When a riot took place and two people were killed, President Hoover ordered the army to get the marchers out of town. The President incorrectly said that Communists and criminals had turned the peaceful protest to one of violence. The shantytown was burned. Those still living in it were driven out with tear gas.

5. Why did the Bonus Marchers come to Washington? What happened to them?

How did life change during the depression?

Hard times affected the way people lived. Family tensions boiled up. Workers who stayed home all day with nothing to do were angry and unhappy. Many families had to double up in single-family houses or apartments.

Young people did not marry because they felt they could not support families. The nation's birth rate fell. Thousands, unable to work, began to wander about the country seeking jobs. At one time more than a million young people were drifting across the country. They hopped on freight trains or thumbed rides along the highways.

In the cities, there were great breadlines where people waited for free food. Shantytowns, called "Hoovervilles," grew up on the edges of towns. There the poor built makeshift houses of packing boxes, scrap iron, or anything else they could find in the city dumps. Homeless people slept in doorways or on park benches and begged for food. Many people moved out of the cities. Between two and three million went back to farms. They hoped to raise at least enough to eat.

It is hard to exaggerate the effects of the Great Depression. It did something to the spirit of the people. Deep gloom and nagging worry ate away at Americans' self-confidence.

Perhaps the greatest change to come out of the depression was the practice of looking to the federal government for help. When Americans realized they could not solve their problems as private citizens, they turned to their city and state governments. But the cities and states were too small to do the job. Finally Americans came to believe that the federal government was responsible for providing jobs for the unemployed, if all other sources failed.

6. What happened to the spirit of the people as the depression dragged on?
7. What important change in people's attitudes toward government came from the depression?

Why was President Hoover defeated?

President Hoover had worked day and night to end the Great Depression. But he did not succeed. He lacked the ability to talk to the common people. He seemed cold and aloof. Hoover couldn't find ways to end the troubled times.

When he ran for reelection in 1932, Hoover explained to the people how he had tried to solve the problems of the times. But in 1932, Americans were not interested in why things had not worked. They wanted things that would work. And they wanted them in a hurry.

Franklin Roosevelt, who ran on the Democratic ticket against Republican Hoover, said he knew how to solve the nation's troubles. All that Americans had to fear "was fear itself," he said. Herbert Hoover's face showed the gloom and fear Americans felt. Roosevelt's wide grin and self-confidence helped him defeat Hoover in 1932.

8. Who were the presidential candidates in 1932?
9. Why wasn't Hoover reelected?

What kind of leader was Franklin D. Roosevelt?

Few men have ever shown greater self-confidence or courage than Franklin D. Roosevelt.

His confidence came naturally. He was born to a rich, old family and grew up on an estate in New York. One of his distant cousins was President Theodore Roosevelt. In fact, the cousins followed much the same path. Both were Assistant Secretary of the Navy, governor of New York, and President of the United States.

Franklin Roosevelt's courage was almost unbelievable. Just when his

Historymaker

Franklin Delano Roosevelt holds the record for having served longer than anyone else as President of the United States. He was elected four times to that office—in 1932, 1936, 1940, and 1944. Just three months after his fourth inauguration, Roosevelt died. But by then he had served twelve years, one month, and eight days. What is more, it is doubtful if anyone—except possibly his fifth cousin, Theodore Roosevelt—ever enjoyed being President more.

There was another important way in which the two Roosevelts were alike. Both overcame serious health problems. TR's health problems surfaced while he was a child. FDR's troubles did not come until he was 39 years old. Then in August 1921, while at the family's summer home, Campobello, he was stricken with polio. Overnight he became a bedridden invalid, completely paralyzed.

A less determined human being might have given up. In fact, his mother, Sarah Delano Roosevelt, wanted FDR to do just that. She told him to come home to her at Hyde Park and forget about ever trying to work again. But Roosevelt would not hear of that. He said, "I don't want to be a useless burden to the rest of my family."

Roosevelt's illness probably did more than anything else to change the course of his life. His wife, Eleanor, later explained why. She wrote:

Little by little, through exercise and wearing braces he learned to walk, first with crutches and with a cane, leaning on someone's arm. The first braces were heavy; later, lighter ones were made. However, for the rest of his life, he was unable to walk or stand without braces and some help. . . .

Franklin's illness was another turning point, and proved a blessing in disguise, for it gave him strength and courage he had not had before. He had to think out the fundamentals of living and learn the greatest of all lessons—infinite patience and never-ending persistence.

Eleanor Roosevelt, *This I Remember* (New York: Harper & Brothers, 1949), p. 25.

Roosevelt set the tone for his presidency on the day he first took office. He said:

This is . . . the time to speak the truth, the whole truth, frankly and boldly. . . . So first of all, let me assert my firm belief that the only thing we have to fear is fear itself. . . . We are stricken by no plague of locusts. Compared with the perils which our forefathers conquered because they believed and were not afraid, we have still much to be thankful for. . . . Happiness lies not in the mere possession of money; it lies in the joy of achievement, in the thrill of creative effort.

Roosevelt plunged into the tasks ahead of him with glee. Though the days were dark and the problems tremendous, he met them all with a wide smile and often with his famed cigarette holder clamped between his great white teeth. The Roosevelt smile

became a favorite subject for cartoonists. His smile and good cheer were something his friends and admirers loved. They felt as though there was someone in the White House who really was in charge and confident about the future.

Despite the complaints of those who disliked him, FDR was the greatest political leader of his time. He was a master of communication. When need be, he went over his opponents' heads and appealed directly to the American people. He told them his side of the story in radio broadcasts which he called "fireside chats." He often called reporters to the White House for press conferences and he relished their give and take. What is more he made news with a nonstop stream of activities. FDR suggested new laws. He traveled all over the country and the world. He planned little surprises. He provoked controversies. And he told jokes about everyone and everything—himself, his family, his enemies, and even his pet dog, a little Scottie named "Fala."

Even in the darkest days of World War II, FDR kept his sense of humor. He also kept a schedule which would have tired someone half his age. Finally the strain of being Commander in Chief, Chief Executive, and leader of the free world began to tell. When FDR ran for a fourth term in 1944, his Republican opponent, Thomas Dewey, publicly charged that FDR was in poor health. The President's response was quick. He drove around New York City in an open car for four hours during a rainstorm. Then he went on to make a major speech.

Roosevelt scored an easy victory at the polls. Most Americans said they did not want to "change horses in midstream." They wanted FDR to guide the nation until the war was won.

But fate was to have it otherwise. Two days after his reelection, FDR left for an important meeting. He conferred with other world leaders at Yalta, a town in southern Russia. When he returned to tell Congress about that meeting, he flashed his famous smile and said, "First of all, I want to say, it is good to be home."

Not only was FDR glad just to be in the United States. He was eager to take a short working vacation. So he went to Warm Springs, Georgia. FDR had gone to Warm Springs time after time during his long bout with polio. There he could swim and relax without the constant glare of publicity. And it was there that he spent the last day of his life, April 12, 1945. FDR began the day as usual by reading several dozen newspapers. Then he tackled the mail which had been flown in from Washington. While FDR worked at his desk, an artist was painting his portrait. Suddenly FDR slumped forward. "I have a terrific headache," he said. Then the voice was still.

As news of his death spread, a silent and bewildered crowd gathered in front of the White House. Who could take his place? All over the world, people blinked back their tears as they paid tribute to the great American leader. In China, a worker read the posters on the wall giving the news. Then he turned away, saying "It was too soon that he died." In India a young woman told an American soldier, "Your President is dead; he was a friend of the poor." The soldier nodded. "We have lost a friend," he said. Then he added, "The world has lost a friend."

political future looked brightest, he was stricken by polio. Determined not to give up, he promised, "I'll beat this thing." Although crippled and unable to stand alone, Roosevelt never used his handicap as an excuse. As he put it, he wanted "no sob stuff." Millions admired a man whose courage was as great as his energy.

As a politician, Franklin Roosevelt has been compared to both the lion and the fox. Some saw and loved his lion-like courage. Others saw and hated his foxy cunning.

Roosevelt had a special appeal for the common people. They felt that he understood them. That in itself is strange, because Roosevelt spoke in language and with an accent unfamiliar to common people. But he certainly knew how to *communicate*.

Roosevelt loved to campaign. He enjoyed a tough political battle. He also liked to tell the people about those battles in radio talks which he called "fireside chats." As a leader, Roosevelt never hesitated to try out new things. If they didn't work, he dropped them. As he put it, "I have no expectation of making a hit every time I come to bat."

As a politician, Roosevelt rolled up an unmatched record. He was the only man to be elected President of the United States four times! (The 22nd Amendment, ratified in 1951, now limits Presidents to two terms.)

Franklin Roosevelt depended greatly upon his wife, Eleanor. Eleanor Roosevelt traveled where her husband could not. She became his eyes and ears outside the White House. She held regular press conferences, wrote a newspaper column, and talked on radio programs. She worked for the poor and neglected. She worked to get more women into politics and government. She also worked for equal treatment for blacks. After her husband's death, Eleanor Roosevelt served as a delegate from the United States to the United Nations under both Presidents Truman and Kennedy.

Eleanor Roosevelt acted as FDR's eyes and ears outside the White House. Here she inspects a coal mine.

10. What qualities made Roosevelt a good politician?

11. What work did Eleanor Roosevelt do?

What new course did Roosevelt set at his inauguration?

Probably no President except Lincoln ever faced a gloomier inauguration day. The nation was in deep trouble. Like Lincoln, Roosevelt asked Americans to look hard at the tough problems at hand.

A shivering crowd stood while the new President spoke from the Capitol steps in Washington on a cold, gray March day in 1933. It was a time, he said, "to speak the truth, the whole truth, frankly and boldly."

As Roosevelt saw it, the country was threatened as surely as if it faced "the emergency of war." If Congress were unwilling or unable to act, he asked for new powers as President. He wanted as much power as "if we were in fact invaded by a foreign foe."

Roosevelt's speech had an almost magical effect on Americans. Congress and most of the people were eager to follow as fast as he would lead.

Some people, however, worried about what Roosevelt had said. Did he want to become a dictator? Would his policies lead the United States to socialism, a system in which the government controls or owns industry?

Both Roosevelt's words and the confident way he spoke them made one thing very clear. As President, he intended to push his powers beyond those of any other President. Desperate times called for desperate actions, he said. It was better to have new powers and programs than to face a revolution. To cure the ills of the nation, Roosevelt offered a program which he called "The New Deal."

12. What powers did Roosevelt ask for in his inauguration speech? Why?

13. Why did Roosevelt's speech have such a great effect on people?

What did Roosevelt accomplish in his first hundred days?

Wasting no time, FDR, as Roosevelt was often called, went into action. The day after he took office, he ordered all banks to take a "holiday." Every bank door was shut all across the nation. Congress was called into special session. Roosevelt asked for a new law to protect the people's money and to let sound banks open again.

A speed record was broken. In just seven hours Congress passed a bank bill and the new President signed it into law. The quick action cheered the country and brought hope for better times to come.

FDR kept up the pace. He pushed Congress hard to get more New Deal programs written into law. In 100 days, Congress passed the 16 major laws which were the backbone of the New Deal.

Roosevelt also went on a talent search. He sought the best people to help him make the New Deal work. Many of them were college professors. Perhaps that is why the group of private advisors FDR gathered were called his "Brain Trust."

Roosevelt also depended on his "Black Brain Trust." Mary McLeod Bethune was an educator. FDR asked her to work with the National Youth Administration. Robert C. Weaver also worked with FDR. Later Weaver became the first black appointed to a cabinet post. He served as Secretary of Housing and Urban Affairs under Lyndon Johnson.

Mary McLeod Bethune was one of Roosevelt's advisors.

14. How many major laws were passed during Roosevelt's first 100 days in office?

15. What was the bank holiday?

16. What were FDR's Brain Trusts?

What were the three major parts of the New Deal?

There were three main parts to the New Deal which began in 1933 and ended in 1938. Those major parts often were called the "Three R's." They were:

1. **Relief.** Food, clothing, and shelter were given immediately to the millions of Americans who were in desperate need.

2. **Recovery.** Laws were passed to cure the "sickness" of the Great Depression and to help the nation "recover" from its economic illness.

3. **Reform.** Long-term action programs were designed to prevent future depressions.

Relief had to begin immediately. People had to have food, clothing, and shelter at once. Even so, Roosevelt did not believe that the government should give money to people who had not worked for it. People lose their self-respect when they take handouts or charity, he said. However, the ugly fact was that some Americans were on the edge of starvation in 1933. These citizens had to be fed and clothed. Congress gave $5 billion to cities and states to use as an emergency relief fund. Then Congress began to set up projects so that these people could be put to work.

Unemployed young men between the ages of 18 and 25 found jobs with the Civilian Conservation Corps (CCC). These young men earned about $30 per month in addition to their room and board. They had to agree to send $25 per month home to their needy families. They lived and worked in camps all over the country. The CCC worked in the national parks and forests. Workers planted trees, drained swamps, and restored battle sites of the American Revolution and the Civil War.

To help young people in school, part-time jobs were opened by the National Youth Administration.

Older unemployed workers found jobs through the Works Progress Administration (WPA). They built dams, roads, bridges, and public buildings. Artists painted murals in public buildings. Musicians gave concerts. Writers wrote local histories and guidebooks. Some scholars did research in history.

All told, nine million people worked at government jobs of one kind or another. Providing these jobs cost the taxpayers $15 billion.

17. What were the "Three R's" of the New Deal?

18. Why was work as well as money given to those needing relief?

How did the New Deal try to speed recovery and push reforms?

The nation was sick with depression. To help the "patient" recover, the New Deal suggested medicines for different groups.

Business people were asked to raise prices and to keep wages up, too. As part of the National Industrial Recovery Act (NIRA), each industry was asked to draw up rules of fair competition. Those which did could put up the sign of the Blue Eagle of the National Recovery Administration (NRA).

Farmers were paid for not growing certain crops and not raising hogs.

Young men from Washington State pose in their CCC camp at Tahoma Creek in Rainier National Forest, Washington. The CCC built trails and worked on forest fire prevention and soil conservation in the forest.

Roosevelt thought that if farmers produced less, prices for their products would go up. Then farmers again would be able to hear the happy jingle of money in their pockets.

Roosevelt knew that the United States could not recover alone. Just as the depression sickness was worldwide, so would recovery have to be worldwide. A new tariff law helped other countries increase trade with the United States.

At the same time that Roosevelt was concerned with recovery, he was interested in reform. He wanted to make sure that the nation would not suffer from future depressions.

To protect people who bought stock and to prevent another crash, Congress set up the Securities and Exchange Commission. It still has power to regulate the stock market.

Roosevelt wanted to see if the federal government could help a whole region. For that reason the Tennessee Valley Authority was started. It covered parts of eight states. (See map, page 476.)

The TVA really changed the lives of people within its giant reach. Dams controlled floods and produced electricity. For the first time, many citizens' homes were lit by electric lights. Factories ran on electric power. Fish and wildlife preserves were started. Soil conservation and fertilizer production were carried on. New recreation areas were opened. With the TVA, the government itself became a "Big Business."

Probably the most lasting reform came with the Social Security Act. This government-run insurance plan is still in operation today. Workers and their employers each contribute money from wages. At a certain age, retired men and women receive monthly payments. States are helped to set up their own unemployment plans under another part of the Act. Social Security would later provide medical and hospital care.

19. What actions to help recovery did the New Deal ask of business?

20. What reforms were started by the New Deal to prevent future depressions?

Why did Roosevelt attack the Supreme Court?

Some Americans did not like Roosevelt's programs. They thought

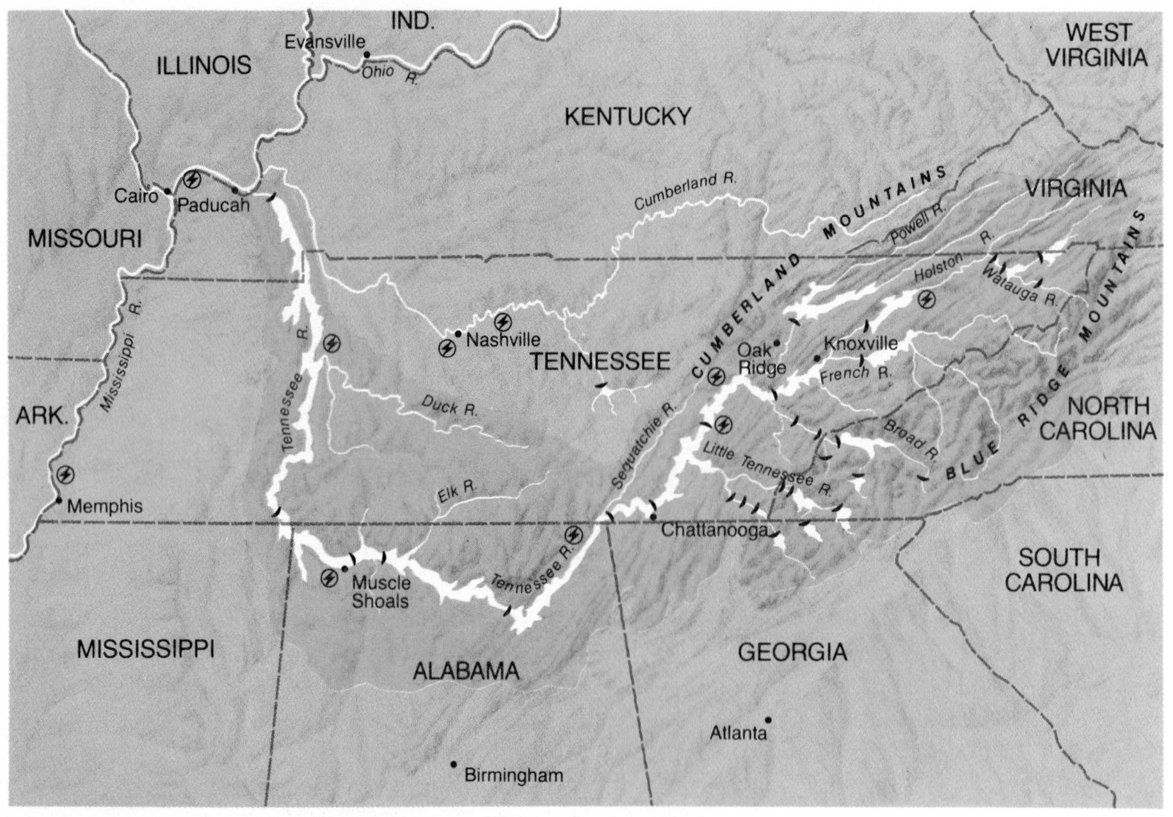

Tennessee Valley Authority

Drainage Basin of the Tennessee River

Major Dams

Major Steam-Electric Plants

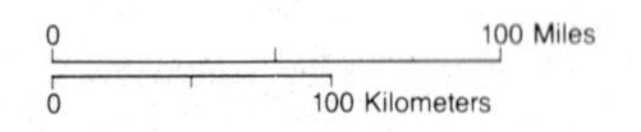

they were close to socialism. Opponents of FDR took their cases to the Supreme Court. Again and again, the Court said that New Deal laws were unconstitutional. The NRA was struck down. FDR grew more angry with every decision of the Court that blocked his programs.

When Roosevelt was reelected in 1936 with majorities in all but two states, he decided to attack the Court. Roosevelt called the justices "nine old men." He said they were out of step with the times. If justices refused to retire at 70, the President wanted power to appoint additional younger justices. Of course he intended to appoint men who believed in the New Deal.

As popular as Roosevelt was, he could not get the American people or Congress to agree with his ideas for changing, or "packing," the Court. Americans worried about upsetting the checks and balances set up in the Constitution. (See page 128.)

Even so, Roosevelt was not beaten. The Court made several decisions in favor of the New Deal. It ruled that the Social Security Act was constitutional. In time, too, several justices retired or died. Roosevelt then got his chance to appoint justices who agreed with him.

21. Why did Roosevelt want to add more justices to the Supreme Court?

22. Who opposed him? Why?

What gains did labor make during the New Deal?

One of the first things Roosevelt did when he took office was to invite Frances Perkins to be Secretary of Labor. At first she said no. She said she was afraid things she wanted to do would cause the President political trouble. Then she explained that she wanted to push for new laws to shorten working hours and abolish night work for women. She wanted more controls on child labor. She thought workers deserved better protection against injuries and unemployment. She also felt that representatives of the public should meet along with employers and union leaders on a regular basis at the Department of Labor.

After listening to her ideas, Roosevelt said he agreed with her. He insisted she take the cabinet post. He promised he would back her in everything she wanted to do. At last, Perkins agreed. In 1933 she became the first woman to hold a cabinet post. She served for twelve years under Roosevelt and continued under President Truman. During her long term of office she was able to work for the things in which she believed.

In 1935, Perkins supported Senator Robert Wagner of New York. Wagner sponsored an important law which bears his name. That law marked a real change in the federal government's feelings toward labor. In the past the government often had taken the side of employers in strikes. (See page 398.) But under the 1935 Wagner Act, employers were told they could not stop workers from joining unions. Men and women who took active parts in union affairs could not be fired for doing so. The Wagner Act also said employers had to meet with union-elected representatives to talk about wages, hours, and working conditions. In other words, the Wagner Act said that employers must bargain collectively with employees.

To watch over the workers' new rights, the National Labor Relations Board was set up. It would hear and settle complaints on unfair practices. Usually the Board sided with labor.

Three years later, in 1938, another landmark labor law was passed by Congress and signed by President Roosevelt. It was the Fair Labor Standards Act, and it proved to be a milestone in American history. The act limited the workweek to forty hours. It set a minimum wage. (The first minimum was 24 cents an hour, to increase over eight years to 40 cents an hour.) The act said that industries in interstate commerce could not employ children.

Naturally labor and labor unions were happy about that act. "Everybody claimed credit for it," Perkins said later. "I cannot remember whether the President and I claimed credit, but we always thought we had done it."

23. Who was the first woman to hold a cabinet post?

24. How did the Wagner Act mark a change in the government's attitude toward labor?

How successful was the New Deal?

Americans have always been deeply divided about the success of the New Deal. Was it worth its great cost?

One serious complaint against the New Deal was that the federal government had grown too big and powerful. Individuals and states were losing their freedom to an "octopus" government. The many arms or tentacles of government were grabbing in every direction.

Focus on Skills

The three graphs which are shown on page 479 are called line graphs. They are especially useful to show trends. A *trend* is a pattern. A trend shows the upward or downward direction of events.

In some ways line graphs are like bar graphs with which you already are familiar. (See pages 297 and 396.) Line and bar graphs have titles. They are plotted on a group of evenly spaced lines, or grids. And they give the reader a lot of information using numbers and very few words.

Line graphs also are unlike bar graphs. Instead of bars, data is recorded on line graphs by dots, or points. Then those dots or points are connected by a line or curve. The direction of the curve shows the trend—upward or downward.

Historians often use line graphs to show economic trends in the Great Depression. Reading those line graphs helps us realize how great the changes of that period really were.

Examine each of the three line graphs shown here. Then show that you understand them by answering the following questions about each one:

1. What is the title of the graph or what information does it offer?
2. What years are represented on the graph?
3. In what year was the highest point shown on the graph? The lowest point?
4. Describe the trend or continuing pattern shown on the graph.

Some critics of New Deal spending felt that it increased inflation and debt.

Defenders of the New Deal argue that it was a great benefit. Saving the human and natural resources of this country was worth any price. If it had not been for the New Deal, Communists or a dictator might have taken over the country in the dark depression days.

25. Why do defenders of the New Deal say it was a great benefit?

26. What complaints against the New Deal have been made?

Why did the New Deal end?

In 1938 many candidates who did not like the New Deal were elected to Congress. They worked with other conservatives to put a brake on Roosevelt's plans.

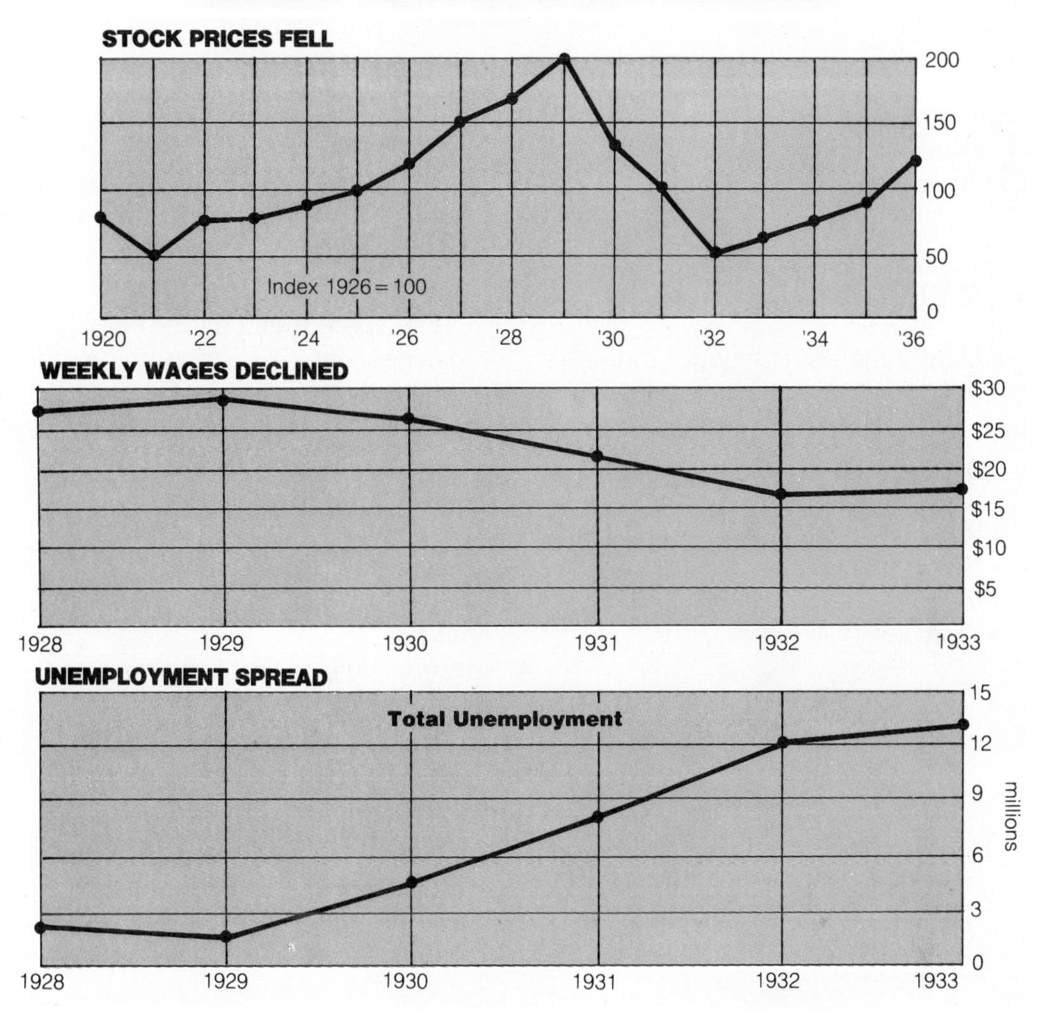

To pay for all the programs, the federal government had borrowed heavily. The national debt had risen higher and higher. At the same time taxes had increased. Yet there were still ten million unemployed Americans! Obviously, the New Deal had not solved one of the country's most serious problems. Although Roosevelt himself remained popular, he had trouble getting more New Deal laws through Congress.

Another important reason for the end of the New Deal was that new threats of war were brewing overseas. Dictators had taken control of Germany and Italy. In Japan, a powerful, warlike government had come to power. The President had to turn attention from problems within the nation to serious international troubles. The New Deal had finally run its course, but its spirit kept the United States free and intact in a time of disaster.

27. What two events caused the end of the New Deal?

Building Your Vocabulary

Select the proper word to fill each blank in the following paragraph.

crash	prosperous	reform
relief	Depression	recover

Many Americans thought the—?—times of the 1920s would never end. But a stock market—?—occurred in 1929, followed by the Great—?—of the 1930s. When Franklin Roosevelt took office as President, he had three great problems with which he had to deal. First,—?—was needed for those people who lacked food, clothing, or shelter. Next, some methods for helping businesses—?—had to be provided. Finally,—?—was needed in order to prevent future depressions.

Recalling What You Have Learned

Match each item in Column A with the correct item in Column B.

Column A	Column B
1. Henry Ford	A. effort to help a whole region
2. the Lone Eagle	B. New Deal
3. Frances Perkins	C. Model-T
4. "Silent Cal"	D. Charles Lindbergh
5. the 18th Amendment	E. first woman cabinet member
6. Bonus March	F. Calvin Coolidge
7. defeated for President in 1932	G. Herbert Hoover
8. Name of FDR's plan to end the Depression	H. veterans' protest in Washington, D.C.
9. Tennessee Valley Authority	I. law to help labor
10. Wagner Act	J. Prohibition

Discussing the Important Ideas in This Chapter

1. Why were the 1920s called "golden" years? Why did the golden years come to an end?
2. What new, or revolutionary, ideas did Henry Ford have? How did Ford use those ideas to help the United States become "a nation on wheels"?
3. How did radio and motion pictures change life for Americans? Why were those changes important?
4. How did life change for American blacks during the 1920s? In the 1930s?
5. What was Prohibition? Why did it fail?
6. What caused the Great Depression?
7. How did the Great Depression change people's feelings about the role of the federal government in their lives?
8. Why was Roosevelt able to get such strong support from the American people?
9. How successful was the New Deal?

Improving Your Map Skills

When Congress created the TVA, it moved to improve living conditions in an entire region.

To provide low-cost electricity and control floods, the government built a vast network of dams. They are shown on the map on page 476. Examine the map. Show that you understand how the TVA changed life in an entire region by answering the questions which follow. All of them are based on the map.

1. With your finger, trace the drainage basin of the Tennessee River. In what state does most of that basin lie?
2. Seven other states have a part of their territory in the drainage basin. Name those seven states.
3. What is the name of the major river in the Tennessee Valley? Rivers flow from mountains or high ground to lower ground. In what two mountain ranges does this major river have its source (start)? Into what other major river does it flow?
4. Find the symbol for major dams shown in the map key. Count the number of major dams constructed in the Tennessee Valley.
5. Use the map key to find the symbol for steam-electric plants. Count the number of major steam-electric plants built in this region.
6. Use the scale shown in the lower left corner of the map. Estimate the distance between Chattanooga and Muscle Shoals. Between Muscle Shoals and Cairo.
7. Write one or two sentences which summarize the changes brought to the area by the TVA.

Improving Your Study Skills: *Research*

On a separate sheet of paper, draw a chart like the one shown below. Now look at the list of events shown on the right. Place those which occurred in the decade of the 1920s on the left-hand side of the chart in their correct chronological order. Put those of the 1930s in the right-hand column, making sure they also appear in correct chronological order.

To discover the year in which each of these events took place, use the index for this book. The index will refer you to the pages on which the events are discussed and their dates given.

Major Events in the Decades of the 1920s and the 1930s

Events of the 1920s	*Events of the 1930s*

List of Events

Stock market crash

Lindbergh flies Atlantic alone

Wagner Labor Law enacted

First radio broadcast

Hoover takes office as President

Vice-President Coolidge becomes President after Harding's death

Frances Perkins becomes first woman cabinet member

New Deal begins

Bonus march

Amelia Earhart disappears on a flight around the world.

Chapter 19

World War II and Its Aftermath

Arizona Memorial, Pearl Harbor, Hawaii

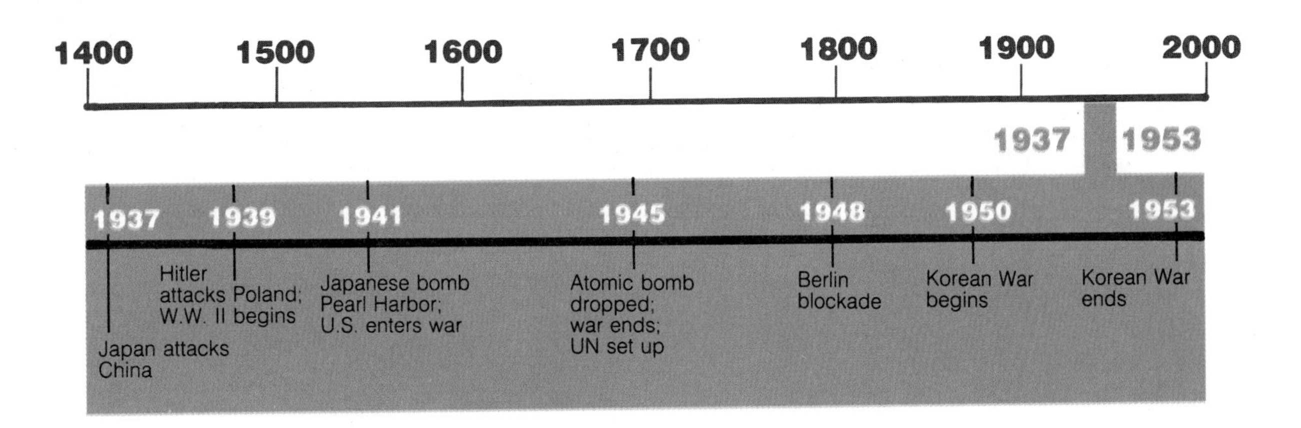

Part One

War Clouds Gather in Europe

Why did dictators in three nations threaten peace?

During the 1930s Americans were most concerned about the Great Depression at home. But they also were alarmed by the rise of dictators in Europe, particularly those in Italy, Russia (the USSR), and Germany. It was obvious that serious trouble was brewing in those three nations.

After World War I, Italy, Russia, and Germany became totalitarian states. In each of them the government took total control of people's lives. Each of those governments was headed by an all-powerful leader, or dictator, who crushed all opposition.

In Italy, Benito Mussolini became dictator. Mussolini told the Italians that democracy was a failure. The strikes, depressions, and violence that rocked Italy after World War I could be stopped easily. Italians needed only to give power to Mussolini.

Mussolini headed the Fascist party in Italy. He was supported in his bid for power by black-shirted Fascists. They believed that individuals had no rights.

Only the state is important, they said. They also believed in war. Mussolini said that peace made weaklings. War brought glory and honor.

Mussolini used every excuse to involve his nation in war. In 1935, Italy attacked Ethiopia in North Africa. Ethiopia became an Italian colony. (See map, above.) One year later, Mussolini sent troops to help Francisco Franco become dictator of Spain. Finally he joined with Germany and Japan to fight in World War II.

In Russia, Joseph Stalin became dictator. He was chosen by the Communist party to head the government. After World War I, the Communists had staged a revolution in Russia. (After the revolution, the official name of Russia was changed to the Union of Soviet

Socialist Republics, or USSR. It is also called the Soviet Union.) The Communists snuffed out all other political parties. So when the leaders of their party met they could name whomever they wished to their top office.

Stalin came into the top spot in 1924. Stalin was not his real name, but it was a good one for him. "Stalin" means "man of steel."

For thirty years, Stalin more than lived up to his name. He was determined to turn the Soviet Union into a great industrial nation. He stopped at nothing, not even lies, torture, or murder. Ruthlessly he snuffed out political, religious, and other human rights.

Stalin was most concerned about what happened in the Soviet Union. But, like other Communists, he also was eager to see communism spread throughout the world.

In Germany, Adolph Hitler became dictator in 1933. After World War I, Germany faced very serious problems. For a time the Germans tried democracy. But the democratic government of Germany was weak and disorganized. Partly as a result of the huge payments required by the Treaty of Versailles, the German economy fell apart. Workers had to be paid every day because the value of the German mark fell daily. Savings were useless in a country where a loaf of bread cost a billion marks. The Germans resented the Treaty of Versailles and the countries that had made it. (See pages 446-448.)

Hitler was watching for a chance to come to power. Like Mussolini, Hitler was a Fascist. But his political party was called the National Socialists, or *Nazis.*

In long, rambling speeches, Hitler began to excite the German people. He told them all their troubles were brought

Adolph Hitler and his followers seized control of Germany in 1933. His mad plans called for German control of Europe.

on by others. They were caused by Jews, international bankers, Communists, old-style German military leaders, and the nations which had made the Versailles Treaty. Hitler urged his listeners to follow him and become Nazis. He would be their *Fuehrer*, or leader. He would make Germany first among the world's nations. His mad plans were heady brew for a people still smarting from their defeat in World War I.

1. Who became dictator in Italy? The Soviet Union? Germany?

2. What did each of those dictators hope to accomplish?

What were Hitler's plans?

Before Hitler became well-known, he had been arrested and put in prison in southern Germany. While he was in jail, he wrote a book called *Mein Kampf*, or *My Battle.* It contained his plans for building a new German empire, or *Reich.* Hitler said that the new *Reich* would last for a thousand years.

It was hard for most people outside Germany to take Hitler's book seriously. They would not or could not believe the things he wrote—for example, that:

The Germans—all those who were not also Jews—were a Master Race. Hitler called "pure" Germans *Aryans*. In time, he said, Aryans would take over the world.

The "final solution" to what he called the "Jewish problem" was to expel all Jews or put them to death.

The only good government was a dictatorship; democracy was nonsense.

Hitler would not rule by truth. Instead he would use what he called "The Big Lie." Because his ideas would seem so outlandish, people would refuse to believe them. Thus, they would be caught off-guard.

In Germany people did not find *Mein Kampf* hard to believe. More and more people read the book. They went to Hitler's rallies. They began wearing the brown shirts and uniforms of the Nazi party.

Hitler became even bolder as the number of Nazis grew. He formed a secret police called the *Gestapo* to arrest anyone who dared oppose him. Jews became his special targets. They were denied citizenship. They were forced to wear yellow stars so that they could be easily recognized. Their property was taken from them. They were beaten and imprisoned. Finally they were marched off to death camps. An estimated six million European Jews died by 1945 in what is called the *Holocaust*.

Ignoring the Treaty of Versailles, Hitler built a bigger army, navy, and air force. He took back land lost to France after World War I. His troops marched into Austria and Czechoslovakia. (See map, page 484.)

Survivors of Dachau, a German concentration camp, greet the American troops who freed them at the end of the war.

Britain, France, and the United States all said Hitler had no right to act this way. But they did not stop him. With Germany firmly in his grasp, Hitler and his Nazis continued to strut, boast, and bully. Hate-filled Hitler gobbled up Europe almost unchallenged.

3. What were some of the main ideas Hitler set forth in *Mein Kampf*?

4. What actions did he take against the Jews? Against other countries?

How did Americans feel about dictators in Europe?

Most Americans had mixed feelings about the events in Europe. Certainly they did not like to see freedom crushed and people killed. But neither did they want to get into a war that they still felt was none of their business.

Once again, as it had many times before in its history, the United States tried to stay neutral. Laws were passed in 1935, 1936, and 1937 which limited trade with countries at war. The sale of arms to either side was forbidden. Americans hoped the oceans around them would protect the United States from foreign dictators.

Some Americans thought European propagandists had fooled the United States in 1917. (See page 441.) Those Americans did not want to be fooled again. Even though the brutal acts of dictators were fact, not fiction, many people just did not want to believe the facts.

Peace movements were in full swing in the United States. Many young people belonged to peace groups. They argued that Americans ought to build a good society at home. They should end the Great Depression. Europe, they said, was not a concern of the United States.

5. Why didn't Americans try to stop Europe's dictators?

When did war begin in Europe?

World War II had been building all through the 1920s and 1930s. The year 1939 saw the fatal buildup. In that year, Germany and Italy signed an alliance. The next year, Japan joined them. These nations became the *Axis Powers.*

Also in 1939, Hitler and Stalin signed an agreement. They promised not to attack each other. Each also promised to stay neutral if the other went to war. That agreement was important to Hitler. He did not want to fight two enemies at once.

Once Hitler had the Soviet agreement in his pocket, he was ready to move. Just a few days later, Hitler demanded part of Poland. Of course, the Poles refused to give up their land.

On September 1, 1939, Hitler opened his attack on Poland. Two days later, Great Britain and France declared war on Germany because they had promised to help Poland. World War II had begun.

6. Who were the Axis powers?

7. Why did the attack on Poland start World War II?

Why did the United States decide to help Britain?

Once World War II began, Hitler moved with unbelievable speed. He launched what was called a *blitzkrieg*, or lightning war. In one year's time, the Nazis took over Poland, Denmark, Norway, the Netherlands, Belgium, and France. They forced factory workers in those countries to help the German war machine. The Gestapo watched the people closely. Any efforts to fight back were immediately crushed. The Gestapo also hunted down Jews in conquered countries. The Jews were marched to concentration camps where they were shot or killed in huge gas chambers.

President Roosevelt was very upset by the speed of the German advance. He was worried because by 1940 Britain was left to stand alone against the Nazis in Europe. Hitler's planes were bombing England nightly.

Roosevelt began to urge Americans to give up neutrality. If the United States did not go to the aid of Britain and democracy, he said, freedom for all people would be lost. "Let no one imagine that America will escape, that it may expect mercy, that this western hemisphere will not be attacked," he warned.

German troops rush through a bombed Polish town. The *blitzkrieg* depended on air power and fast new vehicles.

In November 1940, Roosevelt was reelected President. He began his third term by persuading Congress to vote $17 billion to build up American defenses. For the first time in its history, Congress passed a peacetime draft law. The United States also began sending planes, tanks, food, and raw materials to Britain.

German U-boats (submarines) attacked ships which carried those goods across the Atlantic. When they did, President Roosevelt ordered the United States Navy to provide more protection. Supply ships were to travel in convoys protected by warships. Roosevelt, the Commander in Chief, ordered American sailors to shoot any attackers on sight.

Roosevelt's actions provoked a storm of protest in the United States. Many Americans wanted peace. But the President reminded them that peace does not come just because it is hoped for or wished for. He said that the American nation had to face up to a great question: Could the United States hope to live in peace in a world turned upside down by dictators?

Americans continued to debate that question hotly and loudly, as the Axis dictators marched ever nearer to victory. Americans were still debating and trying to decide what to do as late as December 1941. Then, with dramatic suddenness, the Japanese attacked Pearl Harbor in Hawaii.

8. Why was Britain left to stand alone in Europe against the Nazis?

9. Why did Roosevelt believe the United States should help Britain?

Part Two

Trouble in Asia Brings War to the United States

When were seeds of World War II planted in Asia?

World War II may have started in Asia in 1931. In that year, Japanese troops attacked and conquered Manchuria, a part of China. (See map, page 490.)

Japan wanted Manchuria's natural resources to help build a war machine. As an excuse for taking Manchuria, the Japanese claimed that they needed "more living room." Their own islands were overcrowded, they said.

The United States took the lead in calling Japan's takeover of Manchuria unlawful. But Japan knew that Americans and Europeans were too bogged down in the Great Depression to take any action. Japan ignored the protests. In fact, to show its feelings, Japan calmly walked out of the League of Nations.

At the time, the Philadelphia *Record* said, "The American people don't give a hoot in a rain barrel who controls North China." The Japanese saw they had a green light. No country, including the United States, was going to challenge them as they moved to control Asia.

1. Why did the Japanese move into Manchuria?

2. How did the United States respond to what the Japanese did?

Why did the United States worry about Japan's ambitions?

Japan made no secret of its ambitions in Asia. Military dictators who had taken control in that country loudly proclaimed "Asia for the Asiatics!" They said they were going to build "a new order" in the Pacific. They were going to take control of other countries by force.

On the flag of Japan is a rising sun. The new military dictators hoped that the Japanese sun would rise over all of the Pacific.

Americans watched and worried as Japan began to move in Asia. The Open Door policy (pages 431-432) and the safety of the Philippine Islands were in danger. Even the safety of the United States was threatened by Japan's ambitions.

In 1937, Japan started another war against China. Cities were bombed, civilians were killed, and all of China's coastal cities were overrun. American missionaries and business people in China were badly treated. Even an American gunboat, the *Panay*, was bombed. The United States protested. It accepted an apology from the Japanese and $2 million for the damages.

Americans worried about Japan's actions, but they were unwilling to take a strong stand. In fact, the United States was helping to build Japan's strength. Half the supply of scrap iron and airplane fuel for the Japanese war machine was purchased from the United States.

3. What did the military dictators who came to power in Japan say they wanted to do?

4. How did the United States react?

When and why did Japan become a partner in the Axis?

When the Germans conquered France in June 1940, Japan was sure that Germany and Italy would win the war in Europe. Japan's military dictators called for more action in Asia. They sent troops to take over the French colony of Indochina. (See map, page 490.) If Japan was to make more war, it needed oil and rubber from Southeast Asia.

Japan also decided to become a full partner with Germany and Italy. By signing an agreement to help Hitler and Mussolini, Japan let the world know that it had turned against the United States. Relations between the United States and Japan went from bad to worse.

Americans at last began to see that war with Japan was a real threat. Congress forbade the sale of war supplies to the Japanese.

Meetings were held to try to solve problems between the two nations. But the talks did not get very far. The Japanese were willing to talk, but they

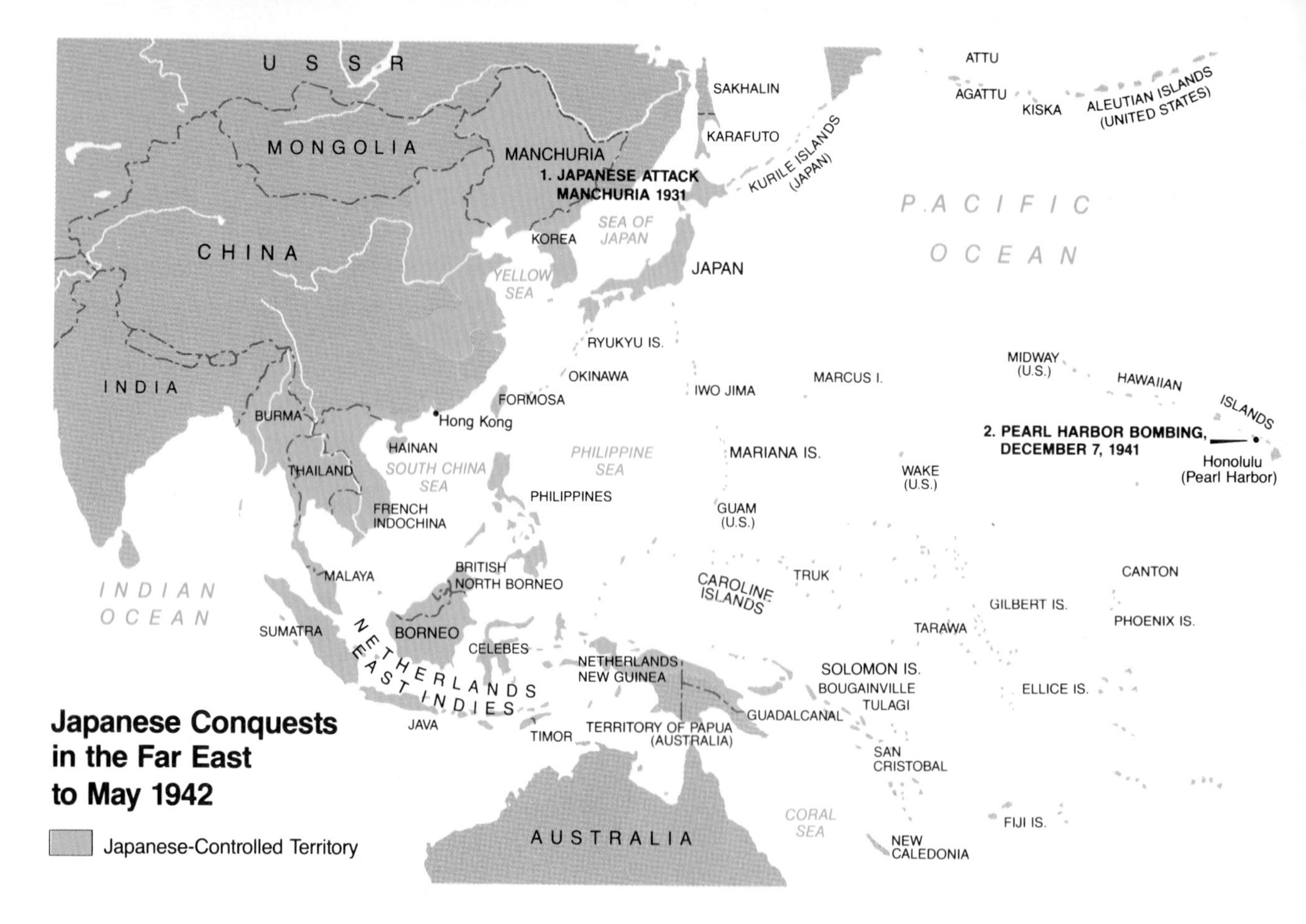

Japanese Conquests in the Far East to May 1942

were not willing to give up any of their aims in Asia.

5. Why did Japan decide to join with Germany and Italy?

6. What did the United States do to try to solve its problems with Japan?

When and where did the Japanese attack the United States?

The Japanese armed forces used a secret code. American experts managed to figure out the code and read it. They knew that the Japanese were about to strike a heavy blow. But just where the blow was to fall remained a mystery.

On Sunday morning, December 7, 1941, American and Japanese representatives were still meeting in Washington. American military leaders were wondering if the Japanese intended to hit Hong Kong or the Dutch East Indies. Then the Japanese put an end to all the talk. A fleet of 191 Japanese warplanes bombed Pearl Harbor, Hawaii. Another fleet of 170 planes followed within an hour with more bombs.

Long lines of American battleships were at anchor in Pearl Harbor. They were in port for the first time since July 4. They made perfect targets for the expert Japanese bombers. Also, most of the warplanes the United States had in the Pacific were at the Pearl Harbor airfield.

The surprise attack on Pearl Harbor took a high toll. American commanders there had made few preparations for an attack.

Five battleships were sent to the bottom of the ocean. Three more were heavily damaged. Almost 2500 Americans lost their lives. Half of them were on the battleship *Arizona* when it

On December 7, 1941, most of the United States Navy's Pacific fleet was caught in the Japanese attack on Pearl Harbor.

exploded. And 150 warplanes were destroyed.

Pearl Harbor itself was a scene of confusion. What had begun as a peaceful Sunday morning had turned into a nightmare. One sailor on watch shouted, "The war is on! No fooling!"

That same day—December 7, 1941—the Japanese also attacked the Philippines, Guam, Hong Kong, and several other points.

7. Why were losses at Pearl Harbor so high?

8. Where else did the Japanese attack on December 7, 1941?

How did Americans react to the bombing of Pearl Harbor?

News of the attack stunned Americans. Radio announcers interrupted programs to give the almost unbelievable information. Could it be true? Had Japan really attacked American territory? People asked each other these questions in amazement.

The next day an angry President Roosevelt stood before Congress. He said,

Yesterday, December 7, 1941—a date which will live in infamy—the United States was suddenly and deliberately attacked by the naval and air forces of the Empire of Japan.

Within four hours, Congress declared war. Only one member voted against the declaration.

Germany and Italy lost no time in joining their partner, Japan. Three days later the European dictators declared war on the United States.

For the first time in the nation's history, there was no real opposition to

Japanese Americans stand in a bleak street of their relocation camp in Heart Mountain, Wyoming.

going to war. Pearl Harbor was probably the worst military defeat in the country's history. But it united Americans as no other event in history had ever done.

There was another quick reaction to the bombing of Pearl Harbor. It was one that most Americans later regretted. In March 1940 the general in charge of West Coast defense began to round up Japanese Americans. There were about 110,000 of these people living in the western parts of Washington, Oregon, California, and Arizona. These people were sent to special camps away from the coast as a "safety measure." They had to sell their homes, farms, and businesses for whatever they could get. At the time, some Americans feared they would be disloyal citizens. There was no evidence that these citizens were disloyal. As it turned out, Japanese Americans were very important to the United States war effort. But not until 1944 did the government begin to release the Japanese Americans from the camps.

As the war continued, Japanese Americans served in many ways. Some made camouflage nets and other supplies. Some volunteered to harvest crops. More than 17,000 served in the army. Many of them volunteered for the "All Japanese" 100th Infantry Battalion which combined with the 442nd Regimental Combat Team. Serving then as one unit, Japanese Americans fought in some of the toughest battles in Italy. That unit probably was the most decorated and honored unit in all United States military history.

9. When did President Roosevelt ask Congress to declare war on Japan?

10. Why were Japanese Americans sent to special camps? How did they help the United States war effort?

Part Three

Victory in Europe and Asia

Why did the United States decide to help defeat Germany first?

After Pearl Harbor, President Roosevelt and Prime Minister Churchill of Britain met to plan the war. They agreed that Germany had to be beaten first because it was the strongest of the Axis Powers.

By June 1941 the Germans had taken control of nearly all Europe except the Soviet Union and Britain. Then Hitler broke his agreement with Stalin and launched a surprise attack on Russia. The Nazi war machine needed Russian oil and wheat. Also the defeat of the Soviet Union was part of Hitler's long-range plan to become master of Europe.

Churchill welcomed the Russians as an ally even though he distrusted the Communists. The goal of beating Hitler was most important. By the time the United States entered the war, the Nazis were deep into Russia.

The long, bloody struggle to regain Europe began first in North Africa. There British troops were able to stop the German drive for the Suez Canal. Allied forces drove the Axis forces out of North Africa. Then they began the bitter task of driving the Axis soldiers out of Italy. (See map, page 494.)

At the same time that land battles raged all over Europe and North Africa, a desperate struggle went on at sea. German submarines roamed the North Atlantic Ocean and even went into the Gulf of Mexico and the Caribbean Sea. Gradually, and at great cost, the Allies turned the tide of battle against these deadly underwater sharks.

1. Why did the Allies agree that it was more important to defeat Germany first?

2. Where did the Allies battle against the Axis forces?

When did Allied forces invade Europe?

D-Day, June 6, 1944. On that fateful day the "second front" in Western Europe was opened. Allied forces were commanded by General Dwight D. Eisenhower. Carefully planned and long awaited, the invasion was known by the code name, "Operation Overlord." Almost three million American and British soldiers had been packed into southern England waiting for the big move. Thousands of bombers pounded German targets in advance.

When the day came, 4600 ships stole out of their hiding places in the harbors and rivers of England. Moving carefully and quietly through the darkness, the biggest fleet ever assembled crossed the English Channel. In those predawn hours, everything from small torpedo boats to huge battleships sailed the rough channel. The coast of Normandy, France, was the goal of this great invasion fleet.

More than a quarter of a million soldiers landed on the beaches that first day. Fighting was savage, especially on Omaha Beach. American troops there suffered terrible losses. But by June 7 the Allies had gained the toehold they needed in Western Europe.

3. Why was D-Day important?

How was France freed?

Within a month after D-Day, more than a million soldiers had poured into Europe through the beachhead on Normandy. Then the Allies broke through the German lines and began a "blitzkrieg" of their own across northern France. Men and women of the French underground rose up to help. Secretly they had been training and waiting for the day when they could strike back.

Other American forces landed on the Mediterranean coast of France. They joined the race to Paris. When they arrived, they found that the French underground had already taken Paris from the Germans. Cheering, crying, laughing, and singing crowds lined the streets to welcome the Allied soldiers.

Soon the Germans were in headlong flight across France with the Allies hot on their heels.

Trucks, guns, equipment and men are unloaded on Omaha Beach on D-Day, June 6, 1944. Within a week, 326,000 men, 50,000 vehicles, and more than 100,000 tons of supplies had been landed.

4. How did Allied forces drive the Germans out of France?

5. Who freed Paris from German control?

How and when did victory finally come in Europe?

While the Allies pounded the Germans in the West, the Russians attacked them all along the Eastern Front. Everywhere the Germans met defeat. Still they would not give up.

The Nazis tried one last desperate attempt to save themselves in a counterattack. They drove a fifty-mile (80 km) bulge into the Allied lines. This "Battle of the Bulge" caused some of the fiercest fighting of the war, but it was no use. The Nazi forces were cut to ribbons.

General Eisenhower's troops reached the Elbe River in April 1945. There they met the Soviets, who had come from the east. The Russians were first to enter Berlin, however.

Hitler could see it was all over. He committed suicide in his underground shelter in Berlin before the Soviets could capture him. Within a week of his death, Germany surrendered.

May 8, 1945, was V-E (Victory in Europe) Day, the day the war in Europe ended. At last, people there could lay down their arms after six long years of death and terror.

There were celebrations all over the world. But joy and relief were mixed with deep sorrow. Millions of people, including six million murdered Jews, were dead. Besides, the final victory against Japan still had to be won.

6. Why was the Battle of the Bulge important?

7. What was V-E Day? When was it?

These rings belonged to Jews killed by the Nazis.

At That Time

"Fresh, spirited American troops, flushed with victory, are bringing in thousands of hungry, ragged, battle-weary prisoners."
(News item)

G.I. Joe and Rosie the Riveter. They were an unlikely pair at the start. But in the end they proved to be an unbeatable team. Joe and Rosie probably were the two most important "persons" in the great cast of characters in the global drama called World War II. They were not real individuals, of course. But Joe and Rosie stood for the millions of American men and women whose efforts made Allied victory possible.

Let's meet G.I. Joe first. The initials "G.I." officially stood for "general issue," or sometimes "government issue," supplies. At the beginning of the war, that nickname was used to describe only the footslogging soldiers of the infantry. By the end of the war, the term "G.I." was used for all of the 15 million men and women in the armed forces.

By law more than 31 million males between the ages of 18 and 45 were required to register for the draft. When their numbers were drawn, they left their jobs as clerks or butchers or teachers. If the United States had not gone to war against the Axis, they probably would have spent their lives in those jobs. They might never have left their hometowns. Instead they were told to report to "induction," or intake, centers. There they were given physical examinations and super-short haircuts. They were issued regulation, look-alike, olive drab uniforms. Then they were scattered about the United States in training camps where they were taught how to shoot—and many other things. They learned to cook, make repairs, give first aid, drive tanks—and to stand in seemingly endless lines. Finally they were sent to do all those jobs in the far corners of the globe.

"Joe, yestidday ya saved my life an' I swore I'd pay ya back. Here's my last pair of dry socks."

G.I. Joes were Americans of all ethnic groups. When Congress passed the Selective Service Act on September 14, 1940, it read: "In the selection and training of men under this Act . . . there shall be no discrimination of any person on account of race or color." As a result the American armed forces reflected all of the peoples who make up this nation. Blacks, Hispanics, Chinese Americans, Italian Americans, Polish Americans, Irish Americans—and more—served side by side.

Life was anything but glamorous for most G.I.'s. No one understood that better than Bill Mauldin, the most famous American cartoonist of World War II.

Mauldin joined the infantry at 18. He fought and drew his way across many battlefields. He invented two famous nonheroes for his cartoons about World War II. Their names were Joe and Willie. They were G.I.'s. The adventures of Joe and Willie showed Americans back home what life "up front" was like.

Joe and Willie were unshaven. They wore soggy fatigue suits. Their shoulders sagged under rain-soaked combat packs. As Mauldin explained, "They don't get fancy pay, they know their food is the worst in the army because you can't whip up lemon pies or even hot soup at the front." Joe and Willie worked 168 hours a week, but "They don't need pity, because you don't pity brave men." Joe and Willie were sometimes rough. But to Mauldin and most Americans they had a certain nobility and dignity despite "the dirt in their ears." Like other G.I's Joe and Willie were "average" Americans who had been put where they were.

They wish they were someplace else, and they wish they would get relief. They wish the mud was dry and their coffee was hot. They want to go home. But they stay in their wet holes and fight, and then they climb out and crawl through minefields and fight some more.

Bill Mauldin, *Up Front* (New York: Henry Holt and Co., 1945), p. 16.

While millions of "Joes" were "up front," millions of "Rosies" swelled the labor ranks at home. When World War II began, there were 14 million women in the work force; when it ended, there were 20 million. Their contributions to the war effort were hailed in a popular song of the era called "Rosie the Riveter."

Women workers prepare the nose cones for fighter planes.

Out of every five women who went to work, most of them previously untrained, two went straight into defense plants. One took up office work. Two others found jobs in restaurants, stores, laundries, and hospitals. The war opened up blue-collar jobs formerly closed to women. The "Rosies" of the United States not only worked at riveting. They assembled small parts, and worked at welding, blueprint reading, on drill presses, milling machines, lathes, and punch and forming presses.

Three groups of women in particular benefited from the war in an economic sense. They were:

1. **Black women.** In 1900 about 95 percent of the black women who worked were employed on farms or as domestic, or household, workers. Their wages were low. Their work was hard. Chances for promotion were nonexistent. But after the war black women were employed in other places previously closed to them. The percentage of black women in domestic work had dropped 42 percent.

2. **Women who joined military units.** Nurses finally were able to become regular commissioned officers. They were eligible for the same wartime benefits given men, instead of serving outside the official military structure as they had during World War I.

3. **Women in the professions.** Opportunities opened for women who were doctors, dentists, and teachers. Eight thousand male reporters and editors who had to leave their jobs to go "up front" were replaced by eight thousand women. For the first time major symphony orchestras began to hire female musicians. And the New York Stock Exchange hired the first woman clerk in its history.

Why did the United States fight a delaying action in Asia?

The Allies' first goal in World War II was to defeat Germany. That meant that they could not make as big a war effort in Asia. In 1942 the United States was not ready to fight a total war in both Europe and Asia.

As a result, the Japanese advanced all over the Pacific practically unchecked. Moving south, they captured island after island until they threatened Australia. A small American army in the Philippines was crushed by the onrushing enemy. The American commander, General Douglas MacArthur, escaped to Australia to carry on the war.

The British could do no better against the Japanese in the Pacific. Their rich islands and other possessions in the Far East were soon lost. Everywhere the Japanese were successful.

8. Why was the war in the Pacific so one-sided in its early stages?

How was the war carried back to Japan?

The first turning of the tide in the Pacific war happened in two naval battles. A Japanese fleet approaching Australia was stopped at the Battle of the Coral Sea in May 1942. Another fleet aiming at Hawaii was defeated shortly afterwards.

General MacArthur then began a policy of "island-hopping" to win the war. Rather than fight on every Japanese-held island, only the most important ones were attacked. Less important islands were skipped over, or bypassed.

Once islands were won, they were used as air bases. Powerful long-range bombers struck at Japan from those bases.

Island by island, the Allies moved nearer to Japan itself. Two important Allied victories were won on the islands of Okinawa (ō kə nä′ wə) and Iwo Jima (ē′ wō jē′ mə).

By the time the European war was over, Admiral William (Bull) Halsey and his fleet were shelling cities up and down the coasts of Japan. Attack by sea and air reduced most of Japan's industrial cities to ruins.

9. How did General MacArthur plan to defeat the Japanese?

When did Harry Truman become President and Commander in Chief?

Americans knew that Franklin Roosevelt was not well when they elected him President for a fourth term in 1944. However, they were not prepared for his death on April 12, 1945, just two and a half months after he was inaugurated.

People all over the world mourned his passing. No one was more shocked than Roosevelt's Vice-President Harry Truman. Truman's own words tell his reaction.

I had been afraid for many weeks that something might happen to this great leader, but now that the worst had happened, I was unprepared for it . . . America had lost a great leader, and I was faced with a terrible responsibility.

Truman asked all Americans to help and to pray for him. But he soon showed that he was no ordinary President. Spunky, down-to-earth Harry Truman carried on as President and Commander in Chief where Roosevelt had left off.

10. When did Roosevelt die?
11. How did Truman react?

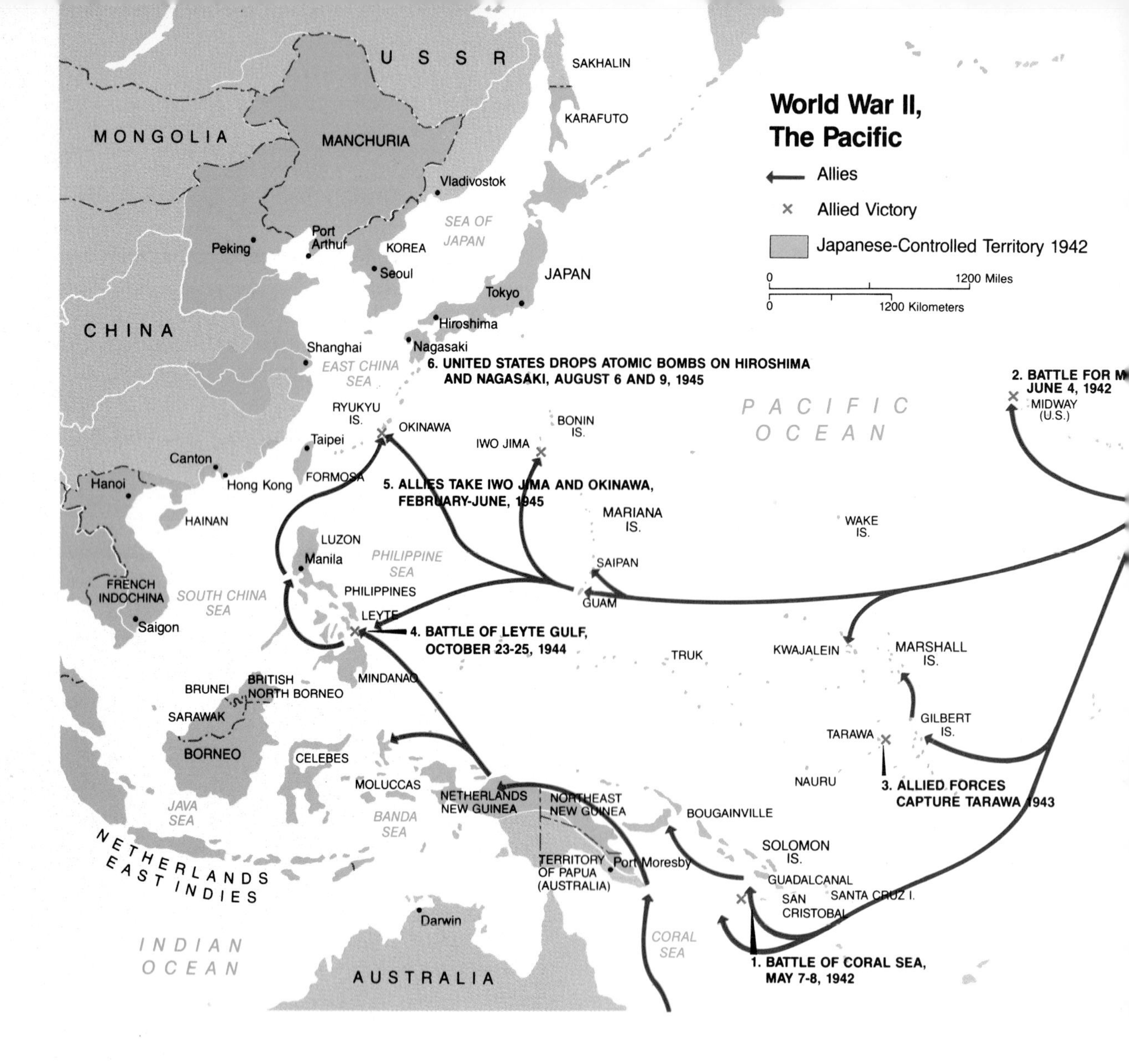

Why did Truman use the atomic bomb?

When Truman became President he learned about an important secret project. It was so secret that, even as Vice-President, Truman did not know about it. It was called the Manhattan Project, and it had been underway for years.

In 1939, even before the Germans had marched into Poland, a famous scientist wrote an important letter to President Roosevelt. Albert Einstein told the President that recent work by other scientists "leads me to expect that the element uranium may be turned into a new and important source of energy in the immediate future." After receiving that message, President Roosevelt started the Manhattan Project to build the first atomic bomb.

Under a football stadium in Chicago, scientists worked for years in the greatest secrecy. Famous refugees from Denmark, Germany, Hungary, and Italy helped in the efforts to develop the bomb. In 1942 they sent a coded message to President Roosevelt. It told him that "the Italian navigator has just landed in the New World. . . ." It meant that the Italian, Enrico Fermi, had succeeded in bringing about the first nuclear chain reaction.

Just after Truman was sworn into office as President, he was told that the scientists were almost ready to complete their first bomb.

The first atomic bomb was tested in a New Mexico desert in the summer of 1945. That bomb had enough power to destroy an entire city. The next question was what to *do* with the powerful new weapon.

President Truman considered that question very carefully. Some of the points he had to consider were:

1. Military leaders said that if the United States had to invade Japan, another million human beings would probably lose their lives.

2. The Empire of Japan still had two million well-armed troops on its home islands. It also had another 5000 kamikaze (kä′ mē kä′ zē: suicide) airplane pilots. They were ready to give their lives for their Emperor to destroy any target.

3. President Truman had sent Japan a stern warning on July 16, 1945. He told the leaders that if they did not surrender, they would face "prompt and utter destruction." The Japanese leaders refused his terms.

4. Truman also sent planes over Japan. He had them shower tens of thousands of leaflets for citizens to read. These leaflets gave the same warning that had been sent to the leaders.

Truman waited a week. Then on August 6, 1945, he ordered an atomic bomb dropped on the city of Hiroshima. When the great mushroom cloud cleared, the city lay in twisted ruins. More than 160,000 people were dead or injured. The warning leaflets had been all too correct.

12. Why did President Truman decide to use the atomic bomb?

13. What actions did he take to try to avoid using it?

When and why did Japan finally surrender?

Japan's leaders knew they were beaten, but they were afraid to tell their people the truth. They hoped that by threatening to fight to the bitter end, Japan would get better peace terms from the Allies.

Some Japanese cabinet members and the Emperor wanted peace. But the more powerful military leaders would not permit it.

Then a series of events which took place in quick succession forced the Japanese to lay down their arms.

Two days after the Hiroshima bombing, the Soviets declared war on Japan. They had promised to enter the war against Japan when the fighting in Europe was over. But they had delayed doing so from May to August 1945.

On August 9, a United States plane dropped a second and even more powerful atomic bomb on the Japanese city of Nagasaki.

At last the Japanese offered to surrender. They asked only that their Emperor be allowed to keep his throne. The Allies agreed, provided the Emperor followed the orders issued by Supreme Allied Commander Douglas MacArthur.

The final terms of surrender were signed on September 2, 1945. The ceremony was held on board the battleship *Missouri* anchored in Tokyo Bay.

President Truman, shown on a happier day in 1949, gave the order for use of the atomic bomb on August 6, 1945. One bomb was dropped on Hiroshima. A few days later another bomb was dropped on Nagasaki. The photograph above shows the ruins of Nagasaki after the bombing. Only one reinforced concrete school building still stands at the foot of the hills in the background. Everything else was blown away.

General MacArthur (left) watches as Japanese delegate Mamoru Shigemitsu signs the surrender. The ceremony was held aboard the *Missouri*, anchored in Tokyo Bay.

14. What two events finally forced Japan to surrender?

15. When and where did the surrender take place?

What were the material and human costs of victory?

World War II was the most far-flung and costly war in history. No one knows for sure what the conflict cost in money. The United States spent more than $330 billion. That was more than ten times the cost of World War I. Or to put it another way, the war cost Americans about a quarter of a billion dollars a day.

The material costs of the war fade when compared to its human costs. No one knows for sure just how many human beings perished. Perhaps as many as 60 million men, women, and children were lost. It is estimated that 18 million Soviets, 4 million Germans, 2 million Japanese, and possibly 22 million Chinese died as a result of the fighting. In addition, some 6 million Jews were killed in German concentration camps.

American losses were not as high as those suffered by other nations. Even so, there were close to 300,000 battle deaths.

The costs of World War II were staggering to all who were involved. But there was no doubt in anyone's mind that it was the power of the United States—material and human—which had made victory possible.

16. What did World War II cost the United States in money?

17. How many people died in World War II? How many Americans died in battle?

Part Four

The United Nations

How did the United States help organize the United Nations?

When World War II ended, the United States was the most powerful nation on earth. It had the greatest navy and air force and one of the two greatest armies in the world. The Soviet Union had the other.

The United States alone knew the secret of the atomic bomb. But all this power brought worldwide responsibilities. And none of those responsibilities was greater than that of trying to insure peace in the future. To do that the United States and its Allies agreed to found a new organization. It was to be called the United Nations. Planning for it began even before the war had ended.

In April 1945, 300 representatives of 50 nations met in San Francisco. They gathered just thirteen days after Roosevelt had died and Truman had become President. Outside the Opera House in San Francisco flags flew at half-mast. Inside the delegates began working out details. For the next two months they argued and they compromised. But at the end of the meeting, all fifty nations signed the charter of the United Nations.

The charter established two important bodies. One was the General Assembly. All member nations—large or small—had one vote in the Assembly, except the Soviet Union. The Soviet Union had three votes (one for Russia, one for Byelorussia, and one for the

Focus on Skills

Without the human and material resources which the United States poured into World War II, victory for the Allies would have been impossible. You can understand better just how great the American contributions to victory were through pictographs. Begin by examining the one shown below. Use the guide questions to help interpret it.

HOW HUMAN RESOURCES WERE USED TO MEET WAR DEMANDS

	Armed Forces	Munitions and Defense Work	Agriculture	Other Industries	Unemployed
1940	.5	4.9	9.5	33.0	8.1
1942	4.0	9.3	9.2	35.2	2.7
Dec. 1944	12.0	12.6	7.8	32.8	.5

(figure) = 2 million

How Human Resources Were Used to Meet War Demands

1. How many millions of Americans were in the armed forces in 1940? In 1944?
2. How great was the decline in agricultural workers between 1940 and 1944? Why do you think that decline occurred?
3. Compare the numbers of workers in "other industries" in 1940, 1942, and 1944. In which year were the smallest number employed in "other industries"? Why do you think that decline occurred?
4. Describe the trend in unemployment from 1940-1944. Why do you think it took place?

Now that you have become more experienced in the use of pictographs, see if you can make a simple one of your own. Use the title and figures below:

Number of Women in the Work Force in World War II

At the beginning of the war: 14 million
At the end of the war: 20 million

Ukraine.) This concession was made to get the Soviets to join.

The second important body was the Security Council. It consisted of eleven (later fifteen) members. Five nations were permanent members. In addition to the United States, they were China, France, the USSR, and Britain. The remaining ten were elected for two-year terms by the General Assembly. The Security Council's main job is peacekeeping. It can investigate disputes which threaten peace. It can and has sent UN troops to "police" trouble spots.

1. When and where was the United Nations born?

2. What are the two most important bodies in the UN?

How quickly did the United States join the United Nations?

The United States became the first official member of the United Nations. Just one month after the delegates finished their work in San Francisco, the UN charter came before the United States Senate for approval. Only two senators voted against it. Polls showed wide public support of the Senate's action. This was very different from the way the Senate had treated the League of Nations proposal after World War I.

When the Senate approved the UN charter, it invited the new world organization to make its permanent home in the United States. The invitation was accepted. John D. Rockefeller, Jr., gave the needed land. It lies along the East River in New York City. Famous architects and artists from many nations gave their talents to make the UN buildings among the loveliest in the world.

3. How did the Senate vote on the proposal to join the United Nations?

4. Who invited the United Nations to make its permanent home in the United States? Where is that home?

What has the United Nations accomplished?

It would be incorrect to say that all the hopes and dreams in the United Nations charter have come true. Like all organizations run by human beings, the United Nations is far from perfect. It has run into many problems trying to keep peace and improve life in the world. But it has also had its successes.

Through special committees and organizations the UN carries on activities to help people all over the world. For example, there are special UN agencies which assist children and refugees. The World Health Organization (WHO) fights disease. The Food and Agriculture Organization sends farming experts and machinery to needy nations. The International Court of Justice hears disputes. In 1980 the United States asked that Court for help in problems it was having with Iran. Iran had seized American citizens and refused to let them go home.

Every President since Truman—Republican or Democrat—has supported the United Nations and its efforts to bring peace and help people. That does not mean that American Presidents have not disagreed with some things the UN has done. But they believe that it is an important and worthwhile organization. They send ambassadors to the UN. Often they appear before the General Assembly in person to present the American side of a subject under debate.

5. How have special committees and agencies of the UN helped people?

6. What has been the attitude of American Presidents toward the UN?

Part Five

An Uneasy Peace Turns into a Cold War

Why did tensions rise between the United States and the USSR?

Americans and Russians had fought on the same side during World War II. The Soviets and the democratic Allies did not believe in the same things. But because they had a common enemy, they worked together.

When the Axis powers were defeated, however, the situation changed. Tensions rose because the Soviet Union failed to keep promises it had made to the Allies. Stalin had agreed that Poland and the other nations occupied by Soviet troops at the end of the war could hold free elections. But this promise was broken. Instead of letting the people in those countries choose their own leaders, the USSR made sure Communists came to power. It established a ring of "satellite" nations along its western border. (A *satellite* is a small body in space that revolves around a larger body.) Estonia, Latvia, and Lithuania, three small nations near the Baltic Sea, were totally swallowed up by the Soviet Union.

President Truman was very disturbed by the Soviets' actions. Just five months after the war ended, Truman wrote, "Unless Russia is faced with an iron fist and strong language, another war is in the making."

Winston Churchill, Britain's wartime leader, also was very disturbed. He came to the United States to make an important speech in Fulton, Missouri. Churchill said the Russians were bringing down an "iron curtain" across Europe. No outside news was allowed behind that curtain. Few people were allowed to come or go. As a result, Churchill said, Europe was being split into two parts. On one side of the iron curtain were democratic nations. On the other side were Russia and its satellites. Churchill said that the Soviet Union must not be allowed to extend its power any further. It must be stopped, or contained, at once. Truman agreed. So did most Americans. In the next months and years, the United States worked out a plan of foreign affairs called the *containment* policy.

1. What promise did the Soviets fail to keep?

2. What was the "iron curtain"? What was the containment policy?

Where was the containment policy first tested?

During World War II the Nazis occupied Greece. They treated the Greek people very cruelly. When the war was over, the Greek people had few jobs and little money. Their government was weak. A group of Communists threatened to take over in Greece. Only support from the British prevented the takeover. But in 1947 Britain said that it could no longer afford to help the Greek government. Nor could Britain afford to continue its help to Turkey.

When Truman heard that news, he decided that the United States must act. He believed that if communism were to be contained, neither Greece nor Turkey could be allowed to fall. So he went before Congress to ask for $400 million in military and economic aid for those endangered countries.

Earlier in our history, President Monroe had warned Europeans to keep "hands off" the western hemisphere. (See pages 186-188.) Now President Truman warned the Communists. The United States, he said, would help any nation in danger of falling under Communist control. That stand was called the Truman Doctrine.

The Truman Doctrine marked a real turning point in American foreign policy. As the President told Americans,

I believe that it must be the foreign policy of the United States to support free peoples. . . in maintaining their freedoms. If we falter [fail] in our leadership, we may endanger the peace of the world—and we shall surely endanger the welfare of our own nation.

Truman faced questions about his new doctrine from all sides. Many people said that the President should have gone to the United Nations. It was not right for the United States to act alone. Besides, they asked, suppose the Communists tried to take over a country that was neither "good" nor democratic. Should we help that country just because it was under Communist attack?

Other Americans worried more about their wallets. They said that the Truman Doctrine would cost the United States too much money.

Thoughtful Americans asked some key questions. What did the new doctrine mean? Did it mean fighting communism everywhere in the world? Would it lead to a third world war?

President Truman said that the United States should take on "limited responsibilities." Certainly communism could not be fought everywhere all over the globe. The United States would act only where there was hope of success.

Money to carry out the Truman Doctrine was approved by both houses of Congress. The President's stand set the pattern for American action against communism.

3. Why did the United States believe it had to act in Greece and Turkey?

4. Why did Truman face questions about the Truman Doctrine?

What was the Marshall Plan?

While the Truman Doctrine gave military help, the Marshall Plan promised economic aid. Secretary of State George Marshall drew up a plan for helping war-torn Europe to rebuild. Unless the millions of war victims were helped, they might turn to communism.

Sixteen European nations took advantage of the Marshall Plan. They used that helping hand to get back on their feet. These countries built factories, produced goods, and traded with each other until they were prosperous again.

By the end of 1949, Western European industries were producing more than they had when World War II started. Farm production increased. Secretary Marshall was right when he called the results a "near miracle."

The Soviets did not like the idea of the Marshall Plan. Nor were they happy with its success. They had been invited to join the plan when it began, but they refused. They would not let their satellites join either. A deep rivalry had grown up between the United States and the Soviet Union. So strong was that rivalry that a new name was used to describe it. It was called the *cold war.* There was no shooting, so it was not a "hot" war. But it was combat just the same.

5. What was the Marshall Plan?

6. What was the cold war?

Why did trouble develop over Germany?

The cold war heated up in 1948 over problems in Germany. At the end of World War II, Germany was divided into four parts, or zones. In the west were the British, French, and American zones. In the east was the Russian zone. The German capital, Berlin, was inside the Russian zone. Even so, that city was divided among the four powers. West Berlin was controlled by the United States, Britain, and France. East Berlin belonged to the Russians. So West Berlin was like an island in the midst of a Soviet sea. (See map, page 507.)

In 1948 the Western nations, led by the United States, announced that they were going to make their zones into a single unit. The Soviets were angry about that plan. It was only seven years since German troops had invaded their country. They feared that West Germany might become powerful and threaten them in the future.

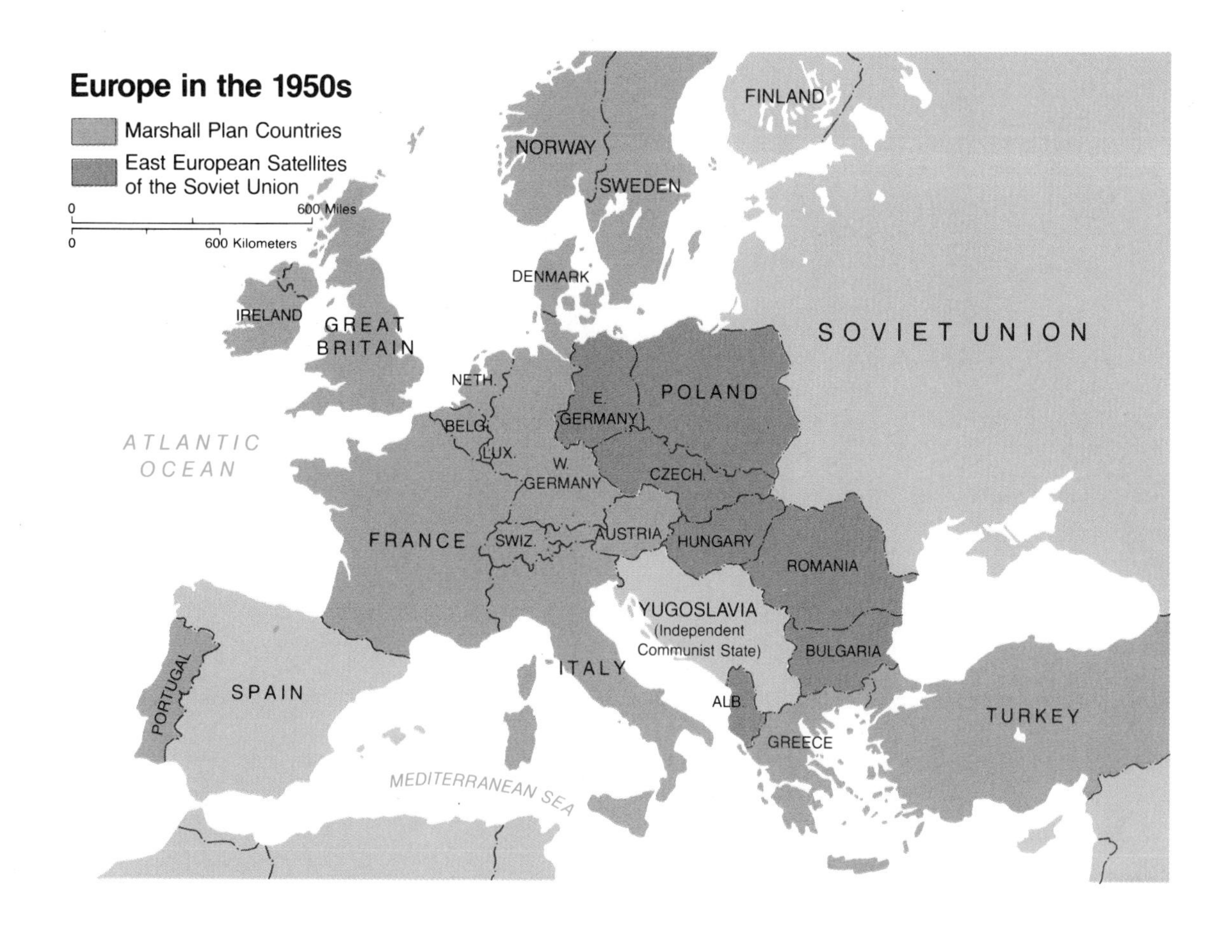

Stalin, still dictator of Russia, reacted quickly. On June 24, 1948, he ordered a blockade of Berlin. All highway, rail, and river traffic was to stop. No supplies were to reach that city from the West.

President Truman decided to meet the Russian challenge. He ordered cargo planes to fly into Berlin. Soon planes filled with food, fuel, medicine, and other supplies were landing every three minutes. The cargo planes continued to land for nearly a year.

Stalin was left with two choices. He could order the cargo planes shot down. But that would turn the cold war into a hot one. Stalin did not want that. Besides, the Soviet Union had not yet

When the Russians blockaded West Berlin in 1948-1949, the Western powers started an airlift.

recovered from its great losses in World War II. It was in no condition to fight. Stalin's other choice was to admit defeat and call off the blockade. He did not want to do that. But he stopped the blockade in June 1949.

When the blockade ended, Britain, France, and the United States went ahead with their plan to combine their zones. In September 1949, they formed the Federal Republic of Germany, or West Germany. The Soviets again responded quickly. They set up the German Democratic Republic, or East Germany. Thus Germany became two nations. It became a symbol of the cold war, the continuing rivalry between the East and West.

7. Why did the Soviets blockade Berlin? How did the United States respond to that blockade?

8. What happened to Germany after the blockade was lifted?

Why did the United States become part of NATO?

The Berlin blockade convinced the United States and Western European nations that they needed to stick together. So they formed NATO. Those four letters stand for North Atlantic Treaty Organization. NATO bound the United States, Canada, and ten European countries as allies. Later, when Greece, Turkey, and West Germany joined, membership in NATO numbered 15. (See map, page 510.)

NATO countries promised to help each other in case of attack. They said they would regard an attack on one member as an attack on all members.

In the cold war, NATO was a turning point as important as the Truman Doctrine. Never before had the United States made a military alliance during peacetime.

An American, General Dwight Eisenhower, was the first commander of NATO forces. Early in 1951 he went to Paris. There he set up what is called SHAPE, or the Supreme Headquarters, Allied Powers in Europe. In 1967, SHAPE headquarters were moved to Brussels, Belgium. The United States is still a member of NATO and looks on it as a chief part of its defense.

9. What is NATO and why was it formed?

10. Who was the first commander of NATO forces?

Part Six

The Korean War

How did the Korean War begin?

While Americans were concerned about the cold war in Europe, important events were taking place in Asia. One of the most important occurred in China in 1949.

For many years China suffered from a weak government and civil war. Many Chinese had become Communists. They fought the national government, or Nationalists. Under their leader, Mao Tse-tung, the Communists finally were able to crush the Nationalists and push them off the mainland. The Nationalists, led by Chiang Kai-shek, escaped to the island of Formosa, now called Taiwan.

Although the United States was not happy to see Communists come to power in China, no military action was taken.

When trouble came to Korea in June 1950, however, the United States immediately became involved.

During World War II, the Allies had agreed that Korea should be made an independent country when victory was won. After the Japanese surrendered, the Soviets occupied all of Korea north of the 38th parallel. American forces moved into the southern part. (See map, page 512.)

Instead of keeping their promise to make Korea one country, the Soviets acted as they had in Germany. They turned North Korea into an armed satellite. In the south, a free country, the Republic of Korea, was set up. The 38th parallel was the boundary between North Korea and South Korea.

President Truman was vacationing at his home in Missouri when he learned that the North Koreans had invaded South Korea. He immediately called on the United Nations to act. Truman said, "If this was allowed to go unchallenged, it would mean a third world war."

Without waiting for the UN, the President also sent American armed forces to help the South Koreans throw back the invaders. Later the UN called on its members to give all possible military aid to South Korea. The UN set

up an army. In time, nineteen nations sent troops or supplies for that army. But Americans made up four-fifths of the troops. American General Douglas MacArthur was given command.

1. When did the Communists take over in China?

2. How did President Truman respond to North Korea's invasion of South Korea?

3. What did the United Nations do?

Why did the United States settle for a "limited war" in Korea?

After a shaky start, the war went well. MacArthur and the UN troops cleared South Korea of Communist soldiers. Almost the entire enemy army was captured or destroyed. MacArthur said that he would unify Korea by occupying North Korea. Both the United Nations and President Truman agreed that MacArthur should advance north.

But a deadly surprise followed. Chinese "volunteer" troops were waiting for MacArthur's armies in the mountains of North Korea. MacArthur ordered his armies to "end the war." However, the Chinese were not about to be beaten. They sent a million soldiers into Korea. Sometimes the Chinese sacrificed thousands of soldiers in mass attacks.

The UN troops were forced to retreat. For a time it looked as though they would be pushed into the sea. In March 1951, the battle line stood where it had started—at the 38th parallel.

General Douglas MacArthur (above), brilliant leader of the army in the Pacific during World War II, headed the U. N. forces in Korea. Two American soldiers (left) bring mail to their unit in Korea via tank.

General MacArthur believed that the best way to win the war in Asia was to attack China. He wanted permission to bomb Manchurian bases and blockade the China coast. However, Truman's advisers were sure that MacArthur was wrong. If China were bombed, the Soviets would certainly come into the war. Europe would then be open to invasion by Russian troops. The danger of an atomic war loomed. General Omar Bradley said it would be "the wrong war, at the wrong place, at the wrong time, with the wrong enemy."

The United States decided to settle for a "limited war." It no longer insisted on a united Korea. It was willing to settle for two Koreas, with the 38th parallel as the dividing line.

4. Who was General MacArthur? What was his plan for winning the war?

5. Why was MacArthur's plan unacceptable to Truman's advisers?

Why did the President fire General MacArthur?

MacArthur did not like the President's decision about fighting a limited war. He wanted to win. General MacArthur criticized the President's decision. MacArthur was warned to stop making public statements. President Truman reminded him that the Constitution puts the President above any general. The President is Commander in Chief of all the armed forces.

MacArthur kept making critical remarks. Finally President Truman stripped MacArthur of his command. General Matthew Ridgeway was sent to replace him. Truman said, "I could do nothing else and still be President of the United States."

People were stunned. The firing of MacArthur was the most dramatic moment of the war. Telegrams by the thousands piled up at the White House. Most of them supported MacArthur.

President Truman's greatest torment came during the days that followed. MacArthur returned home to a hero's welcome. He was invited to speak before Congress. Parades were held in his honor.

At first there was much sympathy for the general. It looked as if he was being punished for doing what Americans like to do—win. But, as the people thought it over, they were not so sure. They wanted to win in Korea, but they did not want to get into a third world war. In the long run, the United States Senate and most historians agreed that Truman was right in limiting the war.

6. Why was Truman able to relieve MacArthur of his command? How did he feel about doing it?

7. How did people react to the firing of MacArthur at first? In the long run?

How and when was the Korean War finally settled?

In June 1951, a year after the invasion of South Korea, peace talks finally began. It was one thing to get the Communists to come to the peace table. It was quite another to get them to really make peace.

The "peace" talks dragged on all through 1952. While the Communists talked about peace, they continued the bloody fighting.

The peace talks deadlocked on the issue of North Korean prisoners of war. Many North Koreans had had their fill of communism. These prisoners wanted to stay in South Korea when the war was over. The United States insisted that no prisoners should be sent back against their will.

Peace talks were at a stalemate. It looked as though they might go on forever.

When Dwight Eisenhower ran for President in 1952, he promised that if he were elected he would go to Korea and settle the war. One month after Eisenhower was elected, he went to Korea. At last, in July 1953, the fighting stopped.

People wondered whether the Korean War was worth fighting. American losses were 35,000 soldiers killed and 103,000 wounded. There is no way of knowing how many hundreds of thousands of Red Chinese were killed.

Some people say that the price was too high for what the war accomplished. Korea is still divided at the 38th parallel. However, defenders of the war argue that all of Asia would have fallen to communism if the United States had not acted promptly.

8. Why did the peace talks drag on? How and when was the fighting finally stopped?

9. Why did Americans disagree about whether or not the Korean War was worth fighting?

Building Your Vocabulary

Match each item in Column A with the correct item in Column B.

Column A	Column B
1. A government which has complete or total control over the lives of people.	satellite
2. A "lightning war."	blitzkrieg
3. A powerful weapon made from uranium.	Fascist
4. Deep rivalry between nations which stops short of a shooting war.	cold war
5. Someone who believes people live only to serve the state and obey its orders.	containment
6. Name of a policy to stop the spread of communism.	totalitarian
7. A small nation which is dominated by a more powerful one.	atomic bomb

---

Recalling What You Have Learned

Choose the best answer for each of the following items.

1. The dictator who headed the Italian government in World War II was (a) Joseph Stalin. (b) Adolph Hitler. (c) Benito Mussolini.
2. Hitler's plans for the German *Reich* were contained in (a) his speeches to the United Nations. (b) letters to Franklin Roosevelt. (c) his book, *Mein Kampf*.
3. World War II began on September 1, 1939, when Germany invaded (a) Poland. (b) Czechoslovakia. (c) Korea.
4. Germany, Italy, and Japan were called (a) the Allied Powers. (b) the Axis Powers. (c) the Central Powers.
5. On D-Day, American and British forces invaded (a) Pearl Harbor. (b) Tokyo. (c) Normandy.
6. The Manhattan Project was (a) a secret plan for invading Japan. (b) a plan to rebuild war-torn Europe. (c) a secret operation to build an atomic bomb.
7. The permanent home of the United Nations is (a) Brussels. (b) New York City. (c) San Francisco.
8. NATO (a) carried out the Berlin blockade. (b) saved Greece and Turkey from becoming Communist nations. (c) was the first military alliance the United States ever made during peacetime.
9. The general whom President Truman relieved of command during the Korean War was (a) Douglas MacArthur. (b) Omar Bradley. (c) Dwight David Eisenhower.
10. The first atomic bomb was dropped on (a) Moscow. (b) Berlin. (c) Hiroshima.
11. The war in Korea finally ended (a) when Douglas MacArthur was sent back to lead the troops. (b) when the North Koreans surrendered. (c) when Eisenhower became President.

Improving Your Map Skills

World War II and the important events which followed it took place on a global scale. Some of those events were centered in Europe. Others took place in Asia. Show that you understand the sequence and location of those important events. The information you will need to complete the exercise is found on the maps in this chapter. Read the maps, map titles, and map keys carefully. On a separate sheet of paper, draw a chart like the one shown below. Select the event from the list at the right which matches each date. Write the name of that event beside the date and in the proper column by continent. The first two have been done for you. Some dates have two events.

Events

West Germany joins NATO

Greece joins NATO

Pearl Harbor bombing

Allies take Iwo Jima and Okinawa

Korean War begins

Atomic bomb dropped on Hiroshima

Berlin Wall is built

Korean War ends

D-Day

Battle for Midway

British stop Axis advance to Suez Canal

MAJOR EVENTS

Events in Europe	Events in Asia
1939 Germany invades Poland	1931 Japanese attack Manchuria
(answer found on map on page 484.)	(answer found on map on page 490.)
1942 ______	1941 ______
1944 ______	1942 ______
1952 ______	1945 ______
1954 ______	1950 ______
1961 ______	1953 ______

Discussing the Important Ideas in This Chapter

1. Why did many people outside Germany find Hitler's plans hard to believe? Why did the United States and other nations fail to take action against Hitler sooner?
2. Why did some Americans approve of Roosevelt's actions to help Britain? Why did some Americans disapprove?
3. How were the seeds of World War II planted in Asia?
4. Why did the Allies decide to defeat Germany first? When and how did the Allies defeat Japan?
5. Why did the use of the atomic bomb change the history of the world?
6. The United States refused to join the League of Nations in 1919, but it helped found the United Nations in 1945. How do you account for this change in attitude?

7. Why did a cold war develop between the United States and the USSR after World War II?

8. Harry Truman was a firm, positive President. He:

   a. sent troops to Korea "because if this was allowed to go unchallenged, it would mean a third world war."
   b. ordered atomic bombs dropped on Hiroshima and Nagasaki. He said, "Let there be no mistake about it. I regard the bomb as a military weapon and never had any doubt that it should be used . . . I made the decision."
   c. fired General MacArthur because "I could do nothing else and remain President of the United States."

Do you agree with Truman's actions? With his reasons?

Improving Your Study Skills: *Reading*

Earlier you learned that news stories contain what are called the five "w's." They tell the reader the who/what/when/where/ and why of any event. (See page 203.)

Below you will find a front-page news story which appeared in many American newspapers on Monday, December 8, 1941. It was written by reporters for INS, or International News Service. Read the story. Then write an answer to each of the questions below. Each question concerns one of the 5 w's.

SEVERE EXPLOSIONS ROCK PEARL HARBOR IN SURPRISE ATTACK

HONOLULU, Dec. 7.—(AP)—Japanese bombs killed at least five persons and injured many others, three seriously, in a surprise morning aerial attack on Honolulu today.

HONOLULU, Dec. 7—(INS)—America's outpost of the Pacific, mighty Pearl Harbor naval base was under enemy attack today.

A number of attacking planes, with red insignia were sighted shortly after 8 a.m.

(In Washington Presidential Secretary Early identified the attacking planes as Japanese.)

Antiaircraft guns opened fire when the planes dived low over the base and released repeated sticks of bombs.

Two warships lying in the harbor were sunk.

The planes later returned to the attack.

The attack was a complete surprise with minimum forces of the Army and Navy on Sunday morning duty.

A pall of heavy black smoke hung over Pearl Harbor.

Army intelligence said:

"Pearl Harbor was subjected to a sporadic air raid. We have no further details."

1. What happened?
2. When did it happen?
3. Where did it happen?
4. Who was involved?
5. This news story does not answer the question "why." Why do you think that question was not answered?

Chapter 20

Years of Change, Years of Challenge

The John F. Kennedy Memorial Library, Boston, Massachusetts

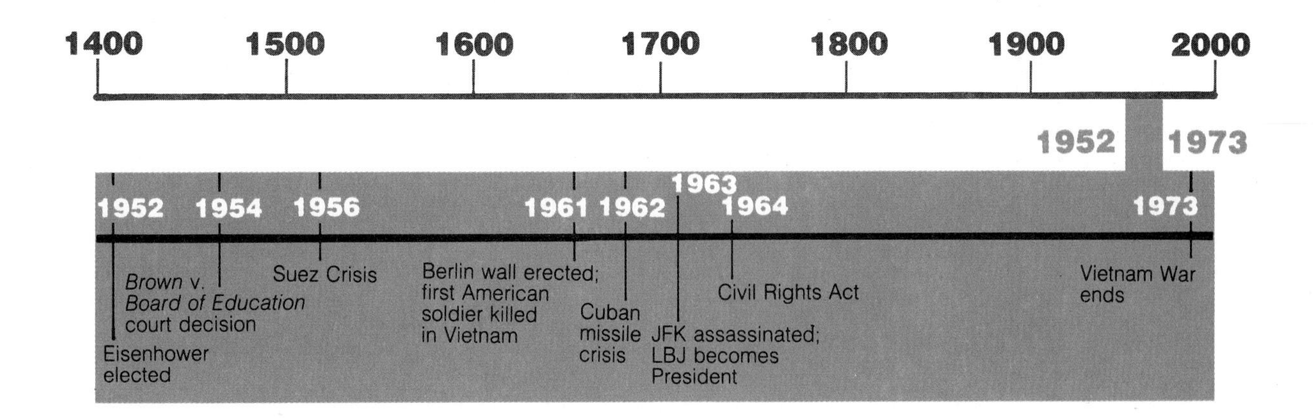

Part One

Changes and Challenges in the 1950s

Why did Americans elect Eisenhower?

By 1952, a presidential election year, Democrats had been in the White House for twenty years. Democrat Franklin Roosevelt had been elected in 1932, 1936, 1940, and 1944. When Roosevelt died, Vice-President Truman took office. Truman, of course, was also a Democrat. He was elected in his own right in 1948. Some people said that twenty years of one party was enough. They were afraid the two-party system was dying out.

In 1952 the Republicans coined a new slogan. They said, "It is time for a change." The Republicans felt they had just the candidate to make some changes—Dwight D. Eisenhower.

Eisenhower, nicknamed "Ike," was a popular hero, a World War II general. Ike had led the Allied invasion of Normandy. His famous grin and his record for service and honesty were known all over the world. Eisenhower was a career soldier. He had grown up on a farm in Kansas. After graduating from West Point, he rose quickly in rank.

Ike, shown here with paratroopers before D-Day, became as popular with voters as he had been with his soldiers.

During World War II, Ike was Supreme Allied Commander in Europe. When he retired from the army, he became president of Columbia University. Then President Truman asked him to return to Europe and serve as commander of NATO forces in Europe.

As a politician, Ike was strictly an amateur. To many Americans that was a point in his favor. Ike was very popular. Probably no presidential candidate since Washington had been better liked. Millions of Americans happily pinned on campaign buttons for Eisenhower in 1952 and again in 1956. The buttons bore just three words: "I Like Ike!" At the polls he won a landslide victory in 1952. Four years later he was reelected with even more votes. In both elections, Ike defeated Democrat Adlai Stevenson of Illinois.

During the 1930s and 1940s, Americans had faced two great challenges: the depression and World War II. They had been forced to make many changes. At the end of the war, Americans longed for a time of peace and plenty. Ike's friendly grin and promise to make government "smaller rather than bigger" made him the people's choice.

1. When was Eisenhower first elected President? When was he reelected?

2. Why did Americans choose Eisenhower to lead the nation in the 1950s?

How did Eisenhower function as President?

Like George Washington, Eisenhower wanted to keep out of the clash of politics. He wanted to bring a new "Era of Good Feelings" to his country. Eisenhower hoped to act like a judge or an umpire instead of a politician.

Unlike Franklin Roosevelt and Harry Truman, who loved a good fight, Eisenhower refused to get into public battles. He organized his White House office along the lines of a military staff. His aides were supposed to work out in detail several plans for what needed to be done. Those plans were brought to Eisenhower. Sometimes he chose the one he thought best. Sometimes he took parts from each of the plans brought to him. For that reason, many of Eisenhower's decisions were compromises.

Although Eisenhower was not an energetic leader, historians praise him as "a humanitarian and a man of peace." A *humanitarian* is a person who is concerned about all human beings.

Eisenhower showed his interest in people by completing the desegregation of the armed forces. He enforced the integration of schools. He helped refugees from communism find new homes in the United States.

Eisenhower also signed a bill passed by Congress that set up a new cabinet office. The Department of Health, Education, and Welfare was the first completely new department added to the President's cabinet in forty years. Oveta Culp Hobby of Texas was asked to be the first secretary of the new department. She had headed the Women's Army Corps (WAC) in World War II. Hobby became the second woman to serve in a presidential cabinet.

HEW was to oversee health programs, food and drug acts, welfare and education programs. It also administered the Social Security program. In 1979 the name of HEW was changed to the Department of Health and Human Services. At the same time, a separate Department of Education was set up.

Peace was very important to Eisenhower, a man who knew a great deal about war. So he worked to see that atomic energy was turned to peaceful uses. In a period of many international crises, he kept calm. Any impatience or carelessness on his part might have touched off an international disaster.

3. How did Eisenhower show that he was a humanitarian?

4. What was HEW? Who was its first head?

What was "McCarthyism"?

The 1950s had barely begun when a little-known senator from Wisconsin first made headlines. Senator Joseph McCarthy made a speech in Wheeling, West Virginia, on February 9, 1950. He told his audience that he was worried about the spread of communism, not only in the world, but in the United States. He hinted that many Americans in high offices were disloyal. McCarthy ended his speech by waving a piece of paper. He claimed that on that paper were listed the names of Communists working in the State Department.

McCarthy quickly became the most well-known person in the Senate. He repeated his charges over and over. A Senate investigation led by Millard Tydings of Maryland found that McCarthy's charges about the State Department were not true. McCarthy became angry. He worked against Tydings in the next election. Tydings lost, as did several others who opposed McCarthy.

McCarthy never proved his charges. Instead, he went on to accuse others of being Communists. He questioned the loyalty of many government officials. He went so far as to question the loyalty of George Marshall and even that of President Truman.

At first some people thought McCarthy was pointing out real dangers to the nation. They did not like his methods, but they did not stand up against him. Just to be accused by McCarthy was enough to ruin a reputation and a career.

One person who did speak out against McCarthy was Senator Margaret Chase Smith of Maine. She had been a representative for 24 years. But she had been a senator only two years when she tangled with McCarthy. In June 1950, she made her first major speech to the Senate. Looking directly at McCarthy she said:

> **I would like to speak briefly and simply about a serious national condition. It . . . could result in . . . the end of everything that we Americans hold dear. . . .**

Then she reminded her listeners that the Constitution "speaks not only of freedom of speech but also of trial by jury instead of trial by accusation."

When Smith finished speaking, McCarthy strode out angrily. During the next several years he tried to get even with her in a number of ways. But he was unsuccessful.

Finally McCarthy destroyed himself. In 1954 he said the United States Army was under Communist influence. Public hearings were held in response to those charges. The hearings were televised. Americans then had a chance to see McCarthy for themselves. They were shocked at his behavior. They disapproved of his total disregard for people's constitutional rights. McCarthy was exposed as a rude bully. Finally the Senate voted to condemn him for conduct unbecoming to a government leader. The people of Wisconsin rejected him at the polls, and he disappeared from view.

One thing remains of McCarthy. It is a new word which was added to the English language. That word is *McCarthyism.* It means accusing someone without having evidence.

5. Who was Joseph McCarthy?
6. What is McCarthyism?

Who were key leaders in the drive for civil rights?

Civil rights are the rights of all Americans to vote and have a fair trial. They include the right to attend public schools and use public facilities. Civil rights mean the chance to live in any neighborhood one can afford. They provide the right to compete for jobs on an equal basis with other citizens. During the 1950s the efforts to obtain full civil rights for blacks were stepped up.

Many organizations and individuals were involved in these efforts. Two were in the forefront, however. They were Earl Warren, Chief Justice of the Supreme Court, and Dr. Martin Luther King, Jr., a black minister from Atlanta, Georgia.

Warren headed the Supreme Court for sixteen years, from 1953 to 1969. The single most important civil rights decision of the Warren Court came in 1954.

The decision involved separate schools for black students. Many students went to schools which were segregated according to race. Just after Warren became Chief Justice, the Court was asked to decide whether segregated schools were legal. The case was called *Brown* v. *Board of Education of Topeka, Kansas.*

In a unanimous decision, the Warren Court struck down that practice. The Court said that it was unconstitutional to make students attend separate schools. In the future, it said, blacks and whites should attend the same schools. The justices said that separate schools for blacks usually were not as good as schools for whites. Blacks, therefore, had been denied the "equal protection" guaranteed them by the Constitution.

Many school districts quietly complied with the law. But trouble broke out in Arkansas. Governor Orval Faubus refused to allow nine black students to attend Central High School in Little Rock, the capital of Arkansas.

President Eisenhower could not allow a federal law to be disobeyed. He sent troops to Little Rock with orders to escort the black students into Central High. The governor then closed all of the public schools in Little Rock. For more than a year their doors remained

President Eisenhower ordered 1000 paratroopers to insure the peaceful opening of Little Rock High School on September 25, 1957. The paratroopers did their job, but in 1958 Governor Faubus closed Little Rock schools for an entire year.

shut. Finally, the Board of Education forced them to reopen. From then on blacks and whites attended school together in Little Rock.

Schools were not the only places in which the races were separated. In the 1950s some cities had laws which required blacks to ride in special sections of busses. If busses were crowded, blacks were expected to give up their seats to whites. But in 1955, Rosa Parks, a black woman on her way home from work in Montgomery, Alabama, refused to give up her seat. She was arrested. Her arrest touched off the Montgomery bus boycott. One of the world's most famous civil rights leaders got his start through the struggle to free Rosa Parks. He was Dr. Martin Luther King, Jr., then just a 27-year-old minister unknown to most Americans.

King asked blacks to refuse to ride busses until the laws were changed. For over a year blacks in Montgomery walked or carpooled or stayed home. They did not ride busses. The boycott dragged on and on. The bus company almost went bankrupt. The stores in Montgomery were losing money because their black customers did not ride the busses to go shopping. Finally, Dr. King and 100 other black leaders were arrested for supporting the boycott. But that did not stop them.

King asked his followers to continue the boycott no matter how many leaders went to jail. He said the struggle was not between whites and blacks, but "between justice and injustice." He urged his followers not to use violence. "Don't ever let anyone pull you so low as to hate them," King warned.

The bus boycott went on until the case reached the Supreme Court in 1956. There the justices ruled that segregated busses were illegal.

At the beginning of the Montgomery boycott, King was unknown. By the end of the boycott he was known all over the world for his leadership.

For many who had thought civil rights were not their concern, Little Rock and Montgomery were turning points. Blacks and whites in increasing numbers joined the struggle for civil rights for all Americans.

7. Who was Earl Warren?

8. Who led the Montgomery bus boycott?

How did the United States respond to challenges from abroad?

While Americans were challenging laws which they believed violated their civil rights, the United States government was responding to challenges in other parts of the world.

In 1956 there was a revolt in Hungary against Soviet-backed Communist rule. Hungarians appealed to the United States for help in their revolt. Some Americans thought the United States should go to their aid. But President Eisenhower disagreed. He said that while Americans sympathized with any people who longed to be free, the United States could not give the Hungarians military aid. Eisenhower did not want to risk a major war with Russia. Soviet troops moved in to crush the revolt. About 200,000 Hungarians fled their homeland. Many of them asked for asylum, or protection, in the United States. They were given asylum.

In that same year another serious problem developed in the Middle East. It concerned the Suez Canal, a vital shipping route. (See map, page 494.) The Suez Canal is in Egypt, but it was built and owned by Britain and France. The President of Egypt, Gamal Abdel Nasser, wanted to build a high dam on the Nile River. Egypt could not pay for the dam. So Nasser tried to get money from all sides—from the Russians, the British, and the Americans. The United States Secretary of State, John Foster Dulles, became angry at what he thought was double-dealing. He withdrew the American offer of money to help build the dam. Britain also withdrew its offer. So Nasser took the Suez Canal by force. He said he would use the tolls which ships paid to use the canal to build the dam.

There was great gloom in Britain and France. Oil for their automobiles and industries came through the Suez Canal. The oil was desperately needed.

Another nation, Israel, also was interested in the canal. Israel was a new country, born in 1948. It was set up in Palestine as a homeland for Jews. Israel was formed to give survivors of concentration camps and other Jews a chance to build new lives. But Egypt and other Arab countries in the Middle East objected to Israel. They said it had been carved out of lands which rightly belonged to Arabs. Nasser said he would destroy Israel. He constantly sent troops on raids into Israel.

Then Israel launched an attack on Egypt. Britain and France joined Israel two days later. They did not tell the United States of their plans. Soon Israel's better equipped and better trained troops reached the banks of the canal. Israel claimed some of the land its troops had crossed.

President Eisenhower was angry about the invasion of Egypt. He went on radio and television to tell the world why. The United States, he said, did not believe that any country had the right to invade another. Not even friends of the United States such as Britain, France, and Israel could be allowed to take such actions.

Nikita Khrushchev, the premier of the Soviet Union, threatened to send troops to help Egypt. He also threatened to attack London and Paris.

The UN took action in the Suez crisis. It called for a cease-fire. Finally, Britain, France, and Israel withdrew.

Egypt kept control of the canal, but it agreed that ships of all nations, except Israel, could use it. UN troops arrived to keep the peace.

9. Why did a crisis develop over the Suez Canal? How did the United States respond to it?

How successful was the Geneva summit conference?

Eisenhower tried to find some way to insure peace in the world. Each time a crisis developed, the danger of an atomic war loomed over the world. Ike proposed a "summit conference" of heads of state to meet at Geneva, Switzerland, in 1955.

At the meeting, Eisenhower suggested that the Soviet Union and the United States should stop arming for war. The two nations should exchange information about all of their military installations. There should be "open skies" above both the United States and Russia. This meant that each country could send airplanes on inspection flights over the other's territory. In that way, no military secrets could be hidden.

Nothing came of Eisenhower's "open skies" proposal. The Geneva conference bogged down with no agreements made. However, the leaders were polite and even friendly to each other.

After the summit, more crises occurred. In the Middle East, Jordan, Lebanon, and Iraq were the scenes of trouble in 1958. Also in 1958 the Chinese Communists began to shell the islands of Quemoy and Matsu near Taiwan. Taiwan was the home of the republican government of Chiang Kai-shek. The United States sent ships to patrol the Straits of Formosa to protect Taiwan. Next, the Soviets called for the Western powers to leave West Berlin. Each of these crises passed without a showdown—without an atomic war.

10. What proposals did Eisenhower make to the Soviets?

11. In what other nations did crises occur in the 1950s?

Why was the 1960 summit meeting cancelled?

President Eisenhower did not stop his efforts to improve relations with the Soviets. In 1959 he invited Khrushchev to come to the United States for a visit. People were surprised when Khrushchev accepted.

The Soviet leader traveled all over the United States. He ate hot dogs, walked in cornfields and on city streets, and spoke to ordinary American farmers and workers.

Later in that same year, Vice-President Nixon was asked to visit Russia. Eisenhower was invited to Russia the following year. But before he could go, the Soviets slammed the door in his face.

Eisenhower and Khrushchev walk past an honor guard shortly after the Soviet leader's arrival in the U.S.

Many Americans moved to the suburbs in the 1950s. This photograph is of moving day in Lakewood, California.

Another summit meeting was due to begin in Paris in 1960 when something unexpected happened. An American spy plane was shot down over the Soviet Union. The plane was a U-2, able to fly at great heights. The pilot was unharmed but was sent to a Russian jail.

Khrushchev was furious over the spying mission. He demanded an apology from Eisenhower and a promise that there would be no more such flights. Eisenhower agreed to stop the flights. But he refused to apologize. The angry Soviet leader then cancelled the summit meeting and Ike's visit. Russian-American relations hit a new low.

12. Why was Eisenhower's visit to Russia cancelled?

13. What did Eisenhower do when the U-2 plane was shot down?

What changes did the 1950s bring to Americans' life-styles?

Life for Americans in the 1950s was not completely taken up with national and international problems. Americans devoted time and energy to changing their own lifestyles.

One of the first changes many Americans made—and liked—was to become great consumers. During the depression most Americans could not afford the things they needed, let alone the luxuries they wanted. During World War II, they could not buy goods even though they could afford them. Factories were busy turning out tanks and guns. Neither time nor material could be spared for items such as record players, baby buggies, or nylon stockings. So in the 1950s demand for such consumer goods was high. People in the growing middle class were eager to spend their paychecks. Americans bought more than six million television sets every year during the 1950s. They also bought automobiles. Between 1945 and 1960 there was a 135 percent increase in the number of motor vehicles registered.

Americans used their new cars to commute from their new homes in the suburbs to their jobs in cities. In 1950, 35 percent of the population lived in central cities while 27 percent lived in suburbs. Growing suburbs changed many central cities. As middle-class white families moved out of cities, blacks

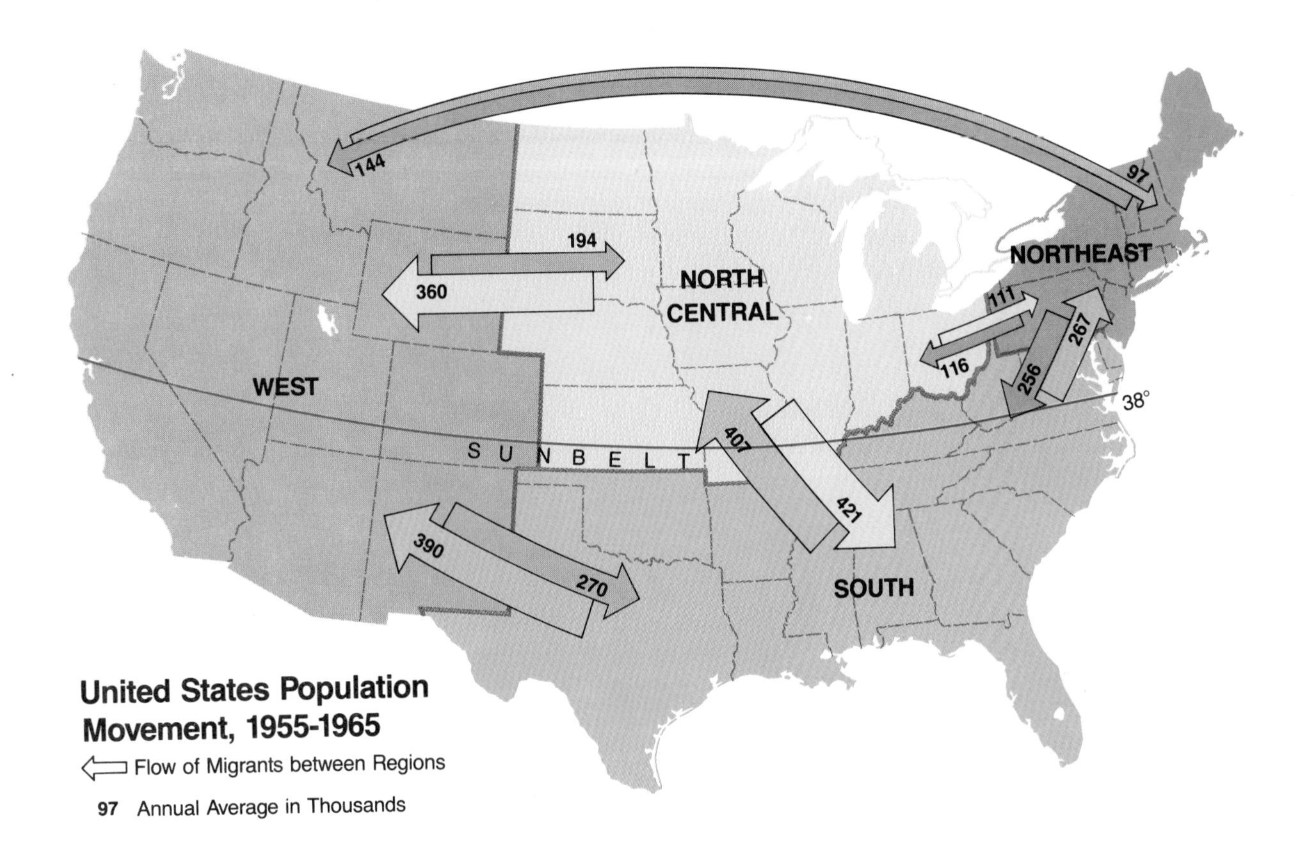

United States Population Movement, 1955-1965

moved in. Take Washington, D.C., for example. In 1940 its population was 72 percent white. By 1960 its population was more than 50 percent black. Other cities experienced similar shifts in population. There were sudden surges in black population in Atlanta, Georgia; Chicago, Illinois; Gary, Indiana; Detroit, Michigan; and Oakland, California.

Not all of the population shifts of the 1950s were from city to suburb, however. Americans often moved from one state or region to another. They moved in great numbers into the states which sometimes are called the "sunbelt." The sunbelt covers the southern part of the United States from southern Virginia in the East to southern California in the West. After World War II, the South and West drew people with job opportunities in aerospace, plastics, and computer industries. The warmer climate of those areas was also a drawing card. Many people, tired of hard winters, went to live year-round in Florida and Arizona. Many other Americans headed for California. By 1964 California had the largest population of any state in the country. Fully half of the residents of the Far West were newcomers from other sections of the United States.

14. Why did Americans become great consumers during the 1950s?

15. How did the shift to the suburbs affect the character of many cities? How did the movement west affect California?

Focus on Skills

Americans were on the move during the decade 1955 to 1965 as the map on page 527 makes clear. To understand where they went, analyze the map. Use these guide questions as aids to your understanding.

1. Name the four major regions of the United States which this map shows.
2. Notice the arrows shown on the map. Consult the key in the lower left corner. What do the arrows indicate? What do the colors of the arrows tell you?
3. Look at the South. Add the figures shown on the green arrows. That sum is the number of people in thousands who left the South yearly during the years 1955-1965.
4. Now examine the arrows which show people moving into the South during 1955-1965. Did more people leave or move to the South during that decade?
5. How many thousands of people left the West during the years 1955-1965? How many moved to the West?
6. Did the North Central region gain or lose population through migration?
7. Did the Northeast region gain or lose population?
8. Which region of the United States shown on this map experienced the greatest increase in population through migration between 1955 and 1965?

Part Two

The New Frontier

Why were voters attracted to John F. Kennedy?

Eisenhower was ready to leave the White House in 1960 after two terms as President. If the 22nd Amendment had not been ratified in 1951, he could probably have won a third term. (See page 614.) After heated primaries, the Republicans chose Vice-President Richard M. Nixon as their candidate. The Democrats chose John F. Kennedy, senator from Massachusetts.

The Kennedy-Nixon campaign featured a series of "great debates." The debates were the first between presidential candidates to be televised. Seventy million Americans watched each of the four one-hour clashes. This was the largest audience ever for a political discussion.

At the start of the debates, Nixon seemed to have the advantage. As Vice-President, Nixon was the better known of the two candidates. He had more experience at the top level of government. Time and again he reminded viewers of just how experienced he was. But Kennedy proved that he knew more about television than Nixon. Kennedy came across well to viewers. While Nixon was somber, Kennedy flashed his great smile. He was handsome, well-dressed, and at ease. Kennedy not only fielded questions well, he held out a new vision of the future to his fellow Americans.

Kennedy faulted Nixon for being satisfied with the country's record of achievements. "I say we can do better," he cried. "Let's get the country moving again. . . . We stand today on the edge of a new frontier—the frontier of the 1960s."

Kennedy pointed to unsolved problems at home and to challenges from abroad. Crowded cities had many troubles. Economic growth had slowed. Blacks and other minorities were not getting their fair share of the nation's wealth. The arms race was a worry. And in Cuba—almost next door—a new dictator with Soviet backing had taken power. Kennedy said that if he were elected, he would tackle those problems.

Kennedy was personally attractive to many Americans. He came from a very wealthy family in Massachusetts. He did not need to work, but he wanted to serve his country. His bravery had been tested in battle. During World War II, Kennedy had served in the United States Navy. When the PT boat he commanded was torpedoed, he tried to rescue his men. In the attempt, he suffered a serious back injury. It caused him pain for the rest of his life, but he endured it without complaint. He went right on with his work. One of his books, *Profiles in Courage*, won the Pulitzer Prize.

Kennedy was a Roman Catholic. Many people thought a Roman Catholic could not be elected President. But the issue of religion played a very small role in the election.

John Kennedy swung many voters to his side during the "great debates." He handled television better than Richard Nixon.

Kennedy seemed to have a vision of a greater, better America. He proposed new government programs which were something like the New Deal. But he called his program the New Frontier.

1. Why was John Kennedy an appealing candidate?

2. What was the New Frontier?

How successful was Kennedy in getting the country "moving again"?

The 1960 election was one of the closest in American history. Out of nearly 70 million ballots, Kennedy received only 118,000 more than Nixon. That was less than a majority of the total popular vote. But Kennedy got 303 electoral votes to Nixon's 219. So Kennedy, or "JFK," as he was called, was the new President.

After his election, Kennedy tried to find "the best and the brightest" people to help him on the New Frontier. One of those to whom he turned was Robert McNamara. He asked McNamara to be Secretary of Defense. As president of the Ford Motor Company, McNamara had been so successful that he was called a "whiz kid." Another of "the best and the brightest" to whom JFK turned was Arthur Goldberg. He asked Goldberg to be Secretary of Labor.

John Kennedy and his wife Jacqueline brought youth and glamour to the White House. Beside them at the Inaugural Ball are John's parents, Joseph and Rose Kennedy, and Lyndon and Lady Bird Johnson.

One appointment caused a great deal of surprise. JFK made history by choosing his brother, Robert, to be Attorney General. JFK brushed aside suggestions that it was improper to name a member of one's family to a cabinet post. The two brothers were very close. "Bobby" had managed the President's campaign.

Getting the country moving again proved to be harder than Kennedy thought it would be. Even with help from members of his cabinet, he could not get Congress to follow his lead. He was able to get only a few of the laws he wanted passed. One such law raised the minimum wage from $1.00 to $1.25 an hour. Another gave aid to "depressed" areas, or parts of the country where unemployment was high. The Senate also approved a nuclear test ban treaty.

On the other hand, Kennedy was turned down when he asked for a Department of Urban Affairs to deal with city problems. His bills to give federal aid to education and medical aid to the elderly were defeated. JFK's plans for tax cuts were also defeated.

3. Who were three of the "best and the brightest" people Kennedy named to his cabinet? Why was one of those appointments controversial?

4. What Kennedy programs did Congress turn down?

What new demands were made for civil rights?

During the time Kennedy was President, blacks pressed strongly for their civil rights. Kennedy declared that "race has no place in American life or law." To prove he meant what he said, Kennedy appointed more blacks to important federal jobs. And he gave protection to those whose civil rights were being violated. One important instance was in the case of James Meredith.

Meredith was the son of a Mississippi farmer. After several years of service in the United States Army, he applied for entrance to the University of Mississippi. But he was refused admission because he was black. A court ordered that Meredith be admitted. But the governor of Mississippi blocked his admission. Finally, Meredith registered for the University. Riots broke out. There were deaths and injuries.

JFK ordered federal troops to Oxford, Mississippi, in October 1962. They were told to protect Meredith at the University.

Federal marshalls had to follow Meredith around the campus and in the classrooms until he graduated. But Meredith's courage, plus the protection he received, helped break the race barrier in southern universities.

Blacks were glad about that victory, but they were not satisfied. They were determined to make increased efforts to obtain full civil rights in 1963. It was a special year. It marked the 100th birthday of the Emancipation Proclamation. (See pages 295-296.) When blacks looked at what had been accomplished in those 100 years, they were not satisfied. As Dr. Martin Luther King, Jr., put it, "In 1963 there arose a great . . . disappointment, and disillusionment, and discontent."

To draw attention to that discontent, King and other leaders, black and white, staged a March on Washington in the summer of 1963. More than 200,000 Americans of all ethnic groups joined in the largest peaceful demonstration in the history of the nation.

At a rally in front of the Lincoln Memorial, the leaders called for action. But it was Martin Luther King, Jr., who best expressed the hopes of everyone present. He said:

> **I have a dream that my four little children will one day live in a nation where they will not be judged by the color of their skin, but by the content of their character.**

Martin Luther King, Jr., "I Have a Dream," *New York Times*, August 29, 1963, p. 17.

Following that demonstration, Kennedy sent a special civil rights bill to Congress. The President said:

> **Surely in 1963, one hundred years after Emancipation, it should not be necessary for any American citizen to demonstrate in the streets for the opportunity to stop at a hotel, or eat at a lunch counter, . . . or enter a motion picture house on the same terms as any other customer.**

But Congress did not act on the civil rights bill right away. Sharp debate continued for eight months. During that time President Kennedy was assassinated. It remained for JFK's successor, Lyndon Johnson, to push the bill through. Later we shall read about how he did that in 1964.

5. What did Kennedy do when James Meredith was denied entrance to the University of Mississippi?

6. What was the March on Washington? How did it trigger a new civil rights bill?

How did the United States offer to assist other nations?

When he took office, Kennedy promised help to "those people in the huts and villages of half the globe struggling to break the bonds of mass misery." He said the United States wanted them to "cast off the chains of poverty." To help them do that, his administration launched two new programs:

1. **The Peace Corps.** Kennedy asked Americans to volunteer to be teachers, farm advisers, librarians, engineers, nurses, and doctors in nations which needed their help. Thousands of Americans—young and old—responded. The first group went to the new

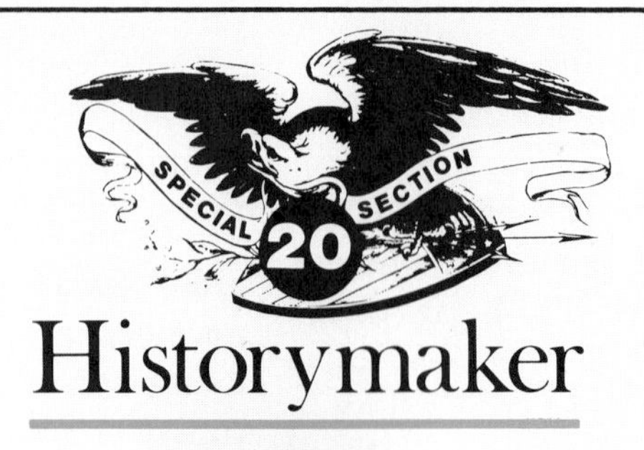

Historymaker

Martin Luther King, Jr.

Martin Luther King, Jr., had no trouble defining courage. According to King, people with courage are those who can stand up for their rights without hitting back.

Certainly King did not believe in ignoring wrongs and injustices. But he did not believe in using violence to correct them either. Instead he urged his followers to use love. Love is so powerful, he insisted, that it can overcome all obstacles. But he was quick to add: "When I speak of love, I am not speaking of some sentimental . . . response which is little more than emotional bosh." King said love was a force, the key to the solution of the problems of the world.

King became America's greatest "apostle," or messenger, of nonviolence. Yet he and his family often were the targets of violence. King was stabbed in New York City. He was stoned in Chicago. He was imprisoned twelve times. His wife and children were threatened. His house was bombed. Finally King's life was cut short by violence. A rifleman lying in wait outside a Memphis, Tennessee, motel shot and killed him on the night of April 4, 1968. King had not yet celebrated his 40th birthday. But he had made his mark on history. As one historian puts it, King was "a giant who strode across our cultural and intellectual and political horizons."

Dr. King was not born to greatness. He began life on January 15, 1929, in Atlanta, Georgia, the son of one Baptist minister and the grandson of another. His other grandfather was a sharecropper.

Martin Luther King, Jr., was a keen student. He won one scholarship after another. First he went to Morehouse College in Atlanta. He graduated when he was just 15 years old. He finished graduate school in Boston in 1953. That year he married Coretta Scott of Marion, Alabama. She was a gifted singer who shared King's ideals. She became a partner in the struggles for civil rights and peace which he was soon to lead.

The Kings returned to the South in 1955. Dr. King became a pastor in Montgomery, Alabama. But he did not remain a quiet pastor for long. Blacks could not use the same drinking fountains, restrooms, swimming pools, or waiting rooms which whites used. Neither could they sit in the same sections of movie theaters or lunch counters. They could not stay at the same hotels. If busses were crowded, they were expected to give up their seats to white passengers. King considered all those restrictions degrading and un-American. So he decided to do something about them. He would bring change by using the great force of love.

In 1955, Rosa Parks was arrested when she refused to surrender her seat on a bus to a white man. Dr. King was upset when he learned what had happened to Rosa Parks. He said that a law which did not apply equally to blacks and whites was unjust, and it should not be obeyed. Dr. King had a chance to test his ideas about bringing change by nonviolent means. He urged the 50,000 blacks who lived in Montgomery to join him in protesting that unjust law by refusing to ride the busses. And for about a year they did. During that time, Dr. King organized voluntary car pools, kept the spirits of the protesters high, and held weekly meetings at churches to instruct people in nonviolent resistance. Finally the bus company had to give in. It promised equal treatment for black customers.

Because he had led the black people of Montgomery to victory, Dr. King was famous. He was asked to head the Southern Christian Leadership Conference (SCLC) and to plan other rights campaigns.

King's next challenge came in Alabama. Blacks made up 50 percent of the population of that state, but in 1965 they were only 1 percent of the voters. When blacks went to register they were forced to wait in long lines. They had to take special tests. And sometimes no one ever appeared to register them. Blacks who did manage to register were often threatened if they dared go to the polls.

So King organized a march, a second big test of his belief in nonviolence and in the power of love. The march was to begin in Selma, Alabama, on March 7, 1965. Protesters were to walk together to the state capital, Montgomery, some 54 miles (86 km) away. They would take their case publicly and directly to the governor and the members of the state legislature. But the marchers had scarcely started when they were brutally turned back. State police used tear gas, clubs, and whips to stop them.

Most Americans, many of whom saw the march on television, were shocked by the turn of events in Selma. President Lyndon B. Johnson went before Congress. In a nationally televised speech Johnson said:

> **At times history and fate meet at a single time in a single place to shape a turning point in [the] unending search for freedom. So it was last week in Selma, Alabama. . . .**
>
> **There is no part of America where the promise of equality has been fully kept. In Buffalo as well as in Birmingham, in Philadelphia as well as in Selma, Americans are struggling for the fruits of freedom.**

President Johnson promised Dr. King and his followers federal protection for another march. It was to begin March 21. People from every state arrived in Selma. Then 25,000 strong—blacks and whites—they made their way peacefully to Montgomery. The eyes of the world were on that citizens' parade. And in the end it spelled victory. Blacks were allowed to register and to vote on the same terms as their white neighbors.

King was awarded the Nobel Peace Prize in 1964. When he accepted the prize in Stockholm, Sweden, King gave a moving speech. He expressed his hope for a world in which the force of love keeps the peace:

> **. . . We have inherited a big house, a great "world house" in which we have to live together—black and white, easterners and westerners, gentiles and Jews, Catholics and Protestants, Moslem and Hindu. . . . Because we can never again live without each other, [we] must learn, somehow, in this one big world to live with each other.**

Martin Luther King, Jr., "Nobel Lecture and Speech" (Stockholm: The Nobel Foundation, 1964).

A Peace Corps volunteer (left) teaches surveying in Sierra Leone. People of all ages joined the Peace Corps.

African nation of Ghana. In time Peace Corps volunteers were at work in more than fifty nations in Asia, Africa, and South America.

Some historians believe that Kennedy's place in history may very well rest on the Peace Corps. They say it was a great unselfish undertaking, unmatched in history. Others are less sure of its success. They doubt the wisdom of sending idealistic Americans to work among people about whom they really know very little. But while the arguments among historians continue about the worth of the Peace Corps, the program still continues. Today many American women and men of all ages continue to volunteer their services abroad.

2. **The Alliance for Progress.** This plan was supposed to do for South America what the Marshall Plan did for Europe. (See page 508.) While the Alliance enjoyed some success, it did not accomplish the near miracles of the Marshall Plan.

The Alliance for Progress called for giving $20 billion over ten years to member nations. With the money, those nations were supposed to provide schools, hospitals, housing, and land for the poor. The United States believed peaceful changes were needed in South America. Otherwise there might be violent revolutions. Communists could come to power. Through the Alliance for Progress it was hoped that needed changes could be brought about. But few reforms were ever made.

7. What is the Peace Corps?
8. What was the Alliance for Progress supposed to do?

What events abroad demanded attention?

While he was President, JFK had to cope with three important events abroad. They overshadowed events at home.

1. The Bay of Pigs disaster. Not long after Kennedy took office, he learned that a number of Cuban refugees were planning to drive Fidel Castro from power in their homeland. Castro had become dictator in Cuba in 1959. He promised the Cubans peace and plenty. Things started out well. He gave land to farmers, built new houses, and opened schools. But he also took over the newspapers and the radio stations. He shut off free speech and refused to hold elections. Hundreds of people were put to death after unfair trials.

The United States was not happy about Castro's actions. Kennedy agreed to give money and arms to the Cubans who planned to overthrow Castro. But he did not give them air support or military personnel.

When 1500 Cubans sailed from Florida and Central America on April 17, 1961, they expected the Cuban people to rise up against Castro. The invasion at the Bay of Pigs (Bahía de Cochinos) on the Cuban coast was a complete failure. The uprising by the people never came. The small force of refugees was no match for Castro's army. After three days the attackers had to surrender.

Castro was angry about the Bay of Pigs affair. He accused Americans of "cowardly aggression." He said that none of the 1200 captured prisoners would be released unless the United States paid a ransom.

President Kennedy accepted blame for the invasion. Later he said he was sorry he had permitted the attack. American citizens collected $53 million. It was sent to Castro in exchange for the prisoners.

2. The Cuban missile crisis. Not long after the Bay of Pigs disaster, Kennedy received disturbing news. American pilots had taken photos showing that the Soviets had set up missiles in Cuba. These missiles were capable of carrying nuclear bombs to important targets in the western hemisphere. They were powerful enough to destroy many of America's largest cities.

Kennedy and his advisers met in secret for several days. Then the President spoke to the world on radio and television. "This secret, swift buildup of

"I've Changed My Mind—Let's Argue on the Bench!"

Communist missiles . . . cannot be accepted by this country," he declared.

To make sure his words were believed, Kennedy readied air and ground forces for action. He sent more troops to Guantanamo Naval Base. American ships were sent to blockade Cuba. Russian ships bringing more missiles to Cuba were to be turned back.

A tense world waited for the next six days. Soviet ships kept on steaming toward Cuba. Work on the missile bases went on. Then suddenly Khrushchev backed down. He sent word from Moscow that he had ordered the Cubans to ship the missiles back to the Soviet Union. In exchange the United States agreed to end the blockade. It promised not to invade Cuba. The crisis was over.

3. The Berlin Wall. President Kennedy had other problems besides those in Cuba. The Soviets interfered with American troop movements to and from West Berlin. There were several ugly incidents. Russia demanded that the Americans get out of Berlin and recognize East Germany.

At That Time

Astronaut Edwin Aldrin, Jr. took this dramatic photograph of Neil Armstrong, his companion on the desolate surface of the moon.

In the 1950s the idea of space exploration seemed like science fiction to most Americans. Many thought that one day human beings would go into space, but they did not think that it would happen in their lifetimes. In October 1957, Americans were shocked to learn that a Soviet satellite was circling Earth. Every 90 minutes a tiny 184-pound (82.8 kg) metal ball made a trip around the globe. Its "beep-beep" radio signals could be heard by scientists all over the world. That small satellite, called "Sputnik," was sending out the message that the space age had begun.

Americans were upset that the pioneer satellite was Russian. Rocket experts had been at work for years in the United States. But they were not yet ready to launch. Suddenly it became important to average citizens that the scientists get ready quickly. Americans were frightened to see the Soviets so far ahead.

The United States increased efforts in space. After one failure, when the rocket carrying a satellite collapsed, the United States did launch a satellite on January 31, 1958. The new National Aeronautics and Space Administration (NASA) was set up to coordinate American efforts in space. Federal money went into a program to improve science education in the schools.

On April 12, 1961, the Russians sent the first man into space.

President Kennedy took up the challenge. In May 1961, he delivered a special message to Congress. He asked Americans to raise their eyes to the stars. He said, "This nation should commit itself to achieving the goal, before this decade is out, of landing a man on the moon and returning him safely to Earth." JFK promised that the United States would land an astronaut on the moon before 1970.

Congress agreed and voted the money needed for a space program. The moon landing cost $25 billion.

For the next eight years hundreds of thousands of Americans worked together through NASA. Test pilots, office workers, scientists—and taxpayers—bent every effort toward reaching the moon. Finally Americans set out for the moon in July 1969. By then Kennedy had been dead for almost six years. LBJ had come and gone from the White House. Nixon had been inaugurated.

The glory of being first to reach the moon was shared by three astronauts. Neil Armstrong, Edwin Aldrin, and Michael Collins had been blasted into space from Cape Kennedy, Florida. For five days they journeyed through space. On July 21, 1969, they reached the moon.

Millions of viewers throughout the world were glued to their television sets. In time they saw a ghostly, white-clad figure slowly descend a ladder. Reaching the bottom rung, the astronaut extended his left foot ever so slowly. Finally, Neil Armstrong put that foot firmly on the fine-grained, powdery surface of the moon. Then he said: "That's one small step for man, one giant leap for mankind."

Minutes later, Edwin Aldrin joined Armstrong. Collins meanwhile was orbiting the ship which would take them back to Earth. For the next two hours and fourteen minutes, Armstrong and Aldrin, the two first moon visitors, enthralled their earthly audience. Sometimes they moved about in a kind of slow motion. Sometimes, in the moon's weak gravity, they bounded about like kangaroos. They set up experiments. They collected rocks. And, like tourists everywhere, they took pictures.

The astronauts appeared to be having a great time. They seemed reluctant to leave the dusty moonscape. Finally the voices at mission control in Houston, Texas, began to urge them to "climb back up that ladder" and return to their rocket ship for their homeward journey.

But before they did, the astronauts planted an American flag on the moon.

As a last act, the astronauts unveiled a plaque. Armstrong read the words on it aloud. Those words were heard by an estimated radio and television audience of 500 million people. Armstrong read: "Here men from the planet Earth first set foot upon the moon, July 1969, A.D. We came in peace for all mankind."

The Brandenburg Gate, a landmark on the border between East and West Germany, is seen through a barbed wire barricade, part of the Berlin Wall.

To ease tensions, Kennedy met Premier Khrushchev in Vienna in June 1961. The Russian leader was tough and aggressive, but Kennedy was equal to him. In a public broadcast Kennedy said, "We cannot and will not permit the Communists to drive us out of Berlin, either gradually or by force." Kennedy's strong, clear statement was cheered by the West Germans.

West Berlin was a constant headache for the Soviets. The Russians insisted that East Berlin was a "workers' paradise." But more and more East Berliners escaped to the West. By the summer of 1961, about 25,000 East German refugees were fleeing from their homeland every day.

To end this public display of failure, the Communists cut off East Berlin from West Berlin. They suddenly built a high wall of concrete, bricks, and barbed wire between the free and Communist parts of the city. Soldiers with searchlights and machine guns patrolled the wall. Guards shot anyone trying to escape.

To this day, Berlin remains a point of tension. The wall still stands. People still try to escape at great risk.

9. Why was the Bay of Pigs invasion a disaster?

10. What happened when Americans and Russians confronted one another over missiles in Cuba?

11. Why did the Soviets build a wall in Berlin?

When and how did the New Frontier end?

Young President Kennedy came to an untimely end. Just one thousand days after he had taken office, he was cut down by an assassin.

Kennedy had gone to Texas because he was unhappy that Congress had passed so few of the laws he felt were needed. So, like many other Presidents, he decided to take his case to the people.

On Friday, November 22, 1963, the President, his wife, Jacqueline, and Governor and Mrs. John B. Connally of Texas were riding through the streets of Dallas. They were enroute to the Trade Mart where the President was to speak at a luncheon. Suddenly rifle shots rang out. The President slumped forward. One bullet had ripped through his neck. Another had lodged in his brain. Governor Connally was wounded. By the time the car carrying the President reached a hospital, JFK was dead.

Television and radio stations interrupted their programs. Announcers, scarcely able to believe the reports, told the nation of the tragic event.

Less than two hours after Kennedy's death, Vice-President Lyndon B. Johnson took the oath of office. He was sworn in by an old friend, Judge Sarah Hughes of Texas, aboard the presidential plane, *Air Force One*.

At almost the same moment that Johnson was sworn in, the police arrested Lee Harvey Oswald. He was charged with firing the bullet which killed Kennedy. Two days later television viewers watched the police preparing to transfer Oswald from one jail to another. Before the eyes of millions, Jack Ruby, a Dallas nightclub owner, stepped out of the crowd. He shot and killed Oswald.

A commission headed by Chief Justice Earl Warren was appointed to investigate the assassination. Ten months after the crime, the commission issued its report. It said Oswald had acted on his own. In the following years, that conclusion has often been challenged. More than sixty books have been written about the assassination. Each of them offers a different account of the tragedy. Each of them has a slightly different idea of how or why it occurred. But about one thing there was certainty. The New Frontier had ended on that dark Friday in Dallas.

12. When and where was Kennedy killed?

13. Who was charged with his death? What happened to that suspect?

Part Three

The Great Society

What was the Great Society?

It would be hard to imagine a sharper difference between two people than between Presidents Johnson and Kennedy. Kennedy was born to wealth and privilege and had been educated in the nation's best private schools. Behind him stood a powerful, loyal, rich family.

Lyndon B. Johnson, on the other hand, came up the hard way. He graduated from country schools in Texas. For two years he taught in a Houston high school. Then he entered politics and became a member of Congress in 1937.

Johnson interrupted his political career to serve in the navy in World War II. After his return, he was elected to the Senate. There he showed such skill that he became Senate Majority Leader.

Different as Johnson and Kennedy may have been, they believed in the same things. They had similar goals for America. Kennedy had not had much success in reaching his goals. Johnson was determined to succeed. He plunged into his work as President with all of the restless energy for which he was famous.

Less than a year after he became President by accident, Lyndon Johnson was elected President in his own right. He won a smashing victory at the polls in 1964. Then "LBJ," as Johnson was known, called on Americans to build a "Great Society."

In spirit and purpose, the Great Society was a plan much like the New Deal and the New Frontier. As LBJ put it,

In a land of great wealth, families must not live in hopeless poverty. In a land rich in harvest, children must not go hungry. In a land of healing miracles, neighbors must not suffer and die unattended. In a land of great learning and scholars, young people must be taught to read and write.

1. How were Presidents Johnson and Kennedy alike? How were they different?

2. To what other plans for improving life in the United States is the Great Society compared?

What new programs did Johnson establish?

LBJ was determined to wage "unconditional war on poverty." He had almost super-human energy. He did not rest, and he did not let Congress rest either until he got the laws he wanted. Johnson asked for—and got—more money for welfare programs from Congress than it had voted in all the twenty years before.

At LBJ's urging, Congress began many poverty programs under the Office of Economic Opportunity. Some of the best known were: (1) The Job Corps to provide training and work experience for unemployed youths. (2) Volunteers in Service to America (VISTA) to do the kinds of things at home that the Peace Corps was doing overseas. (3) Operation Head Start to provide preschool education for poor children.

In 1965 the Great Society scored another triumph. President Johnson pressured Congress until he got a law setting up Medicare, a health insurance plan for the elderly. It is part of the Social Security program.

When Congress passed the Elementary and Secondary Education Act (ESEA), President Johnson was very happy. He had pressed for that program, which was designed to give money to schools with large numbers of poor, educationally disadvantaged students. He flew back to Texas to sign the bill into law. Seated in front of his old, one-room school with his first grade teacher and seven of his own former students at his side, Johnson declared, "No law I have signed or will ever sign means more to the future of the nation."

Finally, Johnson was able to get Congress to create a Department of Housing and Urban Development. That was the department Kennedy had wanted, but was not successful in obtaining. Johnson named Robert Weaver to be its first secretary. Weaver became the first black cabinet member in American history.

Another new department, that of Transportation, was set up. Johnson wanted it to cope with the traffic jams that had developed on the nation's highways and in the airways.

3. What was the name of the health insurance plan for the elderly? The program for preschool children?

4. What two new departments did Johnson persuade Congress to establish?

How did Johnson advance civil rights?

Even before Johnson asked Congress to approve his Great Society programs, he began to push for civil rights bills. Just five days after the assassination, Johnson went before Congress. He spoke of the civil rights bill proposed earlier by Kennedy. It was still stalled. Johnson said, "We have talked long enough in this country about equal rights." Then, looking directly at those with whom he had served for so many years, he declared, "It is time now to write [civil rights] . . . in the books of law."

Congress at last passed the Civil Rights Act of 1964. That act had four major parts:

1. It said that hotels, parks, swimming pools, restaurants, and other public places could no longer be segregated.
2. It tried to protect the right of blacks to vote.
3. Employers were told that they could not discriminate against anyone on the basis of race, color, religion, national origin (birthplace), or sex.
4. The Attorney General could bring law suits against schools or school districts that practiced segregation.

A year later, The Voting Rights Act of 1965 made the use of any tests for voting illegal. (See page 316.)

Three years later, the 1968 Civil Rights Act was passed. That law declared: "It is the policy of the United States to provide, within Constitutional

LBJ poses with his first grade teacher at the ESEA signing (above). The Civil Rights Act of 1964 abolished "separate but equal" facilities like those below.

limits, for fair housing throughout the United States." Discrimination in the sale or rental of most housing because of "race, color, religion, or national origin" was banned.

5. What were the four major provisions of the Civil Rights Act of 1964?

6. What did the Civil Rights Act of 1968 do?

Why did Johnson decide to retire from the presidency?

At first Johnson seemed to be very successful as President. Then, strangely enough, the man elected in 1964 by the largest margin in history became unpopular with the majority of voters before his term was over.

What caused the people to reject Johnson's leadership? There undoubtedly were several reasons. The most important was the Vietnam War, about which more will be said later in this chapter. That war was costing Americans dearly both in lives and money. Many Americans believed that the United States had no business in Southeast Asia. They demonstrated in the streets and on college campuses against the war. Sometimes those demonstrations turned into bloody battles.

Although he worked hard, Johnson did not have Kennedy's ability to attract followers. Johnson had a volcanic temper. Johnson caused doubt, where Kennedy had inspired confidence. LBJ himself was very aware of the Kennedy shadow over his presidency. Two Democrats challenged Johnson for the nomination for the 1968 election. Eugene McCarthy of Minnesota and Robert Kennedy, a younger brother of President Kennedy's, both promised to end the Vietnam War at once.

In March 1968, an old, weary, battered President Johnson went on television. His voice was heavy with emotion. His face was deeply lined. Johnson said that he had ordered a cutback in the bombing in Vietnam. He asked for peace talks.

Then Johnson made this surprising announcement:

> **I shall not seek and I will not accept the nomination of my party for another term as your President. . . . In these times as in times before, it is true that a house divided against itself . . . is a house that cannot stand. There is division among us all tonight. And holding the trust that is mine, as President of the United States, I cannot disregard that peril. . . .**

Those were the words Johnson used to tell the American people that he was retiring from the White House at the end of his term. He promised to use the months he had left to work for peace in Vietnam. But he was unable to achieve it before Republican Richard Nixon took over as President in January 1969.

7. When and how did Johnson tell the American people that he wanted to retire from the presidency?

8. What were some of the most important reasons for his decision?

What judgments have historians made of Johnson?

Historians do not agree about the place Lyndon Johnson will hold in history. Some think he will get a high rating because of the great body of legislation for which he was responsible. Those historians point to the Johnson record for laws that benefited people in education, medicine, and civil rights.

Even those historians admit, however, that he probably mishandled the Vietnam crisis.

Eric Goldman, a historian at Princeton University, believes that Johnson was a tragic figure. At one time Dr. Goldman served as an adviser to LBJ. He says that Johnson was a man of "exceedingly high intelligence," but that he was unable to cope with the strong forces of his time. Johnson was more in tune with times past than with the time in which he lived.

Lyndon Johnson could win votes, enact laws, maneuver mountains. He could not acquire that something beyond, which cannot be won, enacted, or maneuvered but must be freely given. He could not command that respect, affection, and [trust] which alone permit an American President genuinely to lead. In his periods of triumph and of downsweep, in peace as in war, he stood the tragic figure of an extraordinarily gifted President who was the wrong man from the wrong place at the wrong time under the wrong circumstances.

Eric F. Goldman, *The Tragedy of Lyndon Johnson* (New York: Alfred A. Knopf, 1969), p. 531.

Ronald Steel is a historian who disagrees with Goldman. He says:

. . . Though he [LBJ] was not a man of vision, he had a very bold and optimistic view of the United States and of what it could accomplish. He was somebody you felt was in control and who knew what he wanted. Above all, he was able to make government work. He was an effective leader, and if it were not for Vietnam—and that's a big if—he could be considered a great leader.

From "We Are in a Time of Pygmies When It Comes to Leaders," a copyrighted interview with Ronald Steel in *U. S. News and World Report*, October 13, 1980.

9. Why do some historians think Johnson deserves a high rating as President? What do they say was his biggest mistake?

Part Four

Vietnam: The Longest War

When did the war in Vietnam end?

It is strange that a war fought in faroff Vietnam should bring down the presidency of LBJ. He was not very interested in foreign affairs. Once a staff member said, Johnson "wishes the rest of the world would go away and we could get ahead with the real needs of Americans."

But the rest of the world did not go away. Problems in Vietnam kept mounting. And they caused mounting problems within the United States that made it impossible for Johnson to "get on" with what he thought were the country's "real needs."

The war in Vietnam had begun long before Johnson became President. It continued after he left office. Not until January 27, 1973, did one of the most difficult chapters in American history come to an end. That night President Richard Nixon went on television to announce the end "to a long and costly effort."

Nixon was right in saying that it had been a long war. It was the longest war in which the United States had ever

American troops in Vietnam were faced with a new kind of war. There was no battlefront, as there had been in Korea. Instead the Viet Cong controlled much of the countryside. They "hit and ran."

fought. (Since Congress did not declare war on North Vietnam, there is no official date for the start of the war. But 1961 is usually taken as the year of its start. In that year the first American soldier was killed in Vietnam.) The war also had been costly. More than 46,000 American soldiers were killed. That was the fourth largest toll of any war in the nation's history.

In terms of money, the Vietnam War cost taxpayers about $141 billion. There is no way to reckon the costs in human suffering.

How did that long, costly, bitter war begin? Its seeds were planted even before World War II began. Then France owned a colony in Asia. It was called Indochina.

After World War II, the Indochinese rebelled against the French. Under the leadership of Ho Chi Minh, a Communist, the Indochinese finally drove the French out of Southeast Asia. In 1954 Indochina was split into three countries: Laos, Cambodia (Kampuchea), and Vietnam.

But Vietnam never became a united country. It was split into two parts at the 17th parallel. (See map, page 545.) A Communist government under Ho Chi Minh was set up in the North. In the

South, the government was headed by the former emperor of Vietnam. Then, Ngo Dinh Diem was elected premier of South Vietnam in 1955.

The North Vietnamese began to move down into South Vietnam. They wanted to take control of the new republic. The South Vietnamese government resisted the guerilla attacks. It asked for help to remain independent. As time went on, the fighting grew more intense. The United States and other nations grew more concerned.

1. How long and costly was the Vietnam War?

2. Why did the Indochinese rebel against the French? Why did North Vietnam move into South Vietnam?

How and why did the United States become involved?

The United States did not want Communists to take over the Saigon government. President Eisenhower sent American economic aid and military advisers to South Vietnam. He hoped they would help the new republic become strong enough to defend itself.

Seven years later, President Kennedy went even further. He said, "The United States is determined that the Republic of Vietnam shall not be lost to the Communists for lack of any support which the United States can render."

When he took office, there were just 2000 military advisers in Vietnam. But President Kennedy thought more should be done to help the people of South Vietnam stay free. He began to send more troops. By the time Kennedy died, about 16,000 Americans were in Vietnam.

When Lyndon Johnson became President, he, too, continued to send troops. Johnson said:

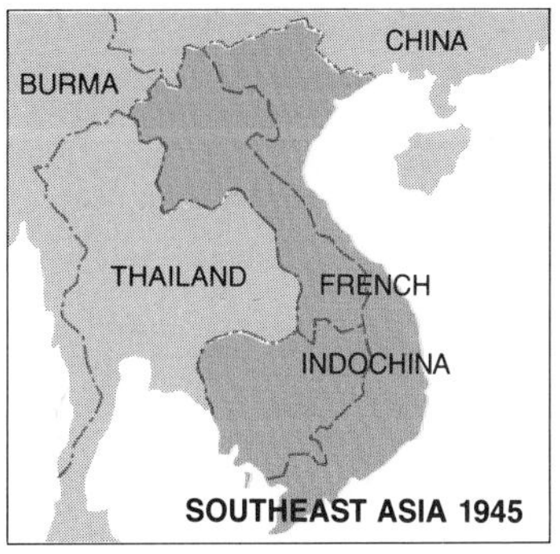

We have a promise to keep. Since 1954 every American President has offered support to the people of South Vietnam. . . . To abandon this small and brave nation to its enemies . . . would be an unforgivable wrong.

Until August 1964, no American forces took part in the actual fighting.

On April 29, 1975, all Americans still in Saigon were evacuated before the city surrendered to the North Vietnamese. Thousands of South Vietnamese were also evacuated.

They acted as teachers and advisers to the South Vietnamese. But then, after attacks by the North Vietnamese on the United States Navy in the Gulf of Tonkin, the United States began to bomb military targets in North Vietnam.

From then on, bit by bit, the United States became more deeply involved in Vietnam. And so did some other nations. The Soviet Union and eight other Communist countries helped the North Vietnamese. By 1968 the stage was set for the most savage fighting of the war. At that time there were more than half a million Americans fighting in Vietnam.

3. How and why did three American Presidents try to aid South Vietnam?

4. What nations helped North Vietnam?

Why did the Vietnam War become unpopular at home?

The war continued to drag on. Losses in combat grew. People at home were troubled by news that civilians in

Vietnam were suffering terribly. Each evening television brought the war into American living rooms. Americans were brought face to face with the war's brutal realities.

For those reasons, support for the war started to lag. Americans began to divide sharply. There were some "hawks" who believed that the United States should fight to win, and win quickly. There were "doves" who argued that the United States should pull out and make peace at any price.

Most Americans were somewhere in the middle. They did not like the war, and they wanted it to end. The trouble was they did not know how to end it.

Meanwhile, more and more demonstrations against the war were taking place in American cities. Sometimes those demonstrations were violent. Antiwar protesters brought pressure on President Johnson to "get out of Vietnam now." In Congress there were many angry debates about the fighting in Vietnam. But President Johnson would not change his stand.

By the time Richard Nixon became President in 1969, most Americans had come to believe that it was wrong to continue to fight. Nixon had promised to end the war if he were elected. He insisted, however, that immediate withdrawal was impossible. The United States had to protect its troops that were still there, and it had to see that American prisoners of war were released.

Nixon began to "wind down" the war by withdrawing troops and stepping up negotiations. But he also ordered American troops to cross the borders into Cambodia. Large-scale secret bombing had been going on in Cambodia for more than a year. Nixon's action brought forth great storms of protest at home. In Paris the negotiators kept trying to make peace at the conference table. But peace was slow in coming. When the North Vietnamese invaded a demilitarized zone in 1972, Nixon ordered more bombing. It was the heaviest bombing of the war.

5. Why did opposition to the war increase?

6. How did President Nixon feel about continuing the war?

How did the war finally end?

For over four years the Paris peace talks were stalemated. But at last the parties reached a cease-fire agreement. It was signed on January 27, 1973. It said that United States troops still in Vietnam were to be withdrawn in ninety days. American prisoners were to be returned to their homes during that time. The Vietnamese were to be allowed to work out their political problems peacefully.

American troops withdrew on schedule. But the Vietnamese did not work out their differences peacefully. Instead North Vietnam launched new, large-scale attacks on South Vietnam during the early months of 1975. On April 20, 1975, South Vietnam surrendered.

Just a few hours before the surrender, the last 1000 Americans remaining in Vietnam got out by helicopter. With the departure of those last government employees and private citizens, the United States withdrawal from Vietnam was complete.

7. What were the provisions of the cease-fire?

8. When and why did the last Americans leave Vietnam?

Building Your Vocabulary

Complete these sentences by selecting the correct word from those listed below.

1. A—?—is a person who is concerned about all human beings.
2. —?—means accusing someone without having evidence.
3. In *Brown* v. *Board of Education of Topeka, Kansas*, the Supreme Court said that schools—?—by race were unconstitutional.
4. When Soviet troops put down the revolt in Hungary, the United States gave—?—to those who asked for it.
5. A meeting which heads of state attend is called a—?—conference.
6. In the 1950s many people moved to the portion of the United States called the—?—.
7. The Voting Rights Act of 1965 made use of any tests for voting—?—.

McCarthyism illegal summit
segregated humanitarian sunbelt
asylum

Recalling What You Have Learned

Match each item in Column A with the correct item in Column B.

Column A	Column B
1. The Great Society	A. Cuba
2. The New Frontier	B. Chief Justice
3. "I Like Ike"	C. Soviet Union
4. Oveta Culp Hobby	D. North Vietnam
5. Margaret Chase Smith	E. Dwight Eisenhower
6. Earl Warren	F. John Kennedy
7. Martin Luther King, Jr.	G. Lyndon B. Johnson
8. Fidel Castro	H. Senator who spoke out against McCarthy
9. Ho Chi Minh	I. First head of HEW
10. Nikita Khrushchev	J. Montgomery bus boycott

Discussing the Important Ideas in This Chapter

1. Both George Washington and Dwight Eisenhower hoped they could stay "above politics" as President. Do you think it is possible for someone to be President of the United States and not be a politician? Explain.

2. When Senator Margaret Chase Smith spoke out against Joseph McCarthy, she said that his actions "could result in the end of everything that we Americans hold dear." Explain what she meant. Do you agree or disagree with her? Why?
3. Why did the United States Supreme Court say in *Brown* v. *Board of Education* that separate schools for blacks and whites were unconstitutional?
4. How important do you think it is to elect a President who has great charm and the ability to attract voters? Explain your answer; give examples.
5. During the 1950s and 1960s television became a great force. In what ways did it affect the election of 1960, the civil rights movement, and people's feelings about the war in Vietnam?
6. For years Lyndon Johnson was successful and happy as a leader in Congress. Why then was he unhappy as President?
7. How and why did the United States become involved in Vietnam?
8. What long-term effects on American foreign policy do you think the war in Vietnam is likely to have?

Improving Your Chart Skills

Study the bar graph below. Notice that it presents in rank order the number of United States war deaths for the seven major wars we have fought. The top bar shows the Civil War, because it had the most deaths.

On a separate sheet of paper, prepare a similar bar graph. Entitle the graph "Length of U.S. Wars." Then order the wars in which the United States has fought according to their length. Across the horizontal axis (the bottom line) indicate the years.

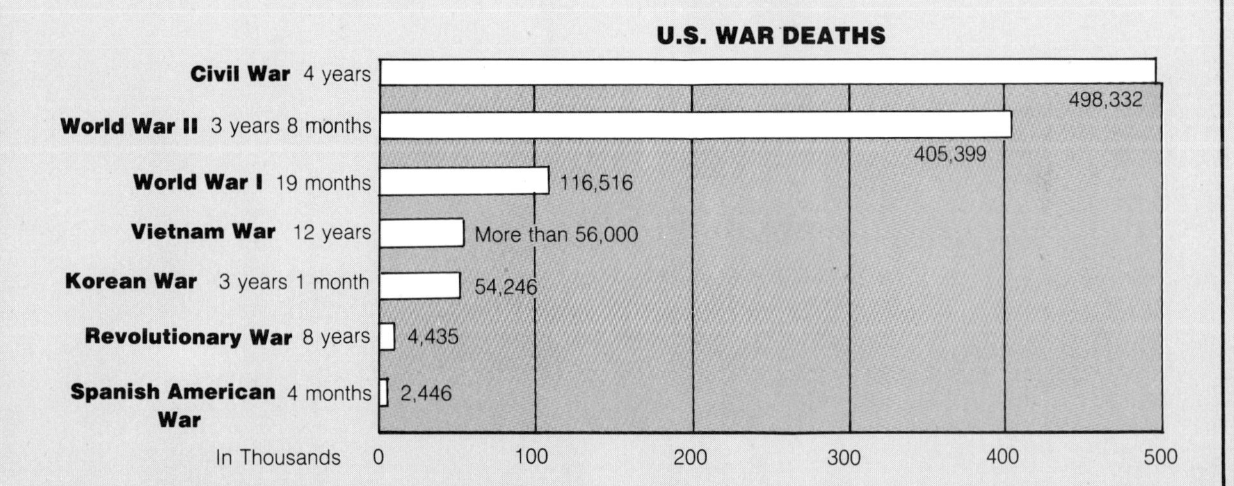

Improving Your Study Skills: *Writing*

The cartoon on page 535 appeared in American newspapers at the time of the Cuban Missile Crisis. Study the cartoon. Reread the description of that crisis on page 535. Then write a short report about it in your own words. In your report tell who was involved, why the crisis arose, how it built to a climax, and how it ended. In your report, explain what the cartoonist felt about the crisis. What did the cartoonist think about Kennedy's handling of the crisis?

Chapter 21

New Directions

The White House, Washington, D. C.

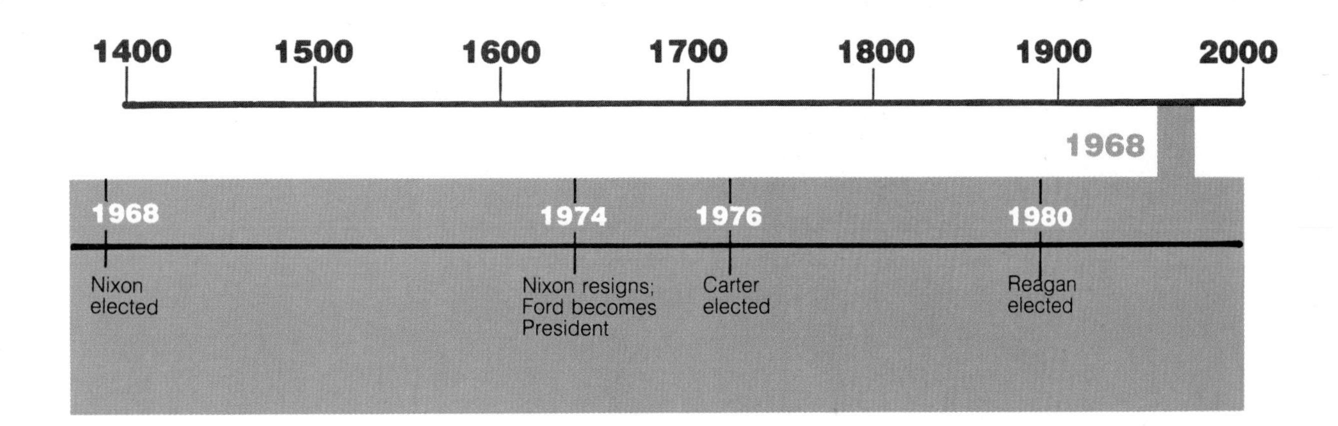

Part One

The Nixon Era Begins

Who were the candidates in the 1968 presidential election?

When Lyndon Johnson announced that he would not run for a second term as President, he opened the door wide to other hopefuls.

George Wallace, former governor of Alabama, ran as the candidate of a third party. It was called the American Independent party. Wallace minced no words in telling Americans where he stood on the issues. He was against the push to integrate the schools. He said that the courts were too easy on criminals. Wallace also said that the United States should fight to win in Vietnam. "I think we've got to pour it on there," he said.

Wallace did not think he could win the presidency. But he thought he might force the election into the House of Representatives. Then his supporters in the House could use their votes to get one of the other candidates to support some of Wallace's goals.

Three candidates ran strongly for the Democratic nomination in 1968. They were:

Hubert Humphrey won the 1968 Democratic nomination, but he could not unite his splintered party.

1. Senator Eugene McCarthy of Minnesota. McCarthy entered the race for the nomination with misgivings. He did not especially enjoy politics and campaigning. But McCarthy believed that he had to come forward to oppose the Vietnam War.

Many of the nation's antiwar college students welcomed McCarthy's candidacy. They rallied behind him. In some states they went door to door to ask voters to support McCarthy in the primaries. The students were bitterly disappointed when McCarthy did not win the nomination.

2. Senator Robert Kennedy of New York. Kennedy enjoyed the advantage of a famous name. He had managed his brother's campaign when John Kennedy ran for President in 1960. "RFK," as he was called, had then served in his brother's cabinet as Attorney General. RFK drove himself to exhaustion on the campaign trail. He pitted himself against McCarthy in California for a crucial primary. On the night he won that race, RFK lost his life. He had gone to a hotel in Los Angeles to thank his workers. Then, tired and hoping to avoid the crowd, he tried to slip out of the hotel through the kitchen. There a man angry about Kennedy's support of Israel was waiting. He shot and killed the senator.

3. Vice-President Hubert Humphrey of Minnesota. Unlike McCarthy and Kennedy, Humphrey, who won the nomination, did not enter any of the primaries. He did not need to. He was well known as Johnson's Vice-President. The leaders of the Democratic party supported him. So, too, did many of the nation's minorities.

The Democratic convention in Chicago was marred by ugly clashes in the streets between demonstrators and police. Humphrey won the nomination on the first ballot. But he was not able to gain the support of many of the Democrats who had worked for McCarthy and Kennedy.

Humphrey was an outgoing, bubbly, talkative person who had loved every minute of his long political career. He wanted to cap that career with the presidency. But, because he was Vice-President, he felt bound to run on Johnson's record. He even defended Johnson's stand on Vietnam. That probably was the reason he lost to the Republican candidate, Richard Nixon.

The Republican convention was orderly and calm, in contrast to the Democratic convention. Richard Milhous Nixon was the Republican party's choice.

Few people have ever wanted to be President as much as Richard Nixon did. And few people in politics have had such mixed fortunes in trying to reach that goal.

Nixon, the son of devout Quaker parents of modest means, worked his way through college and law school. Then he entered politics. In more than a quarter of a century in the public eye, he gathered many admirers, as well as many bitter enemies. Through the years Nixon earned a reputation as a determined man, a hard worker, and a loner.

He was elected to the House of Representatives, the Senate, and then to the vice-presidency. He was a hard-working, widely traveled Vice-President. He had hoped that his record would help him win the race for President against John Kennedy in 1960. But he lost in one of the nation's closest elections. (See page 529.)

On the heels of that defeat came another for Nixon. He lost the election for governor of California in 1962. After that defeat, Nixon announced he was "through with politics" forever. But in 1968 he seized the chance to become the Republican nominee. Nixon chose Spiro Agnew, governor of Maryland, as his running mate.

As he campaigned across the nation, Nixon reminded voters of the "sorry record" of the Johnson administration. If they voted for Humphrey, they would be voting for more of the same, he said. It was time, Nixon said, to put a Republican into the White House. He would curb the high spending of the federal government. He would restore "law and order" and "make the streets safe again." Nixon said that he would bring a swift and honorable end to the fighting in Vietnam.

Nixon defeated Humphrey by a narrow margin. He had the lowest winning majority since Woodrow Wilson in 1912.

1. Who was the independent candidate for President in 1968? Who won the Democratic nomination?

2. What did Nixon promise to do if he was elected President?

Signs and banners on the floor of the 1968 Republican convention proclaim the name of the winner of the nomination—Richard M. Nixon.

How did Nixon deal with major problems at home?

Nixon's main interest was in foreign affairs. But he knew that he must give immediate attention to the major problems at home.

Nixon promised to bring Americans together again. Protests and riots and the bitter campaign of 1968 had shown just how deeply divided the people were. They disagreed—often violently—about the war in Vietnam, the integration of schools, the treatment of those accused of crimes, and many other subjects. Sometimes it seemed as though everyone was talking—or shouting—and no one was listening. So in his inaugural address, Nixon asked Americans "to lower our voices."

"We cannot learn from one another," he said, "until we stop shouting at one another—until we speak quietly enough so that our words can be heard as well as our voices."

Nixon then said, "For its part, government will listen." Nixon promised to listen especially to those whom he called "the silent majority." They were Americans who did not join protest marches or make public speeches. The "silent majority" obeyed the laws, paid their taxes, and worried about three major problems:

1. The growth of government. Nixon agreed that this was a problem. He said, "In this past third of a century, government has passed more laws, spent more money, initiated more programs, than in all our previous history." He warned that "We are approaching the limits of what government alone can do." So Nixon did not propose any big, new federal programs. He asked Congress to turn some powers back to local and state governments.

2. "Law and order." Nixon announced that he would enforce all of the laws of the land. He would see that peace was restored on college campuses and on the streets of the nation's cities. If necessary, he would use the National Guard or the army. He also would appoint judges pledged to deal more severely with those found guilty of crimes.

In 1970 there were student upheavals on many college campuses. They occurred in response to Nixon's orders for stepped-up military action in Southeast Asia. Student discontent climaxed at Kent State University in Ohio. Four students there were killed in a clash with National Guard troops. After a surge of demonstrations, campuses did quiet down.

When vacancies occurred in the courts, Nixon appointed conservative judges. His most important appointment went to Warren Burger as Chief Justice. Although Burger turned out to be much less conservative than Nixon had hoped, he was not as liberal as Earl Warren. (See page 522.)

3. The "overheated" economy. Inflation was a serious problem. Prices kept going up and up. At the same time unemployment was rising. To deal with those twin problems, Nixon announced a ninety-day "freeze" on wages and prices. He was the first President ever to take such action in peacetime.

President Nixon also took steps to discourage Americans from buying foreign goods. Congress put a 10 percent "surcharge," or tax, on imports. That action promoted the sale of American-made products.

Nixon's economic policies proved to be good for the nation. Inflation fell and employment rose.

One of the highlights of President and Mrs. Nixon's visit to the People's Republic of China was a formal Chinese banquet. The host for the meal was Chou En-lai (second from left). During the meal, Nixon and Chou toasted communication between their two countries.

3. Who were "the silent majority"? What did Nixon promise to do for them?

4. What were the three major problems which Nixon had to confront at home? What did he do about each of them?

Why did Nixon visit the People's Republic of China?

Americans were unprepared for the surprise announcement which Nixon made in July 1971. He said he was going to the People's Republic of China, or Communist China. There he would meet with Mao Tse-tung, the leader of government. Nixon was going to try to restore normal relations with the People's Republic of China.

You will recall that Mao had seized control of China in 1949. (See page 511.) When he did, the United States recalled its ambassador. It refused to recognize the existence of Red, or Communist, China. Instead the United States insisted that the Nationalist Government of China which had fled to Taiwan was the real government of China. It was the one which was entitled to sit on the Security Council of the United Nations.

The People's Republic of China had the largest population of any nation in the world. There were more than 800 million people in Red China. It was a leading world power. Nixon thought the time had come to recognize the People's Republic of China.

On February 21, 1972, President Nixon landed in Peking. As television cameras filmed his progress, Nixon and his Secretary of State, Henry Kissinger, strode along the Great Wall. They admired panda bears and raised their glasses in toasts to their Chinese hosts. As a result of Nixon's visit, the United States and the People's Republic of China agreed to exchange ambassadors and to begin trading with one another. The United States also agreed to support Red China in its bid for a seat on the UN Security Council.

President Nixon had made what has been called "the boldest diplomatic move by an American President since Jefferson bought Louisiana." What is more, it is doubtful that any other President could have done what Nixon did. He had fought against communism for years. No one ever had accused him of being sympathetic to Communists.

Then President Nixon packed his bags and headed for Moscow.

While Nixon was in Russia, he signed a series of agreements. Some of them dealt with joint ventures in space. Others were concerned with protecting the environment, and with health and science. But the most important one was an attempt to limit the arms race. It became known as the Strategic Arms Limitation Treaty, or SALT.

Nixon's foreign policy moves may have been the most important acts of his presidency. He reversed what had been American policy since Harry Truman's time. Truman, Eisenhower, and Kennedy had tried to "contain" communism. But Nixon wanted to open direct lines of communication with the two major Communist nations of the world. At the same time, he shrewdly tried to play one off against the other. The Soviet Union and the People's Republic of China were bitter rivals. Nixon let it be known that the United States was willing to work and trade with both of them.

5. Why did President Nixon go to the People's Republic of China?

6. What did Nixon accomplish during his 1972 visit to Moscow?

Part Two

A President Resigns

Why did trouble begin for the Nixon administration?

In 1972 Richard Nixon asked Americans to reelect him as their President. They responded by giving him the greatest popular majority in the history of the United States. Nixon carried 49 of the 50 states.

What started as a happy and successful term did not turn out that way, however. On the evening of August 8, 1974, a grim President Nixon spoke on television. He struggled to control his emotions. In a faltering voice he announced that he was going to do something which no other President had done. "I shall resign the presidency effective at noon tomorrow," he said. If Nixon had not resigned, he almost certainly would have been impeached. He would have been put on trial before the Senate. To understand why, we need to look briefly at a series of events which began with Nixon's reelection campaign.

No one seriously doubted that Nixon would win a second term in the White House. His opponent was Democrat George McGovern. McGovern ran a poor campaign. Many voters could not accept his ideas. Some complained that his proposals had not been carefully thought out. But despite McGovern's lack of popular appeal, Nixon's advisers wanted to make victory absolutely certain.

Some members of the Committee to Re-Elect the President (CREEP) planned a daring—and an unlawful—action. They planned to break into the Democrats' headquarters in Washington. That headquarters was in a building called *Watergate*.

About 1:00 A.M. on June 17, 1972, five burglars slipped into the Democratic headquarters in Watergate. They were not after money. They wanted information. They wanted to find out how the Democrats were planning to carry on their campaign. But while they were trying to install electronic eavesdropping devices, a guard happened by. He called the police. When the police arrested the burglars, they found a card in the pocket of one man. It contained the name and the telephone number of a highly placed member of CREEP who also was on the White House staff. That link later proved to be very important.

The record clearly shows that Richard Nixon did not plan the forced entry of Watergate. In fact, when the President first learned of the burglary, he was very angry.

Soon Nixon learned that those responsible for the break-in were connected with his campaign. Some of his closest and most trusted aides had broken the law. But instead of firing them and telling the American people what they had done, Nixon tried to cover up the affair. That was a very serious mistake. You know from your study of the Constitution that the President is responsible for carrying out the laws of the nation. (See page 127.) The President takes a solemn oath to carry out the laws. But Nixon chose to forget about his responsibilities and his solemn promise. On June 22, 1972, Nixon announced:

On August 8, 1974, a shaken President Nixon announces his intention to resign. His daughter Tricia looks on.

I can say categorically [without question] that no one on the White House staff, no one in this administration presently employed was involved in this very bizarre [unusual] incident.

Most Americans believed the President. They were not very interested in the Watergate affair. They might have forgotten the whole thing had it not been for one newspaper. Robert Woodward and Carl Bernstein, two reporters on the *Washington Post*, were sure there was more to the story. For months they followed one lead after another without success. Then, at last, pieces of what seemed to be a giant jigsaw puzzle suddenly began fitting together. On October 10, the *Washington Post* published a big story. It said the Watergate break-in was just the tip of the iceberg. It was part of "a massive campaign of political spying and sabotage . . . directed by officials of the White House and the Committee to Re-elect the President."

In January 1973, the Watergate burglars went on trial. By this time Congress had become very interested in Watergate. The Senate set up a special investigating committee. Senator Sam J. Ervin of North Carolina was named head of that committee. Its hearings were televised. Americans could see and hear all about Watergate for themselves.

1. Why did burglars enter Watergate? How did the President respond to that forced entry into Democratic headquarters?
2. When and why did Congress take an interest in Watergate?

Why did the Vice-President resign?

In the midst of the Watergate trouble, the Nixon administration was shaken by still another serious problem. In the late summer of 1973 Vice-President Spiro Agnew was charged with wrongdoing. There was evidence that he accepted money from contractors in Maryland for giving them state business. Those payments had gone to Agnew while he was governor. The payments had continued even while he was Vice-President.

Agnew was charged with income tax evasion. He resigned from the second highest office in the land. He was allowed to plead "no contest." This means he did not even try to answer the charges against him. The court sentenced him to three years probation and fined him $10,000.

Acting under terms of the 25th Amendment (see page 614), President Nixon appointed Gerald R. Ford as the new Vice-President. Ford was well known and respected in Congress. He had served continuously in the House of Representatives since 1949. He also had been the Minority (Republican) Leader of the House since 1964. Congress quickly confirmed Ford's nomination.

3. To what charges did Agnew plead "no contest"? What happened to Agnew?
4. Who became Vice-President?

Why did Watergate become a "constitutional crisis"?

As the Senate committee continued its Watergate hearings, it learned about a lot of questionable activities at the White House. Among them were these:

The acting director of the FBI had destroyed records related to the case.

The burglars had been paid large sums of money to insure their silence about the involvement of higher-ups.

The Nixon administration had put wiretaps on the telephones of some of its own officials. It also had tapped the phones of reporters it considered "enemies." It had not asked for or obtained permission from the courts as the law requires.

But the most amazing thing which the Senate committee learned was that some of the cover-up planning was recorded on tape. Nixon, like Presidents Kennedy and Johnson before him, had decided to keep spoken records. The tape recordings of meetings in his office could be used later, if and when the President wanted to write his memoirs.

The Senate committee led by Sam Ervin (center) probed the Watergate affair during five months of televised hearings.

When Congress (the legislative branch) learned that tapes of White House conversations had been made, it demanded them. The President (the executive branch) said the tapes were confidential records and Congress could not order him to give them up.

In the midst of the arguments about the tapes, a committee in the House began to hold hearings. Those hearings, too, were televised. The House committee was to see if there was enough evidence to impeach the President.

So it was that a dramatic crisis developed. It was a constitutional crisis, because it finally involved all three branches of the government and how they "check and balance" one another. (See pages 127-128.) Finally, the Supreme Court (the judicial branch) was asked to decide whether or not the President had to surrender the tapes.

Just before noon on July 24, 1974, Chief Justice Warren Burger announced the Court's decision. He began by reminding Americans that it was "the duty of this Court to say what the law is." He pointed out that the Court believed that a President sometimes needed to keep confidential records about matters which affect the safety or security of the United States. But, Burger continued, the United States has "a historic commitment to the rule of law." No one, not even the President of the United States, can withhold evidence needed in pending criminal cases. Courts must protect the right to a fair trial.

When Nixon heard the Court's decision, he gave in. He agreed to surrender the tapes. They shocked even his strongest supporters, because they showed that he had deceived the American people. One tape made on June 23, 1972, showed that Nixon had known about and ordered the cover-up.

Pressure mounted on Nixon to resign. But he hesitated. He talked about standing trial in the Senate. Three of the nation's most respected Republican leaders went to see him in the White House. They were Senator Barry Goldwater and Representative John Rhodes, both of Arizona, and Senator Hugh Scott of Pennsylvania. They told Nixon that if he were tried, the Senate would convict him. They asked him to consider seriously whether or not he wanted to be the first President to be disgraced in that way.

At last Nixon yielded to advice to step down. He became the first President in history to resign.

During the last months of the Watergate crisis, the eyes and ears of people all over the world were turned to the United States. They wanted to know if the Constitution and the American government could stand up to such a great test. The Constitution and the government passed the test. Watergate proved once again how well designed they are.

5. Why did the Watergate matter become a constitutional crisis?

6. How was the crisis ended? What did it prove?

Part Three

Gerald Ford in the White House

When and how did Ford become President?

Millions of television viewers saw history in the making on August 9, 1974. Early in the morning the Nixon family said an emotional farewell to members of the cabinet and White House staff. Then they began their trip home to San Clemente, California. As Nixon's plane was flying over Kansas, his presidency came to an official end. Meanwhile, back in Washington, Gerald Ford was being sworn in as the 38th President of the United States.

Chief Justice Warren Burger administered the oath of office to Ford at noon. Nixon had nominated Ford to replace Agnew, and Congress had given its approval. So Gerald Ford became the first President to be appointed rather than elected to the highest office in the land.

Ford sought to reassure his fellow Americans in a short speech. He said:

If you have not chosen me by secret ballot, neither have I gained office by any secret promises. . . . I have not sought this enormous responsibility, but I will not shirk it. . . . I will be the President of all the people. . . .

Then he spoke of the crisis through which the nation had just passed. Ford said, "Our long national nightmare is over. Our Constitution works; our great Republic is a government of laws and not men."

Ford's modest manner and his reputation for honesty were as reassuring to Americans as his words. "I'm a Ford, not a Lincoln," he would remind his listeners. He loved his family, enjoyed sports, and was most at home in the smaller communities of the United States.

Although Ford had not run for the office of President, he was well acquainted with Washington and the ways of Congress. He had been elected thirteen times to the House of Representatives. He served in that branch of Congress for a total of 25 years.

After graduating from the University of Michigan, Ford turned down a chance to play football for the Green Bay Packers. Instead he went to Yale where he worked his way through law school. Then he went back to Michigan to practice law.

When World War II started, Ford enlisted in the navy. He saw combat in the Pacific where he served for nearly four years. Then he once again returned to his law practice in Michigan. But two years later he decided to run for Congress.

Ford quickly established himself in Congress as a hard worker. He served on the Warren Commission, which looked into the assassination of President Kennedy. He supported the war in Vietnam, and he worked for the passage of civil rights laws. Ford was the Minority Leader in the House when Nixon nominated him as Vice-President.

When Ford became President, the office of Vice-President once again was vacant. That office was again filled under terms of the 25th Amendment. Ford nominated Nelson Rockefeller, former governor of New York.

Rockefeller was willing, even eager to become Vice-President. But some members of Congress were suspicious. They worried because Rockefeller was a very rich man. "What if some of his business dealings or tax payments had not been proper?" they asked. Although Rockefeller had been a good governor in New York and had served his country under Presidents Roosevelt, Truman, and Eisenhower, they hesitated. Finally, after three months of investigation, Congress could find nothing wrong. Rockefeller was approved. Rockefeller served well as Vice-President. But when Ford ran for President in 1976, he chose Senator Robert Dole of Kansas as his running mate. Later Ford said that bypassing Rockefeller might have cost him the election.

Gerald Ford takes the oath of office as President.

1. What experience in government did Ford bring to the presidency?

2. Why did most Americans feel good about Ford's becoming President? Why did Congress hesitate to approve Rockefeller?

Why did President Ford pardon Nixon?

Just a month after he took office, Ford used an important power which the Constitution gives to the President of the United States. (See Article 2, Section 2, pages 603-604.) He pardoned Nixon for any crimes he may have committed while he was in the White House. Ford told Americans that he had decided to pardon Nixon for four reasons:

1. Nixon and his family had suffered enough already.

2. The ex-President was in poor health.

3. It was doubtful that Nixon could get a fair trial by an impartial jury.

Popular feelings were high. And Nixon had already been "tried" on television, as millions of Americans watched the congressional hearings.

4. Ford was concerned about something more important than what happened to Nixon. He believed his most important task was to restore the nation to health. Americans had to put Watergate behind them. They could not go on living in the angry atmosphere of recent months. The nation's wounds, said Ford, "had festered too long." The time for healing was at hand.

Public reaction to the pardon was immediate and mixed. Many Americans were shocked and angry. They said Nixon ought to stand trial. They also noted that Nixon's top aides had been tried. Some of them had been found guilty and were serving prison sentences. "Why should Nixon be treated differently?" they asked.

Some citizens charged that Nixon and Ford had "made a deal." They suspected that Ford had promised to pardon Nixon if he would agree to resign. But Ford insisted before a congressional committee, "There was no deal!"

As it turned out, the pardon may have been politically costly for Ford. He lost his bid for election to the presidency in 1976. That year Jimmy Carter of Georgia defeated Ford in a very close election. Some observers said that Ford lost because he pardoned Nixon. But Ford said that he would do it again. He was convinced he had done the right thing for his country. He had helped the nation bind up its wounds.

3. What were the four major reasons Ford gave for pardoning Nixon? Which of those reasons did he consider most important?

4. How did the public react to the pardon? Why did Ford say he would do it again?

Why did ethics in government become a concern?

Three major problems faced Americans during the time Ford occupied the White House. None of them was completely solved, although some progress was made on each of them. They are problems which are still with us. They concern three important "e's": *ethics*, *energy*, and *economics*. First, let's explore the issue of *ethics*, or right behavior, in government. Then we will examine the problems of energy and economics.

On the day he became President, Ford talked to his fellow citizens about the importance of ethics. The Watergate scandals, he said, showed that it was time for all Americans to join in "restoring the golden rule to our political process."

Ford not only talked about ethics, he set an example of honesty and openness in government. Some historians consider his "restoring respectability" to the White House as his single greatest achievement.

Congress also showed concern about ethics in the wake of Watergate. It passed several new laws. One of them limited the amount of money any one person could contribute to a political campaign. In the past some people had donated huge amounts of money to a single candidate. In return they expected and sometimes received favors. Congress wanted to prevent such things from happening in the future.

Another law provided federal funds for candidates in presidential primaries and elections. Running for President is expensive. Candidates need money to

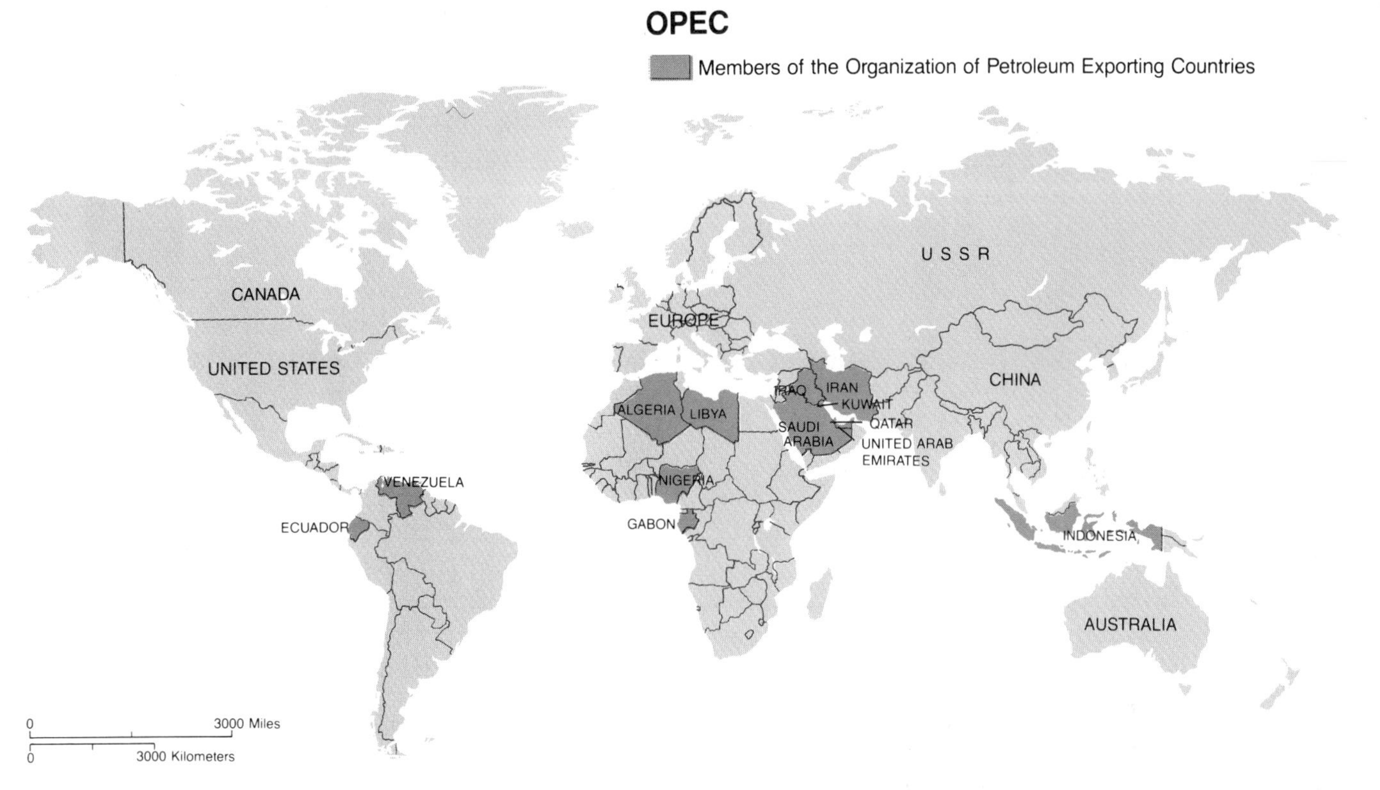

pay for television time, advertisements, campaign staffs, and travel. So Congress said it was time for candidates to get support from the taxpayers. Then they would not have to depend entirely on private contributors.

Still another law gave citizens the right to see information that government agencies had gathered about them. The Watergate scandals had revealed the existence of secret files on some Americans. Congress said that it did not believe in secrecy of that kind. People should have the right to know and to examine files which contain information about them. Americans, Congress insisted, had a right to "freedom of information." Congress also tightened controls on the FBI, the CIA, and other government agencies.

5. What is ethics?

6. What did President Ford say and do about ethics in government? What did Congress do?

Why did energy become a major problem?

When shortages of energy developed during the 1970s, many people were surprised. They thought there was a plentiful supply of fuels. However, the earth has only a limited supply of oil, natural gas, and coal. Those three fossil fuels supply about 95 percent of the world's energy needs. When they are used up, human effort cannot replace them.

Another fact which most people had not realized was that energy demands are rising throughout the world. The United States, with just 6 percent of the population, had been using about a third of the world's energy supply. Until 1953, the United States produced enough oil for its own needs and even for export to other countries. But as demand for oil grew, the United States began to rely on oil imported from other nations.

The event which probably brought the energy problem home to Americans

Gas shortages led to long lines at the pumps during the winter of 1973-1974 and again in 1979.

was the "energy crisis" of 1973-1974. The United States then imported one-third of its oil. Most of it came from Arab countries in the Middle East. Suddenly those oil-rich countries joined to say they would ship no more oil to the United States until their demands were met. They wanted the United States to force Israel to withdraw from land it had occupied. They also wanted higher prices for their oil. The United States faced a shortage of 17 percent of its oil supply. During the winter of 1973-1974, there were long lines of cars waiting for gasoline in the United States.

Eventually the ban was lifted. The lines at the gas pumps disappeared. But prices were raised. And the long-term question of providing energy remained.

By the end of 1974, members of OPEC, the Organization of Petroleum Exporting Countries, were charging more than four times as much for a barrel of crude oil as they had in 1973. The price rise made worldwide inflation even worse.

In 1979 the energy crisis again became critical. A revolutionary government in Iran stopped its flow of oil to the United States. Then OPEC again raised the price of oil.

At present, the United States is trying in a number of ways to decrease its dependence on foreign oil and to conserve energy. It also is trying to increase its own oil supply. Oil reserves in Alaska are being tapped. The oil is flowing to the "lower 48" states—by pipeline to a port where it is loaded on tankers.

More and more coal is being mined from the nation's large reserves. But many people object to coal as a fuel because it pollutes the air. Underground mining is dangerous. Strip mining can spoil the environment. Natural gas is the least harmful fuel to the environment, but it, too, is in short supply.

There are a number of experiments going on to increase use of solar energy, or energy from the sun. Solar power may one day be the answer to the energy problem. At this time, however, it is providing only a small fraction of the industrial and commercial needs of the United States.

Nuclear power appears to be the most likely solution to energy needs in the near future. But nuclear power also has its problems. The cost of building nuclear plants has been much higher than expected. Many citizens who think that nuclear plants are unsafe have raised objections. Their fears have been increased by recent accidents and by information about health hazards. The most serious accident occurred at the Three Mile Island nuclear plant near Harrisburg, Pennsylvania. For about a week in the spring of 1979 there was danger of a major radiation leak from the crippled plant. The problem was brought under control, but the plant was ruined.

7. What was the energy crisis of 1973-1974?

8. Why do Americans face a long-term energy problem?

An accident at the Three Mile Island nuclear plant in 1979 sparked fears about the safety of such plants.

What economic troubles disturbed Americans?

When Ford became President he said that inflation was the nation's number one economic problem. Prices were rising faster than earnings. People complained that everything from gasoline to food to housing "cost too much." If and when they got a raise in their wages, it was more than eaten up by the higher prices they had to pay. Instead of making headway, they actually were losing ground. They were less well off each month.

Ford believed that government itself was responsible for much of the inflation. So he tried to cut government spending. While he occupied the White House, he used his veto power 66 times to turn down programs he thought were too expensive. With each veto he sent a warning to Congress. It should curb expenses, he said. But Congress was unwilling to apply the economic brakes as hard as Ford thought necessary. Few members of Congress were willing to cut back on programs which affected voters in their home states. Even if they favored economy in government, they generally wanted cuts to be made somewhere else.

Unemployment also was on the rise. By the end of 1974 about 9 percent of the labor force, or about 8 million persons, were without jobs. In some states unemployment was as high as 15 percent. Among youths aged 16-22 it was even higher, especially among those who had dropped out of high school. In some cities as many as one-third of those youths were unemployed.

Ford was greatly concerned about unemployment. But he did not think that the long-term solution was the creation of government jobs. That would only add to the burdens of the already overburdened taxpayers. And it would increase inflation, he said. He believed that it was wiser to encourage private businesses and industries to create new jobs.

By the time he turned the presidency over to Jimmy Carter, Ford had

Workers without jobs line up for unemployment benefits. In 1976 the unemployment rate was 8 percent.

begun to make some gains. Inflation, which was 12 percent in 1974, had been reduced by more than half by the Ford administration. It had dropped to less than 5 percent in 1976. Unemployment, however, remained at nearly 8 percent of the work force.

9. How successful was Ford in dealing with inflation?

10. Why was unemployment a serious problem? How successful was the Ford administration in dealing with it?

Part Four

The Carter Years

How did Carter win the presidency?

After Jimmy Carter was inaugurated on January 20, 1977, he and his family headed for the waiting limousines. But they did not get in them for the traditional parade down Pennsylvania Avenue. Instead Carter began to walk hand in hand with his wife and campaign partner, Rosalynn. Alongside them was their pigtailed, 9-year-old daughter, Amy. Immediately following were the rest of the Carter family. Waving, smiling, and pausing so Amy could tie her shoe, they walked to the White House.

That walk and Carter's first televised speech to the nation after taking office were meant to signal some things he thought important. For his first television appearance, Carter wore a sweater and sat before a blazing fire. He was trying to symbolize his desire to "bring the presidency back to the people." Carter was bent on setting a new, informal tone.

Carter had reached the White House by a most unusual route. Unlike Ford, Carter had no previous experience in Washington, D.C. In fact, he had so little experience in government that throughout the long primary campaign, the public kept asking, "Jimmy who?"

"Jimmy" was really James Earl Carter, Jr. But he insisted on being called Jimmy. He was the first President elected from the Deep South since 1849. He was proud of his "common folk" roots in the South.

Carter was born in 1924 in Plains, Georgia, a sleepy little town of 600. After graduating from the local high school, he went on to the Naval Academy in Annapolis, Maryland. Shortly after his graduation he married Rosalynn Smith, also of Plains.

After his father died, Carter left the navy to return to Plains. He and Rosalynn took over his family's peanut business and made it a success. But Carter yearned to get into politics. He ran for a seat in the Georgia Senate. He was elected and reelected. Then he became governor of that state. Finally,

President Carter and his wife Rosalynn walk down Pennsylvania Avenue after his inauguration.

he set out to make himself the Democrat's nominee for President.

In the months that followed, Carter, Rosalynn, other members of his family, and a few backers crisscrossed the country. Bit by bit "Jimmy who" began to build up grassroots strength. By the time the Democratic convention met in New York City in July 1976, Carter had the votes it took for nomination.

Carter ran against President Gerald Ford. During the campaign, they met three times in televised debates. Two important points of difference emerged between them. One issue was whether inflation or unemployment was the biggest economic problem facing the country. Ford said it was inflation. Carter said it was unemployment. The second issue between the candidates was that of experience. Ford reminded voters of his long experience in Washington and pointed with pride to his record as President. Carter was equally proud of his inexperience. He said it was time for an "outsider." He would bring a fresh point of view. He asked Americans to trust him. He would try to make our government

as good and honest and decent and truthful and fair and competent and idealistic and compassionate, and as filled with love, as are the American people.

Time and again Carter repeated that long promise. It had an appealing ring to voters who still remembered Watergate.

As the ballots were counted on election night, victory seemed to seesaw between the candidates. Not until the next morning was the outcome finally certain. It was Jimmy Carter by a hair, 51 percent to 48 percent. The black vote probably put Carter over the top. Only 54 percent of the eligible voters had gone to the polls. That was the smallest turnout since 1960.

1. How did Carter win the Democratic nomination? On what issues did he campaign?

2. How close was the Ford-Carter election?

What were Carter's successes and failures in office?

Carter entered the presidency with high hopes. He worked and drove himself hard. But he was not very well versed in national and world affairs. In the beginning he thought he could solve the nation's energy problems, reduce unemployment, curb inflation, and cut the number of federal agencies to 200. He also thought that by appealing directly to Soviet leaders he could get them to reduce their arms. He hoped he could bring peace to the Middle East by working with Arab and Israeli leaders. Four years later, Carter knew better. His on-the-job training proved to him just how tough all of those problems are.

In domestic affairs Carter had more failures than successes. The unemployment level was at nearly 8 percent in the

President Sadat of Egypt and Prime Minister Begin of Israel signed a peace treaty on the White House lawn in 1979.

fall of 1980. In automobile manufacturing centers, unemployment reached depression levels. Nor was Carter able to control inflation. It zoomed up from the 5 percent level at the end of Ford's administration to 13 percent for 1980.

Carter did enjoy some triumphs at home, however. He moved an "energy package," or a set of laws, through Congress. He also signed into law the Alaska lands bill. It is designed to protect the environment of that largest and most northern state.

Carter's best record was in foreign affairs, but even there it left much to be desired. He was able to bring President Anwar el-Sadat of Egypt and Prime Minister Menachem Begin of Israel together for a peace conference. They met at Camp David, the presidential retreat in Maryland. Carter worked with them for thirteen days, until at last they were able to come to some meeting of the minds. Begin and Sadat signed a peace treaty. But other Arab nations began a boycott against Egypt for its actions. Peace in the Middle East had not yet been achieved.

Carter got the Senate to ratify treaties which returned the Panama Canal to Panama. (See pages 436-437.) Under those treaties the United States will help Panama operate the Canal until 1999. It also will have a permanent right to protect and defend the right of all ships to use that waterway. Latin American nations were cheered by the ratification of those treaties, although some Americans opposed them. Ronald Reagan, who challenged Carter in the 1980 election, was one of the most outspoken opponents.

Carter continued progress in trade and on the diplomatic front with the People's Republic of China. He spearheaded the effort which resulted in the official recognition of that country.

He tried to make human rights the center of American foreign policy. Carter never wavered on the importance of human rights. He said "our support for human rights in other countries is in our own national interest as well as part of our own national character."

Two knotty trouble spots appear on the minus side of Carter's foreign affairs. The first was the long captivity of some Americans in Iran. After a revolution in Iran, student militants stormed the American embassy in Tehran. They seized some fifty Americans there as hostages. For over a year the United States attempted to negotiate with Iran's new, hard-line leaders. It presented the American case to the World Court and to the UN without success. It even tried a daring air rescue. But it failed.

The second trouble spot was Afghanistan. The Soviets invaded that small country which lies across their southern border. Afghanistan was unable to repel the Soviets' 100,000 troops. The Soviets assassinated Afghanistan's political leaders. And they threatened to move still farther south to take over some of the oil-rich lands in the Middle East.

Carter and other Americans were alarmed and outraged by the Soviet action. To bring pressure to bear on the USSR, the United States cut off shipments of grain and electronic equipment. It limited Soviet fishing in United States waters. And it called off American participation in the 1980 Olympic games because they were held in Moscow.

While the Soviets were not happy about those actions, they did not pull out their troops or stop their efforts to reach the oil-rich Persian Gulf countries.

3. What successes did Carter enjoy at home and in foreign affairs?

4. What were Carter's greatest problems at home? In foreign affairs?

What changes did the 1980 election bring?

President Carter easily won the Democratic nomination for the 1980 election. Senator Edward Kennedy, brother of former President John Kennedy, campaigned hard for the nomination, but he did not gain the support of many Democrats.

Several candidates tried for the Republican nomination, but Ronald Reagan, former governor of California, took an early lead. Congressman John Anderson split off from the Republican party and ran as an independent. Reagan won the nomination and selected another candidate, George Bush of Texas, as his running mate.

Reagan's early career gave little clue that he would one day run for President. He was born in Tampico, Illinois. He became a sports announcer after graduating from Eureka College in Illinois. During World War II, Reagan served with the United States Army Air Force. Then he became an actor in motion pictures and television programs. He made over 50 movies.

Reagan became involved in politics only after he retired as an actor. He was elected governor of California in 1966. He promised to cut taxes and control student unrest on college campuses. Reagan served as governor until 1975. He ran unsuccessfully against Nixon for the Republican nomination in 1968. He tried again for the nomination for President in 1976, but lost to Ford.

Reagan campaigned hard in 1980. He took a strong conservative stand on most issues. He blamed Carter's policies for inflation and unemployment. He said government had grown far too large. Reagan promised to trim government spending and cut taxes. He held out a vision to Americans of the United States as "a city on a hill," the same vision that the Puritans had seen two centuries before. (See page 51.)

Carter and his supporters said that Reagan would not make needed compromises in foreign affairs. They said Reagan would be too quick to involve the United States in wars and the use of nuclear arms. Reagan replied that use of arms would always be his last resort. The Democrats hinted that at 69 Reagan was too old for the presidency. If elected, he would be the oldest President in history.

Even on election day, the polls said the race was very close. Many voters were undecided. But when the votes

Ronald Reagan takes the oath as President in 1981. He began at once to trim government spending.

came in, Reagan and the Republican party had won a smashing victory. Reagan won 489 electoral votes to Carter's 49. Carter carried only six states and the District of Columbia.

The voters chose Republicans for Congress, too. For the first time in 25 years, the Republicans captured the majority of seats in the Senate. Several powerful Democrats were defeated, including Senator George McGovern, presidential candidate in 1972. The Democrats held on to a slim lead in the House. Not since 1916 had different parties controlled the House and Senate.

Observers saw the election as a "watershed." They said it marked a definite switch in government policy. They compared the election to the 1932 victory of FDR, which began the New Deal. Voters in 1980 clearly indicated that they wanted a change to more conservative government.

5. Who were the candidates for President in 1980?

6. What did Reagan promise to do as President?

Part Five

Challenges of the Future

What is a minority group?

Since its very beginning, the United States has given its citizens more freedom and liberty than any other country in the world. But as you have seen in your study of American history, various groups of people in the United States have at times experienced discrimination and prejudice. And different groups have at times made strong efforts to obtain their full civil rights.

Although much progress has been made in the United States toward equal opportunity for all citizens, some minority groups are still struggling for their full rights. A *minority group* has less political or economic power than the dominant group in a society. The major minority groups in the United States today are blacks, Hispanics, or Spanish-speaking people, Native Americans, and the handicapped. Women also are considered a minority group. Even though they represent 51 percent of the population, women have less political and economic power than men. In this section we shall look at the progress made by these groups in recent years.

1. What is a minority group?

2. What are the major minority groups in the United States today?

What is affirmative action?

Affirmative action refers to plans and programs aimed at making up for past discrimination. First aimed at blacks, these programs were extended to other minorities. Such efforts give minority persons special advantages in getting jobs, training, promotions, and higher education. In some cases, a certain percentage, or *quota*, became a goal for minority hiring or admission.

Affirmative action got underway in 1961. In that year, President Kennedy signed an executive order. It required firms with federal contracts to increase the number of minority persons doing work for the government. In 1965, President Johnson extended the order to include all operations of those firms.

In the meantime the Civil Rights Act of 1964 had required equal job rights for minorities in any business with 25 or more workers. In 1972 the Equal Employment Opportunity Act pushed this number down to 15 or more workers. It also said that the laws would apply to state and local governments and to schools and colleges. The Equal Employment Opportunity Commission (EEOC), set up under this law, would enforce it. The EEOC could take employers to court to get affirmative action. In some cases, as it turned out, federal judges actually drew up orders that told employers what affirmative action to take. By the early 1970s affirmative action covered millions of the nation's workers.

One big problem grew out of the affirmative action program. Jobs, promotions, or other benefits reserved for blacks or women or other minorities would not be available for white males. Allen Bakke was one of these. He was a white student who had applied for an opening in the medical school at the University of California at Davis. This school had openings for only 100 students per year. But sixteen places were reserved for blacks, Hispanics, or Asian Americans. On entrance tests Bakke scored higher than some minority candidates who were admitted. So Bakke took his case to court.

The number of blacks in colleges and universities has more than doubled since 1960.

Bakke's case finally reached the United States Supreme Court. In 1978 it ruled that the school's affirmative action plan went too far. The decision ruled out rigid quotas but said that race or other minority status could be a factor to take into account in efforts to overcome the effects of past discrimination.

3. What is affirmative action?

4. How did the Supreme Court rule in the Bakke case?

What political progress has been made by blacks?

The black vote has become an important factor in elections. Black voters helped to elect Jimmy Carter in 1976. In 1980 Carter's failure to carry the black vote helped Ronald Reagan to win.

There are fifteen black members of Congress. Thurgood Marshall, the only

Los Angeles Mayor Tom Bradley walks with some friends.

black on the Supreme Court, was appointed by LBJ in 1967. Blacks have been appointed to every level of federal government, including cabinet offices.

Some of the most dramatic gains by blacks have been made on the local level. Over 150 cities have elected black mayors, beginning in 1967 with Gary, Indiana, and Cleveland, Ohio. In 1973 Tom Bradley, a black, was elected mayor of Los Angeles, the second largest city in the nation. At the time of his election, blacks made up only 18 percent of the total population of the city. He said that race was not a significant factor in his election. Bradley won reelection in 1977.

5. Who is Thurgood Marshall?
6. Name three cities which have elected black mayors.

How have Native Americans worked for their rights?

Indians, as you have learned, were living in North America long before the first Europeans and Africans arrived. As the new settlers spread across the continent, the Indians were "cleared away." Many died from diseases brought by the newcomers or in fighting to protect their homelands. Treaties made with the Indians were broken. They became "wards" of the government and were put on reservations. Not until the Snyder Act of 1924 were all Indians born in the United States given full citizenship.

During World War II, 25,000 American Indians served in the armed forces. But after the war, Native Americans still had the least education, the lowest incomes, the highest unemployment, the worst health, the shortest life expectancy, and the highest suicide rate of any large population group in the country.

President Lyndon Johnson, in a special message to Congress in 1968, called the Indian "The Forgotten American." He asked Congress for programs to give Indians a standard of living equal to that of other Americans. Congress voted $510 million for Indian aid programs—the highest amount ever for this group.

Indians themselves began to take action to call attention to their needs. During 1969 a group of 78 Indians seized Alcatraz Island with its deserted prison in San Francisco Bay. They demanded that it be made a cultural center. Finally, they were forced to leave the island by United States marshals in 1971.

More than 200 armed members of the American Indian Movement took over the village of Wounded Knee on the Oglala Sioux Pine Ridge Reservation in South Dakota in 1973. They opposed the local tribal government and demanded other reforms. The occupation continued for two months. Two Indians were killed. They lost their lives in shooting between the Indians and United States government agents.

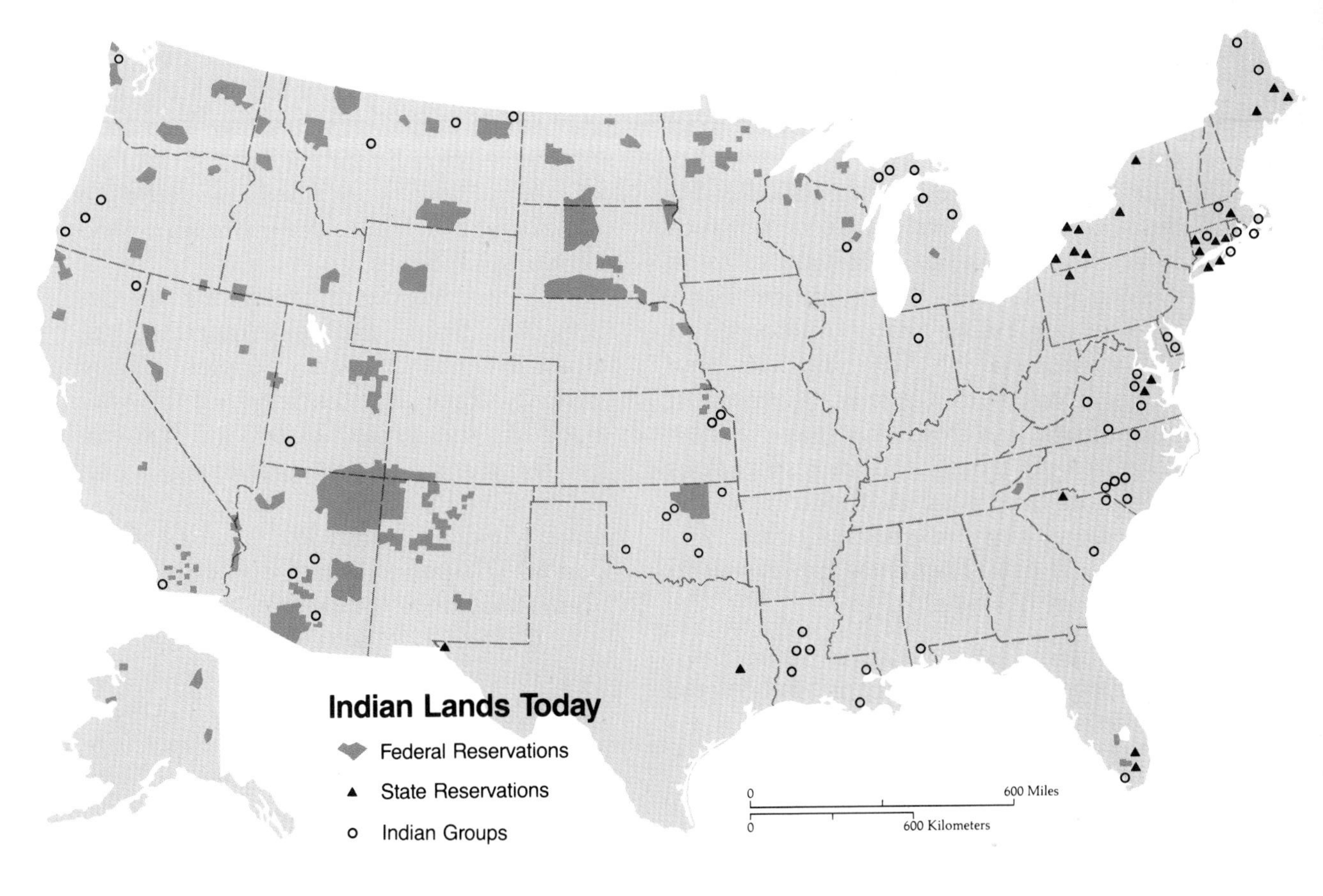

Many Indians rejected the violence of the radicals. They, too, wanted to run their own affairs and see the old treaties carried out. But they felt that the way to gain their rights was through the courts.

The Indian Self-Determination and Education Assistance Act of 1975 assured the Indians of more say on the reservations. During 1977, President Carter created the new post of Assistant Secretary of the Interior for Indian Affairs. A member of the Blackfoot tribe, Forrest J. Gerard, was named to the post.

Many Indians went to court during the 1970s to win the return of lands taken from their ancestors. They also demanded the right to control minerals, water, and grazing on the reservations. They wanted to hunt and fish and to raise their children on the reservations.

An American Indian woman's poster speaks proudly of the advances made by Indians in the 1970s.

Time after time the Indians won in the courts. The state of Rhode Island returned 1800 acres (720 ha) taken from the Narragansets many years before. The Penobscot and Passamaquoddy Indians of Maine were granted thousands of acres and millions of dollars to settle their claims. The Sioux of the Black Hills won a ruling that 7 million acres (2.8 million ha) of their land had been taken from them illegally. Control of their lands and resources gave a new power to the tribes. Indian reservations contained an estimated 16 percent of the nation's energy resources (coal, uranium, and oil). Their new power would come from this wealth.

7. How did Native Americans differ from other Americans after World War II?

8. What success did Indian tribes have in the courts in the 1970s?

Who are the Hispanic people of the United States?

It is estimated that by the year 2000, *Hispanics*, or Spanish-speaking people, will be the largest minority group in the United States. These people have come from many places and at many different times. Some of their ancestors came to America with the Spanish conquerors. Others have come to the mainland United States from Spain, Cuba, Puerto Rico, from Latin American countries, and from the Philippines.

Three-fifths of all the Spanish-speaking people in the United States are Mexican Americans. The ancestors of many of them settled in the Southwest and California in the 1600s and 1700s. These early settlers were followed over the years by millions of others. By 1980 there were at least 7 million Mexican Americans in the United States, and thousands more were entering the country every year. By far the largest number of them have continued to settle in California, Arizona, New Mexico, Colorado, and Texas.

Many Mexican Americans are descended from the intermarriage of Spanish and Indian peoples. They proudly trace their heritage all the way back to the great Aztec and Mayan civilizations. They generally call themselves by a variety of names: Mexican, Mexican Americans, Latinos, Chicanos, Hispanos, and sometimes *La Raza* (meaning "the people").

Originally, almost all Mexican Americans settled in rural areas in the United States. Then, like other Americans, they began moving into cities. Today 80 percent of them live in city neighborhoods, which they call *barrios*.

From the very beginning the differences of religion, language, skin color, and culture between the Mexican Americans and other Americans created conflicts. Mexican Americans were often discriminated against. Great numbers of them ended up in the lowest-paying jobs where no training was needed.

Many Mexicans and Mexican Americans worked as poorly paid farm laborers. Farm workers had always been the most difficult laborers to organize into a union. Since they came to work only for a season and were spread across the countryside, it was hard to bring them together for meetings. But Cesar Chavez succeeded. He had been a farm laborer himself. In 1962 he began to organize migrant laborers into a union. In 1965, 900 Filipino grape pickers in another union went out on strike. Chavez's union decided to go out, too. In

1966, the two unions merged to form the United Farm Workers Organizing Committee.

Chavez, like Martin Luther King, Jr., believed in nonviolence. He firmly insisted on this course in a long strike against the owners of vineyards in Delano, California. This won him public support from many church groups, from other unions, and from leaders like Robert Kennedy.

Chavez organized an effective nationwide boycott of California grapes. Finally, after five years, many owners signed contracts with the union that Chavez had organized.

Chavez himself stayed out of politics, but other Mexican Americans won high office. Both New Mexico and Arizona have had Mexican American governors. Other Mexican Americans have been elected to the United States Senate and the House. President Nixon appointed a Mexican American woman, Romana A. Bañuelos, to be Treasurer of the United States.

Puerto Ricans are different from other Hispanic immigrants because they are citizens of the United States. (See page 427.) They can come and go to the mainland freely. Starting in the 1950s many Puerto Ricans began coming to the mainland. Unemployment was high in Puerto Rico. On the mainland they faced many of the same problems as other immigrants: the language barrier and poverty. Many settled in New York City and worked in the garment industry.

Since 1960 there has been a decrease in the number of Puerto Ricans coming to the mainland. Because economic conditions on the island have improved, Puerto Ricans have not wanted to leave their beautiful homeland.

Cesar Chavez meets with farm workers at Salinas, California. Chavez organized migrant workers in a union.

9. Who is Cesar Chavez?

10. Why are Puerto Ricans different from other Spanish-speaking immigrants?

What laws have helped the handicapped?

Another important minority group in America are the handicapped. In 1978 it was estimated that 35 million Americans were physically handicapped.

The Rehabilitation Act of 1973 forbade discrimination against the physically disabled in any programs,

Focus on Skills

How does the typical or average American live today? No such person exists, of course. Each person is unique, one-of-a-kind. Even so, research points up patterns of living which Americans tend to share. Some of those patterns will be described here. For convenience, they have been grouped, or *categorized*.

Why do people bother to spend the hours and dollars it takes to put together statistics like these? See if you can figure out the answer. For each category of statistics, name at least two groups of people who would be interested in the data.

How Americans Spend Their Incomes

21.7% for food, beverages, tobacco
15.3% for housing
14.7% for household operation
14.3% for transportation
9.8% for medical care
7.9% for clothing
6.7% for recreation
1.4% for personal care

How Long Americans Are Expected to Live

white	
male	70.0 years
female	77.7 years
black and others	
male	64.0 years
female	73.1 years

Homes with Selected Appliances and Vehicle Ownership

radio	99.9%
refrigerator	99.9%
freezer	44.9%
toaster	99.9%
wired for electricity	100%
vacuum cleaner	99%
television (black/white)	99.9%
television (color)	83%
automobile	83%
two automobiles	32%

Americans in the Labor Force

Population (aged 15-64 years) in the labor force	65%
Labor force divisions:	
agriculture	2%
industry	33%
services	15%
information/knowledge (persons who gather and/or disseminate information or knowledge)	50%

Women in the Labor Force

Women make up 26.1% of the total labor force.

Mothers with children under 18 years of age are in the majority (52.9%) of the working women's force.

Women in the labor force are:

professional/technical workers	15.6%
managers/administrators	6.1%
sales workers	6.9%
clerical workers	34.6%
service workers	17.7%

Television Viewing

On a typical Sunday evening one of every two Americans watches TV.

In the average home, the TV is turned on for 43 hours and 52 minutes a week. Women aged 55 or older make up the largest viewing group. Teenagers watch the least amount of television, compared to other age groups.

activities, and facilities supported by federal funds. Other laws aimed to prevent job discrimination against handicapped persons. New federal regulations eased the lives of the handicapped. Every public building had to have at least one main entrance designed for wheelchairs. In public places, too, some telephone booths and toilets had to be provided for use by the handicapped.

To help the blind, the signs in public buildings had to be made with raised letters or numbers. Wherever public warning signals were given by sounds, there also had to be visual signals to warn the deaf. Public meetings

A student in a wheelchair checks out a book in the barrier-free library of Bergen Community College in Paramus, New Jersey. Many handicapped citizens are entering the mainstream of American life.

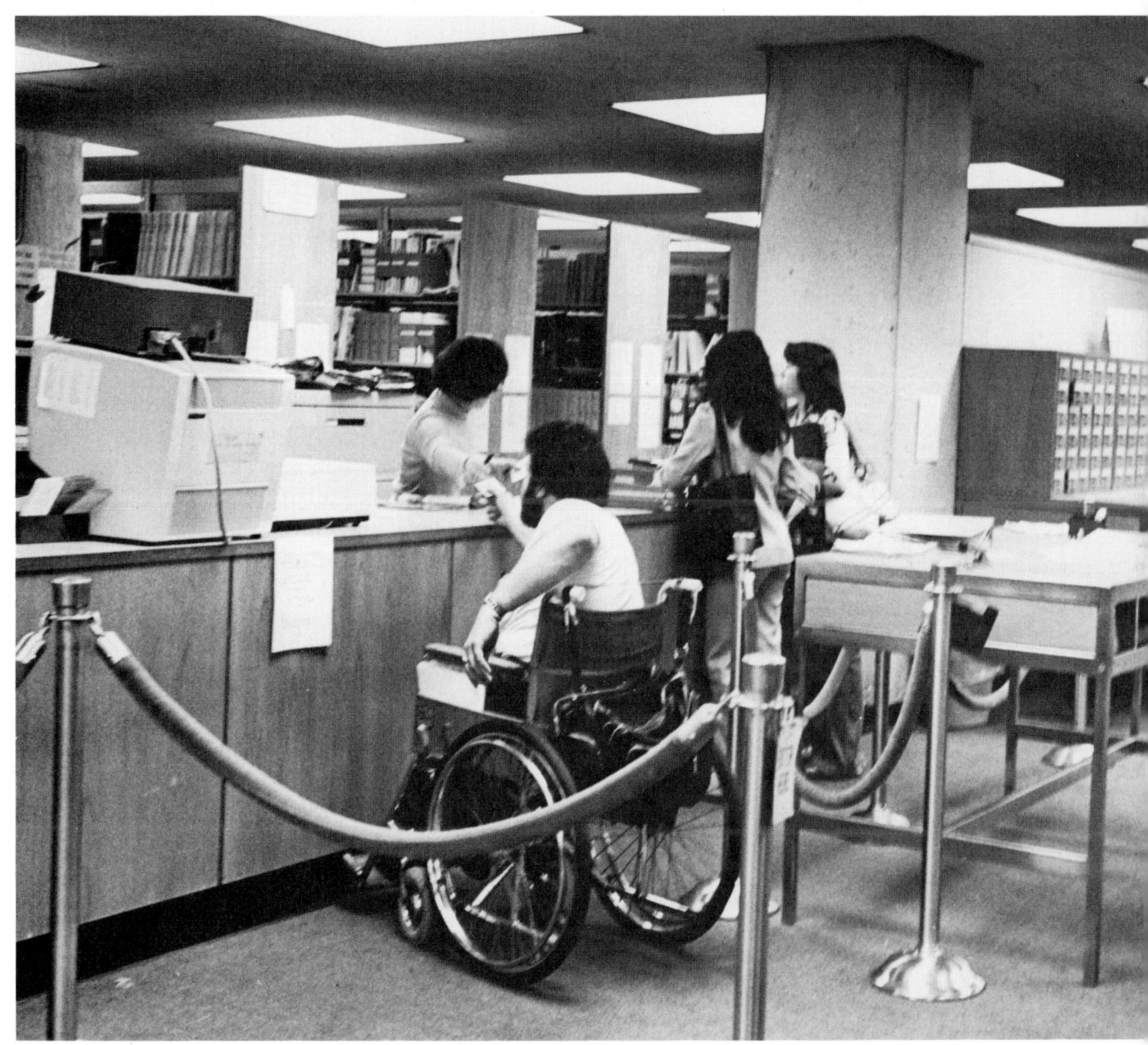

At That Time

It was in the early 1980s that Ung Kong-Mong, his wife, and their four children arrived in the United States. They could not speak a word of English. They had no jobs waiting for them. After paying for their trip, they were almost penniless. Kong-Mong and his wife took the first jobs they could find. Their jobs did not pay well. Nor were they the kind of work that most Americans would accept. After working all day, Kong-Mong and his wife attended night school to learn English. They lived in crowded quarters in the least desirable section of the city.

Were they discouraged or defeated? This is what Kong-Mong said through an interpreter:

We look around, and it is not what we want. But our eye is on the future. We know this will pass. We will become important people in time, good citizens. We are willing to work hard.

This new immigrant came from Southeast Asia.

An old story? Yes, in many ways it is. As someone once said, "People have been forever arriving in America."

The majority of today's immigrants come from Latin America. Almost a million Cubans have arrived by plane and boat. Many have chosen to make their homes in Florida, but some have fanned out into other states. More and more Haitians also have decided to seek a better life in the United States. But the largest group of immigrants comes from Mexico. If the present rate of immigration continues, Los Angeles could have the largest Mexican concentration outside Mexico City by 1984.

Asians account for the second largest group of new immigrants. People from Vietnam, Laos, and Cambodia have claimed every one of the 168,000 places offered to them annually.

The third largest group comes from Europe, particularly Eastern Europe, and from the Middle East.

Earlier you had a chance to meet some newcomers to the United States. Let's meet some of the men and women who have recently arrived.

1. **Ramon Lopez.** Why did I leave Mexico? I didn't have any choice. I had to look for a better way of life, even though it meant being separated from my wife and children for several years. From time to time I went back to see them. Then, at last, I was able to bring them here. Now we are all together again in Houston, Texas.

My wife works as a cook. I'm a gardener. Our oldest son, a machinist, is buying a truck. He hopes to go into business for himself. Our other five children attend school.

I know how it feels to suffer. But the only way to better yourself is to come here to the United States.

2. **Young Lee of Korea.** We Koreans are really the second Puritans in this country. Like the Puritans who came to New England in the 1600s, we are willing to work very hard. Take my wife and me, for example. When we arrived here we had just $200. We worked at any jobs we could find for the first three years. We managed to save enough to open our own service station. Time was our capital. We opened our station at 7 A.M. and closed it at 10 P.M. I slept in the back of the garage for a while.

Today my wife is a teacher's aide, but until recently she worked at the station pumping gas for eight or nine hours a day, seven days a week. I've finally been able to get the kind of work for which I was trained. I'm an engineer.

3. **Anna Davidovitch.** My husband and I spent the first fifty years of our lives in Odessa, USSR. Then we boarded a plane with other Russian-Jewish emigrants. We arrived at Kennedy International Airport in New York with our one-way tickets. We also had the telephone number of a friend of a friend from Odessa. And that's really all we had.

Getting out of Russia wasn't easy. Like other Jews, we had waited for years for permission to leave. We finally were among the lucky ones.

How do we like it here? America is a golden country. We have good food, a good apartment, and a car—more than we ever dreamed. But at first it was hard. We couldn't speak English. We had trouble finding jobs. And we had to adjust to American ways. We couldn't believe that we could change jobs if we wanted to.

and certain television programs were interpreted in signs for the deaf.

Other kinds of handicapped persons—the mentally ill and the mentally retarded—have also gained. Education of the mentally retarded was improved. By 1979 ten states had declared that their handicapped students would have a right to equal education with those not handicapped.

During the 1970s the federal government insisted that education in the nation's schools and colleges should be opened to all qualified mentally and physically handicapped persons. This was called "mainstreaming"—taking the handicapped out of special institutions and bringing them into the mainstream of American life.

11. What laws have been passed to help the handicapped?
12. What is "mainstreaming"?

Why do some women consider themselves a minority group?

It seems strange to think of women as a minority group, since they make up more than half of the population of the country.

But in the 1960s a new movement for women's rights began. In that year, a Commission on the Status of Women, appointed by President Kennedy and headed by Eleanor Roosevelt, found discrimination against women in every part of American life.

In 1966 Betty Friedan founded the National Organization for Women (NOW), which helped organize a nationwide Women's Strike for Equality. NOW urged women to speak up for their equal rights. Women involved in the struggle for women's rights were called *feminists*.

Many conservative Americans—men and women—were irritated by feminists' demands. They found the new feminists to be unladylike and "unfeminine." Others were puzzled because it seemed that in the United States women already had more freedom than women anywhere else.

Statistics confirmed some of the arguments of the new feminists. In 1971, for example, full-time working women were paid only 59 percent as much as men. Women with college degrees earned only half as much as men with similar education. In the 1970s the number of women in the labor force was already 40 percent and was on the rise. The number of working wives and mothers was also increasing. Still, one-third of all female workers were employed in clerical jobs—as secretaries, file clerks, and telephone operators. Few were executives or managers. In the early 1970s women accounted for only 7 percent of the physicians and only 3 percent of the lawyers. But during these years the enrollment of women in medical schools and law schools increased rapidly. By the end of the decade they made up one-fifth of the medical students and one-third of the law students.

The Civil Rights Act of 1964 barred job discrimination on the basis of sex as well as race. In 1972, two-thirds of the members of both houses of Congress approved an "Equal Rights" Amendment and sent it to the states. The proposed amendment read: "Equality of rights under the law shall not be denied or abridged by the United States or any state on account of sex." It was quickly ratified by 22 states. Then it ran into strong opposition.

The feminist movement and the Equal Rights Amendment were opposed by some women and some men because

"Women on the Move," including feminists Bella Abzug (left) and Betty Friedan (right), carry a torch to Houston, Texas, for the first National Women's Conference.

they valued the privileges more than the rights of women. There was no more important work, they insisted, than bearing and raising children. They thought that women were intended by nature for different roles than men. Reformers in the Progressive Era had demanded special laws to protect women in factories. "Equal rights" might mean the end of special protection for women and the end of "alimony" to support them and their children in case of divorce.

Under the Constitution, to adopt the Equal Rights Amendment, ratification by three-quarters of the states is required. In 1979, when the amendment was still three states short of the needed number, Congress extended the deadline for ratification to June 30, 1982. By 1981, 35 states had ratified the amendment. But five of those states had decided to take back their approval. The legality of that action would have to be tested in court.

By the 1980s, though there was still a way to go, women had made great progress. They were found in nearly every occupation. Women now worked as truck drivers, mechanics, business leaders, doctors, lawyers, ministers, and even as astronauts. They were governors, mayors, and cabinet members.

13. What is the ERA amendment?
14. Why do some women oppose the goals of the feminists?

Historymaker

In your study of American history you have met twenty people or groups of people featured as "historymakers." By their actions, these people affected events in their own lifetimes. But their influence is still felt today. What they did still affects the way we live in the world. And their words are quoted in speeches, books, newspapers, and television programs. Motion pictures are made about their lives.

The "historymakers" of the future will be people much like those twenty. Some will overcome handicaps as did Jane Addams, Theodore Roosevelt, and Franklin Roosevelt. Some will work for better lives for the people of their race as did Henri Christophe, John Ross, and Martin Luther King, Jr. Some "historymakers" of the future will run for President. Some will work outside the political arena.

Most of us will not be "historymakers" in the same way as those twenty. Only a few of us will run for President or start great social movements or make important discoveries. Most of us will affect history in less dramatic ways—but we will affect it. We will work, vote, and pay taxes. We may serve in the armed forces. When our actions in these matters are grouped with the actions of many other Americans, we will have decided elections and been part of trends.

But suppose you knew that in the year 2050, when you will be in your eighties, you would be known throughout the world as a "historymaker." What would you want to have done to change the lives of all future Americans?

The possibilities are many. You could be the President who worked out a successful plan for eliminating nuclear arms from the world. You could be the diplomat who brought true peace to the Middle East. You could be the first member of a minority group to be elected President. You could be the inventor who solved the energy crisis.

Pretend for a moment that you did become a "historymaker." Write a short autobiography in which you tell what you did that made you famous—and that will continue to affect the lives of Americans long after your death. Who knows? It might come true.

History is made every day—by leaders and by ordinary citizens. At left, President Reagan meets with his National Security adviser, Richard Allen, and Secretary of State Alexander Haig (center). Above, citizens take part in a movement for lower property taxes.

The space shuttle *Columbia* (left) waits for launch in April 1981 at Cape Canaveral, Florida. Astronauts John Young and Robert L. Crippen piloted the huge vessel on its orbital voyage. Below, some of the 52 hostages who returned from Iran after 444 days of captivity are greeted by a ticker-tape parade in New York City in January 1981. The hostages were seized in the American embassy in Teheran by student militants who were angry because the United States admitted the deposed shah of Iran for medical treatment.

Building Your Vocabulary

Select the word or words from those listed below which best complete each of these sentences.

1. President Nixon made his historic trip to China because he believed it was time for the United States to officially—?—that huge country.
2. The Soviet Union and the People's Republic of China are bitter—?—.
3. Vice-President Spiro Agnew pleaded—?—when he was charged with wrongdoing.
4. Another name for right behavior is—?—.
5. Before Gerald Ford became Vice-President, he was—?—in the House of Representatives.
6. Today the United States is trying to find new ways to meet its—?—needs.
7. A group with less political or economic power than the dominant group in a society is called a—?—group.
8. Programs which aim to make up for past discrimination are called—?—.

ethics	no contest	rivals	affirmative action
Minority Leader	energy	minority	recognize

Recalling What You Have Learned

Choose the best answer for the following items.

1. The Independent candidate for President in 1968 was (a) Jimmy Carter. (b) George Wallace. (c) Hubert Humphrey. (d) Ronald Reagan.
2. About which of these issues was Nixon concerned during his first term in the White House? (a) law and order (b) the growth of big government (c) the overheated economy (d) all of the above
3. The ERA is (a) a proposed amendment to the Constitution which guarantees equal rights for women. (b) the Economic Reform Act of 1980. (c) the Environmental Act of 1978. (d) a proposed amendment to the Constitution which makes the District of Columbia a state.
4. Watergate created a constitutional crisis because it involved (a) the executive branch of government. (b) the legislative branch of government. (c) the judicial branch of government. (d) all three branches of government.
5. Gerald Ford believed his most important job as President was to: (a) bind up the nation's post-Watergate wounds. (b) reduce unemployment. (c) listen to the "silent majority." (d) stop government spending.
6. Jimmy Carter won the Democratic nomination for President by (a) not campaigning in the primaries. (b) building grassroots support. (c) staging a great

parade in Washington, D.C. (d) running as an independent.

7. Which of the following was not a success for Carter? (a) getting the Panama Canal treaties ratified (b) stirring interest in international human rights (c) bringing Israel and Egypt together to try to settle their differences (d) securing immediate release of American hostages in Iran.

8. How did the United States respond to the Soviet invasion of Afghanistan? (a) by limiting Soviet fishing in United States waters (b) by boycotting the Olympic games in Moscow (c) by cutting off shipments of grain and electronic equipment (d) all of the above.

Discussing the Important Ideas in This Chapter

1. Who were the Americans Nixon described as "the silent majority"? Why did he say his administration would listen to them?
2. Nixon's trip to China has been called "the boldest diplomatic move by an American President since Jefferson bought Louisiana." Do you agree? Why?
3. Why do you think the Constitution was able to pass the test of Watergate? What has that test proved?
4. How do you think we should go about meeting our nation's energy needs?
5. Inflation and unemployment long have been serious problems for all Americans. How has your family been affected by those problems? What do you think could/should be done about them?
6. What advances have been made by each of these minority groups: blacks, Hispanics, women, the handicapped? What else needs to be done by and for each of these groups?

Improving Your Chronology Skills

On a separate sheet of paper, copy the timeline exactly as it is shown on page 551. Then add five important events in your own life or in the lives of members of your family. For example, you might list the year you entered school, moved to a new community, won a special honor, or participated in an important activity.

Improving Your Study Skills: *Research*

Many of the issues and problems discussed in this chapter are as yet unresolved. Select one of the topics listed below. Do research in the library on that topic. Use current materials which will help you as you write a short report which will update the information contained in this text. In that report you should:

1. Describe the most recent events in the area you have chosen to study.
2. If possible, tell why recent developments have come about.
3. Tell how people feel about what is happening now.

To prepare your report use resources such as these which you can find in your school or public libraries: *Reader's Guide to Periodical Literature*, *Facts on File*, *New York Times Index*, almanacs for the current year, *Statistical Abstract of the United States*.

Ask your librarian to suggest other sources of current information which also may be available in your school and community libraries.

In addition to the written sources you consult, talk with knowledgeable people in your community. Ask them to tell you how they feel about new developments in the area you have chosen to research.

Suggested Topics

inflation
employment/unemployment
ethics in government
meeting energy needs
the search for peace in the Middle East
Latin American attitudes toward the United States
rights for the handicapped
international human rights
immigration patterns
the United States and the refugee problem
the Equal Rights Amendment
United States/Soviet Union relations
United States/People's Republic of China relations

Appendix

130°
120°
110°
100°
50°
40°
30°
120°
C
A
N
Calgary
Regina
PACIFIC
OCEAN
WASHINGTON
Seattle
Olympia
Tacoma
Spokane
Columbia R.
Columbia R.
Portland
Salem
OREGON
IDAHO
Boise
Snake R.
Pocatello
MONTANA
Helena
Great Falls
Butte
Missouri R.
Yellowstone R.
NORTH DAKOTA
Bismark
SOUTH DAKOTA
Pierre
Sioux Fa
WYOMING
Casper
Cheyenne
NEBRASKA
Platte R.
Linco
CALIFORNIA
Sacramento
San Francisco
Oakland
Los Angeles
San Diego
NEVADA
Reno
Carson City
Humboldt R.
Las Vegas
Great Salt Lake
Ogden
Salt Lake City
UTAH
Colorado R.
COLORADO
Denver
Pueblo
Arkansas R.
KANSAS
Wichita
ARIZONA
Phoenix
Tucson
Colorado
NEW MEXICO
Santa Fe
Albuquerque
Rio Grande
Pecos R.
El Paso
OKLA
Oklahoma City
Amarillo
Fort Worth
TEXAS
Colorado
Aust
Rio Grande
San Antoni
Corpus Christi
USSR
Barrow
Bering Strait
SEWARD PEN.
Nome
BERING SEA
Fairbanks
Yukon R.
KLONDIKE REGION
NUNIVAK ISLAND
Anchorage
PRIBILOF ISLANDS
KENAI PEN.
Seward
ALEUTIAN ISLANDS
Dutch Harbor
ALASKA PEN.
Kodiak
GULF OF ALASKA
CANADA
Juneau
Sitka
Ketchikan
ALASKA
0
750 Miles
0
750 Kilometers
PACIFIC OCEAN
170°
180°
170°
160°
150°
140°
70°
60°
50
160°
22° 30'
KAUAI
NIIHAU
157° 30'
OAHU
Honolulu
Pearl Harbor
MOLOKAI
LANAI
MAUI
KAHOOLAWE
PACIFIC
OCEAN
155°
20°
HAWAII
Hilo
HAWAII
0
100 Miles
0
100 Kilometers

United States
Political
0
1000 Miles
0
1000 Kilometers
A
D
A
90°
80°
70°
50°
40°
30°
20°
80°
Winnipeg
Quebec
St. Lawrence R.
Fredericton
St. John
L. Superior
Sault Ste. Marie
Montreal
Ottowa
MAINE
Augusta
Portland
Burlington
Montpelier
VT.
N.H.
Concord
Manchester
Boston
MASS.
Worcester
Providence
R.I.
Hartford
CONN.
New Haven
Duluth
MINNESOTA
Minneapolis
St. Paul
Mississippi R.
WISCONSIN
Green Bay
Madison
Milwaukee
MICHIGAN
L. Michigan
L. Huron
Grand Rapids
Flint
Lansing
Detroit
Toronto
L. Ontario
Rochester
Hamilton
Syracuse
Buffalo
Albany
NEW YORK
L. Erie
Erie
Scranton
PENNSYLVANIA
Newark
New York
Trenton
NEW JERSEY
Harrisburg
Philadelphia
Wilmington
Pittsburgh
Sioux City
IOWA
Des Moines
Missouri R.
maha
Chicago
Gary
Fort Wayne
Toledo
Cleveland
Akron
OHIO
Peoria
ILLINOIS
Indianapolis
INDIANA
Columbus
Dayton
Cincinnati
Springfield
WEST VIRGINIA
Huntington
Charleston
Washington
D.C.
Baltimore
Dover
Annapolis
MARYLAND
DELAWARE
Kansas City
Topeka
Jefferson City
St. Louis
MISSOURI
Evansville
Ohio R.
Louisville
Frankfort
KENTUCKY
Richmond
Norfolk
VIRGINIA
Raleigh
NORTH CAROLINA
Charlotte
Nashville
Knoxville
TENNESSEE
Chattanooga
Memphis
Tulsa
OMA
Fort Smith
ARKANSAS
Little Rock
Red R.
SOUTH CAROLINA
Columbia
Atlanta
Charleston
Birmingham
ALABAMA
Montgomery
Columbus
GEORGIA
Savannah
MISSISSIPPI
Meridian
Jackson
Dallas
Sabine R.
Shreveport
LOUISIANA
S
Baton Rouge
Mobile
Tallahassee
FLORIDA
Jacksonville
Beaumont
New Orleans
Houston
Tampa
GULF OF MEXICO
Miami
Key West
Straits of Florida
Nassau
BAHAMAS
Havana
CUBA
ATLANTIC OCEAN

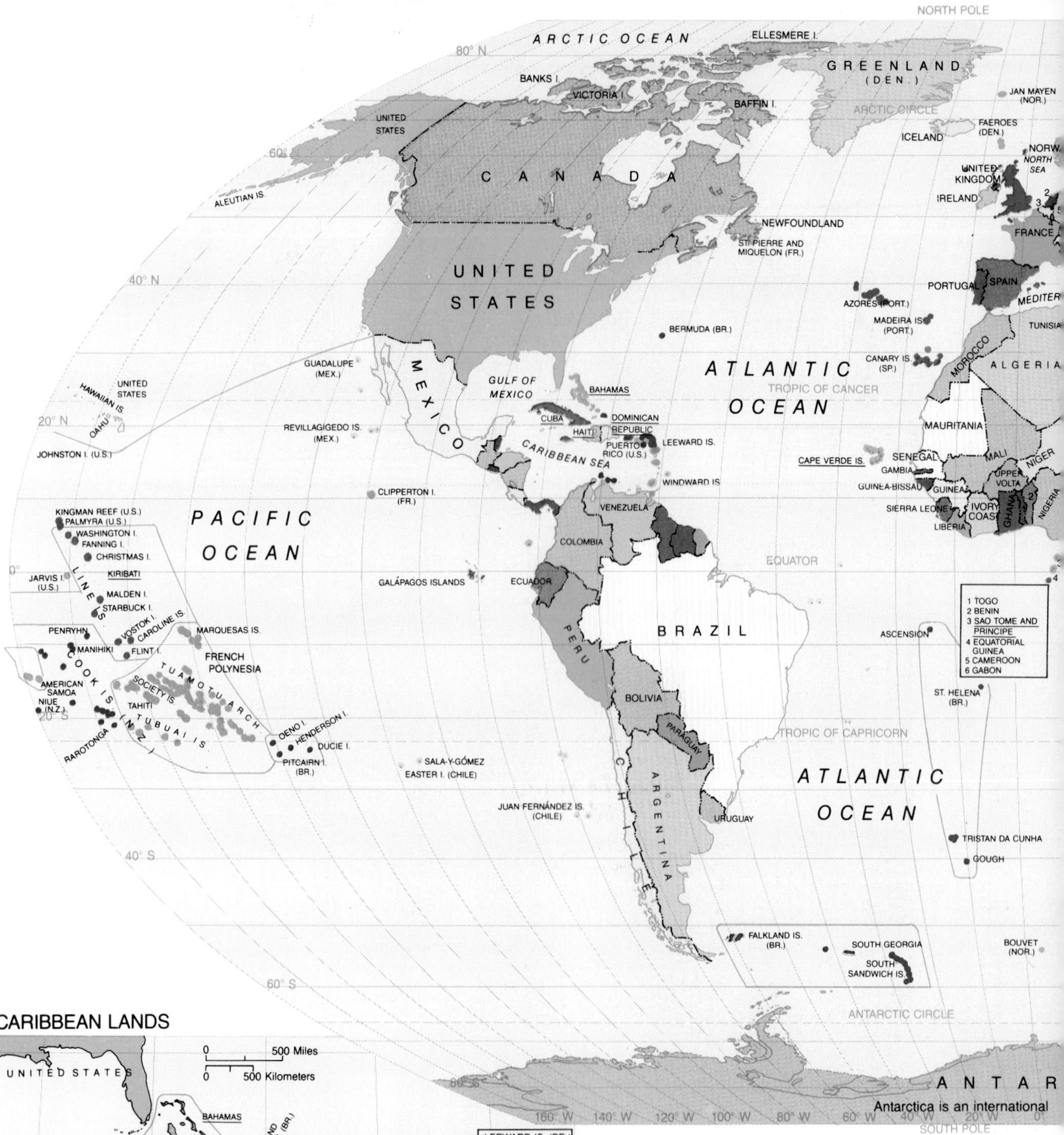

NORTH POLE

ARCTIC OCEAN
ELLESMERE I.
80° N
GREENLAND (DEN.)
BANKS I.
VICTORIA I.
BAFFIN I.
JAN MAYEN (NOR.)
ARCTIC CIRCLE
UNITED STATES
FAEROES (DEN.)
ICELAND
NORW.
NORTH SEA
60°
C A N A D A
UNITED KINGDOM
ALEUTIAN IS.
IRELAND
NEWFOUNDLAND
FRANCE
ST. PIERRE AND MIQUELON (FR.)
40° N
UNITED STATES
PORTUGAL
SPAIN
AZORES (PORT.)
MEDITER
MADEIRA IS. (PORT.)
TUNISIA
BERMUDA (BR.)
GUADALUPE (MEX.)
CANARY IS. (SP.)
MOROCCO
ALGERIA
ATLANTIC OCEAN
MEXICO
GULF OF MEXICO
BAHAMAS
TROPIC OF CANCER
HAWAIIAN IS.
UNITED STATES
OAHU
20° N
CUBA
DOMINICAN REPUBLIC
HAITI
MAURITANIA
REVILLAGIGEDO IS. (MEX.)
PUERTO RICO (U.S.)
LEEWARD IS.
CARIBBEAN SEA
JOHNSTON I. (U.S.)
CAPE VERDE IS.
SENEGAL
GAMBIA
MALI
NIGER
WINDWARD IS.
GUINEA-BISSAU
UPPER VOLTA
CLIPPERTON I. (FR.)
GUINEA
KINGMAN REEF (U.S.)
VENEZUELA
SIERRA LEONE
IVORY COAST
GHANA
NIGERIA
PALMYRA (U.S.)
PACIFIC OCEAN
WASHINGTON I.
LIBERIA
FANNING I.
CHRISTMAS I.
COLOMBIA
EQUATOR
0°
KIRIBATI
JARVIS I. (U.S.)
LINE IS.
GALÁPAGOS ISLANDS
ECUADOR
MALDEN I.
STARBUCK I.
1 TOGO
2 BENIN
3 SAO TOME AND PRINCIPE
4 EQUATORIAL GUINEA
5 CAMEROON
6 GABON
PENRHYN
VOSTOK I.
CAROLINE IS.
MARQUESAS IS.
BRAZIL
ASCENSION
MANIHIKI
FLINT I.
FRENCH POLYNESIA
PERU
COOK IS. (N.Z.)
TUAMOTU ARCH.
AMERICAN SAMOA
SOCIETY IS.
BOLIVIA
ST. HELENA (BR.)
NIUE (N.Z.)
TAHITI
20° S
TUBUAI IS.
PARAGUAY
TROPIC OF CAPRICORN
OENO I.
HENDERSON I.
RAROTONGA
DUCIE I.
PITCAIRN I. (BR.)
SALA-Y-GÓMEZ
EASTER I. (CHILE)
ATLANTIC OCEAN
ARGENTINA
CHILE
JUAN FERNÁNDEZ IS. (CHILE)
URUGUAY
TRISTAN DA CUNHA
40° S
GOUGH
FALKLAND IS. (BR.)
SOUTH GEORGIA
BOUVET (NOR.)
SOUTH SANDWICH IS.
60° S
ANTARCTIC CIRCLE
80° S
ANTAR
Antarctica is an international
160° W 140° W 120° W 100° W 80° W 60° W 40° W 0°
SOUTH POLE

CARIBBEAN LANDS

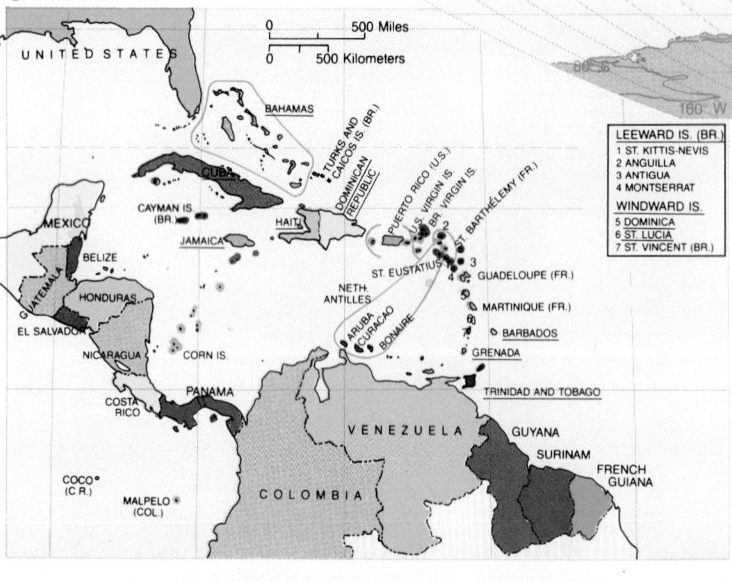

0 500 Miles
0 500 Kilometers

UNITED STATES
BAHAMAS
TURKS AND CAICOS IS. (BR.)
CUBA
DOMINICAN REPUBLIC
MEXICO
CAYMAN IS. (BR.)
HAITI
PUERTO RICO (U.S.)
U.S. VIRGIN IS.
BR. VIRGIN IS.
ST. BARTHÉLEMY (FR.)
JAMAICA
BELIZE
ST. EUSTATIUS
GUADELOUPE (FR.)
NETH. ANTILLES
HONDURAS
MARTINIQUE (FR.)
GUATEMALA
ARUBA
CURACAO
BONAIRE
BARBADOS
EL SALVADOR
NICARAGUA
CORN IS.
GRENADA
TRINIDAD AND TOBAGO
PANAMA
COSTA RICA
VENEZUELA
GUYANA
SURINAM
FRENCH GUIANA
COCO (C.R.)
MALPELO (COL.)
COLOMBIA

LEEWARD IS. (BR.)
1 ST. KITTIS-NEVIS
2 ANGUILLA
3 ANTIGUA
4 MONTSERRAT

WINDWARD IS.
5 DOMINICA
6 ST. LUCIA
7 ST. VINCENT (BR.)

Political Map of the World

Natural Scale 1:100,000,000   Wagner's Near-Equal-Area Projection

—·— International boundaries.

—— Line to show ownership groupings of islands; ocean areas enclosed are mainly international waters.

▫ States or dependencies so small their actual shapes cannot be shown.

—— Island Nations are underlined

0 — 3000 Miles

0 — 3000 Kilometers

The Declaration of Independence

In Congress, July 4, 1776.

Introduction

When, in the course of human events, it becomes necessary for one people to dissolve the political bands which have connected them with another, and to assume, among the powers of the earth, the separate and equal station to which the laws of nature and of nature's God entitle them, a decent respect to the opinions of mankind requires that they should declare the causes which impel them to the separation.

What Americans Believe

We hold these truths to be self-evident:—That all men are created equal: that they are endowed by their Creator with certain unalienable rights; that among these are life, liberty, and the pursuit of happiness. That, to secure these rights, governments are instituted among men, deriving their just powers from the consent of the governed; that, whenever any form of government becomes destructive of these ends, it is the right of the people to alter or to abolish it, and to institute new government, laying its foundation on such principles, and organizing its powers in such form, as to them shall seem most likely to effect their safety and happiness. Prudence, indeed, will dictate that governments long established should not be changed for light and transient causes; and accordingly all experience hath shown that mankind are more disposed to suffer while evils are sufferable, than to right themselves by abolishing the forms to which they are accustomed. But when a long train of abuses and usurpations, pursuing invariably the same object, evinces a design to reduce them under absolute despotism, it is their right, it is their duty, to throw off such government, and to provide new guards for their future security. Such has been the patient sufferance of these colonies; and such is now the necessity which constrains them to alter their former systems of government. The history of the present King of Great Britain is a history of repeated injuries and usurpations, all having in direct object the establishment of an absolute tyranny over these states. To prove this, let facts be submitted to a candid world.

The King's Wrongs

He has refused his assent to laws, the most wholesome and necessary for the public good.

He has forbidden his governors to pass laws of immediate and pressing importance, unless suspended in their operation till his assent should be obtained; and when so suspended, he has utterly neglected to attend to them.

He has refused to pass other laws for the accommodation of large districts of people, unless those people would relinquish the right of representation in the legislature—a right inestimable to them and formidable to tyrants only.

He has called together legislative bodies at places unusual, uncomfortable, and distant from the depository of their public records, for the sole purpose of fatiguing them into compliance with his measures.

He has dissolved representative houses repeatedly, for opposing with manly firmness his invasions on the rights of the people.

He has refused for a long time, after such dissolutions, to cause others to be elected; whereby the legislative powers, incapable of annihilation, have returned to the people at large for their exercise; the State remaining in the mean time exposed to all the dangers of invasions from without, and convulsions within.

He has endeavored to prevent the population of these States; for that purpose obstructing the laws for naturalization of foreigners; refusing to pass others to encourage their migrations hither, and raising the conditions of new appropriations of lands.

He has obstructed the administration of justice, by refusing his assent to laws for establishing judiciary powers.

He has made judges dependent on his will alone, for the tenure of their offices, and the amount and payment of their salaries.

He has erected a multitude of new offices, and sent hither swarms of officers to harass our people and eat out their substance.

He has kept among us, in times of peace, standing armies without the consent of our legislatures.

He has affected to render the military independent of and superior to the civil power.

He has combined with others to subject us to a jurisdiction foreign to our constitutions, and unacknowledged by our laws; giving his assent to their acts of pretended legislation:

For quartering large bodies of armed troops among us;

For protecting them, by a mock trial, from punishment for any murders which they should commit on the inhabitants of these States;

For cutting off our trade with all parts of the world;

For imposing taxes on us without our consent;

For depriving us, in many cases, of the benefits of trial by jury;

For transporting us beyond seas to be tried for pretended offences;

For abolishing the free system of English laws in a neighboring province, establishing therein an arbitrary government, and enlarging its boundaries so as to render it at once an example and fit instrument for introducing the same absolute rule into these colonies;

For taking away our charters, abolishing our most valuable laws, and altering, fundamentally, the forms of our governments;

For suspending our own legislatures, and declaring themselves invested with power to legislate for us in all cases whatsoever.

He has abdicated government here, by declaring us out of his protection and waging war against us.

He has plundered our seas, ravaged our coasts, burned our towns, and destroyed the lives of our people.

He is at this time transporting large armies of foreign mercenaries to complete the works of death, desolation and tyranny, already begun with circumstances of cruelty and perfidy scarcely paralleled in the most barbarous ages, and totally unworthy the head of a civilized nation.

He has constrained our fellow-citizens taken captive on the high seas to bear arms against their country, to become the executioners of their friends and brethren, or to fall themselves by their hands.

He has excited domestic insurrection among us, and has endeavored to bring on the inhabitants of our frontiers the merciless Indian savages, whose known rule of warfare is an undistinguished destruction of all ages, sexes, and conditions.

No End to Injustice

In every stage of these oppressions we have petitioned for redress in the most humble terms; our repeated petitions have been answered only by repeated injury. A prince whose character is thus marked by every act which may define a tyrant is unfit to be the ruler of a free people.

Nor have we been wanting in our attentions to our British brethren. We have warned them from time to time of attempts by their legislature to extend an unwarrantable jurisdiction over us. We have reminded them of the circumstances of our emigration and settlement here. We have appealed to their native justice and magnanimity; and we have conjured them, by the ties of our common kindred, to disavow these usurpations, which would inevitably interrupt our connections and correspondence. They, too, have been deaf to the voice of justice and of consanguinity. We must, therefore, acquiesce in the necessity which denounces our separation, and hold them, as we hold the rest of mankind, enemies in war, in peace friends.

Independence Declared

We, therefore, the Representatives of the United States of America, in General Congress assembled, appealing to the Supreme Judge of the world for the rectitude of our intentions, do, in the name and by the authority of the good people of these colonies, solemnly publish and declare, That these united Colonies are, and of right ought to be, free and independent states; that they are absolved from all allegiance to the British crown, and that all political connection between them and the state of Great Britain is, and ought to be, totally dissolved; and that, as free and independent states, they have full power to levy war, conclude peace, contract alliances, establish commerce, and to do all other acts and things which independent states may of right do. And for the support of this declaration, with a firm reliance on the protection of Divine Providence, we mutually pledge to each other our lives, our fortunes and our sacred honor.

The Signers

DELAWARE
Caesar Rodney
George Read
Thomas M'Kean

MASSACHUSETTS BAY
John Hancock
Samuel Adams
John Adams
Robert Treat Paine
Elbridge Gerry

CONNECTICUT
Roger Sherman
Samuel Huntington
William Williams
Oliver Wolcott

NEW HAMPSHIRE
Josiah Bartlett
William Whipple
Matthew Thornton

NORTH CAROLINA
William Hooper
Joseph Hewes
John Penn

PENNSYLVANIA
Robert Morris
Benjamin Rush
Benjamin Franklin
John Morton
George Clymer
James Smith
George Taylor
James Wilson
George Ross

MARYLAND
Samuel Chase
William Paca
Thomas Stone
Charles Carroll, of Carrollton

VIRGINIA
George Wythe
Richard Henry Lee
Thomas Jefferson
Benjamin Harrison
Thomas Nelson, Jr.
Francis Lightfoot Lee
Carter Braxton

NEW YORK
William Floyd
Philip Livingston
Francis Lewis
Lewis Morris

NEW JERSEY
Richard Stockton
John Witherspoon
Francis Hopkinson
John Hart
Abraham Clark

RHODE ISLAND
Stephen Hopkins
William Ellery

SOUTH CAROLINA
Edward Rutledge
Thomas Heyward, Jr.
Thomas Lynch, Jr.
Arthur Middleton

GEORGIA
Button Gwinnett
Lyman Hall
George Walton

Resolved, That copies of the Declaration be sent to the several assemblies, conventions, and committees, or councils of safety, and to the several commanding officers of the continental troops; that it be proclaimed in each of the United States, at the head of the army.

The Constitution of the United States

Explanations to help you understand the Constitution are printed in blue. The parts of the Constitution printed in gray are no longer in force.

Organization

These are the parts of our Constitution.

Preamble	Tells the aims or purposes of our government.
First Article	Provides for a legislature, Congress, and tells its powers.
Second Article	Provides for a President and Vice-President and tells their powers.
Third Article	Provides for a Supreme Court and other federal, or national, courts.
Fourth Article	Explains how the federal and state governments are to work together. Explains how the states are to cooperate.
Fifth Article	Tells how the Constitution may be amended or changed.
Sixth Article	Says that the Constitution, the laws passed by Congress, and treaties are the highest laws in the land. Requires all government officers to swear to support the Constitution. Says that no religious test needs .to be taken by anyone running for public office.
Seventh Article	Says that when nine states ratify or approve the Constitution, it will go into effect.
The Amendments	Additions to the Constitution—in the order added.

Meaning

1. **We the People** decide what our government will be like.
2. All power belongs to us—**the People.**
3. Government is limited to the power **We the People** have given it.
4. Power is divided among three branches of government which "check and balance" each other.
5. The national and state governments share power in a federal system.
6. All states are equal. Each state must respect the laws of all other states.
7. Each state is guaranteed a republican, or representative, form of government with final authority belonging to us, **the People.**
8. All Americans are equal in their right to be protected by laws.
9. **The People** can change the Constitution.
10. **The People** do not have to obey laws which the Supreme Court says do not agree with the Constitution. The Constitution is our highest law.

The Constitution

Preamble

We the People of the United States, in order to form a more perfect union, establish justice, insure domestic tranquillity, provide for the common defense, promote the general welfare, and secure the blessings of liberty to ourselves and our posterity, do ordain and establish this Constitution for the United States of America.

The Preamble tells *why* our Constitution was written. It is important that the PEOPLE themselves build their own government. There are six important reasons for writing the Constitution:

1. To improve upon the Articles of Confederation.
2. To get fair laws and fair treatment in court.
3. To keep peace and order.
4. To defend ourselves against our enemies.
5. To make life better for everyone.
6. To keep freedom for Americans.

ARTICLE 1—LEGISLATIVE DEPARTMENT

Section 1—Congress

All legislative powers herein granted shall be vested in a Congress of the United States, which shall consist of a Senate and House of Representatives.

Laws for our country are to be made by Congress. Congress is made up of two parts, which are called houses. These houses are the Senate and the House of Representatives.

Section 2—House of Representatives

Election and Term of Members. The House of Representatives shall be composed of members chosen every second year by the people of the several States, and the electors in each State shall have the qualifications requisite for electors of the most numerous branch of the State Legislature.

Representatives are elected every two years by the electors (voters) of the states. Representatives serve a two-year term.

Qualifications. No person shall be a representative who shall not have attained to the age of twenty-five years, and been seven years a citizen of the United States, and who shall not, when elected, be an inhabitant of that State in which he shall be chosen.

To be a representative one must:

1. Be at least 25 years old.
2. Have been a citizen of the United States for seven years.
3. Live in the state that elects him or her.

Apportionment. Representatives and direct taxes shall be apportioned among the several States which may be included within this Union, according to their respective numbers, [which shall be determined by adding to the whole number of free persons, including those bound to service for a term of years, and excluding Indians not taxed, three-fifths of all other persons.] The actual enumeration shall be made within three years after the first meeting of the Congress of the United States, and within every subsequent term of ten years, in such manner as they shall by law direct. The number of representatives shall not exceed one for every thirty thousand, but each State shall have at least one representative; [and until such enumeration shall be made, the State of New Hampshire shall be entitled to choose three; Massachusetts, eight; Rhode Island and Providence Plantations, one; Connecticut, five; New York, six; New Jersey, four; Pennsylvania, eight; Delaware, one; Maryland, six; Virginia, ten; North Carolina, five; South Carolina, five; and Georgia, three.]

The number of representatives is decided by how many people live in that state.

A count, or census, of the population shall be taken every ten years to decide how many representatives each state shall have. Every state gets at least one representative, however, no matter how few people live in it.

Vacancies. When vacancies happen in the representation from any State, the executive authority thereof shall issue writs of election to fill such vacancies.

The governor of a state calls a special election if a representative dies or resigns.

Officers; Impeachment. The House of Representatives shall choose their Speaker and other officers; and shall have the sole power of impeachment.

The House chooses its own officers. The presiding officer is the Speaker. Impeachment means accusing an official so that he or she can be brought to trial.

Section 3—Senate

Number of Senators: Election. The Senate of the United States shall be composed of two senators from each State, [chosen by the legislature thereof,] for six years; and each senator shall have one vote.

The Senate has two members from each state. Senators serve six-year terms. Until 1913 the senators were elected by state legislatures. Now senators are elected directly by the people.

Divided into Three Groups. Immediately after they shall be assembled in consequence of the first election, they shall be divided as equally as may be into three classes. The seats of the senators of the first class shall be vacated at the expiration of the second year; of the second class, at the expiration of the fourth year; of the third class, at the expiration of the sixth year, so that one-third may be chosen every second year; and if vacancies happen by resignation, or otherwise, [during the recess of the legislature of any State,] the executive thereof may make temporary appointments [until the next meeting of the legislature, which shall then fill such vacancies.]

About one-third of the senators are elected every two years. This means that the Senate will never be without members of experience to guide it. If there is a vacancy, the governor of a state may appoint someone to the Senate until a new election is held.

Qualifications. No person shall be a senator who shall not have attained to the age of thirty years, and been nine years a citizen of the United States, and who shall not, when elected, be an inhabitant of that State for which he shall be chosen.

To be a senator, a person must:
1. Be at least 30 years old.
2. Have been a United States citizen for nine years.
3. Live in the state that elects him or her.

President of Senate. The Vice-President of the United States shall be president of the Senate, but shall have no vote, unless they be equally divided.

The Vice-President is chairman of the Senate, but votes only if there is a tie.

Officers. The Senate shall choose their other officers, and also a president pro tempore, in the absence of the Vice-President, or when he shall exercise the office of President of the United States.

The Senate elects a pro tempore (for the time being) president to serve if the Vice-President is absent, or when there is no Vice-President.

Trials of Impeachment. The Senate shall have the sole power to try all impeachments. When sitting for that purpose, they shall be on oath or affirmation. When the President of the United States is tried, the Chief Justice shall preside; and no person shall be convicted without the concurrence of two-thirds of the members present.

Trials for impeachment are held in the Senate. The Chief Justice is in charge if the President is on trial. The Vice-President is in charge of the trials of other officials. Impeaching an officer of the government is a very serious matter. For that reason, the Constitution says that two-thirds of the senators must agree before a person can be put out of office.

Judgment in Case of Conviction. Judgment in cases of impeachment shall not extend further than to removal from office, and disqualification to hold and enjoy any office of honor, trust, or profit under the United States; but the party convicted shall nevertheless be liable and subject to indictment, trial, judgment, and punishment, according to law.

If persons are found guilty, they are put out of office. They cannot hold any other federal office again. If they have broken any laws, they can then be tried in a regular court just as any other people would be.

Section 4—Both Houses

Manner of Electing Members. The times, places, and manner of holding elections for senators and representatives shall be prescribed in each state by the legislature thereof; but the Congress may at any time, by law, make or alter such regulations, except as to the places of choosing senators.

State legislatures make rules on how members of Congress shall be elected. But Congress can pass laws to make national elections honest and fair. Today all states have elections for Congress on the first Tuesday after the first Monday in November. Elections are held in even-numbered years—1982, 1984, 1986, etc.

Meetings of Congress. The Congress shall assemble at least once in every year, [and such meeting shall be on the first Monday in December, unless they shall by law appoint a different day.]

Congress must meet at least once a year. The time Congress meets was changed by Amendment XX. Congress now starts early in January each year.

Section 5—The Houses Separately

Organization. Each house shall be the judge of the elections, returns, and qualifications of its own members, and a majority of each shall constitute a quorum to do business; but a smaller number may adjourn from day to day, and may be authorized to compel the attendance of absent members, in such manner, and under such penalties, as each house may provide.

Each house decides if its members have met the requirements to serve in that house. Each house decides if elections have been honest.

A "quorum" is the least number of people who have to be present so that business can be carried on. Absent members can be forced to attend.

Rules. Each house may determine the rules of its proceedings, punish its members for disorderly behavior, and, with the concurrence of two-thirds, expel a member.

Each house can make its own rules for operating. Each house can punish its members for bad behavior. If two-thirds of the house agree, they can put a member out of office.

Journal. Each house shall keep a journal of its proceedings, and from time to time publish the same, excepting such parts as may in their judgment require secrecy; and the yeas and nays of the members of either house on any question shall, at the desire of one-fifth of those present, be entered on the journal.

A record, or journal, is kept of what happened in both the House and the Senate. In addition, there is a *Congressional Record* containing speeches and notes.

Adjournment. Neither house, during the session of Congress, shall, without the consent of the other, adjourn for more than three days, nor to any other place than that in which the two houses shall be sitting.

Neither house can adjourn, or stop meeting, for more than three days unless the other house agrees. Neither house can decide on its own to move its place for meeting to another location.

Section 6—Privileges and Disabilities of Members

Pay and Privileges of Members. The senators and representatives shall receive a compensation for their services, to be ascertained by law, and paid out of the treasury of the United States. They shall in all cases, except treason, felony, and breach of the peace, be privileged from arrest during their attendance at the session of their respective houses, and in going to and returning from the same; and for any speech or debate in either house they shall not be questioned in any other place.

Senators and representatives are paid by the federal government, not by the state they serve. Members of Congress set their own pay. Members of Congress can be arrested for crimes, but not for other reasons while Congress meets. You cannot sue members of Congress for anything they say while in Congress. Thus they can speak freely.

Prohibitions on Members. No senator or representative shall, during the time for which he was elected, be appointed to any civil office under the authority of the United States, which shall have been created, or the emoluments whereof shall have been increased, during such time; and no person holding any office under the United States shall be a member of either house during his continuance in office.

Members of Congress cannot hold other government jobs during their term in Congress.

Section 7—Method of Passing Laws

Revenue Bills. All bills for raising revenue shall originate in the House of Representatives; but the Senate may propose or concur with amendments as on other bills.

All tax bills must start in the House. The Senate may suggest changes in the bills, however.

How Bills Become Laws. Every bill which shall have passed the House of Representatives and the Senate shall, before it become a law, be presented to the President of the United States; if he approve, he shall sign it, but if not, he shall return it, with his objections, to that house in which it shall have originated, who shall enter the objections at large on their journal, and proceed to reconsider it. If after such reconsideration two-thirds of that house shall agree to pass the bill, it shall be sent, together with the objections, to the other house, by which it shall likewise be reconsidered, and if approved by two-thirds of that house, it shall become a law. But in all such cases the votes of both houses shall be determined by yeas and nays, and the names of the persons voting for and against the bill shall be entered on the journal of each house respectively. If any bill shall not be returned by the President within ten days (Sundays excepted) after it shall have been presented to him, the same shall be a law, in like manner as if he had signed it, unless the Congress by their adjournment prevent its return, in which case it shall not be a law.

When a bill is passed by a majority vote of both House and Senate, it is sent to the President. The President can sign the bill (it then becomes a law) or refuse to sign it. If the President refuses, the bill goes back to the house where it started. The President also sends a letter telling Congress why it wasn't signed. This action is called a "veto." A veto means saying "no" to a bill. Congress can pass a bill over the President's veto. But to do so, a two-thirds vote of each house is needed.

By using the veto power, the President can "check and balance" what Congress does. This is what the Founders intended. Congress, of course, can "check and balance" the President by passing the bill over a veto.

The President can let a bill become a law without signing it. But a bill sent to the President in the last ten days of a session of Congress is "dead" if the President doesn't sign it. The name given this failure to sign is "pocket veto." The President just pockets the bill and forgets about it, so to speak.

Resolutions, etc. Every order, resolution, or vote to which the concurrence of the Senate and House of Representatives may be necessary (except on a question of adjournment) shall be presented to the President of the United States; and before the same shall take effect, shall be approved by him, or being disapproved by him, shall be repassed by two-thirds of the Senate and House of Representatives, according to the rules and limitations prescribed in the case of a bill.

The President must approve any orders or resolutions (except to adjourn) passed by both houses of Congress. In other words, Congress cannot bypass the President by passing laws called by other names.

Section 8—Powers Granted to Congress

Powers of Congress. The Congress shall have power: To lay and collect taxes, duties, imposts, and excises, to pay the debts and provide for the common defense and general welfare of the United States; but all duties, imposts, and excises shall be uniform throughout the United States;

Article I, Section 8, lists the kinds of laws which Congress may make. The first item says that Congress may pass laws to collect taxes for three reasons: (1) to pay the country's debts, (2) to defend the country against its enemies, and (3) to do things for the good of the people.

All federal taxes must be the same in every state.

To borrow money on the credit of the United States;

Congress has power to borrow money for the government to use. Borrowed money must be repaid, so the government must tax the people to pay whatever debts it has. The Constitution does not put a limit on how much money can be borrowed.

To regulate commerce with foreign nations, and among the several States, and with the Indian tribes;

Congress makes rules about trade with foreign countries. It also has power to control trade among the states. This is a very important power because Congress can pass laws which:

1. Forbid business firms to combine in order to overcharge customers.
2. Set the minimum wage (least amount of pay) which employers can pay their workers.
3. State that people cannot be refused a job because of their color.
4. Prevent race discrimination in interstate business.
5. Say that restaurants and hotels cannot refuse to serve people because of their religion or their color.

These few lines in our Constitution give great power to Congress. They have important meaning for every American.

To establish a uniform rule of naturalization, and uniform laws on the subject of bankruptcies throughout the United States;

Naturalization means the rules by which people not born in the United States can become citizens. Bankruptcies happen when people owe more money than they can pay, even by selling all they own. Any laws Congress passes about naturalization or bankruptcies must be the same for all states.

To coin money, regulate the value thereof, and of foreign coin, and fix the standard of weights and measures;

Congress has power to make, or coin, money. Congress sets our system of measurements and weights.

To provide for the punishment of counterfeiting the securities and current coin of the United States;

Congress decides what punishment shall be given people who print imitation money or stamps to defraud.

To establish post offices and post roads;

Post offices and interstate roads are set up by Congress.

To promote the progress of science and useful arts, by securing, for limited times, to authors and inventors the exclusive right to their respective writings and discoveries;

Congress helps scientists and inventors. It encourages writers and artists. These people are given patents or copyrights for their accomplishments. Money made from their work goes to them. No one else may copy or sell their work without permission.

To constitute tribunals inferior to the Supreme Court;

Congress may set up federal courts to serve under the Supreme Court. Congress may not set up any court higher than the Supreme Court. It is the highest court in the land.

To define and punish piracies and felonies committed on the high seas, and offenses against the law of nations;

Congress, not the states, has power over crimes committed at sea. A felony is a serious crime.

To declare war, grant letters of marque and reprisal, and make rules concerning captures on land and water;

Congress has the power to declare war.

Letters of marque and reprisal give permission for private ships to attack enemy shipping. Congress does not use this power today.

Congress decides what to do with enemy property taken on land or sea.

To raise and support armies, but no appropriation of money to that use shall be for a longer term than two years;

To provide and maintain a navy;

To make rules for the government and regulation of the land and naval forces;

Congress votes money and makes the rules for the armed forces.

To provide for calling forth the militia to execute the laws of the Union, suppress insurrections, and repel invasions;

To provide for organizing, arming, and disciplining the militia, and for governing such part of them as may be employed in the service of the United States, reserving to the States respectively the appointment of the officers, and the authority of training the militia according to the discipline prescribed by Congress;

The federal government helps states keep a militia. The militia is the National Guard. The National Guard can be called into service to:

1. See that national laws are obeyed.
2. Put down rebellions or organized attempts to overthrow the government.
3. Drive out enemies who attack us.

To exercise exclusive legislation in all cases whatsoever over such district (not exceeding ten miles square) as may, by cession of particular States, and the acceptance of Congress, become the seat of the government of the United States, and to exercise like authority over all places purchased by the consent of the legislature of the State in which the same shall be, for the erection of forts, magazines, arsenals, dockyards, and other needful buildings;—and

Congress makes all the laws for governing the national capital, Washington, D.C. The capital city is not part of any state government. Congress makes all laws for federal property such as national parks, forests, post offices, etc.

Implied Powers. To make all laws which shall be necessary and proper for carrying into execution the foregoing powers, and all other powers vested by this Constitution in the government of the United States, or in any department or officer thereof.

IMPORTANT! This is the "elastic," or "necessary and proper," clause of the Constitution. All the powers given Congress before this one say quite exactly what may be done. This clause "implies," or suggests, without saying exactly what Congress may do.

This clause does not mean Congress can do any and everything it wants! It does mean Congress can "stretch," or find new ways of using, its rightful powers so that our country can have the kinds of laws it needs.

From time to time, Americans have challenged some of the laws that Congress has passed under this clause. "Congress has gone too far," they have said. In such cases, the Supreme Court has been called on to decide if the law made was really "necessary and proper."

Section 9—Powers Forbidden to the United States

Absolute Prohibitions on Congress. [The migration or importation of such persons as any of the States now existing shall think proper to admit, shall not be prohibited by the Congress prior to the year one thousand eight hundred and eight, but a tax or duty may be imposed on such importation, not exceeding ten dollars for each person.]

Congress could not stop the slave trade before the year 1808. Congress did pass a law in 1808 to prevent slaves from being brought into the United States.

The privilege of the writ of habeas corpus shall not be suspended, unless when in cases of rebellion or invasion the public safety may require it.

Only if our country is in very serious danger can Congress take away a person's privilege of "habeas corpus." If a person in jail or prison believes that no evidence shows that he or she could have committed the crime, the prisoner can ask for a writ of habeas corpus. This is a court order to bring the prisoner into court so that a judge can decide if the person should be held or set free.

No bill of attainder or ex-post-facto law shall be passed.

A bill of attainder is a law to punish a particular person. This is another example of how our Constitution insists that laws be made to apply to all people—not for or against any particular person. An ex-post-facto law would punish people for doing something that was not against the law when they did it.

No capitation, or other direct tax, shall be laid, unless in proportion to the census or enumeration herein before directed to be taken.

This sentence puts a limit on the taxing power of Congress. The 16th Amendment changes the sentence by giving Congress power to pass an income tax.

No tax or duty shall be laid on articles exported from any State.

Goods or products being sent out of any state cannot be taxed.

No preference shall be given by any regulation of commerce or revenue to the ports of one State over those of another; nor shall vessels bound to, or from, one State, be obliged to enter, clear, or pay duties in another.

No laws can be passed which favor one state, or city, or seaport. Ships from any state may go into ports of other states without paying for the privilege.

No money shall be drawn from the treasury but in consequence of appropriations made by law; and a regular statement and account of the receipts and expenditures of all public money shall be published from time to time.

Public money must be spent lawfully. An account of how money has been spent must be published.

No title of nobility shall be granted by the United States: And no person holding any office of profit or trust under them, shall, without the consent of the Congress, accept of any present, emolument, office, or title, of any kind whatever, from any king, prince, or foreign state.

Congress cannot give anyone a title (such as duke, prince, or king). No person working for the United States government may take a gift, payment, job, or title from a foreign country unless Congress approves.

Section 10—Powers Forbidden to the States

Absolute Prohibitions on the States. No State shall enter into any treaty, alliance, or confederation; grant letters of marque and reprisal; coin money; emit bills of credit; make anything but gold and silver coin a tender in payment of debts; pass any bill of attainder, ex-post-facto law, or law impairing the obligation of contracts, or grant any title of nobility.

Certain powers are forbidden to the states for two reasons:

1. These powers belong to the federal government.
2. They are things no democratic government should do.

Conditional Prohibitions on the States. No State shall, without the consent of the Congress, lay any imposts or duties on imports or exports, except what may be absolutely necessary for executing its inspection laws; and the net produce of all duties and imposts, laid by any State on imports or exports, shall be for the use of the treasury of the United States; and all such laws shall be subject to the revision and control of the Congress.

No State shall, without the consent of Congress, lay any duty of tonnage, keep troops, or ships-of-war, in time of peace, enter into any agreement or compact with another State, or with a foreign power, or engage in war, unless actually invaded, or in such imminent danger as will not admit of delay.

Unless Congress agrees, no state may put taxes on goods going into or out of the state. A state may charge a small amount to pay for inspection. Any money collected must go to the federal treasury.

Unless Congress gives permission, no state (1) may tax ships, (2) keep an army or navy, (3) make agreements with other states, (4) make treaties with a foreign country, and (5) go to war unless it is invaded.

ARTICLE II—EXECUTIVE DEPARTMENT

Section 1—President and Vice-President

Term. The executive power shall be vested in a President of the United States of America. He shall hold his office during the term of four years, and, together with the Vice-President, chosen for the same term, be elected, as follows:

Electors. Each State shall appoint, in such manner as the legislature thereof may direct, a number of electors, equal to the whole number of senators and representatives to which the State may be entitled in the Congress: but no senator or representative, or person holding an office of trust or profit under the United States, shall be appointed an elector.

Proceedings of Electors and of Congress. [The electors shall meet in their respective States, and vote by ballot for two persons, of whom one at least shall not be an inhabitant of the same State with themselves. And they shall make a list of all the persons voted for, and of the number of votes for each; which list they shall sign and certify and transmit sealed to the seat of the government of the United States, directed to the president of the Senate. The president of the Senate shall, in the presence of the Senate and House of Representatives, open all the certificates, and the votes shall then be counted. The person having the greatest number of votes shall be the President, if such number be a majority of the whole number of electors appointed; and if there be more than one who have such majority, and have an equal number of votes, then the House of Representatives shall immediately choose by ballot one of them for President; and if no person have a majority, then from the five highest on the list the said house shall, in like manner, choose the President. But in choosing the President, the votes shall be taken by States, the representation from each State having one vote; a quorum for this purpose shall consist of a member or members from two-thirds of the States, and a majority of all the States shall be necessary to a choice. In every case, after the choice of the President, the person having the greatest number of votes of the electors shall be the Vice-President. But if there should remain two or more who have equal votes, the Senate shall choose from them by ballot the Vice-President.]

The President is the leader, or chief executive, of the country. The President holds office for four years. The Vice-President also serves for four years.

The makers of the Constitution thought the President should be chosen by a small, wise group of people, called electors. They did not think the people should vote directly for the President. For that reason, the Constitution says each state shall choose as many electors as it has senators and representatives.

Once political parties began (1796), electors became just "puppets" who did as they were told by the voters. Today, instead of having a small group of electors meet to select the President, each political party chooses electors. When citizens vote today, they really vote for the electors of a particular party. These electors promise to vote for the candidate their party has nominated. Electors almost never break that promise.

The candidate getting the majority of votes for President in each state gets all the electoral votes. Electors really represent an "in-between step" in the way Americans elect a President.

Time of Choosing Electors. The Congress may determine the time of choosing the electors, and the day on which they shall give their votes; which day shall be the same throughout the United States.

The day for presidential elections is the first Tuesday after the first Monday in November. Citizens in all states vote on the same day.

Qualifications of President. No person except a natural born citizen, or a citizen of the United States at the time of the adoption of this Constitution, shall be eligible to the office of President; neither shall any person be eligible to that office who shall not have attained to the age of thirty-five years, and been fourteen years a resident within the United States.

To be a President a person must (1) be a native-born citizen of the United States, (2) be at least 35 years old, (3) have lived in the United States for at least 14 years.

Vacancy. In case of the removal of the President from office, or of his death, resignation, or inability to discharge the powers and duties of the said office, the same shall devolve on the Vice-President, and the Congress may by law provide for the case of removal, death, resignation, or inability, both of the President and Vice-President, declaring what officer shall then act as President; and such officer shall act accordingly until the disability be removed, or a President shall be elected.

Congress has said that after the Vice-President these people shall be next in line for the Presidency:

1. The Speaker of the House.
2. The President pro tempore of the Senate.
3. The cabinet officers in the order in which their departments were set up.

The 25th Amendment says what shall be done if a President becomes too ill to carry out the duties of office.

Salary. The President shall, at stated times, receive for his services a compensation which shall neither be increased nor diminished during the period for which he shall have been elected, and he shall not receive within that period any other emolument from the United States, or any of them.

A President's salary cannot be changed while that person is in office. This law means that Congress cannot try to control a President by threatening to lower the salary or by promising more money. The President also receives an expense allowance.

Oath. Before he enter on the execution of his office, he shall take the following oath or affirmation:—"I do solemnly swear (or affirm) that I will faithfully execute the office of President of the United States, and will, to the best of my ability, preserve, protect, and defend the Constitution of the United States."

Section 2—Powers of the President

Military Powers; Reprieves and Pardons. The President shall be commander in chief of the army and navy of the United States, and of the militia of the several States, when called into the actual service of the United States; he may require the opinion, in writing, of the principal officer in each of the executive departments, upon any subject relating to the duties of their respective offices; and he shall have power to grant reprieves and pardons for offenses against the United States, except in cases of impeachment.

The President is commander in chief of the armed forces and of the National Guard when it is in service.

The President may require written advice from department heads. In practice, department heads also serve in the cabinet.

The President may pardon people, except those impeached.

Treaties; Appointments. He shall have power, by and with the advice and consent of the Senate, to make treaties, provided two-thirds of the senators present concur; and he shall nominate, and by and with the advice and consent of the Senate shall appoint ambassadors, other public ministers and consuls, judges of the Supreme Court, and all other officers of the United States, whose appointments are not herein otherwise provided for, and which shall be established by law; but the Congress may by law vest the appointment of such inferior officers, as they think proper, in the President alone, in the courts of law, or in the heads of departments.

Vacancies. The President shall have power to fill up all vacancies that may happen during the recess of the Senate, by granting commissions which shall expire at the end of their next session.

The President can make treaties with foreign countries, but the Senate has to agree to them. Otherwise such treaties cannot become law.

The President appoints important officials, but the Senate has to approve these appointments. These two rules are part of the way that Congress and the President "check and balance" each other.

The President may appoint people to fill vacancies that happen when the Senate is not meeting. These appointments are good only until the end of the next meeting of the Senate.

Section 3—Duties of the President

Message; Convening of Congress. He shall from time to time give to the Congress information of the state of the Union, and recommend to their consideration such measures as he shall judge necessary and expedient; he may, on extraordinary occasions, convene both houses, or either of them, and in case of disagreement between them with respect to the time of adjournment, he may adjourn them to such time as he shall think proper; he shall receive ambassadors and other public ministers; he shall take care that the laws be faithfully executed, and shall commission all the officers of the United States.

The President must tell Congress about the condition of our country. Presidents always do this at the beginning of each yearly session of Congress in a "State of the Union" message.

The President must recommend laws. The President must suggest laws to change or improve the government of our country.

The President may call either or both houses of Congress back into session if there is an emergency.

If the two houses of Congress cannot agree on a time to adjourn, the President may adjourn Congress. This has never happened, however.

The President meets and talks with ambassadors and other heads of state.

The President is responsible for seeing that all laws of the United States are enforced.

Papers showing the right of officers to hold their jobs must be signed by the President.

Section 4—Impeachment

Removal of Officers. The President, Vice-President, and all civil officers of the United States, shall be removed from office on impeachment for, and conviction of, treason, bribery, or other high crimes and misdemeanors.

If officers of the United States government commit serious crimes or greatly misuse their offices, they can be put out of office.

ARTICLE III—JUDICIAL DEPARTMENT

Section 1—United States Courts

Courts Established; Judges. The judicial power of the United States shall be vested in one Supreme Court, and in such inferior courts as the Congress may from time to time ordain and establish. The judges, both of the Supreme and inferior courts, shall hold their offices during good behavior, and shall, at stated times, receive for their services a compensation which shall not be diminished during their continuance in office.

The Supreme Court is the highest court in the land. Congress may set up lower courts. Judges hold office during "good behavior," which usually means for life. They can be removed by impeachment, or put out of office. Their pay cannot be cut while they are in office.

Section 2—Jurisdiction of United States Courts

Federal Courts in General. The judicial power shall extend to all cases, in law and equity, arising under this Constitution, the laws of the United States, and treaties made, or which shall be made under their authority;—to all cases affecting ambassadors, other public ministers and consuls;—to all cases of admiralty and maritime jurisdiction;—to controversies to which the United States shall be a party;—to controversies between two or more States;—[between a State and citizens of another State];—between citizens of different States;—between citizens of the same State claiming lands under grants of different States; and between a State, or the citizens thereof, and foreign states, citizens or subjects.

These are the kinds of cases which are heard in federal courts:

1. Cases that involve questions under:
   a. the Constitution; b. federal laws; c. treaties; d. laws governing ships.

2. Cases that involve:
   a. ambassadors, consuls, public ministers; b. the United States government itself; c. two or more state governments; d. citizens of different states; e. a state or its citizens against foreign countries; f. citizens of foreign countries.

Supreme Court. In all cases affecting ambassadors, other public ministers and consuls, and those in which a State shall be party, the Supreme Court shall have original jurisdiction. In all other cases before mentioned, the Supreme Court shall have appellate jurisdiction, both as to law and fact, with such exceptions and under such regulations as the Congress shall make.

Some kinds of cases go directly to the Supreme Court. These are cases that involve one of the states or a foreign country. If a case begins with the Supreme Court, we say the Court has "original," or first, jurisdiction. Jurisdiction means the right to decide.

Cases tried by lower courts can be appealed, or heard again, in the Supreme Court if there is reason to think justice was not done. The right to decide cases on appeal is called "appellate jurisdiction."

Trials. The trial of all crimes, except in cases of impeachment, shall be by jury; and such trial shall be held in the State where the said crimes shall have been committed; but when not committed within any State, the trial shall be at such place or places as the Congress may by law have directed.

All crimes (except those involving impeachment) shall be tried by a jury in the state where the crime is said to have taken place. This section on how trials shall be held is made stronger by the Bill of Rights, especially Amendment VI.

Section 3—Treason

Treason Defined. Treason against the United States shall consist only in levying war against them, or in adhering to their enemies, giving them aid and comfort.

No person shall be convicted of treason unless on the testimony of two witnesses to the same overt act, or on confession in open court.

Punishment. The Congress shall have power to declare the punishment of treason, but no attainder of treason shall work corruption of blood, or forfeiture, except during the life of the person attainted.

Treason means making war or helping those who make war against the United States. No one can be punished for treason without confessing in court or unless at least two witnesses say they saw an act of treason take place.

Congress may punish persons found guilty of treason, but not members of their family. Death or imprisonment and fines are now the punishments for treason.

ARTICLE IV—RELATIONS OF THE STATES TO EACH OTHER

Section 1—Official Acts

Full faith and credit shall be given in each State to the public acts, records, and judicial proceedings of every other State. And the Congress may by general laws prescribe the manner in which such acts, records, and proceedings shall be proved, and the effect thereof.

States must respect each other's laws, records, and legal decisions. This is important especially in cases of marriage, divorce, wills, etc.

Section 2—Privileges of Citizens

The citizens of each State shall be entitled to all privileges and immunities of citizens in the several States.

This wise provision grants "interstate citizenship." In other words, a citizen can move from one state to another without losing any rights and privileges as an American citizen. But states can require new residents to live in them for a time before they can vote, receive welfare payments, etc.

Fugitives from Justice. A person charged in any State with treason, felony, or other crime, who shall flee from justice, and be found in another State, shall, on demand of the executive authority of the State from which he fled, be delivered up, to be removed to the State having jurisdiction of the crime.

A person accused of a crime in one state cannot flee to safety in another state. The governor of the second state has the power to return the accused person to the first state for trial.

Fugitive Slaves. [No person held to service or labor in one State, under the laws thereof, escaping into another, shall, in consequence of any law or regulation therein, be discharged from such service or labor, but shall be delivered up on claim of the party to whom such service or labor may be due.]

This section, no longer in force, was used to get back runaway slaves.

Section 3—New States and Territories

Admission of States. New States may be admitted by the Congress into this Union; but no new State shall be formed or erected within the jurisdiction of any other State; nor any State be formed by the junction of two or more States, or parts of States, without the consent of the legislatures of the States concerned as well as of the Congress.

Congress has the right to add new states to the United States. Note that there is no way under the Constitution for any state to leave the Union, however.

New states cannot be made by dividing or putting together old states unless both Congress and the states involved agree. In our history two new states have been made by dividing a state. Maine was made from part of Massachusetts in 1820. In 1863, West Virginia was made from part of Virginia. When Texas was admitted to the Union, the law said it could later be divided into five states.

Territory and Property of United States. The Congress shall have power to dispose of and make all needful rules and regulations respecting the territory or other property belonging to the United States; and nothing in this Constitution shall be so construed as to prejudice any claims of the United States, or of any particular State.

Congress governs new territories added to the United States. Congress also manages national parks, military bases, and other public property.

Section 4—Protection of the States

The United States shall guarantee to every State in this Union a republican form of government, and shall protect each of them against invasion, and on application of the legislature, or of the executive (when the legislature cannot be convened) against domestic violence.

The federal government is responsible for seeing that every state has a government run by the people of that state. A republic is a government which gets all its power from the people. A republican government is one run by representatives elected by the people. If a state is invaded by an enemy, or troubled by riots from within, the federal government can send troops to restore order.

ARTICLE V—AMENDMENTS

How Proposed; How Ratified. The Congress, whenever two-thirds of both houses shall deem it necessary, shall propose amendments to this Constitution, or, on the application of the legislatures of two-thirds of the several States, shall call a convention for proposing amendments, which, in either case, shall be valid to all intents and purposes, as part of this Constitution, when ratified by the legislatures of three-fourths of the several States, or by conventions in three-fourths thereof, as the one or the other mode of ratification may be proposed by the Congress; provided [that no amendment which may be made prior to the year one thousand eight hundred and eight shall in any manner affect the first and fourth clauses in the ninth section of the first article;] and that no State, without its consent, shall be deprived of its equal suffrage in the Senate.

All amendments have been suggested by a two-thirds vote of each house of Congress. However, the Constitution does say that amendments can be suggested by a convention requested by two-thirds of the state legislatures. Amendments must be ratified by three-fourths of the states before they become part of the Constitution. No amendment can take away from a state its equal vote in the Senate.

ARTICLE VI—GENERAL PROVISIONS

Public Debt. All debts contracted, and engagements entered into, before the adoption of this Constitution, shall be as valid against the United States under this Constitution, as under the Confederation.

Money owed by our government before the Constitution was adopted was to be paid in full. The United States would not turn its back on its debts just because a new Constitution had been written.

Supremacy of Constitution. This Constitution, and the laws of the United States which shall be made in pursuance thereof; and all treaties made, or which shall be made, under the authority of the United States, shall be the supreme law of the land; and the judges in every State shall be bound thereby, anything in the Constitution or laws of any State to the contrary notwithstanding.

The Constitution, federal laws, and treaties are the highest law of the land. Judges in every state must obey them.

Official Oath; Religious Test. The senators and representatives before mentioned, and the members of the several State legislatures, and all executive and judicial officers, both of the United States and of the several States, shall be bound by oath or affirmation to support this Constitution; but no religious test shall ever be required as a qualification to any office or public trust under the United States.

All public officials—state and national—must swear to support the Constitution. No one can be asked to take a religious test in order to hold a public office. Americans believe that church and state, or religion and government, should be separate.

ARTICLE VII—RATIFICATION OF THE CONSTITUTION

Ratification. The ratification of the Conventions of nine States shall be sufficient for the establishment of this Constitution between the States so ratifying the same.

The Constitution was to go into effect when nine states approved it.

Done in convention, by the unanimous consent of the States present, the seventeenth day of September, in the year of our Lord one thousand seven hundred and eighty-seven, and of the independence of the United States of America the twelfth. In witness whereof, we have hereunto subscribed our names.

George Washington, PRESIDENT, AND DEPUTY FROM VIRGINIA

NEW HAMPSHIRE
John Langdon
Nicholas Gilman

MASSACHUSETTS
Nathaniel Gorham
Rufus King

CONNECTICUT
William Samuel Johnson
Roger Sherman

NEW YORK
Alexander Hamilton

NEW JERSEY
William Livingston
David Brearley
William Paterson
Jonathan Dayton

PENNSYLVANIA
Benjamin Franklin
Thomas Mifflin
Robert Morris
George Clymer
Thomas Fitzsimons
Jared Ingersoll
James Wilson
Gouverneur Morris

DELAWARE
George Read
Gunning Bedford, Jr.
John Dickinson
Richard Bassett
Jacob Broom

MARYLAND
James M'Henry
Daniel of St. Thomas Jenifer
Daniel Carroll

VIRGINIA
John Blair
James Madison, Jr.

NORTH CAROLINA
William Blount
Richard Dobbs Spaight
Hugh Williamson

SOUTH CAROLINA
John Rutledge
Charles C. Pinckney
Charles Pinckney
Pierce Butler

GEORGIA
William Few
Abraham Baldwin

ATTEST: *William Jackson, Secretary*

AMENDMENTS

These first ten amendments to the Constitution are known as the Bill of Rights. They were added to the Constitution by the first Congress and ratified by the states.

AMENDMENT I

Religion, Speech, Press, Assembly, Petition. Congress shall make no law respecting an establishment of religion, or prohibiting the free exercise thereof; or abridging the freedom of speech, or of the press; or the right of the people peaceably to assemble, and to petition the government for redress of grievances.

Congress may not:
1. Set up an official church;
2. Pass any laws that limit freedom of religion, speech, or press;
3. Keep people from meeting peacefully to talk about anything they like;
4. Keep people from asking the government to correct things they think are wrong.

AMENDMENT II

Militia. A well-regulated militia being necessary to the security of a free State, the right of the people to keep and bear arms shall not be infringed.

The federal government must not interfere with the rights of states to arm and drill state militias. This amendment does not say that individual citizens have an absolute right to keep guns for their own personal use. Congress can and has put limits on owning sawed-off shotguns or carrying hidden weapons. States have the right to require citizens to get licenses for guns.

AMENDMENT III

Soldiers. No soldier shall, in time of peace, be quartered in any house, without the consent of the owner; nor in time of war but in a manner to be prescribed by law.

Citizens cannot be forced to take soldiers into their homes in peacetime. Even in wartime, Congress must pass laws requiring citizens to give room and board to soldiers.

AMENDMENT IV

Unreasonable Searches. The right of the people to be secure in their persons, houses, papers, and effects, against unreasonable searches and seizures, shall not be violated, and no warrants shall issue, but upon probable cause, supported by oath or affirmation, and particularly describing the place to be searched, and the persons or things to be seized.

No federal officer may arrest or search people or their houses without proper legal papers, or warrants. Judges are not to give out warrants unless they are very sure they are necessary to catch a criminal.

AMENDMENT V

Legal Protection of Accused Persons. No person shall be held to answer for a capital, or otherwise infamous crime, unless on a presentment or indictment of a grand jury, except in cases arising in the land or naval forces, or in the militia, when in actual service in time of war and public danger; nor shall any person be subject for the same offense to be twice put in jeopardy of life or limb; nor shall be compelled in any criminal case to be a witness against himself, nor to be deprived of life, liberty, or property, without due process of law; nor shall private property be taken for public use, without just compensation.

A person arrested for a serious crime cannot be brought to court until a grand jury looks over the evidence and decides that a trial is needed. Persons cannot be tried twice for the same crime once any court has freed them. People cannot be forced to answer questions about crimes that they are accused of. People cannot be put to death, locked up in prison, or fined, except as punishment after they have had a fair, public trial.

Government may not take away people's property unless they are paid a fair price for it.

AMENDMENT VI

Right to Trial. In all criminal prosecutions, the accused shall enjoy the right to a speedy and public trial, by an impartial jury of the State and district wherein the crime shall have been committed, which district shall have been previously ascertained by law, and to be informed of the nature and cause of the accusation; to be confronted with the witnesses against him; to have compulsory process for obtaining witnesses in his favor, and to have the assistance of counsel for his defense.

In criminal trials, the accused has these rights:

1. A speedy, public trial is promised;
2. A fair, or impartial, jury is guaranteed;
3. The trial must take place where the crime supposedly happened;
4. A person must be informed, or told about, what he or she is accused of doing;
5. Witnesses must give evidence in open court so that the accused can answer their charges;
6. Defense witnesses can be called at public expense;
7. The accused has the right to have the help of a lawyer at public expense.

AMENDMENT VII

Suits at Common Law. In suits at common law, where the value in controversy shall exceed twenty dollars, the right of trial by jury shall be preserved, and no fact tried by a jury shall be otherwise reexamined in any court of the United States than according to the rules of common law.

Jury trial is guaranteed in damage suits when the matter amounts to more than $20.

AMENDMENT VIII

Bail, Punishments. Excessive bail shall not be required, nor excessive fines imposed, nor cruel and unusual punishments inflicted.

An unreasonable amount of money cannot be asked as bail before a person can get out of jail. Bail is money the accused puts up while waiting to be tried. If the person accused appears in court the bail is returned.

Unreasonably large amounts of money cannot be set as fines. A person could not be asked to pay a million dollars, for example, as punishment for a small robbery.

Cruel or unusual punishment cannot be given. No one could be tortured or be starved to death, for example.

AMENDMENT IX

Reserved Rights. The enumeration in the Constitution of certain rights shall not be construed to deny or disparage others retained by the people.

The Constitution cannot list all the rights Americans have. Just because a right is not listed does not mean that citizens don't have that right.

AMENDMENT X

Reserved Powers. The powers not delegated to the United States by the Constitution, nor prohibited by it to the States, are reserved to the States respectively, or to the people.

The states or the people themselves keep all the rights and powers they have not given the federal government in this Constitution. This amendment points out a very important principle of our government. The federal government has only those powers given to it. THE PEOPLE give the power to the government. This is very different from countries in which the people must beg government for some rights or powers.

AMENDMENT XI

Suits against States. The judicial power of the United States shall not be construed to extend to any suit in law or equity, commenced or prosecuted against any of the United States by citizens of another State, or by citizens or subjects of any foreign state.

A citizen in one state cannot sue another state in a federal court. The case must be tried in the courts of the state being sued. This amendment was adopted because the states were afraid of the powers of the federal government.

AMENDMENT XII

Method of Electing President and Vice-President. The electors shall meet in their respective States, and vote by ballot for President and Vice-President, one of whom, at least, shall not be an inhabitant of the same State with themselves; they shall name in their ballots the person voted for as President, and in distinct ballots the person voted for as Vice-President; and they shall make distinct lists of all persons voted for as President, and of all persons voted for as Vice-President, and of the number of votes for each, which list they shall sign and certify, and transmit sealed to the seat of the government of the United States, directed to the president of the Senate;—the president of the Senate shall in the presence of the Senate and House of Representatives, open all the certificates, and the votes shall then be counted;—the person having the greatest number of votes for President, shall be the President, if such number be a majority of the whole number of electors appointed; and if no person have such majority, then from the persons having the highest numbers not exceeding three on the list of those voted for as President, the House of Representatives shall choose immediately, by ballot, the President. But in choosing the President, the votes shall be taken by States, the representation from each State having one vote; a quorum for this purpose shall consist of a member or members from two-thirds of the States, and a majority of all the States shall be necessary to a choice. And if the House of Representatives shall not choose a President whenever the right of choice shall devolve upon them, [before the fourth day of March next following], then the Vice-President shall act as President, as in the case of the death or other constitutional disability of the President. The person having the greatest number of votes as Vice-President, shall be the Vice-President, if such number be a majority of the whole number of electors appointed; and if no person have a majority, then from the two highest numbers on the list, the Senate shall choose the Vice-President; a quorum for the purpose shall consist of two-thirds of the whole number of senators, and a majority of the whole number shall be necessary to a choice. But no person constitutionally ineligible to the office of President shall be eligible to that of Vice-President of the United States.

This amendment changed the old way of voting for President and Vice-President. Electors now vote for President and Vice-President on separate ballots so that there will be no chance of a tie, as in 1800.

If no candidate for President gets a majority of the votes, the House of Representatives chooses a President from the three highest. Each state gets one vote.

If no candidate for Vice-President wins a majority of the votes, the Senate chooses between the two highest.

The Constitution's requirements for becoming President are the same for becoming Vice-President.

AMENDMENT XIII

Slavery Abolished. Section 1—Neither slavery nor involuntary servitude, except as a punishment for crime whereof the party shall have been duly convicted, shall exist within the United States, or any place subject to their jurisdiction.

Section 2—Congress shall have power to enforce this article by appropriate legislation.

No one in the United States or its territories may be held as a slave. People cannot be made to work against their will unless they have been found guilty of crimes after fair trials.

AMENDMENT XIV

Blacks Made Citizens; Protection of Citizens. Section 1—All persons born or naturalized in the United States, and subject to the jurisdiction thereof, are citizens of the United States and of the State wherein they reside. No State shall make or enforce any law which shall abridge the privileges or immunities of citizens of the United States; nor shall any State deprive any person of life, liberty, or property, without due process of law, nor deny to any person within its jurisdiction the equal protection of the laws.

Former slaves are declared citizens. States are told to give equal privileges to all citizens.

IMPORTANT! Protections in the Bill of Rights now apply to states as well as to the federal government. This is the famous and important "due process clause." It guarantees fair treatment under the law to everyone in the United States, no matter where they live.

Section 2—Representatives shall be apportioned among the several States according to their respective numbers, counting the whole number of persons in each State, excluding Indians not taxed. But when the right to vote at any election for the choice of electors for President and Vice-President of the United States, representatives in Congress, the executive or judicial officers of a State, or the members of the legislature thereof, is denied to any of the male inhabitants of such State, being twenty-one years of age, and citizens of the United States, or in any way abridged, except for participation in rebellion or other crime, the basis of representation therein shall be reduced in the proportion which the number of such male citizens shall bear to the whole number of male citizens twenty-one years of age in such State.

Any state which denies adult male citizens the right to vote may have the number of its representatives in Congress reduced.

Section 3—No person shall be a senator or representative in Congress, or elector of President or Vice-President, or hold any office, civil or military, under the United States, or under any State, who, having previously taken an oath, as a member of Congress, or as an officer of the United States, or as a member of any State legislature, or as an executive or judicial officer of any State, to support the Constitution of the United States, shall have engaged in insurrection or rebellion against the same, or given aid or comfort to the enemies thereof. But Congress may, by a vote of two-thirds of each house, remove such disability.

This section was aimed at Southerners after the Civil War. No former federal or state official who had once sworn loyalty to the United States, and had then fought for the South in the Civil War, could hold public office again. But Congress soon pardoned these people.

Section 4—The validity of the public debt of the United States, authorized by law, including debts incurred for payment of pensions and bounties for services in suppressing insurrection or rebellion, shall not be questioned. But neither the United States nor any State shall assume or pay any debt or obligation incurred in aid of insurrection or rebellion against the United States, or any claim for the loss or emancipation of any slave; but all such debts, obligations, and claims shall be held illegal and void.

Section 5—The Congress shall have power to enforce, by appropriate legislation, the provisions of this article.

The United States would pay the federal Civil War debt, but not the debts of the Confederate states.

AMENDMENT XV

Blacks Made Voters. Section 1—The rights of citizens of the United States to vote shall not be denied or abridged by the United States, or by any State, on account of race, color, or previous condition of servitude.

Section 2—The Congress shall have power to enforce this article by appropriate legislation.

No one can be denied the right to vote because of race, beliefs, color, or because that person was once a slave.

AMENDMENT XVI

Income Tax. The Congress shall have power to lay and collect taxes on incomes from whatever source derived, without apportionment among the several States, and without regard to any census or enumeration.

Congress can tax incomes.

AMENDMENT XVII

Direct Election of Senators. The Senate of the United States shall be composed of two senators from each State, elected by the people thereof for six years; and each senator shall have one vote. The electors in each State shall have the qualifications requisite for electors of the most numerous branch of the State legislature.

When vacancies happen in the representation of any State in the Senate, the executive authority of such State shall issue writs of election to fill such vacancies: Provided, that the legislature of any State may empower the Executive thereof to make temporary appointments until the people fill the vacancies by election as the legislature may direct.

This amendment shall not be so construed as to affect the election or term of any senator chosen before it becomes valid as part of the constitution.

The people themselves, instead of the state legislatures, will elect senators.

AMENDMENT XVIII

National Prohibition. [Section 1—After one year from the ratification of this article the manufacture, sale, or transportation of intoxicating liquors within, the importation thereof into, or the exportation thereof from the United States and all territory subject to the jurisdiction thereof for beverage purposes is hereby prohibited.

Section 2—The Congress and the several States shall have concurrent power to enforce this article by appropriate legislation.

Section 3—This article shall be inoperative unless it shall have been ratified as an amendment to the Constitution by the legislatures of the several States, as provided in the Constitution, within seven years from the date of the submission hereof to the States by the Congress.]

It was illegal to make, sell, or carry liquors while this amendment was in effect.

In 1933, the 21st Amendment canceled this amendment.

AMENDMENT XIX

Woman Suffrage. Section 1—The right of citizens of the United States to vote shall not be denied or abridged by the United States or by any State on account of sex.

Section 2—Congress shall have power to enforce this article by appropriate legislation.

Women are given the right to vote in all states and in national elections.

AMENDMENT XX

"Lame Duck" Amendment. Section 1—The terms of the President and Vice-President shall end at noon on the twentieth day of January, and the terms of senators and representatives at noon on the third day of January, of the years in which such terms would have ended if this article had not been ratified; and the terms of their successors shall then begin.

Section 2—The Congress shall assemble at least once in every year, and such meeting shall begin at noon on the third day of January, unless they shall by law appoint a different day.

Section 3—If, at the time fixed for the beginning of the term of the President, the President-elect shall have died, the Vice-President-elect shall become President. If a President shall not have been chosen before the time fixed for the beginning of his term, or if the President-elect shall have failed to qualify, then the Vice-President-elect shall act as President until a President shall have qualified; and the Congress may by law provide for the case wherein neither a President-elect nor a Vice-President-elect shall have qualified, declaring who shall then act as President, or the manner in which one who is to act shall be selected, and such person shall act accordingly until a President or Vice-President shall have qualified.

Section 4—The Congress may by law provide for the case of the death of any of the persons from whom the House of Representatives may choose a President whenever the right of choice shall have devolved upon them, and for the case of the death of any of the persons from whom the Senate may choose a Vice-President whenever the right of choices shall have devolved upon them.

Section 5—Sections 1 and 2 shall take effect upon the fifteenth day of October following the ratification of this article.

Section 6—This article shall be inoperative unless it shall have been ratified as an amendment to the Constitution by the legislatures of three-fourths of the several States within seven years from the date of its submission.

This amendment changed the time when the President takes office. A presidential term now begins on January 20 instead of March 4. Congress now meets once a year beginning January 3. This amendment was passed to shorten the time between the election and the time of taking office. This is the so-called "lame duck amendment." A "lame duck" is an official who serves out a term though not reelected. Congress has made rules to take effect if the President-elect should die before taking office.

AMENDMENT XXI

The Repeal of Prohibition. Section 1—The Eighteenth article of amendment to the Constitution of the United States is hereby repealed.

Section 2—The transportation or importation into any State, Territory, or possession of the United States for delivery or use therein of intoxicating liquors, in violation of the laws thereof, is hereby prohibited.

Section 3—This article shall be inoperative unless it shall have been ratified as an amendment to the Constitution by conventions in the several States, as provided in the Constitution, within seven years from the date of the submission hereof to the States by the Congress.

This amendment canceled the Eighteenth Amendment.

Section 2 says that states themselves may forbid sale and use of liquors if they choose to do so.

AMENDMENT XXII

Presidential Term. No person shall be elected to the office of the President more than twice, and no person who has held the office of President, or acted as President, for more than two years of a term to which some other person was elected President shall be elected to the office of the President more than once. But this article shall not apply to any person holding the office of President when this article was proposed by the Congress, and shall not prevent any person who may be holding the office of President, or acting as President, during the term within which this article becomes operative, from holding the office of President or acting as President during the remainder of such term.

A President may serve only two terms. A person who serves more than two years of a previous President's term may be elected only once.

AMENDMENT XXIII

Electors for the District of Columbia. Section 1—The District constituting the seat of Government of the United States shall appoint in such manner as the Congress may direct:

A number of electors of President and Vice-President equal to the whole number of senators and representatives in Congress to which the District would be entitled if it were a State, but in no event more than the least populous State; they shall be in addition to those appointed by the States, but they shall be considered, for the purpose of the election of President and Vice-President, to be electors appointed by a State; and they shall meet in the District and perform such duties as provided by the twelfth article of amendment.

Section 2—The Congress shall have power to enforce this article by appropriate legislation.

The District of Columbia is given three electoral votes. For the first time, people living in Washington, D.C., received the right to vote for President and Vice-President.

AMENDMENT XXIV

Poll Tax. Section 1—The right of citizens of the United States to vote in any primary or other election for President or Vice-President, for electors for President or Vice-President, or for Senator or Representative in Congress, shall not be denied or abridged by the United States or any State by reason of failure to pay any poll tax or other tax.

Section 2—The Congress shall have power to enforce this article by appropriate legislation.

No federal or state laws can make people pay a tax in order to vote for President and Vice-President of the United States or for members of Congress.

AMENDMENT XXV

Presidential Disability and Vice-Presidential Vacancy. Section 1—In case of the removal of the President from office or his death or resignation, the Vice-President shall become President.

Section 2—Whenever there is a vacancy in the office of the Vice-President, the President shall nominate a Vice-President who shall take the office upon confirmation by a majority vote of both houses of Congress.

Section 3—Whenever the President transmits to the President pro tempore of the Senate and the Speaker of the House of Representatives his written declaration that he is unable to discharge the powers and duties of his office, and until he transmits to them a written declaration to the contrary, such powers and duties shall be discharged by the Vice-President as Acting President.

Section 4—Whenever the Vice-President and a majority of either the principal officers of the executive department or of such other body as Congress may by law provide, transmit to the President pro tempore of the Senate and the Speaker of the House of Representatives their written declaration that the President is unable to discharge the powers and duties of his office, the Vice-President shall immediately assume the powers and duties of the office as Acting President. Thereafter, when the President transmits to the President pro tempore of the Senate and the Speaker of the House of Representatives his written declaration that no inability exists, he shall resume the powers and duties of his office unless the Vice-President and a majority of either the principal officers of the executive department or of such other body as Congress may by law provide, transmit within four days to the President pro tempore of the Senate and the Speaker of the House of Representatives their written declaration that the President is unable to discharge the powers and duties of his office. Thereupon Congress shall decide the issue, assembling within 48 hours for that purpose if not in session. If the Congress, within 21 days after receipt of the latter written declaration, or, if Congress is not in session, within 21 days after Congress is required to assemble, determines by two-thirds vote of both houses that the President is unable to discharge the powers and duties of his office, the Vice-President shall continue to discharge the same as Acting President; otherwise, the President shall resume the powers and duties of his office.

1. If the President dies, resigns, or is removed from office, the Vice-President becomes President.
2. Whenever there is a vacancy in the office of Vice-President, the President shall appoint someone to fill the office. Such an appointment would have to be approved by a majority vote in both houses of Congress.
3. A President who is unable to serve because of illness must send a letter to Congress. The Vice-President would then serve as "Acting President" until the President is well again.
4. If the President is ill but will not admit it, the Vice-President and the majority of the cabinet may declare the President unable to serve. The Vice-President then becomes Acting President immediately.
5. When the President is well, he notifies Congress and goes back to work. If the Vice-President and the cabinet do not agree that he is well, they tell Congress within 48 hours. Congress must then vote on the question within 21 days.
6. Two-thirds of Congress must agree that the President has not recovered from the illness, or the President continues in office.

AMENDMENT XXVI

Voting Age. Section 1—The right of citizens of the United States, who are eighteen years of age or older, to vote shall not be denied or abridged by the United States or by any state on account of age.

Section 2—The Congress shall have power to enforce this article by appropriate legislation.

This amendment became effective July 1, 1971. It was sent to the states for ratification on March 23, 1971. In just four months time, the necessary number of states approved. Prior to this amendment, the required age for voting varied from 18 to 21 in the various states.

Since winning the right to vote, young adults in the 18 through 20 age bracket have been given many other legal privileges in almost all of the 50 states. Some states, as well as the federal government, have lowered the age for service on juries to 18.

Presidents and Vice-Presidents of the United States

	President	Years in office	Party	Born	Died	State Born/Home	Vice-President
1	George Washington	1789–1797		1732	1799	Virginia	John Adams
2	John Adams	1797–1801	Federalist	1735	1826	Massachusetts	Thomas Jefferson
3	Thomas Jefferson	1801–1809	Republican	1743	1826	Virginia	Aaron Burr
							George Clinton
4	James Madison	1809–1817	Republican	1751	1836	Virginia	George Clinton
							Elbridge Gerry
5	James Monroe	1817–1825	Republican	1758	1831	Virginia	Daniel D. Tompkins
6	John Quincy Adams	1825–1829	Nat. Rep.	1767	1848	Massachusetts	John C. Calhoun
7	Andrew Jackson	1829–1837	Democratic	1767	1845	S.C./Tenn.	John C. Calhoun
							Martin Van Buren
8	Martin Van Buren	1837–1841	Democratic	1782	1862	New York	Richard M. Johnson
9	William Henry Harrison	Mar. 1841	Whig	1773	1841	VA./Ohio	John Tyler
10	John Tyler	1841–1845	Whig	1790	1862	Virginia	
11	James K. Polk	1845–1849	Democratic	1795	1849	N.C./Tenn.	George M. Dallas
12	Zachary Taylor	1849–1850	Whig	1784	1850	VA./La.	Millard Fillmore
13	Millard Fillmore	1850–1853	Whig	1800	1874	New York	
14	Franklin Pierce	1853–1857	Democratic	1804	1869	New Hampshire	William R. D. King
15	James Buchanan	1857–1861	Democratic	1791	1868	Pennsylvania	John C. Breckinridge
16	Abraham Lincoln	1861–1865	Republican	1809	1865	Ky./Ill.	Hannibal Hamlin
							Andrew Johnson
17	Andrew Johnson	1865–1869	Republican	1808	1875	N.C./Tenn.	
18	Ulysses S. Grant	1869–1877	Republican	1822	1885	Ohio/Ill.	Schuyler Colfax
							Henry Wilson
19	Rutherford B. Hayes	1877–1881	Republican	1822	1893	Ohio	William A. Wheeler
20	James A. Garfield	1881	Republican	1831	1881	Ohio	Chester A. Arthur
21	Chester A. Arthur	1881–1885	Republican	1830	1886	Vt./N.Y.	
22	Grover Cleveland	1885–1889	Democratic	1837	1908	N.J./N.Y.	Thomas A. Hendricks
23	Benjamin Harrison	1889–1893	Republican	1833	1901	Ohio/Ind.	Levi P. Morton
24	Grover Cleveland	1893–1897	Democratic	1837	1908	N.J./N.Y.	Adlai E. Stevenson
25	William McKinley	1897–1901	Republican	1843	1901	Ohio	Garret A. Hobart
							Theodore Roosevelt
26	Theodore Roosevelt	1901–1909	Republican	1858	1919	New York	Charles W. Fairbanks
27	William Howard Taft	1909–1913	Republican	1857	1930	Ohio	James S. Sherman
28	Woodrow Wilson	1913–1921	Democratic	1856	1924	Va./N.J.	Thomas R. Marshall
29	Warren G. Harding	1921–1923	Republican	1865	1923	Ohio	Calvin Coolidge
30	Calvin Coolidge	1923–1929	Republican	1872	1933	Vt./Mass.	Charles G. Dawes
31	Herbert C. Hoover	1929–1933	Republican	1874	1964	Iowa/Cal.	Charles Curtis
32	Franklin D. Roosevelt	1933–1945	Democratic	1882	1945	New York	John N. Garner
							Henry A. Wallace
							Harry S Truman
33	Harry S Truman	1945–1953	Democratic	1884	1972	Missouri	Alben W. Barkley
34	Dwight D. Eisenhower	1953–1961	Republican	1890	1969	Tex./N.Y., Pa.	Richard M. Nixon
35	John F. Kennedy	1961–1963	Democratic	1917	1963	Massachusetts	Lyndon B. Johnson
36	Lyndon B. Johnson	1963–1969	Democratic	1908	1973	Texas	Hubert H. Humphrey
37	Richard M. Nixon	1969–1974	Republican	1913		Cal./N.Y., Cal.	Spiro T. Agnew
							Gerald R. Ford
38	Gerald R. Ford	1974–1977	Republican	1913		Neb./Mich.	Nelson A. Rockefeller
39	Jimmy (James Earl) Carter	1977–1981	Democratic	1924		Georgia	Walter F. Mondale
40	Ronald Reagan	1981–	Republican	1911		Ill./Cal.	George H. Bush

Some Facts about Our States

	State	Date of admission	Capital	Area (sq. mi.)	Land area	Population (1980)	Cities 100,000+
1	Delaware	1787	Dover	2,057	1,982	595,225	—
2	Pennsylvania	1787	Harrisburg	45,333	44,966	11,866,728	4
3	New Jersey	1787	Trenton	7,836	7,521	7,364,158	6
4	Georgia	1788	Atlanta	58,876	58,073	5;464,265	4
5	Connecticut	1788	Hartford	5,009	4,862	3,107,576	5
6	Massachusetts	1788	Boston	8,257	7,826	5,737,037	4
7	Maryland	1788	Annapolis	10,577	9,891	4,216,446	1
8	South Carolina	1788	Columbia	31,055	30,255	3,119,208	1
9	New Hampshire	1788	Concord	9,304	9,027	920,610	—
10	Virginia	1788	Richmond	40,817	39,780	5,346,279	7
11	New York	1788	Albany	49,576	47,831	17,557,288	6
12	North Carolina	1789	Raleigh	52,586	48,798	5,874,429	4
13	Rhode Island	1790	Providence	1,214	1,049	947,154	1
14	Vermont	1791	Montpelier	9,609	9,267	511,456	—
15	Kentucky	1792	Frankfort	40,395	39,650	3,661,433	2
16	Tennessee	1796	Nashville	42,244	41,328	4,590,750	4
17	Ohio	1803	Columbus	41,222	40,975	10,797,419	8
18	Louisiana	1812	Baton Rouge	48,523	44,930	4,203,972	3
19	Indiana	1816	Indianapolis	36,291	36,097	5,490,179	6
20	Mississippi	1817	Jackson	47,716	47,296	2,520,638	1
21	Illinois	1818	Springfield	56,400	55,748	11,418,461	3
22	Alabama	1819	Montgomery	51,609	50,708	3,890,061	4
23	Maine	1820	Augusta	33,215	30,920	1,124,660	—
24	Missouri	1821	Jefferson City	69,686	68,995	4,917,444	4
25	Arkansas	1836	Little Rock	53,104	51,945	2,285,513	1
26	Michigan	1837	Lansing	58,216	56,817	9,258,344	7
27	Florida	1845	Tallahassee	58,560	54,090	9,739,992	8
28	Texas	1845	Austin	267,338	262,134	14,228,383	10
29	Iowa	1846	Des Moines	56,290	55,941	2,913,387	2
30	Wisconsin	1848	Madison	56,154	54,464	4,705,335	2
31	California	1850	Sacramento	158,693	156,361	23,668,562	20
32	Minnesota	1858	St. Paul	84,068	79,289	786,690	2
33	Oregon	1859	Salem	96,981	96,184	2,632,663	1
34	Kansas	1861	Topeka	82,264	81,787	2,363,208	3
35	West Virginia	1863	Charleston	24,181	24,070	1,949,644	—
36	Nevada	1864	Carson City	110,540	109,889	799,184	1
37	Nebraska	1867	Lincoln	77,227	76,483	1,570,006	2
38	Colorado	1876	Denver	104,247	103,766	2,888,834	2
39	North Dakota	1889	Bismarck	70,665	69,273	652,695	—
40	South Dakota	1889	Pierre	77,047	75,955	690,178	—
41	Montana	1889	Helena	147,138	145,587	786,690	—
42	Washington	1889	Olympia	68,192	66,570	4,130,163	3
43	Idaho	1890	Boise	83,577	82,677	943,935	—
44	Wyoming	1890	Cheyenne	97,914	97,203	470,816	—
45	Utah	1896	Salt Lake City	84,916	82,096	1,461,037	1
46	Oklahoma	1907	Oklahoma City	69,919	68,782	3,025,266	2
47	New Mexico	1912	Santa Fe	121,666	121,412	1,299,968	1
48	Arizona	1912	Phoenix	113,909	113,417	2,717,866	2
49	Alaska	1959	Juneau	589,757	569,600	400,481	1
50	Hawaii	1959	Honolulu	6,450	6,425	965,000	1
	Dist. of Columbia		Washington	67	61	637,651	1
	Puerto Rico		San Juan	3,435	3,421	3,187,566	
	Guam		Agana		209	105,861	
	American Samoa		Fagotogo		76	32,395	
	Virgin Islands		Charlotte Amalie		132	95,214	

Glossary

abolitionists people who worked for an immediate end to slavery.
alien a person who is not a citizen of the country in which he or she lives.
alliance a formal agreement among nations to help each other in war or national defense.
ally a nation joined in an alliance.
anarchists people who believe in little or no govermental authority and seek to overthrow existing government.
annex to join or add to a larger thing: especially, to add territory to a nation or state.
armistice a cease-fire; an agreement to stop fighting.
arsenal storage place for arms and ammunition.
autobiography a written story of the author's own life.

bankruptcy state of being legally declared unable to pay one's debts; the court divides the property of a bankrupt person among his or her creditors.
blitzkrieg "lightning war"; German strategy of quick attack during World War II.
blockade a military or naval attempt to keep supplies from the enemy.
blue-collar worker industrial or factory worker.

cabinet department heads in the executive branch of our federal government who advise the President.
caravel small sailing ship of 15th century Portuguese design.
carpetbaggers Southern term for Northerners who went to the South to seek private gain from the Reconstruction governments.
caucus a closed meeting of political leaders, usually of the same party, to choose candidates or to decide on policy.
cede to give up or hand over to another, especially to give up territory.
checks and balances means by which the separate branches of our government check each other to prevent one branch from assuming too much power.
civil rights rights guaranteed to all citizens of the United States by our Constitution.
civil service system in which government employees are hired using the merit system.
collective bargaining negotiation between organized workers and their employer.
colony a settlement by citizens of an established nation who keep their ties to that nation.
cold war a deep bitterness between nations which stops short of a shooting war; the situation between the USSR and its satellites and the West after World War II.
combine a machine which reaps, threshes, cleans, and bags grain in one operation.
compromise give and take between parties to reach agreement.
communism an economic and political system based on government ownership of land, factories, and other means of production. Communism emphasizes the overthrow of existing social systems by revolution and the control of the new system by a single political party.
confederation a very loose union of equals.
conquistadores Spanish conquerors.
conservative a person who does not want major changes in government or society; one who believes in limited government.
constitution a written plan of government.
containment name of a policy to stop the spread of communism adopted by the United States after World War II.
convention a meeting held for some purpose, usually by delegates from one or more organizations.

delegate a representative.
democracy a government that is run by its citizens either directly or indirectly through elected leaders.
depression a time of serious reduction in business activity resulting in failing businesses and high unemployment.
dictator person in absolute authority in a nation, especially one who seizes such control.
doctrine a statement of beliefs.
duty tax on imported goods.

economy the system of producing, distributing, and using goods and services.
elector a person elected to the electoral college, which formally elects the President and Vice-President.
elevateds steam and electric trains that run on overhead tracks.
emancipation freedom, especially from slavery.
embargo the forbidding of trade with another nation.
empire a nation and its colonies.
epidemic outbreak of contagious disease.
era a long period of time.
ethics right behavior.
excise tax a tax levied on goods offered for sale.
executive the branch of government that carries out the laws; the branch headed by the President.
exports goods sent out of a country for sale in another country.

federal system of government in which power is divided between the national and state governments.
forty-niners prospectors who went to California in 1849 to find gold.
freedmen term used after the Civil War for ex-slaves.
frontier an outpost on the edge of the wilderness.

goods items for sale which can be seen and touched.
grange an organization of farmers formed in 1867.

hemisphere one-half of the surface of the earth.
homesteader pioneer; especially a person who acquired land under the Homestead Act of 1862.

impeach officially accuse a public official of wrong conduct during office.
imports goods brought in from another country.
inauguration ceremony in which the President or other high government official takes the oath of office.
inflation sharp increase in prices, often resulting from too great an expansion of bank credit or paper money.
injunction a court order to stop an action.
interchangeable parts identical parts of a manufactured item. Any of the identical parts may be used to assemble the finished item.
iron curtain imaginary line separating the USSR and its satellites from the United States and other nations after World War II.

judicial the branch of government that interprets and applies the law through a system of courts.

legislature the branch of government that makes the laws; Congress is the legislature of the federal government.
liberal a person who favors reforms and large government.
literacy the ability to read and write.
loyalist during the American Revolution, a colonist who sided with the British.

manifest destiny a common belief during the 19th century that the United States was destined to expand to the Pacific Ocean.
massacre a bloody killing.
McCarthyism accusing someone of wrongdoing without having evidence to support the accusation.
militia a volunteer citizen army.
minority less than half of a group; a group having less political or economic power than the majority in a society.
monopoly control of a product by one company or group of companies that results in the elimination of competition.
muckrakers writers who exposed corruption in business and government during the late 19th and early 20th centuries.

natural resources things found in nature which are useful for producing goods.
neutral taking neither side in a conflict.
nomads wanderers.
nullify cancel.

ordinance a law.

patent a government guarantee which gives a person the exclusive rights to an invention for a certain number of years.
patriots during the American Revolution, colonists who favored a complete break with England.
platform the statement of the ideas of a political party.
plantation a large southern estate or farm, usually spread over thousands of acres.
proclamation announcement.
progressives reformers of the period between the turn of the century and World War I who believed in strong government.
prohibition laws or laws against selling alcoholic liquors; *Prohibition* is the period between 1919 and 1933 when it was illegal to make or sell alcoholic liquors anywhere in the United States.
propaganda the selection and use of facts which support only one side of a story.
prospector a person who explores for minerals, such as gold or silver.

quartering providing housing, food, and other necessities, especially by private persons to soldiers.
quota a set limit.

radical one who wants to make sweeping changes.
ratify to approve.
raw materials natural materials which can be used to manufacture various products.
rebel a person who fights against authority.
reformer a person who wants to bring about change for the better.
repeal to withdraw or call back; to cancel a law.
republic a government where the people elect their leaders.
reservation land set aside by the state or federal government for the Indians.

satellite nation after World War II, a nation dominated by the USSR.
secede to withdraw; to leave the Union.
sedition action inciting rebellion.
segregation the practice of separating people on the basis of race or color.
self-determination the right of a people to choose their own government.

separation of powers the policy by which the powers of the federal government are divided among the three branches of government: executive, legislative, and judicial.
serf a person in medieval Europe who was bound to the soil with no freedom to move to some other place or job.
services tasks which people perform for one another.
sharecropper a person who lives and farms on another's land and gives part of the crop to the landowner as payment for use of the land.
sod the top layer of the soil containing grass and plant roots.
spoils system the system of rewarding followers with government jobs or other advantages.
squatters people who settle on land they do not own.
strike an organized work stoppage by labor groups.
suffrage the right to vote.
suffragists women who worked for women's right to vote.
sunbelt southern part of the United States from southern Virginia to southern California.

tariff tax on imports.
temperance movement to stop the manufacture and sale of alcoholic beverages.
tenement a substandard apartment house.
ticket list of a political party's candidates.
transcontinental across the continent; coast to coast.
treason betrayal of one's country.
trust separate businesses under the control of trustees whose purpose is to control an industry and eliminate competition.

underground railroad escape trail for slaves from the South to Canada.
union a group of workers joined together to improve wages and working conditions; the *Union*, the United States of America.

veto the executive's power to refuse to sign a bill passed by the legislature.
vigilantes citizens who take law and order into their own hands.

ward voting district in a city.
white-collar workers people who work in offices and stores.

yellow journalism sensational stories in newspapers; style of journalism used widely before the Spanish-American War.

The pronunciation of difficult words is shown in the text just after the word, in this way: **abbreviate** (ə brē′vē āt). The letters and signs used are pronounced as in the words below. The mark **′** is placed after a syllable with primary or heavy accent, as in the example above. The mark ′ after a syllable shows a secondary or lighter accent, as in **abbreviation** (ə brē′vē ā′shən).

Some words, taken from foreign languages, are spoken with sounds that do not otherwise occur in English. Symbols for these sounds are given in the key as "foreign sounds."

a hat, cap
ā age, face
ä father, far

b bad, rob
ch child, much
d did, red

e let, best
ē equal, be
ėr term, learn

f fat, if
g go, bag
h he, how

i it, pin
ī ice, five

j jam, enjoy
k kind, seek
l land, coal
m me, am
n no, in
ng long, bring

o hot, rock
ō open, go
ô order, all
oi oil, voice
ou house, out

p paper, cup
r run, try
s say, yes
sh she, rush
t tell, it
th thin, both
ᴛʜ then, smooth

u cup, butter
ů full, put
ü rule, move

v very, save
w will, woman
y young, yet
z zero, breeze
zh measure, seizure

ə represents:
a in about
e in taken
i in pencil
o in lemon
u in circus

foreign sounds

Y as in French *du.* Pronounce (ē) with the lips rounded as for (ü).

à as in French *ami.* Pronounce (ä) with the lips spread and held tense.

œ as in French *peu.* Pronounce (ā) with the lips rounded as for (ō).

N as in French *bon.* The **N** is not pronounced, but shows that the vowel before it is nasal.

H as in German *ach.* Pronounce (k) without closing the breath passage.

Index

A

C

H

I

M

N

Q

R

S

T

U

V

W

Y

Z

Credits

Abby Aldrich Rockefeller Folk Art Collection, Colonial Williamsburg: 62,210; ACTION: 534; American Antiquarian Society: 53, 102L, 290,307; American Archaeological Institute: 10; American Museum of Natural History: 5 b; Amon Carter Museum, Fort Worth: 173, 253; Anne S. K. Brown Military Collection, Brown University Library: 284; Archivo general de Indias de Seville: 38; Argosy Galleries: 196; Peter Arnold: 577; Bancroft Library, University of California: 9; H. K. Barnett: 518; Benjamin Harrison House: 210; The Bettmann Archive: 14, 406, 410, 428, 463, 473; Bibliotheque Nationale, Paris; 111 R; Black Star: 509 (Fenno Jacobs), 530, 559 (Fred Ward), 564, 565 (Robin Moyer), 568 (Fred Ward) 572, 575 (Bob Fitch), 583 BR; Bodleian Library, Oxford: 15; Senor A. Boulton, Caracas, Venezuela: 186L; British Museum: 16B, 40 (all); Brooklyn Museum: 141; Brown Brothers: 240, 242, 381, 382L, 406, 432, 442B, 450, 461; Burton Historical Collection, Detroit Public Library: 120; California Historical Society: 263; California State Library: 269; Camera 5: (Ken Regan); Carolina Art Association: 47; Charleston Library Society: 76; Chicago Historical Society: 148, 170, 178, 288L; Cincinnati Art Museum: 220, 280; Civico Museo Storico, G. Garibaldi, Como: 20; Colonial Williamsburg: 90; Colorado Historical Society: 250R; Colour Library International: 45, 66; Corcoran Gallery of Art: 123; Culver Pictures: 151, 208, 233, 234, 270, 279, 303, 309, 311, 312, 341 (both), 375, 376, 378, 382R, 384, 399, 404, 405, 412, 430, 434, 462, 473; Daughters of the Republic of Texas Library, The Alamo, San Antonio: 255B; Delaware Art Museum: 100; Denver Public Library, Western History Division: 248, 250; J. Doyle De Witt Collection, University of Hartford: 210, 288R, 451; Edison National Historic Site: 322; Enoch Pratt Free Library, Baltimore: 48; Richard Erdoes: 24; J. R. Eyreman, *Life* Magazine, © 1953: 526; F.P.G.: 393; Field Museum of Natural History, Chicago: 179; Fort Pulaski National Monument: 110; F.D.R. Library: 164; George Eastman House: 409; Thomas Gilcrease Institute: 328, 351; Giraudon: 11; The Granger Collection: 109, 282, 333L, 397, 409, 442T; Greensboro Historical Museum: 183; Hancock Shaker Village: 239TR; Harvard University Portrait Gallery: 153; Henry Francis duPont Winterthur Museum: 113; Henry Huntington Library, San Marino, California: 155, 325, 329, 348; Historical Pictures Services, Chicago: 55, 478; Historical Society of Pennsylvania: 9, 44; The Image Bank: 8T (Harold Sund), 36 (John Louis Stage), 88 (John Louis Stage), 116 (John Louis Stage), 156 (Chuck Place), 245 (David Hiser), 345 (Gerald Brimacombe), 421 (Charles Weckler), 482 (Gabe Palmer), 550 (Nick Nicholson); Imperial War Museum, London: 445B, 447, 495T; Independence National Historical Park: 110R, 129, 176; Kunsthistoriches, Vienna: 33L; Le Pelley, *The Christian Science Monitor*, October 29, 1962: 535; Liason: 573 (Dirck Halstead), 580 (Keza); Library of Congress: 72T, 93, 193, 213, 268, 292, 295, 296, 304, 308, 315, 337, 339, 361, 386, 400, 425, 475; Robert Llewellyn: 138; Lyndon Baines Johnson Library, University of Texas, Austin: 541; Magnum: 541, 553 (Miller) 555; Maryland Historical Society: 188; Fred Maroon: 275; Massachusetts Historical Society: 93, 198, 228; Mauldin, Bill, *Up Front*, Henry Holt and Co., 1944: 496, 497, 498; Metropolitan Museum of Art: 95, 228, 286, 436; David Muench: 2, 27; Munson-Williams-Proctor Institute, Utica, N.Y.: 190; Museo Historico Nacional, Buenos Aires, Argentina: 186R; Museum of the American Indian: 9; Museum of the City of New York: 96, 192, 368, 370, 372 (both), 388; Museum of Fine Arts, Boston: 61, 94, 260; NASA: 536, 537, 583BL; National Archives: 162, 355, 491, 492; National Collection of Fine Arts: 356; National Gallery of Art: 102R, 130, 133; National Maritime Museum, Greenwich, England: 16T (Michael Holford); 32 (Michael Holford), 78; National Portrait Gallery, Washington, D.C.: 42; Nebraska Historical Society: 352, 356T; New Orleans Museum of Art, Gift of Colonel and Mrs. Edgar Garbisch: 184; New York Historical Society: 60, 111BR, 181, 215 (both), 237; New York Public Library: 24B, 46, 57, 77, 230, 261; New York Public Library, Prints Division: 99, 147L; New York Public Library, Rare Book Division: 43, 52, 70, 252; New York Public Library, Schoemberg Collection: 169, 231, 445T; New York State Historical Association: 74; North Carolina Museum of Art: 226; Oakland Museum: 423, 445L; Oklahoma Historical Society: 363; Old Sturbridge Village: 69, 79; Peabody Museum of Salem: 433; *Pennsylvania Almanac* 1795: 146; Philadelphia Museum of Art, E. W. and B. C. Garbisch Collection: 105; Phillips Collection, Washington, D.C.: 465: Photo Researchers: 5 (George Holton), 5B (George Gerster), 6 (Victor Englebert), 204 (Fred Maroon); Photo Trends: 502; Photri: 147R, 300; Polk Home, Columbia, Tennessee: 258; Puerto Rican Government Tourist Office: 427; San Jacinto Museum of History: 256; Scala/EPA: 6, 23, 33; Shostal: 167, 458; Frank Siteman: Title page; Smith College Library: 232; Smithsonian Institution: 9, 129, 359; Society of Antiquities, London: 39; Southwest Museum: 361 R; State Historical Society of North Dakota: 174; State Historical Society of Wisconsin: 85, 403, 413; State of Illinois: 239TL; State of South Carolina: 108; Stock/Boston: 51, 55; William Strode: 224, 239B; Sygma: 546 (J. A. Pavlovsky), 561 (J. P. Laffont); Time, Inc., The Old West, *The Spanish West*, photograph by Frank Lerner, Time-Life Books Inc., Publishers, 158; Tuskegee Institute: 333; Union Pacific Railroad: 327; United Press International: 468, 471, 472, 488, 513, 567; University of New Mexico: 9; University of North Carolina Library: 39; John de Visser: 8B, 12; Walter Hampden Memorial Library: 464; West Point Museum: 266; Wide World: 485, 486, 495, 502R, 513L, 520, 523, 525, 529, 538, 557, 559, 570, 579; Woolaroc Museum: 218; Woodfin Camp: 366 (Dan Budnik) 566, 583BR (Jim Anderson), 583TL (W. McNamee); Yale University Art Gallery: 133L, 144, 200 (Mabel Brady Garvan Collection).

BCDEFG 085432
Printed in the United States of America